Why Do You Need This New Edition?

If you're wondering why you should buy this new edition of *Research Methods: A Tool for Life*, here are six good reasons!

1. Each chapter now features a **concept map** that helps students connect the important ideas in the chapter. The concept maps show how the complex ideas in each chapter connect with one another, so students can form coherent schemas to help integrate the information.
2. The updated chapters use the most **recent, interesting research** to illustrate the concepts. Students will find the examples highly engaging and relevant to many issues that they face in their own lives and issues they see in the news.
3. The new examples in the book feature **interesting and important social issues** addressed in recent psychological research. These examples help students learn how psychology can have a significant, positive impact in helping society deal with complex problems.
4. **Data sets for in-class data collection have been expanded.** Instructors can combine data from their own classes with the existing data sets. These data sets let students provide their own data and, with the large data sets available, conduct data analyses that have enough power to spot significant effects.
5. **New end-of-chapter test questions** and discussion questions will test student knowledge and stimulate discussion. These questions allow the student to focus on the important issues and to recognize the type of detail they need to know to maximize their success in the course.
6. Complex material in the chapters has been **revised** for maximum clarity and greater student understanding.

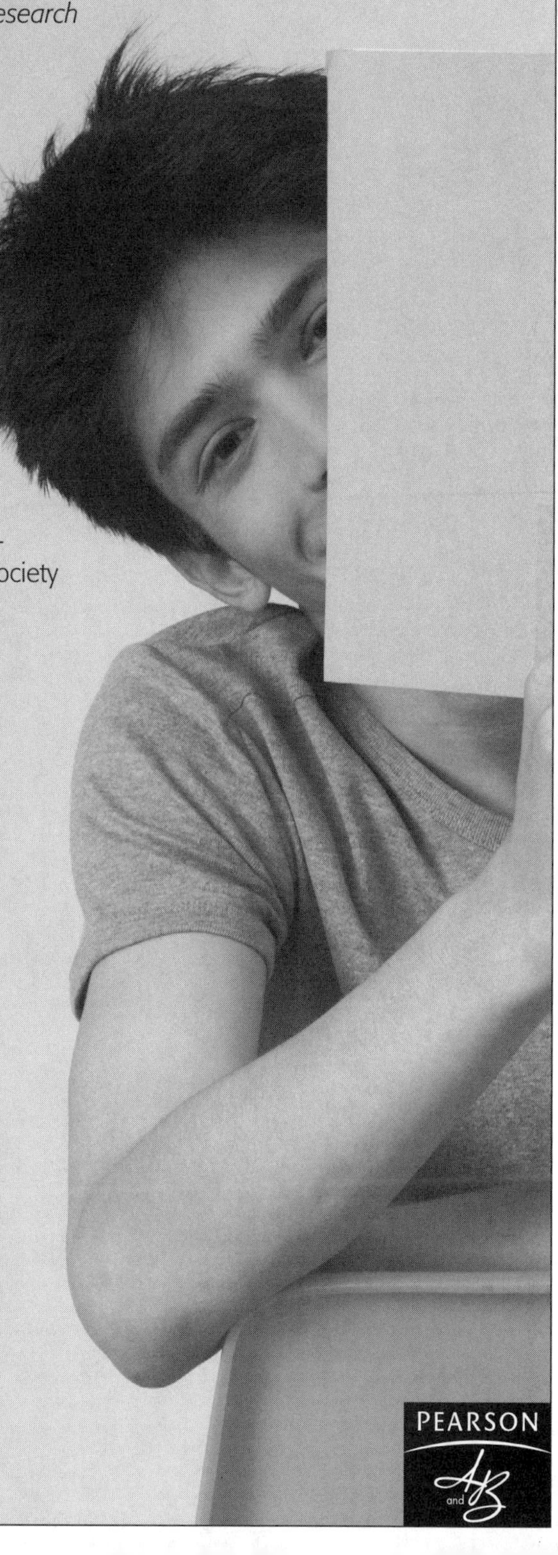

SECOND EDITION

RESEARCH METHODS
A Tool for Life

BERNARD C. BEINS

Ithaca College

Boston New York San Francisco
Mexico City Montreal Toronto London Madrid Munich Paris
Hong Kong Singapore Tokyo Cape Town Sydney

For Linda, Simon, and Agatha, still the center of my universe.

Acquisitions Editor: *Michelle Limoges*
Editorial Assistant: *Christina Manfroni*
Marketing Manager: *Kate Mitchell*
Production Supervisor: *Beth Houston*
Editorial Production Service: *Publishers' Design and Production Services, Inc.*
Manufacturing Buyer: *JoAnne Sweeney*
Electronic Composition: *Publishers' Design and Production Services, Inc.*
Cover Administrator: *Kristina Mose-Libon*

For related titles and support materials, visit our online catalog at www.pearsonhighered.com.

ISBN-13: 978-0-205-53506-4
ISBN-10: 0-205-53506-2

Library of Congress Cataloging-in-Publication Data

Beins, Bernard.
Research methods : a tool for life / Bernard C. Beins.—2nd ed.
p. cm.
Includes bibliographical references and index.
ISBN-13: 978-0-205-53506-4 (alk. paper)
ISBN-10: 0-205-53506-2 (alk. paper)
1. Psychology—Research—Methodology. I. Title.
BF76.5.B439 2009
150.72—dc22 2008031390

Printed in the United States of America

10 9 8 7 6 5 4 3 2 1 13 12 11 10 09 08

CONTENTS

CHAPTER SEVEN
Experiments with One Independent Variable 169

CHAPTER EIGHT
Experiments with Multiple Independent Variables 195

CHAPTER NINE

Expanding on Experimental Designs: Repeated Measures and Quasi-Experiments 217

CHAPTER TEN

Principles of Survey Research 246

CHAPTER ELEVEN

Correlational Research 271

CHAPTER TWELVE

Studying Patterns in the Natural World: Observational Approaches 295

CHAPTER THIRTEEN

Research in Depth: Longitudinal and Single-Case Studies 321

CHAPTER FOURTEEN

People Are Different: Considering Cultural and Individual Differences in Research 349

PREFACE

Writing the first edition of this research methods textbook was an interesting and challenging task. Trying to improve it in the second edition was just as daunting a task. All complex work requires the author to make decisions about what to include or exclude and about where to place certain types of information. In this edition, I think I have made the book more pedagogically sound by the addition of updated material and the exclusion of other material that I believe did not foster student learning.

New features in this edition include a concept map that gives an overview of the main concepts in each chapter and how they relate to one another. It should give the reader a good sense of how the ideas fit into a coherent schema. I also included practice test items in each chapter. These practice tests will give students a preliminary view of how well they have learned the information in each chapter.

One feature that continues in this edition is the material on controversies that relate to the various chapters. These controversies are intended to give the student an awareness that research projects lead to discussions and differences of interpretation, which itself can lead to new research. Psychologists do not address their questions in a vacuum. Social and societal factors are always present to influence what research is done, how it is done, and what interpretations result.

After learning the material in this book, students will have the ability to set up their own research, involving experiments, surveys, correlational designs, and naturalistic observation.

Throughout my work, I benefited from the help of Michelle Limoges and Christina Manfroni; I appreciate their attention to the important matters that I may have initially neglected. I also thank Kathy Whittier for her eagle eye in catching small details that I overlooked.

Once again, I would like to thank the reviewers of this edition for their time and input: Heather Hill, University of Texas at San Antonio; Merry Sleigh-Ritzer, Winthrop University; C. Mark Wessinger, University of Nevada; and Bonnie Wright, Gardner Webb University.

I also acknowledge important figures in my education, starting with Jim Kwiatkowski, then John Jahnke at Miami University and Arthur Reber and Brooklyn College of CUNY. They helped me in myriad ways they probably don't even recognize.

It is important to recognize that students who read this book will be the next generation to produce interesting and useful research. The most compelling reason I can think of for doing psychological research is that is it enjoyable and meaningful to their lives.

Finally, as before, I would be remiss if I didn't acknowledge the importance of my wife, Linda, and my two children, Simon and Agatha, who have always provided support and good humor.

CHAPTER ONE

PSYCHOLOGY, SCIENCE, AND LIFE

CHAPTER OVERVIEW

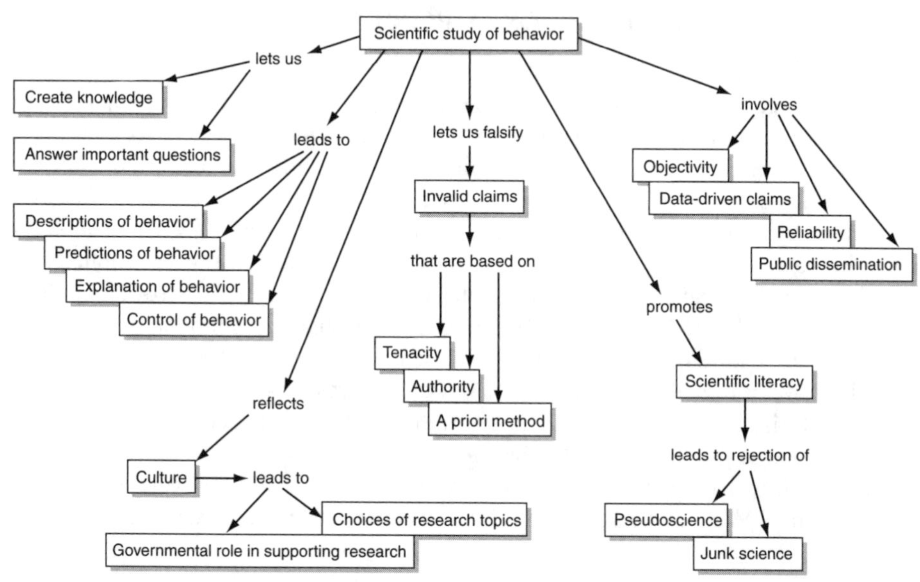

KEY TERMS

a priori method, p. 9
Authority, p. 9
Control, p. 7
Data driven, p. 11
Description, p. 5
Empirical, p. 11
Explanation, p. 5
Falsifiability, p. 6
Junk science, p. 20
Objective, p. 10
Peer review, p. 12
Prediction, p. 7
Pseudoscience, p. 18
Public, p. 12
Replicable, p. 11
Scientific approach, p. 9
Tenacity, p. 9
Verifiable, p. 11

CHAPTER PREVIEW

You probably know a great deal about people and some interesting and important facts about psychology, but you probably know relatively little about psychological research. This book will show you how research helps you learn more about people from a psychological point of view. You can be certain of one thing: There are no simple explanations.

When you read through this chapter, you will learn that there are different ways of knowing about behavior. As a beginning psychologist, you will get a glimpse about why some types of knowledge are more useful than others. In addition, you will see that people can be resistant to changing what they believe. For instance, a lot of people believe in ESP or other paranormal phenomena, even though the scientific evidence for it just isn't there. One reason for such beliefs is that most people don't approach life the same way that scientists do, so the evidence they accept is sometimes pretty shaky.

Finally, this chapter will introduce you to some of the cautions you should be aware of when you read about psychological research in the popular media. Journalists are not scientists and scientists are not journalists, so there is a lot of potential for miscommunication between the two.

WHY ARE RESEARCH METHODS IMPORTANT TOOLS FOR LIFE?

The great thing about psychology is that people are both interesting and complicated, and we get to learn more about them. As you learn more, you will see that there can be a big difference between what we think we know about behavior and what is actually true. If people were easy to figure out, we would have done it by now. That is why you need this course. Your course on research begins the process of learning about how psychological knowledge emerges. This knowledge can be useful when applied to people's lives. For instance, even four years after a domestic terrorist destroyed a federal building in Oklahoma City, killing 168 people, about half the survivors were still suffering from some kind of psychiatric illness (North et al., 1999). Those most at risk refused to think about the devastation and isolated themselves socially. Other characteristics associated with the development of post-traumatic stress disorder (PTSD) are the previous existence of psychiatric problems and the degree to which the individual was directly involved or had friends or relatives who were injured; women were also at higher risk than men. We may be able to use this research to help people who survived the tragedy and devastation of Hurricane Katrina, the horror of the terrorist attacks on the World Trade Center, or other traumatic events that may occur.

We don't have to rely on such extreme examples of the use of psychological research. Scientists have suggested that some people suffer from addiction to indoor tanning (Zeller, Lazovich, Forster, & Widome, 2006). Other investigators have demonstrated that some people showed withdrawal symptoms when the researchers experimentally blocked the physiological effects of tanning (Kaur et al., 2006)

The only way to address such issues is to do research, which means that we need to create knowledge where it does not already exist. It might sound strange to think of "creating" knowledge, but that is exactly what happens in research. You end up with information that didn't exist before. This is one of the exciting parts of doing research: When you complete a study, you know something that nobody else in the world knows.

Creating Knowledge

In reading textbooks or journal articles, we might get the impression that we can carry out a research project and an explanation jumps clearly out of the results. In reality, there is always uncertainty in research. When we plan our investigations, we make many decisions about our procedures; when we examine our results, we usually have to puzzle through them before we are confident that we understand what we are looking at. In textbooks and journals, we only see the end product of ideas that have worked out successfully, and we do not see the twists and turns that led to those successes.

In this course, we will see that we need to use imagination, creativity, and ingenuity in developing knowledge. If we want to address the question of indoor tanning addiction (or any other behavior), we need to understand how we can create knowledge, which is what a course in research methods is all about.

Your course in research methods will also help you prepare for a possible future in psychology. If you attend graduate school, you will see that nearly all programs in psychology require an introductory psychology course, statistics, and research methods or experimental psychology. Most programs do not specify much more than that. Your graduate school professors want you to know how psychologists think; research-based courses provide you with this knowledge. Those professors will provide courses that will help you learn the skills appropriate for your career after you develop the basics. As a psychologist, you also need to understand the research process so you can read scientific journals, make sense of the research reports, and keep abreast of current ideas. Even if you don't choose a career as a researcher, you can still benefit from understanding research. Many jobs require knowledge of statistics and research.

In addition, every day you will be bombarded by claims that scientists have made breakthroughs in understanding various phenomena. It will be useful for you to be able to evaluate whether to believe what you hear. One of the purposes of a course in research is to help you learn how to think critically about the things people tell you. Is their research sound? Is the conclusion they draw the best one? Do they have something to gain from getting certain results? This process of critical thinking is a hallmark of science, but it is also a useful tool in everyday life.

Answering Important Questions

There are many important scientific questions in need of answers. The journal *Science* (Kennedy & Norman, 2005) listed what some scientists see as the top twenty-five questions that society needs to address. At least five of these are associated with issues that psychologists can help address:

- What is the biological basis of consciousness?
- How are memories stored and retrieved?
- How did cooperative behavior evolve?
- To what extent are genetic variation and personal health linked?
- Will the world's population outstrip the world's capability to accommodate 10 billion people?

These questions deal with behavior, either directly or indirectly. As such, psychologists will need to be involved in providing portions of the answers to each of these questions.

Of the next 100 important questions, thirteen are psychological and behavioral, at least in part. These questions appear in Table 1.1, along with the areas of psychology to

TABLE 1.1 Psychological Questions Listed Among the Top Unanswered Questions in *Science* Magazine and the Areas of Psychology Associated with Them (Scriven & Paul, 2005)

Area of Psychology	Question
Social psychology	What are the roots of human culture?
Cognitive psychololgy	What are the evolutionary roots of language and music?
Biological bases of behavior/Cognitive psychology	Why do we sleep?
Personality/Learning	Why do we dream?
Biological bases of behavior	What synchronizes an organism's circadian clocks?
Comparative psychology/Learning	How do migrating organisms find their way?
Social psychology/Biological bases of behavior	What is the biological root of sexual orientation?
Abnormal psychology	What causes schizophrenia?
Developmental psychology	Why are there critical periods for language learning?
Personality theory/Biological bases of behavior	How much of personality is genetic?
Biological bases of behavior	Do pheromones influence human behavior?
Developmental psychology/Biological bases of behavior	What causes autism?
Personality theory	Is morality hardwired into the brain?

which they relate. As you can see, regardless of your specific interest in psychology, you will be able to find important questions to answer.

After you complete this course in research methods, you will be able to apply your new knowledge to areas outside of psychology. The research skills you pick up here will let you complete solid psychological research projects, but they will also help you understand life better.

WHY WE DO RESEARCH

People are curious, social beings. As a result, most of us are interested in what others are up to and why. By the time you read this book, you have been observing others since childhood. You have probably become a sophisticated observer of others' behaviors and can predict pretty well how your friends will react if you act a certain way, at least some of the time. How did you gain this knowledge? Throughout your life, you have done things and then you observed the effect you had on others. Although you probably have not gone through life wearing the stereotypical white lab coat worn by some scientists, you have acted like a scientist when you discovered that "When I do this, they do that." One of the differences between scientific and nonscientific observation, though, is that scientists develop systematic plans, and we work to reduce bias in recording observations. In the end, though, curiosity and enjoyment in finding out about behavior underlies the reason why researchers do their work—they think it is fun.

As curious scientists, we generally work toward four increasingly difficult goals based on our observations: **description**, **explanation**, **prediction,** and **control** of behavior.

Description

Our tendency to act and then to observe others' reactions fulfills what seems to be a basic need for us: describing the world around us. In fact, when you can *describe* events around you, you have taken the first step in scientific discovery. In research, description involves a systematic approach to observing behavior

Description—A goal of science in which behaviors are systematically and accurately characterized.

In your course on behavioral research, you will learn how, as scientists, we systematically begin to understand why people act as they do. The biggest difference between what you do in your everyday observations and what scientists do is that scientists pay attention to a lot of details that we normally think of as unimportant. Unlike most of us in everyday, casual observation, researchers develop a systematic plan for making objective observations so we can generate complete and accurate descriptions.

Explanation

This leads to the second goal of science, *explanation.* When we truly understand the causes of behavior, we can explain them. This is where theory comes in. A theory helps us understand behavior in a general sense. In scientific use, a theory is a general, organizing principle. When we have enough relevant information about behavior, we can

Explanation—A goal of science in which a researcher achieves awareness of why behaviors occur as they do.

develop an explanatory framework that puts all of that information into a nice, neat package—that is, into a theory.

In order to develop a theory, we look at the facts that we believe to be true and try to develop a coherent framework that links the facts to one another. The next step is to test the theory to see if it successfully predicts the results of new research. So we generate hypotheses, which are educated guesses, about behaviors, and we test those hypotheses with research. The research shows us whether our hypotheses are correct; if so, the theory receives further support.

If enough of our hypotheses support a theory, we regard it as more useful in understanding why people act in a certain way; if those hypotheses do not support the theory, we need to revise or abandon the theory. When we conduct research, we should have an open mind about an issue; we might have preconceived ideas of what to expect, but if we are wrong, we should be willing to change our beliefs

Falsifiability—A characteristic of science such that any principle has to be amenable to testing to see if it is true or, more specifically, if it can be shown to be false.

When we test hypotheses, we make them objective and testable. This means that we define our terms clearly so others know how exactly what we mean, and we specify how our research will assess whether a hypothesis is valid. One of the important elements of the scientific method is **falsifiability.** That is, we will test hypotheses to see if we can prove them wrong. If a hypothesis doesn't have the potential to be tested for its validity, it isn't useful scientifically.

For decades, people have used Freudian (psychodynamic) or behavioral theories to try to understand behavior. Both approaches have generated useful ideas about human behavior and have been accepted, at least in part, by the general public. You can see the impact of Freudian theory if you consider some of Freud's terms that have gained currency in everyday language, like repression, penis envy, or Freudian slips.

Some psychologists believe that many of Freud's ideas are not scientifically valid. In fact, when Freudian ideas have been subjected to experimentation, they often have not stood up well. In a perspective as complicated as psychodynamic theory, though, there is still disagreement about the scientific status of ideas such as unconscious processing of information, and some psychologists maintain that Freudian ideas have received support from research (Westen, 1998).

Behavioral terms have also made their way into everyday language, as when people talk about positive or negative reinforcement. In the case of behaviorism, most psychologists affirm that it is a truly scientific approach. The ideas are objective and testable; in a wide variety of research programs, the utility of behavioral ideas has been well established.

In research, we use hypotheses to make predictions about behavior; theories are useful for helping us explain why our predictions are accurate. As psychologists, we use theory to explain behavior. Our explanations differ from the ones we generate in everyday life in that scientific explanations involve well-specified statements of when behaviors will or will not occur.

Prediction

After you describe what people are likely to do in a certain situation, the next logical step is to expand your knowledge beyond simple description. The third step is to *predict* behavior. Suppose you tell a joke. You are likely to make a prediction about how your friends will react to it. They may laugh, cry, show sympathy, or walk away in disgust. In considering whether to tell the story, you are making a prediction about their responses. Every time you tell a story, you are engaging in a kind of experiment, making a prediction about the outcome. Naturally, you are sometimes wrong in your prediction because people are not easy to figure out.

Prediction—A goal of science in which a researcher can specify in advance those situations in which a particular behavior will occur.

Similarly, in behavioral research, we sometimes make poor predictions. When that happens, a scientist will try to figure out why the predictions were wrong and will attempt to make better ones next time. A big difference between casual and scientific predictions is that scientists generally specify in great detail what factors led to a given outcome. For most of us in everyday life, we have a vague notion of what behaviors to expect from others and, as a result, will accept our predictions as true if somebody behaves in ways that are roughly approximate to what we expected. There is a lot of room for error.

In our relationships with others, we find it helpful to describe and to predict their behaviors because it gives us a sense of control; we know in advance what will happen. At the same time, most of us want to know even more. We want to know *why* people act as they do. This is a difficult process because people's behaviors arise for a lot of reasons. Sigmund Freud believed that behaviors arise from multiple causes. As such, he said they were overdetermined. Even psychologists who do not believe in Freud's ideas generally agree that behaviors do not emerge from a single cause.

Control

The final step in the scientific study of behavior is *control.* Some people may ask whether it is right for us to try to control others' behaviors. Most psychologists would respond that we affect others' behaviors, just as they affect ours. It is not a matter of *should* we control behavior, but rather *how* does it happen. For example, parents try to raise children who show moral behavior. It would be reassuring to parents if they knew how to create such behavior in their children.

Control—A goal of science in which a researcher can manipulate variables in order to produce specific behaviors.

In order to exert control of behavior effectively, we need to understand why the behavior occurs as it does. To understand the elements of control, we need to have well formulated theories. At this point, we don't have a single theory of behavior that can capture the variety of human experience.

Psychologists with different theoretical orientations may use similar statements in describing behavior, but they will begin to diverge when making predictions, become even more different regarding explanation, and even more so with respect to control. Table 1.2 summarizes the four different goals of science and how psychologists have used them at various points in their research programs.

TABLE 1.2 Table 1.2 Example of the Goals of Research and How They Relate to the Development of Knowledge

Description	One evening in 1964, a woman named Kitty Genovese was attacked and murdered while walking home from work at 3 A.M. in Queens, New York. Thirty-eight people saw what was happening from their apartment windows, but nobody helped; nobody even called the police. Two psychologists (e.g., Latané & Darley, 1970) wondered why this might happen. Their first step in understanding this phenomenon was to describe what happened. Based on descriptions of the initial event, Latané and Darley (1970) investigated some of the implications of Genovese's murder as they relate to helping behavior. This event was so striking that it led to an enormous amount of research and analysis (e.g., Cunningham, 1984; Takooshian & O'Connor, 1984) and stands as a prime example of research that results from something that occurs outside the laboratory. (See Cialdini, 1980, for a discussion of using naturally occurring events as a basis for behavioral research.)
Explanation	Once we can document and predict events, we can try to explain why behaviors occur. Psychologists have identified some of the underlying factors that may help us understand why people do not help others. As Darley and Latané (1970) have noted, when there are more people around, we are less likely to notice that somebody needs help, and even when we notice, we are less likely to offer aid. Part of this failure to act involves what has been called diffusion of responsibility; that is, when others are around, we can pass blame for our inaction to them, assuming less (or none) for ourselves.
Prediction	We can try to determine those conditions where helping behavior is likely to occur. Helping occurs as people try to avoid feeling guilty (Katsev, Edelsack, Steinmetz, Walker, & Wright, 1978), and helping diminishes if people have been relieved of guilt (Cialdini, Darby, & Vincent, 1973). In addition, if people believe that another individual is similar to them, they will help (Batson, Duncan, Ackerman, Buckley, & Birch, 1981). Helping behavior involves complicated dynamics, so it will be difficult to identify precisely those conditions in which helping will occur, but we have identified some variables that allow us to make generally accurate predictions.
Control	Once we are confident of our predictions, we can ultimately control behavior. Behaviors in everyday life are seldom controlled by a single variable, but we can control behavior to a degree by manipulating the relevant variables. Programs to help poverty-stricken people often rely on guilt or empathic pleas. Depending on the particulars of the circumstances, we may help others if our mood is positive because we tend to generalize our good mood to everything around us (Clark & Teasdale, 1985); or we may help if our mood is negative, but we think that helping somebody will improve our mood (Manucia, Baumann, & Cialdini, 1984). Knowledge of these effects can help us control behaviors.

WHAT CONSTITUTES SCIENTIFIC KNOWLEDGE?

There are different paths to factual knowledge in our lives. We will see that not all roads to knowledge are equally useful. The nineteenth-century U.S. philosopher Charles Sanders Peirce (1877) identified several ways of knowing, which he called **tenacity**, **authority**, the **a priori method**, and the **scientific approach**. Others have added **experience**.

Tenacity involves simply believing something because you don't want to give up your belief. People do this all the time; you have probably discovered that it can be difficult to convince people to change their minds, concluding that they are simply being stubborn. But they are probably thinking exactly the same about you. If two people hold mutually contradictory beliefs, both cannot be true. According to Peirce, in a "saner moment," we might recognize that others have valid points, which can shake our own beliefs.

Tenacity—The mode of accepting knowledge because one is comfortable with it and simply wants to hold onto it.

Authority—The mode of accepting knowledge because a person in a position of authority claims that something is true or valid.

a priori method—The mode of accepting knowledge based on a premise that people have agreed on, followed by reasoned argument.

Scientific approach—The mode of accepting knowledge based on empirically derived data.

Experience—A way of knowing that uses personal experience as the means of deciding what is true about behavior.

An alternative to an individual's belief in what is true, Peirce thought, could reside in what authorities say is true. This approach removes the burden from any single person to make decisions; instead, one would rely on an expert of some kind. Peirce talked about authorities who would force beliefs under threat of some kind of penalty, but we can generalize to any acceptance of knowledge because somebody whom we trust says something is true. As Peirce noted, though, experts with different perspectives will hold different beliefs. How is one to know which expert is actually right?

Belief: If a child ate a hot dog and got sick, he or she would likely avoid hot dogs in the future for fear of getting sick again. Everybody has probably had the experience of eating a particular food and later becoming ill, so that we associate the food with illness. This is such a powerful experience that when it happens, we develop a firm belief that we should not eat that food. Such a feeling is remarkably resistant to change; we don't eat a food, even though we might know that the food is usually safe.

We probably persist in not eating the food because our bodies have developed the strategy to avoid foods that lead to sickness. Animal pests, like rats, are very good at drawing the same conclusion about food and illness, leading to a phenomenon called "bait shyness." If we put out poisoned food, they will sample a little of it. If they get sick, they will avoid that food in the future. This is a wise decision for the animals, even if it frustrates people.

Experience can lead us to an erroneous conclusion about a certain food. Coming up with a general belief based on a single episode is not a very effective way to gain knowledge. Single episodes may not represent reality in general. We might have great confidence in our beliefs based on experience, but confidence does not equate with truth.

Peirce also suggested that people might fix their knowledge based on consensus and reasoned argument, the *a priori* approach. The problem here, he wrote, was that reasons for believing something may change over time, so what was seen as true in the past may change. If we want to know universal truths, he reasoned, the most valid approach is through science, which is objective and self-correcting. Gradually, we can accumulate knowledge that is valid and discard ideas that prove to be wrong.

One of the major differences between scientific knowledge and other kinds of knowledge is that scientific work is much more systematic than casual observation. In addition, researchers abide by certain general principles in deciding what to believe. Our scientific knowledge relies on the fact that our observations are objective, data-driven, public, and potentially replicable. We will see shortly what this means, but what it all comes down to is the fact that, as scientists and as good decision makers, we need to evaluate how well research has been done. If we decide that the investigators have done everything correctly, we should be willing to change our minds about what we believe to be true, even if we don't like the truth. As it turns out, people are so complicated that a single research study will never lead to a complete change in beliefs; the process is incremental, with a series of small steps rather than a giant leap.

Science Is Objective

What does it mean for our observations to be **objective**? One implication is that we define clearly the concepts we are dealing with. This is often easier said than done. Psychologists deal with complex and abstract concepts that are hard to measure. Nonetheless, we have to develop some way to measure these concepts in clear and systematic ways. For example, suppose we want to find out whether we respond more positively to attractive people than to others.

Objective—Measurements that are not affected by personal bias and that are well-defined and specified are considered objective.

To answer our question, we first have to define what we mean by "attractive." The definition must be objective; that is, the definition has to be consistent, clear, and understandable, even though it may not be perfect.

Researchers have taken various routes to creating objective definitions of attractiveness. Wilson (1978) simply mentioned that "a female confederate . . . appearing either attractive or unattractive asked in a neutral manner for directions to a particular building on central campus at a large Midwestern University" (p. 313). This vague statement doesn't really tell us as much as we would like to know. We don't have a clear definition of what the researchers meant by "attractiveness." Juhnke, Barmann, Cunningham, and Smith (1987) varied the attire of people who seemed to be in need of help. The researchers defined attractiveness based on clothing. Unattractive people, that is, those wearing less desirable clothing, received help, even though they did not look very attractive.

On the other hand, Bull and Stevens (1980) used helpers with either good or bad teeth. In this case, attractive was defined as having good teeth, whereas unattractive was defined as having bad teeth. In this study, it didn't matter whether a person had good teeth. People were just as likely to help those with bad teeth, although they were willing to do so for a shorter length of time.

If the different research teams did not report how they created an unattractive appearance, we would have a harder time evaluating their research and repeating it exactly as they did it. It may be very important to know what manipulation the researchers used. Differences in attractiveness due to the kinds of clothes you are wearing may not lead to the same reactions as differences due to unsightly teeth.

Interestingly, Stokes and Bikman (1974) found that people may be less willing to ask help *from* attractive people than from unattractive people. In their study, they defined attractiveness on the basis of physical appearance as rated by other people. This strategy relies on a clear and consistent method of defining attractiveness. Because attractiveness can be defined in many ways, we need to tell others what we mean when we use the term, which is what we mean by objectivity.

Science Is Data Driven

Our conclusions as scientists must also be **data driven.** This simply means that our conclusions must follow logically from our data. There may be several equally good interpretations from a single set of data. Regardless of which interpretation we choose, it has to be based on the data we collect.

To say that science is based on data is to say that it is **empirical**. Empiricism refers to the method of discovery that relies on systematic observation and data for drawing conclusions. Psychology is an empirical discipline in that knowledge is based on the results of research, that is, on data.

Data driven—Interpretations of research that are based on objective results of a project are considered data driven.

Empirical—Relying on systematic observation and data collection for guidance on drawing conclusions.

The critical point here is that if we are to develop a more complete and accurate understanding of the world around us, scientific knowledge based on data will, in the long run, serve us better than intuition alone. Don't discount intuition entirely; quite a few scientific insights had their beginnings in intuitions that were scientifically studied and found to be true. We just can't rely on it entirely because it is not always right.

Science Is Replicable and Verifiable

Our scientific knowledge has to be potentially **replicable** and **verifiable.** This means that others should have the opportunity to repeat a research project to see if the same results occur each time. Maybe the researchers who are trying to repeat the study will generate the same result; maybe they will not. We do not claim that *results* are scientific; rather, we claim that the *approach* is scientific. Any time somebody makes a claim but will not let others verify it as valid, we should be skeptical.

Replicable—When scientists can recreate a previous research study, that study is replicable.

Verifiable—When scientists can reproduce a previous research study and generate the same results, it is verifiable.

Why should one scientist repeat somebody else's research? As it turns out, there is a bias among journal editors to publish findings that show differences across groups and to reject studies showing no differences. So a relatively large number of research reports may describe differences that occurred accidentally. That is, groups may differ, but not for any systematic or reproducible reason. If the researcher were to repeat the study, a different result would occur.

Ioannidis (2005), referring to genetic and biomedical research, noted that "there is increasing concern that in modern research, false findings may be the majority or even the vast majority of published research claims" (p. 696). His conclusion comes, in part, from a recognition that journal editors and researchers are more impressed by findings that show that something interesting occurred but not by findings that do not reveal interesting patterns. Ioannidis's speculation may be true for psychological research, just as it is for biologically based studies.

Psychologists have recognized this problem for quite some time (e.g., Rosenthal, 1979). Fortunately, when a research project is repeated and when the same outcome results, our confidence in the results increases markedly (Moonesinghe, Khoury, & Janssens, 2007). The reason that replication of research is such a good idea is that it helps us to weed out findings that turn out to be false and to strengthen our confidence in findings that are valid.

Sometimes even when researchers follow a completely scientific path, there can be great controversy in the conclusions about what the research is telling us. For instance, in the controversy surrounding the cause of rape, there are at least two distinctly different schools of thought. One approach invokes the ideas of evolutionary psychology. The other is more socially oriented. Both groups have data and theory to support their ideas, although both are clearly still incomplete.

In the Controversy on rape on page 21, you can see two very different theoretical approaches to the study of why rape occurs. The arguments are heated, and each camp believes that it has useful insights into the problem.

Science Is Public

Public—Scientists make their research public, typically by making presentations at conferences or by publishing their work in journal articles or books.

Peer review—A process in which researchers submit their research for publication in a journal or presentation at a conference to other experts in the field who evaluate the research.

When we say that our research is **public,** we mean this literally. Scientists only recognize research as valid or useful when they can scrutinize it. Generally, we accept research as valid if it has undergone **peer review.** For instance, when a psychologist completes research, the next step is often to write the results in a journal article and submit it for publication in a research journal. The editor of the journal will send the manuscript to experts in the field for their comments. If the editor and the reviewers agree that major problems have been taken care of, the article will appear in the journal. Otherwise, the article will be rejected. Among major journals in psychology, about a quarter or fewer of all manuscripts submitted are published. Another approach to making our research public involves submitting a proposal to a research conference for a presentation. The process for acceptance to a conference resembles that for acceptance by a journal. In some cases, researchers may initially present their ideas at a conference, then follow up with a published article.

THE INTERACTION OF SCIENCE AND CULTURE

Many people undoubtedly think of science as happening in laboratories remote from the lives of real people. Nothing could be farther from the truth. Scientists live in communities and go to the same movies you do, coach their children's soccer teams, and worry about the same things that you do. Not surprisingly, culture shapes the research conducted by many scientists because our culture shapes the way we think.

For example, after the terrorist attacks in the United States, some person or persons sent anthrax spores through the mail, infecting a number of people and killing some of them. This spurred increased scientific attention to anthrax.

In addition, in an energy crisis, researchers in psychology, biology, physics, and chemistry are motivated to study patterns of energy-using behavior, the development of biofuels, creation of efficient technologies, and conservation of energy. When environmental issues loom, those in the natural sciences may be predisposed to focus on ecological issues. With the AIDS crisis, medical researchers have often concentrated on issues related to it. Psychologists are as much a part of the community as anyone, so it should come as no surprise that our research reflects the needs and concerns of our society.

Discussion of research ideas are also affected by social attitudes. After Thornhill and Palmer (2000) proposed their evolutionary suggestions about rape in *The Sciences* (in the Controversy on rape), the consequent letters to the editor took an overwhelmingly negative tone (Jennings, 2000; Müller, 2000; Steinberg, Tooney, Sutton, & Denmark, 2000; Tang-Martínez & Mechanic, 2000).

Can it be that not a single scientist, or even any reader of *The Sciences*, supported Thornhill and Palmer's ideas? It is more likely that people have refrained from writing letters in support of the evolutionary argument because they know that a great many people will take them to task for it. We can easily imagine that fear of reprisal might lead some people to avoid conducting research in the area. As such, research that might clarify the issue may never take place because nobody is willing to pursue it.

The Government's Role in Science

Societal issues often dictate scientific research, in part because of the way money is allocated for research. The federal government funds a great deal of the research that occurs in colleges and universities, where most scientific developments occur. As such, the government plays a large role in determining what kind of research takes place. How does the government decide which areas of research should have priority in funding? Ultimately, the decision makers pay attention to issues of pressing importance to taxpayers. This view simplifies the dynamics of how federal money is allocated for research; even in the so-called pure and abstract sciences, societal demands affect the types of questions that scientists ask. If researchers do not get funding for asking one question, they will ask a different question for which they can receive financial support.

In the United States, the federal government actively directs some scientific research. For instance, the highly secretive National Security Agency employs more mathematicians than any other organization in the world (Singh, 1999). These people work on finding ways to create and break secret codes that affect political, economic, and military activities. Many mathematicians who research the use of codes do so because the government encourages it.

Further, the U.S. government has affected social research indirectly, sometimes through questionable means. Harris (1980) noted that beginning in the 1930s, the Federal Bureau of Investigation (FBI) engaged in surveillance and kept files on the American Psychological Association (APA) and the Society for the Psychological Study of Social Issues, now a division of APA. The FBI used informants who reported on colleagues. One incident that Harris cited involved an individual who informed on a colleague who had spoken out against racism at the 1969 APA convention. The result of such activities by the government, according to Harris, may have been to lead psychologists to abandon some lines of research (e.g., on racial attitudes) because they were too controversial.

Cultural Values and Science

Even when governmental interference is not an issue, there are still cultural aspects to our research. For example, some people feel strongly that a woman should remain at home raising her children rather than taking them to a daycare center while she works. An examination of the amount of research effort devoted to the effects of childcare outside the home reveals that few behavioral scientists showed much interest in the question until the past decade or so. In fact, a search through the primary psychological database on research, PsycINFO©, reveals that the first citation with the term "childcare" in an abstract did not occur until 1927; for a long time, the use of that term was often associated with orphanages. In the early 1900s, the social issue of childcare was nonexistent. Work then was more likely to center around the home, and the primary caregivers, the mothers, were less likely to work outside the home. Thus, the issue of the effects of childcare centers on the development of children was irrelevant to society.

In contemporary life, women's work has moved from inside the home to outside, and there are more single parents who must have paying jobs. The increase in research on the effects of childcare centers has become important to many people, including psychologists, spurring an increase in psychological research on the topic. The issues are complex, and different researchers have generated conflicting results, so we still see considerable controversy surrounding the topic. Until the issue is resolved, this important societal concern will receive continued attention.

Another example of the effect of culture on research involves a commonly used technique to assess attitudes and opinions. Psychologists regularly ask people to rate something on a scale of one to seven. (Technically, this is called a Likert-type scale, named after the U.S. psychologist Rensis Likert, who pioneered this popular technique.) The use of such a scale may not be appropriate for people in cultures different than ours because it calls for a certain mindset that others don't share with us (Carr, Munro, & Bishop, 1995). People in non-Western cultures may not think it makes sense to assess a complex concept on a simple rating scale. We tend to assume that others think as we do, but such an assumption may lead to research results that lack validity. Greater numbers of psychologists are addressing these concerns and focusing more systematically on cultural issues in research (see Matsumoto, 1994; Price & Crapo, 1999).

A person's culture determines not only what behaviors are of interest, but how those behaviors are studied. Cultural perspective also influences how scientists interpret their data. An interesting example of the way that societal topics affect research occurred as Hugo Münsterberg (1914) decided to study whether women should be allowed to participate on juries. This topic is irrelevant now, but in the early 1900s, it was controversial. Some people thought that women wouldn't do as good a job on a jury as men did. The Controversy on female jurors presents the issues, which sheds light on how attitudes change as cultures change.

CONTROVERSY: Should Women Serve as Jurors?

Psychologists are affected by the times in which they work. Their research ideas reflect the social milieu. This point is important here because the research that people view as important in one time may not carry over to another era. For instance, in the first decade of the twentieth century, Hugo Münsterberg, one of the most prominent psychologists in the United States, reported the results of investigations of the question of whether women show the appropriate mental processes that would allow them to take part in jury deliberations (Münsterberg, 1914). He presented a group of men and a group of women a pair of displays that had different numbers of dots and asked them to vote on which display contained more dots. After a group debate of the issue, they voted again.

What does this simple procedure have to do with the way trials are conducted and whether women should serve as jurors during those trials? According to Münsterberg (1914), the psychologist studies "thoughts and emotions and feelings and deeds which move our social world. But . . . he must simplify them and bring them down to the most elementary situations, in which only the characteristic mental actions are left" (pp. 186–187). As a researcher you need to simplify complex situations so you can study each important issue individually, without being affected by complicating factors. We still do this today in psychological research; in fact, scientists in every discipline do this because reality is too complex to be studied in its fullest extent in a single study.

In Münsterberg's research, at a final vote, the percentage accuracy for the men went from guessing (52%) to reasonably accurate (78%). Women, on the other hand, began at 45 percent correct and stayed unimproved at 45 percent.

Münsterberg concluded that women were too stubborn to benefit from group discussions; they would not change their minds when confronted with evidence. He asserted that the difference in the way men and women respond to debate "makes the men fit and the women unfit for the particular task which society requires from the jurymen" (p. 198). When he published his conclusions, quite a number of people argued against them, including many women.

A few years later, another psychologist, Harold Burtt (1920) conceptually replicated Münsterberg's study. Burtt asked women and men to try to detect when people were lying to them in a laboratory study involving simulated trial witnesses. The participants then discussed the veracity of the witness and decided again. Burtt found that men and women were equally proficient in their ability to use debate to arrive at a reasonable conclusions.

Burtt's conclusion was that women were as suitable for jury work as men were. In fact, he reported that men were more willing to attribute lies to simulated witnesses who were actually telling the truth. Does this suggest that women are more appropriate for jury deliberation than men are? Because our society holds men in such high regard, the research that might answer this question might never be done.

It is interesting and important to be aware that neither Münsterberg nor Burtt ever hinted that they should ask the question of whether men should sit on juries. This is an important fact because it reveals that the social environment influences what questions are asked as well as what questions are *not* asked. If we intend to use our research to help answer real life problems, we need to remember that no single experiment is going to answer a complex social question, but each one provides a small part of the answer. Our decisions will be better if we base them on sound research, but we also need to remember that we have to evaluate the research to see if it adequately answers the questions we are asking.

Questions for Discussion: Do you believe that research projects like those of Münsterberg and Burtt could potentially contribute answers to social questions? Should we conclude that women are unfit for jury duty?

SCIENTIFIC LITERACY

Even if you don't engage in research yourself, it is important to be scientifically literate in our society. News about science abounds on the Internet, on television, and in newspapers and magazines. In addition, voters must decide about scientific issues, like whether the federal or state governments should fund stem cell research or should act to prevent possible global warming. In order to understand the issues, citizens need to understand the nature of scientific research.

Scientific literacy is a specialized form of critical thinking, which involves developing clear and specific questions, collecting and assessing relevant information, identifying important assumptions and perspectives, and generating effective solutions to problems (Scriven & Paul, 2007). These are all goals associated with conducting research.

Are people as scientifically literate as they should be? Unfortunately, research has suggested that about 28 percent of Americans qualify as being scientifically literate (Miller, 2007a, b). This figure is low, but it actually represents progress. In the 1980s and early 1990s, only about 10 percent were scientifically literate.

How can you develop scientific literacy? One way to foster such literacy is to learn about and to conduct research (Holmes, Beins, & Lynn, 2007). Knowledge of the process of doing research appears to facilitate an awareness of the scientific process. More specifically, training in psychological research prepares a person for the kind of thinking associated with scientific literacy and critical thinking as well as or better than training In other scientific disciplines (Lehman, Lempert, & Nisbett, 1988).

Science and Pseudoscience

Various people believe in phenomena that scientists reject as being invalid. For instance, many patients and some medical practitioners believe that homeopathic medicine is effective in treating physical illness. According to mainstream medical workers, homeopathy not effective and is not even scientifically based.

Homeopathic medicines contain ingredients that have been so diluted that a dose may not even have a single molecule of the substance. Furthermore, controlled scientific studies have demonstrated a lack of effectiveness of homeopathic treatments. The few studies that show an effect generally reveal weak effects and may be methodologically flawed. Why do such people refuse to change their beliefs about this approach? There are many reasons, but one of them is that believers do not approach homeopathy from within a scientific framework. their belief in homeopathy stems more from a reliance on tenacity or authority.

Belief in paranormal phenomena like ESP, astrology, mental telepathy, and ghosts is perhaps more prevalent in the United States than belief in homeopathy. Although scientists firmly reject the existence of such phenomena, surveys have revealed that nearly three-quarters of all Americans believe in at least some of these things (Moore, 2005). If you look at Figure 1.1, you will see the disconnect between the general public and scientists. Why do so many people lend credibility to these ideas when the majority of scientists who have studied these things have found essentially no support for

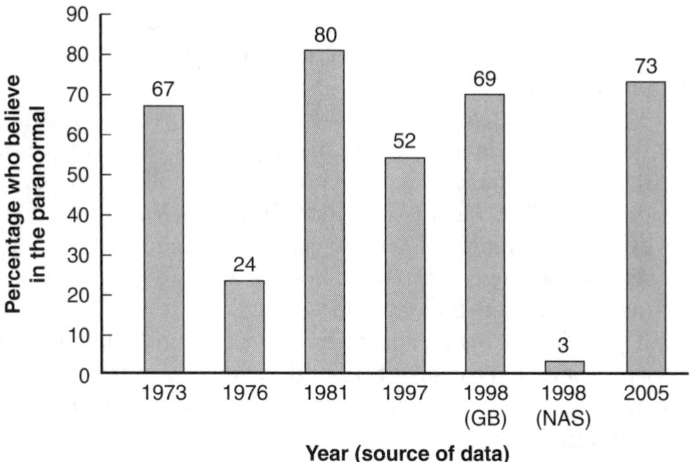

FIGURE 1.1 Percentage of respondents who claim to believe in some kind of paranormal phenomenon in different studies.

Sources:

[a]1973 and 1998 (GB): Radford (1998), nonrandom samples from Great Britain.
[b] 1976 and 1997: Nisbett (1998), random samples from the United States.
[c] 1981: Singer and Benassi (1980), random samples from the United States.
[d] 1998 (NAS), sample of members of the National Academy of Sciences in the United States.
[e] 2005: Random sample from the United States.

them? A number of years ago the magician James Randi (whose stage name is The Amazing Randi) issued a challenge that he would award $1,000,000 to anybody who could demonstrate paranormal phenomena that he could not successfully disprove through rigorous testing. To date, nobody has been able to do so, although some people have tried.

Most scientists reject the notion that paranormal phenomena exist. The most notable reason for scientific skepticism is that, under controlled conditions, the evidence for phenomena like ESP or mental telepathy remarkably disappear. Before we do the research, we should have an open mind about the issue, but we need to abandon such beliefs if research shows no evidence of their existence.

Another basis for rejection of paranormal phenomena is that most of the explanations offered for such events are inconsistent with the physical laws that scientists recognize. If there is no way to explain a phenomenon, scientists are reluctant to accept it as valid. So sometimes researchers have failed to accept new ideas because they could not explain those ideas; it may take a while for theory to catch up to fact. Regarding paranormal phenomena, the well-established laws of physics that have led to our current marvels of technology cannot explain something like ESP. The failure to explain how the paranormal could occur and the inability to document these phenomena in the laboratory have made scientists reluctant to embrace them.

From the viewpoint of many psychologists, the term "parapsychology" is seen as unfortunate because it links our scientifically oriented discipline with **pseudoscience.**

Pseudoscience—A domain of inquiry that has the superficial appearance of being scientific but that does not rely on the critical scientific principles of objectivity, verifiability, empiricism, and being public.

We regard a discipline as pseudoscientific when it claims that its knowledge derives from scientific research but fails to follow the basic principles of science.

Many scientists have worked to dispel pseudoscientific myths (e.g., Radner & Radner, 1982; Zusne & Jones, 1989), as have other critical thinkers, like James Randi. There are also publications that foster critical thinking about such issues, like *The Skeptical Inquirer.* This periodical exists to examine and debunk claims of paranormal phenomena. When scrutinized, these claims don't hold up well. Table 1.3 reflects some of the major characteristics of pseudoscience.

In general, pseudosciences are characterized by a reliance on flimsy and questionable evidence, a resistance to change or further development of theory, a lack of ways to test the ideas, avoidance of contradictory information, and a lack of critical thought about ways to develop the theory.

Warning Signs of Bogus Science

As a consumer of research, you can spot some of the issues associated with claims that appear to be based on science but that are not. Even if you are not knowledgeable about the technical issues associated with a scientific topic, there are some warning signs that you should be dubious about facts that others claim are true, as noted by physicist Robert Park (2003).

The first warning sign is when an investigator publicizes claims in the popular press rather than in a scientific journal. If an article appears in a journal, it will have undergone careful scrutiny by professionals in the field. Scientists are skeptical when a research claim first appears in the news because other scientists have probably not assessed its validity.

Second, when somebody claims that the scientific establishment is trying to suppress research findings, you should be careful. It may be difficult to publish radically new findings in a journal, so valid claims may need a higher standard of proof, but if the findings result from valid scientific approaches, journals will publish new work.

A third sign to be cautious is when a researcher's findings are difficult to detect, thus difficult to verify by an independent judge. A fourth problem appears when the only data for a discovery involve anecdotes, or stories, that other researchers cannot investigate more fully. One of the problems with anecdotes is that they can lead to powerful, emotional responses, so people are likely to accept claims about the stories as being valid. An unusual occurrence may take place, but scientists are unwilling to accept it as being real if they cannot investigate how general the phenomenon is.

A fifth warning sign is the claim by the investigator that a phenomenon is real because people have known about it for centuries. Simply because people have made claims for a long time does not indicate that their claims are correct. For hundreds of years, people thought that the earth was only a few thousand years old; we know now that this claim is not true.

The next sign that you should be wary of is that the investigator worked alone and discovered an important phenomenon that nobody else had happened upon. New find-

TABLE 1.3 Characteristics of Pseudoscience

General Characteristics	Example
Pseudoscientists believe that there is no more to be learned; they fail to generate testable hypotheses or to conduct objective tests of theory. There tends to be no advancement of knowledge in the field, which is resistant to change. There are few tests of previous claims.	Homeopathic medicine makes claims about cures that are not based on research. The ideas never change and believers do not conduct systematic tests that would disconfirm their ideas.
Pseudoscience is based on dogma and uncritical belief; there may be hostility in the fact of counterevidence or disagreement.	Creationism is accepted by some as a matter of faith. There is no attempt to subject its tenets to scientific scrutiny. In addition, when disagreements arise, believers often show antagonism toward the individual without dealing with the evidence.
There is a suppression or distortion of unfavorable data; selective use of data, including looking only for supportive information (confirmation bias).	People who believe that psychics can foretell the future will accept just about any statement that seems correct but will ignore errors in predictions.
Many ideas are not amenable to scientific evaluation; ideas are subjective and can't be tested objectively.	There have been claims that we have an undetectable aura surrounding us. If it is undetectable, there is to way to verify its presence.
There is an acceptance of proof with data of questionable validity; the lack of evidence is taken as support that a claim *could* be true.	Some people conclude that there is evidence for the existence of UFOs on the basis of anecdotal reports in the popular media or ancient myths. There is little or no independent evaluation of ideas, but more a reliance on evidence that is not questioned.
Personal anecdotes and events that cannot be tested systematically are used to provide evidence; there is often a reliance on "experts" with no real expertise.	Anybody who claims an experience about foretelling the future or who relates a supposed experience with aliens becomes an expert whose statements are not to be questioned.
Pseudoscience involves terms that sound like scientific ideas, but the terms are not clearly defined. Often the ideas violate known scientific principles.	Varieties of extrasensory perception include phenomena like *telekinesis*, which sounds scientific. In reality, it is a poorly defined (and undocumented) notion. Paranormal phenomena do not conform to known physical laws, such as the fact that for all known forms of energy, the force exerted declines over distance, which is not the case for ESP, according to its adherents.
Pseudoscientific phenomena are "shy" or "fragile" in that they often disappear or weaken noticeably when subjected to well-designed experiments, especially with nonbelievers.	The ability to identify stimuli that are not visible is sometimes striking when two believers conduct a study; when independent scientists conduct the study, the effect is often attenuated or eliminated.

(continues)

General Characteristics	Example
Pseudoscience involves looking for mysteries that have occurred rather than trying to generate and test explanations for the phenomena.	Sometimes people solicit incidents from people who seem unusual. For instance, mystery hunters look might look for instances when a person seems to have foretold the future in a dream, ignoring the fact that if you look at enough dreams, you can find coincidental patterns that resist normal explanations.
Pseudoscientists engage in explanation by scenario. They identify a phenomenon and provide an explanation that fits the facts after they are known, but doesn't provide a means for making predictions in advance.	Some years ago, Julian Jaynes suggested that, historically, the two hemispheres in the human brain were not connected as they are now. Thus, brain activity in the right hemisphere was perceived to be the voices of gods. Unfortunately for this explanation, there is no credible evidence that it is true. In fact, given what we know about evolution, there is no realistic way that our brains could have evolved as Jaynes suggested.

ings are almost invariably the result of the accumulation of ideas. Contemporary science almost involves a community of researchers or, at least, an awareness by a single researcher of the work of others.

Finally, if a researcher makes a bold claim of an entirely novel finding, the researcher must be able to propose a physical or scientific law that can account for the phenomenon. If a finding does not accord with the natural laws that scientists have established, the researcher must develop a coherent and believable explanation for the phenomenon.

Junk Science

Sometimes people, including scientists, use scientific research to promote their own causes. When they use science inappropriately, they may make claims that look good on the surface but that are really not valid. The term for such uses is called **junk science**. This term is as much a rhetorical term as a scientific one; that is, it is a term related to making arguments to support one's beliefs. A person using junk science is more interested in winning the argument than in presenting sound, valid scientific information.

Junk science—The use of scientific research for nonscientific goals, a term with negative connotations suggesting a problem with the way scientific research is used.

Sometimes people making arguments with junk science will call upon data and research results of questionable validity. For instance, according to the Union of Concerned Scientists, people may make use of data that have not gone through peer review, meaning that experts in the field have not had the opportunity to examine the research procedures or the data. Another hallmark of junk science is the use of simple data from complex research projects to generate a solution to a complicated problem. If the problem is complicated, it is not likely that a solution will emerge based on simple data.

There is no clear definition of what constitutes valid science versus junk science. Sometimes it is a matter of perspective by the person using it and the person hearing it.

CONTROVERSY: Why Do Men Rape?

The act of rape constitutes one of the most horrific invasions of one's person. Most rapes, as we know, are committed by men against women. Psychologists have investigated such crimes, trying to figure out why they happen. Not surprisingly, rape is a complex issue, and we do not yet have a clear understanding of its dynamics.

At the same time, at least two very different views have emerged about why rape occurs. These two theoretical perspectives both deal with the same phenomenon; that is, they both describe the same behavior. The two theories begin to differ, though, in their consideration of predicting when the behavior will occur. They bear little resemblance to one another when it comes to explaining why rape occurs. Finally, they also provide contrasting pictures of how to control (i.e., prevent) rape.

One model to explain the occurrence of rape has as its basis the notion that a rapist learns his attitudes through social processes. Further, these psychologists believe that rape represents an act of power and control, not an act of sex. As such, theorists who subscribe to this notion rely on a model that rape can be prevented through adequate control of educational and learning processes.

A second model arises from evolutionary psychology, which suggests that some of our behaviors are, in part, genetically triggered. Some behavioral scientists (e.g., Thornhill & Palmer, 2000) assert that education alone is not enough to prevent rape because sexual behavior, even if it involves coercion, is part of our evolutionary, genetic sexual makeup. These theorists claim that rape is not about power and control, but rather precisely about sex. With such different views about the underlying nature of rape, we should not be surprised that the two groups argue heatedly with one another.

How can competent, knowledgeable, and intelligent scholars differ so much with one another? Both groups have objective data arising from replicable research. The answer is that any time you try to explain complex behavior patterns, you have to rely on a lot of information that might be conflicting and that is certainly incomplete. We don't know everything that we need to know.

In short, we believe things that we are predisposed to believe or that we want to believe. Scholars can legitimately differ in their interpretations, each believing in a theory that makes most sense to them. It is important to remember, though, that what is sensible to one person may be senseless to another. Nobody can generate a theory that does not rely on personal and cultural biases and predispositions.

At this point, we need to remember what theories are good for. A theory is used after we have a good idea of how to describe behaviors of interest and can make accurate predictions about them. The theory is an overall explanation that puts together as much of the information about our topic as possible.

In the present controversy about why rape occurs, some psychologists believe that a social learning model is the best explanation. Other psychologists believe that evolutionary ideas provide the best explanation. What we ultimately hope for is that we can generate enough data to help us figure out which explanation is best.

When we look at this controversy, it becomes clear that our cultural biases can influence the conclusions we draw. Many people don't want to believe the evolutionary explanation because it may be inconsistent with their personal beliefs about people and the control of their behavior.

When considering theory in this light, we can easily see why a theory is actually a very practical thing. Depending on your theory of rape, you might consider very different ways of controlling behaviors so rape does not occur. Or you might use your theory to plan therapy to help rape victims. If your theory is not the best way to understand the behavior, your ability to control the behavior will suffer.

Questions for Discussion: Why is description not controversial here, but prediction, explanation, and control are very controversial? Is it realistic to think that people with very different perspectives can discuss and resolve the controversies so they agree on explanations about rape?

Nonetheless, by understanding the context in which the data were generated, whether the research followed the scientific method, and the relation between the data and the question at hand, you can begin to ask the right questions about whether you are on the receiving end of real science or junk science.

SUMMARY

Research exerts a large impact on our lives, so we are better off as citizens when we can examine research claims that people make. Knowing how to ask critical questions is also a useful skill in many other facets of our lives.

When psychologists engage in research, we do what other scientists do: We look for ways to describe behavior accurately, to establish a basis for predicting behavior, to explain why people act as they do, and ultimately to know how to control behavior. The best way to accomplish these goals is to study behavior scientifically.

Research is considered scientific when it conforms to certain game plans. Researchers strive to make objective measurements and to define precisely what they have done in their work. This allows others to evaluate the credibility of the research and to do further work to extend knowledge. After creating a research plan, psychologists collect data and draw conclusions from the data. We hope that when scientists make a claim, they can support their arguments based on objective data, not on opinion.

Another critical component of scientific research is that it must be public. The knowledge we gain in research doesn't help us advance what we know unless researchers publicize their work, usually in the form of professional papers that appear in journals or in conference presentations attended by other scientists. Only by making clear statements about what research is all about and what discoveries the scientist has made can others verify the validity of the claims made by the investigator and attempt to reproduce those results in other research projects.

We rely on the scientific approach for the study of behavior because other ways of finding out about people's thoughts, feelings, and acts are not as reliable. Sometimes we can use intuition to understand the world around us, but too often intuition leads to poor judgments. Similarly, we can ask people who are authority figures; unfortunately, they are like the rest of us—sometimes they make mistakes. We can also use logic, but all of us know that people's behaviors often don't seem to follow any logic we can detect. Finally, all of us make judgments based on our own experience. The problem with using our own experiences is that they may not reflect general principles. These other ways of understanding the world have their place, but the systematic and scientific study of behavior provides us with the best overall picture of the human condition.

As researchers investigate human behavior, they gather information and collect data. This is often the easy part. The complex part is trying to interpret what the information means. People do research for reasons that relate to their social and cultural outlook, and they interpret their results from within their own cultural framework. Sometimes people disagree vigorously on how to interpret research in all of the scientific disciplines; this reflects that science is just another type of human activity.

Finally, learning about research is one way to increase one's scientific literacy. Research promotes critical thinking about how to ask and answer questions systematically and objectively. Unfortunately, the majority of Americans show low levels of scientific literacy, which may account for acceptance by some people of certain types of pseudoscience that scientists firmly reject.

REVIEW QUESTIONS

Multiple Choice Questions

1. Researchers recently documented the fact that after a terrorist attack, people who refused to think about the horrible events and isolated themselves were at greater risk than others of developing post-traumatic stress disorder. This fact relates to which goal of science?
   a. Control
   b. Description
   c. Explanation
   d. Prediction
2. Researchers with different theoretical beliefs are likely to differ greatly with respect to their statements regarding the ___________ of behavior.
   a. explanation
   b. testability
   c. falsifiability
   d. description
3. When colleges use high school grades and SAT or ACT scores to determine whether to admit a student, they are using the tests scores as a measure of the likelihood of student success in college. This is related to which goal of science?
   a. Control
   b. Description
   c. Explanation
   d. Prediction
4. After gaining an understanding of why behaviors occur as they do, a scientist interested in applying this knowledge would be interested in what goal of science?
   a. Control
   b. Description
   c. Explanation
   d. Prediction
5. Researchers test the strength of a theory by seeing at what point it breaks down. This activity relates to
   a. control.
   b. explanation.
   c. falsifiability.
   d. proof.
6. If a person drew a conclusion about some topic based on opinion and prior beliefs, a researcher would claim that such a conclusion was not scientific because it was not
   a. objective.
   b. intuitive.

c. data driven.
d. predicted.

7. A scientist who decides to repeat an experiment to see if the results are the same is interested in what characteristic of scientific knowledge?
a. Objective
b. Data driven
c. Public
d. Verifiable

8. Beliefs based on intuition or on common knowledge that people hold firmly and are simply reluctant to abandon are based on what kind of knowledge?
a. Tenacity
b. Experience
c. Authority
d. a priori method

9. When your professor informs you of fact and theory based on research, you develop a belief system that is consistent with that information. Your beliefs are based on
a. authority.
b. experience.
c. a priori method.
d. science.

10. One of the problems associated with knowledge based on experience is that
a. our own experiences might not generalize to others.
b. the use of logical deductions does not work in predicting behaviors.
c. common knowledge might be erroneous, even if many people believe in it.
d. experiential knowledge and scientific knowledge are usually very different from one another.

11. In planning scientific research, psychologists' choices of topics
a. have generally been directed by theory, but seldom by cultural values.
b. have not been influenced by the actions of the government.
c. are most productive when they are removed from controversial topics.
d. often reflect cultural values that they hold.

12. The effects of culture on research are reflected in the fact that
a. the government tries to stay out of the personal choices of researchers.
b. researchers may avoid controversial topics because of the reactions of others to their research.
c. research methodologies in psychology tend to remain constant across virtually all societies.
d. psychologists tend to study the same topics in the same ways across the decades.

13. Reports of scientific "breakthroughs" in the popular media
a. let the audience know when truly revolutionary research results have been obtained.
b. generally occur when an investigator turns toward a new area of study and manages to spot trends that others cannot.

   c. usually involve a small set of studies that an independent investigator conducts away from others in the field.
   d. are really reports of a continuous body of research that has been ongoing over a relatively long period of time.

14. A belief in parapsychology (e.g., ESP)
   a. is fairly uncommon in the general public, contrary to common belief.
   b. is typical of most scientists.
   c. has been documented in over half the general public in a number of surveys over several decades.
   d. is at the same level for scientists as it is for the general public.

15. Scientists become suspicious of scientific claims about new phenomena when the people raising the new ideas
   a. insist on publicizing their research in scientific journals instead of in the mainstream press where more people can view it.
   b. claim that the scientific establishment is actively working to suppress their new ideas.
   c. are unable to provide solid anecdotal evidence and specific examples of the phenomenon in everyday life.
   d. do not want to be limited by existing scientific data and theory in providing explanations of the phenomena.

Essay Questions

16. Identify and describe the four goals of scientific research. Include in your description how the four goals build on one another.
17. Identify and describe the five ways of knowing described by the philosopher Charles Sanders Peirce and others.
18. How do scientists and pseudoscientists differ with regard to the evidence that they will accept to support their ideas?

ANSWERS TO REVIEW QUESTIONS

Multiple Choice Questions

1. b	6. c	11. d
2. a	7. d	12. b
3. d	8. a	13. d
4. a	9. a	14. c
5. c	10. a	15. b

Essay Questions

16. Identify and describe the four goals of scientific research. Include in your description how the four goals build on one another.
   Suggested points:
   a. Description—the process of documenting the existence of behaviors of interest.
   b. Prediction—the ability to predict behaviors given knowledge of prior conditions.

c. Explanation—identifying reasons for the occurrence of a behavior.
d. Control—using knowledge of a phenomenon to predict when it will occur and being able to explain the reasons for the behavior in such a way as to control that behavior.

17. Identify and describe the five ways of knowing described by the philosopher Charles Sanders Peirce.
    a. Tenacity (the obvious/intuition)—knowing something because "everybody knows it is true" or because "it is obvious" so that people are comfortable and simply refuse to abandon that knowledge.
    b. Authority—reliance on an expert or authority figure.
    c. A priori method—use of deductive logic or logical proof.
    d. Experience—use of one's own life as a measure of what is generally true.
    e. Scientific method—reliance on empirical methods that are objective, empirical, public, and replicable.
18. How do scientists and pseudoscientists differ with regard to the evidence that they will accept to support their ideas?

    Ideally, scientists continually revise their ideas based on empirically based evidence. In addition, they are willing to develop theories to accommodate new findings, to update their methods to improve on the quality of research, and to question new information critically.

    On the other hand, pseudoscientists rely on flimsy and questionable evidence; they are not willing to question information that supports their ideas. At the same time, they avoid contradictory information that fails to support their ideas. In addition, pseudoscientists show a resistance to change in their ideas and they are unlikely to seek further development of theory; in fact, they tend to avoid testing their ideas critically.

CHAPTER TWO

ETHICS IN RESEARCH
Following the Golden Rule

CHAPTER OVERVIEW

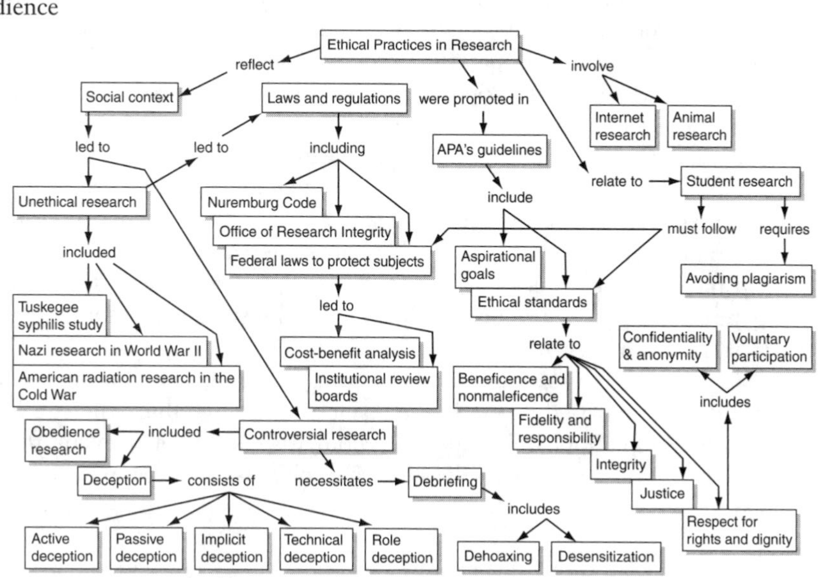

KEY TERMS

Active deception, p. 45
Anonymity, p. 48
Aspirational goals, p. 33
Beneficence, p. 33
Confidentiality, p. 48
Cost-benefit analysis, p. 41
Cover story, p. 44
Debriefing, p. 45
Dehoaxing, p. 45
Desensitization, p. 45
Ethical standards, p. 33
Fidelity, p. 33
Institutional review board (IRB), p. 39
Integrity, p. 33
Justice, p. 33
Naturalistic observation, p. 44
Nonmaleficence, p. 33
Nuremberg Code, p. 37
Passive deception, p. 45
Plagiarism, p. 30
Respect for people's rights and dignity, p. 34
Responsibility, p. 33
Role playing, p. 47
Simulation, p. 43

CHAPTER PREVIEW

Most psychological research poses little physical or psychological risk to participants. Nonetheless, because some researchers in the past have conducted notorious and unethical projects, laws and guidelines have been developed for the protection of research participants. Another problem is that researchers made up data, invented entire experiments, and misrepresented their data in published journal articles.

Researchers generally become very interested and excited in their programs of research. Sometimes this means that they focus very narrowly in their work and forget to consider the implications of what they are doing. In this chapter, you will see that investigators may get so caught up in their research that they may endanger the people who participate in their studies.

The American Psychological Association has developed a set of guidelines that has evolved over the past half century. Many researchers in disciplines other than psychology rely on these guidelines. We must also follow legal requirements that federal and state governments have enacted for the protection of human participants in research.

Students sometimes mistakenly believe that the APA approves or vetoes research. It would be impossible for any single organization to oversee as much research as psychologists conduct. Ethical supervision occurs under the oversight of institutional review boards (IRBs) that evaluate proposed projects; this takes place in the colleges and universities where the research is carried out.

In discussing ethics in psychological research, the famous research of Stanley Milgram (1963) and Philip Zimbardo (1973) comes to mind. Milgram's research participants thought they were delivering electrical shocks to another person, often to the extent that the other person might have died. Zimbardo created a prison simulation that led participants, all of them students, to treat one another very brutally. This type of research is very rare in psychology, which is why the most illustrative examples of ethically controversial research occurred over thirty years ago.

We can categorize research in two groups for our discussion. In one category, involving clinically based research, the result of ignoring ethical dictates is potentially very serious. People approach clinical psychologists because of problems that need to be resolved. If clinical research involves ethical problems, those people could be seriously harmed.

Our second category involves basic research in academic settings. Most psychological research has fairly minor risk-related implications for participants. Some psychological research can involve more than minimal risk, but most psychological research on topics like learning, motivation, social processes, and attitude change would virtually never lead to long-term, highly negative outcomes, no matter how incompetent or unethical the researcher. To decide whether a project is appropriate, we conduct a cost-benefit analysis; if the risk exceeds the benefit, we should not do the research; if the benefit exceeds the risk, the research may be acceptable. Before we conduct research, we need to assess the relative risk of the research compared to the benefits for two main reasons. First, it is the ethical and moral thing to do. Second, there are legal requirements that we do it. There has been an unfortunate history of abuse on the part of researchers; some of it is due to carelessness, some due to callousness, and some due to unconscionable social and governmental policies. We hope to avoid such problems in our research.

UNETHICAL RESEARCH PRACTICES—PAST AND PRESENT

Ethical Problems in the Early Years of the Twentieth Century

Through the past century, shameful episodes of unethical research practices have occurred, in many cases leading to extreme suffering and death. The troublesome decisions made by researchers have led to the Nuremburg Code and to the various federal laws designed to protect people.

Among the most egregious examples include the investigations done by the Nazis during World War II. For example, according to Lifton (1986), the Nazi Carl Clauberg researched techniques for sterilizing women by injecting them with what was probably Formalin, which consists of formaldehyde and methanol (a kind of alcohol). Both substances are poisonous, and formaldehyde is an extreme irritant; survivors reported that the pain was excruciating. Clauberg injected this substance into the women's cervix, with the aim of destroying the fallopian tubes that are necessary for carrying an egg to the uterus for implantation. This kind of research clearly reflects a pathological society that we want to believe could not happen anywhere else.

As you will see, there have been violations in medical and psychiatric research that go beyond the bounds of good judgment and indicate a callous, sometimes horrific disregard for a person's right to be treated with dignity and fairness. The Nazis did not corner the market on such research. Beginning in the 1930s and continuing for several decades, researchers at the Tuskegee Institute in the United States purposely withheld treatment from black patients in order to study the progress of syphilis. It is true that when the study began, knowledge of the specific course of the disease and of effective treatment was minimal, but within a short period of time, the evidence was clear that lack of treatment was devastating. Syphilis can lead to blindness, organically caused psychosis, and death. The negative effects on its patients were all too clear decades before the research ceased, and the research continued after treatment with penicillin was standard practice.

A report (Research Ethics and the Medical Profession, 1996) has documented a number of problematic studies that occurred during the 1950s and 1960s in the United States. In many cases, the guidelines that had existed regarding informed consent and voluntary participation were ignored.

Examples of harmful and unethical research included cases in which researchers at the University of Cincinnati, in conjunction with the U.S. military, subjected uninformed, terminally ill cancer patients to whole-body radiation to see how it affected those people (Rothman, 1994). Further, in separate projects in the decades after World War II, researchers at the Massachusetts Institute of Technology (funded by the National Institutes of Health, The Atomic Energy Commission, and the Quaker Oats Company) and investigators at Harvard Medical School, Massachusetts General Hospital, and Boston University School of Medicine administered radioactive substances to mentally retarded children living in facilities for the developmentally disabled (ACHRE Report, n.d.).

Ethical breaches in medical research continued to occur into the 1960s and 1970s such that Congress created regulations to prevent physicians from abusing their relationships with patients.

Many of the episodes of notorious research come from the 1970s or earlier. Does this mean that we have solved the problems associated with unethical research practices? Or do ethical problems continue in research programs?

Unfortunately, questionable practices still exist. For example, dozens of experiments with human participants came to a halt at Duke University Medical Center in 1999 when the federal government discovered ethical lapses in the projects involving protection of research participants. One development occurred with a participant in a NASA-sponsored study who underwent testing in a chamber designed to simulate the pressure that you would feel at 30,000 feet above sea level. The man began to lose sensation in his limbs and, after treatment, became semi-conscious. On the positive side of the ledger, as soon as a rare and unexpected problem occurred, the researchers terminated the study to protect a research participant; on the negative side, some ethicists questioned whether the project's risks had been adequately studied and whether the participant had received appropriate informed consent (Hilts & Stolberg, 1999).

Beyond this potentially harmful research from the past, recent investigators have engaged in potentially troublesome behaviors. In a recent survey, up to a third of respondents who had received grants from the National Institutes of Health reported engaging in some type of ethically questionable practices, including falsifying and fabricating data, plagiarism, having potentially inappropriate relationships with students or research participants, circumventing minor aspects of human-subject requirements, and others (Martinson, Anderson, & de Vries, 2005; Wadman, 2005). Sometimes researchers have even invented studies that they did not conduct (Mendoza, 2005) or add their names to reference citations, making it appear that they co-authored published papers when they had not (Case summaries, 2004).

One of the few controversies involving psychology related to a paper whose authors failed to cite important research leading to the research in question (Liston & Kagan, 2002). Kagan and Liston did not plagiarize any earlier material, they just failed to cite it. Their article was brief, limited to just 500 words, they noted, so they had to

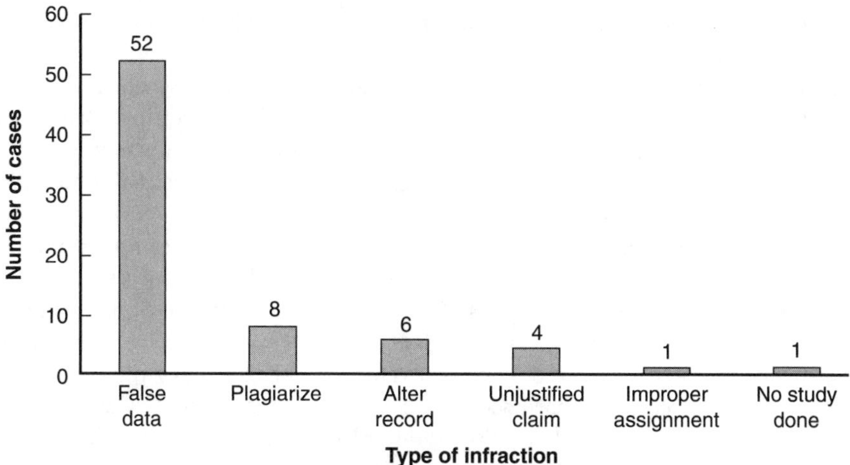

FIGURE 2.1 Cases of ethics violation in research as examined by the Office of Research Integrity (2001–2006).

leave out a lot of important material. Nonetheless, they received criticism regarding how appropriate their behavior was (Farley, 2003).

In an attempt to monitor scientists' behaviors, the U.S. federal government's Office of Research Integrity (ORI) investigates claims of scientific misconduct in research associated with federal grants. Between 2001 and 2006, the office concluded that seventy-two researchers were guilty of misconduct related to data collection, analysis, and presentation. Although such fraud is very troublesome, the number of cases identified by the government is relatively small. Naturally, we don't know how often fraud goes undetected, but if one-third of respondents on a survey reported unethical behavior (Martinson et al., 2005; Wadman, 2005), one might assume that the proportion is higher, given that scientists may be reluctant to report on their ethical lapses. Figure 2.1 shows the types of cases investigated by ORI in that time period. As you can see, most cases involved falsifying or fabricating data and plagiarism, but there are several other severe problems that also occurred.

Ethical Questions in Corporate Research

The federal office that deals with unethical research practices, ORI, only looks at cases involving grants from the government. Questionable practices can occur in the private sector, too. Decades ago Congress took action because physicians were conducting research for pharmaceutical companies, unbeknownst to their patients. The federal legislation was supposed to have put a stop to the practice.

Unfortunately, history has a way of repeating itself. Several years ago, *The New York Times* (Eichenwald & Kolata, 1999) reported that one particular physician, Peter Arcan, recommended to a patient that he (the patient) might want to join a study of a new drug to shrink enlarged prostates. Suspiciously, the patient did not have an enlarged prostate gland. The doctor insisted that the drug might prevent future problems, so the patient agreed.

In reality, the pharmaceutical company, SmithKline Beecham PLC, paid the doctor over $1,600 for each patient enrolled in the study. In addition, physicians sometimes receive highly coveted authorship on published research papers merely for recruiting enough patients. This pattern seems to have involved hundreds of thousands of patients, according to the *Times*.

Further, sometimes the drug companies employ physicians to do research in areas outside their realm of expertise. Eichenwald and Kolata reported, for example, that asthma specialists have dispensed experimental psychiatric drugs, while psychiatrists have investigated Pap smears, which are gynecological tests. There seem to be a number of physicians involved who possess little knowledge of or training in research.

More recently, pharmaceutical companies have received criticism for hiring physicians after state medical boards had discovered that those doctors had engaged in troublesome behaviors. For instance, one psychiatrist was sanctioned by the Minnesota Board of Medical Practice after he showed "reckless, if not willful, disregard" for forty-six patients; five of them died while in his care or shortly thereafter (Harris & Roberts, 2007, ¶ 1). According to a *New York Times* report, the doctor discharged a patient from a psychiatric facility, supposedly because the patient would not participate in a study funded by a drug maker. The patient committed suicide two weeks later. The U.S. Food and Drug Administration had concluded that "the psychiatrist had violated the protocols of every study that they audited and reported inaccurate data to drug makers, . . . and once hospitalized a patient for the sole purpose of enrolling him in a study" (Harris & Roberts, 2007, ¶ 34).

Most of the research associated with such problems has been biomedical in nature. The risks associated with it may involve life and death issues. Your research in psychology is likely to have less impact. However, the behavioral research you complete also has to conform to certain ethical principles and is bound by the same laws that professional researchers must follow.

Finally, you might ask why individuals engage in these unethical behaviors. As you've just seen, receipt of money is obviously one reason. In addition, according to a researcher who has investigated why scientists cheat, there are four other basic reasons:

- Intense pressure to publish research and to obtain grants.
- Inadequate mentoring.
- Some sort of mental disorder.
- Scientists from outside the United States who learned standards that differ from those in the United States (Charges of fake research, 2005).

ETHICAL GUIDELINES CREATED BY THE AMERICAN PSYCHOLOGICAL ASSOCIATION

Researchers are not exempt from some of the same lapses in good judgment that beset the rest of us. In psychology, we are fortunate that the serious breaches of ethics are rare.

Aspirational goals—General set of ethical principles that guide psychologists in their research and other professional activities.

Ethical standards—A set of enforceable rules created by the American Psychological Association and by legal authorities that relate to moral values of right and wrong.

Beneficence and nonmaleficence—Acting to promote the welfare of the people a psychologists deals with (beneficence) and avoidance of harm to them (nonmaleficence).

Fidelity and responsibility—Psychologists must act professionally in ways that support the discipline of psychology and benefit their community, especially regarding the well-being of the people with whom they interact professionally.

Integrity—Psychologists should promote the honest and truthful application of the discipline in science, teaching, and practice.

Justice—Psychologists must recognize the implications of their professional activity on others and strive to make the best professional judgments they can.

Long before the general public learned of the excesses of some researchers, the American Psychological Association had formulated a set of principles that would guide psychologists in their work. Some research disciplines have yet to develop such codes (Scientists should adopt, 2007). We will discuss primarily those guidelines that relate to research, although APA's guidelines pertain to all areas of psychological work, including therapy. The principles associated with ethics in providing psychotherapy are vitally important in the therapeutic realm, but are of less interest to us here. When the two worlds of therapy and research merge, psychologists must attend carefully to the ethical guidelines both for therapy and for research. This is an especially difficult area because it is not always clear that psychiatric patients are able to make informed decisions about participating; in part, they may be unable to understand the implications of their participation.

The first set of APA's ethical principles appeared in 1953, the most recent in 2002, and they continue to be refined. As stated in a recent version, psychologists should incorporate the rules as an integral part of their professional lives. "The development of a dynamic set of ethical standards for a psychologist's work-related conduct requires a personal commitment to a lifelong effort to act ethically" (American Psychological Association, 2002, p. 1062).

The General Principles espoused in the standards reflect "**aspirational goals** to guide psychologists toward the highest ideals of psychology" (p. 1061), whereas the **Ethical Standards** involve enforceable rules of conduct. When psychologists violate these rules, they face possible loss of certification to work in their field of expertise. Such offenses are relatively rare and, when they occur, generally involve the areas of clinical and counseling psychology rather than research. Every year a small number of psychologists suffer such action for their violations of the ethical guidelines. Fortunately, most psychologists, like most of you, approach their work with integrity; the relatively small numbers that face censure are vastly outweighed by those whose work is creditable and valuable.

Aspirational Goals and Enforceable Rules

The six General Principles of the ethical guidelines appear in Table 2.1. As you look at them, you can see that the principles reflect the high moral character that we prize in people around us. In part, (a) **beneficence** and **nonmaleficence** relate to maximizing the positive outcomes of your work and minimizing the chances of harm. Psychologists must also act with (b) **fidelity** and **responsibility** in dealing with others. Psychologists should also strive for (c) **integrity** in promoting themselves and their work accurately. As psychologists, we should also aspire to (d) **justice**, recognizing

TABLE 2.1 General Ethical Principles and Examples of Violations

Beneficence and Nonmaleficence	A psychologist would be in dangerous territory in conducting research in which he or she has a financial interest because that interest could cloud professional judgment to the detriment of the participant and others. Further, psychologists who are aware that they are experiencing mental health problems may be acting unethically with clients if their own mental health may lead to poor judgment.
Fidelity and Responsibility	A psychologist would violate ethical principles by engaging in dual relationships with patients. One of the most notable transgressions occurs when a therapist engages in sexual relations with a person while providing therapy to that individual. Also a psychologist who knows that a colleague is engaging in unethical behavior would himself or herself be acting unethically by not taking steps to prevent further such behavior.
Integrity	Psychologists who intentionally misrepresent their research results or who falsify data are engaging in ethical misconduct because they are not striving to maximize gain to the scientific and professional community, but rather are simply trying for personal gain. In addition, psychologists who knowingly use their knowledge to mislead others, such as in courtroom testimony, are engaging in unethical conduct. In this case, they are not using their professional expertise responsibly or contributing to the welfare of society in general.
Justice	A psychologist who is not trained in the use of a test like the Minnesota Multiphasic Personality Inventory but who uses it in his or her research or with clients might be engaging in unethical behavior because the validity of test interpretations may be low.
Respect for People's Rights and Dignity	Psychologists who violate the confidentiality of their research participants act unethically. This means that if you are doing research, you may not discuss with others how a particular participant responded during a testing session. (Such a discussion could be appropriate, however, if you discuss a research session with a colleague who is also working on that project and you need to resolve a methodological problem.)

Respect for people's rights and dignity—Psychologists must recognize the dignity and value of all people and, to the fullest extent possible, eliminate biases in dealing with people.

our biases and the limitations to our expertise as they affect others. Finally, we need to show (e) **respect for people's rights and dignity**.

We recognize that one of our goals is to promote human well-being. In addition, one of the critical aspects of such responsibility is that the public will lose faith in the work of psychologists and in the value of psychology if we don't act with the highest morals. The enforceable ethical standards consist of ten categories related to different aspects of professional, psychological work. These standards are listed in Table 2.2. Of these categories, the one that pertains most to us here involves research.

It probably never occurred to you, but if your professors are members of the American Psychological Association, they are ethically bound to educate and train you well. For example, the Ethical Principles of Psychologists (American Psychological Association, 2002) specify that psychology teachers make sure that syllabi are meaningful and that students be informed about grading procedures.

TABLE 2.2 General Standards of Ethical Behavior for Psychologists

Section 1–Resolving Ethical Issues

Psychologists need to recognize problematic ethical situations and work to resolve them on an individual level when possible. Sometimes it may be necessary to seek formal remedies to perceived unethical conduct. When there are legal issues that pose a conflict between ethical guidelines of psychologists and the law, the psychologist should work to minimize the conflict. When a conflict cannot be resolved, it may be appropriate to defer to legal authorities.

Section 2–Boundaries of Competence

Researchers, including you, may conduct research only within the boundaries of their competence. You need to pay attention to this, although most research you are likely to carry out will not be problematic. In certain circumstances, though, such as if you planned on using psychodiagnostic tests, you might be in a gray area because many such instruments require specialized training for adequate administration and interpretation. One potential problem is that you would expose your research participants to risk if you interpreted test results in a way that changed their behaviors for the worse.

Section 3–Human Relations

Psychologists must strive to minimize discrimination or harassment of people with whom they have a professional relationship. Exploitation of another by use of power or authority is unethical. For example, if a psychologist has power over others (e.g., a professor over a teaching or lab assistant, a resident assistant, etc.), he or she should take care that not to coerce people when recruiting their participation for research. Psychologists should also avoid multiple relationships, one of the most egregious being sexual relationships with students or clients. Clients and research participants should also provide informed consent for research or therapy.

Section 4—Privacy and Confidentiality

You should not discuss the behavior or responses of research participants or clients with those outside your project or treatment setting if not seeking professional consultation. Your participants have a right to expect that their responses will be confidential and anonymous to the fullest extent possible.

Section 5–Advertising and Other Public Statements

Psychologists should not make fraudulent or misleading professional statements when presenting their work to the public. Nor should they misrepresent their professional expertise or credentials.

Section 6–Record Keeping and Fees

Psychologists must document their research and maintain their data so that they are available for legal or other reasons.

Section 7–Teaching, Training Supervision, Research, and Publishing

Psychologists are responsible for competent education and training of students and for accurate descriptions of education and training programs. Teachers must avoid exploiting those over whom they have authority.

(continues)

Section 8–Research and Publication

With respect to research, it must be approved by an IRB. Participants should give informed consent and be debriefed (dehoaxed and desensitized). In informed consent, you have to provide them with the following information:

- The nature of the research.
- Their right to decline to participate and to withdraw at any time without penalty.
- The foreseeable consequences of their participation, such as risks and discomfort.

Some research projects involving anonymous questionnaires, naturalistic observation, and some archival research do not require informed consent. If you think this applies to you, you need to check with your local IRB or its representatives. Table 2.4 provides relevant information about this.

Deception in research is acceptable only if other alternatives are not available or appropriate. Presentation of results should accurately reflect the data.

Psychologists must give appropriate credit to those involved in research but should not give credit to an individual whose work on the research was minimal.

Sections 9 and 10–Assessment and Therapy

Psychologists must use contemporary assessment and therapeutic techniques and the psychologists must be adequately trained to use them. This complex realm is most relevant to doctoral level psychologists who provide service to clients.

As the ethical guidelines pertain to research, psychologists have certain responsibilities to provide research participants with informed consent, to minimize the use of deception in research, to report research results accurately, and to correct any errors in reporting. One further mandate is that researchers must be willing to share their data with other researchers, provided it does not violate the confidentiality promised to research participants.

There are a few areas that are of special relevance to researchers. You will have to consider them when you plan your own research because you must present a proposal to your school's Institutional Review Board (IRB) or to delegated representatives of that committee before you can carry out your proposed research. The committee members may approve your research as proposed, but they may require changes before you can begin. Depending on the nature of the regulations at your school, you may have to wait for a month or longer to receive permission. Your IRB will consider your research proposal based on the relevant state and federal regulations.

Ethical Standards as They Affect You

The General Principles developed by the American Psychological Association cover a wide range of psychological activities (see Table 2.1). At this point in your life, many of them will be completely irrelevant to you because you do not provide therapy for clients, engage in professional consultation, or perform psychological assessments. As a psychology student, however, you may carry out research projects, at which time the Principles will definitely apply to you.

Your research activity may not be ethically troublesome, but you need to avoid crossing the line into the realm of unethical behavior. The major points appearing in

Anonymity—The practice of maintaining records so that nobody can identify which individual is associated with a certain set of data.

Confidentiality—The practice of making sure that nobody outside a research project has access to data that can be identified with a specific individual.

Plagiarism—An ethical breach in which a person claims credit for another person's idea or research.

Table 2.2 do not exhaust the Principles; they merely highlight many of the points relevant to you. You should ultimately be aware of the American Psychological Association's Code of Conduct (American Psychological Association, 2002), as well as the relevant legal considerations. You should also become familiar with the changes in ethical guidelines as they evolve.

Among the most important practical issues you will face if you conduct research are those associated with informed consent—that is, making sure that your participants know what they are going to do and understand the nature of the research. In addition, you must provide debriefing in which you inform participants of any deception involved in the research, called dehoaxing, and you make sure that you eliminate any potential sources of negative feelings by the participants, called desensitization. If you think that there are likely to be any long-term consequences for your participants after they complete your research, you need to engage in compensatory followup, which means that you arrange for those problems to be remedied.

An additional requirement when you conduct research is that you must protect the **anonymity** and **confidentiality** of your research participants. It is desirable that, after a study is over, you cannot link people's behaviors in a research project with them personally. If there are no identifying characteristics in the data that allow you to know whose data you are examining, the data are anonymous. In some cases, you will not be able to separate a person's identify from the data. For example, if you are tracking people over time, you have to be able to link their current data with past data. In such a case, you need to make sure that nobody outside the research project has access to that information. When you do this, you are making sure that the data are confidential.

Finally, when you develop research ideas or when you write up a report of your project, you must avoid claiming credit that belongs to others. When an investigator asserts that he or she came up with an idea, but that idea was really developed by another person, this is **plagiarism**. It is considered a very serious breach of ethics. If an investigator has received research money from the federal government, plagiarism can lead to severe sanctions.

Nuremberg Code—A set of legal principles adopted by the international community after the Nazi atrocities in World War II to ensure fair and ethical treatment of research participants.

LEGAL REQUIREMENTS AND ETHICS IN RESEARCH

Shortly after World War II, the international community recognized the need for laws concerning research with people. These laws are known as the **Nuremberg Code**, named for the German city where they were developed. The ten points of the Code appear in Table 2.3.

As you look at the Code, you might wonder why anybody had to enact such a code. All of the points seem to involve little but common sense. Unfortunately, the Nazi atrocities alerted people to risks to research subjects. The Nazis victimized many people in research; the Nuremberg code formalized a set of rules that could be used by researchers with integrity when they planned their studies that involve people.

TABLE 2.3 Ten Points of the Nuremburg Code

Point	Comment
1. Research on humans absolutely requires informed consent.	You cannot do research on people who are not able to give voluntary, informed consent. This requires that they be sufficiently aware of their rights to be able to make a choice that is good for them. You are also not allowed to use undue influence or power you have over a person. The individual must know what risks might be involved.
2. The experiment must have the possibility of contributing to our body of knowledge.	You should not perform research that has no chance of being useful to society. This does not mean that an investigation has to produce major results, but the outcome should add to the accumulation of knowledge about human and nonhuman behavior.
3. Researchers should be informed about the topic they investigate to maximize the likelihood that the results will be useful.	Especially for biomedical research, scientists should design their research based on previous work that has been conducted using animals. In addition, the scientist must be competent enough to design a study whose results will justify the experimentation.
4. The experiment should avoid unnecessary physical and mental suffering.	Sometimes research by its nature involves discomfort of some kind (e.g., a study of sleep deprivation). Researchers should design their work to minimize the extent of the discomfort should it be necessary. Embarrassment and frustration are examples of mental suffering that might be associated with psychological research.
5. No experiment should be conducted if there is good reason to believe that death or serious injury will occur.	When an investigation involves high levels of potential risk, this restriction can be relaxed if the researchers serve as participants in this research.
6. The degree of risk must be less than the potential gain from the research.	Scientists must perform a cost-benefit analysis. If the costs exceed the potential benefits, the research is inappropriate.
7. Prior arrangements must be in place for responding to an emergency that occurs during a research project.	The investigators must make provisions for emergencies that they can reasonably foresee. Sometimes a participant may suffer harm because of an entirely unforeseen circumstance. In such a case, the researcher might not be seen as acting unethically. Points 2 and 3 relate to this–a researcher should be sufficiently well informed to know what risks are likely.
8. The investigator must have appropriate training to conduct the research.	Researchers have to know what they are doing. If a researcher fails to anticipate dangers that an expert would recognize in advance, that researcher might be judged as acting unethically. Researchers must also ensure that workers subordinate to them are qualified to carry out the tasks assigned to them.
9. Research participants must be free to terminate their involvement at any time.	When an individual has reached the point that he or she no longer feels comfortable participating in research, the person has the right to leave without penalty.
10. The experimenter must terminate a research project if he or she believes that continuing the study will lead to injury or death.	The investigator has to be aware of the dynamics of the research situation. If he or she recognizes that there is an elevated level of risk, the investigator must end the study.

Although most people would not come anywhere near the Nazi atrocities, the code is helpful because having a well-articulated set of principles to guide research might keep us from being blinded by our enthusiasm for our own research.

In addition to the internationally recognized Nuremberg Code, the U.S. government has also passed laws to protect human subjects. These procedures were initially implemented in 1966 and have evolved over time (Reynolds, 1982).

Institutional Review Boards

Changes in the regulations appear in the *Federal Register*, which reports on congressional activities of all kinds. One of the major provisions of the federal regulations mandates an **institutional review board (IRB)**, a committee that consists of at least five people, including a member of the community who is not a researcher. The IRB reviews research proposals for ethical problems and either approves or disapproves projects that investigators want to carry out. Although the official term for this group is the institutional review board, people often refer to it as the human subjects committee.

Institutional review board (IRB)—A committee that reviews research projects to make sure that the projects are in compliance with accepted ethical guidelines. An IRB is required for every institution receiving federal funding in the United States.

Most research must receive approval from an IRB, but there are exceptions, as listed in Table 2.4. Federal regulations stipulate that an IRB must document that research does not require formal review. These exceptions exist because the experts who work for the government recognize that not all research carries significant risk. For example, you are allowed to conduct some survey research and simple observational research in a public area without IRB approval. The reason is that those you survey or observe do not experience greater risk because you are studying them when compared to the risks of everyday life. Survey research that probes sensitive issues may require IRB approval.

One of the most important issues associated with research with people is that you need to inform them about the risks and benefits of the project. One way of recording the fact that you informed the participants and that they voluntarily agreed to take part in the study is through the informed-consent form. This form lays out the nature of the study, including potential risks for participating. Unfortunately, people may have difficulty understanding informed-consent forms. Sometimes IRBs have specific formats that they want researchers to follow; in addition, institutions sponsoring research may use these forms as legal documents.

Researchers have found that the readability level of the forms is often higher than IRBs mandate, even if the IRBs have created the forms. Likewise, the forms that some institutions use can be very legalistic and, to a typical reader, uninformative. The prose in the average form was between the tenth- and eleventh-grade reading level, but the half of the U.S. public reads at the eighth-grade level or below (Paasche-Orlow, Taylor, & Barncati, 2003). This research involved medical informed consent, which is likely to be more complex and technical than behavioral research, but the important point is that research participants need to be able to understand what you are telling them in order for their consent to participate is truly voluntary.

Ironically, Keith-Spiegel and Koocher (2005) have argued that when researchers believe that they have not received fair treatment from an IRB, they may engage in

TABLE 2.4 Types of Research Most Relevant to Psychology That Do Not Require Approval by an Institutional Review Board

In general, research activities in which the only involvement of human subjects will be in one or more of the four following categories are exempt from review by an IRB.

1. Research conducted in established or commonly accepted educational settings, involving normal educational practices, such as
   a. research on regular and special education instructional strategies, or
   b. research on the effectiveness of or the comparison among instructional techniques, curricula, or classroom management methods.
2. Research involving the use of educational tests, survey procedures, interview procedures, or observation of public behavior. The exemption does not hold (and IRB approval is required) if
   a. information obtained is recorded in such a manner that human subjects can be identified, directly or through identifiers linked to the subjects; and
   b. any disclosure of the human subjects' responses outside the research could reasonably place the subjects at risk of criminal or civil liability or be damaging to the subjects' financial standing, employability, or reputation.
3. Research involving the use of educational tests, survey procedures, interview procedures, or observation of public behavior is exempt as listed in paragraph (2) above; in addition, research is exempt from IRB approval if
   a. the human subjects are elected or appointed public officials or candidates for public office, or
   b. federal statute(s) require(s) without exception that the confidentiality of the personally identifiable information will be maintained throughout the research and thereafter.
4. Research involving the collection or study of existing, publicly available data, documents, records, pathological specimens, or diagnostic specimens; in addition, the research is exempt from IRB approval if the information is recorded by the investigator so that subjects cannot be identified, directly or through identifiers linked to the subjects.

behaviors designed to deceive the IRB. The investigators may conclude that their research is truly ethical and that they need to identify ways to get around elements of the ethics review process on which the IRB treats them unfairly.

THE IMPORTANCE OF SOCIAL CONTEXT IN DECIDING ON ETHICS IN RESEARCH

Consider this: A participant volunteers to help with research. He is told that he will be in the role of the teacher, delivering electrical shocks to another person, also a volunteer, every time that person makes a mistake in a learning task. With each mistake, the strength of the shock will increase, up to a level on a panel marked "Danger: Severe Shock," followed by a mysterious higher level of shock simply labeled "XXX." The learner remarks that he has a heart condition, but the experimenter replies that it won't matter. The learner is strapped into a chair in another room and connected to the apparatus that will deliver the electrical shocks.

After the learner makes several mistakes and receives shocks, he demands to quit, but the experimenter simply says the experiment must continue. Shortly thereafter, the learner (who allegedly has a heart problem) becomes completely silent, but the researcher encourages the teacher to continue to deliver electrical shocks if the learner doesn't respond because a nonresponse is the same as a wrong answer.

Stanley Milgram's Research Project on Obedience

Suppose you were the participant. Would you continue shocking the learner? Or would you stop? If you were like the majority of people who took part in some of Stanley Milgram's (1963) experiments on conformity, you would have persisted in shocking the learner. How would you have felt afterward, knowing that you had delivered shocks to somebody with a heart condition, somebody who became utterly silent after a while, somebody you might have killed by shocking him?

As you may already know, the victim never received shocks. Milgram employed deception to induce participants to feel personally involved in what they thought was a real set of conditions.

Milgram (1974) described a variety of studies in his extensive research project that subjected his volunteers to this situation. Knowing what you know about the ethics of research, would you consider this ethical research? This experimentation has generated voluminous commentary. Some psychologists and ethicists believe that the studies were simply unethical (e.g., Baumrind, 1964). On the other hand, Milgram (1964) defended them as being within ethical boundaries.

The Ethical Issues

What are some of the important issues to consider here? If psychologists legitimately differ in their conclusions, it is pretty certain that we are in a gray area here. You might conclude that the research was acceptable, or you might condemn it. In the end, we need to make a judgment call using the best wisdom we can muster.

An IRB decides whether any given research project would subject people to undue risk. Formally, the IRB is supposed to weigh the risks (physical and psychological harm) against the benefits (increased knowledge and applications) of the research. If the risks are greater than the benefits, the research should not be done; if the benefits exceed the risks, the research can be defended on ethical grounds. This type of assessment is often known as a **cost-benefit analysis**. In essence, if the risks (costs) are great, they outweigh small and, maybe, even large benefits; as such, the researcher should not conduct the research. On the other hand, if the benefit is large, then small or maybe medium level risks are tolerable. The difficulty arises when the risks and the benefits are both high. A decision may not be easy to reach, and different people may arrive at different, but legitimate conclusions.

Cost-benefit analysis–An evaluation of the relative risks that research participants face in a study (the cost) relative to the potential benefit of the outcome of the research.

Unfortunately, before researchers carry out their studies, nobody knows for sure what risks exist or what benefits will actually accrue. In advance, we are talking about possibilities, not actualities. Before a study takes place, we can guess at costs and benefits, but not until after investigators complete their work can we identify either the risk-associated problems that arose or the actual benefits of the research.

Criticisms of Milgram's Research. With this uncertainty in mind, we can ask whether Milgram violated the rights of his participants. Among others, Baumrind (1964) asserted that Milgram's obedience research should not have been done. She said that the "dependent attitude" (p. 421) of the participants rendered them more susceptible to the manipulations of an authority figure, that is, the experimenter. She also named several ethical problems, asserting that Milgram did not show concern for participants' well-being, that the cost (i.e., degree of psychological distress and having been lied to) exceeded the benefits of having done the research, that the participants' long-term well-being was negatively affected, and that their attitudes toward authority figures would in the future be more negative. She also noted Milgram's statement that fourteen of the forty participants showed obvious distress and that three suffered seizures.

Baumrind (1964) did not accept Milgram's statement that the distress was momentary and that the gain in psychological knowledge outweighed the negatives: "I do regard the emotional disturbance described by Milgram as potentially harmful because it could easily effect an alteration in the subject's self-image or ability to trust adult authorities in the future" (p. 422). She also stated that Milgram's debriefing and dehoaxing processes would not have remedied the situation.

Milgram's Defense of His Research. Not surprisingly, Milgram (1964) responded to Baumrind's criticisms. He disagreed with her assessments, saying that he tried to predict in advance how the participants would respond and had been confident that they would not engage in the shocking behavior very long. He went to great lengths, asking psychiatrists and others to estimate how often the participants were likely to engage in blind obedience. The experts thought that participants would not administer severe shocks. Thus, at the outset, Milgram firmly believed that virtually everybody would refuse to engage in extreme behavior. As a result, he felt that the risk to his participants would be minimal. As it turned out, the estimates that the experts gave were wrong—people did administer what they thought were severe electrical shocks.

Milgram also noted that he debriefed and dehoaxed the participants, trying to ensure that they departed with no ill effects. Further, at his request, a psychiatrist interviewed forty participants after a year. There seem to have been no problems at that time. In fact, Ring, Wallston, and Corey (1970) specifically examined participants' reactions to a Milgram-like study. These researchers reported that people may have felt distressed during participation, but the effects were short-lived. A large majority of the people responded that they were happy that they participated. Further, when Ring et al. debriefed their participants after using an approach like Milgram's, the level of tension by participants dropped relative to that of no debriefing.

Baumrind raised critically important points. According to the data we have, though, many or most of the problems she cited did not seem to materialize. Both Milgram's and Baumrind's predictions were off the mark. This is another good example of how experts can be wrong, and why we should not simply rely on authority for the "truth."

The Social Context

We might want to consider the social context in which Milgram did his work. His studies took place from 1960 to 1963, which was not long after the end of World War II. The Nazis carried out numerous experiments that no normal person could ever justify.

In some very famous cases, the perpetrators of those acts claimed that they were merely following orders, that is, simply being obedient. Milgram, like many others, was greatly affected by the reports of these atrocities. In fact, when Milgram gave an overview of his research in his book *Obedience to Authority* (1974), he referred directly to the Nazi crimes in the very first paragraph of the book.

The United States, where Milgram did his research, was still in the process of recovering from the war, like citizens in many countries. In addition, people were worried about the possibility that communists would try to conquer the world, turning people into blindly obedient automatons. War was clearly on people's minds. It was reasonable that we would try to understand how seemingly normal people could commit the wartime acts of the Nazis, behaving with blind obedience. An experimental psychologist might try to reproduce the dynamics of obedience in the laboratory to find out how and why people defer to authorities. This is precisely what Stanley Milgram did.

As members of our society, we continually decide whether behaviors are acceptable. In the early years of the century, many people felt entirely comfortable discriminating against people of color in all aspects of life. Society has changed, and the number of people who agree that such discrimination is acceptable has diminished. In a similar vein, people in the post-war years may have been very comfortable with the idea of Milgram's research because the effects of blind obedience were still fresh in people's minds. Society has changed, and the number of people who would support such research has undoubtedly diminished. The question of blind obedience is no longer as relevant as it was in the aftermath of World War II. It is unlikely that an IRB would approve such research today. But in a different era, people might consider it acceptable or even desirable.

Incidentally, Milgram's application to become a member of APA was initially questioned on the basis of the ethics of his research. Ultimately, though, the organization accorded him membership, judging that he had not violated ethical guidelines in his work.

WHAT YOU NEED TO DO IF YOUR RESEARCH INVOLVES DECEPTION

For decades, deception was very prevalent in social psychological research (Adair, Dushenko, & Lindsay, 1985). This means that many psychologists have accepted it as a reality of their research. As

Figure 2.2 suggests, deception may have been more routine into the 1970s compared to today. Nonetheless, in spite of the criticisms leveled by opponents of deception, psychological researchers have not embraced alternate methodologies like **role playing**, **naturalistic observation**, or **simulation**.

When many people argue against deception, they do so because they see it as immoral. In addition, a second area of concern involves the risk for participants who are deceived. In such a case, a person cannot give informed consent about his or her willingness to participate. We cannot ignore this important notion of informed consent. It is a critical component of national and international laws. Fortunately, there is good reason

Role playing—An approach to research in which participants act as if they were participating in a study so the investigator can avoid using potentially unethical strategies that might lead to physical or psychological harm to the participants.

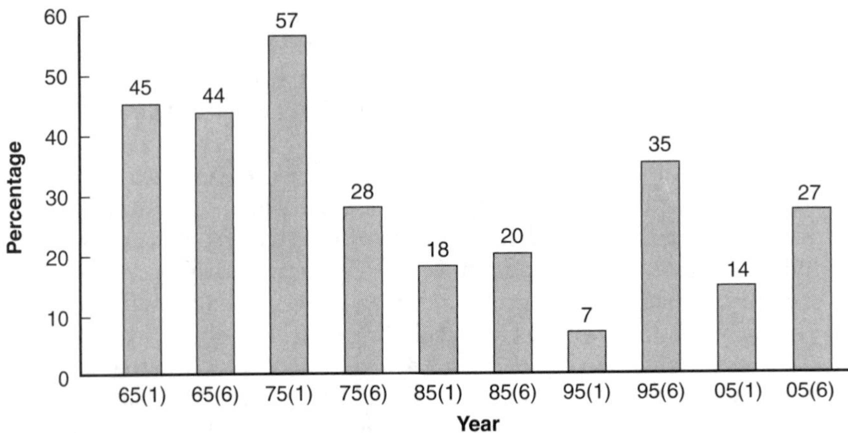

FIGURE 2.2 Percentage of studies using deception in a sample of articles from *Journal of Personality and Social Psychology* from 1965 to 2005. The articles appeared in issues 1 and 6 of the journal from each year represented.

Naturalistic observation—A research technique in which the investigator studies behavior as it naturally occurs, without any manipulation of variables or intervention into the situation.

Simulation—An approach to research in which the investigator creates an environment similar to one of interest in order to study behaviors in a realistic way. This approach is also known as the simulated environment.

Cover story—The story a researcher creates to disguise the actual purpose of a study when deception is considered necessary to conduct a study.

to believe that keeping participants ignorant of some aspects of the research has negligible effects on them in general (e.g., Bröder, 1998).

A very different type of criticism of the use of deception is that people will develop negative attitudes or suspicion toward psychology and psychological research (Orne, 1962). There is credible evidence, however, that people regard the science and practice of psychology very positively, even after learning that a researcher had deceived them (e.g., Soliday & Stanton, 1995). Christensen (1988) even reported that research participants believed that it would be undesirable if we failed to investigate important topics that might require the use of deception.

Some Research Requires Deception

The dilemma about using deception in research is that some research projects virtually require a level of deception. If you want participants to act naturally, you might have to create a **cover story** that keeps them from acting in a self-conscious manner during the study. If, after careful consideration, you conclude that you need to use deception, you must keep two points in mind.

First, you should minimize the amount of deception involved. You need to make sure that you do not withhold critical information that would make a difference in a person's decision about whether to participate in your research. As Fisher and Fyrberg (1994) noted, we can characterize different kinds of deception, depending on the degree to which we actually provide incorrect information to participants. For example, we can distinguish between active and passive deception.

Active deception—The process of misinforming a research participant about some aspect of a study so that the individual is not aware of the investigator's intent in the project.

Passive deception—The failure to provide complete information to a research participant about some aspect of a study so that the individual is not aware of the investigator's intent in the project.

Debriefing—Informing research participants at the conclusion of a research project of the purpose of the research, including disclosure of any deception and providing an opportunity for participants to ask questions about the research.

Dehoaxing—The process of telling research participants of any deception or ruses used in a study.

Desensitization—The process of eliminating any negative aftereffects that a participant might experience after taking part in a project.

In **active deception**, you would actively mislead the participants by providing them with information that is not true. In **passive deception**, you would not actually tell a lie. Instead, you would withhold information that might give clues to the participants about the purpose of the study. That is, you give them incomplete information.

All research involves telling our volunteers less than we know. Participants would probably not be terribly interested in all the details of our research. At the same time, with passive deception, you intend to keep the participants in the dark, so your intent is clearly to deceive. One relevant question involves the extent to which you see an ethical difference between active and passive deception. This depends on your own point of view; psychologists differ in their beliefs in the matter.

Furthermore, you need to debrief your participants adequately after the session ends. There are two components to **debriefing**. One element involves **dehoaxing**, which means that you tell the individuals what you did, how you deceived them, and why it was necessary. The second element involves **desensitization**, which means that you eliminate any potential sources of negative feelings by the participants.

We have to make sure that when we explain to participants that they were deceived, the dehoaxing does not, in and of itself, lead to discomfort. Would people feel even worse knowing that they were deceived and would there be psychological risk simply because of the debriefing itself? One problem you face is that debriefing itself might lead to problems; a participant might feel worse after learning about a deception. In rare cases, one might refrain from debriefing a participant, but this should be a last resort that has received approval from an IRB.

The Effects of Debriefing on Research

Most psychologists debrief their participants immediately after a testing session concludes. Practically, this is the easiest approach. If a researcher decides to postpone the debriefing, it takes extra effort to contact the participants. One drawback to immediate debriefing is that participants might discuss our research with others. If you deceived them in order to make sure they acted naturally, there are obvious problems if your participants talk to others who later take part in your study.

How often will participants actually discuss the research with others? According to Marans (1988), of fifty participants in a debriefing-disclosure study, ten (20%) reported discussing the experiment with other potential participants. If 20 percent of participants disclose the nature of a study to others, this could pose a serious problem to the validity of research that relies on the naïveté of participants. On the other hand, Diener, Matthews, and Smith (1972) discovered that only eleven of 440 potential participants had learned about the deceptive elements of an experiment for which fellow students had volunteered. Diener et al. concluded that leakage of information is not a serious concern.

Further, Walsh (1976) reported that when researchers asked people not to disclose any information about the research, the participants refrained from discussing the study more than when such a request was not made. These results suggest that researchers must evaluate the potential problems of immediate debriefing on a study-by-study basis. If the investigator is worried that a participant might talk about the study and forewarn other potential participants of the nature of the study, the researcher might decide to defer debriefing until the end of the project. This would solve one problem: People remain naïve about the study. At the same time, this solution itself introduces a different problem, having to contact people later, which is not always easy.

Psychologists have asked the question of whether debriefing actually serves its purpose. That is, does it remove any negative responses of the participants? Although there is controversy (see Rubin, 1985), there seem to be few noticeable effects of deception when researchers take debriefing seriously. Gruder, Stumpfhauser, and Wyer (1977) studied the effects of feedback. These researchers provided participants with false feedback about poor performance after having taken an intelligence test. Gruder et al. wondered if there would be a difference in performance in a subsequent testing session depending on whether the participants learned about the false feedback in a debriefing session.

The results showed that when participants learned that the feedback was not accurate, their later performance on another test improved; there was no comparable trend among participants who were not debriefed. This suggests that false feedback about poor performance has a real effect on participants. On the other hand, debriefed participants were able to cast away the negative information readily. There are clear implications about the beneficial effects of debriefing and potential risks if it is not done or is not done well.

CONTROVERSY: On Deception

Do you like it when people lie to you? If you do, you are probably fairly unusual. Most people are upset when others lie to them. Over the years, psychologists have used deception in their research. Do people object to being lied to in these research settings? Or do you think that people are unconcerned? The answers to these questions are difficult because there are few absolute standards.

For instance, people in different cultures may show different responses to issues like deception in research. U.S. students are more likely to be bothered by it than are Malaysian students, although neither group appears terribly concerned about the issue of protecting research participants. Because of a greater tendency on the part of Malaysians to defer to the judgments of respected authorities, they may feel comfortable relinquishing an individual right to decline to participate in research (Bowman & Anthonysamy, 2006). So if you were interested in determining the ethics of a research project, your decision would be culturally based.

If you were to search for published articles on ethics in psychological research, you would find that a great deal of it would relate to the use of deception. Some psychologists (e.g., Ortmann & Hertwig, 1997) have condemned the use of deception in research, calling for the outlawing of the practice, in part on purely moral grounds. In response, other psychologists have argued that moral philosophers do not agree that deception is unambiguously wrong (Korn, 1998), that the "social contract" between researchers and participants may permit behaviors that might elsewhere be considered unethical (Lawson, 1995), and that participants themselves do not condemn such an approach (Christensen, 1988).

Fisher and Fyrberg (1994) asked potential participants (i.e., college students) to evaluate research scenarios involving three types of deception, implicit deception, technical deception, and role deception. Implicit deception involves having participants complete their tasks for a purpose of which they are unaware; in this case, Fisher and Fyrberg (1994) used this type of deception to manipulate mood by means of an imagery task.

Technical deception involves misrepresentation of the use of equipment; Fisher and Fyrberg technically deceived participants by telling them that equipment had broken down when it hadn't. Finally, role deception involves misrepresenting the role of another individual in the testing session; the researchers induced participants to believe that they had damaged another person's belongings.

The results suggested that people don't see much problem with implicit deception. Ninety percent of the students participating in Fisher and Fyrberg's study thought that the benefits of the research outweighed the costs. On the other hand, just over 70 percent of the students were comfortable with technical and role deception.

It might be informative to figure out why some research situations could lead to negative reactions. Psychologists who study embarrassment note that we feel embarrassed when we think somebody may evaluate us unfavorably (Miller, 1995). If we feel that we have been fooled in the presence of someone, we might be embarrassed because we feel that the person might think less of us. Thus, in a situation like technical deception or role deception, you might be annoyed at having been deceived. On the other hand, in implicit deception, the participants may not feel they are really interacting with another during the deception, so they don't feel uncomfortable.

If participants do not particularly mind implicit deception in a research study, does that relieve psychologists of the responsibility to consider the ethics of their actions? If participants do not mind being deceived, it means that one of several issues becomes less controversial.

Fisher (2005) has proposed that we consider deception on several dimensions. Her discussion related to research with children, but the three questions discussed here have validity for any project involving deception:

- Will alternative methodologies produce data of equal validity to that involve deception?
- Does deception permit the research participant to make an informed consent thereby minimizing potential harm?
- Will debriefing eliminate the potential for risk or could it cause problems in and of itself?

The question of using deception is complex. As Fisher and Fyrberg (1994) pointed out, participants are partners in research, not merely objects of study. As such, we have to balance the potential risks of psychological harm (e.g., embarrassment or anger at being deceived) with the potential benefits of research. We have to consider whether hiding the truth means that participants will not be able to make informed judgments about participation.

Question for Discussion: Under what conditions do you think it is acceptable for researchers to deceive participants?

ETHICAL ISSUES IN SPECIAL CIRCUMSTANCES

Ethics and Internet Research

A new challenge that we face as researchers involves ethical issues associated with using the Internet. Neither researchers nor IRBs have much experience with this approach. Still, we must protect our participants from risk, even those at remote sites.

We are in uncharted territory with web research. The community of psychological researchers has had a century to figure out how to complete in-person research; we have had well over a quarter of a century to come up with legally sanctioned protections for participants. But with web research, some very tricky questions arise about how to deal with the issues of confidentiality and anonymity (especially regarding sensitive topics), informed consent, protecting participants from unforeseen negative consequences, debriefing them, and how to arrange compensatory followup if it is needed (which we may never know).

A sizable amount of web-based research in psychology involves questionnaires. These are generally regarded as being fairly benign, so the risks associated with them are minimal. An added protection for the participants is that they can quit any time they want if they feel frustrated, overwhelmed, or otherwise uncomfortable. However, suppose a researcher wants to know about serious, private issues in a person's life. Two notable concerns appear here. First, it is absolutely required that the researcher guarantee that nobody can intercept the responses of the participant. Experts in the field of ethics will have to join experts in technology in certifying secure data transfer.

Second, merely filling out a questionnaire may trigger an emotional response; if it happens in a laboratory, the researcher can try to deal with any problems and can get help for the individual if necessary. The researcher can also arrange to contact the individual at a later point to make sure that there were no lasting problems. Nobody may ever know about the unfortunate consequences for remote people who participate online.

The research community recognizes these concerns and has begun to address them. Major national organizations have entered the discussion. The Board of Scientific Affairs of the American Psychological Association, the American Association for the Advancement of Science, and the federal government's National Institutes of Health are trying to generate solutions to these ethical questions (Azar, 2000a).

Finally, an ethical consideration that involves researchers, not participants, has arisen. With web research, it would be both possible and easy for an unscrupulous researcher to steal the ideas of another person (i.e., commit plagiarism), conduct a similar project, then claim priority for the ideas. Unfortunately, it could be difficult to know if somebody stole another's ideas.

Internet research has become a hot topic, so it would not be surprising that two people would generate similar research projects. How could we distinguish between simultaneous discovery and chicanery (i.e., cheating)? It could be possible by examining the records of the researchers, but the issue is not easy and could besmirch the reputations of honest scholars.

Ethics and Survey Research

All research carries the requirement of ethical behavior on the part of the investigator. With regard to survey research, we have to pay particular attention to two critical, related considerations—anonymity and confidentiality.

It is standard practice to completely guarantee both the anonymity and confidentiality of responses. This means that nobody who is not part of the research will have access to information about whether an individual participates or what his or her responses might have been.

If a researcher is tracking whether people have responded and wants to send a reminder to those who have not completed a survey, some kind of identification is necessary. In the rare event that an investigator needs to keep identification information over a long period of time, the data cannot be anonymous. There is nothing wrong with such procedures in and of themselves, although at the end of the project, the researcher should destroy any information that could link a respondent with participation in the study.

When researchers cannot guarantee anonymity, they can at least assure respondents that participation will be kept confidential. Confidentiality means that nobody will be able to connect a given person with participation in a study. This is typically assured by reporting the data only in aggregate, that is, in a summarized form so that nobody can tell who responded in one way or another. For surveys that ask sensitive questions, you must provide such assurances because your respondents will either decline to respond or will not tell the whole truth.

Ironically, if you make a big point of assuring confidentiality and anonymity, it may arouse suspicions in those you survey (Singer, Von Thurn, & Miller, 1995). In a situation involving mundane questions, it might be more reasonable to play down the confidentiality and anonymity aspects because they may distract a participant from the real purpose of the study. If you are going to ask sensitive questions about topics like sexual abuse, sexual behavior, drug or alcohol use, cheating, or behaviors that are otherwise disapproved of, you should make sure that the person knows about confidentiality and anonymity.

A further ethical constraint is that your respondents must know that they do not have to participate in your research and that they can terminate their responses at any time, without any penalty. This constitutes voluntary participation. If you stand over their shoulder or are even in their presence, you may be influencing a person's behavior; your respondent may feel compelled to enter answers because you are watching. You may be acting unethically and unprofessionally. You may also pay a price in the data. People may not respond honestly.

You can see in Table 2.5 the professional code of the Council for Marketing and Opinion Research. This code provides good guidance about ethical behavior in survey research. Naturally, you would want to follow APA's ethics code and state and federal laws as well.

Ethics and Research with Animals

Psychologists have studied animal behavior for the past century. Much of the work has involved laboratory rats and pigeons that have learned to perform tasks in different conditions. Even though the study of animal behavior constituted one of the pillars of psychology, not all people have agreed on its value. Some have criticized animal research as being of limited applicability to human behavior and restricted mostly to one variant of one species, namely, the Norway rat (Beach, 1950). This is an important question: Can we learn about people by studying animals? The answer is definitely yes, although we cannot learn everything from animals.

Table 2.5 The Ethics Code Promulgated by the Council for Marketing and Opinion Research

What Are Your Rights If You Are Surveyed?

Your participation in a legitimate marketing or public opinion research survey is very important to us, and we value the information you provide. Therefore, our relationship will be one of respect and consideration, based on the following practices:

- Your privacy and the privacy of your answers will be respected and maintained.
- Your name, address, phone number, personal information, or individual responses won't be disclosed to anyone outside the research industry without your permission.
- You will always be told the name of the person contacting you, the research company's name, and nature of the survey.
- You will not be sold anything, or asked for money, under the guise of research.
- You will be contacted at reasonable times, but if the time is inconvenient, you may ask to be recontacted at a more convenient time.
- Your decision to participate in a study, answer specific questions, or discontinue your participation will be respected without question.
- You will be informed in advance if an interview is to be recorded and of the intended use of the recording.
- You are assured that the highest standards of professional conduct will be upheld in the collection and reporting of information you provide.

A second group of people has condemned research with animals as being unethical. There are several aspects to their arguments. For instance, animal rights activists maintain that we do not have the right to keep animals in laboratory captivity. Some also believe that the animals are treated inhumanely. Over the past few decades, there has been growing sentiment against use of animals in research in society, although a majority of people still believe that if such research benefits humans, it is not unethical (see Plous, 1996a, for a discussion of these issues).

The use of animals in psychological research has diminished notably over the past several decades in the United States, Canada, and western Europe. According to Plous (1996a), a quarter to a third of psychology departments have either closed their animal laboratories or are giving it serious consideration. Further, there is a remarkable decrease in the number of graduate students in psychology who conduct animal research (Thomas & Blackman, 1992, cited in Plous, 1996a).

Plous has found that psychologists, as a group, show overwhelming support (over 85%) for naturalistic observation, which does not involve animal confinement, somewhat less support for studies involving laboratory confinement (over 60%), and little support for research involving pain or death (17 to 34%). He has also discovered that undergraduate psychology majors are highly similar to their mentors in the attitudes they hold toward the use of animals in psychological research (Plous, 1996b). He also noted that among the general public, there is significant support for research involving rats (88%), but less for dogs (55%).

If a person's own moral principles imply that it is unethical to use animals in research, then no arguments about the benefit to people will persuade that individual to accept such research. That person has the right to hold his or her moral principles and others must recognize that right. At the same time, the majority of Americans accept animal research as being beneficial, as long as the investigations might be beneficial to human welfare and do not expose the animals to unreasonable distress. We must rely on knowledge and common sense to make the best decision. If we are either to criticize or to defend research with animals, we need to know the truth of the animals' treatment at the hands of the scientists.

Arguments and Counterarguments. According to Coile and Miller (1984), some animal rights activists made claims about the plight of animals in psychological experiments that would make most of us wonder if the research is justified. The claims include the idea that animals receive intense electrical shocks that they cannot escape until they lose the ability to even scream in pain, that they are deprived of food and water, and suffer until they die.

Coile and Miller discussed six points raised by the activists (Mobilization for Animals, 1984, cited in Coile & Miller, 1984). Coile and Miller's arguments are two decades old but are probably still reasonably valid, especially given the changes in the nature of psychological research away from the animal model. Coile and Miller examined the previous five years of psychological journal articles that commonly report the use of research animals, like *Journal of Experimental Psychology: Animal Behavior Processes* and *Journal of Comparative Psychology*. They only looked at psychological journals; other disciplines, like biology, also rely on animals to varying degrees.

The claims of some activists were simply wrong regarding psychological research. The alleged intense electric shocks, severe food and water deprivation, smashing of bones and mutilation of limbs, and pain designed to make animals psychotic never appeared in research reported in the most prestigious psychology journals.

The fact that the claims about the research are false does not mean that the animals do not experience pain or distress in some studies. In fact, various experiments clearly involve discomfort, some of it intense. Research on learned helplessness, for example, involved such an approach.

Coile and Miller argued that there can be good reason for engaging in this type of research, particularly in the biomedical realm. For example, experimental animals have been used to investigate treatments for such maladies as cancer and AIDS in people and distemper in animals and to study ways to relieve the chronic pain that some people live with. Researchers who seek to further our understanding of depression sometimes use electrical shock as a treatment; however, as Coile and Miller pointed out, depression can lead to suicide, which is the third leading cause of death in young adults.

Miller (1985) further amplified some of the benefits of animal research for people suffering from problems like scoliosis, enuresis (bed wetting), anorexia, loss of the use of limbs due to nerve damage, chronic pain, stress, and headaches. Many people would consider it justifiable to study animals in order to ease the plight of people suffering from such problems.

As Plous (1996a, b) has found, psychologists and psychology students hold quite similar attitudes about the use of animals in research. The general public also shows sympathy toward animal research; there is widespread support regarding the use of rats in biomedical research. People do not like to see animals exposed to intense suffering or distress, though. According to the findings of Coile and Miller, psychologists do not regularly expose their research animals to the kind of treatment that people find objectionable. In some ways, however, the issue may become less pressing in psychology because the use of animals in research is on the decline.

SUMMARY

Scientists who study people usually show consideration for the well-being of the individuals they study. After all, scientists are just like everybody else in most respects. Unfortunately, however, there have been cases in which researchers have shown a reprehensible lack of concern about the people who participate in their studies.

Probably the most notorious violators of ethics in research are the Nazi doctors who tortured people in the name of research. Unfortunately, they are not the only ones who have violated ethical standards. For instance, U.S. researchers studying men with syphilis for several decades beginning in the 1920s withheld treatment to see the course of the disease. The men thought they were receiving appropriate levels of treatment.

In order to protect human participants, the American Psychological Association was one of the first organizations to promulgate ethical standards in research. APA has developed a set of aspirational goals and enforceable rules that members of APA must follow. It is the responsibility of each researcher to be aware of these rules. Student researchers are just as responsible for ethical treatment of participants as professional researchers are.

Among psychologists, Stanley Milgram is undoubtedly the most famous person whose research was questioned on ethical grounds. He deceived his participants into thinking they were shocking another individual. The controversy over whether he should have conducted his projects persists. In the end, the decision about ethics involves complex issues that differ for each instance we consider.

After the Nazi atrocities, an international body created the Nuremburg Code, which specifies the basic rights of human participants in research. It is an internationally recognized code. In the United States, there is federal and state legislation similarly protects the welfare of participants. One of the newest areas that is receiving scrutiny is web-based research. There are questions of informed consent and invasion of privacy that have yet to be addressed and resolved.

Another aspect of research ethics that has received considerable attention in the past few decades involves the treatment of animal subjects. Some people condemn any use of laboratory animals in research, regardless of the type of projects. Other people feel that if such research will ultimately benefit people, some degree of discomfort or harm is acceptable. Medical researchers are more likely to inflict pain or distress in animals; psychological research is usually more benign and may involve little, if any, discomfort for the animals. The controversial issues associated with animal rights is still an evolving field.

REVIEW QUESTIONS

Multiple Choice Questions

1. Researchers at the University of Cincinnati wanted to investigate how much radiation military personnel could be exposed to and still function. In order to study the effects of radiation, they
   a. gave food with radioactive substances to developmentally disabled children.
   b. withheld treatment from patients who had been accidentally exposed to radiation.
   c. exposed psychiatric patients to radiation without informed consent.
   d. subjected cancer patients to whole-body radiation without informed consent.
2. In recent psychological research that has received criticism on ethical grounds, the authors (Liston & Kagan, 2002)
   a. failed to cite research by other psychologists that was important and relevant to the development of their ideas.
   b. claimed to have completed a study but they did not actually carry it out.
   c. subjected participants to high levels of pain without first obtaining informed consent.
   d. published a figure that originally came from the research of other psychologists that had appeared in a different journal.
3. According to research by the U.S. Office of Research Integrity, the most frequently occurring ethical offenses involved
   a. departing from protocols for randomly assigning participants to groups.
   b. falsifying or fabricating data.
   c. plagiarizing by claiming that another researcher's data were the offender's own data.
   d. completely fabricating (i.e., making up) details of studies that were never actually conducted.
4. Pharmaceutical companies have come under criticism on ethical grounds by researchers because the companies
   a. have made so much money researching and producing drugs for the very ill.
   b. have waited much too long to release drugs that would benefit people who have no other effective drugs.
   c. have hired medical personnel to supervise drug research after those people had been accused of serious ethical violations in research and treating patients.
   d. regularly fail to receive informed consent by the patients they study.
5. The enforceable rules of conduct associated with the ethical principles developed by the American Psychological Association are
   a. aspirational goals.
   b. principles of responsibility.
   c. ethical standards.
   d. ethico-legal principles.

6. A psychologist who is providing therapy for a person should not develop a close friendship with the client because such dual relationships can compromise the success of the therapy. This problem relates to which General Ethical Principle of the American Psychological Association?
   a. Beneficence and nonmaleficence
   b. Respect for people's rights and dignity
   c. Justice
   d. Fidelity and responsibility
7. In resolving ethical situations involving legal issues and confidentiality, a psychologist
   a. can never reveal what a client has disclosed in a therapeutic session.
   b. may appropriately defer to legal authorities, even if it involves violating confidentiality.
   c. is obligated to keep information confidential if revealing it would cause embarrassment.
   d. is allowed to reveal confidential information only when a client gives written permission.
8. If you have deceived participants during the course of a study, you need to debrief them. When you tell them about the deception, you are engaging in
   a. dehoaxing.
   b. desensitization.
   c. ethical standards.
   d. informed consent.
9. When participants in Stanley Milgram's obedience studies left the research session, they had been told that they had been deceived about the nature of the study. Because the participants might have experienced potentially serious distress after the study, Milgram arranged for visits with a psychiatrist. This process was called
   a. dehoaxing.
   b. desensitization.
   c. compensatory followup.
   d. informed consent.
10. The Nuremburg Code of ethics in human research arose because of
    a. the failure to provide medical treatment in the research on syphilis done at the Tuskegee Institute.
    b. the addition of radioactive substances in children's food at a home for the developmentally disabled.
    c. Milgram's obedience studies.
    d. Nazi research in World War II.
11. Research may not require approval by an Institutional Review Board if
    a. it occurs in a commonly accepted educational setting and assesses instructional strategies.
    b. it involves only passive deception.
    c. a similar study has already been done elsewhere with no ethical problems.
    d. it involves studies of children.

12. Research on how people respond to informed consent forms has revealed that
    a. many Americans don't read well enough to understand what they are reading on the informed consent forms.
    b. many people do not bother to read the informed consent forms because they trust the researchers.
    c. the informed consent forms often omit information important for people to understand the research
    d. people are often upset after learning what they will have to undergo if they participate in the research.
13. The criticism of Milgram's obedience research by psychologist Diana Baumrind (1964) included the claim that the research
    a. did not include compensatory followup.
    b. should have been preceded by an attempt to estimate how many participants would be willing to give high levels of shock.
    c. did not include either dehoaxing or desensitization.
    d. costs in terms of participant distress were not outweighed by the benefits.
14. Milgram's obedience research was important at the time he conducted it because
    a. behavioral theories of the time predicted one outcome but Freudian theory predicted very different outcomes.
    b. the Nazi atrocities of World War II that were based on blind obedience was still fresh in people's memories.
    c. Milgram's studies were among the first to study the effect of obedience on racist behaviors.
    d. earlier studies of obedience had erroneously predicted how people would behave under stressful conditions.
15. Milgram defended his research by pointing out that he
    a. did not intend to harm anybody.
    b. engaged both in debriefing and in dehoaxing of participants after the study ended.
    c. paid participants well enough to overcome any discomfort they had experienced.
    d. the research was so important that it was acceptable, even if a few people were harmed.
16. Studies about participants' reactions to being deceived in research have revealed that
    a. most participants are offended when they learned that they have been lied to.
    b. deception leads participants to be skeptical or suspicious about psychological research.
    c. participants regard the science and practice of psychology positively, even after learning that they have been deceived.
    d. they agree that ethical guidelines should prohibit deception in psychological research.
17. When you decide to tell participants something false about a research session in order to mislead them, you are using
    a. naturalistic observation.

b. role playing.
c. active deception.
d. dehoaxing.

18. If volunteers complete an Internet-based survey on a sensitive and potentially distressing topic, one of the ethical considerations that is hard to deal with is
a. debriefing the participants after they complete their responses.
b. providing any necessary compensatory followup.
c. reaching people who might not take distressing topics seriously.
d. informing the participants that they can leave the study at any time.

19. Some psychologists have criticized research with animals on ethical grounds. They have claimed that
a. animal research cannot be used to understand or ultimately provide the basis for control of human behavior.
b. psychological research with animals has doubled about every ten years.
c. keeping animals in captivity is unethical in and of itself.
d. moral arguments are not a sufficient basis to justify ending animal research.

20. When psychology students evaluate research with animals, students
a. usually have very negative attitudes about the use of cats, dogs, and rats.
b. are very similar to their faculty mentors in their attitudes toward such research.
c. support such research for their own studies, but not for the research of others.
d. are very likely to agree that animals are necessary for their own research.

21. When participants complete a task for a purpose of which they are unaware, the researchers are using
a. technical deception.
b. implicit deception.
c. role deception.
d. naturalistic deception.

22. Participants are often uncomfortable when they learn that a research study has involved ____________ deception.
a. role
b. passive
c. implicit
d. active

23. If researchers provide negative, false feedback to participants, the performance of those participants may worsen. According to research, subsequent debriefing
a. leads to improved subsequent performance compared to participants who are not debriefed.
b. often results in anger on the part of the deceived participants.
c. makes no difference to the participants in subsequent behavior.
d. leads to later frustration on the part of the participants.

24. When considering the ethics of survey research, an investigator should
a. ensure that all responses are anonymous and confidential.
b. let respondents know from the very beginning that once they begin their participation, they need to continue with the project.

c. remember that if the researcher makes a big point of assuring confidentiality and anonymity, it may needlessly arouse suspicions among respondents.
d. avoid asking questions of a sensitive nature.

25. In their defense of research with animals, Coile and Miller argued that
    a. even though animals were often seriously harmed, the overall benefit to people was high enough to justify the pain.
    b. animals do not really suffer pain as intensely as people do, so the issue of pain in animal research is a minor issue.
    c. some day in the future, we will discover the benefits of research on animals, even if they have suffered.
    d. animals research has increased understanding of serious problems like chronic pain, depression, and anorexia.

Essay Questions

26. Identify the six general principles regarding ethical conduct and what behaviors they pertain to.
27. What types of research can be exempt from Institutional Review Board (IRB) consideration, according to U.S. federal law?
28. When people oppose the use of animal research, what arguments do they produce?

ANSWERS TO REVIEW QUESTIONS

Multiple Choice Questions

1.	d	10.	d	19.	c
2.	a	11.	a	20.	b
3.	d	12.	a	21.	b
4.	c	13.	d	22.	a
5.	c	14.	b	23.	a
6.	d	15.	a	24.	c
7.	b	16.	c	25.	d
8.	a	17.	c		
9.	c	18.	b		

Essay Questions

26. Identify the six general principles regarding ethical conduct and what behaviors they pertain to.

    Competence—Engaging in professional work for which one has adequate training and knowledge.

    Integrity—Refraining from engaging in inappropriate relationships with clients, colleagues, and research participants.

    Professional and scientific responsibility—Upholding ethical principles in one's own behavior and working to maximize it in colleagues.

Respect for people's rights and dignity—Treating people with respect, obeying laws and regulations, maintaining anonymity and confidentiality when appropriate.

Concern for others' welfare—Acting in ways that minimize the possibility of physical or psychological harm to others.

Social responsibility—Using psychological knowledge for the benefit of people and animals.

27. What types of research can be exempt from Institutional Review Board (IRB) consideration, according to U.S. federal law?

    Research conducted in established or commonly accepted educational settings, involving normal educational practices can be exempt from approval, such as the effects of different instructional strategies.

    Research involving the use of educational tests, survey procedures, interview procedures, or observation of public behavior. Surveys and interviews on sensitive or controversial topics may require IRB approval, though.

    In addition, research involving public officials or political candidates can be exempt from IRB approval.

    Research involving the collection or study of existing, publicly available data, documents, records, pathological specimens, or diagnostic specimens is exempt if the personal identity of those providing the data is protected.

28. When people oppose the use of animal research, what arguments do they produce?

    Some people argue from a practical standpoint, saying that we don't learn very much about people from studying animals, so keeping animals confined to laboratories reduces the quality of the animals' lives and doesn't produce useful research results.

    Other people argue from a moral standpoint, maintaining that we don't have the right to keep animals captive or to treat them inhumanely.

CHAPTER THREE

PLANNING RESEARCH

Generating a Question

CHAPTER OVERVIEW

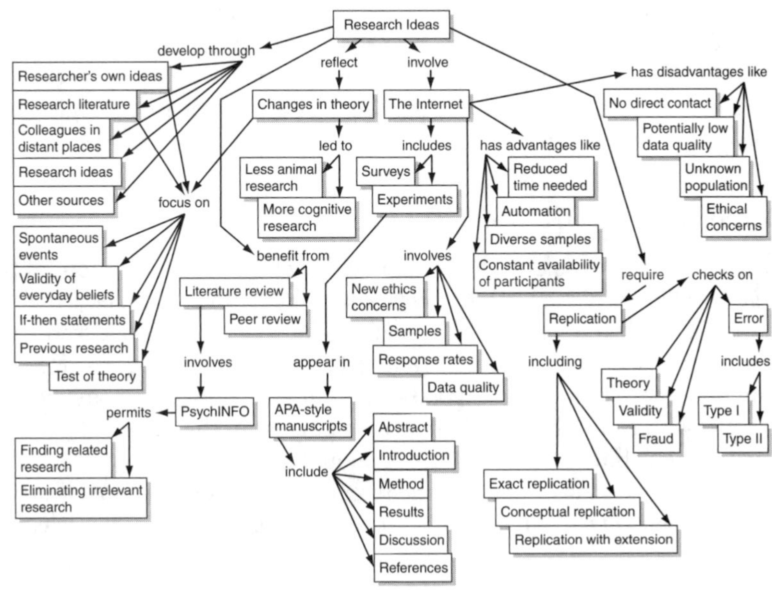

KEY TERMS

CHAPTER PREVIEW

Research questions come from a variety of sources and motivations, most of them arising from the investigator's curiosity. At the same time, our ideas develop within a social context. The questions we consider important develop because of the combination of our personalities, our histories, what society values, and other factors that may have little to do with the scientific research question per se.

Ideas arise in different ways. Sometimes, researchers notice an event that captures their interest, and they decide to create research to study it. At other times, researchers have a specific question to address or a problem to solve that leads to a research project. In some cases, researchers develop research ideas to test theories. No matter how the idea develops, researchers have to figure out the best way to investigate their questions.

To generate good research, investigators should be aware of the work of other scientists. This allows the investigator to advance knowledge and to avoid simply repeating what others have done. Such knowledge will also help a researcher generate new questions. Sources of information include scientific publications and presentations at research conferences. As your exposure to research expands, you will learn effective and efficient means of searching for prior work that relates to your own research question.

Electronic databases provide easy access to descriptions of research in psychology. By conducting a systematic literature review, psychologists can learn about the work of others, devise their own research questions, and ultimately publish research articles or make presentations at professional conferences.

New research questions are being asked using a convenient new technology: the Internet. We are just beginning to explore the best ways to collect data online. The future of such research looks very promising, but some methodological questions have to be resolved in this area.

HOW DO RESEARCH IDEAS DEVELOP?

If we read journal articles or listen to psychologists give presentations of their research, we get a coherent picture of what led them to do their research, how they accomplished it, and what their results mean. The final product is a nice package whose ideas flow logically; we can see how the ideas developed and how they progressed. Researchers who communicate well can weave a good story. But where do the research ideas come from?

Why do researchers study topics ranging from thinking and problem solving to social relationships to personality development? The answer is fairly simple: The researchers are curious and doing the research is fun. Research involves solving puzzles and getting answers, so why shouldn't it be enjoyable? Scientists like what they are doing even when they study serious and complex issues. Further, the social context of researchers' lives affect the types of questions they ask and how they ask them.

For example, people who are familiar with conventional birth control pills know that a woman takes a pill each day for three weeks out of the month. The pills in the fourth week are placebos that allow menstruation to occur. The reason for the development of this strategy is that the developer of the first birth control pill, John Rock, was a Catholic who wanted the form of contraception to be "natural," thus acceptable to his religious authorities. As such, his plan included monthly menstruation, even though it was not necessary or maybe even desirable (Gladwell, 2002). This episode provides a good example of how a researcher's religious beliefs led to his scientific approach. It would be an interesting exercise to speculate on what might have occurred if the strictures of the Catholic church had not been part of the picture. The nature of birth control may have gone through an entirely different development. In fact, the week of placebos may disappear as new contraceptive medication develops.

Let's consider an example of how simply thinking about an interesting social topic can lead to research questions. For instance, consider a topic that has captured the interest of the U.S. public: handgun control. Some people support control; some oppose it. Using surveys, researchers have investigated how often people protect themselves with their guns.

The picture is complex, which is why there is still debate on the topic. Data collected by Kleck and Gertz (1995) suggested that Americans use their guns for self-defense about 2.5 million times a year in various emergency situations. According to Hemenway (1997), those surveys reflected overestimates of protective gun use. In this debate, there are valid data supporting contradictory claims. Both sides approach the research carefully and look for valid information. But the topic is very complex, and each answer to a research question raises new questions. As a result, the research on the topic continues. Because of the complexity of the issue, the data don't point to a single, clear answer regarding whether handgun ownership is, on balance, a positive or a negative phenomenon.

One of the reasons that researchers have a hard time answering questions definitively is that the issues are so complex. Beyond that, though, whenever you ask people for information, they may mislead you without even knowing it. People think their memories are accurate, but there are many gaps and errors in what they recall. According to Wentland and Smith (1993), people are not as accurate as you might suppose in responding to easy questions, such as whether they own an automobile, a home, a driver's license, or a library card. We should not be surprised that answers to hard questions are more problematic. It would be an interesting research project to discover the situations in which we should accept people's reports of behaviors and those situations when we should not.

In essence, any time we encounter a behavior that we do not fully understand, there is potential for a research project.

Informal and Formal Sources of Ideas

There are various ways that research ideas develop. We can characterize them on a continuum as being more or less formal. Figure 3.1 presents this continuum and the kind of question that leads to more research.

Informal			**Formal**
"This is interesting. I'd like to know more about it!"	"We have a problem to solve. Let's figure out the best way to do it."	"Our earlier project answered some of our questions, but there are still some unanswered questions."	"The theory says people should act this way. Let's test the theory."

FIGURE 3.1 Continuum representing the development of research ideas.

The Continuum of Research Ideas. Sometimes a research question will arise because a psychologist observes something in everyday life and decides that he or she would like to research it. The idea does not derive from theory or from previous research, only from curiosity about some behavior that takes place. This approach represents a very informal and idiosyncratic way of generating research ideas. If it weren't for the fact that the psychologist happens to notice something worth investigating in a particular situation, the research might not take place.

One step toward the more formal or systematic end of the continuum involves solving practical problems. That is, in a particular situation, you might look around and say, "We can do this better." The next step would be to design a program to test your ideas. Psychologists who work in organizations or in industry often specialize in solving such applied problems. Their approach is not based only on personal observation and curiosity, but it comes from a question that relates to the workplace. This strategy is somewhat more formal than deciding to study a behavior because it catches your eye. At the same time, it does not develop from other research or from a theory; it might be idiosyncratic to a particular time or place. The research takes place because the psychologist is in the position to solve practical problems as they arise in a particular setting.

A third point on the continuum involves researchers who evaluate the work of others or who are in the middle of a research program. Already completed research has some loose ends, so the investigator takes the partial answers and tries to extend our knowledge. This is a more formal approach to research because the ideas that led to a particular project are embedded within a research context and help answer a question that others are also investigating.

At the most formal end of the continuum, a research idea can develop from a well-defined theory. That is, a theory predicts certain behaviors, so the psychologist tries to see whether the behaviors follow from theoretical predictions. This would represent the most formal approach because theoretical expectations may dictate the nature of the research. The questions to be answered are not the result of a single, unsystematic event, but rather unfold from a well-defined and systematic set of ideas. Most research ideas develop in the middle of the continuum. That is, old ideas lead to new ideas that we can test empirically.

According to Glueck and Jauch (1975), researchers in the natural and physical sciences tend to develop their projects based on a combination of their own insights and the results of previous research. Clark (cited in Glueck & Jauch, 1975) agreed that productive psychologists also tend to generate their research ideas based on earlier work. We see what others have done and we try to clear up the loose ends.

Table 3.1 presents how researchers say they develop their ideas. Figure 3.2 illustrates the difference in importance. As you can see, investigators generate ideas on their own, from the research literature, and in conjunction with colleagues in their field at different institutions. Colleagues in their own institutions are seen as less helpful, probably because most departments have people with very different research interests.

Research ideas often arise from the personal interests of the investigators. For example, the noted psychologist Robert Sternberg of Tufts University became interested in issues of intelligence because of his own experience with taking tests. Sternberg, who was elected president of the American Psychological Association and has written or edited dozens of books and has authored hundreds of scientific journal articles, did not score very well on standardized intelligence tests. There is a clear discrepancy between the message given by his test scores ("he isn't very smart") and his remarkable achievements ("he is very smart"). Sternberg has spent a considerable part of his career studying the various forms intelligence can take. He currently directs a center that actively investigates intelligence and knowledge and how we can assess them.

The Effect of Theory

The dominant theoretical perspective affects the kind of research questions that investigators ask. We can see this pattern occurring in psychology now as it relates to animal research. From the early 1900s until well into the 1960s, psychologists studied animal behavior to help understand all behavior, including that of humans. This meant creating research questions that could be asked with nonhuman subjects.

TABLE 3.1 Different Sources of Ideas for Research in Order of Frequency of Occurrence, as Reported by Active Scientists

The more frequent sources appear first in the table (Glueck & Jauch, 1975).

Source of Research Ideas	Comment
Researcher's own ideas	People have more interest in their own ideas, so they are more likely to invest time and resources in studying those ideas.
Research literature	Reading others ideas can give you an idea for an extension to fill in the gaps in knowledge; it can also lead to an idea for trying to disprove a claim.
Distant colleagues	Researchers build up a network of contacts across the country or the world. Discussions with these colleagues provides stimulation to develop new ideas.
Departmental colleagues	In most science departments in colleges and universities, there may not be much overlap in specialized, professional interests among faculty in a department. It can be hard to develop joint research ideas because local colleagues very often have different interests.
Research team	In many laboratories, students carry out the research program of the director, who may develop most of the research ideas.
Local colleagues outside the department	It is rare that researchers can provide significant ideas to others outside their own area of expertise.

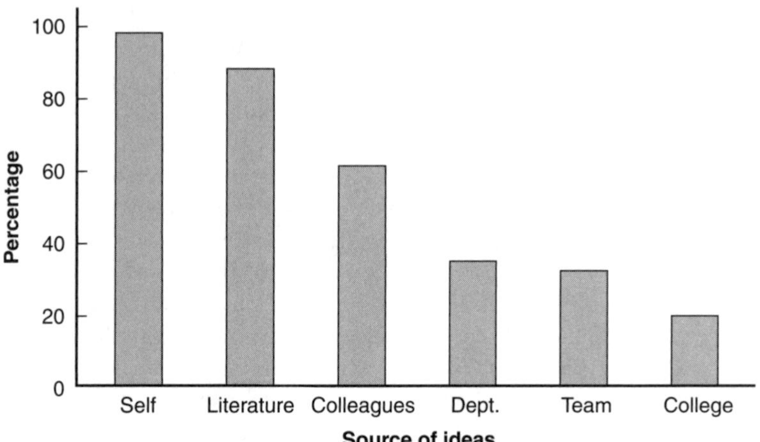

FIGURE 3.2 Percentage of the time that scientists get ideas for their research from various sources at least some of the time. [Note: *Colleagues* refers to researchers at different institutions.]

Source: W. F. Glueck & L. R. Jauck (1975). *The Journal of Higher Education, 46*, 103–114. Copyright © 1975 by The Ohio State University Press. All rights reserved. Adapted with permission.

Over the past few decades, though, there has been a notable change in the way psychologists do research. For example, in Great Britain, the amount of animal research has declined precipitously. The number of doctoral dissertations by young researchers in psychology that involve animals has declined by 62 percent over the past twenty-five years (Thomas & Blackman, 1992, cited in Plous, 1996a). We haven't exhausted the entire repertoire of research questions involving animals, we have just focused our attention differently.

As we have seen in the discussion of ethics in research, many people have noted that ethical concerns led them away from research with animals. There are other significant factors as well. Social forces are complex, and major changes in the way people think reflect multiple underlying causes.

Reasons for Decreases in Animal Research. Several reasons can help account for these changes. One reason is that there are more women earning doctorates in psychology. In general, women seem to be interested in different topics—those that don't involve animals.

A second possibility is that, as a society, we have become more sensitized to the ethical issues associated with animal research. Even though psychologists may support the use of animals in research, as we have seen in Chapter 2, these same psychologists may choose not to involve animals in their own professional work.

Behaviorism—A theoretical approach in psychology that focused on studies of observable behaviors rather than internal, mental processes.

Another reason for the decline in animal research is that we have changed theoretical perspectives. For the first seven decades of the last century, the dominant paradigm was **behaviorism**. One of the fundamental tenets of behaviorism is that a few simple principles of learning and behavior can explain the behavior of virtually any organism of any species. Thus, it does not matter if you study people or rats; the specific behaviors may differ, but the principles of learning, reinforcement, and punishment hold true across species, according to the behaviorists. Thus, what is true for rat behavior would be true for human behavior.

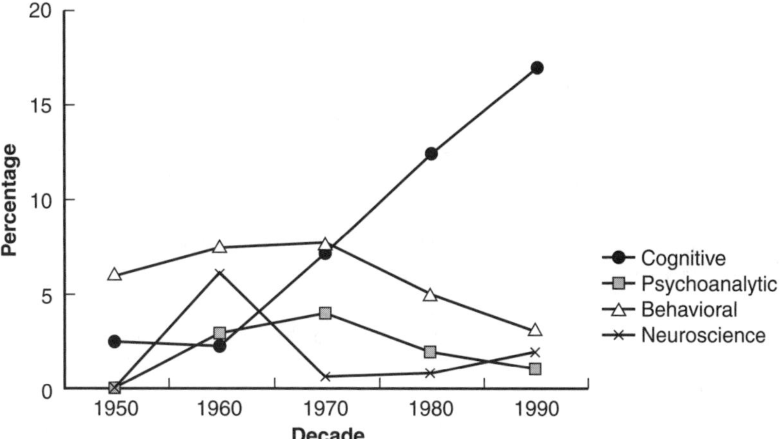

FIGURE 3.3 Percentage of articles by decade published in key psychology journals that include keywords associated with cognitive, behavioral, psychoanalytic, and neuroscience perspectives.

Source: R. W. Robins, S. D. Gosling, and K. H. Craik (1999). An empirical analysis of trends in psychology. *American Psychologist*, *54*, 117-128. Copyright American Psychological Association. Reprinted with permission.

Psychologists have expanded on this simple set of rules and have developed new ideas to explore more complex behavior and thought. Behaviorism has not been shown to be false; indeed, its principles have led to some very useful outcomes. With the new cognitive orientation, though, we have begun to ask different kinds of questions.

The Effect of the Cognitive Revolution. What does this movement away from behaviorism and animal studies mean about the nature of the research we publish? As Figure 3.3 reveals, some striking patterns emerge. The so-called "cognitive revolution" in psychology is clear from the amount of research that is cognitive in nature. According to Robins, Gosling, and Craik (1999), the percentage of articles using words related to cognition have has risen dramatically since the early 1970s.

During the past three decades, the use of behavioral terms (e.g., reinforcement, punishment, discriminative stimulus) has declined. (Even though behavioral terms have decreased in use, the principles of behaviorism still account for some of the most generally useful principles of behavior.) Also, in spite of the excitement about neuroscientific approaches in psychology, researchers have seldom included terms related to it in the past half century; it falls one short step ahead of the even more scant references to psychoanalytic approaches. These trends allow us to make predictions about the dominant patterns of psychological research in the future. It will likely be psychologically based and largely human, rather than biologically based and animal.

HOW CAN YOU DEVELOP RESEARCH IDEAS?

Professional researchers have an easier time developing a research project than a beginning student researcher because professionals have more knowledge and a greater sense of the field in which they work. In addition, once a person establishes a research program, new ideas often emerge easily.

How should you begin to select a problem for yourself? The first step is to acquire as much knowledge as you can about as many different areas as you can. The greater your scope of knowledge, the more likely you will be able to bring together different ideas into a unique project.

TABLE 3.2 Approaches to Generating Research Ideas and Some Examples of Ideas That Could Develop into Research Projects (McGuire, 1983)

Types of Phenomena	An Idea That You Could Develop
Studying spontaneously occurring events	
Intensive case studies	Study the behavior of a friend who consistently scores well on tests. Try to find out why and see if the technique works for others.
Extrapolate from similar problems already studied	Psychologists have investigated the credibility of expert witnesses. One question that remains to be answered, though, is whether jurors respond similarly to female and male expert witnesses.
Studying the validity of everyday beliefs and when these beliefs break down	
Reverse the direction of a commonsense hypothesis	Many common sayings, like "Opposites attract," suggest behavioral hypotheses. You could investigate whether opposites really do attract, by studying to see if similar people are more likely to date or form friendships.
Evaluating formal if-then statements	
Use the hypothetico-deductive method of saying that "if A is true, then B should be true"	Psychologists have discovered in laboratory research that people learn better with multiple, short sessions than in single, long sessions. Conduct a survey in which you test the hypothesis that "if students study in multiple, short sessions, they should perform better in classes than students who study in single, long sessions."
Using previous research as a stepping stone	
Bring together areas of research that originally did not relate	Research on people with physical disabilities and research on sport and exercise psychology can come together for investigators who would like to apply knowledge on sport and exercise to a new population that has not been connected to this domain in the past (Crocker, 1993).
Tests of theory	Piagetian theory generally does not support the idea that children regress to previous levels of cognitive development; test children under difficult conditions (e.g., when they have a limited time to complete a long task) to see if they do regress.

McGuire (1983) has developed a set of useful techniques that you could use to generate research questions. His suggestions span the continuum from very informal to very formal. At the most personal and informal level, he suggested that you introspect about your own experiences and use your thoughts to generate research questions. At the more formal level, he proposed that you can look at research in a particular area and try to adapt some of those ideas to a new area. Table 3.2 presents a list of research possibilities that you could implement; the research questions may be relatively simple, but they can lead to productive ideas.

Generating Research Hypotheses

McGuire (1983) suggested that too many people erroneously believe that generating research questions involves creativity that cannot be taught. If this were true, highly creative individuals would use their innate gift to generate research, and for the unfortunate people with less creativity, the likelihood of engaging in good research would be low. McGuire disagreed with this pessimistic view. He proposed a set of approaches to generating research questions.

Table 3.2 illustrates that it isn't always difficult to generate research ideas. One suggestion is to evaluate commonsense ideas to see when they hold true and when they don't. You may hear that "opposites attract" as a principle of human behavior. This maxim leads to testable hypotheses. Once you define what you mean by "opposites" you can find out if we tend to select people opposite to us. You may find instead that "Birds of a feather flock together."

You could also combine previously unrelated topics. For instance, research on sports and physical disabilities don't usually fall together. You might be able to generate some interesting research projects by connecting them. It is important to remember that the more practice you get in developing ideas and the more knowledge you gain in a particular area, the easier it is to come up with new research projects.

Many of the ideas that you generate at first will probably have been studied already. The reason for this is that if the idea is obvious to you, it will probably be obvious to others. You may have to revise your initial plan. This can be a frustrating experience for students because you may not have enough background knowledge to be able to figure out how to proceed, so you feel that all the good ideas have been taken. This is where you can rely on professionals in the field (including your professor).

Sometimes researchers make suggestions for future projects. For instance, Goodman-Delahunty (1998) provided a set of questions of particular relevance to psychologists interested in the interface between psychology and the law. Goodman-Delahunty reported that studies of sexual harassment typically involve college students as participants. Further, the research may not employ accurate legal definitions of sexual harassment. The mock trial transcripts are also not very complex, unlike real life. What would happen if you did a study with people from the working world? What about using more realistic scenarios? We don't know what would happen because researchers have not yet investigated these questions. Table 3.3 presents further topics for study. These examples involve psychology and the law, but you can use the same process for just about any other area of study.

TABLE 3.3 Examples of Potential Research Projects on Gender and Law That Are Based on Existing Research and Legal Questions

Current Situation: Sexual harassment creates a hostile working environment, but there are differences in people's conceptualizations of what constitutes harassment. Studies of gender differences in perception of sexual harassment are complex and inconsistent (Goodman-Delahunty, 1998).

Recommendations for Related Research:

- Do results differ when we use accurate, legal definitions of sexual harassment in research, which is not always done?
- Do simple, fictitious cases result in different outcomes than rich and complex scenarios that occur in actual legal cases?
- Do convenience samples consisting of college undergraduates produce results different from studies using other people?

Current Situation: Jurors have to evaluate the credibility and the evidence presented by expert witnesses. Are female and male experts regarded the same by different participants in trials related to battered women who kill their spouse (Schuller & Cripps, 1998)?

Recommendations for Related Research:

- What happens if we vary the sex of the expert witness as well as the nature of other testimony and evidence?
- Can we identify different mannerisms and characteristics of expert witnesses that may add or detract from their credibility and that may be confused with gender effects?
- Does gender of an expert witness make a difference in more versus less serious offenses?

Current Situation: Most sexual harassment claims are made by women against men, but on occasion, men are the victims of such harassment. Those inflicting the harassment may be either female or male, although men report fewer negative reactions to these experiences (Waldo, Berdahl, & Fitzgerald, 1998).

Recommendations for Related Research:

- Given that harassment might take different forms for female and male victims, do people show parallel criteria pertaining to women and to men?
- Can we identify whether male jurors will defer to female jurors during debate, or vice versa?
- Do juries take harassment of men as seriously as they do harassment of women? Gay men versus straight men?
- Will a jury deal with the questions of the severity of the harassment differently for men and women?

Current Situation: In research settings, aggressive defense attorneys seem to gain acquittal for clients more than passive attorneys do. Male attorneys are more successful than female attorneys (Hahn & Clayton, 1996).

Recommendations for Related Research:

- Do aggressive attorneys achieve the same acquittal rate with adult witnesses and child witnesses?
- Do female attorneys achieve equal success when they question female and male witnesses?
- Do female and male prosecuting attorneys have comparable success in winning convictions?

You are likely to experience greater success if you pick a small research question. Even professional researchers investigate small questions, accumulating a great deal of knowledge bit by bit.

THE VIRTUAL LABORATORY: RESEARCH ON THE INTERNET

Some psychological research requires specialized laboratory space and equipment. Whenever we want to measure specific behaviors or responses just as they occur, we must be in the presence of the people (or animals) we measure. It is hard to imagine that a behavioral researcher could study reinforcement or punishment without having direct contact with whomever is being observed. If developmental psychologists want to see whether an infant will cross a visual cliff, parents must bring the infant to the laboratory.

However, psychologists may be easily able to accomplish research at a distance that involves judgments of opinion and attitude. For such studies, it is common to bring participants to the laboratory and administer surveys and tests to them or to mail the materials. (Unfortunately, people often do not mail them back.) With the advent of easy access to the Internet, we no longer need to be in the physical presence of those who agree to participate in such research, and we don't need to go to the trouble and expense of mailing anything. The concept of the laboratory is undergoing adjustment; it can be worldwide in scope. Table 3.4 presents some examples of actual web-based research. As you can see, survey research involves attitudes and their relations to behavior. There are also experiments that involve manipulations. Creative researchers should be able to use the Internet to good effect.

Research using the Internet poses special considerations because it is a relatively new methodology. Just as researchers had to identify critical aspects of telephone sur-

TABLE 3.4 Samples of Web-Based Research

Survey Research

Topic: Romantic relationships
Researcher: Manuela Thomae (University of Kent at Canterbury, UK)

Topic: Personal standards in early, middle, and later adulthood
Researchers: J. Stoeber (University of Kent, UK) and F. S. Reschke (University of Halle, Germany)

Topic: Differences in the ways people think and behave in everyday life
Researchers: Erica Hepper and Constantine Sedikides (University of Southampton, UK)

Experimental Research

Topic: Implicit attitudes and stereotypes regarding people of different races or ethnicities
Researchers: Nosek, Banaji, and Greenwald (2002)

Topic: Judgments and decision making about causing harm when aiding somebody
Researchers: Royzman and Baron (2002).

veys forty years ago, now we have to figure out how to collect data most effectively on the Internet. This concern holds true for other types of research as well.

Ethical issues provide a good starting point for the discussion of Internet surveys. We should follow the ethical guidelines that professionals have developed, such as those of the American Association of Opinion Research and of the American Psychological Association. But we have to consider the issues a little differently here.

Some people believe that Internet research has the potential for greater invasion of privacy than other modes of data collection. They contend that sending unwanted surveys via email invades the personal space of recipients; when people pay for their email access according to length of time they spend online (e.g., when they are in an Internet cafe), unwanted email has a real monetary cost. Another type of privacy that Internet surveys can violate is called informational privacy, which relates to information about an individual that is sent on the World Wide Web. It could be used for sending additional email to the unsuspecting person. Many respondents share this fear and claim to have lied on surveys (Cho & LaRose, 1999).

There is also the ethical (and legal) question of sending a research instrument to a minor via the World Wide Web. One of the prime conditions of research is that it be voluntary and that the person be informed about the nature of the research. Legally, minors cannot volunteer on their own. Further, children may not realize the implications about the information they provide, so their consent would not be truly informed.

Regarding adult participation, sometimes people read personal email at their work, which might violate company policies. Sending an email or Internet survey to a person who gets it at work might be ethically questionable, even though it is the recipient who has decided to violate company rules. In addition, organizations may intercept some email messages or may even store anything a person sends. Thus, the content of the response may endanger the person both physically (e.g., loss of the job) and psychologically (e.g., embarrassment because of some responses to survey questions).

Internet Research

Some aspects of Internet research mirror those in traditional formats. For instance, changing fonts and text size, including a lot of bold and italic type and lack of contrast between the text and the background reduce the usability of paper surveys; the pattern will likely hold true for Internet surveys. If researchers take care of these formatting considerations, computerized testing (including the Internet) seems to lead to comparability with other formats (Gosling, Vazire, Srivastava, & John, 2004; Vispoel, 2000).

It would be nice to know exactly who is likely to complete online surveys. We do have a partial picture of who is connected to the Internet. Table 3.5 gives a breakdown of who is using the Web. The picture is still incomplete, but you can see that the demographic characteristics of Internet users do not mirror those of the general population in the United States. As of several years ago, people with incomes under $30,000 represented about one-third of all households, but they constituted less than one-tenth of the Internet traffic; at the other end of the continuum, web users with over $100,000 income constituted about one-tenth of the population, but they represented twice that proportion of those who are online. Currently, the incidence of Internet use in low-income households has risen, but people in these households are connected at lower rates than

TABLE 3.5 Demographics of Internet Users

Numbers reflect the percentage of each group who used the Internet in early 2007.

Total Adults	71%
Women	70
Men	71
Age	
18–29	87
30–49	83
50-64	65
65+	32
Race/Ethnicity	
White, Non-Hispanic	73
Black, Non-Hispanic	62
English-speaking Hispanic	78
Geography	
Urban	73
Suburban	73
Rural	60
Household Income	
Less than $30,000/yr	55
$30,000–49,000	69
$50,000–74,999	82
$75,000+	93
Educational Attainment	
Less than high school	40
High school	61
Some college	81
College +	91

Source: Demographics of internet users (2007). Pew Internet & American Life Project, February 15-March 7, 2007 Tracking Survey. www.pewinternet.org/trends/User_Demo_6.15.07.htm. Reprinted with permission.

people in higher-income homes. Accessibility to the Internet is also associated with age, race, where people live, and educational level (Demographics of Internet Users, 2007).

Not only do we have to consider who is online, but we also have to pay attention to how much time they spend on the Web. Teens spend more time on the Web than they did a few years ago. In fact, the average teen, aged 12 to 17 years, spent an average of almost 45 minutes online every day in 2006, a 19 percent increase over the previous year (The Score: Teens highly engaged online, 2006). Teens and young adults use the Internet much more than older adults, although as current users age, this discrepancy may diminish or disappear.

One of the major problems concerning the representativeness of online studies is that we are never sure exactly what population such surveys pertain to because there is no exhaustive specification of the population (Schillewaert, Langerak, & Duhamel, 1998). In fact, the international nature of the Internet means that researchers have even less knowledge about the population of potential respondents than in other modes.

If you decide to conduct a study online, you want to maximize the return on your work. What is the best way to get people to respond? This is not a question with an easy answer.

One study of Internet surveys led to minuscule response rates of 0.18 percent when notices of the survey appeared in a print magazine, requiring readers to switch to a computer to complete the survey. When a person was able to use a hyperlink to access a survey, the response rate was somewhat higher, 0.68 percent, but still extremely low. When a posting appeared in newsgroups, the response rate was estimated to be 1.68 percent. Finally, when respondents were emailed individually three times, the return rate was 31 percent, which is a respectable figure. You can see the magnitude of the difference in Figure 3.4. Not surprisingly, persistence and a personal approach provide the best results.

An advantage to the email technique is that responses arrive very quickly, much more so than the other approaches. Further, the quality of the data (i.e., how complete the responses were) seems to be comparable, regardless of the means of notifying respondents (Schillewaert, Langerak, & Duhamel, 1998).

Online surveys aren't noticeably worse than other approaches, and they have some practical advantages. It's not unreasonable to expect their frequency to increase as researchers become familiar with the characteristics of successful Internet surveys and the approaches that work best.

Respondent Motivation

It doesn't help a researcher if a potential respondent receives but ignores the information. For instance, over the past few decades, the response rate for surveys in general has decreased, and email surveys have lower response rates than mail and telephone surveys (Cho & LaRose, 1999).

You can try to motivate people to comply by using incentives. However, the motivating factors that work in mail surveys may not translate to the computer. Researchers have not yet determined the functional equivalents of mail incentives, which include money in mail surveys (Martinez-Ebers, 1997) and in face-to-face surveys (Willimack, Schuman, Pennell, & Lepkowski, 1995), and even tea bags (which don't work; Gendall, Hoek, & Brennan, 1998).

Another potential problem is that there is so much research on the internet that it is unlikely that any single researcher's work will stand out. Scientific investigators tend to be cautious in their approaches, which includes creating credible-looking, but not flashy, web pages. Such websites have a hard time competing with the more glittering marketing or entertainment pages.

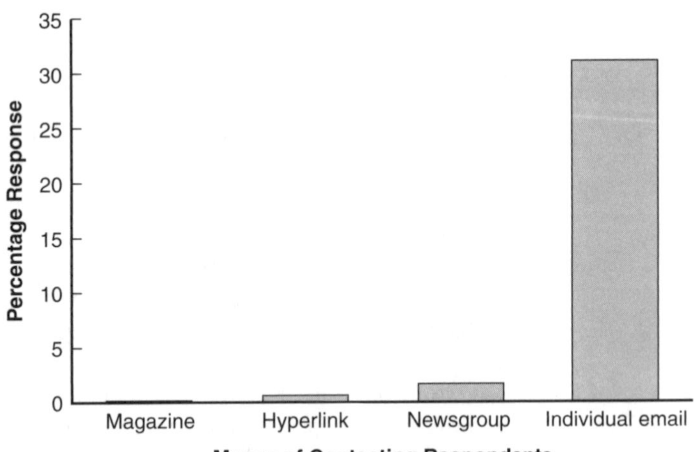

FIGURE 3.4 Response rates to online surveys for various means of contacting potential respondents (Schillewaert, Langerak, & Duhamel, 1998).

For instance, the website by Mister Poll (www.misterpoll.com) presents entertainment polls on a variety of topics. Fortunately, the owner of the site does include a disclaimer about what the results mean: "Mister Poll is interested in what you think about anything and everything. He maintains a directory of the most interesting and topical polls created by his staff and independent pollsters for your general entertainment. None of these polls are 'scientific,' but do represent the collective opinion of everyone who participates." It is hard for serious researchers to compete with such entertainment. An example of some questions from an environmentally oriented poll that used to appear on that website appears in Table 3.6.

The environmental poll may be fun to complete and submit, but it would be risky to draw any conclusions from it about people's feelings on the environment. For instance, how many people would seriously claim that they do not care about the environment? In addition, the misspellings in the table (which came from the survey itself), reduce its credibility. As mentioned before, this kind of poll is fun and entertaining, but it is not scientifically valid. Other, more serious polls appear on the such sites as the

TABLE 3.6 Example of an Entertainment Poll as the Questions Appeared on the Mister Poll Website (www.misterpoll.com)

Question	Comment
Are you for the Enviroment?* ☐ Yes ☐ No ☐ Yes, but I'm not a radical	How many people do you know that would claim that they are against the environment. In addition, the question suggests that if you claim to be for the environment, you are likely to be a radical.
Do you support the work of the EPA and the GDC? ☐ Yes ☐ No ☐ Yes, but only the EPA ☐ Yes, but only the GDC	Do you know what "GDC" stands for? If not, can you say whether you support it?
What activitys do you enjoy? ☐ Computer ☐ Fine Arts ☐ Television ☐ Hiking and camping ☐ Sports ☐ Traveling ☐ Cooking ☐ Reading	What does this question have to do with the environment? When irrelevant questions appear on a survey, the credibility of the survey may diminish. This is the kind of item that appears on a marketing instrument, not in scientific research.
Which of these settings is the most beatiful to you? ☐ The Television Screen ☐ The Veiw from you porch ☐ The graduer of Nature ☐ Watching smog rise from a stack	This humorous item can clearly be seen as meant for entertainment. Would it change your opinion about the rest of the survey?

*Note: These questions (including misspellings) came directly from the Mister Poll website and are used for illustrative purposes only.

Cable News Network (CNN) website. They too are clearly marked as being nonscientific, reflecting only those who choose to participate. Would you prefer to complete a one-question survey on a serious topic, a longer entertainment survey, or a still-longer serious scientific survey? This is an important question for researchers.

Advantages to Web-Based Research

We can see four clear advantages to web research. The first involves the amount of time required to test a single participant. In traditional research it takes a lot of time for a researcher to test people individually; the investigator needs to arrive at the testing site in advance in order to set up the experimental apparatus and materials. Then the researcher waits for the participant to show up. People do not always honor their commitments, though; they may forget where to go or when to show up. If the participant appears, the session runs its course for perhaps 15 minutes up to an hour. Then the researcher needs to collect all the data forms, informed consent forms, and put away any equipment.

For some projects, it would not be unreasonable to expect the time commitment to be an hour per person. Web-based research requires the initial time to create a web page, but this time commitment probably would not exceed the time required to put together the in-the-lab, paper version of the study. Over time, a web-based project could involve significantly less time per person than a laboratory-based project because there is no required laboratory setup for each new person. In fact, it can be remarkably easy to create an online survey through websites like SurveyMonkey (www.surveymonkey.com), which provides the ability to create surveys easily and to post them online with little technological knowledge.

A second advantage of web-based research is that the investigator does not need to be available when a participant is interested in engaging in the task. The web is open all day, every day. Data collection occurs at the convenience of the participant, not at the inconvenience of a researcher who has to set aside time from a busy schedule to be in the lab.

A third advantage of web research is that data collection is automatic and accurate. In the traditional version of research, an investigator has to transfer information from an original data sheet to some other form so data analysis can take place. When the amount of data from a single person is large, it takes a long time to enter and record data, and there are more opportunities for error. When research occurs on the web, the investigator can create a means by which the data are automatically transferred to a file for data analysis. The chance for error diminishes drastically.

A fourth advantage is that we can generate a sample of participants that extends beyond college students; any interested person of any age who is living anywhere in the world can take part.

Potential Problems with Web-Based Research

As you will see throughout this book, any solution to potential problems in conducting research introduces its own problems. We want to make sure that we eliminate major difficulties and that the limitations that remain are as minimal as possible. In the case of web-based research, we eliminate the disadvantages of having to schedule participants to test in person, to code and transfer data, and so forth. At the same time, we introduce potential problems.

One concern is that, although the research can take place in the absence of the investigator, we also lose the advantage of having a person who can help a participant who is uncertain of how to proceed, who might misunderstand directions, or who might have a question. Thus, although the investigator does not have to be present (an advantage), it is also true that the researcher cannot be there (a disadvantage). The question that we need to address is whether we gain or lose more through data collection in the laboratory versus on the web.

Second, the gain in accuracy in data collection can be offset if remote participants provide poor data. If they do not take the research seriously or if they return to the website for repeated testing, the quality of the data will suffer. Once again, because of the remote nature of the procedure, the investigator may never know about the problem. Fortunately, research on the quality of data collected on the web suggests that the quality is high (Azar, 2000b; Vadillo, Bárcena, & Matute, 2006). For instance, Vadillo et al. presented their participants with a learning task that was either online or that used paper and pencil. The degree and pattern of learning were similar for both groups, leading to a sense of confidence that participants engage in the same types of behaviors and thought processes online as they do in a traditional laboratory setting.

In general, according to Krantz and Dalal (2000), the results of traditional laboratory studies with college students correspond quite closely to web-based research, and the Internet samples are broader than the typical college student sample. This should provide some comfort to us as researchers because the behaviors of the larger group, computer users, resemble those of college students.

Third, there may be differences between computer users and the population as a whole. When we venture into the realm of online research, we can't be sure that the population of participants that we reach are always comparable to the usual samples we use. Thus, for some tasks, like Vadillo et al.'s learning task, people may learn through the same processes, regardless of who they are. So an Internet sample would reflect a typical laboratory sample. But if a study involves some topics for which different types of people show different patterns, like healthcare issues, the online population may be different from the general population.

For instance, Couper, Kapteyn, Schonlau, and Winter (2006) studied an online population of older adults who provided information about their health, income, where they lived, their level of education, and so forth. These researchers discovered that less healthy, poor, and nonwhite populations were underrepresented in the online survey. If the researchers drew generalized conclusions about the health and well-being of the older population based on their online survey, those conclusions could be seriously inaccurate because of the nature of the people who have computer access and the inclination to participate in online surveys.

A fourth consideration involves the ethics of Internet research. As researchers, we need to act ethically, providing informed consent and debriefing, making sure that there is no immediate or long-term harm to participants, making sure that participants are of legal age, and so forth. When a participant is at a remote location, it may not be easy to guarantee ethical safeguards.

Finally, a fifth, fairly new concern relates to the fact that an increasing number of people access the Internet via cell phones (Mobile web audience, 2007). In fact, some segments of the population, most notably those under 35, expect advanced features, like Internet access, on their cell phones (Consumers in the 18-to-24 age segment, 2007). A survey on the small screen of a cell phone, combined with potentially slow access, might make a survey difficult to complete, leading either to nonresponse, satisficing, or acquiescence. As technology changes, the nature of these problems may change, or the problems may disappear.

The Future of the Internet in Psychology

Increasingly, psychologists are bringing research to the world at large. As we have seen, there are limitations to the kind of research that is possible, and we face new ethical concerns, but there is potential for increased contact with populations that we have previously ignored. The samples generated by Internet research will not involve random selection, which is an ideal that psychological research seldom achieves. Internet-based studies are likely to be broader than the typical, college-student samples that most research includes, even if we still don't know how well the samples represent the populations that interest us. Given the ease with which we can conduct such projects, Internet studies are almost certain to increase in size and scope.

We must remember that the research results we obtain via the Internet will only be as good as the methodology we develop. The same careful attention to detail is important for Internet research as in any other research. Once the details of the investigation are in place, there are ways to enhance the likelihood of success in a project. Table 3.7 presents some tips for creating successful web pages for research.

TABLE 3.7 Guidelines for Creating Internet-Based Research

1. **Become familiar with related research.** You can take cues from the work others have done and avoid simply repeating research that others have already done, perhaps with a better methodology than you would have developed on your own.
2. **Keep your web page simple, but attractive.** Try not to keep your potential participants waiting as they access lengthy web pages. At the same time, you should develop an attractive, professional-looking site.
3. **Follow the regulations regarding ethics in research.** The same rules and regulations about ethics in research pertain to Internet-based research. Several important points stand out; you need to check out all aspects of the approval process, however.
   - Virtually every academic institution has an Institutional Review Board (IRB) to evaluate the degree of potential risk associated with participation in your research. All research, whether by students or by professional researchers, requires approval by the IRB. Most schools have a specific form to complete.
   - You need to ensure that participants understand the concept of informed consent. It will be crucial to let people know that participation is voluntary and that, by sending you their responses, they agree to let you include their responses in your analysis. You must tell them that they can terminate their participation at any time.
   - The law regards some people as unable to provide informed consent. That is, legally they are barred from volunteering to participate without approval of parents or guardians. For instance,

people under the age of 18 may be legally unable to volunteer on their own. You should highlight this restriction.

- Naturally, if there is any deception, you need to debrief your participants, but the best means of doing this is not clear at this point.

4. **Give an adequate description of your research.** It will also generate goodwill if you provide some means by which the participants can learn about the results of your research. You can gain cooperation from potential participants by educating them about the importance of your research. Tell them what questions you are addressing, how long their participation will take, and how you will protect their confidentiality. It would be ideal to keep their participation anonymous, so that nobody knows they took part.
5. **Check out your newly created website thoroughly.** If you create a website, you will be familiar with it, so some of the snags in using it may not be clear to you. It will help to get naive people to test your page. In addition, you can minimize problems if you check your web page on as many different computers as possible. Not all machines display information identically; pretesting the web pages can reduce the frustrations that your participants experience and can result in data that are more valid.
6. **Find out how to disseminate information about your study.** Several websites that list ongoing research and various electronic discussion groups may allow you to post announcements about your research.

CHECKING ON RESEARCH: THE ROLE OF REPLICATION

Behavior is complicated and multifaceted, so any single study cannot answer all of our questions about a topic definitively. In addition, no matter how well a researcher designs a study, problems can occur with the results. The participants might have been an unusual group, or the assignment of those participants to different conditions may have led to nonequivalent groups. The wording of questions asked may have misled people. Or the selection of the variable to be measured might have been inappropriate. If any of these problems occurred, the **validity** of the results would suffer. These types of problems can and do occur; you have to learn to anticipate problems as well as possible to deal with them and to recognize that you cannot eliminate them all.

Validity—A property of data, concepts, or research findings whereby they are useful for measuring or understanding phenomena that they are of interest to a psychologist. Data, concepts, and research findings fall on a continuum of usefulness for a given application.

This may sound like a pessimistic view, but with enough systematic research on a topic, we can identify the problems and take them into account. Ideally, researchers will replicate their research, which means to repeat the investigations to see if the same results emerge. **Replications** can take three basic different forms. In exact replication, a researcher repeats an earlier investigation exactly. In replication with extension, the experimenter asks the same question, but adds something new. The advantage of the replication with extension is that you don't spend your time merely repeating what we think might be true and that we already know; you are advancing beyond the initial knowledge. In a conceptual replication, the researcher attacks the same basic question, but does it from a different approach.

Replication—In research, the act of recreating or reproducing an earlier study to see if its results can be repeated. The replication can reproduce the original study exactly or with some modifications.

Type I error—In statistics, erroneously deciding that there is a significant effect when the effect is due to measurement error.

Type II error—In statistics, erroneously failing to decide that there is a significant effect when it is obscured by measurement error.

Construct validity—The degree to which a measurement accurately measures the underlying concept that it is supposed to measure.

Replication serves several important functions. First, it can check on the reliability of research results and help us avoid seeing things that aren't there (**Type I errors**) and failing to see things that are there (**Type II errors**). That is, if an initial project erroneously suggested that some behavioral pattern was real, replications could confirm or deny that claim. Or if research seemed to indicate erroneously that some behaviors were likely, replications could show that to be false.

Second, replication can provide additional support for theories. Each replication whose results confirm a theory's predictions increases our confidence in that theory. Or replications may fail to support the predictions, which can lead to new ideas that may be better than the old ones.

A third advantage of replication is that we can increase the **construct validity** of our concepts. This means that when we are dealing with complicated and abstract concepts, such as anxiety or depression, we develop more confidence in what they involve by making diverse measurements of the same concept.

A fourth effect of replications is to help protect against fraud. If researchers who might cheat know that their work will be put to the test, they may be less likely to engage in that fraud. If they have engaged in fraud, replications can call the earlier research into question. One of the stated functions of replication is to identify whether research can withstand close scrutiny.

Even with such clear positive aspects of replication, simple replications seldom occur; replications with extension are more prevalent, but they appear in research journals with considerably less frequency than original research reports.

We can identify several reasons as to why researchers advocate replication but do not do it. In the end, all the reasons come down to the relative payoff for the time and energy devoted to the replication. Scientists prefer to conduct original, novel research because it generates new knowledge, for which the rewards are greater. Doing a replication is like finishing second in a race. Nobody cares about the person or remembers who it was. Familiar people in the history of psychology, like Sigmund Freud, have often worried a great deal that they would not get credit for their ideas. Outside of psychology, people are no different.

The meager reward for replications dissuades most researchers from attempting them. Ross, Hall, and Heater (1998) have identified several specific reasons for the lack of published replications in nursing and occupational therapy research. The same principles hold for all behavioral research. First, they suggest, journals are reluctant to publish replications. Second, researchers may be reluctant to submit replications because they contain little that is new. Third, colleagues and professors encourage original research. Fourth, funding for replication research may be very limited. Fifth, in writing up the initial research, investigators may not provide enough detail for others who want to replicate. None of these barriers is insurmountable, but they certainly need to be overcome.

A good example of how a widely publicized research project led to subsequent attempts at replication and the correction of erroneous information involves the so-called Mozart effect (Rauscher, Shaw, & Ky, 1993, 1995). Other investigators repeated the research, but were unable to generate the same results. The Controversy on music shows how our knowledge in this area increased as one set of research questions led to new ones.

Don't Reinvent the Wheel: Reviewing the Literature

All researchers recognize that replicating previous research is a good idea, but we also recognize that it is more useful to replicate with extension than simply to replicate. That is, it is important to develop and test new ideas as we verify the old ones. And it pays greater dividends if we can generate new knowledge in our research.

CONTROVERSY: Music–Does It Make You Smarter?

Does music make you smarter? Rauscher et al. (1993, 1995) reported that listening to Mozart's music could increase intelligence; the researchers determined that scores on a standardized test increased significantly, about 8 or 9 points. The public was enthralled. The implications were remarkable. People envisioned a populace that was suddenly smarter.

Other researchers were immediately interested. First, there were practical implications. Could we do something to make our children smarter? One plan proposed by the governor of Georgia was to give a tape of this music to each family of a newborn baby in the state. The payoff could be great, but so could the cost if the effect turned out to be imaginary.

A second reason for interest was that scientists were interested in finding out why intellectual functioning would improve. What was the actual cause? This is an interesting scientific question in its own right. Further, perhaps there were other, even more effective, means of enhancing thought processes.

Unfortunately, the first published report provided insufficient detail on the methodology, so it was difficult to replicate the study because the details were unavailable. The second report presented that information.

When details became available, Carstens, Haskins, and Hounshell (1995) found that listening to Mozart, compared to a silent period, had no effect on test performance. Then Newman et al. (1995) also reported a failure to replicate the original results. Surprisingly, they discovered that people with a preference for classical music actually showed lower test scores than others after listening to music. As the puzzle grew, Rauscher, Shaw, and Gordon (1998) proposed more arguments to support their original conclusions.

Subsequently, Steele and his colleagues (Steele, Bass, & Brook, 1999; Steele, Dalla Balla, et al., 1999) extended the methodology even further. They found no Mozart effect. Subsequently, Thompson, Schellenberg, and Husain (2001) varied the types of music to which participants listened, finding that arousal levels and mood accounted for the so-called Mozart effect. Higher arousal and positive mood were associated with better test scores, not specifically having listened to Mozart.

This sequence of studies illustrates how effective the scientific approach, with replication, is self-correcting and leads to more complete knowledge. Although it is exciting to think that we can get smart by listening to music, it is important to know the truth—that increases in test performance are more likely to result from arousal and high levels of motivation, perhaps from positive mood, and certainly through hard work.

Question for Discussion: What would have been the practical implications if researchers had not replicated the original "Mozart effect" research?

In order to maximize the gains in our research projects, it pays to know what researchers have already done. No matter what topic you choose for a research project, somebody has undoubtedly paved the way already. There is no doubt that they had to solve problems in developing a methodology that satisfied them. You do not need to repeat their mistakes. In fact, researchers consider it completely legitimate to borrow ideas from others, as long as we give appropriate credit to them and don't pass the ideas off as our own.

You are allowed to borrow somebody else's methodology for your own purposes. If it worked for them, it might work for you, and it has the advantage of having been pretested. A journal article has generally been evaluated by experts in the field and further reviewed by the journal editor. The article will not appear in print unless these experts agree that both the methodology and the ideas are sound. You can learn a lot about what to do (and what not do to) by reading the work of respected professionals.

What Is a Literature Review?

In order to find out what has been done in an area that interests you, you should conduct a **literature review**. When we talk about literature in everyday language, we generally hear about writers like Alice Walker, F. Scott Fitzgerald, Charles Dickens, and others in the pantheon of writing. People presume that any work penned by these authors is worthwhile. On the other hand, people may minimize the importance of other writers, like the horror novelist Stephen King. The enormous success of his popular and compelling work tells us that many people enjoy it. So why is his work not "literature"? In reality, it all depends on your definition of "good writing."

Literature review—An overview of published journal articles, books, and other professional work on a given topic.

Among researchers, the term "literature" refers to the body of work that is considered to be of high enough quality to appear in technical journals. Psychology has its own pantheon of writers whose words (and research) have had an impact on the field. Psychology has its own versions of Stephen King as well, whose work might be considered highly valuable by one group, but minimized by another.

At the other end of the continuum are those authors who produce temporarily popular books like romance novels. These works capture an audience, but the books (and their ideas) themselves have short lives. There is a comparable group among psychologists. Radio talk show hosts like "Dr. Laura" are popular but are not taken seriously by the psychological community. Although people may ask "Dr. Laura" for advice, she is neither a psychologist nor a psychiatrist.

When researchers prepare a literature review for a journal article or for a conference presentation, they usually discuss relevant previous studies. Because many areas of research have generated a lot of studies, authors do not present an exhaustive listing of every study that has appeared in journals or books. The amount of information would be too great. Consequently, they write about the studies that have had greatest impact on the project currently underway and about research that psychologists consider very critical in the area. Most of the research in a literature review is fairly recent, although classic and important older articles generally receive attention as well.

The Effect of Peer Review on the Research Literature

As a researcher, you need to differentiate among the various levels of writing that constitute our psychological literature. This is often a judgment call, but articles that appear in **peer-reviewed** journals have been taken seriously by experts. A peer-reviewed journal publishes articles that have undergone careful scrutiny and may have been revised by the authors several times until they have eliminated any major problems. This process is a stringent one. Among the best psychology journals, the rejection rate may be around 70 percent or more. Thus, the editor accepts only 30 percent or fewer of the articles that are submitted.

Peer review—A process in which scientific research and ideas are evaluated by experts in a field so that obvious errors or other problems can be spotted and corrected before a work is published or presented at a research conference.

One of the reasons for such a low acceptance rate is that in psychology, our ideas are very complex and abstract. We often have to develop clever operational definitions of our concepts because we cannot observe and measure them directly. It takes considerable diligence to create and conduct a well-designed study that deals with the ideas successfully. There are many ways for ambiguities and uncertainties to creep in, so reviewers and editors frequently request an author to do additional work to take care of these problems.

In disciplines that are more descriptive, such as botany or other areas of biology, the acceptance rate for major journals is often much higher than in psychology. The ideas they work with are often more straightforward and obvious, so the research is easier to design. (The tools and techniques of the natural and physical sciences may be difficult to master, but so are those in the behavioral sciences. In any case, we shouldn't confuse the concepts of a science, which are the most important elements, with the tools, which are merely tools.) The differences between psychology and other disciplines in this regard do not imply that one domain is more or less important or useful; it simply means that different areas of research make different demands on researchers.

HOW TO CONDUCT A LITERATURE REVIEW

Researchers publish an enormous amount of research each year. In fact, there are over a thousand journals that publish psychology-related articles. Most libraries will have no more than a tiny fraction of them on hand, so even if you wanted to browse through each one of them, you would not be able to.

So how do you find out what has appeared in print? The easiest way is to use an electronic database that lists psychological research. The most useful database for psychologists is PsycINFO®, which is published by the American Psychological Association. It references over 1,300 journals published in twenty-five languages, and in its most complete version, PsycINFO cites articles going back to 1887.

Electronic Databases

PsycINFO is a modern successor to Psychological Abstracts (PA), which appeared in a paper version until 2006 when they were discontinued. PsycINFO is extremely easy to use compared to PA. The basic strategy is to select a term of interest to you and to tell PsycINFO to search for published articles related to that term. There are strategies that you can use to maximize the likelihood of finding what you are seeking without also generating a long string of less relevant material. On the flip side, there are ways to expand the number of citations you generate so you can get a more complete picture of the research in anarea.

Using PsycINFO is easy, but you need to learn how to do it if you want to maximize the return on your time. In the following sections, you will learn about useful strategies for searching databases. Keep in mind that we will be focusing on PsycINFO. If you use other databases, the particulars of your search may differ somewhat, but once you learn PsycINFO, you can adapt your search strategies to other databases.

Starting Your Search

A first step in searching for information is to decide on a relevant term that matches your interest. This is an important first step because it will determine the nature of the articles listed in your output.

The number of published articles listed in PsycINFO continues to increase because researchers keep publishing their work. Thus, any specific examples that appear here will become outdated over time. Nonetheless, you can get an idea of how to generate worthwhile search strategies.

Suppose that you are interested in finding out about psychological aspects of adopting children. You could type the word adoption and begin the search. In early 2007, entering the word *adoption* resulted in a list of 16,112 references. Obviously, it would be impractical to read every source, but you would not want to in any case because there are many citations that do not relate to your topic in the least. The reason that a search of adoption generates irrelevant references is that if you type in a word, PsycINFO will search for the word, regardless of the way that word is used.

For example, in the search for the word *adoption* the PsycINFO listings, twenty-eight of the first thirty listings had nothing to do with adopting children. In fact, there were more citations regarding colorectal cancer than there were about adopting children. Table 3.8 gives the titles of the first five. None of them relate to adopting children. PsycINFO does not know what meaning of the word *adoption* you intend without some help from you. If the article relates to adopting some strategy or plan, the database will include it.

You can further reduce the number of irrelevant citations. Table 3.9 illustrates the steps you can take to narrow your search to be more productive. One involves using the PsycINFO thesaurus to identify a narrower term than you are using; another pertains to setting limits on the search process, like a restricted range of years in which articles were published, types of studies (theoretical versus empirical), and populations (adults, children, women, men, etc.). There are quite a few ways to set limits to restrict the scope of your search.

If your search produces too few hits, there are ways of expanding it. One strategy is to insert a "wild card" in your search. For instance, in PsycINFO, you can use an asterisk (*) to expand the search. When you enter the subject of your search as adopt*,

TABLE 3.8 Titles of the First Five (of 9,932) Articles Produced by PsycINFO for *adoption* Anywhere in the Citation and the Use of the Word *adoption* in Those Citations

Reference	Reason for Inclusion in a Search for *Adoption*
Horst, M., Kuttschreuter, M., & Gutteling, J. M. (2007). Perceived usefulness, personal experiences, risk perception and trust as determinants of adoption of e-government services in The Netherlands. *Computers in Human Behavior, 23*, 1838-1852.	Are people willing to **adopt** information provided on the Internet by the government?
Lee, S., Kim, K-J. (2007). Factors affecting the implementation success of Internet-based information systems. *Computers in Human Behavior, 23*, 1853-1880	What are the factors that affect the **adoption** of technology in business services?
Hsu, C-L., & Lu, H-P. (2007). Consumer behavior in online game communities: A motivational factor perspective. *Computers in Human Behavior, 23*, 1642–1659.	The word **adoption** appears in the titles of several citations in the reference list.
Ikazaki, S. (2007). Lessons learned from i-mode: What makes consumers click wireless banner ads? *Computers in Human Behavior, 23*, 1692–1719.	The word **adoption** appears in the titles of several citations in the reference list.
Segal, N., McGuire, S., Havlena, J., Gill, P., & Hershberger, S. (2007). Intellectual similarity of virtual twin pairs: Developmental trends. *Personality and Individual Differences, 42*, 1209–1219.	The word **adoption** appears in the titles of several citations in the reference list.

TABLE 3.9 Examples of Strategies to Reduce the Number of Irrelevant Citations in a PsycINFO Search

Search for References to Adoption	Strategy to Narrow the Search	Number of References
Adoption anywhere in the citation		16,111
Adoption as the Keyword of the reference	Choose "Word Appears in Keyword." (You could also select "Author" if you want to name an author who has studied adoption.)	6,672
Only work published since 1980	Choose "Set Other Limits" and indicate publication year of 1980 to the current year (or whatever time span you want).	1,625
Only work published in the English language	Choose "Set Other Limits" and select English as the only language.	1,538
Only work published in books or journals	Choose "Set Other Limits" and select material in journals. This eliminates hard-to-access material like doctoral dissertations.	1,082
Only empirical studies (i.e., original research reports)	Choose "Set Other Limits" and select Publication Type = Empirical Studies.	515
Only work involving females in the adoption process	Choose "Set Other Limits" and select Population = Female.	273
Only work on adoption of children	Choose "Set Other Limits" and select Age Group = Childhood.	110

TABLE 3.10 Strategies for Expanding the Number of Relevant Citations in PsycINFO®

Strategy to Expand the Search	Result
Use the *Suggest* option and enter "Adopt*" or "Adoption"	You get a list of terms that relate to your topic, like Adoptive, Adoptive Children, Biological Family, Interracial Adoption. You can use these as subjects for your search.
Use the *Thesaurus* option and enter "Adopt*"	You get a list of categories that PsycINFO uses that are related to adoption.
Use the *Index* and enter "Adopt*" or "Adoption"	You get at least a dozen subject categories to search.
Example: Use the Thesaurus terms "Adopted-Children," "Adoptees," "Adoption-Child," "Interracial Adoption," and "Adoptive-Parents" connected by OR (i.e., Adopted-children OR adoptees OR adoption-child OR interracial-adoption OR adoptive-parents).	You get 156 citations that relate to the thesaurus terms and that still follow the limits set in Table 3.7. Using OR tells PsycINFO to access any citation that uses any of your terms. If you connected them with AND, PsycINFO would only access those citations that include all those terms at the same time, which would restrict the search greatly. In fact, a single journal article is unlikely to fall into all these categories.

PsycINFO will look for any subject beginning with adopt, such as adopt, adoption, and adoptive. You can also use the database's thesaurus, which tells you what terms to use when searching for a given concept. Table 3.10 gives a glimpse of the possibilities for expanding your search. By experimenting, you may be able to figure out alternate strategies for increasing the number of hits.

HOW TO READ A JOURNAL ARTICLE

When you first begin reading scientific writing, it may seem like it has been written in another language, and the organization of the information can seem convoluted. After you get used to the style of research reports, your task of reading journal articles will be easier. There is a reason for the organization of journal articles, and there is a skill involved in understanding scientific writing. Most likely, for your psychology courses, you will be reading articles written in a format often called APA style. This means that the authors have followed the guidelines set forth in the *Publication Manual of the American Psychological Association* (American Psychological Association, 2004). This style differs from others that you may have encountered, like MLA (Modern Language Association, 1995) for the humanities, or various formats for each of the scientific disciplines. APA style may seem complicated, but the primary rules are fairly easy to learn. The *Publication Manual* is over 400 pages long, though, so you can expect that there is a lot of detail about specific formatting and writing issues.

Understanding the Format of a Research Paper

When you pick up a research article written in APA style, you will be able to figure out very quickly where to look to find the information you seek. Writers divide their man-

TABLE 3.11 Concepts That Are Clarified in the Different Sections of a Research Report

Introduction

- What is the general topic of the research article?
- What do we know about this topic from previous research?
- What are the authors trying to demonstrate in their own research?
- What are their hypotheses?

Method

***Participants*—Who took part in the research?**

- How many people (or animals) were studied?
- If there were nonhuman animals, what kind were they?
- If there were people, what were their characteristics (e.g., average and range of age, gender, race or ethnicity, were they volunteers or were they paid)?

***Apparatus and Materials*–What did the researchers need to carry out their study?**

- What kind of stimuli, questions, etc. were used?
- How many different kinds of activities did participants complete?
- What instrumentation was used to present material to participants and to record their responses?

***Procedure*–What did the people actually do during the research session?**

- After the participants arrived, what did they do?
- What did the experimenters do as they interacted with participants?

Results

- What were patterns of behaviors among participants?
- Did behaviors differ when different groups were compared?
- What type of behaviors are predictable in the different testing conditions?
- What were the results of any statistical tests?

Discussion

- What do the results mean?
- What explanations can you develop for why the participants responded as they did?
- What psychological processes help you explain participants' responses?
- What questions have not been answered fully?
- How do your results relate to the research cited in the introduction?
- How do your results relate to other kinds of research?
- What new ideas emerge that you could evaluate in a subsequent experiment?

References

- What research was cited in the research report (e.g., work published in journals or other written sources, research presentations, personal communications)?

uscripts into six sections as a rule. The actual number of sections will differ, depending on the complexity of the research report. Regardless of the exact number of sections, there are specific reasons why information appears where it does. Table 3.11 presents an overview of the different sections of a research report written in APA style and some of the questions addressed in those sections. Table 3.11 can serve as a worksheet to guide you in reading journal articles. If you write a brief answer to each of the questions in the table, you will have a pretty complete summary of the work that was done, why it was done, and what the authors think it means.

Abstract. In the **abstract**, the authors give an overview of the entire paper; this section is fairly short, usually fewer than 120 words. It presents a preview of the research question and hypotheses, the methodology, the results, and the discussion. The abstract is kept short so the reader can get a quick glimpse into the nature of the research.

Abstract—The part of a research report that summarizes the purpose of the research, the methodology, the results of the study, and the interpretations of the research.

Introduction—The part of a research report that gives an overview of the field to be investigated and the investigator's hypotheses about the outcome of the research.

Method—The part of a research report that provides information about those who participated in the study, how the research was actually carried out, and the materials and apparatus used for it.

Participants— subsection of the Methods section that details the nature of the humans or nonhumans who took part in the research. Nonhuman animals are often referred to as *Subjects*, whereas humans who took part are called *Participants*.

Introduction. After the abstract comes the **introduction**, which provides background information so you can understand the purpose of the research. When the research involves specific tests of hypotheses, the authors will generally present these hypotheses here. This section also gives a general preview of how the researchers have conducted their project. The purpose of the introduction is to clarify the purpose of the study and show how relevant ideas developed in previous research. You will virtually never see a journal article that does not refer to previous research on which the current article is based.

As you read through the introduction, you will see that the first ideas are relatively broad. These ideas relate to a more general depiction of the field of interest to the researchers. As the introduction progresses, the scope of the material narrows. The authors will describe and discuss in more detail the research that relates most closely to their own project. Finally, the authors will present their own ideas. They may outline how they will clarify confusions from earlier research, correct problems, and test hypotheses. By the time you finish reading the introduction, you will have a clear picture of the logic that led from the ideas of previous researchers to those of the authors.

Method. Following the introduction is the **Method** section. This section should allow an independent researcher to reproduce the project described in the article. The methods section contains an extreme amount of detail. Very often, students regard this section as not being very important. In some ways, they are right: Without it, they can understand why the researchers conducted the study and what results occurred. In another way, though, if they do not read this section, they might miss out on important details that affected the research outcome. This section is absolutely critical for those who want to replicate the original research.

Participants. Writers subdivide the methods section into three or four sections. The first one, **participants**, characterizes those who took part in the study. It describes how many were there, what were their ages, racial and ethnic backgrounds, etc. This subsection provides the reader with enough information to understand if the nature of the participants may have influenced the outcome of the research in some way.

Materials and apparatus—A subsection of the Methods section that details what implements and stimuli were used to carry out the study. Sometimes the materials and apparatus appear in separate subsections.

Materials and Apparatus. The next subsection, **materials and apparatus,** provides details about what you would need to carry out the study. Sometimes writers will create separate subsections for the materials and apparatus if there is a need.

Procedure—A subsection of the Methods section that provides extensive detail about the actual process used to carry out the study.

Procedure. After the description of the implements of the study, the authors will describe the **procedure**. In the procedure subsection, they describe exactly what occurred during the research session. As a rule, the procedure subsection includes only what occurs during the data collection session. Based on the information in this section, an independent researcher could follow the steps that the original researchers took.

Results—The part of a research report that details the quantitative and qualitative results of an investigation, including results of statistical analyses.

Results. After the data collection is complete, scientists typically present the outcome in a **Results** section that usually includes statistical tests. Although choosing a statistical test seems to be a pretty straightforward task, there are actually controversies in some cases about the best approach to data analysis. If you chose one approach, you might end up with one conclusion; if you took an alternate approach, your conclusion might be different. This issue has such great implications that the American Psychological Association created a task force that issued guidelines about research methodology and statistics. The task force wrote an important article that highlights some of the controversies associated with statistics (Wilkinson & the Task Force on Statistical Inference, 1999).

The results section details the outcome of the study. For example, if a researcher compares two groups, the results section tells whether they differed and by how much. The results section also presents the results of any statistical tests that the researchers conducted. This part of a research report can be very complicated because you have to translate technical materials and terminology into comprehensible English.

One way to make sure that you understand what you are reading is to keep track of the different research questions that the investigators have asked. You can do this by making note of them when you read the introduction. Then when they present the statistics, you can try to figure out the particular question that goes along with the statistic.

You will also encounter figures and tables in the results section. The purpose of these graphic elements is to provide an overview when the results are complicated. By creating a figure or chart, the authors can combine a large amount of information into a single picture.

Discussion—The part of a research report that provides an interpretation of the results, going beyond a simple description of the results and statistical tests.

Discussion. The data do not mean anything until we, as researchers, decide what they mean. When we ask a research question, our task is to take complicated data about a question that we are the first to ask and see what the data tell us. Because nobody else has done what we have, we are the ones who have to figure out what it all means. A successful investigation generates new information that has to be interpreted and placed in the context of earlier research.

This final section involving treatment of the research ideas is the **Discussion** section, which provides closure to the project. That is, the investigators tell you what their

References—The part of a research report that contains complete reference information about any work cited in the research report, that is, where the work was published or presented and the source of any work that has not been published or presented.

results mean. Unlike the results section, which says what happened, the discussion tells you why it happened. Another way to characterize the distinction is that the results section provides fact, whereas the discussion section provides interpretation, explanation, and speculation. The results of a study are incontrovertible; they are what they are. What may be controversial, however, is the interpretation of the results.

References. At the very end of the paper, the **References** section appears. This section simply gives information on where a reader can find the ideas that others generated and that you cited in your paper.

APA style dictates a specific format for virtually any kind of reference, including references from the World Wide Web. The details are quite specific. With practice, they are not hard to master.

SUMMARY

Research ideas come from many different sources. Ultimately, it boils down to the fact that somebody has a question and wants to find an answer. Sometimes the source of a research project begins with an "I wonder what would happen if . . ." type of question. In other cases, there is a problem to be solved, and an investigator will use research skills to devise an answer that can be applied to the situation. In still other cases, a theory makes a prediction that a scientist can test through research.

Regardless of the source of ideas, the scientists who investigate them take their cues from the society around them. Scientists are members of their community and share the same attitudes and values as many others in our society. Thus, social issues are important in determining what a particular researcher will think important. This consideration is true for any scientific discipline, but it is especially true in the study of human behavior.

In our current social context, the Internet has become important in research. Psychologists are studying how to use the Internet as a research tool. A number of important issues need to be addressed before web-based research can flourish, but scientists are working on the question.

Regardless of the topics of research or how the data are collected, we want to have confidence in the results. We want them to be meaningful. One way to ensure that scientific findings are useful is through replication, that is, repetition of the research by different investigators in different contexts. When the same results appear regularly, we can have greater confidence that our conclusions are warranted.

When you generate a research project, you can get guidance about how to conduct it by reading what others have done. This usually involves a literature review of published studies. Without such a review, you run the risk of simply repeating what others have already done. Such a replication may give you more confidence in the phenomenon you are studying, but most researchers want to include novel features in their research so they can advance the field with new knowledge. One way to increase what we know about the behaviors we study is through publication of the results in scientific journals and through presentations at research conferences.

Finally, if you conduct research, you may write it up in a formal report. You are likely to follow the style of presentation set forth in the *Publication Manual of the American Psychological Association*.

REVIEW QUESTIONS

Multiple Choice Questions

1. When researchers develop projects to test how well competing theories predict behaviors, their ideas
   a. tend to fall more toward the formal end of the continuum of ideas.
   b. usually end up testing ideas that arise from practical issues.
   c. rely on informal and idiosyncratic approaches.
   d. are seldom based on previous ideas and research.
2. When scientists develop their ideas for research projects, which of the following is most often the source of their ideas?
   a. Colleagues in different departments within their own institutions
   b. Colleagues in their own department
   c. The existing research literature
   d. Discussions within their research teams
3. When the dominant theory in psychology was behaviorism, researchers
   a. used behavioral observation to study cognitive processes.
   b. believed that you could learn just about anything regarding human behavior with animal models.
   c. used neuroscientific approaches to understand brain processes that affect behavior.
   d. capitalized on the effects of the cognitive revolution to understand behaviors.
4. When you come across an interesting research idea accidentally when dealing with some other issue, you are experiencing
   a. construct validity.
   b. replication with extension.
   c. exact replication.
   d. serendipity.
5. If you want to discover whether "Haste Makes Waste" or "He Who Hesitates Is Lost" is a better description of the effects of human behavior, you could make an experimental test. According to McGuire's (1983) description of the development of research ideas, such an approach would involve
   a. studying spontaneously occurring events.
   b. studying the validity of everyday beliefs and when they break down.
   c. evaluating formal if-then statements.
   d. using previous research as a stepping stone to new ideas.
6. Generating a research idea by finding an individual who acts in different or interesting ways would use which of McGuire's (1983) approaches to generating research ideas?
   a. Studying spontaneously occurring events
   b. Studying the validity of everyday beliefs and when they break down

c. Using an intensive case study
d. Using previous research as a steppingstone to new ideas

7. There are differences in the way we conduct laboratory and Internet-based research. The differences include the fact that
   a. actually carrying out the study on the Internet requires less time on the part of the experimenter than a laboratory study does.
   b. for Internet studies, the researcher has to be available more frequently because Internet users can access the research on the Internet just about any time of the day, so the researcher needs to be available to answer questions.
   c. laboratory research generally leads to more accurate recording of data because paper data sheets are right in front of the researcher who can enter them into a computerized database.
   d. because anybody can access the research on the Internet, an investigator can't be certain that the sample is representative of the population, whereas this isn't a problem with laboratory studies.
8. One of the problems with research on the Internet is that
   a. because many people can access the research, the samples differ from typical psychological research samples, so the results are often different.
   b. because of the remote nature of the research, the investigator might never know about problems that occur during the course of the study.
   c. the investigator usually has to commit more time for data collection than in laboratory studies.
   d. participants who have difficulty with the study are likely to contact the investigator at any time of the night or day to ask questions.
9. One practical issue in Internet-based research is that
   a. displays of the research web page might be very different for people on different types of computers.
   b. sample sizes might become so large that the study becomes impractical to conduct.
   c. it is very difficult to create good descriptions of Internet-based research because it reaches so many people.
   d. it is almost impossible to guarantee that participation in such research will be anonymous and confidential.
10. Research on how to conduct studies on the Internet has revealed that the lowest rate of return occurs when the investigator contacts potential respondents through which of the following?
    a. Hyperlinks on websites
    b. Sending information to newsgroups
    c. Individual email messages
    d. Announcements of the surveys in major magazines
11. The technical differences among computers on which people complete Internet surveys
    a. are minimal with the standard Internet formatting of surveys.
    b. can lead to very different displays of the same survey.

c. require that researchers avoid using colors that may not be the same on different computers.
d. make constant response formats difficult to implement.

12. When a researcher repeats an earlier experiment but includes some novel elements, this process is called
a. assessment of validity.
b. replication with extension.
c. conceptual replication.
d. construct validity.

13. Replicating research so we can develop more confidence in our understanding of complex and abstract concepts helps us
a. increase our construct validity.
b. avoid both Type I and Type II errors.
c. perform replication with extension.
d. develop conceptual replication.

14. The process by which scientists try to guarantee that only high-quality research results appear in journals involves getting experts to evaluate the work and is called
a. construct validity.
b. peer review.
c. the literature review.
d. conceptual review.

15. A literature review in a research article generally includes
a. an exhaustive listing of just about every study published about the topic being reviewed.
b. a discussion of what has been written by psychologists as well as by more popular authors.
c. the ideas that are favorable to the researcher's theory.
d. a discussion of research that is important but that has not yet been published.

16. If you wanted to understand the theoretical reasons that led researchers to conduct a project that appeared in an APA journal, you would read which section of their article?
a. abstract
b. introduction
c. discussion
d. references

17. The results section of an APA style report will contain
a. information about the statistical tests used to analyze the data.
b. a statement about the research hypotheses.
c. the number and types of participants.
d. an integration of the data with theory.

Essay Questions

18. Where on the continuum of formality of ideas will a beginning student's research likely fall? Explain your answer.

19. Explain how changes in psychology and changes in society have affected psychologists' use of animals in research.
20. Why could it be more profitable for a beginning researcher to do an exact replication, while it would be more profitable for a seasoned researcher to do a conceptual replication?
21. What are the advantages of a literature review of research related to your own investigations?

ANSWERS TO REVIEW QUESTIONS

Multiple Choice Questions

1.	a	7.	a	13.	a
2.	c	8.	b	14.	b
3.	b	9.	a	15.	a
4.	d	10.	d	16.	b
5.	b	11.	b	17.	a
6.	c	12.	b		

Essay Questions

18. Where on the continuum of formality of ideas will a beginning student's research likely to fall? Explain your answer.

    Students are likely to pose research questions that arise from their own experiences, that is, from less formal points on the continuum. Students' levels of knowledge are going to be less than those of experienced researchers, so students will be less familiar with research to replicate, although after some preliminary study, they might be able to do so. Beginning students are unlikely to come up with significant tests of theory because they are just learning about the content of psychology.

19. Explain how changes in psychology and changes in society have affected psychologists' use of animals in research.

    Some psychologists have speculated that decreases in the amount of animal research has resulted, in part, from a change in theoretical perspectives, from behaviorism to cognitivism. Behaviorists were willing to generalize to people from animals, cognitive psychologists less so.

    A second reason is that psychologists have turned their attention to different research questions, ones that are less likely to be answered through animal research. Part of this may be due to the increasing number of women in psychology.

    A third reason is that people, including psychologists, are more sensitive to the ethical issues associated with animal research.

20. Why could it be more profitable for a beginning researcher to do an exact replication, while it would be more profitable for a seasoned researcher to do a conceptual replication?

    Beginning researchers can benefit from learning how to carry out research by following the well-specified procedures of earlier research. This will help them avoid overlooking important potential problems because most of these problems will have been ironed out by the original researchers. Seasoned researchers who can anticipate potential problems can be more confident that they will be able to create well-structured studies that go beyond the original studies.

21. What are the advantages of a literature review of research related to your own investigations?
    a. You can learn what experts in the area are interested in.
    b. You can get clues about how to conduct your own study, avoiding mistakes that might have beset earlier researchers.
    c. You can see how other researchers have defined their concepts and made their measurements.

CHAPTER FOUR

PRACTICAL ISSUES IN PLANNING YOUR RESEARCH

CHAPTER OVERVIEW

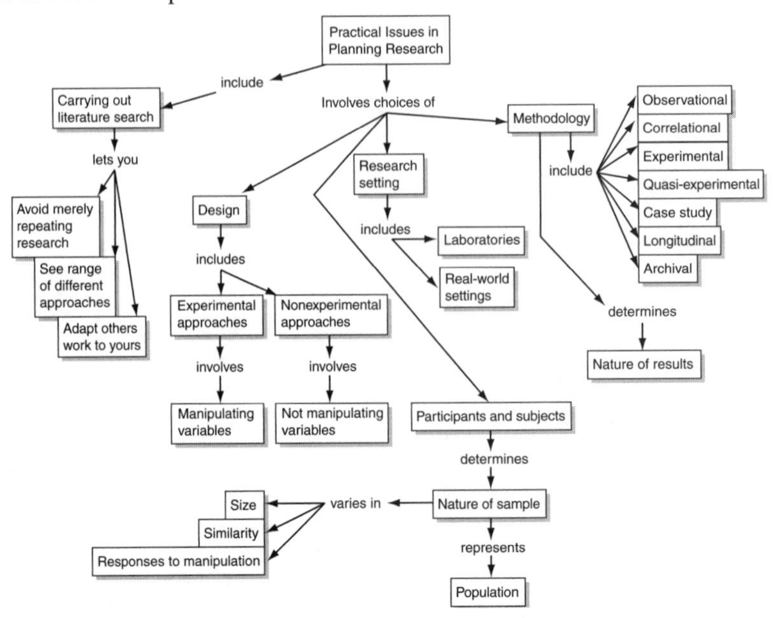

KEY TERMS

Applied research, p. 100
Archival research, p. 103
Basic (theoretical) research, p. 101
Case study, p. 102
Correlational research, p. 102
Experimental approach, p. 102
Longitudinal study, p. 103
Observational approach, p. 101
Population p. 126
Quasi-experiment, p. 102
Representative sample, p. 107
Sample, p. 107

CHAPTER PREVIEW

When most students are learning about research, they typically are not aware of how many decisions are made in putting a project together. You will find that when you read a journal article, you learn only what the researchers finally did, not what they tried that didn't work. The reason for this lack of information is that journal space is in short supply. There is always more to print than the journals have space for. As a result, authors omit just about everything not entirely germane to the topic they are studying. The authors report only what was successful. Another result is that as a reader, if you want to plan your own research project, you can use the information in published work, but you have to fill in a lot of details on your own.

The researchers leave out information on false starts, procedures that did not work out, and judgments that led to an unsatisfactory outcome. You can be sure that in virtually every research project ever conducted, the researchers made choices that caused them to stop and evaluate what they were doing and to make changes to improve the research design.

Some of the tasks associated with completing a study include describing in concrete terms the concepts you are interested in, figuring out how to measure them, identifying those you will test in your study, carrying out the project itself, looking at and understanding the results, then interpreting what you've discovered. If you make poor choices or conclusions at any step along the way, your research will be less meaningful than it could otherwise be.

In each case, the choices you make will each take you in a slightly different direction than some other choice. Each of these steps will involve making quite a few decisions that, you hope, will provide you with a clear answer to your original question.

PRACTICAL QUESTIONS IN PLANNING RESEARCH

When you read about successful research projects either in a scientific journal or in a popular magazine or when you see a report on television, the reporter makes the research sound as if it were put together perfectly and that there was only one reasonable way to have conducted it. In reality, if you were to follow a research project from beginning to end, you would see that the researchers had to make a great number of decisions about the study.

We investigate concepts that are very complex and abstract. This means that we need to simplify the complex ideas so our research doesn't become unmanageable. We also have to take abstract ideas and generate concrete ways to measure them. For example, sadness is an idea that can help us understand why people act as they do. But what is sadness? It is a complex set of emotions that we don't have an easy way to measure.

If we consider the goals of science, we can see that we could try to describe what it means to be sad. To do so, we have to identify what behaviors reflect sadness. If we don't describe sadness well, we can't move to the more difficult goal of predicting when it will occur. How can you predict what you can't describe? Beyond that, we will not be able to understand when it occurs, or how to control it.

In other areas of science, researchers frequently engage in descriptive research. They may count the number of plants that live in a particular type of field, or the number of animals born with deformities due to the presence of toxic substances. In this research, the concepts are fairly obvious and easy to measure. In some areas, the research may require complex tools to answer the scientists' questions, but although the tools are complex, the concepts are relatively simple. In psychology, we use tools that may be easy to develop (e.g., measuring behaviors on a scale of 1 to 10), but the concepts are complex.

Once you decide on a research question, you need to fill in the details about how you will carry out your project. This aspect of your task is not necessarily difficult, but you need to consider carefully myriad details. These details are the subject of the rest of this book. A research project can take many different paths; you have to decide how you want yours to proceed so that you arrive at the best answer to your question.

UNDERSTANDING YOUR RESEARCH

If your research is going to be data driven, you have to measure something. After you decide the topic you want to study, one of the next steps is to figure out what you will be observing. Because psychologists study complex ideas, the question of measurement sometimes poses difficulties. For instance, if you wanted to study depression, you could do so in any number of ways.

Social psychologists who study depression might investigate the extent to which a depressed person has social ties in the community. A researcher interested in family dynamics would focus on parents, siblings, and partners. Someone interested in psychological testing and assessment might try to identify tests that are most effective in identifying somebody who shows signs of depression. A neuroscientist could study the role of neurotransmitters in depression. All of these psychologists would tell you that they were studying depression, but each one would be doing it in a different way. Depending on how you approached the study of depression, you would define and measure that concept in different ways. In order to find out how to do that, your best first step would be to search the literature to see what others have already done.

You can see in Table 4.1 that investigators gather a lot of information from previously published research. The number of references cited is considerable, providing some confidence that the investigators have a firm grasp of the issues they are dealing with and that they know how the major researchers in the area have done their work. In your own research projects, it is unlikely that you will have the forty-seven references that the

TABLE 4.1 Examples of Participants Included in Different Studies in Three Major Psychology Journals

***Journal of Experimental Psychology: Applied* (2000, Vol. 6, No. 1)**

Topic of Research	Description of Participants as Given in Journal Article
Effects of characteristics of negotiators in reaching settlements in disputes	173 undergraduates
Participants' reactions to changes in the nature of auditory displays	184 undergraduates
Effects of verbal and spatial tasks on eye movements in driving	12 adults with at least two years driving experience; 7 women, 5 men
Personal characteristics and completion of time-critical tasks	30 students
Effects of sleep loss on reasoning and eyewitness identification	93 students; 45 women, 48 men
Children's use of anatomically correct dolls in reporting genital touching in medical examinations	84 children, average age = 3 years

***Journal of Experimental Psychology: General* (2000, Vol. 129, No. 1)**

Topic of Research	Description of Participants as Given in Journal Article
Backward inhibition in cognitive processing	118 students
Memory for annoying sounds	134 undergraduates
Personality effects, frontal lobe mechanisms, and error monitoring	42 students
Differences in visuospatial and verbal memory	110 undergraduates
Remembering and classifying stimuli	104 students
Identification of visually presented stimuli	34 students; 17 women, 17 men
Vividness of imagery and memory	112 adults

***Journal of Applied Psychology* (2000, Vol. 85, No. 1)**

Topic of Research	Description of Participants as Given in Journal Article
Nature and correlates of ethnic harassment	167 students; 91 women, 76 men; approximately 80% Hispanic
	110 school district employees; 81 women, 9 men; 50% Hispanic
	295 graduate students; 194 women, 101 men; 48% Hispanic

(*continues*)

TABLE 4.1 continued

Journal of Experimental Psychology: Applied (2000, Vol. 6, No. 1)	
Topic of Research	**Description of Participants as Given in Journal Article**
Identification of departure of international participants	58 international employees; 95% men 70 workers in 40 countries; 95% men
Comparison of standardized math test results and reading accommodations	1500 randomly sampled Kansas students
Using response times to assess guilt	72 undergraduates
The effects of reinforcement on children's mundane and fantastic claims regarding wrongdoing	120 children, ages 5–7
Influence of job familiarity and impression management on self-report and response time measurements	116 undergraduates; 87% men; 84% white; 198 job applicants; 92% men, 73% white
Examination of self-reported stress among managers	841 managers; 91% men; 96% white
Evaluating social sexual conduct at work	200 workers recruited from newspaper ads; 100 women, 100 men; 76% white
Behaviors of female and male executives as they "climb the corporate ladder"	137 executives; 68 women, 69 men
Group trust and workplace conflict	380 workers; 81% men; 95% white
Comparing mechanical and computer-driven systems of creating facial composite pictures	24 undergraduates; 75% women
Openness to change in workplace reorganization	130 workers
Comparing different types of test items	1969 freshmen; 915 women, 1054 men (from archival data set)

typical article in *JEP: Applied* does. You are a beginning researcher without the background that professional researchers have gained in their work. It may be acceptable to include many fewer references as you develop a narrower focus in your first projects.

Carrying Out a Literature Search

Suppose you wanted to study stress levels and the effects they have on students. This is not an easy area to investigate because the concept of importance here, stress, is not directly observable. It is an internal, psychological state. You can observe only the behaviors and reactions associated with it. To understand it, you should find out what others have already learned. You do this by conducting an initial literature search.

A literature search serves several particularly important purposes. First, by learning about what other researchers have discovered, you can avoid merely repeating what they have done. It is always more exciting to create a study that generates knowledge that nobody knew before you did.

A second advantage of searching through the research literature is that you find the vast range of approaches that previous researchers have already used. With this knowledge, you can begin to identify the approach that might be most useful to you in answering your own question.

Third, you can see what approach others have used and how they defined their variables. This lets you see what worked for them. When planning research, there is absolutely nothing wrong with adopting the methods that others have used. If you think back on the concept that scientific knowledge is cumulative, you will recognize that researchers expect others to follow up on their work, just as they have followed up on the work of others.

CONDUCTING YOUR STUDY

Another important choice in creating a research project concerns whether you intend to manipulate and control the situation or whether you will simply observe what occurs naturally. In experimental research, we actively manipulate what we expose the research participants to. In other research, we may not be able to manipulate variables for ethical or practical reasons.

Suppose you wanted to investigate the effects of stress on people. You could choose a descriptive approach in which you observed behaviors without interacting with the people you monitor. For example, you could look at behavior during stressful periods, like final exam week, compared to other less stressful times. This approach would enable you to describe stress-related behaviors that emerge during periods of differential stress.

A second method to study stress might involve administering a questionnaire that inquires about sources of stress and looks at their possible effects. If you used such an approach, you would not have to worry about the ethics of increasing stress levels in already stressed students. Miller and Rahe (1997) took the approach of developing a survey technique to study stress. They used a questionnaire to assess the amount of change in people's lives and the resultant changes in stress. These researchers found that apparently trivial events, even positive ones like going on vacation, contributed to overall stress levels that have an effect on one's health.

A third strategy is to identify existing stress levels in your research participants, then see how they respond to some manipulation. Investigators (e.g., Cohen et al., 2006; Cohen, Tyrrell, & Smith, 1991) did exactly this. They used nose drops to introduce either viruses or an inactive saline (i.e., saltwater) solution into the body and quarantined the people so they were not exposed to any other viral agents. These researchers found that people with higher levels of stress in their lives were more likely to come down with colds and, if they did, their colds were more severe. They also found that people with more positive emotional styles were less susceptible to colds.

Finally, you could bring research participants to a laboratory and induce stress, but as you have learned in Chapter 2, there would be ethical questions about that strategy (just as there would be if you exposed your participants to a virus). Few researchers actively induce stress in people; if they want to control stress levels directly, they often use laboratory animals. (For an example of a study on stress and learning using animals, see Kaneto, 1997.)

The important point here is that you could study stress and its effects in a number of different ways. Each approach involves asking slightly different questions about stress and results in a slightly different portrayal of its effects. All approaches are methodologically valid, and each has its own strengths and weaknesses.

When you decide how you want to conduct your study, you must consider ethical issues. When we consider research on stress, we have to pay attention to the effects it will have on research participants, both human and nonhuman, and balance those effects against the gains from doing the research. Studying the effects of stress on people's lives is certainly worthwhile. If we gain a more complete understanding of when stress reactions are likely to occur (i.e., description and prediction), why the stress builds up (i.e., explanation), and how we might avoid them (i.e., control), a lot of people will lead healthier lives. On the other hand, can we justify what we put our participants through in the research?

Determining the Research Setting

Once we decide on a research question and define our variables, we have to establish the location in which we will actually carry out the study. Some research almost by necessity requires a formal laboratory setting. If an investigation involves highly specialized equipment or a highly controlled environment, the researcher has few options other than the laboratory. For example, if you decided to study a behavior that is affected by many variables, you might want to use a laboratory to eliminate some of the variables so you can see the effect of the other variables. This approach is typical in theoretical research in which some variables have large effects that can obscure a variable that has a small effect on behavior. To study the factor that has a small effect, you need a controlled environment to offset the effects of the unwanted variables.

If the research question involves an application relating to a particular environment like a business, the investigator needs to conduct the study in a business setting. In many cases, the investigator can choose from a wide variety of locations, including laboratories, large classrooms, small seminar rooms, or even busy public areas.

Another decision is whether to test people one by one or in groups. If people are tested in groups rather than individually, they might perform differently on their tasks. Social psychologists have found that people perform differently when they think others are observing them. Zajonc (1965) reported that even rats and ants work differently when in groups. If you are conducting your own study, it makes a difference whether your participants are alone or in groups, but you often do not know whether their performance changes for the better, for the worse, or in ways that are irrelevant to what you are measuring.

Applied research—Research that attempts to address practical questions rather than theoretical questions.

Very often, **applied research** takes place in a natural environment where people are acting as they normally do. **Basic (theoretical) research** is more likely to occur in a laboratory or other controlled set-

Basic (theoretical) research—Research that tests or expands on theory, with no direct application intended.

ting. The reason for choosing a natural environment for research is that it represents the actual question you want to answer: How do people behave in a particular situation? On the other hand, when psychologists conduct theoretical research, we often want to simplify the situation so we can identify the effect of a single variable that might get lost in a complex, real-world setting.

CHOOSING YOUR METHODOLOGY

After you have operationally defined your concepts and variables, you can establish your methodology. Psychologists have developed many techniques to study a wide variety of behaviors. Each approach has its own strengths and weaknesses and, no matter how hard you try, you can never eliminate all the weaknesses in any single study. You simply have to make choices that maximize the amount of useful information your study provides, while minimizing the number of problems you experience.

When we actively make changes in a situation to see the effect of those alterations, we are likely to be using an experimental or quasi-experimental approach that looks at groups created specifically for comparison in a study. A quasi-experiment is like an experiment in some ways, but involves somewhat less control over some variables. If we are content to monitor events as they naturally unfold, we could adopt observational or survey techniques.

Sometimes we are interested in an getting an extensive amount of information from our research participants. In using a detailed case study of one or a few individuals, we gain a rich and complex base of information. We can also study people repeatedly over time, using longitudinal studies.

If we are interested in a more holistic depiction of people, their attitudes, and their feelings rather than numerical information, we can use a more holistic approach known as qualitative research. Qualitative research typically does not rely on manipulating variables or measuring behavior quantitatively. Rather, a qualitative researcher observes behavior patterns and tries to interpret the behaviors without resorting to numerical analysis.

Finally, sometimes we can find out about behaviors and attitudes by studying existing records or other materials, which constitutes archival research. Ultimately, they all provide part of the picture of behavior that we can combine for fuller understanding.

Approaches to Psychological Research

Observational research—Investigation that relies on studying behaviors as they naturally occur, without any intervention by the researcher.

Let's take a specific example. Suppose you wanted to see if stress level is associated with learning. Given that students report high stress levels, this could be a very important question. One decision you must make pertains to whether you would manipulate a person's stress level directly or whether you would simply measure the stress level as it naturally occurs.

If you decided not to actively manipulate a person's stress level for ethical or other reasons, you could make use of **observational research**, noting how people or animals behave in situations that are likely to lead to stress responses. By choosing simply to observe behaviors, psychologists engage in descriptive research. There are varied ways to conduct such studies. They all involve specifying particular behaviors and the behavioral and environmental contexts in which they occur.

An alternative strategy would be to measure a person's existing stress level and try to relate it to the amount of learning that takes place. This method involves **correlational research**. This strategy would avoid the ethical dilemma of elevating stress, but the downside is that you wouldn't know if changes in stress actually cause changes in the amount that a person learns.

Correlational research—Investigation meant to discover whether variables covary—that is, whether there are predictable relationships among measurements of different variables.

Consider the situation of a student who is taking classes for which she is not prepared; she might have difficulty learning the material. When she recognized that fact, it could lead to stress. There would be a relationship between stress and learning, but the causal factor is not the stress; in this example, the stress is the result.

On the other hand, people with naturally high stress levels may not learn well because they can't concentrate well. In this case there would still be a relationship between stress and learning, with the stress being the cause of poor learning.

The problem is that with a correlational design, there may be a predictable relationship between stress level and learning, but you do not know if stress affected learning, if learning affected the stress level, or if something else affected them both. If you don't actively manipulate stress levels experimentally (which could put people at risk), you can describe and maybe predict the connection between stress and learning, but you can't explain the causal mechanism.

If you actively manipulate stress to see how it affects behavior, you will be using **experimental research**. With an experiment, you control the research situation, which is clearly an advantage. In this approach, you would randomly assign participants to groups, expose them to different treatments, then see if the people in the groups behave differently from one another. In this example, you would manipulate stress level to see what effect your manipulation has on some other behavior. The measured behavior that might change depending on stress level is the amount of learning that occurs.

Experimental research—Investigation that involves manipulation and control of an independent or treatment variable with the intent of assessing whether the independent variable causes a change in the level of a dependent variable.

Sometimes you might wish to compare groups to see if they differ in their learning as a result of different levels of stress, but you use existing groups, like women and men or older and younger people. Such a design would resemble an experiment but, because people come to your experiment already belonging to a certain category, there is no real manipulation by the experimenter. We refer to such a design as a **quasi-experiment**.

Quasi-experiment—A research study set up to resemble a true experiment but that does not involve random assignment of participants to a group or manipulation and control of a true independent variable, instead relying on measuring groups based on pre-existing characteristics.

You could also choose other approaches, such as a **case study**, in which you study a single individual's stress levels and the grades that person earns in classes. You can study the person in great depth over a long

Case study—An intensive, in-depth study of a single individual or a few individuals, usually without manipulation of any variables to see how changes affect the person's behavior.

period of time. You end up with a lot of information about that person, which helps you put together a more complete picture of the behavior. Unfortunately, with such an approach, you do not know if this person's behavior is typical of other people. Case studies can be useful in formulating new research questions, but we have to consider whether it is prudent to use the behavior of a single individual as a model for people in general. Psychologists typically study groups rather than individuals, so case studies are relatively rare in the research literature.

The value of case studies (or case reports, as they are sometimes known) has been the subject of debate. One prestigious medical journal, *Journal of the American Medical Association*, does not publish case studies. Other journals, like the *New England Journal of Medicine* and *The Lancet* appear to regard such reports as educational or as teaching tools.

Rare conditions may be of little use to practitioners and clinicians because of that rarity—most psychologists or medical personnel never see them. On the other hand, a report of unusual characteristics of a more frequent condition may be of greater use to practitioners.

Investigations of the frequency with which researchers cite case reports in their published studies reveal that those investigators do not cite case studies as frequently as they do other types of research. Nonetheless, a new journal, *The Journal of Medical Case Reports*, has begun publishing articles. It limits its articles to case studies (Gawrylewski, 2007a).

When we want to gather a lot of information about development over a period of time, we use **longitudinal studies**. Longitudinal research generally involves studying groups of people rather than individual people. This approach requires patience because observations can continue for months, years, and even decades. One of its advantages is that we could see the long-term effects of stress on learning; long-range changes in learning due to stress might be quite different than short-term effects.

It is even possible to study people's behaviors without ever being in contact with those people. Sometimes investigators engage in **archival research** in which they look at existing records to answer their questions. For instance, studying crime reports during periods of social unrest may provide some insights into the link between stress due to social circumstances and educational attainment.

Longitudinal study—A research project in which a group of participants is observed and measured over time, sometimes over many decades.

Recently, psychologists have increased the use of qualitative research. This approach doesn't rely on numerical information but often uses complex description to characterize the way people respond to a situation or experience it. Analyses of behavior in qualitative studies often involve discussions of how people experience and feel about events in their lives. So a study of stress and learning with qualitative research might focus on how people react to a situation when they are trying to learn and they feel stressed.

Archival research—Investigation that relies on existing records like books or governmental statistics or other artifacts rather than on direct observation of participants.

Table 4.2 presents some of the methodologies that psychologists use to study behavior. These do not exhaust all possibilities, but they represent the major strategies in our research.

TABLE 4.2 Major Methodologies That Psychologists Use to Study Behavior

Methodology	Main Characteristics	Advantages	Disadvantages
Experiments	Variables are actively manipulated and the environment is as controlled as possible.	You can eliminate many extraneous factors that might influence behavior, so you can study those of interest. Consequently, you can draw conclusions about causes of behavior.	You may create an artificial environment, so people act in ways that differ from typical. Sometimes, there are ethical issues about manipulating variables.
Quasi-experiments (and ex post facto studies)	The design of the study resembles an experiment, but the variables are not manipulated. Instead the researcher creates categories based on pre-existing characteristics of participants, like gender.	You can eliminate some of the extraneous factors that might influence behavior (but less so than in true experiments). You can also spot predictable relationships, even if you do not know the cause of behaviors.	Because you do not control potentially important variables, you cannot affirm cause-and-effect relationships.
Correlational studies	You measure variables as they already exist, without controlling them.	You can spot predictable behavior patterns. In addition, you do not strip away complicating variables, so you can see how behavior emerges in a natural situation.	You cannot assess what variables predictably cause behaviors to occur.
Surveys, tests, and questionnaires	You ask for self-reported attitudes, knowledge, statements of behavior from respondents.	You can collect a significant amount of diverse information easily. In some cases, you can compare your data with established response patterns from other groups who have been studied.	You do not know how accurately or truthfully your respondents report their behaviors and attitudes. You cannot spot cause-and-effect relationships.
Case studies	You study a single person or a few people in great depth, so you know a lot about them.	You can study people in their complexity and take their specific characteristics into account in trying to understand behavior.	You may not be able to generalize beyond the person or small group. One subject may not be representative of people in general.

TABLE 4.2 continued

Methodology	Main Characteristics	Advantages	Disadvantages
Observational research	You study behaviors in their natural settings without intervening (in most cases).	You can study life and behavior in its complexity.	There are so many factors that influence behavior in the natural world that you cannot be sure why people act as they do.
Longitudinal research	You study people's behaviors over a long period of time.	You can see how behaviors change over time, particularly as an individual develops and matures.	This research may take weeks, months, or years to complete. In addition, people may change because society changes, not only because of their personal maturation.
Archival research	You use existing records and information to help you answer your research question, even though that information was gathered for other reasons.	You can trace information historically and use multiple sources to address your research question.	The information was gathered for purposes different than yours, so the focus may be different. You also do not know how accurate the records are or what information is missing.
Qualitative research	You study people in their natural environment and try to understand them holistically. There is reliance on descriptive rather than quantitative information.	You can gain useful insights into the complexity of people's behaviors. Very often the focus is on the meaning of text or conversation, rather than on its subcomponents.	This research often takes considerably longer than quantitative research and can involves painstaking analysis of the qualitative data. Some researchers do not like the fact that numerical analysis is not critical to this approach.

Selecting Research Materials and Procedures

The details of your research include the materials and apparatus that you use to carry out your project. For example, if you are investigating the connection between stress and learning, you need to develop materials that people will try to learn; your choice of the type of stimuli (complex or abstract ideas, classroom materials, nonsense syllables, words, pictures, foreign words, etc.) may affect your outcome. For example, researchers have known since your grandparents were children that more meaningful material is easier to remember than less meaningful information (Glaze, 1928).

In connection with stress, the choice of material to be learned could be critical. For example, Gadzella, Masten, and Stacks (1998) reported that when students were stressed, they didn't think very deeply about material to be learned. As such, if you wanted to see if stress affected learning, you might get a different result by using simple versus complex material. Similarly, Heuer, Spijkers, Kiesswetter, and Schmidtke (1998) found that stressors impaired the performance of more or less automatic, routine tasks, but not tasks that required more attention. Once again, your results might differ dramatically if you chose a learning task that required considerable attention.

Why Methodology Is Important

How you decide to test your participants is critical. For instance, psychologists have studied how easy it is to learn lists of frequently occurring words versus relatively rare words. Do you think it would be easier to remember common words or uncommon words? Some creative, excellent psychological research has revealed that more common words are remembered better. Other just as creative and excellent psychological research has shown that less common words are easier to remember.

These conflicting results do not make much sense until you know about the details of the research. There are several ways to test a person's memory. One of them is to ask the person to recall as many words from a list as possible. When we do this, people tend to recall more common words better than less common words (Wallace, Sawyer, & Robertson, 1979).

On the other hand, we could give a test of recognition memory. In this case, we would present a large group of words and ask the individual to identify which words had occurred during the learning phase of the study. Thus, the learners do not need to search through memory; they simply have to identify the words they saw before. This methodology leads to better memory for less frequent words (Underwood & Freund, 1970).

Generations of students know about the relative ease of recognition compared to recall. "College students are aware of this fact and notoriously rely less on thorough preparation for objective (multiple choice) tests than for tests which demand recall. Recognition makes no demands upon availability of items," as Deese and Hulse (1967, p. 378) noted over forty years ago.

When you think about it, it makes sense that a recall task favors common words, whereas recognition favors less frequently occurring words. When you try to recall information, you have to search through memory for possibilities. For instance, if you can't find your keys, you may try to locate them by asking yourself where you have been. You need to generate the possibilities yourself until you identify the correct location. If you fail to think of the correct location, you will not find your keys. It would be much easier if somebody gave you a list of places you have been; all you would have to do is to select the correct one because you know the answer is in front of you.

Regarding your memory for words, you can recall more frequent words because they are easier to generate as possibilities in the first place. You have a harder time with infrequent words because you are less likely to generate them, so you don't consider them as possibilities.

As this example shows, your research methodology is important to the development of your ideas. The conclusions you draw from your research result from the way you do your research. No matter what kind of research project you plan, if you overlook the importance of your methodology, you will not have a full understanding of the question you want to answer.

CHOOSING YOUR PARTICIPANTS OR SUBJECTS

Fifty years ago, psychologists studied the behaviors of rats as much as the behaviors of people. Psychologists who studied rats were often referred to as "rat runners." At the time, researchers felt that they could explain the behaviors of just about all animals, human or not, with a single set of behavioral principles. So it did not make much difference to them what kind of organisms they studied. We are in a different era now and we ask different questions, so we mostly study human behavior (Plous, 1996a).

Population—The entire set of people or data that are of interest to a researcher.

Sample—A subset of the population that is studied in a research project.

Representative sample—A subset of the population in a research project that resembles the entire population with respect to variables being measured.

The group that we are interested in understanding constitutes our **population**. It varies in different research projects. If we are interested in stress and learning in college students, then college students constitute the population. If we are interested in how the "typical" person learns, our population consists of college students and many others. If we want to study animal behavior, then a type of animal may constitute our population.

Other than in a census, we seldom have access to the entire population, and it would be too costly to observe the entire group even if we could get to them all. So we use a subset of the population, our **sample**. When the sample is similar to the population, we say we have a **representative sample**.

The decisions we make about studying people involve such questions as who we will study, how we will recruit them for our research, how many we will test, and in what conditions will be study them. We make some very practical choices. The decisions that we make depend in many cases on exactly what questions we want to ask.

The Nature of Your Participants

In general, psychologists do research with organisms that are easiest to study. Can you figure out some of the characteristics of these organisms? This question is important because it determines the type of research questions you can ask.

The typical research subject turns out to be a young, highly educated, cooperative, motivated, female psychology student. Wouldn't you want to work with people with those characteristics? Professional researchers are like you—they want to do their work with the greatest efficiency and the least inconvenience.

Rosenthal and Rosnow (1975) investigated volunteering rates for women and men; they discovered that women tend to volunteer more than men, although the nature of the research project affects this tendency. Rosenthal and Rosnow looked at research during an era in which men were likely to outnumber women in psychology classes; the reverse is true today, so the number of female volunteers will typically outnumber the number of males by a wide margin. For very practical reasons, having access to such a population of willing volunteers (i.e., students in psychology classes) means that psychologists are going to rely on that group of people.

The good news is that when students volunteer to participate in research, they will show up and do what you tell them. The bad news is that we don't always know whether such female participants from psychology classes at a single college or university resemble the entire population. Do older people or younger people act the same way? Do men act the same way? Do less well-educated people act the same way? Do people from other parts of the country act the same way?

We don't know the answers to these questions. So why do we continue to rely on this very restricted population? The answer is because they are there. It would be more time consuming and difficult to locate a more diverse group who might not want to participate in a research study anyway.

Table 4.3 presents participant characteristics typical of research in some journals and the types of research reported in those journals. As you can see, experimental work typically features students, generally undergraduates. Experimental journal articles provide very little detail about the characteristics of the participants. Traditionally, experimental psychologists assumed that we could study any population in order to understand behavior in general; they reasoned that the details of particular groups might differ, but the patterns would be valid across all of them. We now recognize that this could be a problem if we want to know about generalizing results to different populations.

Investigators studying more applied questions usually give greater detail about the people they study, including age, gender, and ethnicity. This makes sense if you consider the point of much applied research, which is to identify answers to questions related to specific situations or well-defined groups.

Deciding How Many Participants to Include

After we identify our participant population, we need to decide how many people we will study. The greater the sample size, the more time and effort it will take to complete the research. At the same time, if we test small samples, we diminish the chance of finding statistically significant results and increase the relative size of error in generalizing our results to our population. Berkowitz (1992) has commented that, in social psychology, research typically relies on sample sizes that are too small. Researchers may miss potentially important and interesting findings as a result. The larger your sample, the more likely you are to spot differences that are real, even if they are small. With smaller samples, we may detect large differences, but miss the small ones.

One of the other principles that should guide you in determining how many people to include in your research project involves variability. When you measure people, they will naturally produce different scores. Some of the discrepancy results from the fact that people differ due to intelligence, motivation, energy levels, and other personal char-

TABLE 4.3 Differences in Research Methodologies in Psychology Journals

Journal	Average Number of Participants per Study	Percentage of Different Methodologies	Percentage of Studies in Different Settings	Percentage of Articles Using Different Statistical Tests	Number of References per Article
Journal of Applied Psychology[a]	(85 Articles; 96 Studies) Mean = 784[d]	44% Survey 23% Experimental 1% Interview 19% Archival 5% Meta-analysis 2% Theoretical	22% Workplace 20% Lab 4% Classroom 22% Other 31% N/A or unknown	27% ANOVA 49% Correlation 19% t-test 18% Chi-square 18% Other	Mean = 54 Range = 21–113
Journal of Experimental Psychology: Applied[b]	(24 Articles; 54 Studies) Mean = 39	96% Experimental 4% Theoretical	75% Laboratory 9% World Wide Web 16% Other 4% N/A	92% ANOVA 38% Correlation 33% t-test 12% Other	Mean = 47 Range: 8–124
Journal of Experimental Psychology: General?[c]	(34 Articles, 26 empirical; 103 Studies) Mean = 156	76% Experimental 24% Commentary	100% Laboratory	85% ANOVA 31% Correlation 54% t-test 8% Chi-square	Mean = 59 Range = 13–121

[a]Volume 85(1-6), 2000.

[b]Volume 5(4),1999 through Volume 5(3), 2000.

[c]Volume 129(1-4), 2000.

[d]One study of military personnel surveyed 29,346 participants. If this highly unusual study is removed, the mean number of participants equals 427, with a median of 236.

acteristics. As a result, when you test them in a research setting, differences will emerge independent of any variables you are interested in. The greater the amount of variability among your participants to begin with, the harder it will be to spot changes in behavior due to different treatments. If you separated them into groups, they would show some differences regardless of whether you treated them differently. With groups of very different types of people, you might wind up with two groups that look very different only because the people start out different.

Consider this situation: Suppose you wanted to manipulate a variable and create a treatment group and a control group. You could assemble your sample and assign each person to one of the two conditions. Then you would expose one group to the treatment and leave the other group untreated. Finally, you would measure them to see if the two groups behaved differently.

If your participants were fairly similar to one another at the beginning, the effect of any treatment would be easier to spot because any differences in behavior would probably be due to that treatment. On the other hand, if the people were quite different before your manipulation, you might not know if any differences between groups were due to initial differences or to your manipulation.

The similarity among your participants is not the only factor influencing the sample size in your research. An additional consideration involves whether you think your manipulation will have a big or a small effect. The effect of your treatment might be real and consistent, but it might be small. For instance, if a teacher smiled at students in one class as they entered a classroom to take a test, it might relax them so their performance increased. The improvement would probably be fairly small, reflecting a small treatment effect. In order to be able to see a difference in scores because of a smiling teacher, you would need a large group of students.

On the other hand, if the teacher announced in advance that there would be particular questions on a test, this manipulation would have a big effect. You would not need such a large sample to see the effects of the information given to the students.

If your research manipulation is likely to have a large effect, you can get away with smaller samples, especially if your participants are relatively similar to begin with. If your manipulation has only a small effect, you will need larger samples to spot differences between groups, particularly if your participants differ from one another noticeably before the experiment begins. You cannot always know in advance how big your effect size will be, although the more you know about the research that others have done, the better your prediction will be. You also do not know how homogeneous your samples are, but if you test college students in your research, your population is likely to be more homogeneous than the population as a whole. They are similar to one another, even if they differ from the vast array of people in general. The bottom line is to test as many people as possible so even small effects show up if they exist.

CONTROVERSY: Comparing Animal and Human Stress

Psychologists have had a long tradition of studying animals and then generalizing the animal behaviors to humans. Over the years, some people have objected to characterizing people as susceptible to the same factors that affect animals. So it is an important and interesting question as to whether studies of animals in a laboratory pertain to human behavior.

It would be helpful if we knew more about how to deal with stress responses so that, when tragedies occur, people can receive treatment. In order to devise maximally effective treatment, it is necessary to know how and why the responses develop.

Such researchers have found that mice who experience stressors that they cannot control (e.g., being forced to swim for 10 minutes) experience changes in the limbic system and affect the rate of extinction of fear responses conditioned to a tone. That is, they develop fear but cannot extinguish it. Additional research with animals has demonstrated that rats that experience chronic stress show less extinction of fear response than rats who are not stressed (Miracle et al., 2006; Schultz, Buddenberg, & Huston, 2007). In addition, in rats bred to show characteristics of learned helplessness, extinction of fear responses is retarded (Schulz et al., 2007).

On the other hand, investigators have also found that other substances can foster extinction of fear responses in mice (Cai et al., 2006; Varvel et al., 2007) and fish (Barreto, Volpato, & Pottinger, 2006).

All of the research just cited involves animals. Because it would be unethical to induce chronic stress in humans or to conduct experiments that might worsen symptoms of stress, psychologists have resorted to studying stress in animals. The big question is whether what is true for rats, mice, and fish also holds true for people.

There is evidence that the same patterns of failure or success in extinguishing fear responses that occur in trout (e.g., Barreto et al., 2006), in mice (e.g., Cai et al., 2006), and in rats (e.g., Miracle et al., 2006) may be at work in people (Felmingham et al., 2007). The same kinds of processes in the brain seem to be occurring in people and in animals who experience anxiety and stress (e.g., Rauch, Shin, & Phelps, 2006). Researchers appear to have reached consensus that animal models can provide the basis for the development treatment of anxiety and stress disorders in people (Anderson & Insel, 2006).

Thus, research with animals like rodents and fish have given us clues about the development and treatment of psychiatric disorders. Such developments are important because of the high levels of stress many people experience. For instance, after the terrorist attacks in the United States in 2001, many people had significant stress reactions, even if they were not directly affected by the attacks (Melnik et al., 2002). In addition, evidence suggests that students also experienced stress reactions (MacGeorge, Samter, Feng, Gillihan, & Graves, 2004). With constantly occurring stress events, we probably should not expect a reduction in psychological problems, particularly in light of data showing that stress and anxiety among college students at one institution increased by 73% between 1992 and 2001 (Benton et al., 2003).

It seems that we can use all the help we can get from the animals studied by researchers.

Question for Discussion: How can researchers gain confidence that their research results with animals pertain to people?

DIFFERING APPROACHES IN DIFFERENT AREAS OF PSYCHOLOGY

When psychologists plan research projects, we often use methods that others before us have developed. It is easier to use a strategy that somebody else has adopted successfully and reported in a journal article than to create your own.

The advantage of relying on the research procedures of others is that they have worked through the problems that arise in developing a new approach. In addition, the previous researchers have developed appropriate materials. As a result, we don't have to repeat the initial errors and false starts of other investigators.

Different Approaches in Different Journals

It is instructive to look at the published work of psychologists, that is, the literature of psychology, to see what decisions they have made in their work. If you look at Table 4.3 on page 109, you will see that the articles that appear in different journals reflect different decisions by scientists as they develop their research projects. Because the American Psychological Association is the largest group of psychologists in the world, with about 150,000 members, and because APA publishes some of the most prestigious journals in psychology, you should expect that the articles in those journals reflect mainstream thinking in our field. As you can see in the table, journals have established different traditions.

Even journals with similar titles have different traditions. For example, *Journal of Experimental Psychology: Applied* (*JEP: Applied*) and *Journal of Applied Psychology* (*JAP*) are very different. Articles in *JEP: Applied* involve true experimental approaches and are more likely to take place in laboratories. On the other hand, articles in *JAP* are more likely to be correlational, to rely on survey methods, and to take place in settings outside the laboratory. As such, researchers who publish their work in *JEP: Applied* are more likely to be able to identify causes of behavior in applied fields.

In contrast, in *JAP*, the correlational articles are such that the researchers can identify patterns of behaviors that occur in natural settings, but are less likely to be able to identify causes. These two journals may publish reports describing different methodologies, but the journals reflect the common interests of the authors, namely applications of psychological knowledge in people's lives. The investigators simply make different decisions regarding how to answer their research questions.

If you examine *Journal of Experimental Psychology: General*, you will find that the authors favor experimental approaches, although these researchers study very different topics than do authors of articles in *JEP: Applied.* They tend to use the same type of experimental approach that allows them to conclude that the level of an independent variable actually causes changes in the level of the dependent variable. Articles that appear in *JEP: General* are also much more likely to be laboratory-based.

The statistical approaches also reveal an interesting picture. Applied research often relies on correlational analysis, whereas experimental, laboratory research typically implies the use of analysis of variance (ANOVA) and t-tests that help us spot differences across groups. It is interesting that *JEP: Applied* resembles the other two journals in some ways but also differs in others.

Different Types of Participants in Different Journals

Another difference in the articles across journals involves the participants. Articles in the realm of applied psychology often employ more and diverse participants. Laboratory studies typically involve many more women than men, mostly students. Applied, workplace studies often have as many or more men than women, especially studies of managers.

Studies in the workplace are likely to be correlational rather than experimental; they are often survey studies. As a result, it is relatively inexpensive to get information from more people. As you can see in Table 4.3 (page 109), the sample sizes are much larger for *JAP* than for *JEP: General* articles.

The greater the diversity among participants, the more confidence we have when we state that our research results will extend to different people. Especially for applied psychological research, we want our results to relate (i.e., to generalize) to others. Generalizability allows us to feel confident that our findings are not specific to a single group of people. Experimental approaches typically rely on undergraduate students, usually psychology students. We need to consider whether the results of such research would be the same if the investigators relied on a different sample. We often do not know the answer to these questions.

Making Choices in Your Research Design

As a researcher, you have only so much time, energy, and money, so it is often not possible to conduct a laboratory study and a field study. Consequently, you choose one and try to get the greatest amount of information from it.

At this point, it should be clear why it is important that scientific research be public. If you read about an experimental study done in a lab, you might question whether the same behaviors would occur in a more realistic setting. You could take the idea and develop a similar approach in the workplace. Most likely, the managers of the work setting are not going to let you disrupt their business with experimental manipulations, so you have to rely on correlational approaches. In the end, two projects relate to a common question, each with a different methodology.

We hope that both studies lead to similar conclusions. When they do, psychologists say that the research results have a type of validity called convergent validity. If not, we try to figure out why the two approaches led to different conclusions, which means doing more research. Because so many variables influence human behavior, we can be assured that each research project will provide only a small piece of the puzzle and that we will need many different projects and many different methodologies in order to assemble a complete picture of the behavior.

If you use a jigsaw puzzle as an analogy to research, you might say that we have a puzzle consisting of a great number of pieces and that occasionally we find that somebody has thrown pieces from another puzzle into our box. We often don't know that the odd piece has come from another puzzle until we spend a lot of time trying to make it fit. When we become aware that the stray piece belongs to a different puzzle, we toss it out. The good news is that we become aware of another interesting puzzle to work on later.

SUMMARY

Once you decide the general nature of your research question, you have to make a lot of practical decisions about how exactly to conduct your study. These practical decisions can make a big difference both in the shape your research takes and the conclusions you draw. Researchers studying similar questions often take very different paths to their answers.

A good place to begin any project is through a literature search. By investigating how others have approached research like yours, you can avoid having to reinvent techniques that have already worked for others. If you find useful ways of creating and measuring variables of interest to you, it only makes good sense for you to use them if they are appropriate. This is perfectly acceptable as long as you give credit to the researchers who developed the ideas initially. In some cases, however, you might want to create different ways of approaching the question because you might not be able to find anybody else who approached your question quite the way you would like. This is an example of the kind of practical decision you will make when setting up your project.

A different decision is to identify the group of people you will study. You will have to decide how you will contact them and how to convince them to participate. Psychologists very often solicit participation from students in beginning psychology classes who receive extra credit for their participation. It can be harder to get participants from other populations. The risk in using student samples is that you are not sure that your results generalize beyond that particular type of person.

Finally, it is important to remember that psychologists with different specialties will approach related questions very differently. Various areas of psychology have developed their own traditions regarding methodological approaches.

REVIEW QUESTIONS

Multiple Choice Questions

1. When you complete a literature search, you can
   a. avoid engaging in replication with extension.
   b. identify the different approaches used by various researchers to address the same question.
   c. ensure that you do not use a similar means to identify and create variables.
   d. make sure that you do not use measurements that everybody else has.
2. Because psychology involves trying to understand complex and abstract concepts, researchers need to develop __________ in order to make useful measurements of those concepts.
   a. operational definitions
   b. hypothetical constructs
   c. literature searches
   d. independent variables
3. When psychologists develop their experiments, they will decide what they want to manipulate as part of the experimental procedure. The variable controlled by the experimenter is the __________ variable.

a. hypothetical
b. construct
c. extraneous
d. independent

4. When you choose your operational definitions in the research you conduct, you have to remember that
   a. there is usually a single best way to deal with complex concepts.
   b. there is usually a great deal of controversy associated with selecting an operational definition.
   c. it is important to operationally define your variable so that it is meaningful across a wide range of cultures.
   d. different operational definitions of the same concept lead to different research questions and can generate different results.
5. If psychologists wants to study the interactions among children on a playground, they are likely to choose
   a. experiments.
   b. quasi-experiments.
   c. observational research.
   d. correlational research.
6. If a journal article has a title like "The relation between political beliefs and activism in students," it is likely to be
   a. observational research.
   b. correlational research.
   c. experimental research
   d. longitudinal research.
7. If an investigator wanted to study the differences in speed of problem solving in young versus old adults, the approach is likely to be
   a. observational research.
   b. correlational research.
   c. case study research
   d. quasi-experimental research.
8. Researchers have studied the effects of traumatic events, like experiencing devastating hurricanes, on children over an extended period of time. Such research is
   a. observational research.
   b. qualitative research.
   c. experimental research
   d. longitudinal research.
9. The systematic elimination of extraneous variables other than those you are interested in can be eliminated in what research design?
   a. Qualitative research
   b. Correlational research
   c. Experimental research
   d. Longitudinal research

10. Research involving a single person who is studied in great depth is characteristic of
    a. survey research.
    b. longitudinal research.
    c. case studies.
    d. qualitative research.
11. If a sample in a study is generally the same as the population, we say the sample is
    a. representative.
    b. reliable.
    c. constructed.
    d. dependent.
12. When an experiment makes use of a small number of participants, the results
    a. are easier to replicate than when there are many participants.
    b. may miss potentially important findings because research with small samples is not very sensitive.
    c. small differences between groups are easier to spot than with large numbers of participants.
    d. are seldom valid.
13. It is easier to spot differences among groups when research involves small samples if
    a. the investigator uses probability sampling.
    b. the participants are homogeneous regarding the behavior to be studied.
    c. the effect sizes for the behavior to be studied are also small.
    d. the hypothetical constructs are operationally defined.
14. Research articles that appear in the *Journal of Applied Psychology* are likely to be
    a. laboratory based.
    b. experimental.
    c. basic.
    d. correlational.
15. When research projects on a given topic lead to similar conclusions, the measurements show
    a. convergent validity.
    b. criterion validity.
    c. interrater validity.
    d. construct validity.

Essay Questions

16. Why is applied research often conducted outside a formal laboratory, whereas theoretical research generally takes place in a laboratory?
17. We hope to be able to generalize our research results to people other than those who actually participated in our research. For the typical psychology study, why is it hard to determine the people to whom our research will generalize?

ANSWERS TO REVIEW QUESTIONS

Multiple Choice Questions

1. b
2. a
3. d
4. d
5. c
6. b
7. d
8. d
9. c
10. c
11. a
12. b
13. b
14. d
15. a

Essay Questions

16. Why is applied research often conducted outside a formal laboratory, whereas theoretical research generally takes place in a laboratory?

    Applied research very often answers a specific question about behaviors in a natural setting. As such, it may be important to study behaviors in the environments in which they typically occur, rather than in a restricted and somewhat artificial atmosphere of the lab.

    On the other hand, in theoretical research, investigators are frequently interested in the effect of a variable that has a consistent, but small, effect on behavior. In such a situation, it makes sense to eliminate variables that have big effects on behavior that will obscure the effects of variables that have smaller effects. One way to get rid of the larger effects of variables you aren't interested in is to control the environment very carefully, which is easiest to do in a lab.

17. We hope to be able to generalize our research results to people other than those who actually participated in our research. For the typical psychology study, why is it hard to determine the people to whom our research will generalize?

    Most psychological research with people involves undergraduate psychology students, the majority of whom are female. So we are likely to be able to generalize to other young, educated women, although it isn't always clear if we can generalize to men or to people younger or older than the female college students. For some measurements, the participants we use may be representative of many other people, but for other measurements (e.g., attitudes), the participants may not be like older or younger people or men, or even female students at other schools or in different parts of the country or in other countries.

    The issue is complicated because, for some measurements, our participants produce very similar results to many other groups (e.g., speed of learning one type of material versus another), whereas for other measurements (e.g., attitudes toward abortion), participants in a single location may not be like others.

CHAPTER FIVE

MEASUREMENT AND SAMPLING

CHAPTER OVERVIEW

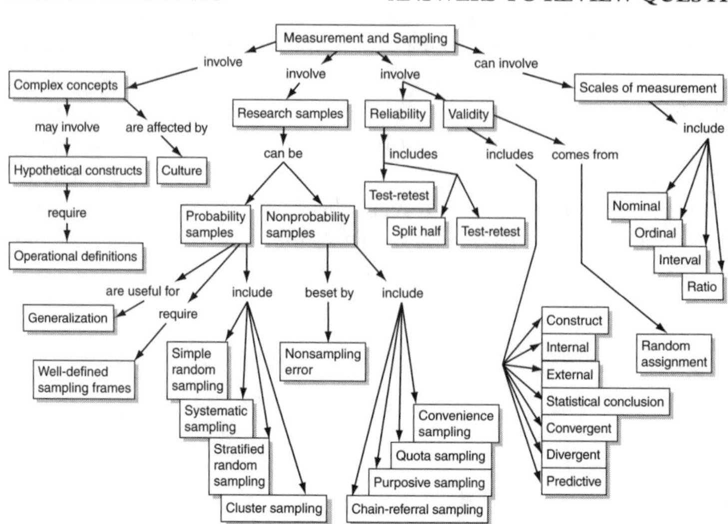

KEY TERMS

Chain-referral sampling, p. 131
Cluster sampling, p. 128
Construct validity, p. 133
Convenience sampling, p. 129
Convergent validity, p. 140
Divergent validity, p. 140
External validity, p. 138
Generalization, p. 126
Hypothetical construct, p. 123
Internal validity, p. 136
Interrater (interobserver) reliability, p. 132
Interval scale, p. 144
Measurement error, p. 131
Nominal scale, p. 143
Nonsampling error, p. 128
Operational definition, p. 123
Ordinal scale, p. 143
Probability sampling, p. 126
Purposive (judgmental) sampling, p. 130
Quota sampling, p. 130
Random assignment, p. 136
Ratio scale, p. 144
Reliability, p. 132
Simple random sampling, p. 127
Split-half reliability, p. 132
Statistical conclusion validity, p. 140
Stratified random sampling, p. 127
Systematic sampling, p. 127
Test-retest reliability, p. 136
Validity, p. 133
Variable, p. 123

CHAPTER PREVIEW

Psychological concepts are often abstract and complex. As a result, researchers create operational definitions that make these difficult concepts easier to measure. The operational definitions provide a concrete set of definitions that different researchers can understand and, in most cases, agree on.

When creating operational definitions to use in research, the investigators have to keep culture and context in mind. People from different backgrounds may respond in different ways to the same stimulus. So concepts may take on different operational definitions in different cultural contexts.

In addition to specifying operational definitions, researchers must also decide who they are going to sample and how they are going to do it. One general classification is called probability sampling. This approach requires identification of the population of interest and a well-specified means of selecting individuals for the research. The simplest and most well-known type is simple random sampling in which every person in the population has an equal chance to participate in the research. But there are also complicated designs involving probability sampling. The benefit of these approaches is that researchers can be confident that the sample represents the population.

A more common approach in psychology is to use nonprobability samples. The main nonprobability approach is to use convenient samples, often of college students. Although these samples are quite convenient, there is some concern that the results may not pertain to a wider population.

After researchers collect their data, they must face the question as to whether their measurements and their results are reliable. That is, if the investigators were to conduct another similar study, would they obtain the same results? If measurements and results are reliable, they may also be valid. That is, the measurements and results might help answer the researchers' questions. There are multiple forms of reliability and validity that are relevant in different circumstances.

Finally, when researchers collect their data, the results are sometimes qualitative, involving how many observations fall into a category. At other times, the results are quantitative, leading to various types of statistical analysis. Depending on the type of measurement, some researchers believe that certain statistical tests may be inappropriate, but this is a controversial issue that has spawned considerable disagreement.

PSYCHOLOGICAL CONCEPTS

In an experiment, a researcher manipulates and controls at least one variable. A variable is a construct whose measurement can result in different values, and it is typically contrasted with a constant, which is something that stays the same. A score on a test to measure the severity of depression would be a variable because the score can vary from one person or time to another.

Every discipline that deals with complex issues has its own set of hypothetical constructs. For instance, in physics, the concept of gravity is a hypothetical construct. We can see the effects of gravity, and knowing about it helps us function in everyday life, but we still don't really know what it is.

We measure overt behaviors, but we assume that the behaviors reflect mental and emotional processes that we can't observe. Even if we can't define exactly what cognitive or neural processes associated with depression, intelligence, motivation, or other constructs entail, our sometimes imprecise measurements have nonetheless led us to a better understanding of people.

Measuring Complex Concepts

Just about every realm of psychology deals with complex and abstract concepts. Think of the different domains that psychologists investigate. Forensic psychologists might deal with the results of a polygraph, the so-called lie detector; they don't know if a suspect is telling the truth, but can only observe the person's behaviors. Similarly, psychologists interested in intelligence can only identify behaviors that they think are related to intelligence. If developmental psychologists want to know if a child understands the world, they may see if the child shows conservation (e.g., the ability to recognize that the amount of a substance doesn't change simply because its shape does). The researchers will observe the child's response but will have to make educated guesses about cognitive processes.

What we need in our research are reasonable ways to measure complex concepts like the "truth" that the forensic psychologists seek, the "intelligence" that the cognitive psychologists want to measure, or the sophistication of thought that the developmental psychologists hope to understand.

Table 5.1 presents how psychologists measured some of these hypothetical constructs. Consider the hypothetical construct of motivation. Bell and Brady (2000) investigated the tendency of street sex workers (e.g., prostitutes) to go to health clinics depending on whether they were given motivation to do so. In this research, the investigators defined the sex workers as being motivated when they were offered monetary rewards for going to the clinic; in contrast, the researchers defined the workers as not motivated when there was no such incentive. The hypothetical construct of motivation was defined in terms of money the sex workers received.

TABLE 5.1 Examples of Operational Definitions of Hypothetical Constructs

Independent variables (IV) reflect manipulated variables used for creating groups to compare; dependent, or measured, variables (DV) reflect variables that are either pre-existing or are the result of manipulation of the independent variable. Some variables are not amenable for use as true IVs, such as intelligence, which can't be manipulated by the experimenter.

Concept	Operational Definition and Research Topic	References
Depression	1. Score on Beck Depression Inventory (DV)–Relation between positive life events and depression 2. The mental state a person is in after reading negative or positive statements (IV)	1. Dixon & Reid (2000) 2. Velten (1968); Bartolic, Basso, Schefft, Glauser, & Titanic-Schefft (1999)
Intelligence	Score on Kaufman Assessment Battery for Children (DV)–Cognitive Processing of Learning Disabled children Score on Raven's Progressive Matrices Test (DV)–Cognitive functioning of immigrants	1. Teeter & Smith (1989) 2. Kozulin (1999)
Happiness	1. Self-report score; amount of smiling and facial muscle activity (DV)–Happiness in people with severe depression 2. Score on Depression-Happiness Scale (DV)–(a) Subjective well-being; (b) religiosity 3. Behavioral observations of happiness (DV)–Happiness in people with profound multiple disabilities 4. Mental state of a person after listening to fearful, sad, happy, and neutral nonverbal vocalizations (IV)–Neural responses to emotional vocalizations	1. Gehrick & Shapiro (2000) 2. (a) Lewis, McCollam, & Joseph (2000); (b) French & Stephen (2000) 3. Green & Reid (1999) 4. Morris, Scott, & Dolan (1999)
Motivation	1. Score on Achievement Motives Scale (DV)–Motivation in athletes 2. Score on Aesthetic Motivation Scale (DV)–Aesthetic motivation and sport preference 3. Scores on Thematic Apperception Test (DV)–Peer group influence in levels of motivation 4. Whether participants received monetary incentives (IV)–(a) Enhancing attendance at clinics for street sex workers; (b) time spent on different tasks in the workplace	1. Halvari & Kjormo (2000) 2. Wann & Wilson (1999) 3. Novi & Meinster (2000). 4. (a) Bell & Brady (2000); (b) Matthews & Dickinson (2000)

On the other hand, Novi and Meinster (2000) defined motivation in terms of the score a participant achieved on the Thematic Apperception Test, a projective test involving ambiguous pictures that an individual tries to interpret.

In both research projects, these investigators were interested in motivation, but they defined motivation differently. These ways of measuring hypothetical constructs are not perfect, but they work to advance our knowledge. In the future we will undoubtedly have different operational definitions, but these are moving us in the right direction now.

As you see, in order to measure an abstraction, we need something with which to make a measurement. That sounds simple, but in practice, it is often quite difficult. For instance, how do you know if somebody is depressed? How do you know the extent to which the person is depressed?

To work with depression, we need a measurement that is reliable. That is, we want a measurement that will produce about the same result every time we measure the depression level of an individual (assuming that the person's level of depression hasn't changed). We need more than reliability, though. We also need a measurement that is valid, that is, a measurement that will help us make accurate predictions about a depressed person's behavior.

Operational Definitions

How would you go about measuring depression or any other hypothetical construct? You have to start with an operational definition. When we use an operational definition, we discuss an abstract concept in terms of how we measure it. For example, a clinical psychologist can't just look at an individual and know the degree of depression the person is experiencing. Some diagnostic measurement tool is necessary. The score on a test would be our operational definition. We would define a high score as reflecting greater depression and a low score as reflecting less.

Researchers regularly use the Beck Depression Inventory (BDI) to assess levels of depression; a high test score indicates more severe depression, whereas a lower score suggests a lower level. Dixon and Reid (2000) used the BDI to assess the depression levels of college students having varying numbers of positive and negative life events; Sundblom, Haikonen, Niemi-Pynttaeri, and Tigerstedt (1994) used the BDI to examine the effects of spiritual healing on chronic pain, which can lead to depression.

A simple self-report test like the BDI is not perfect, but it provides valuable information. One important point to remember is that the score on the BDI is on a continuum and can be low or high. Although there can be a cutoff for "depressed" versus "not depressed," this criterion is arbitrary.

In a research project, using a BDI score to measure an existing level of depression is helpful. But suppose a researcher wants to manipulate an individual's mood, creating a temporary, mild state that resembles depression. The researcher could use the experimental paradigm to start with nearly identical groups, treat one of them in a certain way (like inducing depression in the participants), then measure their behaviors to see if there are any differences in behaviors across groups.

Quite a few researchers have studied the effects of depression on behavior by inducing such a version of depression. For instance, Velten (1997) asked participants to read a series of statements that would either elevate or depress their mood. In this research, he operationally defined depressed as having been exposed to the depressing statements.

DEFINING AND MEASURING VARIABLES

As you plan your project, you need to translate your general ideas into concrete terms. In considering research on stress, this involves creating an **operational definition** of stress, which is our variable of interest here. A **variable** is a something of interest to us that can take on different values.

Operational definitions are important in psychology because we deal with concepts that are hard to define in concrete terms. For instance, most people would agree that stress is a real psychological state. Unfortunately, it is completely internal, a set of feelings and responses that are hard to measure. It is a **hypothetical construct** because we are hypothesizing that it is psychologically real. In just about every area of psychology, we deal with hypothetical constructs for which we need adequate measurements and operational definitions.

Operational definition—A working definition of a complex or abstract idea that is based on how it is measured in a research project.

Variable—An element in a research project that, when measured, can take on more than one value.

Hypothetical construct—An idea or concept that is useful for understanding behavior, thought, and attitude but that is complex and not directly measurable.

If you intend to study stress, you have to figure out what observable measurements can represent this concept meaningfully. Holmes and Rahe (1967) decided they would measure stress through the amount of change a person experiences in his or her life. Think about what they had to do. They had to ask people how much change the people had experienced. This is not an easy issue. First of all, what does it mean to go through change? There are big changes and there are little changes. There are good changes and there are bad changes. What kind of change is worth mentioning? In addition, how far back should people go in their lives when they think of change? Holmes and Rahe had to answer these questions (and more) in deciding how to measure change.

They created the Social Readjustment Rating Scale (SRRS) that indicates the level of change in one's life. For instance, the death of a spouse equaled 100 change units. An outstanding personal achievement contributed 28 change units. A change in eating habits was worth 15 change units. To identify stress, they posed 43 potential episodes reflecting some kind of change in people's lives.

Miller and Rahe (1997) updated the SRRS, finding somewhat different degrees of perceived stress in current society. For reasons we don't understand, people report that the same events today invariably generate higher levels of stress than they used to. The researchers also found gender differences in ratings of the degree of stress of various events, a finding that did not occur in the original scale. Table 5.2 shows the relative amounts of stress associated with various behaviors. As you can see, change can be for the better or for the worse, but it all contributes to stress. Further, it can vary depending on the cultural context.

Subsequent research has shown that SRRS scores constitute a useful predictor of negative outcomes, like an increased likelihood of brain lesions in people with multiple sclerosis (Mohr et al., 2000) and hair loss among women (York, Nicholson, Minors, &

TABLE 5.2 Relative Amounts of Stress Associated with Different Events

Event	Relative Stress (1967)	Relative Stress (1997)	Presumed Valence for Most People (Positive/Negative)
Death of a spouse	100	119	Negative
Jail term	65	79	Negative
Marriage	50	50	Positive
Pregnancy	40	66	Positive
Sex difficulties	39	45	Negative
Death of a close friend	37	70	Negative
Change in work responsibilities	29	43	?
Change in schools	20	35	?
Change in recreation	19	29	?
Change in sleeping habits	16	26	?
Change in eating habits	15	27	?
Christmas	12	30	Positive

Source: Reprinted from Holmes, T. H., & Rahe, R. H. (1967). The social readjustment rating scale. *Journal of Psychosomatic Research, 11,* 213–218; and Miller, M. A., & Rahe, R. H. (1997). Life changes scaling for the 1990s. *Journal of Psychosomatic Research, 43,* 279–292. Copyright © 1967 and 1997, with permission from Elsevier Science.

Duncan, 1998). On the other hand, SRRS scores do not predict frequency or intensity of headaches, which are more predictable from the severity of a person's daily hassles (Fernandez & Sheffield, 1996).

When psychologists create experiments, one kind of variable they define is the independent variable. This is the variable that they manipulate in order to see if changes in this variable will affect behavior. Thus, if a researcher wants to see whether research participants give more help to a person with a tattoo or without a tattoo, the independent variable is presence or absence of the tattoo. In such a study, the researcher might measure how long the person provides help. This measurement, which may change depending on whether somebody who asks for help has a tattoo, is called the dependent variable. When Strohmetz and Moore (2003) conducted this study, they discovered that when the person with a tattoo was dressed in sweatshirt and jeans, that person received more help than when the person was dressed more formally.

The Importance of Culture and Context in Defining Variables

It is important to remember that not everybody reacts the same way to a given change; in fact, in different cultures, the same amount of change leads to quite different amounts of stress. In the United States, the death of a spouse leads to much greater relative adjustment than it does in Japan (Ornstein & Sobel, 1987).

Subsequently, Renner and Mackin (1998) created a scale more suitable for many college students. The original SRRS included items involving dealing with in-laws, having mortgages, and other aspects of life that do not pertain to all students. So Renner and Mackin created a list of fifty-one events of relevance to students. These include being raped or finding that you are HIV-positive, which have the greatest impact weight of any items on the scale; difficulty with a roommate; maintaining a steady dating relationship; getting straight As; and attending a football game. This new scale has not been evaluated for validity, but it contains items that students associate with stress.

If you were studying stress and people's responses to it, you could measure stress levels through either of these scales. Change in a person's life is not exactly the same as stress, but a score on the scale would serve as a reasonable operational definition of stress. Like any operational definition, it is not perfect, but it should work within the cultural context in which it was developed. When used with people from different backgrounds, however, it may be less useful.

People from different groups may show varied types and degrees of stress in their lives, so we have to use caution in the statements we make about the effects of stress. For example, Broman (2005) investigated the relation between stress and substance abuse among college students. He discovered that you have to factor in both race and gender to understand alcohol use as it relates to stress. Black men showed fewer alcohol problems in reaction to stress when compared to Black women and to White men and women. Furthermore, White women show a greater extent of problems with alcohol than White men and Blacks following traumatic stress. Traumatic experiences are associated with heavy episodic drinking for White women only.

MULTIPLE POSSIBLE OPERATIONAL DEFINITIONS

You could measure stress in many ways. If you took a physiological approach, you might measure the amount of cortisol in a person's bloodstream because this chemical results when an individual experiences stress. The advantage of using this particular operational definition is that you can measure the substance very accurately and immediately. The disadvantage is that such an approach would cost a lot of time and money, and it would be invasive for the person who provided the blood. Luckily, we can measure cortisol more easily with modern technology. The chemical can be measured through the simple means of getting a sample of a person's saliva. It would still be costly, but less invasive. You could also measure stress through a questionnaire, as Miller and Rahe (1997) and Renner and Mackin (1998) did. This measurement of stress would be less precise than cortisol level, but it would be cheaper. A questionnaire can also measure long-term stress.

One fact to remember here is that cortisol level does not characterize a psychological response, only a biological response. It might help you understand about biological responses to stress, but not about the psychological experience of stress.

As a researcher, it is up to you to decide how you will define your concept. There is no perfect way; there are simply multiple ways that have their own strengths and weaknesses. Depending on the question you want to ask, you choose one over another. You could use Holmes and Rahe's scale or Renner and Mackin's, or you could find out how other researchers have decided to measure stress and adapt their strategies. In the end you have to select a method that you think will work for you.

PROBABILITY SAMPLING

Probability sampling is the gold standard of sampling. In its simplest definition, probability sampling means that everybody that you are interested in, your population, has an equal chance of participating in your study. Unfortunately, outside of some survey research, psychologists typically don't employ it because it would be very costly. If we were interested in how people in general behave, we would need to test people from every country, of all ages, with diverse backgrounds. For all of its desirability, researchers forego probability sampling in favor of less costly approaches, like the samples of college students that most research employs.

Probability sampling—A method used in research whereby any person in the population has a specified probability of being included in the sample.

We know that psychology students are not typical of people in general on a lot of dimensions; they are younger, more educated, female, etc. A critical question is whether the differences are important in your research. If you are studying reaction times to the appearance of a visual stimulus on a screen, college students may be very similar to other people. On the other hand, if you want to study voting preferences, college students may be dissimilar to people not in college. In our research, we often do not know how well our sample mirrors the population of interest.

Generalization—The property of research results such that they can be seen as valid beyond the sample involved in a study to a larger population.

When the sample is similar to the population, we can be confident in **generalization** of our results from the sample to the population. We hope that if our experimental and control groups consisting of students differ by some amount, then other groups will show a similar difference. We will be satisfied most of the time if we can establish patterns of behavior, even if we can't make precise predictions.

One of the difficulties in probability sampling is purely practical. We don't have enough resources to test people who are far away; we even miss out on nearby people whose schedules are such that they don't have time to take part in our research. So we don't bring them into the lab to test them or go out into the field to track them down.

Another difficulty associated with probability sampling is that, in order to use it, we have to be able to define our population of interest. In theory, we would have to be able to list every member of the population so we could pick our participants from the list. In much of our research, it is not really clear that we could do this, even in theory.

You are most likely to encounter probability sampling in survey research like political polls. In this research, the investigators can identify their population (e.g., registered voters) pretty well and can contact a random subset of the entire population. The population is well-defined and a random sample is reasonably easy to create.

There are four general strategies for probability sampling. They result in simple random samples, systematic samples, stratified random samples, and cluster samples.

Simple Random Sampling

Simple random sampling (SRS) involves identifying your population precisely, then identifying some probability that each person in it will appear in your sample. (We often refer to this approach just as random sampling.) In SRS, each person has an equal chance of being selected. In professionally conducted polls, the researchers use randomly selected telephone numbers, so each household with a phone has an equal chance of being called. The result is likely to be a sample that reflects the entire population.

Simple random sampling—A process of sampling in research that specifies that each person in a population has the same chance of being included in a sample as every other person.

It is important to remember that even with a random sample, you may not have a truly representative sample; sometimes pollsters get unlucky. For instance, if the voters they get in touch with are home because they are unemployed, the sample might show certain biases because such people hold different attitudes than those who are working. But the more people you call, the less likely you are to have a sample that is quite different from the whole population when you use random sampling.

Systematic Sampling

If you have a list of the entire population from which you will sample, you might decide to sample every tenth, twentieth, hundredth, etc. name after selecting a random position to start. This process will generate a **systematic sample**. Some (e.g., Judd, Smith, & Kidder, 1991) have argued that such a technique deviates from randomness because if you started with the fifth name, then went to the fifteenth, twenty-fifth, etc., then the fourteenth and sixteenth names (for example) have zero probability of being chosen. The counterargument is that empirical studies have shown the results of SRS and systematic sampling to be virtually identical, particularly if your list of people is in a random order to begin with; further, in many cases systematic sampling is simply easier to do (Babbie, 1995).

Systematic sampling—A process of sampling in which an apparently unbiased but nonrandom sample is created, such as by creating a list of every element in the population and selecting every nth member from the population.

Stratified Random Sampling

On occasion, you might decide that you want certain groups to be included in your sample in specific proportions. For instance, if you wanted to survey your college so that you could get responses from first-year students, sophomores, juniors, and seniors in equal proportions, you probably would not want to use SRS because you are likely to sample more first-year students because, in most schools, there are more of them; the less interested or able students have not yet dropped out, as they have with upper-level students. As a result, you could employ **stratified random sampling**, in which you identify the proportion of your total sample that will have the characteristics you want.

Stratified random sampling—A process of sampling in which groups of interest (e.g., male and female; young and old; Democratic, Republican, and Independent) are identified, then participants are selected at random from these groups.

Theoretically, stratification can be appropriate for virtually any variable you could think of. You can stratify by age, gender, socioeconomic status, education level, political affiliation, geographical location, height, weight, etc. In practice, though, some stratification is easier than others because you may not be able to identify in advance the members of your population according to some variables (e.g., height or weight) as easily as others (e.g., sex—by using the person's first name as a guide).

Cluster Sampling

Finally, sometimes a strategy like simple random sampling will be too cumbersome to be practical, especially if you have a sampling domain whose elements you cannot list. For instance, if you wanted to survey teachers' attitudes in elementary schools, you might have so many schools in an area that it would be too time consuming to engage in simple random sampling. One alternative is **cluster sampling**.

Cluster sampling—A process of sampling in which a number of groups (or clusters) are identified in a population, then some clusters are randomly selected for participation in a research project.

In this approach, you would randomly select some number of schools, then sample from within each school chosen. In this method, large chunks of the population will be ruled out. You should still have a random sample, though, because your selection of schools was nonsystematic, that is, nonbiased, and the subsample is also nonsytematic. So in advance, there is no built-in bias in the sample, and you should have some confidence that your sample will represent the entire population.

In all of these probability sampling approaches, you have a good chance of ending up with samples that describe the population pretty well. As always, we should remember that we are dealing with probabilities, not certainties, so any given sample might not be useful for depicting the population. Still, this is the most certain of any strategy short of using the entire population. If you look at the results of surveys by professionals, it is clear that their techniques work very well.

NONPROBABILITY SAMPLING

Most psychological research does not involve probability sampling. The implication is that we often do not know to whom our research results generalize. This means that we can say that a particular result applies to students like the ones we study, but we don't know if our results also pertain to people younger or older, less or more educated, poorer or richer, or any other characteristics.

Among the greatest problems with nonprobability samples is **nonsampling error**. This problem occurs when people who should be included in a sample are not. It results in a nonprobability sample that is not representative of the population as a whole. The end result is that a researcher doesn't know to whom the survey results apply.

Nonsampling error—A problem in sampling that leads to a nonrepresentative sample because some members of the population are systematically excluded from participation.

To ignore nonsampling error is to jeopardize the validity of a research project's results. For instance, Wainer (1999) notes an interesting result from a historical set of data. In the mid-nineteenth century, the Swiss physician H. C. Lombard examined over 8,000 death certificates and tallied each individual's cause of death and each individual's profession. The profession generating greatest longevity was that of furriers at 70.0 years.

Surprisingly, the group with the shortest life expectancy was that of student, at 20.2 years. Has life changed so much in a century and a half? The problem, of course, is that students are typically fairly young, so if they die, their life span has been short. After they finish being students, they engage in various occupations, so they don't have the chance to die as students at age 70. This is a clear example of a nonsampling error: There is no opportunity to sample old students because they go into other categories before they die. The conclusion that being a student is dangerous clearly makes no sense, which the original researchers recognized.

The problem is less obvious in some research because you don't always know who you are surveying and who is being left out. For instance, in research on bulimia, investigators often study people referred from medical doctors. It turns out that, compared to bulimics in the community in general, bulimics referred for treatment by a doctor show a greater incidence of self-induced vomiting, greater likelihood of misusing laxatives, and a more severe eating disorder in general (Fairburn et al., 1996). The difficulty here is with nonsampling error. Thus, conclusions about the characteristics and behavior of people suffering from bulimia will differ, depending on how a sample is drawn. If researchers rely on referrals from doctors, the sample will consist of people with more severe problems compared to a randomly drawn sample from the community.

The sampling approaches that psychologists use, particularly in laboratory studies, include convenience samples, quota samples, purposive (judgmental) samples, and respondent-driven (chain-referral) samples. Unfortunately, all of these approaches have limitations because of the people who do not participate in research.

Convenience Sampling

As you saw in Table 4.3, the journals of experimental psychology involve students almost exclusively. Fifty years ago, psychologists hoped to generalize about behavior from the activity of white rats in Skinner boxes. Rats were easy to obtain and were always there when the psychologists wanted to study them. Today, we have the same hope of generalizing from college students, who are also easy to obtain and generally pleasant to work with. As you learned before, when researchers rely on such a population because it is easy or available, we refer to **convenience sampling**.

Convenience sampling—A nonrandom (nonprobability) sampling technique that involves using whatever participants can conveniently be studied, also known as an accidental sample and a haphazard sample.

Unfortunately, in many cases, we don't really know how well our research findings generalize from our samples. At the same time, when we create experimental groups and compare them, we may not be interested in precise measurements of differences between the groups, but rather patterns of differences. For instance, Recarte and Nunes (2000) investigated how students performed in a driving task when asked to complete verbal and spatial imagery tasks. Students are probably younger, on average, than the typical driver. Do you think this would matter when we discuss the effects of verbal versus spatial thought among drivers? Students may be better or worse in their driving than older people, but will the verbal-spatial comparison differ between the two groups? When researchers conduct this type of study, they hope not.

When psychologists test theories, they may not care about the specifics of the samples they work with. In fact, in experimental journals, the researchers report very little detailed information about the participants. The philosophy is that if the theory generates certain predictions, those predictions should come true, regardless of the population tested. If the psychologists are working to develop the details of the theory, they hope the characteristics of the sample are not all that important. On the other hand, if the researchers are hoping to be able to apply their findings to a particular population, characteristics of the sample are very important.

In the end, we have to use our best judgment when deciding how important the demographics of our samples are. Sometimes, using students is just fine; sometimes, it isn't. This is where judgment and experience become important.

Quota Sampling

Quota sampling is analogous to stratified sampling in that, in both, the researcher attempts to achieve a certain proportion of people of certain types in the final sample. Suppose an investigator wants to know if less able students differ from better students in their political beliefs.

The researcher could recruit volunteers from a class, asking the students to indicate name, contact information, and grade point average. Then the researcher could make sure that the proportion of students with low averages in the final sample matches the proportion of students below a certain grade point average in the population, with the proportion of good students in the final sample matching the proportion of better students in the population. In this example, the researcher would need some way to establish the relevant grade point averages, like contacting the Registrar's Office on his or her campus.

Quota sampling—A nonrandom (nonprobability) sampling technique in which subgroups, usually convenience samples, are identified and a specified number of individuals from each group are included in the research.

This type of quota sampling is a variation on convenience sampling. The sample is not random, so the researcher does not know to whom the results generalize.

Purposive (Judgmental) Sampling

At times, a researcher may not feel the need to have a random sample. If the investigator is interested in a particular type of person, say somebody with special expertise, the investigator may try to find as many such people as possible and study them. The result is descriptive research that may say a lot about this group of experts.

For instance, if you were interested in how engineers develop products so that consumers can use them easily, you could get in touch with people who create consumer products. Then you could find out what factors they consider in making the products they create trouble-free when consumers get them home.

Purposive (judgmental) sampling—A nonrandom (nonprobability) sampling technique in which participants are selected for a study because of some desirable characteristics, like expertise in some area.

The problem with such a sample is the same as with any other nonprobability sample—you don't know who, beyond your sample, your results relate to. At the same time, you may wind up with a general sense of the important issues associated with the group of interest. This approach is sometimes called **purposive (judgmental) sampling** because it relies on the judgment of the researcher and a specific purpose for identifying participants.

Chain-Referral Sampling

Sometimes it is difficult to make contact with some populations because they might not want to be found (e.g., drug users, sex workers, illegal immigrants). They are not likely to be conveniently listed with their phone numbers. As a result, researchers have to use creative approaches to contact them. Investigators have developed several techniques to study such groups, which are sometimes called hidden populations; the broad term for these techniques is **chain-referral** methods. As a rule, these strategies are more likely to be practical for survey and interview research than for experimental studies.

Chain-referral sampling—A nonrandom (nonprobability) sampling technique in which a research participant is selected who then identifies further participants that he or she knows, often useful for finding hidden populations.

In these approaches, the researcher may use a contact in the group of interest to provide references to others who, in turn, provide other names. Another chain-referral technique involves finding where members of the group congregate, then sampling the individuals at that location. A third approach is to use a member of the group to recruit others; there may be an advantage to this technique because a known person of the group solicits participation, not an unknown and anonymous researcher. A final approach involves finding a key informant who knows the population of interest; rather than questioning members of the population, the researcher talks with a person knowledgeable about the group.

MAKING USEFUL MEASUREMENTS

Psychologists have spent a lot of time devising reliable and valid ways of measuring concepts that we cannot observe directly. So we may devise a test that gives good information about mental states that we cannot see. Difficulties arise when we try to measure something we can't see; we may make generally good, but imprecise, measurements. Scientists refer to this as **measurement error**.

Measurement error—An error in data collection based on poor measuring instruments or human error that leads to invalid conclusions.

Measurement error does not mean that the investigator has made a mistake. The researcher may carry out his or her tasks flawlessly. The error arises because the measurement device is imperfect, and the participant may also be imperfect in providing data.

For example, if you were interested in knowing if fast readers can identify individual words more quickly than poorer readers, you could present a single word and ask a participant to press a "Yes" button if the item is a word (e.g., crow) and a "No" button if the item is a nonword (e.g., corw). You are studying word recognition skill, which is a complex, internal process. For any given trial, the respondent may respond more slowly than usual because of fatigue; this is measurement error. On another trial, the person may respond more quickly because he or she just saw the word before coming to the laboratory and it was fresh in memory. This is also measurement error.

In general, we say that measurement error occurs when something affects behavior other than the variable you are investigating. In the first example above, you would call slow responses due to fatigue measurement error because you are not studying fatigue—it has just gotten in the way. In the second example, we call the quick response due to familiarity with the word results in measurement error because the study is not focusing on word familiarity—it has just gotten in the way.

Every science faces measurement error. That is why the sciences use statistics; they help us understand the magnitude of the error that we can expect in our measurements.

Reliability

Reliability—A measure of the consistency or reproducibility of data collected using the same methodology on more than one occasion; across different, but related test items; or by different individuals.

Test-retest reliability—A measure of the consistency of data collected at different points in time.

Split-half reliability—A measure of the consistency of data across subgroups when the data from a test or other measuring instrument are broken down into smaller segments.

Interrater (interobserver) reliability—A measure of the consistency of observations of a single situation made by different people.

Because measurement error is a fact of life, psychologists have spent a lot of time developing the notion of **reliability**. If a measurement is reliable, then repeated measurements on the same person should result in similar outcomes each time. Reliability relates to consistency and repeatability in the results. If you completed an intelligence test, then repeated it later, you would probably get a different score each time, but they would likely be fairly similar. The similarity occurs because standardized intelligence tests are generally reliable. Just because an intelligence test is reliable, we shouldn't automatically assume that it shows validity, that is, that the test is useful. Tests can be reliable without giving us any useful information. For example, we could use your height as an estimate of your intelligence; the measurement would be reliable, but it wouldn't be valid. Similarly, standardized tests might be reliable, but we don't always know how valid they are.

When a measurement yields similar results with repeated testing, we say it shows **test-retest reliability**. There are other types of reliability as well.

If questions from subcomponents of a test lead to similar results, the test may have **split-half reliability**.

Another aspect of reliability involves how consistently different investigators record behaviors that they observe independently of one another. If data from two observers tend to agree, their measurements show **interrater (interobserver) reliability**.

Reliability is not an all-or-none situation; different measuring instruments are more or less reliable. Regardless of the type of reliability in question, if measurements are to help us answer questions about behavior, they must show appropriate levels and types of reliability.

Validity

The concept of reliability differs from that of validity. Validity relates to the question of whether measurements provide information on what we really want to measure. Is the measurement really useful for what we want? In order for a measurement instrument to be valid, it must be reliable. You can get consistent (i.e., reliable) scores, but they may not give useful (i.e., valid) information. Just because scores are reliable, we don't know if they are valid.

CONSIDERING VALIDITY IN RESEARCH

As researchers, we want our work to be meaningful. That means creating research designs that relate the independent variable (IV) meaningfully to the dependent variable (DV). Another, more technical way of saying that research results are meaningful is to say that they are valid.

Validity—A property of data, concepts, or research findings whereby they are useful for measuring or understanding phenomena that are of interest to a psychologist. Data, concepts, and research findings fall on a continuum of usefulness for a given application.

There are several different types of **validity**; some are particularly relevant in experimental research. Some types involve the nature of variables; others relate to the structure of an experiment; yet another pertains to the statistics used to analyze the data. They are summarized in Table 5.3.

Validity is not an all-or-none situation. Rather, a measurement may show less or more validity, and its validity may legitimately and predictably change in different situations. Further, an experiment may show high levels of some types of validity, but lower levels of different types.

Construct Validity

When investigators develop an operational definition of a variable, they work to create a measurement that shows **construct validity**. This means that the abstract, underlying concept is being defined, or operationalized, in a way that is useful in understanding that concept. Fortunately, we can often use measurements that others have already created.

Construct Validity—The degree to which a measurement accurately measures the underlying concept that is supposed to be measured.

We can measure intelligence, depression, and other psychological concepts in multiple ways. There may be no need to create a new measurement when other adequate tools are already available. So why should you try to develop something else? Most of the time there is no need unless you are breaking new ground, studying a topic that nobody before you has investigated or studying an existing topic in a new way.

We can get a glimpse of how we can apply the concept of construct validity in the measurement of depression. Depression is complex, which is why psychologists need to study it extensively in order to begin to understand it. As you will see, doing research on depression well requires paying close attention to the details.

Psychologists generally accept the construct validity of the Beck Depression Inventory (BDI) because it is useful in dealing with depressed people. According to many research findings, the BDI has useful psychometric properties, which means that it can distinguish those with depression from those without, and it can document an individual's level of depression (Dozois, Dobson, & Ahnberg, 1998). Steer, Rissmiller, Ranieri, and Beck (1994) reported that the BDI can reliably differentiate patients with mood disorders from those with other kinds of psychological problems.

TABLE 5.3 Different Types of Validity and How They Affect Research

Construct Validity	How well do your operational definitions and procedures capture the hypothetical constructs you want to study? *Example:* If you want to study intelligence, you can administer an IQ test. It will be reasonably high in construct validity if you are interested in educational abilities, but lower in construct validity if you are interested in problem solving in daily activities.
Convergent and Divergent (Discriminant) Validity	Are there positive correlations between your variable and variables that are supposed to be positively correlated? If several different variables that are all related give you the same information, you have convergent validity. Are there negative correlations between your variable and others that are supposed to be unrelated? *Example:* Research on the topic of emotional intelligence has shown that measures of emotional intelligence and personality are related. This suggests that the measures of emotional intelligence overlap with personality traits and are not being measured separately from personality (Davies, Stankov, & Roberts, 1998). There is a lack of divergent validity here. The results do not remove the possibility that emotional intelligence reflects specific skills, it only means that we haven't figured out how to measure it if it does exist.
Internal and External Validity	Is your research set up so that you can draw a firm conclusion from your data? Or are there other potential interpretations that arise because of limitations in your research design? If you have eliminated extraneous and confounding variables from your methodology, your study will have internal validity. *Example:* Mexican American students expressed preference for a Mexican American over a European American counselor. The researchers identified a social response bias, however, that led to the stated preference. When this confound was eliminated, the difference in preference disappeared (Abreu & Gabarain, 2000). Are your results meaningful beyond the setting and the participants involved in your research? If your findings will generalize to new people, new locations, and a different time, they show greater external validity. If your results pertain only to the context of your research project, they will have lower external validity. *Example:* In order to generalize his research results on obedience, Stanley Milgram studied nonstudents from an office building in downtown New Haven, CT. He obtained similar results as with college students, suggesting that his findings have external validity.
Statistical Conclusion Validity	Have you used the proper statistical approaches to analyzing your data? If you employ the wrong statistical model, your conclusions will be less valid. This is particularly relevant for complex approaches like complex analyses of variance, structural equation modeling, or other analyses involving multiple variables.

The BDI also appears to be useful cross-culturally when used with Portuguese (Gorenstein et al., 1999) and with German speakers (Richter, Joachim, & Bastine, 1994). It can also be useful with elderly people who are clinically depressed (Steer, Rissmiller, & Beck, 2000). Thus, we can conclude that for applications like these, the BDI's construct validity is just fine.

At the same time, the BDI may not be appropriate for all types of research on depression. Wagle, Ho, Wagle, and Berrios (2000) have provided evidence that it is not ideal for measuring depression in Alzheimer's patients, and it may perform less well than therapists' judgments in severely depressed people (Martinsen, Friis, & Hoffart, 1995). This means that the BDI is a highly valid instrument for many situations, but not for all.

In the research just mentioned, the investigators were interested in depression as an outcome or measured variable. Sometimes researchers use depression as a manipulated IV. They may induce a mildly depressed state in participants by using simple laboratory techniques, then observe the effect. An important question is whether the lab techniques used to create depression are valid.

One widely known approach was developed by Emmet Velten, who asked his participants to read positive or negative statements in order to elevate or depress their mood. By doing this, he could actively manipulate mood state and see what effect it had on a subsequent behavior of interest.

Does Velten's induced depression resemble naturally occurring depression? That is, does depression as Velten operationalized it have construct validity? Researchers have questioned the validity of the Velten mood induction procedure because there is no guarantee that reading a series of statements induces a realistic version of depression. If the result of this manipulation does not relate to depression, construct validity will be low or nonexistent.

There is reason to believe that Velten's version of depression shows adequate construct validity. For example, Bartolic and colleagues (1999) investigated whether brain activity differs depending on mood. They reasoned that positive (euphoric) and negative (dysphoric) emotional states produce different patterns of activity in the frontal lobes of the brain.

So they used Velten's mood induction procedure to change research participants' emotional states and found that the euphoric state leads to enhanced verbal performance, whereas dysphoric states lead to better figural processing. Their findings are consistent with previous studies of depression. These results suggest that experimental participants are in an emotional state that resembles depression. That is, we see evidence of reasonable levels of construct validity.

On the other hand, sometimes people who are actually depressed behave differently from those whose depression has been induced by the Velten statements (Kwiatkowski & Parkinson, 1994). Once again, when we deal with complex topics, we have to be careful that we are measuring what we think we are. Thinking about research you might do, you can often use the same operational definitions that others have used, but you also need to be aware that you can't adopt them blindly.

Internal and External Validity

The next types of validity we will consider are internal validity and external validity. When research shows **internal validity**, it means that you started your project with groups that were comparable with respect to the DV (or equated them using statistical procedures), eliminated confounds and extraneous variables, manipulated a variable that possessed construct validity, held everything but the IV treatments constant across your groups, and measured your participants' behaviors accurately on another variable that had construct validity.

Internal validity—The degree to which an experiment is designed so that a causal relationship between the independent and dependent variable is demonstrated without interference by extraneous variables.

In order to have external validity, your experiment has to be meaningful in a context outside of your laboratory with people (or animals) other than the ones who took part in your study. In other words, would your findings be replicable in another setting with different participants and at a different time?

Internal Validity. An example of a strategy of assigning people to groups that could very easily lead to bias is as follows. Suppose you were going to test two groups of participants with ten in each group. You could assign the first ten who showed up to Group 1 and the second ten to Group 2. The first ten people might be more eager, more motivated, more energetic, more cooperative, and so on. That's why they got there first. You could end up with two groups that consisted of very different types in each group. Any difference in behavior after your experimental manipulation could be due to their eagerness, motivation, energy, cooperation, or other factors, rather than to the manipulation. This strategy is easy but not advisable.

In contrast, the chief means that scientists use to create similar groups in an experiment is to use random assignment of participants to groups. Random assignment means that any single individual can end up in any group in the experiment and that the individual is placed in the group on the basis of some objective and unbiased strategy. No approach to assignment guarantees that in a single experiment, the groups to be compared would have equivalent scores on the DV at the start of the study. Sometimes an experimenter is simply beset by bad luck. But, in the long run, **random assignment** is an effective way to create equivalent groups.

Random assignment—The process in which participants in a research study are nonsystematically placed in different treatment groups so those groups are equivalent at the start of an experiment.

You can randomly assign participants to groups by using a random number table. Figure 5.1 illustrates how you could assign ten people to two groups on a random basis. In this case, if you took numbers from a random number table and used them to assign people to conditions, you could match the random numbers on the order in which people arrived at the lab, alphabetically, by height, by IQ score, by grade point average, or by any other means. As long as one of the lists is random, the grouping is random.

Across many experiments, this process is the most valuable in creating groups that don't differ systematically at the start. In any given experiment, you might be the victim of bad luck, so that all the smart, tall, nervous, friendly people are in one group instead of being evenly distributed across conditions. Unfortunately, there is nothing you can do about it. You have to decide on a process of randomization (random number table, drawing names out of a hat, rolling dice, etc.) then follow it and live with the results. In the long run, random grouping of participants will lead to the most valid results.

FIGURE 5.1 Steps to take to randomly assign participants to groups.

1. Go through a random number table and write down the numbers from 1 to N (your sample size) in the order in which they occur in the table. In this example, we will move down the columns, choosing the first two digits of the column in each block of numbers. The critical numbers are shaded for this example.

2. Place your participants in order. (The actual order of listing of participants isn't critical here; any ordering will do–alphabetical, in order of arrival to the lab, etc.)

3. Pair each person with the random numbers as they occur.

4. Put each person paired with an odd number into Group 1 and each person paired with an even number into Group 2.

Example of Random Number Table

91477	29697	90242	59885	07839
09496	48263	55662	34601	56490
03549	90503	41995	06394	61978
19981	55031	34220	48623	53407
51444	89292	10273	90035	04758
66281	05254	35219	96901	38055
08461	61412	53378	13522	80778
36070	12377	52392	67053	49965
28751	01486	54443	01873	02586
64061	22061	10746	84070	71531

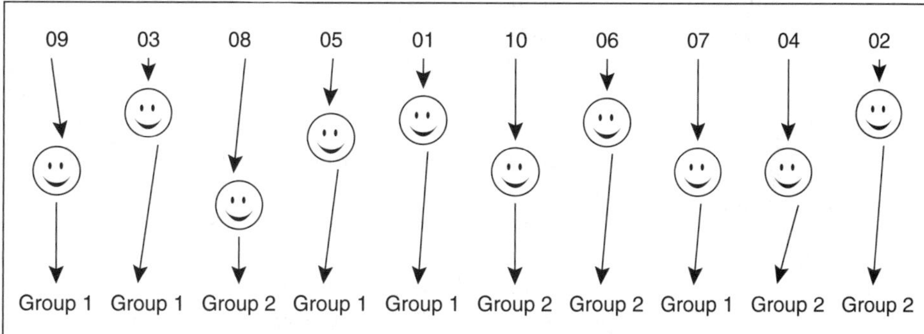

As experimental procedures get more complicated and you add groups, you will have to adjust your randomization techniques. If you plan to create three groups with ten participants randomly assigned to each group, you need to change your assignment strategy a little. Your first step would be to identify your participants and randomly order them.

Then using the random number table in Figure 5.1, you could identify two-digit numbers starting at the upper left of the list. If you have 30 participants, you will only need to pay attention to values in the table of 01 to 30. The first number in the table is 91, which you ignore because it is greater than 30. Moving down the column, we see the next number is 09; you would put the ninth person to show up in Group 1. The next number is 03; the third person would go in Group 2. The next number between 01 and

30 is 19; so the nineteenth person would go in Group 3. You would continue until each of the 30 participants would be assigned to one of the three groups. This approach would remove systematic bias in assigning participants to groups.

Random assignment of participants to groups keeps us from introducing systematic bias into the process of creating groups. Consequently, we can have confidence that any group differences after a treatment are due to the treatment. This produces a greater level of internal validity.

The internal validity of a research project is critical to the level of confidence you have in your conclusions. The greater the internal validity, the more you can have faith that you know what factors cause an individual to act in a certain way.

External Validity. In addition to random assignment, there is another randomization process sometimes used in research. In some research, mostly surveys, investigators make use of random selection. When researchers use this technique, it means that everybody in the population has a specified probability of being included in the research.

The goal of random selection is to increase the representativeness of the sample. With random selection, a scientist can have confidence that the sample used in the research is generally similar to the population as a whole. If your sample is like the population, you can conclude that the results from your sample will be similar to what would happen if you measured the entire population. When you can generalize beyond your sample, your results show external validity.

In terms that you should be familiar with, random assignment relates to internal validity, the degree to which an experiment is structured so that its results can be interpreted unambiguously. On the other hand, random selection relates to **external validity**, the degree to which the experiment pertains to those other than the participants in the study. In experimental research, it is typical to have random assignment of participants to groups, but not to have random selection because it is easier to use convenience samples, usually college students.

External validity—The property of data such that research results apply to people and situations beyond the particular sample of individuals observed in a single research setting.

In some cases, using college students will lead to low levels of external validity. On the other hand, college students are people, and you are interested in people. In many ways, they are going to be like other older and younger people who come from the same socioeconomic and ethnic groups. As such, their behaviors during experiments might very well reflect the behaviors of others from the same background.

If you use animals in your research, you are likely to use rats, mice, or pigeons. Traditionally, psychologists who studied learning processes have used rats or pigeons; researchers studying genetics have used mice. These creatures are very different from other animals; they have been bred for laboratories and are likely to be more docile than rats that you might see in the wild. Domesticated mice, for instance, are larger than wild mice and reach sexual maturity quicker. But domesticated mice are physically weaker and have poorer vision than their wild counterparts. Mice, like all domesticated animals, show more chromosomal breakage than wild animals (Austad, 2002).

Can you generalize from white lab rats, from pigeons, or from mice to other rats, pigeons, and mice? to other animals? to people? These are not questions that are always easily answered. You have to use good judgment and expert opinion, plus a lot of caution, when you generalize across species.

When psychologists discuss generalization, we are interested in whether our research results will pertain to other organisms, other settings, and other times. Given the success that psychologists have had in applying research results to contexts outside the laboratory, we can conclude that levels of external validity are often acceptable, even if not perfect.

In any case, Mook (1983) has suggested that asking about the generalizability of research results may not really be the best question to ask. He proposed that we may want to test a set of ideas or a theory in the lab. For purposes of testing a theory, internal validity is critical, but external validity (and generalization) aren't relevant.

To illustrate his point, Mook used Harry Harlow's classic studies of young monkeys that could turn in a time of distress to either a soft and cuddly, artificial "mother" or an uncomfortable, wire "mother" from which the monkey got its milk (from a baby bottle). Drive-reduction theory would lead to the prediction that the animal would turn to the wire mother. Harlow tested this assumption and found that, in times of distress, the monkey preferred warm and cuddly.

The experimental setup was very artificial. The monkeys were probably not representative of baby monkeys in general; after all, they had been raised in a laboratory. They were certainly not like people.

The important issue here is that Harlow's results further weakened a dying theory and helped replace it with a different theory. In some ways, it doesn't matter, Mook explained, whether the results would generalize to people. The critical issue in some cases is development of ideas to test a theory.

Statistical Conclusion Validity

After you complete your experimental procedure, it is typical to conduct a statistical analysis of the results. In an introductory statistics course, everything seems pretty straightforward with regard to the selection of an appropriate statistical procedure.

In reality, there are times when it is not clear which test is most appropriate. As psychological methods become more complex, new statistical approaches are developed. They may be better than older ones in some cases.

Psychologists also maintain that nominally and ordinally scaled variables do not lend themselves to tests like the Student's *t*-test or the analysis of variance (ANOVA). They assert that you should not use the *t*-test or ANOVA for such variables. Statisticians have never thought that scale of measurement was a particularly critical issue.

When the noted psychologist S. S. Stevens (1946) invented the concepts of nominal, ordinal, interval, and ratio schedules, he decided that different statistical tests were appropriate for different scales of measurement. It wasn't long before others spotted the flaws in Stevens's arguments. For instance, Lord (1953) showed that in some cases, it might be entirely appropriate to use a t-test with football numbers, which are on a nominal scale. Later, Gaito (1980) further argued that Stevens had confused the numbers and the concepts that they were supposed to represent. Even Stevens (1951) recognized that his earlier proclamations could keep researchers from answering important questions

Statistical conclusion validity—The characteristic of research results such that the conclusions drawn from the results are valid because the appropriate statistical analyses were used.

appropriately. More recently, Velleman and Wilkinson (1993) have articulated arguments about cases in which scales of measurement are or are not particularly meaningful. The traditional prohibitions against using parametric tests with ordinal data often don't really have a solid theoretical or mathematical basis.

The important thing to remember is that you should give adequate consideration to your statistical tests. If you are uncertain, ask somebody who knows. Researchers do this all the time, especially when they are engaged in research techniques that are new to them. If you use the appropriate statistical test, and use it accurately, your results will have **statistical conclusion validity**.

There have been recent discussions about what constitutes adequate statistical conclusion validity in research reports. The American Psychological Association constituted a task force to deliberate the issues. The final report noted that traditional tests of statistical significance were appropriate in many cases, but that they needed to be supplemented by other statistics, like measures of effect size and confidence intervals (Wilkinson et al., 1999). The task force also recommended using the simplest statistic that will answer the question the researcher poses.

Convergent validity—The degree to which two measurements that attempt to measure the same hypothetical construct are consistent with one another.

Divergent validity—The degree to which two measurements that should be assessing different constructs lead to different values.

Convergent and Divergent Validity

One way to have confidence in our findings is through **convergent validity**, which means achieving similar results with different methodologies. If two different approaches to a given question lead us to the same conclusion, our confidence in our methodology and results will increase. Similarly, we can gain confidence through **divergent validity**, which means that when two measurements that should be unrelated actually are unrelated. (Divergent validity is also called discriminant validity.)

The SAT: Questions of Reliability and Validity

The SAT is reasonably reliable, but the question is whether it is useful in predicting how well students will perform in college. If the SAT is useful for answering this question, we say it has predictive validity. We have a predictor variable, the SAT scores, that we use to predict the criterion variable, which is what we are really interested in. In a general sense, SAT scores do predict how well students perform in their first year in college, but it does not provide enough information by itself to make good predictions about college performance. Admissions offices must use SAT information in conjunction with other data if they are to make the best decisions about students who have applied to their institutions.

Another type of validity relates to the actual items that appear on a measurement instrument. For instance, a classroom test that has questions that assess how well students have learned a particular body of material will show content validity. If a measurement of an abstract concept (like academic strength, for example) really seems to assess that hypothetical construct, we say that the measurement shows construct validity. Depending on what we try to measure, we may be interested in different kinds of validity.

You can see the importance of validity in Controversy on Head Start. Depending on how researchers have measured the effectiveness of the program, they have arrived at opposite conclusions about how effective Head Start has been. The easy-to-measure variables suggested low effectiveness. Longer-term, but more important (and valid)

CONTROVERSY: Intelligence

One very widely used operational definition is the Intelligence Quotient, or IQ score. What is intelligence? We don't really know; we can only see the results of intelligence level as people function well or poorly in various aspects of their lives. Still, if we are going to predict behavior based on a person's intelligence level, we have to come up with an operational definition of this concept; we have to measure it somehow.

Traditionally, intelligence has meant an IQ score. In everyday life, many people do not recognize any difference between the concept of intelligence and the IQ score. In truth, though, an IQ score is a pale representation of intelligence. Standardized intelligence tests are fairly good at indicating how well a person is likely to perform in school. However, they don't necessarily say much about the individual's abilities in nonscholastic domains that are major components of Gardner's (1999; Gardner, Krechevsley, Sternberg, & Okagaki, 1994) theory of multiple intelligence or about some of the analytical, practical, and creative components of intelligence that are major elements of Sternberg's (1985, 1999) triarchic theory of intelligence.

This means that when we consider a complex hypothetical construct like intelligence, there are going to be different operational definitions that will be useful in different situations.

A recently developed hypothetical construct is that of emotional intelligence (Goleman, 1996). Basically, emotional intelligence is said to relate to a person's ability to be emotionally sensitive or attuned to others. In order for this construct to be useful for psychologists, we have to be able to measure it. There should be some test that generates scores that will differentiate people with different levels of such intelligence.

A test of emotional intelligence should also be unrelated to other constructs. For instance, if IQ score and emotional intelligence were correlated, we might assume that emotional intelligence is simply part of "regular" intelligence. If we are going to consider emotional intelligence as something that exists on its own, it should not overlap with other constructs very greatly.

As of now, it is not clear whether emotional intelligence will be a useful construct in psychology in the long run. Mayer, Salovey, Caruso, and Sitarenios (2001) reported their work to devise an independent measurement of it, the Multi-Factor Emotional Intelligence Scale (MEIS); they demonstrated some empirical support for it. On the other hand, Roberts, Zeidner, and Matthews (2001) claimed that the MEIS may not provide sufficient evidence for emotional intelligence as a valid construct. Further, Davies, Stankov, and Roberts (1998) reported that some attempts to measure emotional intelligence have led to low reliability.

The arguments get complicated, but some psychologists have argued that the tests of emotional intelligence do not have divergent validity because measurements that should be unrelated turn out to be related. So the different measurements are actually tapping the same underlying concept, not different constructs. If so, the current instruments designed to measure emotional intelligence have failed. This conclusion doesn't necessarily mean that emotional intelligence isn't real, just that we haven't come up with a reliable measurement of it yet.

Question for Discussion: How could you set up a research project to measure emotional intelligence?

measurements reveal that Head Start has met many of its goals. Some research has not documented long-term academic gains, but enough studies have done so. Consequently, many educators believe that Head Start has lived up to its promise.

CONTROVERSY: The Head Start Program

Researchers have to decide how they are going to complete their study. The choices reflect the way they define their concepts. This set of choices can be of paramount importance. To examine the effect of choices, let's consider the Head Start program, a federal program that provides educational opportunities for children deemed at risk for educational difficulty because of social and cultural factors. It would be nice to know whether it is effective because, as a country, we spend millions of dollars on it each year.

One of the choices a researcher would make in studying Head Start is how to define "effective." One way is to look at later IQ scores, which are easy to measure. Or you could look at students' grades during their elementary school years, which are also easy to measure. (One of the factors that arises repeatedly in research design is how easy it is for the investigator to carry out a project. If it is too costly or difficult, the researcher will most likely simplify or abandon it.)

Evaluation of the Head Start program reveals that the children in the program might initially show gains in IQ scores, but those gains are not permanent (Barnett, 1998). If you relied solely on IQ scores, you might conclude that Head Start and programs like it are not particularly useful. Fortunately, Barnett reviewed other measures of effectiveness, like graduation rates and school achievement. On both of these measures, children who experienced early childhood education programs showed success in the long term, into adulthood.

Thus, a conclusion based on IQ scores would be that the program was ineffective; one implication would be to discontinue the program. When you think about it, though, why are IQ scores so important? What do they tell us that is so important? Academic success and graduation lead to long-term benefits. Barnett concluded that the benefits significantly outweigh the costs of such programs.

Some studies suggest that the long-term improvements are small or nonexistent, even though most researchers have found support for the effectiveness of Head Start. When we deal with complex research, it isn't surprising to find contradictions in the research literature. Whenever we deal with complex issues, it often takes a lot of research to resolve discrepancies, especially when researchers study different samples and use different measurements in their studies. Each study that we do resolves some of the contradictions and provides another piece to the puzzle.

This example is important because it shows how important your decisions can be about your methodology. If "effective" is defined as IQ scores, the Head Start program seems ineffective. That is, the children are no better off afterward than they would have been without it. On the other hand, if you define "effective" as long-term benefit leading to becoming a productive member of society, the program clearly meets its goals. In this research, it took a decade for the beneficial effects of Head Start to become apparent. Most of us don't want our research programs to last a decade, so we generally look at short-term effects. As we see in this situation, such decisions can lead to radically different conclusions.

Question for Discussion: How could planning differ depending on how effectiveness is defined in the research on Head Start?

SCALES OF MEASUREMENT

The highly respected psychophysicist, S. S. Stevens (1951), argued that the numerical information provided by the data we collect depends on the type of measurements we make. Some data are relatively crude, providing information about categories in which observations fall. Other data are more mathematically sophisticated, permitting more complex algebraic manipulation.

As such, he reasoned, some data are appropriate for a given psychological test, but other data are not. His arguments have had significant impact on the way psychologists analyze data, even though there are compelling reasons to believe that Stevens overstated his case greatly (Lord, 1953; Gaito, 1980; Velleman & Wilkinson, 1993). Nonetheless, controversies and misunderstandings about the issues Stevens raised still persist.

Nominal Scales

Stevens labeled four different scales of measurement. At the simplest level, **nominal scales** involve simple categorization. People are generally recognized to come in two sexes, female and male (although there is some argument on that count, too, Fausto-Sterling, 1993). When we categorize people or things, we are engaging in the simplest form of measurement. As we conclude that one person is female and another is male, we are measuring them on a nominal scale.

Nominal scale—Measurement that involves putting observations into qualitatively different categories.

Usually, we talk about measurement in the context of "real" numbers, not categories, but assigning people to categories involves a simple variety of measurement. There isn't much arithmetic we can do with these numbers other than counting. We can tally the number of people who fall into categories of interest. With nominal data, though, we can differentiate among the categories themselves only descriptively.

Although we can tally different numbers of observations in each category, as when we say that there are more female psychology majors than male psychology majors, we can't compare any two measurements (e.g., one male, one female) and say that they differ quantitatively, that is, numerically. We can only say that the observations differ, but we can't give an amount by which they differ because these measurements are don't fall on a number line.

Ordinal Scales

When our measurements do fall on a number line, we are dealing more quantitatively, not only descriptively and categorically. When we are able to compare two measurements and have the ability to decide that they differ (e.g., perhaps one is larger than the other), but we can't say how large the difference is, we are dealing with an **ordinal scale**.

Ordinal scale—Measurement that involves ranking data according to size.

In this case, we have some quantitative information, but only enough to say that one measurement falls above or below another on the number line. An absolute measure of the difference isn't possible on an ordinal scale. A typical example of measurements on an ordinal scale are ranks. Somebody who ranks first is ahead of somebody who ranks second; the second place person is, in turn, ahead of the third ranked person. But we don't know by how much they differ. First and second could be very close, with third very far away. On the other hand, first might be well ahead of second and third, who are close.

Ratio and Interval Scales

As we have seen, sometimes we use data that permit us to identify two people or things as being the same or different, which involves a nominal scale. These data may also allow us to identify which of two measurements is larger (or smaller) when they do differ; this involves an ordinal scale.

In many cases, we can go beyond ranking and assess an amount of difference between two measurements. When we are using such measurements and when the measurement system has an absolute zero (i.e., it will not permit negative numbers), we have a **ratio scale**. If the zero point on the scale is arbitrary (i.e., it will allow negative numbers), we have an **interval scale**. Practically speaking, we don't need to differentiate between interval and ratio scale numbers in our discussion here.

Ratio scale—Measurement that shows the characteristics of an interval scale but that has an absolute zero point.

Interval scale—Measurement that involves data organized from large to small for which any two adjacent values are the same distance from one another as any other pair of adjacent values.

In both of these scales, a fixed difference (e.g., 10 points) means the same thing regardless of where the number falls on the number line. The difference between 50 and 60 and the difference between 90 and 100 is 10 in both cases, and that difference means the same thing.

Remember that for ranks, the difference between finishing first and second, a difference of one place, doesn't reflect the same as the difference between last and next to last. If you have ever been to a track meet, you will have seen close battles between first and second in a race, but the time of the last and next to last runners might be considerable. The difference in ranking is the same, but the difference in their times is quite another matter.

There are arguments that some data we use in psychology look like interval or ratio data, but are really ordinal data. A common example in which there is disagreement about the scale of measurement involves intelligence as represented in IQ scores. The difference in behavior between somebody whose IQ score is 80 and somebody whose score is 90 may be quite noticeable, whereas the difference between people whose scores are 140 and 150 might be minimal. This pattern suggests that the difference of 10 points between members of each pair isn't really the same. This would be characteristic of an ordinal scale of measurement. That is, there are differences, but just as we don't know how big the differences are when people differ by a rank of one, we also don't know how big the real behavioral differences are when people differ in IQ scores by a fixed amount.

The importance of the issue, to the extent that it is important at all, is that some researchers identify one set of statistical tests that we can use when data are on an interval or ratio scale, and different sets of tests for each of nominal and ordinal scales.

Some researchers think that if IQ scores are really on an ordinal scale of measurement, the logical implication is that we should not be using certain statistical tests with them. Other researchers advance arguments to the contrary. In practice, psychologists may argue against using parametric tests with data like IQ scores, but most researchers use them anyway with no apparent problems.

SUMMARY

One of the first steps that researchers engage in while preparing to conduct a study is to make sure that their variables are well defined and measurable. The complex, abstract hypothetical constructs of interest to psychologists are often difficult to measure directly, so researchers rely on operational definitions that are clear and objective; these operational definitions are never perfect ways to measure concepts, but they are useful.

Once the concepts are defined, researchers have to decide whom they are going to sample. If the overall population of interest is well specified, researchers can use probability sampling that leads to groups of people that are likely to be representative of the entire population. Unfortunately, random sampling is virtually impossible for most psychological research, so investigators rely on convenience sampling. The people in these samples do not always behave in the same ways that the overall population does. In spite of this limitation, though, psychologists believe that research with convenience samples can often generalize to the population.

In the end, the usefulness of research will depend on whether measurements are reliable and valid. Reliability refers to whether the same results occur with repeated measurement or across different measurements. Validity refers to how well the measurements tap into the concepts that researchers are trying to measure. Measurements can be reliable but not valid. By definition, if measurements are valid, they must be reliable.

When we are able to control for outside factors that affect the behavior of research participants, we can maximize the internal validity of our studies. Sometimes we are more concerned with internal validity, that is, the structure of the experiment itself. At other times, though, we are more concerned with external validity, the extent to which our results make sense outside the confines of our own research setting.

There are other types of validity as well, including construct validity, which relates to how well we operationally define our hypothetical constructs. We also pay attention to convergent and divergent validity, the degree to which measurements are associated with related constructs or differ from unrelated constructs. Finally, statistical conclusion validity relates to whether a researcher uses statistical tests that lead to the most meaningful conclusions possible.

REVIEW QUESTIONS

Multiple Choice Questions

1. The complex abstract concepts that we cannot observe directly but that we study in psychology are
   a. manipulations.
   b. variables.
   c. main effects.
   d. constructs.

2. When we discuss hypothetical constructs in terms of how we measure them, we are using
   a. quasi-experimental variables.
   b. operational definitions.
   c. task variables.
   d. factorial designs.
3. When psychologists develop their experiments, they will decide what they want to manipulate as part of the experimental procedure. The variable controlled by the experimenter is the _____ variable.
   a. hypothetical
   b. extraneous
   c. independent
   d. construct
4. If a research project is set up so everybody in the population of interest has an equal chance of being included, the research involves
   a. quota sampling.
   b. judgmental sampling.
   c. probability sampling.
   d. convenience sampling.
5. Suppose a researcher created a list of the names of everybody in a population of interest and selected every tenth name in order to get a list of participants. This means of sampling is
   a. simple random sampling.
   b. systematic sampling.
   c. quota sampling.
   d. cluster sampling.
6. You could create a stratified random sample by
   a. breaking the population into subgroups and randomly selecting from each subgroup.
   b. randomly selecting participants from the names of everybody in your population.
   c. creating clusters of people in the population and selecting everybody from randomly chosen clusters.
   d. using chain-referral sampling.
7. The research on bulimia often involves participants who are referred by doctors to the researchers. This means that those suffering from bulimia not requiring medical intervention are missed. This problems reflects
   a. measurement error.
   b. nonsampling error
   c. a quasi-experimental design.
   d. participant sampling.
8. If you conducted research that relied on students from introductory psychology classes who volunteered to participate, you would be using a
   a. quota sample.
   b. stratified sample.
   c. systematic sample.
   d. convenience sample.
9. Purposive sampling involves
   a. using research participants from specifically identified subpopulations.
   b. making sure that critical subgroups are included in your research sample.
   c. identifying people with particular characteristics of interest to you and testing them.
   d. systematically sampling every n^{th} person in the population.

10. Suppose a researcher measures a behavior in a research sample, then repeats data collection to see if the results are the same. If the data provided by each person is very similar on the two occasions, the measurement shows
    a. reliability.
    b. validity.
    c. generalizability.
    d. low nonsampling error.
11. A test shows split-half reliability if
    a. the test is split into small components and people respond similarly to each part.
    b. the test leads to similar results more than 50 percent of the time.
    c. the hypothetical constructs have adequate operational definitions.
    d. the predictor and criterion variables are related.
12. If a measurement of depression on a standardized depression inventory is useful in understanding an individual's depression, that measurement is said to
    a. show good reliability.
    b. eliminate nonsampling error.
    c. be representative.
    d. have validity.
13. Construct validity refers to how well
    a. your operational definitions relate to the underlying concepts you are trying to measure.
    b. your measurements agree with the measurements of others.
    c. your statistical tests help you answer your research questions.
    d. your measurements correlate with one another.
14. If you want to generalize the results of your research to a different population, your measurements should show
    a. convergent validity.
    b. construct validity.
    c. external validity.
    d. internal validity.
15. When laboratory research settings are created to resemble the real-life situations they are investigating, the effect is to lead to
    a. the Hawthorne effect.
    b. causal ambiguity.
    c. random selection.
    d. mundane realism.

Essay Questions

16. Describe how three different types of psychologists (e.g., social psychologist, developmental psychologist) could study a concept like happiness.
17. Identify two major reasons why psychological research typically does not involve probability samples.
18. If you have to sacrifice either internal validity or external validity, which would be better to sacrifice? Why?

ANSWERS TO REVIEW QUESTIONS

Multiple Choice Questions

1. d	4. c	7. b	10. a	13. a
2. b	5. b	8. d	11. a	14. c
3. c	6. a	9. c	12. d	15. d

Essay Questions

16. Describe how three different types of psychologists (e.g., social psychologist, developmental psychologist) could study a concept like happiness.

    A social psychologist could study how interactions with others influence happiness.
    A psychometrician would try to figure out ways to define and measure happiness.
    A neuroscientist could study what areas of the brain are involved in feelings of happiness.
    A developmental psychologist could monitor patterns of happiness through the lifespan.
    A clinical psychologist could investigate how people with emotional disturbances regain feelings of happiness.

17. Identify two major reasons why psychological research typically does not involve probability samples.

    We generally don't have the resources necessary to sample randomly. It would take considerable time, money, and energy to collect information from diverse groups of people. So we take the easier route most of the time, using college students. It is an imperfect strategy but it does yield useful results.
    We may not be able to identify our population specifically enough to be able to develop a sampling strategy that would generate a probability sample.
    When psychologists engage in theoretical research, the population may not be of great interest. The test of a theory should produce the expected results, regardless of the nature of either the sample or the population.

18. If you have to sacrifice either internal validity or external validity, which would be better to sacrifice? Why?

    Depending on your goals, one type of validity may be preferable if you have to sacrifice. If you are testing a theory, internal validity is more critical because you are assessing whether your theoretical ideas lead to good predictions about behavior and what causes it. If you are trying to find the effect of a single variable on behavior, internal validity will be critical.

    If you are interested in applying results of research to a real-world setting, external validity might be more important. You might lose some confidence in your statements of causation, but you might have more confidence in your ability to make predictions accurately.

CHAPTER SIX

CONDUCTING AN EXPERIMENT

General Principles

CHAPTER OVERVIEW

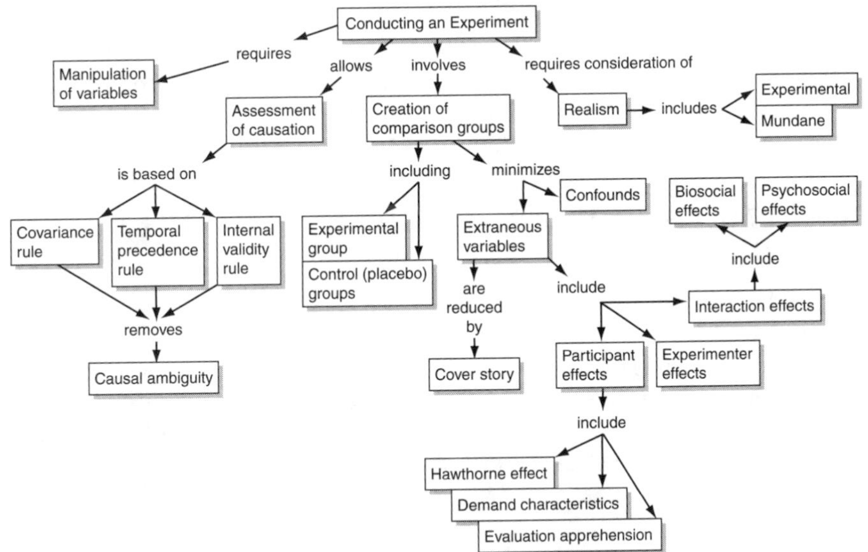

KEY TERMS

Biosocial effect, p. 163
Blind study, p. 161
Causal ambiguity, p. 153
Confound, p. 156
Control group, p. 153
Covariance rule, p. 152
Cover story, p. 161
Demand characteristics, p. 161
Double blind study, p. 161
Evaluation apprehension, p. 161
Experiment, p. 150
Experimental realism, p. 164
Experimental group, p. 153
Experimenter bias, p. 160
Extraneous variable, p. 156
Hawthorne effect, p. 161
Internal validity rule, p. 152
Mundane realism, p. 164
Placebo group, p. 153
Psychosocial effect, p. 163
Single blind study, p. 161
Temporal precedence rule, p. 152

CHAPTER PREVIEW

If you want to study behavior, it is helpful to be able to describe and predict behavior, but it will be more satisfying to know why people act they way they do. It is relatively easy to observe different kinds of behavior and, from there, to make predictions about other behaviors. Most of us have a general sense of how people are going to act in certain circumstances (although we are fooled often enough). The real goal is to understand the causes of behavior.

In research, we choose experimental designs when we want to discover causation. Descriptive approaches can be quite useful for making predictions about behavior, but they do not inform us about the underlying reasons for those behaviors.

In the simplest experiment, the researcher creates a treatment group that will be compared to an untreated, or control, group. If the two groups start equal but end up different, we presume that the treatment made a difference. In practice, most studies employ more than two groups, but the logic is the same regardless of the number of groups.

Complications arise in any research project because small details of the research situation often have effects on participants' behaviors that we don't anticipate or even recognize. Further, because an experimental session involves an interaction between people—an experimenter and a participant—social effects can contribute to changes in behavior.

Nonetheless, we try to construct our research design to have maximal reliability and internal validity. We create an experimental approach that others can repeat and obtain the same pattern of results; we also put together a study whose results provide meaningful answers to our questions.

CHOOSING A METHODOLOGY: THE PRACTICALITIES OF RESEARCH

In psychology, the word **experiment** has a specific meaning. It refers to a research design in which the investigator actively manipulates and controls variables. Scientists regard experimental methods of research as the gold standard against which we compare other approaches because experiments let us determine what causes behavior, leading to the ultimate scientific goal—control. In general, researchers often prefer experiments over other methods such as surveys, observational studies, or other descriptive and correlational approaches.

Experiment—A research project in which the investigator creates initially equivalent groups, systematically manipulates an independent variable, and compares the groups to see if the independent variable affected the subsequent behavior.

It is important to understand the difference between an experiment and other ways of carrying out a research project. It can be confusing sometimes because in everyday language people often refer to any data collection project as an experiment. In fact, until the middle of the 1900s, psychologists, like other scientists, referred to any research project as an experiment. Since then, however, psychologists have used the term in a specific way.

An experiment is a methodology in which a researcher controls variables systematically. As the researcher alters the level, intensity, frequency, or duration of a variable, he or she will examine any resulting change in behavior in the person or animal being studied. As such, research is experimental only when the investigator has control over the variable that might affect a behavior. By controlling and manipulating variables systematically, we can determine which variables influence behaviors that we are studying.

Given that we recognize the advantage of the experimental approach, why would we bother to consider other types of research strategies? The answer is that ethical and practical considerations dictate the approaches we use. For example, suppose we wanted to know whether the amount of sleep a pregnant woman gets affects a baby's weight at birth. It would be unethical to force a woman to get a certain number of hours of sleep each night. It would also be impossible to do. You can't force people to sleep. In addition, in the course of living a life, people don't always stick to the same schedule every day. There are too many inconsistencies in people's lives to permit strict control over sleeping schedules.

An investigator who wanted to see the relation between amount of sleep women get and their newborn babies' weights would have two basic options: to experiment with nonhuman animals or to use a nonexperimental method.

In some areas of psychology, the experimental approach predominates. In other domains, researchers choose other methods. In the end, the choice of research strategies depends on the practicalities of the project. Sometimes experiments are possible and feasible, sometimes they are possible but not realistic. Sometimes they are simply impossible. Psychologists have to use good judgment and creativity in deciding what will work best in their research.

DETERMINING THE CAUSES OF BEHAVIOR

Describing behavior is fairly easy. Predicting behavior is usually more difficult. Understanding exactly why people act as they do and controlling behavior is fiendishly difficult, especially because our ideas of causation may be affected by our favored theory or our cultural perspective. Nonetheless, one of the ultimate goals of most sciences is to be able to exert control over events in our world.

Trying to Determine Causation in Research

Research psychologists who want to know what factors lead to a certain behavior follow a logical plan in the experiments they devise. The details of different studies vary widely, but the underlying concept is consistently very simple. In the simplest situation, we identify a factor that, when present, affects the way a person acts (or increases the probability of a certain behavior) but that, when absent, results in the person's acting differently.

For instance, we know that depressed people have typically experienced more stressful, negative life events than nondepressed people. Positive life events may lessen depression that already exists (Dixon & Reid, 2000). This fact may be quite relevant to you because college students seem particularly prone to stress and to symptoms of depression (Affsprung, 1998; Benton et al., 2003; Shannon, Neibling, & Heckert, 1999).

Could we find out if positive experiences would make a difference in level of depression? We might expose depressed students to different levels of positive feedback. If those who received the most feedback showed lower levels of depression, we could conclude that more positive feedback causes lower levels of depression.

Requirements for Cause–Effect Relationships

In simple terms, if three particular conditions are met, we conclude that a variable has a causal effect. The first condition for claiming causation involves the **covariance rule**. That is, two variables need to be correlated (i.e., to vary together in predictable ways—to covary) so you can predict the level of one variable given the level of the other. In the example of depression, you can predict the degree of depression from the number of positive life events. More positive life events are associated with lower depression (Dixon & Reid, 2000).

Covariance rule—One of the criteria for assessing causation such that a causal variable must covary systematically with the variable it is assumed to cause.

Temporal precedence rule—One of the criteria for assessing causation such that the variable assumed to have a causal effect must precede the effect it is supposed to cause, that is, the cause must come before the effect.

Internal validity rule—One of the criteria for assessing causation such that the variable assumed to be causal must be the most plausible cause, with other competing variables ruled out as the cause.

Knowing that the two variables are correlated does not establish causation. As virtually all statistics students learn, correlation does not equal causation. But you need correlation if there is to be causation; correlation is one requirement for determining causation, even though it is not sufficient by itself. As Dixon and Reid pointed out, depression could be a causal variable, not the effect. People who were depressed might have sought out fewer positive situations.

In order to determine causation, we need to satisfy two other conditions. A second critical element is the **temporal precedence rule**; that is, the cause has to precede the effect. This makes sense based on our everyday experience. An effect occurs only after something else causes it to occur.

If covariance and temporal precedence hold, we need to meet one further criterion. We have to rule out other causal variables, satisfying the **internal validity rule**. Some unknown factor may be affecting the depression and also the number of positive life events. For instance, perhaps a person finds himself or herself socially isolated. This might cause depression; it might also cause a person to have fewer positive life events. Thus, it could be the social isolation that actually influences the degree of depression as well as the number of positive life events.

Establishing internal validity is extremely difficult *because* our behaviors are influenced by multiple factors. Even in a well-controlled experiment, it is not unusual for participants to be affected in ways the

Causal ambiguity—The situation of uncertainty that results when a researcher cannot identify a single logical and plausible variable as being the cause of some behavior, ruling out other possible causal variables.

experimenter doesn't know. Later in the chapter, you will see how some of these extraneous variables affect our research.

In summary, the only time we are safe in determining a causal relationship between two variables is when (a) two variables covary, (b) the causal variable precedes the effect, and (c) we can rule out any other variables that could affect the two variables in question. Unless these three criteria are met, we are in a state of **causal ambiguity**.

Experimental group—The group (or groups) in an experiment that receives a treatment that might affect the behavior of the individuals in that group.

Control group—The group in an experiment that receives either no treatment or a standard treatment with which new treatments are compared.

Placebo group—In medical research, the comparison group in an experiment that receives what appears to be a treatment, but which actually has no effect, providing a comparison with an intervention that is being evaluated.

THE LOGIC OF EXPERIMENTAL MANIPULATION

The logic of an experiment is simple, even for complex studies. Most psychological experiments involve comparison of more than two groups, but describing research with two groups involves the same logic. So we'll start with a discussion of research with two sets of people (or other animals). If you understand the idea here, you can understand the structure of any experiment.

The basic idea of our simple, hypothetical experiment is this: You start with two groups that are the same, then you do something to one group that you don't do to the other. The group that experiences the manipulation is called the **experimental group**; the group that doesn't is called the **control group**. (In medical research, this approach is called a randomized clinical trial, or RCT, and may use a control group called the **placebo group** if it receives a sham, or fake, treatment.) If the two groups behave differently afterward, whatever you did to the experimental group must have caused the change. The scheme for the simplest experimental design appears in Figure 6.1.

If you understand the logic of this approach, you can comprehend more complex designs. Experimental designs usually involve multiple groups that receive different experimental manipulations; most of the time there is no control group as such. Rather, each group receives a different treatment. The simple questions that would allow us to create meaningful two-group studies have often been answered; we need to

FIGURE 6.1 Logic of an experiment.

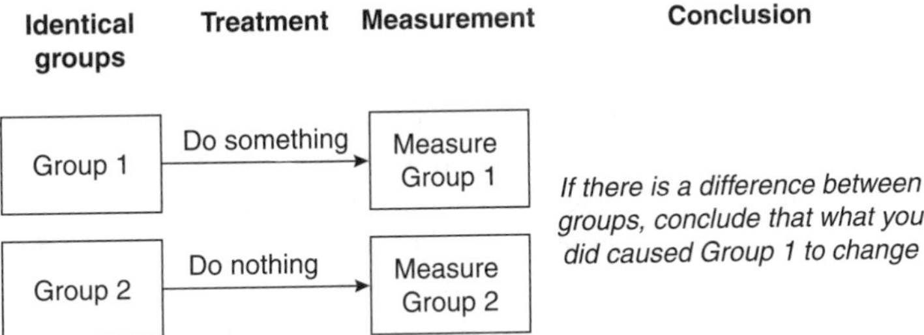

create more complex designs in order to advance our knowledge. In this chapter, you will learn about the principles and the practicalities of each component of the logic presented in Figure 6.1.

ETHICS IN EXPERIMENTAL CLINICAL RESEARCH

Let's consider for a moment the ethical issues of conducting research on people who are seeking medical or psychiatric treatment. If you were seriously ill, would you agree to participate in a research project in which one group of people received medical treatment and the other did not? In such research, the participants do not have a choice of which group they are assigned to. Would you take a risk that you were in the control or placebo group and received no actual treatment? Or the group receiving an untested treatment?

Suppose a clinician wants to assess whether a new treatment works. Is it ethical to withhold standard treatment for the sake of research? This is an important question that has no easy answer. In the Controversyy on withholding treatment, you will see an example involving medical interventions and some dilemmas associated with them. The same concerns that surface in those examples are relevant in clinical and counseling psychology and in psychiatry.

Before clinical research can begin, an Institutional Review Board (IRB) has to approve it, as you read in Chapter 2. Then, at the beginning of the study, each patient must learn about any risks associated with participating in the research, including the fact that the person might be in a placebo group or might be receiving a new treatment that is not known to work as well as the standard treatment. The new treatment might work better, it might work the same, it might not work at all. Nobody knows the answer, which is why the investigator is doing the research.

In some cases, the IRB may approve the research only if the investigators use patients who have not responded to traditional treatment or who have exhausted all other treatments. This guarantees that only the most seriously ill patients will participate, a group whose improvement or recovery is questionable no matter what approach is taken.

On occasion, the effectiveness of a new treatment will be so superior to the standard treatment that the study will be halted in the middle, and the new treatment will be given to all participants. In such a situation, it would be unethical to continue the study because it would deprive the control group of treatment that appears to be most appropriate in the best judgment of the researchers.

EXPERIMENTAL CONTROL

If you keep the basics of experimental research in mind, it becomes apparent why it is critical to control the research environment very carefully. The essence of good experimental research is the control that an investigator has over the situation and the people in it. When researchers create a solid experiment, they minimize the presence of factors other than the treatment variable that affect participants' behaviors, and they are able to measure a meaningful outcome.

It is easy to specify on paper that you are going to manipulate a variable and measure the effect on a person's behavior. But it is safe to say that most experiments involve

CONTROVERSY: Withholding Treatment in Medical Research

One possible protocol for testing new medical treatments involves an experimental group that receives a new treatment and a placebo group that appears to be getting treatment but is not. For many maladies, people improve on their own, without any medical intervention. In the experimental/placebo design, the researchers are interested in the difference in rate of recovery or severity of symptoms between the two groups.

A critical question is whether people should be denied treatment for the sake of research that might benefit people later on, but not the patient now. Ethical guidelines prohibit sacrificing a person's health now for a future set of people. On the other hand, many current medical interventions have not been tested empirically to see if they actually work. Physicians often prescribe treatments because somebody taught them to, not because there has been research on the topic. For instance, for decades, physicians used lidocaine to prevent heart attacks even though there is evidence that it doesn't help (Olkin, 1992).

Further, many medical treatments in some specialties (up to 63%) have not been subjected to randomized clinical trials. (Many of these interventions are based on other kinds of evidence, though.) Still, the published research on the degree to which treatments have been empirically tested reveals that just under a quarter of them have not received scrutiny regarding their effectiveness (Imrie & Ramey, 2000).

We have a dilemma here. If we can't use a placebo group in research, we can never perform research to establish if a treatment works. This has troublesome implications. For example, in the 1950s, premature babies were given oxygen to help them breathe. This sounds reasonable, but the oxygen caused blindness in many of the babies. For ethical reasons it would have been unthinkable to withhold oxygen or even to lower the dosage in a research study.

As it turns out, though, premature babies of poor mothers were given lower levels of treatment, including less oxygen. These infants did not suffer the blindness that babies given standard treatment did.

It is interesting that we would not consider it ethical to withhold treatment for the babies in a research project, yet society as a whole does not think it is unethical to withhold treatment for poor babies due to economic factors. Ironically, in the case of the premature babies in the 1950s, this natural experiment showed the benefit of giving less oxygen or no oxygen; for once, those on the lower end of the economic continuum benefitted.

Currently, ethical guidelines in medical research on new treatments are such that the design typically involves comparing a new approach to a standard medical treatment, so there may not be a true placebo group.

Question for Discussion: If it is unethical to withhold treatment, how can researchers figure out if a given treatment actually works?

problems and surprises that the researcher has not anticipated. People may stop paying attention to their task, they forget instructions, they fail to show up for a lab session that requires group participation, equipment breaks down, and so on.

The problem is that surprises can arise at many different points during an experiment. For one thing, try as we might to create comparable groups, we are not always able to do so. When we administer the experimental treatments, initial differences that we might not know about affect the participants' behaviors.

Further, researchers may inadvertently treat people differently, leading to changes in behavior that have nothing to do with the treatment variable. Furthermore, when we measure the outcome, we can make mistakes in recording the data or we might use a behavior that is not a very good measurement of what we are interested in. Finally, when we analyze the results of the research, we might use a statistical approach that is not the best one available, and we might interpret it incompletely or inaccurately.

Even though life tends to throw us curve balls, there are steps we can take to maximize the likelihood that research results will be meaningful and accurate.

LACK OF CONTROL IN EXPERIMENTAL RESEARCH: EXTRANEOUS VARIABLES AND CONFOUNDS

When you think of all the factors that can influence people's behaviors, you can appreciate how hard it can be to control all the variables that might influence the behavior you want to observe and measure. Factors other than your intended treatment that affect the outcome are called **extraneous variables**. They are variables that make unambiguous interpretation of your results impossible: You don't know if your results are due to the effect of an independent variable or to the extraneous variable.

Extraneous variable—A variable that is not of interest to a researcher and that may not be known by the researcher that affects the dependent variable in an experiment, erroneously making it seem that the independent variable is having an effect on the dependent variable.

One particular type of extraneous variable is called a **confound**. A confounding variable systematically affects participants in one group differently than it affects those in other groups. As a result, when groups differ at the end of a study, it may be because a confounding variable, not the treatment variable, affected one group. If researchers aren't aware of the confound, they may attribute differences to the treatment.

A confound may also obscure real differences between groups by raising or lowering the scores in a group affected by that confound. A group that might ordinarily perform poorly on a task could, because of a confound, show high scores. So that group could have an average that is not much different from a group that is really more proficient. As a researcher, you would conclude that your treatment did not make a difference when it really did. The problem is that the confound helped the poorer group, obscuring a real effect of the treatment. Thus, extraneous variables can erase the difference between two groups that should differ. Or extraneous variables can make a difference appear where none should be.

One example of published research illustrates how even experienced researchers rely on public scrutiny of their work in spotting extraneous variables. Such scrutiny leads to advances in knowledge that go beyond the original study. Quinn, Shin, Maguire, and Stone (1999) investigated whether using night lights for children under the age of 2 years will lead them to become nearsighted (myopic) later. Previously, scientists studying chickens noted that the birds developed visual problems if they did not experience a period of darkness each day. These researchers wondered whether nearsightedness in people might be related to the incidence of light throughout the day and night. Figure 6.2 shows the percentage of children who became nearsighted according to whether they slept with nighttime illumination or without.

Confound—A variable that is not controlled by an experimenter but that has a systematic effect on a behavior in at least one group in an experiment.

As you can see, the results are shocking. When children had slept with their rooms illuminated, the incidence of myopia was very high. The

FIGURE 6.2 Incidence of myopia and normal vision according to whether a child's room is illuminated at night.

Source: G. E. Quinn, C. H. Shin, M. G. Maguire, & R. A. Stone. (1999). Myopia and ambient lighting at night. *Nature, 399*, pp. 113–114. Reprinted by permission from *Nature*, copyright 1999 Macmillan Magazines Ltd.

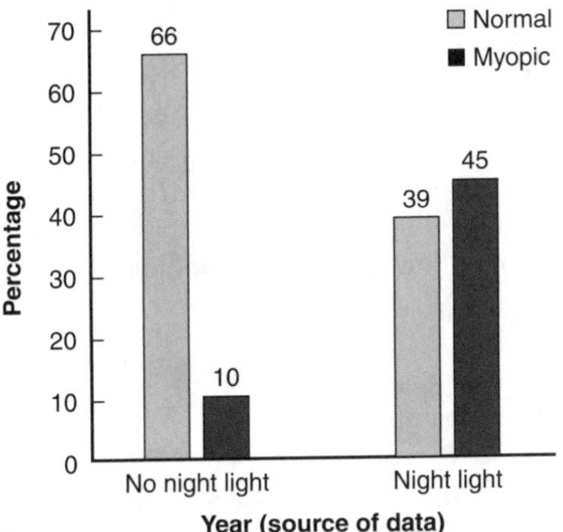

researchers knew that their findings were preliminary and, given the correlational nature of the data, not appropriate for cause–effect analysis (Quinn, Shin, Maguire, & Stone, 1999). Still, the findings were intriguing and Quinn et al. offered their results to the research community.

Subsequently, researchers have been able to identify some potential extraneous variables at work here. First, it may be that parents with myopia, which they can pass on to their children, may prefer to have night lights so they themselves can see when they enter their infant's room at night. (Stone noted that their preliminary analysis of parental vision did not reveal problems for the research.)

Second, the study was done in an eye clinic, which makes it likely that the children who were studied did not reflect children in general. Characteristics of the sample other than whether they had night lights may have affected the results.

Third, the study relied on parental memory from an average of six years before the study. Such memories are notoriously unreliable. It could be that parents with poor vision simply remember about night lights, which help them see, whereas parents with normal vision might be less attuned to such memories.

Subsequent to the publication of the Quinn et al. research, other research provided reassurance that nighttime illumination would not cause myopia (Gwiazda, Ong, Held, & Thorn, 2000; Zadnik et al., 2000).

In some studies, we may not be able to spot confounds and extraneous variables based on research reports. Fortunately, in the Quinn et al. work, because they provided enough detail about their methodology, others could continue to investigate their ideas.

Problems may also arise because research is a human enterprise. If there are two groups to be compared and if a researcher acts differently toward the people (or animals) in each group, the resulting behaviors may be different because of the way the participants were treated rather than because of the IV.

Rosenthal and Fode (1966) demonstrated that visual and verbal cues by an experimenter have an effect on participant behavior. Most researchers are aware that they may have an effect on the way experimental participants act. At the same time, the cues may be so subtle that the researchers (or their assistants) don't know what changes they are causing in participant behaviors.

Consider the effect of small wording changes on behavior. Elizabeth Loftus was among the first researchers to document the effect of "leading questions," that is, wording that may lead a respondent in a particular direction. Experimenters can unknowingly use leading questions or other wording that affects the way participants behave. Loftus (1975) showed her participants a film clip of an automobile accident, then asked them one of two questions:

1. How fast was Car A going when it ran the stop sign? or
2. How fast was Car A going when it turned right?

A final question asked "Did you see a stop sign for Car A?" When participants had been asked Question 1, they were significantly more likely to respond that they had seen a stop sign. When the experimenter planted the seed of a memory, participants nourished that memory and began to believe in it. There actually was a stop sign in the film clip. Nonetheless, it was clear that the change in wording affected how people responded to later questions. There has subsequently been ample research demonstrating that false memories can be planted successfully (e.g., Mazzoni & Loftus, 1998; Loftus, 1997) and that slight changes in wording or even simply exposing a person to an idea can change later responses (Loftus, 2003). These effects are very important for you to understand because they can alter the way participants behave in an experiment, unbeknownst to the researcher.

An additional source of extraneous influences in an experiment can be the stimulus materials. When investigators change materials across different groups, subtle differences in the nature of the materials can make a notable difference in the outcome of the research.

Sometimes we are able to spot confounds and sources of error in research, but it is possible that we may not recognize that research has subtle problems that lead to poor conclusions. One area of research that has been beset by a potentially very important confound involves whether women show fear of success (FOS). Psychologists have identified FOS in women with a variety of tasks. Over two decades after the initial research appeared, though, some hidden problems became apparent.

Fortunately, scientific research is done so that problems can be corrected. As a result, we have overcome one stumbling block in studying FOS. It is clear now that FOS is not a function of sex alone, as you can see in Controversy on fear of success.

The problem with extraneous variables and confounds is that no experiment has complete control over what a participant experiences in the lab or over any of the participant's life experiences. If you set up an experiment as outlined in Figure 6.1, there are

CONTROVERSY:
Do Women Fear Success?

Research across the past thirty years has suggested that women fear success. A typical experimental strategy was to give participants an essay to read and then to ask them to write about it. Horner (1968, cited in Kasof, 1993) gave male participants a story in which the main character was a man; female participants read stories in which the main character was a woman. A critical sentence in the essay was "After first-term finals, John (Anne) finds himself (herself) at the top of his (her) medical school class." Horner reported that women wrote more negative essays, which the researcher interpreted to indicate that women were more fearful of success than men were.

Subsequent to this research, investigators studied such topics as sex discrimination, sex stereotypes, and fear of success by altering experimental stimuli for women and men by changing the name of the protagonist in a story. In many instances, stimuli with female characters were rated lower than stimuli with male names.

We could debate Horner's original interpretation about women's fear of success, but there was a fundamental problem with the fear of success research that lay hidden for two decades. According to Kasof (1993), the names of the characters in the experimental stimuli were not comparable across sexes.

The tendency among researchers was to use male and female versions of a name, such as John and Joan or Christopher and Christine. Kasof reported that, in as many as 96 percent of the studies, the female names tended to be more old-fashioned, connoted lower intelligence, and were associated with being less attractive compared to male names.

As he pointed out, dependent variables in sexism studies often relate to intellectual competence (e.g., who is more competent, John or Joan). Some names are associated with lower intelligence, even though we know that how smart you are has nothing to do with what your parents named you.

In the past decade, the attractiveness of the names seems to be more nearly equal. Not surprisingly, during this period researchers have learned that fear of success has little to do with sex per se and more to do with whether a woman holds a traditional view of sex roles (Basha & Ushasree, 1999; Krishnan & Sweeney, 1998; Kumari, 1995) and careers (Hay & Bakken, 1991), and whether she is gifted (Hay & Bakken, 1991).

In addition, women who are concerned about being evaluated negatively because they are "too successful" may show higher levels of fear of success. It's not that they actually fear success; they are just sensitive to social evaluation (Exline & Lobel, 1999). Further, being a successful woman entails taking risks, and women may be less likely to engage in risky social behavior (Byrnes, Miller, & Schafer, 1999).

Sometimes, apparently small changes in the way an experiment is set up (e.g., the stimulus names) introduce extraneous variables that can be more important than the IV. Now that we are aware of the effect of stimulus names, we may be able to identify more precisely who fears success. Sometimes it can be men (Rothman, 1996).

Question for Discussion: How could replication with extension have helped overcome the problems with this research? Why do you think it took so long to discover the problem?

many variables other than the IV that could affect the outcome of your project. Conducting a sound study requires attention to detail and a good grasp of how researchers in the past have overcome the problems they faced.

EXPERIMENTER EFFECTS

One source of difficulty in research involves **experimenter bias**, the tendency for the researcher to influence a participant's behavior in a certain direction. If the experimenter thinks that one group will perform better on a task than another, the investigator may inadvertently lead the participants to act in the expected way.

Experimenter bias—The tendency of researchers to subtly and inadvertently affect the behaviors of participants in a study, obscuring the true effect (or lack thereof) of the independent variable.

How big a problem is such behavior on the part of the researcher? It is hard to tell, although when surveyors were studied to see how often they departed from the directions they were supposed to follow in administering questionnaires, the results showed that there were notable deviations from the standardized protocol (Kiecker & Nelson, 1996).

One of the most common departures involved rephrasing or rewording a question; the interviewers reported that, on average, they had done this about 18 percent of the times in their last hundred sessions. (The standard deviation was 27.2%, indicating that some interviewers may have changed the wording around half the time.)

These data suggest that, in an attempt to be helpful or to clarify a question, the surveyors regularly rephrased questionnaire items. Given the results of research like Loftus's (1975, 1997), the changes in wording may very well have affected the survey results. We don't know how often comparable behaviors occur in experiments or how big the effects might be, but the survey results suggest that researchers deviate from their directions regularly.

Interestingly, Kiecker and Nelson (1996) reported that surveyors rarely fabricated an interview that never took place. Thus, even though their behaviors could have changed people's responses, we can infer that they were trying to be helpful to the respondents. You may remember from Chapter 2 that, in a number of cases, investigators created nonexistent interviews and falsified data. The motivation to engage in those ethical problems are probably much more likely when the researchers are working on or attempting to obtain large federal grants.

PARTICIPANT EFFECTS

The majority of psychological research with people involves college students. Students generally have some very desirable characteristics, three of which are a high degree of education, a willingness to cooperate, and a high level of motivation. These are helpful traits most of the time. Unfortunately, in the context of an experiment, they might pose some problems.

It isn't unusual for a student who participates in a study to try to figure out what the experimenter "wants." This can be a problem because the experimenter really wants the person to act naturally.

How might we keep participants from reliably picking up on clues? One means is to use automated operations whenever possible. If the participant reads the instructions, then carries out a task on a computer, there is less risk that the experimenter will influence the person's behavior.

Cover story—A fictitious story developed by a researcher to disguise the true purpose of a study from the participants.

Blind study—A research design in which the investigator, the participants, or both are not aware of the treatment that a participant is receiving.

Single blind study—A research design in which either the investigator or the participant is not aware of the treatment a participant is receiving.

Double blind study—A research design in which neither the investigator nor the participant is aware of the treatment being applied.

Hawthorne effect—The tendency of participants to act differently from normal in a research study because they know they are being observed.

Demand characteristics—The tendency on the part of a research participant to act differently from normal after picking up clues as to the apparent purpose of the study.

A second strategy is to use a convincing **cover story**. This is a story about the study that either conveys the actual purpose of the study or successfully hides the true nature of the research. Some people object to deceptive cover stories, but others have argued that the nature and level of the deception is trivial. If you carry out your own research projects, you will have to decide on your own whether deception is warranted and appropriate.

Another solution is to use a **blind study.** In such an approach, the participants do not know the group to which they have been assigned, so it will be harder for participants to know what treatment they receive, so they are less likely to try to conform to expectations. When either the participants or the researchers do not know to which group the participants are assigned, we call it a **single blind study**. When the participants in different groups are blind, which is how single blind studies usually proceed, they don't have systematically different expectations that they might try to fulfill. When the investigators who actually conduct the study are blind to which group a person is in, it keeps a researcher from unintentionally giving clues to a participant. When neither the investigator nor the patient knows which group the patient has been assigned to, it is called a **double blind study**.

The Hawthorne Effect

When people change their behavior because they know they are in a scientific study, showing higher levels of motivation, they can produce results that lack validity. The behaviors are due to the motivation rather than to the IV. This phenomenon is often referred to the **Hawthorne effect**. This phenomenon is controversial and has been discussed at great length. It is also not particularly well described in textbooks.

The effect got its name because, in the 1920s and 1930s, researchers concluded that workers at Western Electric's Hawthorne plant near Chicago increased their output because they felt special, having been included in a research project. In reality, the studies were methodologically troublesome, including confounding variables (Adair, 1984). Further, some of the apparent improvement in weekly worker performance arose because the workweek was lengthened (Bramel & Friend, 1981), not necessarily because the workers performed more effectively. In addition, in one case, a poorly performing and disgruntled employee withdrew from one of the studies. The replacement was a very productive worker. It's no surprise that the average output went up. Nonetheless, the term Hawthorne effect remains in use to describe an individual's change in behavior while trying to be helpful to the researcher.

In addition to the Hawthorne effect, a commonly described participant effect involves **demand characteristics**. When participants actively try to figure out the purpose of the study and act in ways they think are helpful, they are said to be showing demand characteristics. It should come as no surprise that people are active participants in a research setting; they try to figure things out, just as they do in any other aspect of their lives.

One compelling example of a situation involving demand characteristic was provided by Orne and Scheibe (1962). These researchers told individual participants that they might experience sensory deprivation and negative psychological effects while sitting in a room. When the researchers included a "panic button," the participants tended to panic because they thought it would be an appropriate response in that situation. When there was no panic button, the participants experienced no particular adverse effects. The inference we can draw here is that when the participants concluded that a highly negative psychological condition would emerge, they complied with that expectation. When the expectation wasn't there, neither was the negative response.

Evaluation apprehension—The tendency to feel inadequate or to experience unease when one is being observed.

Another source of bias associated with participants is **evaluation apprehension**. This bias arises because people think others are going to evaluate their behaviors. As a result, the participants are on their best behavior. This is something we do all the time. Many people will litter as they walk or drive down the street, but not if they think somebody (even a stranger) is going to see them and, presumably, evaluate their littering behavior negatively.

This evaluation apprehension is not always so benign. Researchers have shown that when people begin thinking about stereotypes applied to them, their behavior changes. Thus, women may perform less well on mathematics tests because women "aren't supposed" to be good at math (McGlone & Aronson, 2007; Spencer, Steele, & Quinn, 1999), African Americans may perform less well on academic tests because blacks "aren't supposed" to be as strong academically as whites (Steele & Aronson, 1995), and poor people "aren't supposed" to be as proficient as rich people (Croizet & Claire, 1998).

The effects of stereotyping hold true for people from different cultural backgrounds, including Italian (Muzzatti & Agnolik, 2007), German (Keller, 2007), French (Croizet & Claire, 1998), Chinese (Lee & Ottati, 1995), and Canadian (Walsh, Hickey, & Duffy, 1999). Fortunately, though, appropriate messages can mitigate them (McGlone & Aronson, 2007).

Surprisingly, even groups of people who are demonstrably proficient in an area can suffer from stereotype threat. Aronson et al. (1999) showed that math-proficient white males could be induced to perform more poorly than expected on a test of math skills if they were compared to a group that is expected to perform even better than they, namely, Asians.

As such, evaluation apprehension can exert notable effects on results in an experiment, making it seem that the IV has affected behavior when, in reality, a confounding variable has made the difference. This particular type of bias is likely to be more pronounced when the experimenter is examining participant (subject) variables, that is, the effects of predetermined characteristics like sex, race, age, and so on.

Comparisons between men and women, black and white, young and old, rich and poor, and many other participant variables may result in distorted results because one group acts differently because they are "supposed to." Too many conclusions have probably been drawn about differences across groups because of effects related to evaluation apprehension in one form or another.

INTERACTION EFFECTS BETWEEN EXPERIMENTERS AND PARTICIPANTS

Research projects are social affairs. This may not be obvious at first glance, but whenever you get people together, they have social interactions of various kinds. However, when you are carrying out a research project, you don't want either experimenters or participants to communicate in ways that will compromise the study.

In a research setting, behaviors that we generally take for granted as normal (and maybe even desirable) become problematic. Consider the following situation: A college student agrees to participate in an experiment and, when arriving there, finds a very attractive experimenter. Isn't it reasonable to suppose that the student will act differently than if the experimenter weren't good looking? From the student's point of view, this is a great opportunity to show intelligence, motivation, creativity, humor, etc. In other words, the research project is a social affair.

Just as the experimenter and the participant bring their own individual predispositions to the lab, they bring their own interactive, social tendencies. Research results are affected not only by experimenter bias and participant bias, but also by interactions between experimenter and participant.

Biosocial effect—The type of experimenter bias in which characterictics of the researcher like age, sex, or race affect the behavior of the participant.

Psychosocial effect—The type of experimenter bias in which attitudes of the researcher affect the behavior of the participant.

If a participant responds to some "natural" characteristic of the researcher, we may have a distortion of experimental results due to a **biosocial effect**. For instance, if the experimenter seems too young to be credible, the participant may not take research seriously. Or if the participant is overweight, the experimenter may be abrupt and not be as patient in giving directions. Other examples of factors that could induce biosocial effects could include race, ethnicity, nationality, and religion. Obviously, these are not strictly biological characteristics, as the term "biosocial" implies. Nonetheless, these characteristics all pertain to what people may see as fundamental about another individual.

A different, but related, bias involves **psychosocial effects**. This type of bias involves psychological characteristics, like personality or mood. Researchers with different personality characteristics act differently toward participants. For instance, researchers high in the need for social approval smile more and act more friendly toward participants than those lower in this need (Rosnow & Rosenthal, 1997).

It is clear that the way an experimenter interacts with a participant can affect the outcome of a study (Rosenthal & Fode, 1966). For instance, Malmo, Boag, and Smith (1957, cited in Rosnow & Rosenthal, 1997) found that when an experimenter was having a bad day, participants' heart rates were higher compared to when the experimenter was having a good day.

Realism in Research

A potential weakness of the experimental approach is that it is usually a stripped-down version of reality. In an effort to create groups that are virtually identical except for differences on one dimension, scientists try to simplify the experimental setting so that anything that will get in the way of a clear conclusion is eliminated.

When we use simple laboratory situations for our research, the result is often a reduction in **mundane realism**. When a situation has mundane realism, it resembles the normal environment you live in on an everyday basis. If you have ever volunteered to participate in a laboratory study, you probably saw pretty quickly that the environment was different from what you encounter normally.

Mundane realism—The characteristic of a research setting such that it resembles the kind of situation that a participant would encounter in life.

The low level of mundane realism sometimes makes researchers wonder if their experimental results are applicable to normal human interaction. The simple version of reality in a laboratory can give us useful information about human behavior if the tasks of the participants have **experimental realism**. This type of realism relates to whether the participants engage in their tasks seriously.

Experimental realism—The characteristic of a research setting such that the person participating in a study experiences the psychological state that the research is trying to induce, even if the research setting is artificial, like a laboratory.

An example of a series of studies that has little mundane realism is Stanley Milgram's obedience studies. He asked people to shock others if they made a mistake in a learning task in a laboratory. This is not something that most of us will ever do in our lives. As such, the mundane realism is fairly low. On the other hand, the research participants acted like they were very engaged in the task, showing nervousness and extreme discomfort in many cases. This behavior suggests a high level of experimental realism. When research shows good experimental realism, the research results may pertain to the real-world behaviors the researcher is investigating.

The critical element regarding realism is that we want our research participants to be in the psychological state of interest to us. The nature of the setting, regardless if whether it is a laboratory, may not be relevant. We are more interested in whether the person is engaged in the task in the way that will provide insights into behaviors we are studying.

SUMMARY

The single most important advantage associated with experiments is that they allow you to determine the causes of behavior. Not only can you predict the behaviors, but you can also control them.

The basic idea behind the experiment is that you start with two groups that are equivalent and apply a treatment to one of them. If differences appear after you do that, you can assume that your treatment made a difference.

If life were this simple, we would not need to pay as close attention to the details of research as we must. Characteristics of experiments, participants, and the context of the research can all affect the outcome of a research project in subtle but important ways. For instance, extraneous variables that you don't know about can affect the DV, so you mistakenly think that your IV is responsible for differences across groups. One particular type of extraneous variable is the confounding variable, which affects at least one group in systematic ways.

It is also important to remember that experiments involve social interactions among experimenters and participants. These interactions can affect the outcome of research in predictable ways, although the problem is that researchers are often not aware of these effects in their own studies.

REVIEW QUESTIONS

Multiple Choice Questions

1. The research approach that involves changing the level, intensity, frequency, or duration of an independent variable is
   a. correlational.
   b. observational.
   c. experimental.
   d. validational.
2. Psychologists have speculated that having more acquaintances leads to better health. Research has supported this connection. Which principle of causation is met in this relation between acquaintances and health?
   a. Internal validity rule
   b. Covariance rule
   c. Causal ambiguity rule
   d. Temporal precedence rule
3. If we want to conclude that a given variable has a causal relation with a second variable, we have to be able to rule out other possible causal variables. The principle of causation involved here is the
   a. covariance rule.
   b. internal validity rule.
   c. causal ambiguity rule.
   d. temporal precedence rule.
4. In a research project, a group that experiences the manipulated independent variables is called the
   a. independent group.
   b. experimental group.
   c. control group.
   d. placebo group.
5. Researchers have discovered that children experiencing Attention-Deficit Hyperactivity Disorder (ADHD) show improvements if they attend classes on involving behavioral and social skills, compared to a group of ADHD children who did not attend the classes. The group of children who attended the classes constitute the
   a. experimental group.
   b. independent group.
   c. control group.
   d. placebo group.

6. In medical research, groups sometimes undergo an experience that resembles the experimental manipulation but does not actually involve that manipulation. Such a group is called the
   a. independent group.
   b. experimental group.
   c. control group.
   d. placebo group.
7. Extraneous variables
   a. tend to be problems in single blind studies, but not double blind studies.
   b. tend to reduce the degree of external validity in a study.
   c. can be avoided through random sampling.
   d. can sometimes be dealt with by using control groups.
8. A group of researchers discovered that people who slept with nightlights as children were more likely to be nearsighted than were children who did not have nightlights. In the end, the nightlights didn't seem to be the cause; rather, parental nearsightedness was. Parental vision, which affected the DV, not the nightlights, reflected the presence of
   a. a single blind design.
   b. a confound.
   c. lack of mundane realism.
   d. lack of experimental realism.
9. In a double blind study, an experimenter cannot influence participants' behaviors differently across groups. As such, we should expect that there will be little
   a. Hawthorne effect.
   b. external invalidity.
   c. placebo effect.
   d. experimenter bias.
10. If a researcher deceives a participant by telling the individual that a study is about one thing, but it is really about something else, the researcher is using
    a. a double blind study.
    b. a cover story.
    c. experimental realism
    d. demand characteristics.
11. When a researcher sets up a study so that the participants do not know to what condition they have been assigned, we refer to this design as
    a. a blind study.
    b. a cover story design.
    c. a control design.
    d. an externally valid design.
12. People often change their behavior when they know they are being observed in a scientific study, a phenomenon called
    a. mundane realism.
    b. experimental realism.

c. the Hawthorne effect.
d. external validation.

13. When psychologists Orne and Scheibe gave research participants a "panic button" in the event that they began to experience negative psychological effects while sitting in a room, the participants showed panic responses. When there was no mention of a panic button, the participants experienced no negative effects. Orne and Scheibe were documenting the existence of
    a. experimenter bias.
    b. mundane realism.
    c. demand characteristics.
    d. evaluation apprehension.
14. Participants sometimes act differently than normal in a research project because of the race or ethnicity of the experimenter. This change in behavior occurs because of what psychologists call
    a. psychosocial effects.
    b. biosocial effects.
    c. stereotype effects.
    d. experimenter bias effects.
15. Initial studies of fear of success included descriptions of fictitious characters with corresponding male and female names, like John and Joan, who were engaged in activities that could lead to success. The researchers did not realize that
    a. research participants tended to relate those names to actual people they knew.
    b. women were seen as being high in fear of success but were really high in expectation of failure.
    c. the names used as stimuli in the research were associated with different levels of achievement, with female names being associated with less success.
    d. over time, fear of success became less meaningful among men but not among women.

Essay Questions

16. Why is research involving already existing groups rather than randomly assigned groups prone to the effects of extraneous variables?
17. Explain how demand characteristics and evaluation apprehension affect participant behavior in research.

ANSWERS TO REVIEW QUESTIONS

Multiple Choice Questions

1. c	6. d	11. a
2. b	7. d	12. c
3. b	8. b	13. c
4. b	9. d	14. b
5. a	10. b	15. c

Essay Questions

16. Why is research involving already existing groups rather than randomly assigned groups prone to the effects of extraneous variables?

    When you use existing or intact groups, you don't have a guarantee that they are equivalent; that is, if you were to measure then on the DV, they might differ from the start. If you didn't know about this difference, you would mistakenly attribute a difference at the end of the study to the IV.

    When groups are created by random assignment, there is less chance that the groups will differ systematically because differences that could be critical are spread out randomly across groups.

17. Explain how demand characteristics and evaluation apprehension affect participant behavior in research.

    With demand characteristics, the participants react to the perceived demands of the situation, that is, what they think the experimenter expects of them. As such, they don't act naturally. Instead, they respond to clues in the environment to direct their behaviors.

    Evaluation apprehension affects participants as they act differently because they know they are being observed. They may act in a particular way in order to look better in the eyes of the researcher, for instance.

CHAPTER SEVEN

EXPERIMENTS WITH ONE INDEPENDENT VARIABLE

CHAPTER OVERVIEW

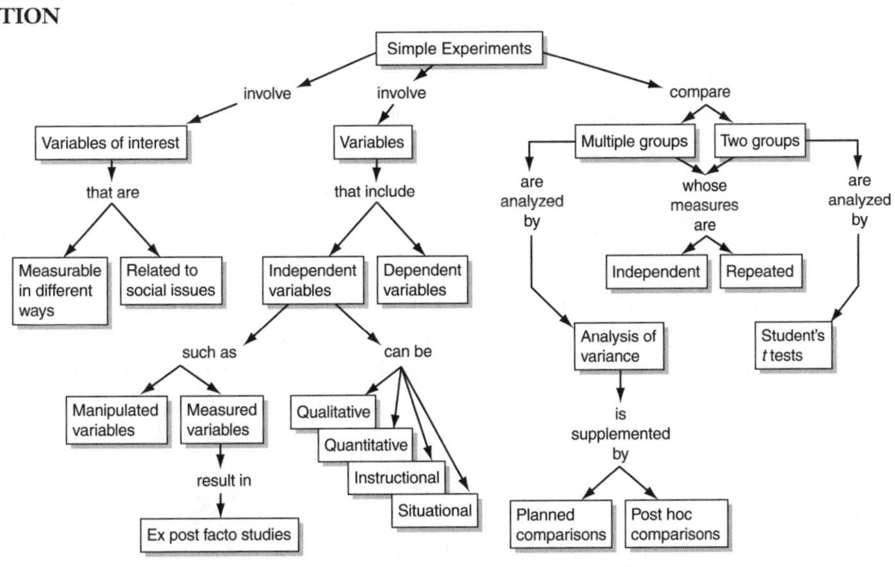

KEY TERMS

CHAPTER PREVIEW

When you create experiments, you are trying to find the causes of behavior. In order to establish causation, you manipulate one variable to see its effect on another. Many of the concepts that psychologists deal with are complex and abstract; consequently, we are forced to create working definitions of variables that represent concepts that we cannot measure directly.

When you create a research project, there are many possible ways to set it up. You have to decide on which variables are relevant to your research question, then you have to narrow down the number of variables you will manipulate so that your methodology is manageable. There are always more variables that would be of interest than you could deal with in a single experiment.

Psychologists have devised many different ways to develop independent variables (IVs) and dependent variables (DVs). No matter how researchers define their variables, it is very important that the variables be objectively measurable. This allows others to understand how research has proceeded and how the methodology used by the investigators may have affected the outcome of the study.

Sometimes psychologists create simple studies with a single IV; most such studies in psychology have several comparison groups. In other cases, researchers manipulate more than one IV in a single experiment. The advantage of a multifactor study is that we can get a better look at the complex interplay of variables that affect behavior. After all, in our lives, most of what we do is a result of more than a single cause.

After we finish conducting an experiment, we complete data analysis that helps us understand our results. There are several standard statistical tests that we use, but data analysis is an evolving field and new techniques and approaches are emerging.

DETERMINING VARIABLES OF INTEREST

One of the first things that researchers learn is that there is no single way to define psychological concepts for the purpose of doing research. In addition, most of the time, there is no best way to set up a study to answer a research question. The way you set up your experiment is determined by many theoretical and practical considerations. Your choice of variables will reflect the specific question you want to address, the variables others have used, and the compromises you make between what you would like to do and what you actually can do.

As you will see, there are always many more variables that relate to a research question than you can possibly manipulate. On a practical level, if you want to manipulate many variables, it can mean that you need an unreasonably large sample size in order to carry out the study, or it can mean that a research session is too long and complicated to be realistic. In this section, we will consider the types of choices researchers have made in one particular area of psychology and the law, the accuracy of eyewitness testimony. The discussion here will illustrate how many different research variables you could consider; in your work, you have to limit your focus to only a few variables in a single study.

This area has generated considerable interest because of its importance in society. Before we outline the way researchers adopt independent and dependent variables, though, we will see how this type of research provides a good example of how societal influences can direct or retard the progress of research.

The Interaction of Society and Science

Alfred Binet, who achieved greatest recognition because of his work that led to intelligence testing, suggested over a century ago that we bring psychological science into the legal system. Unfortunately, his idea did not gain traction in his home country of France.

However, German psychologists dabbled in the area and, in the United States, the psychologist and German expatriate Hugo Münsterberg successfully advocated for research in psychology and the law. But when the first World War broke out, the public was not favorably inclined toward Germans. Consequently, Münsterberg's credibility and influence in the United States diminished, and there was only a trickle of research for the next several decades.

It was not until Elizabeth Loftus's influential book, *Eyewitness Testimony* (Loftus, 1979), appeared that psychologists in significant numbers began to investigate the interface between psychology and the law. More recently, research has been stimulated as we have become aware of the fact that the majority of people who have been convicted of crimes but subsequently exonerated by DNA evidence were convicted on the basis of mistaken eyewitness identification (Wells, Memon, & Penrod, 2006).

There is a growing list of people identified by eyewitnesses who have been shown to be innocent as a result of DNA testing. Unfortunately, the type of crime in which biological evidence is available is quite limited, generally involving sexual assault. Few cases of murder, robbery, or aggravated assault produce useful DNA. Nonetheless, people accused of such crimes can be victimized by mistaken eyewitness testimony (Wells at al., 2006).

In our discussion of the variables that psychologists have investigated, it is obvious that the researchers know who is "guilty." They stage the crime, so they have all the relevant details. In real-world crime, the problem is that nobody knows for sure that the suspect is guilty, even though people may feel certain about it.

In addition, the relatively high accuracy rates (at least in some circumstances) in laboratory studies may be artificially high because the research participants tend to be college students who typically show good memory and visual acuity, are highly educated, and are less suggestible than many people; furthermore, the laboratory studies typically involve low stress situations. As Wells et al. (2006) have suggested, the significant degree of error among relatively accurate college students does not bode well for the accuracy of eyewitness testimony in the complex and highly stressful environment of the criminal justice system.

Variety of Research Variables

It would seem that people should be able to recognize somebody they saw commit a crime, but the data show that what people consider a straightforward task is actually quite difficult. In fact, in a high-stress situation, 50 percent of soldiers were unable to identify a person who had been interrogating them for 40 minutes (Morgan et al., 2004). Researchers have used different approaches to address the question of eyewitness behavior. The process of identification is complex; so is the research on the topic.

For example, psychologists have measured how confident people are in identifying a supposed perpetrator in a lineup. Wells et al. (2006) have noted that this is one of the "most researched questions in the study of eyewitnesses" (p. 65). This issue is critical because of the value that jurors place on confidence, a judgment accepted by the U.S. Supreme Court.

As it turns out, there is a significant, but imperfect, correlation between accuracy and confidence in judgment. That is, if you ask people how confident they are in their recognition of a supposed criminal, you can't always count on their accuracy. In order to understand the accuracy-confidence relationship better, you also have to know about other variables, like the similarity between the suspect and others in a lineup, the nature of viewing conditions, whether the eyewitness has been given feedback on correctness, and whether the eyewitness has been coerced into identifying a suspect.

Experimental participants who express high confidence tend to be more accurate in eyewitness identification. But even with the significant connection between confidence and accuracy, those with high accuracy may still be wrong a quarter of the time (Brewer, Keast, & Rishworth, 2002).

It also turns out that how researchers structure the identification task can make a difference in an eyewitness's decision. In research on lineups, it makes a difference if the investigator includes two conditions, one in which the target is present and on in which the target is absent. If the investigator only used a lineup having the target, the result would be an inflated estimate of the accuracy of eyewitnesses. So including the suspect (usually called a "target") may or may not be present. When the target is present, the experimental witness is generally right more than wrong. But if the research involved a condition in which the target was absent, there is a high likelihood that an "innocent" person would be chosen.

Researchers have also found that it makes a difference if people in a lineup appear all at once (as in most television shows) or sequentially (i.e., one at a time). Studies have shown the superiority of sequential lineups in reducing mistaken identifications (Steblay, Dysart, Fulero, & Lindsay, 2001), although sequential lineups may also lower correct identification of the target (Meissner, Tredoux, Parker, & MacLin, 2005).

In addition to measuring how confident experimental witnesses are, researchers have studied eyewitness accuracy by measuring another variable, response time to identify a suspect in a lineup. It turns out that people who make faster identifications tend to be more accurate than people who are slower (Dunning & Perretta, 2002). Unfortunately, what constitutes a fast or slow response changes in different viewing circumstances (Weber, Brewer, Wells, Semmler, & Keast, 2004). So, theoretically, response latency could be useful in assessing the accuracy of eyewitness identification; practically, however, response latency may not be very useful at all.

As you can see, the experimental research on the accuracy of eyewitnesses involves a lot of intersecting variables. This brief review shows how one small area of research involves an enormous number if potential variables. If we are to understand the conditions in which we can trust eyewitness testimony, we will have to research many different variables. There are many other variables that were not mentioned here that are important. When psychologists investigate eyewitness behavior, they have to choose which variables to include in a given study and which to ignore.

In this chapter, we will be talking about research with a single independent variable, which is always a good place to start. But it does not take long before the issues become very complex and require multiple independent variables. In the next chapter, you will see how researchers combine in a single study several independent variables of the type discussed here.

INDEPENDENT AND DEPENDENT VARIABLES

The best way to begin your study of any psychological topic is to make sure you understand your concepts. Then you can come up with ways to measure them. After a while, these measurements that are critical to research are taken for granted, but they have to be developed.

Let's consider the way psychologists have measured depression in different projects associated with depression and memory. Investigators have regularly found that depressed people show poorer memory than others. As you have read, one way to assess depression is to use a score on the Beck Depression Inventory (BDI). You could define the amount of information in a person's memory simply as the number of words he or she recalls from a list of words. These two operational definitions are straightforward. However, if you want to assess a causal relationship between depression and memory, you cannot simply administer the BDI and see the relationship between the BDI score and a person's ability to recall a list of words. In this example, the BDI score and the number of words recalled may very well covary. Depressed people may remember less than nondepressed people. But it takes more than covarying (i.e., correlation) for us to conclude causation.

The second criterion for causation is temporal precedence; that is, the cause (depression) must precede the effect (memory). If you bring participants into your

Subject (participant) variable—An independent variable that resembles a true IV but that is created on the basis of some pre-existing characteristic of the participant, as in a quasi-experiment.

Manipulated variable—A true independent variable that is manipulated by an experimenter, with assignment of participants to groups according to some system rather than on the basis of pre-existing characteristics like sex, age, etc.

Measured variable—A variable that is used to create groups to be compared, but assignment of participants to groups is on the basis of characteristics of the participants rather than according to a system created by the researcher.

Quasi-experiment—A research project resembling a true experiment that involves comparison of groups that are not formed by random or systematic assignment by the investigator, but rather on the basis of participant characteristics.

Ex post facto study—A research project resembling a true experiment but using existing grouped data that did not involve random assignment of participants to conditions.

laboratory and measure their BDI score and then assess their memory, you can conclude that the depression score came first. This still isn't enough to determine cause and effect.

The third criterion stipulates that you have to be able to rule out other causal variables. In this instance, perhaps if a person has a very catastrophic experience, he or she might show signs of depression and also have poorer memory because the flashbacks of the experience constantly distract him or her from remembering. We can't rule out such an explanation.

An optimal strategy is to use an experimental approach, inducing depression in one group and leaving a second group unaffected, then assessing their memory. If you did this, you would be investigating two variables, (a) presence or absence of depression, the IV, and (b) amount of material recalled, the DV.

For this research involving depression, a true experimental manipulation would involve creating two groups by inducing different emotional states in them, then measuring the DV for each person. This design would make use of a true IV that is controlled by the experimenter. Sometimes we can't actively manipulate a variable.

Subject (participant) variables like age, sex, political affiliation, and so on are beyond the control of the experimenter and are not true IVs. We cannot create women and men on the spot. A person's gender comes with the person. You can measure the variable of gender; that is, you can determine if a person is a man or a woman, but you can't manipulate it.

Many researchers will treat existing depression, gender, and similar variables as true IVs for the purpose of designing research, but in reality when they study differences based on such variables, the research design is correlational, which does not permit us to conclude causation.

If a researcher manipulates the variable, like induced depression, the IV is a **manipulated variable**. On the other hand, if the value of the variable comes with the person, like gender, the IV is a **measured variable**. Manipulated variables lend themselves to cause and effect explanations; measured variables do not. Studies involving measured variables are often referred to as **quasi-experiments**; they look like experiments, but they really aren't. We'll cover quasi-experiments in detail in the next chapter.

Sometimes when researchers use existing data to create groups, like using psychiatric patients with high versus low BDI scores to create comparison groups, the approach is called an **ex post facto study**. The data may have been collected during diagnosis and not originally intended for research. It may resemble a true experiment because groups are created and compared, but it is also really correlational because variables have not actually been manipulated. Table 7.1 gives some examples of manipulated and measured variables.

TABLE 7.1 Examples of Manipulated and Measured Variables in True Experiments and Quasi-Experiments.

Research Question	Independent and Dependent Variable
Measured Variables (Quasi-Experimental)	
Question: Does fitness level predict injury better than sex? (Bell et al., 2000). **Results**: Initial fitness level predicts the prevalence of injury better than the person's sex does.	**IV:** Physical fitness level at the start of army training: five levels, ranging from least fit to most fit **DV:** Incidence of injury during training
Question: Do dysphoric (i.e., depressed) people show better memory than euphoric people? (Murray, Whitehouse, & Alloy, 1999) **Results**: Depressed people remembered fewer positive words than nondepressed people did.	**IV:** Depressed versus nondepressed, based on scores on the Beck Depression Inventory **DV:** Number of positive and negative words remembered from a previously presented list
Question: Do brain waves of women and men differ after sleep deprivation? (Armitage et al., 2001) **Results:** Women showed more dramatic increases in slow waves after sleep deprivation.	**IV:** Participant's sex **DV:** Incidence and amplitude of slow waves during sleep as measured with EEGs
Manipulated Variables (Experimental)	
Question: Does the drug temazepam improve sleep of mountain climbers at an altitude of 17,400 ft (5,300 m)? (Dubowitz, 1998) **Results:** Temazepam improved sleep in climbers at high altitudes.	**IV:** Treatment (temazepam versus placebo) **DV:** Self-reported sleep; amount of oxygen in the blood
Question: Does treating patients for pain before surgery affect pain and recovery after surgery? (Gottschalk et al., 1998) **Results:** Treating patients for pain before surgery begins led to less pain and quicker recovery after the surgery.	**IV:** Type of presurgical pain treatment (epidural narcotic, local anesthesia, no presurgical pain medication) **DV:** Pain levels after surgery; activity level after surgery
Question: Does suggestion change people's memories of the past? (Mazzoni & Loftus, 1998) **Results:** Dream interpretations can induce people to change the way they remember their past.	IV: Suggestion given to participant (dreams are indicators of prior experience versus no suggestion that dreams are indicators of prior experience) DV: Amount of agreement that nonevents had actually occurred

Researchers rely on measured IVs because they have to. After all, you can't change a person's sex, age, political affiliation, and the like in your experiment. Sometimes, though, you can create a manipulated variable when you would normally expect a measured variable. As you have seen, depression, usually a measured variable, has been studied experimentally.

TYPES OF INDEPENDENT AND DEPENDENT VARIABLES

Psychologists have shown considerable creativity in generating diverse independent variables. The need for a vast array of IVs is clear when you think of all the different areas of research in psychology.

Researchers make their decisions about their IVs based on what others have already done and on current circumstances. When you make use of ideas of other researchers, you can save yourself a lot of effort in generating new variables. If a process worked for another researcher, it might very well work for you.

Qualitative and Quantitative Independent Variables

There are different ways of considering IVs. One way is according to the type of measurement involved in measuring the IV. Another dimension of IVs is the nature of the experimental manipulation. We will consider these separately.

Qualitative variable—A variable whose different values are based on qualitative differences (e.g., female and male) rather than on numerical differences.

Quantitative variable—A variable whose different values are based on numerical differences, like differences in amount, size, duration, and the like.

A **qualitative variable** involves variation on a nominal scale. That is, the change from one condition to another relies on a difference in categorization. In some cases, investigators use IVs whose groups are qualitatively, rather than quantitatively, different. For instance, Fosse, Strickgold, and Hobson (2001) studied the incidence of hallucinatory images in varied states of waking and sleeping. These researchers asked participants to report what was going through their heads at various times during the day and when they awakened at night. The reports of these volunteers were later coded by raters who were blind to the participant's state when giving the report. The investigators then recorded the percentage of the time each person's reports included hallucinations. As you can see in Figure 7.1, there were notable differences among the various states of consciousness.

A second type of manipulation in an experiment can relate to **quantitative variables**. Quantitative variables change along a continuum and will differ in amount, intensity, frequency, or duration. One clever experiment using a quantitative variable that tells us something interesting and important about ourselves was performed by Ross, Lepper, and Hubbard (1975). They demonstrated how we can persist in believing things that, in some sense, we know are not true. They showed student participants pairs of fake suicide notes and told them that one was real; the participants were supposed to identify the real one. After going through 25 pairs of these notes, the researchers deceived the participants, telling them that they had either identified 24, 17, or 10 correctly. In this study, the IV was the number of correct guesses the participants were told they had made; it varied from high to medium to low. The experimenters had randomly assigned participants to one of the three groups in advance. The "24 correct" group was really no different from the "17 correct" or "10 correct" groups.

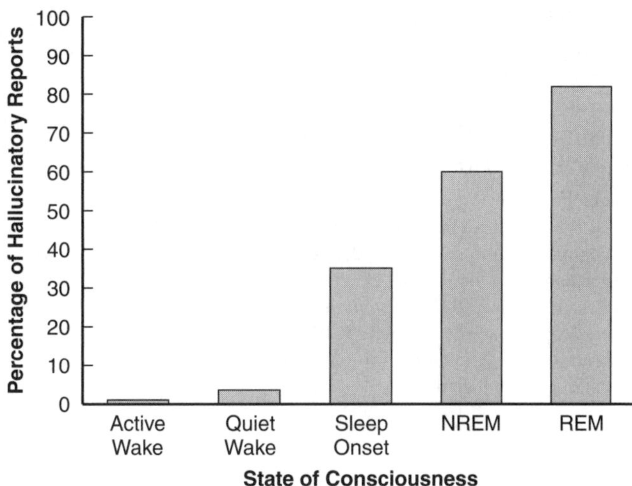

FIGURE 7.1 Example of a single-factor study with a qualitative independent variable. In this study, the researchers recorded the number of hallucinatory reports in qualitatively different mental states.

Source: Fosse, R. Strickgold, R., & Hobson, J. A. (2001). Brain-mind states: Reciprocal variation in thoughts and hallucinations. *Psychological Science, 12*, 30–36. Reprinted with permission from American Psychological Society.

This is a quantitative IV because the experimenters created three groups of participants who differed in a quantitative way—the number of correct responses they thought they had made.

The researchers then told the participants about the deception and that the feedback they were given was totally unrelated to their actual performance. The researchers then asked the participants to guess how many they really had gotten correct. The participants ignored the fact that the feedback on their performance was completely inaccurate, persisting in their belief that their actual accuracy matched the randomly assigned condition. That is, those who had thought they identified 24 of 25 correctly still thought they were above average, whereas those who thought they had identified only 10 of 25 still felt that they were below average. As the research showed, once people believe something about themselves, they become remarkably good at ignoring evidence to the contrary.

In this study, the IV had three levels, meaning three conditions, that differed numerically. One advantage of research with quantitative variables is that you can see whether more (or less) is better. You can also find out if there is a maximum effect when your manipulation occurs on a continuum. For instance, one example would be to see the effect of increasing dosage of a particular drug on people's or animals' behaviors. For instance, Evans et al. (2001) administered different amounts of the drug methylphenidate to students diagnosed with attention-deficit hyperactive disorder (ADHD) to get an idea of the dosage that would lead to optimal performance and behavior in school. These researchers found that a "more is better" approach is not necessarily optimal. In fact, a relatively low dose of the drug led to a very promising outcome, and improvements with higher dosages were not reliable across all students. The results of this single factor, multiple group design appear in Figure 7.2.

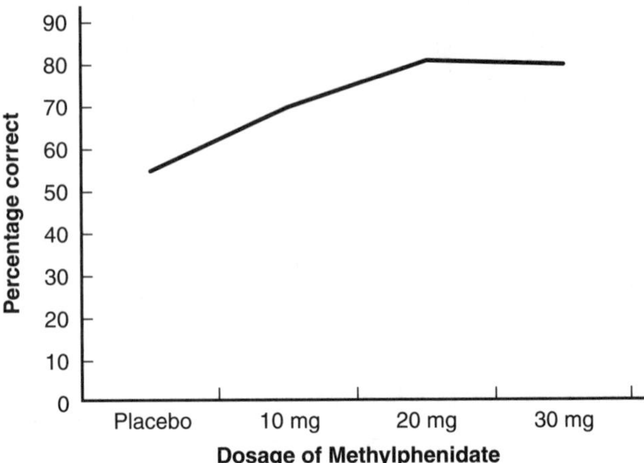

FIGURE 7.2 Results of a multiple group, single factor study. The results show the effect of a drug on performance on history worksheets among students diagnosed with ADHD. The IV here is a quantitative variable.

Source: Evans, S. W., et al. (2001). Dose-responsive effects of methylphenidate on ecological valid measures of academic performance and classroom behavior in adolescents with ADHD. *Experimental and Clinical Psychopharmacology, 9*, 163–175. Reprinted with permission of the American Psychological Association.

You can see the advantage of this research design. There are many possible dosages of the drug that could be prescribed. If Evans et al. had created a study with only two groups, it would have been impossible to get a good sense of how to use the drug most appropriately.

Some experiments lend themselves to qualitative variables, some to quantitative. You can also have a mixture of the two. Depending on the nature of your research question, you decide which approach to take. Table 7.2 presents some examples of qualitative and quantitative IVs and how they vary. As you can see in the table, researchers use qualitative variables like presence versus absence of a manipulation. For instance, Mennella and Gerrish (1998) wanted to find out whether the presence or absence of alcohol in breast milk made a difference in infants' sleep.

Why would anybody add alcohol to an infants' milk to see if it would sleep differently? Some people believe that alcohol enhances sleep. It would be worthwhile to find out if there is any benefit to an infant's being exposed to alcohol; unless there are clear positive effects that outweigh any negatives, we probably don't want to give an infant such a drug. As summarized in the Table 7.2, the benefit of alcohol is questionable indeed.

You can also see how investigators use quantitative variables in Table 7.2. Schul and Goren (1997) varied the strength of evidence in a mock trial to see how participants would evaluate evidence that was supposedly strong or weak. Sometimes results can be surprising. In the mock trial, the pretend jurors were able to discount persuasive evidence of guilt when they were told to do so.

Independent Variables Created by Different Types of Manipulations

Another dimension on which we can identify independent variables is according to how the IV is created. The IV can relate to the instructions that participants receive, the tasks they engage in, the situation, and the personal characteristics of the participant.

TABLE 7.2 Examples of Qualitative and Quantitative Independent Variables and the Different Levels Used in Research Projects

Research Question	Independent and Dependent Variable
Qualitative Independent Variable	
Question: Do infants sleep any differently when breast milk has alcohol in it? (Mennella & Gerrish, 1998) **Results**: Babies exposed to alcohol sleep less and showed less movement (i.e., active sleep).	**IV:** Presence or absence of alcohol in breast milk that had been expressed into a bottle **DV:** Amount of time the babies slept; movement during sleep as recorded on a device that measured leg activity
Question: Do bilingual people remember differently when asked questions in different languages? (Marian & Neisser, 2000) **Results**: Russian-English bilinguals displayed better memory for events experienced while speaking Russian better when quizzed in Russian; they remembered English-related events better when quizzed in English.	**IV:** Language of stimulus words (Russian versus English) **DV:** Number of events remembered when prompted with a word either in Russian or in English
Quantitative Independent Variable	
Question: Do jurors respond differently to strong evidence versus weak evidence? (Schul & Goren, 1997) **Results:** Strong evidence led to higher judgments of guilt unless participants were instructed to ignore it. When instructed to ignore strong evidence, participants did so.	**IV:** Strength of evidence (based on witness's confidence, age of witness, and abnormality of defendant's actions) **DV:** Judgment of guilt
Question: Does caffeine affect blood pressure and heart rate in workers? (Lane, Phillips-Bute, & Pieper, 1998) **Results:** Higher levels of caffeine intake produced higher blood pressure and heart rate in workers.	**IV:** Dose of caffeine (50 milligrams—equal to about half a cup of coffee)—versus 250 milligrams (equal to about two and a half cups of coffee) **DV:** Blood pressure and heart rate as measured by a portable monitor
Question: Does a particular drug (methylphenidate) affect classroom performance and behavior in adolescents with ADHD? (Evans et al., 2001) **Results:** The drug caused increases in academic performance, with the largest increase arising from the smallest dosage tested.	**IV:** Dose of methylphenidate (placebo, 10 mg, 20 mg, or 30 mg) **DV:** Measurement of accuracy of classroom note taking, number of grammatical errors detected in writing, independent grading of writing assignments, on-task and disruptive behavior, and others

(*continues*)

TABLE 7.2 continued

Research Question	Independent and Dependent Variable
Question: Do older Alzheimer's patients perform differently than other older adults in their ability to recognize when they have seen a given visual image before? (Budson, Desikan, Daffner, & Schacter, 2001)) **Results:** Alzheimer's patients are less able to correctly distinguish between new pictures and pictures they have already seen than are a comparison group of older adults.	**IV:** Degree of similarity of visual images–high versus medium versus low as rated by independent participants; type of person (Alzheimer's patient versus healthy person)
Question: Are people likely to recall syllables in a list when those syllables are repeated? (Soto-Faraco & Sebastián-Gallés, 2001) **Results:** When syllables were presented quickly and in close sequence, participants were less likely to remember both of them, showing "repetition deafness."	**IV:** Whether syllables in a list to be learned occurred one or twice **DV:** Proportion of critical syllables recalled by each participant across 288 lists

Task variable—An independent variable whose different conditions involve differences in a task performed by participants.

Instructional variable—An independent variable whose different conditions involve different instructions given by the researcher to participants.

Situational variable—An independent variable whose different conditions involve different environments or contexts for different participants.

A **task variable** refers to an IV used to create groups that engage in somewhat different tasks. For example, in a study of the effect of expertise, Rowe and McKenna (2001) asked participants to watch a video of a tennis player and to try to anticipate which play would involve a point-winning stroke. Sometimes the participants merely watched the video, whereas sometimes they engaged in a distracting task, generating a random stream of letters of the alphabet while they watched the video.

Thus, the participants engaged in two different tasks, one involving simple monitoring of the video, the other involving monitoring the video while generating letters.

An **instructional variable** is one in which the different groups of participants receive different instructions or types of information that might affect their responses. In the Ross et al. (1975) study described above involving the persistence of false beliefs, the IV was an instructional variable because the college students who took part in the study received different information depending on the group to which they were assigned. That is, they learned that they were correct on 10, 17, or 24 trials in differentiating between a genuine and a fake suicide letter.

A **situational variable** involves changing the situation or context of the experiment for different groups. For instance, researchers conducted a study to find out whether inner city residents could be educated to engage in safer sexual practices (The NIMH Multisite HIV, 1998). Participants either engaged in intensive, small group discussions of their sex lives and what they might want to change, or the participants listened to lectures and viewed a film on safe sex. All participants met twice a week for three weeks.

In this experiment, the IV was situational: The participation involved different situations, the discussion versus the lecture. The outcome was that those people in the discussion groups experienced a lower incidence of sexually transmitted disease compared to the group that saw a film and listened to lectures.

A subject variable is used to compare people who differ on important characteristics at the beginning of a study. (Because the term *participant* has replaced the term *subject* in psychological research with people, researchers also call these variables participant variables). When you compare people on existing characteristics, this is not a true experimental manipulation; rather, it is quasi-experimental. Most researchers treat these subject variables as legitimate IVs, even though we know that we cannot attribute causation based on these IVs.

For example, the incidence of injuries among females in sports is higher than that for males (Bell et al., 2000). Some people have concluded that there is something about being female that predisposes women to injury or that there is something about being male that predisposes men to protection from injury. This is a good example of how a quasi-experiment could be set up: Look at men and women across some time period and monitor the number of injuries.

Recently, additional evidence has arisen that the picture regarding women's and men's injuries may be more complex than previously thought. Bell et al. studied female and male army trainees in the United States for an eight-week period. Women were two and a half times more likely to incur serious injury than the men. However, when the researchers grouped the participants according to level of fitness at the beginning of training, sex ceased to be a significant predictor of injuries. The investigators concluded that level of fitness is a better predictor of injury than sex is. The Bell and colleagues study was also quasi-experimental, but it provides a reminder that we need to be careful in assigning causation when using quasi-experimental approaches.

Similarly, researchers who have studied changes in the elderly have found a decreased sense of taste (Stevens, Cruz, Hoffman, & Patterson, 1995), but Schiffman (1997) suggested that it may be disease and medications that cause loss of taste abilities. When older adults are not on medications, she argued that their taste sensitivity doesn't decline. Age is another example of a subject variable that may speciously look like a causal variable. We are just too willing to believe that the elderly should be in a state of decline, so we attribute changes in taste sensitivity to age, ignoring other possibilities. This type of problem is always present with subject (participant) variables.

Types of Dependent Variables

Just as independent variables can come in many varieties, so can dependent variables. DVs can be categorized as either qualitative or quantitative, for instance. They can also involve measures of amount, intensity, frequency, or duration.

When DVs are qualitative, researchers investigate whether a manipulation leads to different categorical outcomes. Suppose you were on a jury that had to decide on the guilt or innocence of a defendant. Your decision would depend on the nature of the evidence regarding guilt and innocence. It would involve a categorical outcome on a nominal scale; the defendant would fall into one of two categories: guilty or not guilty.

Psychologists have investigated the variables that influence jury responses. A typical approach is to present a fictitious trial transcript that varies in content to see if the change in content affects jury decisions on guilt and innocence.

CONTROVERSY: Studying Race

Researchers have identified differences in pain responses in people of different races. One finding was that Blacks experience greater pain unpleasantness, emotional response to pain, and pain behavior than Whites, although pain intensity did not differ across groups (Riley et al., 2002). These types of comparisons will only be useful if the researchers are comparing groups whose members are meaningfully categorized. This same caution is true for the other behavioral differences that researchers have examined across racial and ethnic boundaries. There are several potential problems with research that investigates racial differences.

First of all, psychologists have increasingly questioned the categorization process. For instance, Helms, Jernigan, and Mascher (2005) pointed out that in much research, the investigators do not indicate the basis on which they included people in different groups. Operational definitions of the process of categorization are absent.

Second, investigators have convincingly argued that race is more a social than a biological phenomenon (Goodman, 2000). If this claim is valid, discussions based on race as a biological concept are bound to be invalid. Furthermore, genome research has shown remarkably little difference in genetic makeup across racial groups, with more variability within groups than across groups. In addition, Ossorio and Duster (2005) have pointed out that seemingly Black people can show genetic profiles resembling those typically occurring among Europeans, and seemingly White people can show genetic profiles associated with Africans. In light of this situation, Edwards, Fillingim, and Keefe (2001) have suggested that genetic research leads to the conclusion that race may be a meaningful construct only for discussion of behavioral and social issues, not biological or medical ones.

Third, there may be cultural differences in the ways that people within particular groups respond to pain. That is, those differences may be social rather than biological.

Fourth, social factors like discrimination and degree of access to healthcare may affect perceived pain. And factors like prolonged stress may affect a person's ability to cope with pain, leading to differences in responses to the pain.

Fifth, journal articles often do not mention the race and ethnicity of the experimenter. Research has revealed that the sex of the experimenter can affect pain responses (Levine & De Simone, 1991). It may be the case that the race or ethnicity of the experimenter may affect pain responses of patients and research participants.

These cautions are important because differences that appear with invalid grouping are, at best, hard to interpret. At worst, they may be entirely misleading. Given that a person may be assigned to a given category on one occasion and a different one on another occasion is problematic (Helms et al., 2005). Even more distressing is the fact that racial categories are often based on what has been termed "folk taxonomies," that is, groupings based on social and stereotypical factors rather than scientific ones (Sternberg, Grigorenko, & Kidd, 2005).

Question for Discussion: If many researchers do not think that race is a valid scientific construct, why do people still study it?

On the other hand, quantitative DVs measure on an ordinal, interval, or ratio measurement scale. If participants in jury research assigned different monetary damages in a fictitious lawsuit based on different types of testimony, such a decision would involve a quantitative DV. Investigators using quantitative DVs are often interested in amount of change or direction of change in a score.

USING EXPERIMENTS TO DETERMINE CAUSATION

The advantage of conducting a true experiment is that you can determine causation. For instance, several research projects have established the link between depression and poor memory. For example, Croll and Bryant (2000) found that women experiencing postnatal depression (i.e., depression after having given birth to a child) had poorer memories for events in their own lives and that it took them longer to retrieve memories compared to nondepressed women. In addition, adults over 50 years of age with unipolar major depression showed memory impairment that was unusual in a group that age (Lockwood, Alexopoulos, Kakuma, & Van Gorp, 2000). These studies are correlational, however, so they are not useful for finding causes.

It is not clear in advance that depression is causing the memory impairment. It could be that when people's memory begins to falter, they become depressed because of their memory difficulties. In order to experimentally explore this question of whether depression actually causes poorer memory, you have to define depression and develop some way to define thinking and problem solving. Then you have to induce depression in one group of people and not in another. Finally, you have to see whether the induced depression leads to worse cognitive processing.

Consider the research by Ellis, Thomas, and Rodriguez (1984). They induced depression in participants in one condition and did not alter the mood of people in a second group. Participants in the depressed group read a series of increasingly negative statements while the neutral participants read a series of very innocuous statements, the methodology devised by Velten (1968). In the Ellis and colleagues study, the participants with induced depression showed poorer recall of words than those in a neutral mood. (This is a good illustration of a case in which the researchers decided to use another psychologist's methodology rather than creating their own.)

In this study, the researchers operationally defined depression as the state an individual was in after reading mood-depressing statements. They measured thinking in terms of the number of critical words the participants could recall. It is important in your research to make sure that you define your variables specifically in terms of how you measure or create them. Simply talking about "depression" or "thinking" is too vague.

Others researchers have defined thinking differently. For example, Bartolic and colleagues (1998) defined thinking as the amount of brain activity, measured through electroencephalograms (EEGs), that took place when participants worked on a problem. Bartolic et al. also used Velten's methodology to induce depression in one group and to induce an elevated mood in a second group.

The research by Ellis et al. (1984) and Bartolic et al. (1998) led to the same general conclusion—that depression leads to changes in cognitive processing. Previous work had established a correlation between depression and poor memory, but the Ellis and colleagues experiments helped reinforce our confidence that the depression was causing poorer memory. The results from Bartolic et al. reinforced the idea that induced depression leads to similar brain activity as naturally occurring depression does.

Both of these experiments involved one IV and one DV. Ellis et al. (1984) studied the individual's mood (either depressed or not—IV) and degree of recall (number of words recalled—DV); Bartolic et al. (1998) investigated the individual's mood (depressed or elevated mood—IV) and cognitive activity (amount of EEG activity in different parts of the brain—DV). Their independent and dependent variables are clearly defined and obviously measurable. This makes it easier to understand and interpret their work.

CONTROVERSY: Studying Depression Experimentally

In an experiment, the researcher creates a situation so that every participant in a given group is in the same psychological state with respect to the concept being studied.

If a scientist wants to see whether people in a depressed state act differently from those who aren't, the researcher depresses the people in the treatment group and compares them to people who have not been depressed by the experimenter.

This raises a dilemma and a question. First, is it acceptable to depress research participants to see if they behave differently from a control group? That is, is it ethical? As you already know, the ethical guidelines for research specify that a researcher should not put research participants at risk by exposing them to physical or emotional harm. You might argue that by inducing a state of depression, you could harm participants.

Second, if it is ethical to induce depression, how could you do it realistically? When people are depressed, it is often as a result of an accumulation of negative experiences. How could a researcher operationally define depression for the purposes of an experiment?

As it turns out, researchers have effectively used different means to induce depression in research participants without endangering them. For instance, Velten (1997) asked people to read statements that would depress their mood, like "Every now and then I feel so tired and gloomy that I'd rather just sit than do anything." Others read statements like "If your attitude is good, then things are good, and my attitude is good," which elevated their moods.

These statements had the desired effect, which was to induce different psychological states. The operational definition of depression here is the state a person is in after reading Velten's statements.

Is it fair to the participants, though? Was he exposing them to psychological or physical harm? Velten (and many other researchers using mood-changing manipulations) have asked this question and have used their expertise to anticipate the answer. Mood manipulations have weak and temporary, but consistent, effects. As a result, the researcher can induce a mood change that will not be very strong or last very long and that is easily reversed.

So it appears that we can safely and effectively induce a lowered mood. It is, fortunately, a pale copy of true depression, but we can use such changes in emotional states to study mental states related to depression. The good news is that such techniques are not harmful to participants when used carefully and can be used ethically to provide us with useful information about what happens when people are depressed.

Question for Discussion: If you wanted to induce a state of mild depression in participants, what ethical issues would you have to contend with?

Because these two studies used different methodologies but produced similar results, they have a good case for claiming good convergent validity in their discussion of the effect that depression has on thinking. Convergent validity is further established by the fact that the majority of published experimental research has shown the depression–memory link.

The issue is complex, though, and some research deviates. For instance, Hertel (1998) found that depression produced no worse memory than a nondepressed emotional state when participants thought neutral thoughts, but people in the depressed state showed poorer memory when asked to focus their thoughts on themselves. Further, Kwiatkowski and Parkinson (1994) found that induced depression was associated with lower recall, but naturally occurring depression was not. The majority of research shows the depression–poor memory link, but investigators still have questions to answer.

COMPARING TWO GROUPS

If you have seen the movie *Legally Blonde*, you might recall a scene in which the attractive main character, Elle Woods, watches two women reject the advances of a male student. She then puts on an act in front of the other women to make them think that she finds him attractive. Afterward, those two women seem to find him more attractive. Is this purely fiction, or is there some reality to it?

Several researchers have carried out experiments to address this issue. Some of this research involves comparison of two groups. In a number of cases, the investigators have not studied people. Instead, they have observed the behaviors of birds and fish. This may sound like an odd strategy to learn about mating, but it has provided some insights into the way that organisms, including people, choose mates.

In many animal species, the female selects the mate with whom she will reproduce. According to evolutionary theory, she develops a strategy that helps her pick the mate with the best genes, presumably so that her offspring will have the greatest chance of survival. (Males of many species are generally less selective and will mate with as many females as possible.) One question that scientists have investigated is how those organisms choose one another for mating.

An interesting question in this area is to ask what causes a female fish to find a male fish attractive enough to want to mate with it. A number of investigators have researched this topic, with surprising results. For example, Hill and Ryan (2006) placed a female sailfin molly, a type of fish, in an environment in which she could choose to swim with either of two male mollies. The researchers recorded the amount of time the female spent with each male. They then let the female observe the less-preferred fish male fish interacting with another female sailfin molly. The next time she had the choice of which of the two fish to swim with, she spent more time with the formerly less-preferred fish, presumably because she had seen him with another female. That is, the researchers concluded, when the female saw a potential mate with another attractive female fish, that male became suddenly more attractive.

In this research, the investigators recorded the length of time that the female fish spent with the less-preferred male fish. Then they recorded the amount of time the

Repeated measures design—A design in which a single participant is observed and measured on more than one level of an independent variable rather than measuring different individuals on each level of the independent variable.

female fish spent with that male after she had seen him with another female. In this case, the researchers defined the DV, *attractiveness*, as the amount of time the female spent with the male fish. Obviously, we can't directly assess what a fish thinks is attractive, but experts in this area agreed that the time spent with the male fish is a reasonable indicator of how attractive the female finds the male.

In this example, the researchers used what is called a **repeated measures design**. They measured the DV twice for each fish–before the female saw the male fish with another female and again afterward–and looked for a change in the amount of time spent with the male. According to the logic of research, changes that occur after a treatment are likely to be due to that treatment. For this study, the researchers concluded that the female fish found the male fish more attractive because she had seen him with another female. (We will discuss the advantages of repeated measures designs more fully in the next chapter.)

This so-called mate copying behavior is not limited to fish. Researchers have found the same pattern with birds, too. In fact, even in bird species where birds are monogamous (i.e., two birds mate for life), there is a tendency among females to be attracted to males seen in the presence of other females (Swaddle, Cathey, Correll, & Hodkinson, 2005). In this research with birds, the DV was the amount of time the female bird spent in courtship display with the male.

Does the behavior of fish tell us anything about human behavior? Does it tell us anything about the behavior in *Legally Blonde*? It is a legitimate question to ask whether we can generalize from bird and fish behavior to human behavior. Referring to somebody as "bird brained" suggests that the person has a small brain and isn't very smart. When it comes to selecting mates, are humans any smarter than birds or fish?

Apparently, we may not be. A group of researchers (Jones, DeBruine, Little, Burriss, & Feinberg, 2007) showed women pairs of pictures; one picture was of a man paired with a second picture of a women. The man's face was shown from the front; the woman's face was shown in profile, as if she were looking at the man. In one condition, the woman in the picture had a neutral expression; in a second condition, the woman was smiling. The question was whether the female participant would find the man more attractive, depending on the woman's expression in the picture. For this study, the researchers could not use the same DV as the investigators did with the fish and birds—that is, the time spent with the male. The human participants were only looking at pictures. (There are also ethical issues associated with fostering and observing reproductive behavior of people who participate in research.) So the investigators needed a different DV; they chose a common measurement, a score on a rating scale. The participants rated the man's attractiveness on an eight-point scale.

The participants were in one of two conditions. In one condition, the woman in the picture was smiling; in the second condition, the women in the picture had a neutral expression. Thus, the IV here was type of facial expression of the women in the picture; there were two groups for the IV, smiling face and neutral face.

The results showed a higher rating of attractiveness of men in the pictures when a woman appeared to be smiling at them. The researchers concluded that the IV (type of facial expression of the woman in the picture) affected the DV (the rating of the man's attractiveness). The investigators' interpretation of the results was that preferences for men were subject to social factors. The picture of a smiling woman next to a picture of a man increased the man's attractiveness for the same reason, the researchers concluded, that the attractiveness of male fish and birds increased—another female found him attractive, so he must have positive characteristics. Other research (Hazlett & Hoehn-Sarin, 2000) had revealed that women smile more when looking at pictures of attractive men. So when participants saw women smiling in the direction of a man's picture, the participants may have picked up cues about the man's suitability as a possible mate. In that research, the DV was the amount of movement of the muscles used in smiling; women smiled more when looking at pictures of men who were judged to be attractive.

Interestingly, when male participants rated the pictures of the men, the ratings were lower when the women was smiling. The researchers interpreted this to mean that the male participants unconsciously saw the man in the picture as competition.

In this study, the investigators used a slightly more complex design than described here, but one of their comparisons involved a simple comparison of two groups. As mentioned previously, most behavioral research involves more than a simple two-group comparison, but such comparisons can be a significant component of the results.

Generalizing Research Results

So can we conclude that the scene in *Legally Blonde* is more truth than fiction? Perhaps. We can recognize parallel behaviors across species, and we can identify behaviors caused by factors that we are unaware of. But we also need to recognize that there are limitations to the research cited here. One limitation here is that just because a woman sees a man as attractive, it does not necessarily follow that she will choose him as a reproductive mate. Second, there is a big difference between a female fish or bird's spending time with a male and providing a rating of attractiveness. Third, humans undoubtedly take into consideration many factors in deciding on a mate.

On the other hand, some preferences appear to be associated with biological factors that we cannot control and may not be aware of. For example, when women rated pictures of other women in one study, the ratings of the attractiveness of the women in the pictures depended on the estrogen levels of the female participants (Fisher, 2004). Women with high estrogen levels, reflecting maximal fertility, rated pictures of other women lower than did women with low estrogen levels.

What is clear here is that there are some parallels between the behavior of fish and birds and the behavior of humans. At the same time, we need to recognize that people make decisions based on more than attractiveness. Simply because attractiveness may change depending on the social context, it does not mean that people blindly follow hidden urges. Many other factors, including learned social norms, affect our behaviors.

The picture is complex, but sometimes simple experiments involving a comparison between two groups can provide insights into human behavior. Because our behaviors are not controlled by a single variable, though, we need to use caution in drawing conclusions based on a single experiment.

COMPARING MULTIPLE GROUPS

Sometimes a simple two-group experiment is too simple to answer a researcher's question. It may be necessary to create more than two groups in order to address an issue. Beins et al. (2007) conducted a followup study to previous research (Wimer & Beins, 2000). The earlier research involved presenting jokes to participants after they had learned to expect jokes that fell into one of the following categories: (a) horribly unfunny, (b) very unfunny, (c) very funny, and (d) hysterically funny. There was also a neutral category in which participants did not have any particular expectations.

In the earlier research, Wimer and Beins (2000) found that participants rated the jokes differently, depending on the message. When primed to expect mildly unfunny or mildly funny jokes, the participants gave lower and higher ratings, respectively. The neutral group was in the middle. The participants ignored the extreme messages entirely. (This earlier research was subsequently written for publication [Wimer & Beins, in press].)

In the followup research, Beins et al. (2007) used cartoons rather than jokes and primed the participants to expect mildly funny or unfunny cartoons; there was also a group of participants who did not receive any message about how funny the cartoons were. So there were three groups to be compared. Figure 7.3 shows how the groups rated the cartoons. As you can see, there is a consistent increase toward more favorable ratings of jokes as you move from the prime to expect jokes that are not very funny, to the control group, to the prime about very funny jokes.

This humor research shows the advantage of having multiple groups. You can see how patterns emerge and gain a more complete understanding of what is going on in participants' heads. A simple, two-group study is useful, but a multiple-group study with

FIGURE 7.3 Results of a multiple-group study in which the researchers compared the ratings of cartoons across three different conditions.

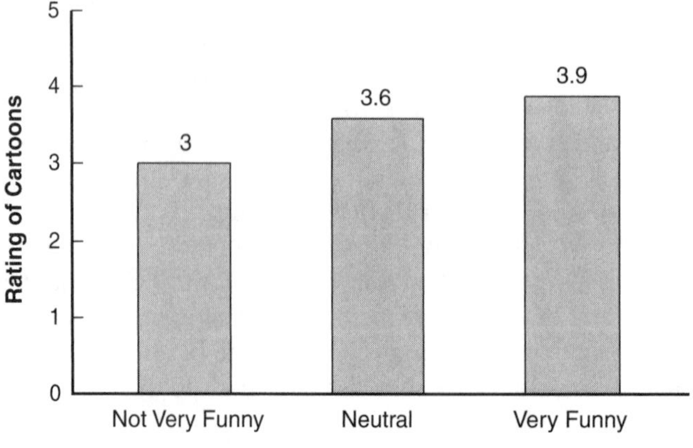

one independent variable lets you expand the amount of information you get from your research.

DATA ANALYSIS

Many tests are available for analysis of experimental data. When data are normally distributed, there are about equal sample sizes, and the variances of the different groups are equal, we typically use a group of tests referred to as parametric tests. When the data do not meet these criteria, we use nonparametric statistics.

The parametric tests predominate by a great margin. If you look at virtually any journal dealing with experimental methods in psychology, you will see great use of the Student's t-test, the analysis of variance, and Pearson's correlation, all of which are parametric. The tests are useful even when there are departures from the usual criteria for their use. You can see applications of the most commonly used tests in the statistics appendix.

Experiments with Two Groups

Researchers have traditionally used the **Student's *t* test**, more often simply called the *t*-test, for comparing two groups. This test was invented in the early 1900s by William Gossett, who performed research for the Guinness Brewery. (The Guinness Brewery did not allow its employees to publish their work, so he published a paper about the statistic anonymously; he used the pseudonym Student in his article. This is why his test is called Student's *t*). At the time, it was the most advanced statistical technique available for experimental designs. We still use *t*-tests for such simple experiments.

Student's *t* test—A statistical test that compares two group means or compares a group mean to a population mean to assess whether the differences between means are reliable.

There are three different *t*-tests, two of which are relevant here. The repeated measures *t*-test lets us compare two set of scores in which the scores are paired, as in a before-and-after design. The other relevant *t*-test is the independent groups *t*-test. It lets us compare scores in two groups when there is no connection between a score in the first group and any other score in the second group. When researchers randomly assign participants to different groups, this *t*-test is appropriate. (The third type of *t*-test is useful when a single group's mean is compared to a population mean. Researchers very rarely use this.)

Experiments with Multiple Groups

Analysis of variance—A family of statistical tests that compares group means to assess whether differences across means are reliable.

When researchers use designs that call for multiple groups, the most commonly employed test is the **analysis of variance** (ANOVA), also known as the *F*-test. It was named after Ronald Fisher, who invented it. Recently, researchers have increased their use of regression analysis where they would formerly have used an ANOVA. In many cases, the two approaches give the same basic information.

The advantage of the ANOVA over the *t*-test is that the ANOVA permits comparison of multiple groups with a single test. It also keeps

Planned comparison—A comparison of differences across levels of an independent variable when the researcher decides during the design of the study to make the comparison rather than waiting until after preliminary data

Post hoc comparison—A comparison of differences across levels of an independent variable when the researcher decides make the comparison after a preliminary data analysis.

the probability of incorrectly rejecting the null hypothesis at the level the researcher sets, which is usually .05. That is, the ANOVA lets you compare multiple groups without increasing the chance that you mistakenly conclude there is a difference between means.

If you compute an ANOVA and find that there is a significant difference between means, you don't know where the difference falls. For instance, in the research by Beins et al. (2007) in which there were three groups that received different messages about how funny a set jokes was, the significant *F*-value revealed that some of the groups differed from some others, but it didn't indicate which groups differed, only that there was a difference somewhere.

When you have multiple groups, you have options for comparing them after computing an ANOVA. When you know in advance which groups you want to compare, you conduct **planned comparisons**. When you look at your results and then decide to make a comparison between two groups, you use **post hoc comparisons**. There are different statistical assumptions associated the two approaches. Without going into detail, it is enough at this point for you to know that the different statistics are designed to keep your Type I error rate from getting bigger than the .05 value you will probably use.

The philosophy underlying all of these tests is that your null hypothesis specifies that there is no difference between groups. The alternative hypothesis specifies that not all groups are equal. Supplemental tests can inform you about which groups differ if you conclude that not all are equal.

SUMMARY

In this chapter, you have seen how researchers create experiments. Psychologists recognize the importance of producing well-defined and objective definitions of the concepts we study. We have to develop concrete working definitions because many psychological topics involve very abstract ideas that are hard to study directly.

So in order to answer experimental questions, we set up one or more independent variables to see how they affect a subsequent behavior, the dependent variable. Independent variables can take many forms. The groups we study can differ quantitatively or qualitatively. Other types of IVs involve manipulations of situations, instructions, or tasks.

Dependent variables are also quite diverse in different experiments. Most experiments involve manipulation of one to three independent variables. It is not unusual for some experiments to have multiple dependent variables as well.

The advantage of comparing multiple groups at one time is that we can see how patterns emerge across several groups, particularly with quantitative variables. Furthermore, some questions are complicated enough that simply comparing two groups will not give us all the information we would like from a single study. So we add more groups to get a more complete picture of the behaviors that interest us.

After an experiment is complete, we analyze the results statistically to see if there are any significant effects. When researchers compare two groups, they typically use a Student's *t*-test, although there are some cases in which the analysis of variance (ANOVA) is appropriate. For experiments involving comparisons of more than two groups, researchers use the ANOVA. Finally, we have to decide what the results mean as we interpret the data and relate it to behavior.

REVIEW QUESTIONS

Multiple Choice Questions

1. The complex, abstract concepts that we cannot observe directly but that we study in psychology are
   a. manipulations.
   b. variables.
   c. main effects.
   d. constructs.
2. A group of psychologists studying humor reaction studied participants' enjoyment of jokes by recording how many times the participants grinned, smiled, and laughed. These measurements of grinning, smiling, and laughing to represent enjoyment involve
   a. manipulated variables.
   b. main effects of humor enjoyment.
   c. logistic analysis.
   d. an operational definition of laughter.
3. When a researcher manipulates the environment to see if changes affect participants' behaviors, the behaviors that are measured for change are considered
   a. factorial variables.
   b. dependent variables.
   c. manipulated variables.
   d. repeated measures variables.
4. A variable that cannot be truly manipulated by a researcher, like sex or age of the participant, is called a
   a. dependent variable.
   b. qualitative variable.
   c. measured variable.
   d. situational variable.
5. When researchers use existing data to create groups for comparison, the approach is known as
   a. ex post facto.
   b. experimental.
   c. operational.
   d. quasi-experimental.
6. An independent variable whose groups differ on amount or frequency of some measurement is called

a. task variable.
b. quantitative variable.
c. quasi-experimental variable.
d. subject variable.

7. An independent variable
   a. has at most two levels.
   b. can have any number of levels.
   c. is never a manipulated variable.
   d. cannot be a qualitative variable.
8. Psychologists Marian and Neisser (2000) found that people fluent in both Russian and English had better memories for events experienced while speaking Russian if they were quizzed in Russian; they had better memories for events experienced while speaking English if they were quizzed in English. In this study, the independent variable was
   a. measured.
   b. instructional.
   c. qualitative.
   d. quasi-experimental.
9. When research participants listen to different types of instructions that might change their behavior regarding the dependent variable, we know that the independent variable is
   a. a situational variable.
   b. a subject variable.
   c. an instructional variable.
   d. a participant variable.
10. A study conducted by the National Institute of Mental Health revealed that when participants received a message about safe sex practices in a discussion format, they changed their sexual practices. In this study, the independent variable was
    a. a subject variable.
    b. a situational variable.
    c. an instructional variable.
    d. a measured variable.
11. Researchers who study differences in behaviors across races have discovered that
    a. differences in the sex of a researcher and a participant affect behavior more than differences in the race of the researcher and the participant.
    b. a person's social history, such a experiences of racism, may affect behavior, so differences in behaviors across races may not be due to race itself.
    c. racial categorization in older research was not objective, but new research has made categorization more accurate.
    d. genetic research has shown that racial categories are more useful for studying medical or biological phenomena and less useful for studying behaviors.
12. Researchers have wanted to set up studies to see if depression affects memory. To see if people who are depressed differ from those not depressed, researchers
    a. have induced mild states of depression in some participants but not others, then tested their memory.

b. have typically given mild drugs to participants to simulate depression temporarily.
c. have not discovered an effective way to induce, then remove, depression in research participants.
d. cannot ethically induce a state that resembles depression.

13. Researchers who study depression experimentally have tried to induce mild states of depression in participants. This type of research
    a. has been considered unethical because of the psychological harm to participants that could result.
    b. has been able to induce depression but researchers have found it difficult to reverse the process.
    c. has shown that some procedures seem to induce mild depression in a way that has construct validity.
    d. has shown that experimental models of depression seldom match actual depression in useful ways.
14. The Student's *t*-test is typically used
    a. in comparing two groups to see if their means differ.
    b. when analyzing the results of a correlational design.
    c. as a followup to designs using case studies.
    d. in educational research.
15. Supposed you have conducted an analysis of variance in a design with multiple groups and obtained evidence of a significant difference among means. If you decided to investigate which means differed significantly, you would use what test(s)?
    a. Multiple *t*-tests
    b. Planned comparisons
    c. Logistic regression
    d. Post hoc comparisons

Essay Questions

16. Why do we have to rely on operational definitions to study abstract hypothetical constructs?
17. How can a variable, like depression, be used either as an independent or as a dependent variable?
18. Identify and describe the four types of independent variables according to type of manipulation.

ANSWERS TO REVIEW QUESTIONS

Multiple Choice Questions

1. d
2. d
3. b
4. c
5. d
6. b
7. b
8. c
9. b
10. b
11. b
12. a
13. c
14. a
15. d

Essay Questions

16. Why do we have to rely on operational definitions to study abstract hypothetical constructs?

    Abstract hypothetical constructs are hard to characterize because they are not concrete. So we have to find out some objective way to measure them. Any measurement we choose is not going to be exactly the same as the underlying concept, but we need that measurement to represent the hard-to-define idea we want to deal with.

17. How can a variable, like depression, be used either as an independent or as a dependent variable?

    If an experimenter wanted to see if level of depression affected some behavior, the researcher would manipulate the depression level in participants to see if behavior changed. In this case, depression level would be the IV, the manipulated variable.

    If the experimenter wanted to see if some manipulation affected a person's level of depression, the researcher would manipulate an IV and see the result in terms of a person's depression level. In this case, depression would be a DV, or an outcome behavior.

18. Identify and describe the four types of independent variables according to type of manipulation.
    a. Task variable—The independent variable is set up so that participants in different conditions engage in different tasks.
    b. Instructional variable—The IV is set up so that participants in different conditions receive different instructions about what they are going to do.
    c. Situational variable—The IV is set up so that the context or setting of the experiment differs across groups.
    d. Subject variable—The IV is set up so that comparisons are made between two groups of people who differ in some pre-existing way (e.g., sex, political affiliation)

CHAPTER EIGHT

EXPERIMENTS WITH MULTIPLE INDEPENDENT VARIABLES

CHAPTER OVERVIEW

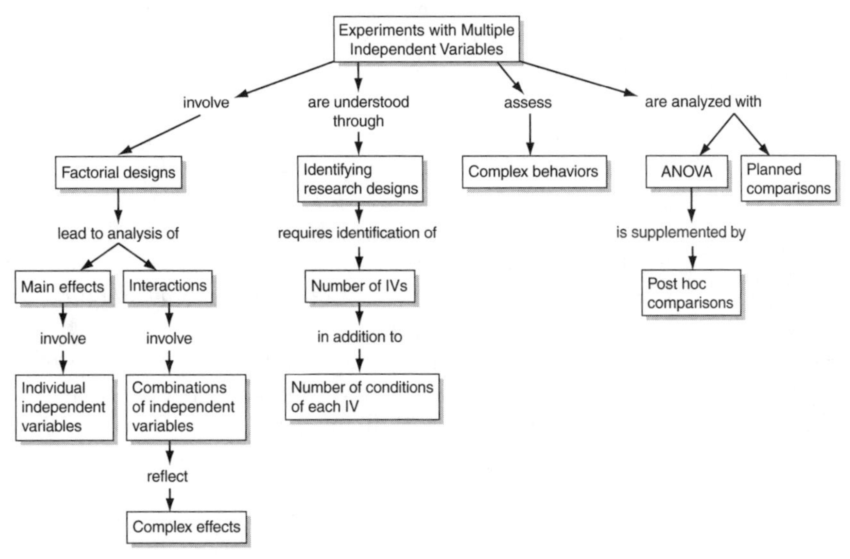

KEY TERMS

Analysis of variance (omnibus F-test), p. 208
Factorial design, p. 196
Higher order interaction, p. 200
Interaction effect, p. 200
Main effect, p. 198
Planned comparison, p. 196
Post hoc comparison, p. 196
Repeated measures design, p. 207

CHAPTER PREVIEW

Sometimes psychologists create simple studies with a single IV; most such studies in psychology have several comparison groups. In other cases, researchers manipulate more than one IV in a single experiment. The advantage of a multifactor study is that we can get a better look at the complex interplay of variables that affect behavior. After all, in our lives, most of what we do is a result of more than a single cause.

Planned comparison—A comparison of differences across levels of an independent variable when the researcher decides during the design of the study to make the comparison rather than waiting until after preliminary data analysis.

In this chapter, you will learn about experiments involving multiple IVs. The benefit of this approach is that we can examine individual IVs, but we can also see how different variables interact to produce unexpected results.

With these more complex designs, we use various statistical tests. The most common approach is the analysis of variance (ANOVA), which is sometimes supplemented by **planned** or **post hoc comparisons**. For studies with multiple DV, we typically use a multivariate ANOVA, followed by a standard ANOVA, called a univariate ANOVA.

RESEARCH WITH MULTIPLE INDEPENDENT VARIABLES

In the last chapter, you saw how researchers compare two or more groups using a single independent variable (IV). A lot of interesting psychological questions are too complicated to be answered by comparing only two groups, maybe too complicated for a single IV.

Post hoc comparison—A comparison of differences across levels of an independent variable when the researcher decides make the comparison after a preliminary data analysis.

An expansion on the simplest design involves experiments that manipulate more than one IV. The advantage of this approach is that you can get a more detailed picture of behavior because you are observing more complex conditions.

Beyond multiple group studies, many experiments in psychology involve more than one factor, that is, more than just a single IV. One reason for using multiple IVs is that many psychological questions are too complicated to answer with a single independent variable. Another reason is that we often gain more than twice as much information from a two-factor study than we do from a single-factor study. And, even better, we may not have to expend twice as much energy and time when we use multiple IVs in a single study.

Factorial design—A design of a research study in which the investigator manipulates more than one independent variable in a single study, with each level of one IV crossed with each level of all other IVs.

When an experiment uses multiple IVs, if each level of one variable is crossed with every level of the other variables, the approach is referred to as a **factorial design**. If there are two variables, A and B, and if A has two levels (A_1 and A_2) and B has three levels (B_1, B_2, and B_3), we would have a factorial design if A_1 is paired with each of B_1, B_2, and B_3 and A_2 is paired with each of B_1, B_2, and B_3. Table 8.1 schematically illustrates a 2×3 design.

In theory, there is no limit to the number of factors you can study in an experiment. Three IVs is not unusual, and occasionally you will see four. Realistically, though, you won't encounter more than four except in extremely rare instances.

To see how experimenters might create a study with multiple IVs, consider this situation: You hear somebody laugh, but you can't see him or her. What about the laughter would lead you to be more or less likely to want to meet that person?

Bachorowski and Owren (2001) played recorded laughter from either a woman or a man. This represents a qualitative variable because the voices differed by the category of the laugher—female or male. The researchers were not trying to assess the difference in behavior as a result of a numerical difference in the level of the IV, but rather on the basis of sex.

In this study, the participants provided a rating of their interest in meeting the person whose recorded laughter they had heard. The results showed that, on average, participants were about equally likely to want to meet women and men after hearing them laugh.

The researchers also manipulated a second qualitative IV in the experiment. This was whether the laugh was "voiced" like a real laugh; as the investigators explained, the voiced laughs were "harmonically rich" (p. 253). The second type of laugh was "unvoiced," including "grunt-, cackle-, and snortlike sounds" (p. 253). Participants were much more interested in meeting the people who had produced the voiced laughs.

In this study, there are two IVs; both are qualitative. One IV is gender of the laugher; it has two levels, female and male. The second IV is type of laugh, voiced and unvoiced. When you report your research, it will help your audience if you identify both the IV as a general concept and also the levels or conditions. The researchers here created qualitative IVs. The change from one group to another involves changing the quality of the stimulus, not a quantity.

TABLE 8.1 Schematic Example of a Factorial Design Involving Two Independent Variables, A and B

Each level of an IV is paired with each level of the other IV. In this example there are six conditions because the two levels of A are paired with the three levels of B, creating a 2×3 design. In factorial designs, the total number of conditions is equal to the number of levels of the variables multiplied together.

	B_1	B_2	B_3
A_1	A_1B_1	A_1B_2	A_1B_3
A_2	A_2B_1	A_2B_2	A_2B_3

MAIN EFFECTS

When we use factorial designs, we look at each IV individually. We temporarily isolate each IV and assess it as if it were the only one in the study. When we determine whether it has affected the DV, we are looking at a **main effect**. We monitor whether there is a significant main effect for each IV separately. So if the research design involves three IVs, we would test for three main effects.

Main effect—In a factorial design, differences among groups for a single independent variable that are significant, temporarily ignoring all other independent variables.

Let's consider a study that links self-esteem, past experiences, and a concept called subjective distance. Ross and Wilson (2002) investigated how far in the past certain experiences felt depending on whether those experiences were positive or negative.

Specifically, Ross and Wilson randomly assigned students to a condition in which they were supposed to recall a college course in which they either performed well or poorly. The investigators also recorded the students' level of self-esteem as measured on a self-esteem inventory (Rosenberg, 1965) and how long ago the recalled course had taken place.

Consequently, we have three IVs of interest to us here. One IV is the Grade Condition, whether the student recalled a class that involved a good grade or a poor grade. This is a true manipulated IV because the researchers randomly assigned students to the groups.

The second IV is the students' self-esteem level, a measured variable rather than a true, manipulated IV. The third IV is how long ago the course in question had taken place, also a measured IV. Ross and Wilson included a fourth IV that isn't relevant to our discussion here. The DV we are interested in here is the subjective distance from the class in question. That is, how far in the past did that class seem to the participants?

Ross and Wilson discovered a significant main effect of time since the last class. More recent classes felt more recent. This offers no surprise. In fact, the researchers might have worried about their results if the students had consistently concluded that recent events seemed more remote than the remote events.

In addition, the investigators found a significant main effect of Grade Condition. Students who recalled classes in which they had earned poor grades tended to think of them as more remote; classes with good grades had the feel of being more recent. It's as if we keep good memories close and send bad memories to the attic. There was no main effect of self-esteem. That is, students with high and low self-esteem were comparable in their judgments of subjective distance.

In this discussion we can see that two IVs were related to students' feelings of how remote certain classes felt. Classes that students had completed in the most distant past felt remote, as we might expect. In addition, classes in which the student performed more poorly also seemed more remote. As such, there were two significant main effects—actual time since the class and the type of class the student recalled. On the other hand, students with high self-esteem made the same judgments of remoteness as did students with low self-esteem. This main effect—level of self-esteem—was not significant.

INTERACTIONS BETWEEN VARIABLES

Ross and Wilson's assessment of the main effects was interesting, but they also found some intriguing results when they examined the IVs together rather than in isolation. Remember that courses with good grades seemed closer. This was a significant main effect. Further, self-esteem was unrelated to subjective distance. However, these patterns weren't always present. Figure 8.1 illustrates the findings. High-grade courses were seen as being subjectively closer, but only for high self-esteem students. Students with low self-esteem tended to keep both successes and failures equally close, while high self-esteem students kept good memories close, shuffling less pleasant memories to a distance.

By looking at the effects of IVs together, you are examining interactions. In this study, Ross and Wilson found a significant interaction between grade condition and self-esteem. This means that in order to understand the effect of grade on subjective distance, you have to know whether the student showed low or high self-esteem.

Any time you need to know something about a second variable in order to understand the first variable, you have an interaction. Here we have to know about level of self-esteem in order to predict accurately whether students keep their negative experiences subjectively close or far.

Let's summarize what you need to do with a factorial study involving two IVs. When you study two variables in a single experiment, you assess the effect of the first

FIGURE 8.1 Subjective distance as affected by memory for a class resulting in good or poor grade and student's self-esteem. The interaction suggests that high self-esteem students distance themselves from poor performance but not from good performance, whereas low self-esteem students react to good and poor performance comparably.

Source: M. Ross & A. E. Wilson. (2002). It feels like yesterday: Self-esteem, ralence of personal past experiences, and judgments of subjective distance. *Journal of Personality and Social Psychology*, 32, 797. Copyright © American Psychological Association. Used with permission.

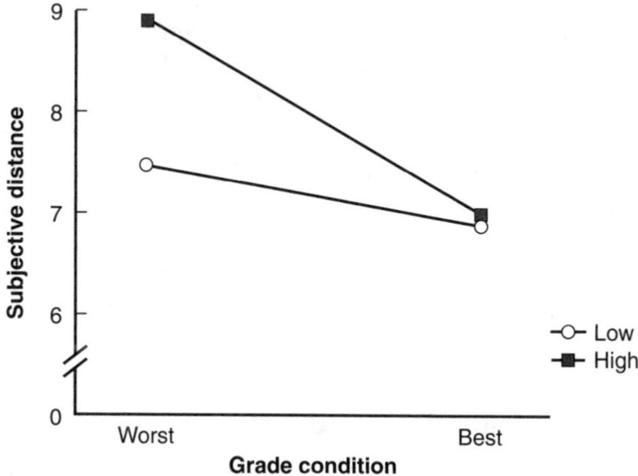

variable on the DV—that is, the main effect associated with the first IV. You also assess the effect of the second variable on the DV, seeing if there is a main effect of the second IV. Further, you see if the two variables, considered together, produce a combination of effects that is not predictable from either one alone, that is, the interaction effect. Some researchers recommend investigating interactions first.

Interactions can be hard to understand because they reflect a level of complexity one step up from main effects. Interactions may reflect the fact that people may engage in different thought processes or behaviors when exposed to slightly different conditions.

With interactions you have to pay attention to more than one IV at a time. In addition, you have to pay attention to each level of each IV because data in a single cell may be responsible for a significant interaction. Because interactions are important and because they can be difficult to grasp, we will deal with different patterns of interactions in the discussion that follows.

What Do Interactions Mean?

Interactions reflect an element of complexity in behavior when we move from simple to more complicated investigations. In interpreting them, you need to ask yourself why a change in the level of one IV leads to a different change in behavior when paired with a second IV.

In our examples of interactions here, we are going to concentrate on two-way analyses—that is, designs that involve two independent variables. Such interactions are easier to conceptualize in two-dimensional graphs.

Some psychologists assert that, if there is a significant interaction, you should pay attention to the interaction effects first because the main effects, regardless of whether they are significant, might be irrelevant or they might not be particularly informative. This view has validity, but sometimes the main effects themselves can be important and interesting, even when there is an interaction.

As the number of IVs increases, the number of potential interactions to examine grows quite dramatically. If you have two IVs, there is a single interaction. If you have three IVs, there are four possible interactions. With four variables, there are six. The difficulties in interpretation often arise with the higher order interactions, that is, the interactions involving greater numbers of IVs. If you have a three-way interaction, it means that you need to look at every combination of three IVs combined. Gaining an understanding of what **higher order interactions** means can very difficult. You can see the number of interactions that are possible in different designs in Table 8.2. The rare five-variable design would require consideration of twenty-six potential interactions.

Higher order interaction—An interaction in a factorial design that involves the joint effects of more than two independent variables.

Interaction effect—In a factorial design, differences across groups of a single independent variable that are predictable only by knowing the level of another independent variable.

Examining Main Effects and Interactions

We will discuss several patterns of results that lead to **interaction effects**; when we graph those results, each one will look slightly different. Graphs indicate whether an interaction might exist. As you can see in Figure 8.1,

TABLE 8.2 The Number of Possible Main Effects and Interactions in Designs with 2, 3, and 4 Independent Variables

Number of IVs	Two-way Interactions	Three-way Interactions	Four-way Interactions
2 (A, B)	**1**	—	—
	A × B		
3 (A, B, C)	**3**	**1**	
	A × B	A × B × C	
	A × C		
	B × C		
4 (A, B, C, D)	**6**	**4**	**1**
	A × B	A × B × C	A × B × C ×D
	A × C	A × B × D	
	A × D	A × C × D	
	B × C	B × C × D	
	B × D		
	C × D		

the lines in the graph are not parallel. In fact, they nearly intersect. When lines are parallel, there is no interaction. When lines are at an angle to one another, there may be an interaction. You need a statistical test to see whether the interaction is significant.

When interactions are present, it can mean that participants are engaged in different psychological processes in the different conditions. For instance, Fisher (2004) studied how women perceived attractiveness in other women. She presented female participants with pictures of women and of men, and the participants rated how attractive they found the person in each picture.

Fisher found a significant main effect of the sex of the person in the picture. The participants rated the women in the pictures as being more attractive, on average, than the men in the pictures. The ratings differed slightly depending on the estrogen level of the female participants, with lower ratings by women with high estrogen levels and higher ratings by women with low estrogen levels.

What is particularly interesting here is the interaction between sex of the person in the picture and the female participant's estrogen level. As you can see in Figure 8.2, women with high estrogen levels rated pictures of females as less attractive than did women with low estrogen levels. The participant's estrogen level had no relation to ratings of pictures of men. Fisher observed from these data that when women are at more fertile points in their ovulation cycles, they see other women as less attractive compared to when the participants are at less fertile points. In comparison, the rated attractiveness of men did not differ as a function of estrogen level, though.

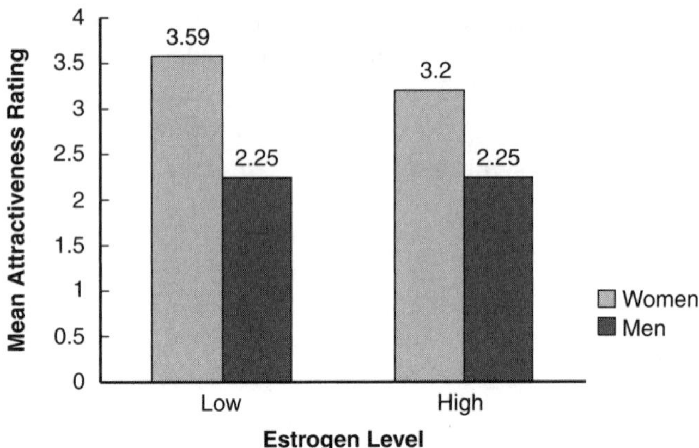

FIGURE 8.2 Illustration of an interaction in which the pattern of responses on the dependent variable for a given IV differs depending on the level of a second IV. In this study, women rated the attractiveness of females (white bars) and males (black bars) in pictures. The relative estrogen level was associated with different average ratings of women when estrogen levels differed.

Source: Fisher, M. L. (2004). Female intrasexual competition decreases female facial attractiveness. *Proceedings of the Royal Society of London*, *271*, 5283–5285. Used with permission.

These results reveal a clear interaction effect. If you want to know how much more attractive women rate a group of women in pictures than a group of men, you can't answer accurately without knowing about the estrogen level of the women doing the rating.

This research involves some important points. First, one of the variables, estrogen level, is a measured variable. Thus, we have to be cautious in talking about causation. Fisher pointed out that evolutionary theory predicts her results, so she appears confident in drawing a causal conclusion.

A second important point is that Fisher did not measure estrogen levels directly. Rather, she asked the female participants to identify how many days it had been since menstruation. She classified women who were between 12 and 21 days since the beginning of menstruation as being high in estrogen (i.e., in the most fertile point of the ovulation cycle) and those outside that range as being low in estrogen.

She also eliminated some potential participants, excluding 38 because they were using contraceptives that could affect estrogen level, 28 because of antidepressant use, 23 because they had missed an ovulation cycle within the past year, and 8 because they were not heterosexual (Fisher, 2004, p. S283). This elimination of participants was meant to avoid including women as participants whose estrogen levels may not have followed a typical pattern across the ovulation cycle.

If Fisher had decided to conduct two separate studies, each with only one IV, she would have arrived at a less informative conclusion. If she had paid attention only to the first IV, estrogen level, she would have missed the interaction between estrogen level and sex of a person being evaluated. Similarly, if she had only looked at the sex of the person being rated, she would also have missed the importance of a woman's estrogen level.

Only by looking at the entire both variables in combination could she see this interesting pattern emerging. The advantage of using a factorial design is that you can see how the variables work independently, but you can also see their combined effects.

Patterns of Interactions

When you assess your results, in some interactions, you might look individually at each level of an IV and see how the DV changes as you move across groups on the second IV. There might be a consistent increase or decrease in scores on the second variable for both levels of the first one, but one group might change more than the other.

Consider the research by Rowe and McKenna (2001), who wanted to know if expert tennis players could anticipate a winning shot better than novices. The researchers created a video of a tennis player hitting the ball in a simulated match. The participants were supposed to identify which shot was likely to be the winning one before seeing the outcome of the shot.

Some of the participants were experts, whereas some were novices. If you look at the results in Figure 8.3a, you will see that novices are always worse at anticipating a winning shot than experts are. Another way of saying this is that experts can predict the future in ways that novices can't.

The researchers included a second variable in their study, a distracting task. If they had not included this second variable, the results would still have shown that experts were better at anticipating winning shots than novices. The effect of the second independent variable, the presence or absence of a distracting task, is apparent in Figure 8.3b. You can see that the distraction, which involved saying aloud random letters in the alphabet while watching the tennis video, led to consistently lower performance.

You can again see the "It depends" statement about interactions here. If you asked how much a distraction hampers performance, the answer is that it depends on whether you are talking about novices or about experts. One group, the novices, shows a greater decline in the presence of a distracter.

The advantage of this factorial design is that, as Figures 8.3a and 8.3b reveal, Rowe and McKenna showed that experts are better than novices all the time and distractions always lead to worse performance. But the figures also show that with distraction, the novices' performance shows more deterioration than the experts'. That is, whereas experts might perform less well when they are distracted, novices might fall apart completely. You can translate these results into everyday life. If you are playing tennis or golf or basketball, or if you are driving a car, a distraction will worsen your performance; if you aren't very good to begin with, you get very bad.

A final example of a different pattern of results that leads to an interaction occurs when there is no difference among most groups, but a single condition that departs from the rest. For example, in a study of prejudice against Black defendants in trials, Sommers and Ellsworth (2001) created fictitious trials in which they varied the cases in several ways. For our discussion, we are interested in two specific independent variables: race of the defendant (Black versus White) and type of trial (race is emphasized versus race is not emphasized in the trial summary).

The researchers asked the participants to recommend a sentence when the defendant was found guilty. As you can see in Figure 8.4, in three of four conditions, the jurors (who were White adults solicited for participation at an airport) recommended sentences of nearly equal length. The one exception involved the condition with Black defendants when the trial summary did not emphasize race.

FIGURE 8.3 Two graphs of an interaction effect based on the same data. Each one highlights a slightly different aspect of the data. Figure 8.3a emphasizes the difference between novices and experts, whereas Figure 8.3b emphasizes the difference when participants engage in an additional, distracting task.

Source: R. M. Rowe & F. P. McKenna. (2001). Skilled anticipation in real-word tasks: Measurerment of attentional demands in the domain of terms. *Journal of Experimental Psychology: Applied*, 7, 65. Copyright © 2001 American Psychological Association. Used with permission.

(a)

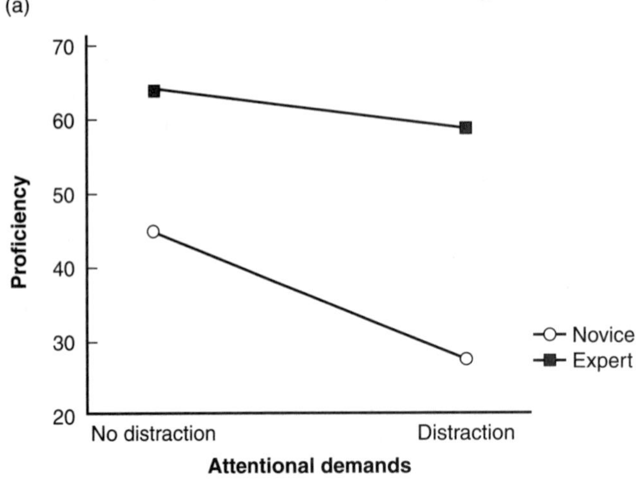

(b)

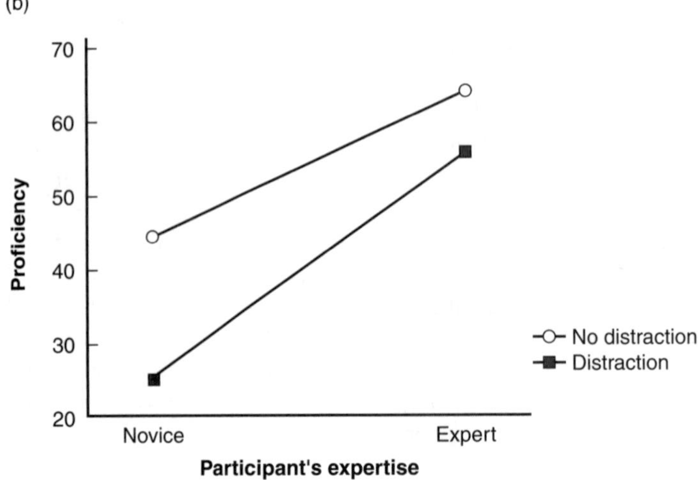

This is another instance in which a factorial design is critical. If race had been emphasized in a mock trial with the only comparison being sentences recommended for White versus Black defendants, there would have been no effect of the IV because the average sentence lengths for Black and for White defendants were about equal. Or if race had not been emphasized at all, it would have appeared that Black defendants received harsher sentences, which is not always the case.

FIGURE 8.4 Interaction showing nearly equal responses for one group (White defendants), regardless of race salience, but a difference in the second condition (Black defendants). The line graph and the bar graph are based on the same data.

Source: S. R. Sommers & P. C. Ellsworth. (2001). White juror bias: An investigation of prejudice against black defendants in the American courtroom. *Psychology, Public Policy, and Law*, 7, data from Table 1, p. 218. Copyright © 2001 American Psychological Society. Used with permission.

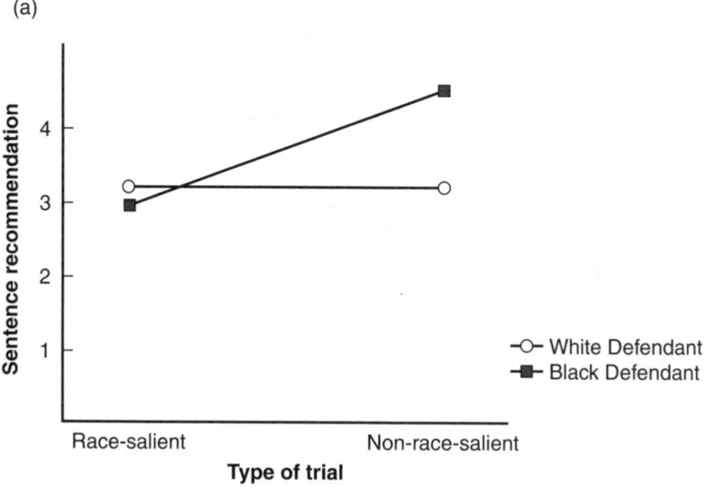

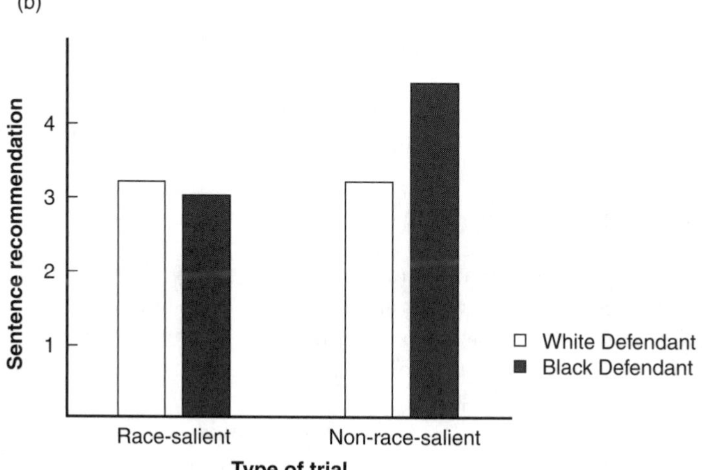

CONTROVERSY: Prejudice

Just about everybody agrees that prejudice is undesirable. It would be hard to argue that it is desirable for people to make judgments about others without having any information about them. Further, common sense would dictate that we could identify racially prejudiced people by observing their behavior toward another person from another group.

As it turns out, though, this viewpoint is too simplistic. Sechrist and Stangor (2001) identified the prejudice level in their student participants, all of whom were White. The researchers then created a situation in which the participant would have to choose how far to sit from a Black confederate. You would probably predict that high prejudiced people would sit farther from the Black confederate than the low prejudiced people. In fact, this is what generally happened.

When the participants thought that others on their campus agreed with them in racial matters, low prejudiced people sat quite close to the confederate, whereas highly prejudiced people sat quite far from the confederate. That is, if they thought "everybody thinks like I do," the distance they chose to sit from the confederate strongly reflected their underlying attitude. There is no real surprise here.

An interesting complication was revealed by a significant interaction effect, however. When the high prejudice participants thought that most other students did not share their racial attitudes, they sat somewhat closer to the confederate than when they thought everybody believed as they did. That is, when participants thought they were in the minority in their racial attitudes, their seating behavior appeared less prejudiced. On the other hand, when low prejudiced participants thought most students had prejudicial racial attitudes, they sat farther from the Black confederate.

The data suggest that if people are aware that others do not share their prejudices, those people will act with less prejudice. Unfortunately, if low prejudice people think that most others are racially biased, the opposite may occur.

These results give us an indication of how we might reduce undesirable behavior. If we can convince those who are racially biased that others don't share their ideas, we may be able to change behaviors for the better; perhaps attitudes will follow. The worst situation will be to allow prejudice to continue because we let others believe that everybody around them is also prejudiced.

Question for Discussion: Do you think the Sechrist and Stanger (2001) research has external validity? That is, do you think it would tell us about behaviors in nonlaboratory situations?

The Controversy on prejudice illustrates research that shows that the situation may be more complex than we might think.

IDENTIFYING RESEARCH DESIGNS

When you create an experiment, you need to specify very clearly your IVs and your DVs. Similarly, when you read about another study, you should identify each IV and DV. If you don't have a firm idea of what you are manipulating, you will have a hard time setting up your study; if you don't understand what somebody else did, you won't be able to understand and interpret those results.

Once you establish an IV, you should determine how many treatments were involved and the nature of the IV. For example, as you discovered in Table 7.1, Murray et al. (1999) wanted to know if people in a depressed state remembered more words from a list than nondepressed people. The IV here is Psychological State, and it has two levels, dysphoric (depressed) and euphoric (nondepressed). In that experiment, Psychological State was a manipulated variable because the researchers induced either a dysphoric or a euphoric state in participants randomly assigned to one of the two groups. The DV was the number of words remembered from a list. It was the only dependent measure involved.

Repeated measures design—A design in which a single participant is observed and measured on more than one level of an independent variable rather than measuring different individuals on each level of the independent variable.

However, their experiment involved a little more complexity. They also investigated whether the participants remembered different numbers of positive and negative words. Thus, they employed a second IV, Word Type; it had two levels, positive words and negative words.

All participants were exposed to positive and to negative words during the learning phase of the study. This approach involves a **repeated measures design**, which means that participants are tested on all levels of at least one IV.

The design in the Murray et al. study is consequently called a 2 × 2 (which is read as "two by two") factorial design. Sometimes in journal articles, you will see such a design described as a "2 (Psychological State) × 2 (Word Type) factorial design with repeated measures on the second factor."

In a more general way of talking about a design, we would say that this experiment involved an A × B design. This tells us that there are two IVs, Variable A and Variable B. A and B are each associated with the number of conditions; in our example here, A = 2 and B = 2. So the A × B design in the Murray et al. study is a 2 × 2 design. A 2 × 2 design has four conditions because, as simple arithmetic tells you, 2 times 2 equals 4.

An example of a 2 × 3 design comes from the work of Budson et al. (2001); the design is outlined in Table 8.3. They compared Alzheimer's patients and healthy older adults on their ability to differentiate between pictures of nonsense shapes they either had or had not seen before. Some of the new shapes were very similar to the old ones, some of medium similarity, and some of low similarity.

TABLE 8.3 An Example of a 2 (Type of Person) × 3 (Similarity of Image to Original) Factorial Design with Repeated Measures on the Second Factor

A 2 × 3 design implies that there are six different conditions (Budson, Daffner, Desikan, & Schacter, 2001).

	Low Similarity	**Medium Similarity**	**High Similarity**
Alzheimer's Patient	Alzheimer's Patient/Low Similarity	Alzheimer's Patient/Medium Similarity	Alzheimer's Patient/High Similarity
Healthy Elderly Person	Healthy Elderly Person/Low Similarity	Healthy Elderly Person/Medium Similarity	Healthy Elderly Person/High Similarity

Healthy adults were more easily fooled by new shapes that were similar to the old because they had been able to encode the previously seen shapes into memory. For the Alzheimer's patients, because their memories were generally poor, they were not fooled into thinking that they had seen a particular shape even if it was similar to ones they had actually seen because they didn't remember the similar ones to begin with.

The design was a 2 (Type of Person—Healthy versus Alzheimer's adult) × 3 (Similarity of Image—low, medium, or high) factorial design with repeated measures on the second factor. There were a total of 6 conditions (because 2 × 3 = 6). You can see the conditions in Table 8.3. Their dependent measure was the proportion of new images that the participants incorrectly identified as old.

DATA ANALYSIS

Many tests an available for analysis of experimental data. When data are normally distributed, there are about equal sample sizes, and the variances of the different groups are equal, we typically use a group of tests referred to as parametric tests. When the data do not meet these criteria, we use nonparametric statistics.

The parametric tests predominate by a great margin. If you look at virtually any journal dealing with experimental methods in psychology, you will see great use of Student's *t*-test, the analysis of variance, and Pearson's correlation, all of which are parametric. The tests are useful even when there are departures from the usual criteria for their use. You can see applications of the most commonly used tests in the statistics appendix.

Factorial Designs

Data analysis in factorial designs typically involves the analysis of variance (ANOVA). This statistic permits the researcher to compare each IV individually and the interaction between them.

Analysis of variance (omnibus F-test)—A statistical analysis that permits simultaneous evaluation of differences among groups in research using multiple groups and multiple independent variables.

The first step for researchers typically involves what is called an **omnibus *F* test,** commonly called **analysis of variance** (ANOVA). (There are related tests like the Multiple Analysis of Variance, MANOVA, and the Analysis of Covariance, ANCOVA, as well. They are variations on the ANOVA.) An omnibus *F* tells you whether the main effects are significant and whether any interactions are significant. After the omnibus *F*-test, researchers have several options. One is to discuss all main effects and interaction effects individually.

Researchers also use planned contrasts when analyzing their results. This can involve using *t*-tests to see whether individual pairs of conditions differed from one another. If you decide before collecting any data to compare certain pairs of conditions, you should use planned comparisons. On the other hand, if you collect your data and conduct an ANOVA, then discover a potentially interesting comparison among groups, you should use post hoc comparisons.

You will probably be seeing greater use of confidence intervals and measures of effect size in the future. The most recent edition of the *Publication Manual of the Amer-*

CONTROVERSY: Cell Phones and Driving

Cell phones are popular means of communication. By 2005, there were more cell phones in the United Kingdom than there were people (CIA–The World Factbook, 2007); in the United States there were 219 million cell phones for about 300 million people. Mobile phones allow people to be in contact virtually on demand, even when they are driving.

One important question that researchers have addressed is whether driving while talking on a cell phone is safe. Preliminary data using records from traffic accidents suggested that talking on a cell phone impairs people to the same degree as driving while drunk (Redelmeier & Tibshirani, 1997). Those data were archival, not experimental, though; they relied on cell phone records and reports of accidents while drivers were (or were not) talking on the phone, so it is not easy to spot cause-and-effect relations. In order to assess whether there is a causal link between cell phone use and unsafe driving, investigators have created experiments that are useful for cause-and-effect explanations.

The research on the impact of cell phone use and driving has required varied approaches, each with its own strengths and weaknesses. For one thing, it would be unethical to create a situation in which a research participant was driving dangerously on roads and highways, so investigators have used laboratory-based driving simulators. One limitation of such studies is that participants know they are not on the road, so their driving behavior may not represent their behavior in a real-world situation. In this case, we hope that the experiments have experimental realism; that is, we hope that the participants are taking the research seriously and engaging in the same types of behaviors they normally do. With a driving simulator, there may actually be a high level of mundane realism as well, which is why psychologists use them to study behavior (e.g., Strayer, Drews, & Crouch, 2006).

On the other hand, some researchers have taken drivers on actual roads. For example, Harbluk, Noy, Trbovich, and Elizenman (2007) asked participants to drive on a busy four-lane city road while talking on a cell phone and engaging in easy and difficult tasks. In this study, the researchers included an emergency brake that the passenger, one of the investigators, could operate if necessary.

In this section of the chapter, you will see how different researchers investigated the question of impairment of driving performance due to cell phone use. There are many ways to address the same question. Each provides another piece to the puzzle.

Question for Discussion: If people were made aware of the research on cell phone use and driving, do you think they would reduce this behavior?

ican Psychological Association specifies greater use of these statistics. You can refer to a statistics text for greater detail, but confidence intervals give you a sense of the range of scores that contains the true population mean from which your sample scores came, and measures of effect size inform you about whether your IV accounts for a small to a large amount of the difference across groups.

Illustration of a 2 × 3 Repeated Measures Design

To address the issue of cell phone use and the ability to attend to visual signals, Strayer and Johnston's (2001) participants either repeated words they heard on a cell phone or generated a word beginning with the same letter as a word they heard. In addition, the participants had to track (i.e., follow) a visual stimulus on a screen with a joystick and respond when they saw a specific target stimulus. This study involved two independent variables (IV). One IV was the difficulty of the tracking task, with two levels: easy and difficult. The second IV was the type of distracting task, with three levels: only the tracking task, repeating what the participant heard on the cell phone while tracking, and generating a word beginning with the letter of a word heard on the cell phone while tracking. In addition, every participant experienced the easy and difficult task and all three distraction conditions. Thus, the study involved a 2 × 3 design with repeated measures on both IVs.

In their two studies, Strayer and Johnston (2001) found that when participants were listening on the cell phone, they made twice as many errors as when not talking on the cell phone and took longer to react when they did spot a signal. In addition, when participants had to engage in a task requiring them to generate a word rather than just repeating a word they heard, they made more errors.

This study indicates that people who engage in tasks that involve some complexity, like coming up with a word beginning with a given letter, they are less able to attend to stimuli around them. The word-generation tasks is somewhat similar to generating words in a conversation that requires some thought. At the same time, this study did not actually investigate a driving situation. It was a laboratory-based test of attention on a nondriving visual task. So it adds to our suspicions about possible decrement in performance while driving and talking on a cell phone, we have to consider whether the effects generalize to real driving tasks.

Illustration of a 2 × 2 Design with Repeated Measures on One Factor

In another experiment, Strayer, Drews, and Johnston (2003) used a driving simulator to represent real-world situations. There were two IVs in this study. Participants either drove without a cell phone or while engaged in a conversation with another person on a topic of interest to the participant. Each person drove with no cell phone in use half the time and with cell phone use the other half. In addition, there were two traffic-density conditions, simulations of low traffic density and high traffic density. Thus, this study involved a 2 × 2 design with repeated measures on one factor. The appropriate statistic here would be a 2 × 2 analysis of variance.

Consistent with the earlier study by Strayer and Johnston (2001), the results of this experiment showed that cell phone use was detrimental to driving performance. Strayer and Johnston measured how long it took drivers to apply the simulator's brakes while talking on the cell phone, to release the brake pedal after using it, and to get back to normal driving speed after slowing down. All of these measurements showed poorer performance during cell phone use.

Strayer, Drews, and Johnston (2003) conducted a second study in which they compared only two groups. Participants engaged in a simulated driving task either with or without a cell phone conversation taking place. After the driving task, they received a surprise test of their memory for billboards that had been present during driving. Performance was worse in the cell-phone condition; participants using cell phones were about half as likely to recognize a billboard as having been present during their simulated driving. Strayer et al. referred to this inability to attend to stimuli as *inattention blindness*.

These studies had mundane realism; the investigators hoped it had experimental realism, such that participants were taking the task seriously. But they were laboratory studies, so we can't be absolutely confident that it reflected real driving behavior.

Illustration of a 2 × 2 × 2 Design with Repeated Measures on All Factors

Some researchers actually took participants on the road to see the effects of cell phone use on driving (Recarte & Nunes, 2003). The participants drove about 186 miles (300 kilometers), a task that took about four hours.

At different points during the driving, participants had to learn some abstract information or some concrete information. At other points, they had to produce either abstract or concrete information. And during the trip, sometimes they had to engage in a detection task and sometimes there was no such detection task. The study involved a 2 × 2 × 2 design with repeated measures on all factors.

Their study involved numerous dependent variables. One DV was the extent to which drivers shifted their gaze during driving, that is, the extent to which they surveyed the road ahead of them. The analysis of the gazing behavior showed, among other things, that drivers restricted their gaze when they had to generate responses as opposed to the simpler task of learning some material. The data support the results generated by Strayer and Johnston (2001) in a nondriving, laboratory-based study. The data of Recarte and Nunes (2003) also support Strayer, Drews, and Johnston's (2003) results in a laboratory-based driving simulator.

One possible limitation to this real-road study was that the researchers could not control the driving situation. There were different drivers on the road for each participant, and the road conditions might have been slightly different. Other, hidden differences may also have been at work. The limitations may not be problematic, though, because other on-the-road research led to the same results and conclusions (Harbluk et al., 2007).

Illustration of a One Variable Design with Repeated Measures on All Factors

Further research has suggested that driving while talking on a cell phone is about as dangerous as driving while drunk. Strayer, Drews, and Crouch (2006) looked at driving performance in a driving simulator when participants were in a control condition, while talking on a cell phone, and after having drunk an vodka-orange juice cocktail. In the alcohol condition, the blood alcohol level was 0.08%, which is a commonly used threshold for being labeled as driving while intoxicated.

Drunk drivers showed different patterns of disrupted driving (e.g., they were more aggressive in their behavior) than did cell-phone-using drivers (e.g., they were slower to respond). But both showed deteriorated abilities compared to the situation with no alcohol and no cell phones. This design involved repeated measures, so we can be assured that the participants in all conditions had the same level of competence at driving to begin with: They were the same people in each condition. The manipulation (cell phone, alcohol, neither cell phone nor alcohol) must have been responsible for differences in performance.

In this study, cell phone users showed the same deficiencies compared to nonusers as in other studies. They were slower to brake, they applied more force to the brake when they did slow down, they showed longer following distances, took longer to resume normal speed after braking, and had more accidents. The researchers concluded that the relative danger each group poses is about the same. This conclusion based on experimental research is consistent with that generated a decade previously in archival research (Redelmeier & Tibshirani, 1997). There seems to be no evidence that using a hands-free cell phone makes any difference (e.g., Redelmeier & Tibshirani, 1997).

It would be interesting to know if novice drivers are differentially affected by cell phone use compared to experienced drivers. It could be that, as people become better drivers (i.e., more experienced), they are able to drive well even if they talk on the phone.

Kass, Cole, and Stanny (2007) studied new drivers aged 14 to 16 and more experienced drivers aged 21 to 52. The investigators monitored performance in a driving simulator. The dependent variables included such behaviors as number of collisions, the number of pedestrians hit, speeding violations, stop signs missed, and center line crossings. Novice drivers made more overall errors than experienced drivers, but the differences between novice drivers with and without cell phones was similar to the difference between experienced drivers with and without cell phones. Thus, being an experienced driver did not mean that people were able to drive well while talking on the phone.

This study involved two comparison groups, novice and experienced drivers, which makes it a static group design. It would have been impossible for the researchers to randomly assign people to conditions because the participants came to the study at a given age. So there could be important initial differences between the younger and the older people. It is not clear, though, why we would expect differences between the novices and experienced drivers that would influence the results; still, there might be differences that we don't know. The good news is that results make sense. You would expect novices to make more mistakes. And all the research suggests that everybody is hampered by cell phone use. So the possible limitations of this study are probably not troublesome.

The Conclusion

The results of all the studies support the same conclusion: Talking on a cell phone while driving impairs a driver's ability. Each study had its own limitations, but other studies do not suffer from that same limitation. In the end, we have good convergent validity, with all the data pointing to the same conclusion.

One final situation in which cell phone use can be problematic involves pedestrians. That is, Hatfield and Murphy (2007) have demonstrated that pedestrians with cell phones engage in behaviors that may not be safe. These researchers monitored the behavior of people crossing streets while using or not using cell phones. The results were somewhat complicated, and there were differences in patterns of behaviors for women and for men, but the researchers found that using a cell phone while crossing a street is associated with unsafe behaviors, like not looking at traffic before venturing into a crossing and crossing more slowly compared to non-users. One conclusion is that some cell phone users may not be able to walk and talk at the same time.

SUMMARY

Behavior is complex, so studying behavior is complex. Experiments sometimes require more than one IV in order to provide answers to interesting research questions. Studies with multiple IVs are often referred to as having factorial designs. The advantage of factorial designs with multiple IVs is that a researcher can study behavior in greater detail and identify patterns of behavior that change when another variable is present.

When researchers create more complex designs, they investigate the effects of single IVs, just as researchers do in simple experiments. Each IV in a factorial study receives independent analysis. In addition, however, investigators assess what happens when they manipulate more than one variable in a single study. Sometimes variables interact to produce behaviors that are not predictable when the researcher examines them individually. These complex patterns are called interaction effects.

When you read about experiments or actually create your own, you need to identify your research design. You specify the number of IVs and the number of levels within each IV. Factorial designs are very common in psychological research, with most studies investigating the effects of two to four IVs.

The most common type of statistical analysis for factorial designs is the analysis of variance (ANOVA). The ANOVA permits the researcher to assess the effect of each IV and of each combination of IVs. Psychologists also supplement the ANOVA with either planned comparisons or post hoc comparisons of individual conditions within the factorial design. In the future, statistical analysis is likely to include more systematic presentation of confidence intervals and effect sizes, and estimates of the probability that a result will be reproduced if an investigator replicates the study.

REVIEW QUESTIONS

Multiple Choice Questions

1. An advantage of a using multiple levels of an independent variable includes the fact that
   a. you generally can obtain more data from fewer participants.
   b. you can spot quantitative differences in behaviors more easily.
   c. you can treat a qualitative variable as if it were a quantitative variable.
   d. you can identify changes in patterns of responses across different amounts of an independent variable.
2. If a researcher reported that there was a significant difference between groups on one variable but not on a second variable, that researcher would be talking about
   a. main effects.
   b. interaction effects.
   c. measured effects.
   d. dependent effects.

3. In an experiment involving three independent variables, it is possible for the results to show
   a. more than three main effects.
   b. a factorial design.
   c. higher order interactions.
   d. extraneous variables.
4. Suppose you conducted a study using a factorial design and somebody asked you about the results for Variable A. If you replied that, to answer their question, they have to know which level of Variable B was involved, your experiment involved
   a. main effects.
   b. logistic analysis.
   c. measured variables.
   d. an interaction.
5. Budson et al. (2001) compared healthy adults and Alzheimer's patients regarding their memory. The people in the study were tested on their memory for nonsense shapes of three types: shapes they had seen, shapes they had not seen, and shapes that were similar to ones they had seen. This design involved
   a. planned comparisons.
   b. quantitative variables.
   c. repeated measures.
   d. situational variables.
6. Student's *t*-test is typically used
   a. in comparing two groups to see if their means differ.
   b. when analyzing the results of a factorial design.
   c. as a followup to designs using logistic regression.
   d. in place of the correlation coefficient.
7. Supposed you have conducted an analysis of variance in a design with multiple groups and obtained evidence of a significant difference among means. If you decided to investigate which means differed significantly, you would use what test?
   a. Multiple *t*-tests
   b. Planned comparisons
   c. Logistic regression
   d. Post hoc comparisons
8. If your data analysis revealed that you have a significant interaction,
   a. your design involved a single-factor, multigroup design.
   b. you used a factorial design in your study.
   c. your design involved manipulated variables.
   d. your design involved only measured variables.
9. Strayer and Johnston (2001) created a study in which participants engaged in either an easy or a difficult task while trying to track a visual stimulus on a screen. In addition, there were three types of distracting tasks. The researchers measured how many errors the participants made in spotting visual stimuli. This research
   a. could not have involved a repeated measures design.

b. involved five different conditions.
c. involved only measured variables.
d. used a 2 × 3 design.

10. Strayer, Drews, and Johnston (2003) tested participants in a driving simulator while they either talked on a cell phone or did not. Afterward, participants received a surprise test of their memories for billboards that had appeared. The design of this study
    a. was correlational.
    b. involved a 2 × 1 design.
    c. was a factorial design.
    d. could lead to analysis by a *t* test.
11. Recarte and Nunes (2003) tested participants who drove for about four hours on a highway. During that time, the participants had to learn either abstract and concrete information, had to generate abstract and concrete information, and drove either with or without distraction. This design involved
    a. repeated measures on all factors.
    b. a correlational design.
    c. a partial factorial design.
    d. a main effect design but not an interaction design.
12. A study that compared novice drivers and experienced drivers with respect to the relative number of driving errors they made while using a cell phone or not using a cell phone resulted in the same amount of deterioration in both groups. This type of design
    a. is appropriate for analysis with a *t* test.
    b. involved two manipulated variables.
    c. used a static groups design.
    d. used a reduced factorial design.

Essay Questions

13. Traditionally, what statistical test has been used for a single variable, two-group design? Why is it not appropriate for multiple groups or multiple variables?
14. In the Sommers and Ellsworth (2001) experiment on the effects of race on a trial verdict, explain how the interaction provided important information. Were the independent variables qualitative or quantitative? the dependent variables?
15. On a practical level, why wouldn't a researcher be likely to create an experiment with a 2 × 3 × 4 × 5 design?

ANSWERS TO REVIEW QUESTIONS

Multiple Choice Questions

1. d
2. a
3. c
4. d
5. c
6. a
7. d
8. b
9. d
10. d
11. a
12. c

Essay Questions

13. Traditionally, what statistical test has been used for a single variable, two-group design? Why is it not appropriate for multiple groups or multiple variables?

    When there are multiple independent variables or more than two groups, you can use the analysis of variance. It has the advantage of being a single test that can let you compare all the groups at one time. In addition, an ANOVA can result in a lower rate of Type I errors.

14. In the Sommers and Ellsworth (2001) experiment on the effects of race on a trial verdict, explain how the interaction provided important information. Were the independent variables qualitative or quantitative? the dependent variables?

    In the Sommers and Ellison experiment, there was no difference in sentencing for Black defendants when a mock trial involved a specific statement about racial issues. On the other hand, when race was not mentioned, Black defendants received longer sentences than White defendants. If there had been only one variable, the investigators would not have seen the complex pattern of results.

    That is, if the researchers had only compared sentences of Black and White defendants in race-salient trials, they would have concluded that race was unimportant on sentence length. If the researchers had only compared sentences of Black and White defendants in non-race-salient trials, they would have concluded that race did make a difference. The truth is more complex: Race sometimes makes a difference, but sometimes it doesn't. You need a factorial design to see this complexity.

15. On a practical level, why wouldn't a researcher be likely to create an experiment with a $2 \times 3 \times 4 \times 5$ design?

    An experiment with this design would include 120 conditions. That would mean that, with a between groups design, you would need 120 people to provide a single person in each condition, and you would never want a single person. If you wanted 10 people, which is still small, it would involve 1,200 people. If you used a repeated measures design, each person could, in the extreme, be involved with 120 conditions, which wouldn't be practical.

    In addition, it could be very difficult to interpret the interactions, especially if there were higher order interactions (e.g., three- or four-way interactions).

CHAPTER NINE

EXPANDING ON EXPERIMENTAL DESIGNS

Repeated Measures and Quasi-Experiments

CHAPTER OVERVIEW

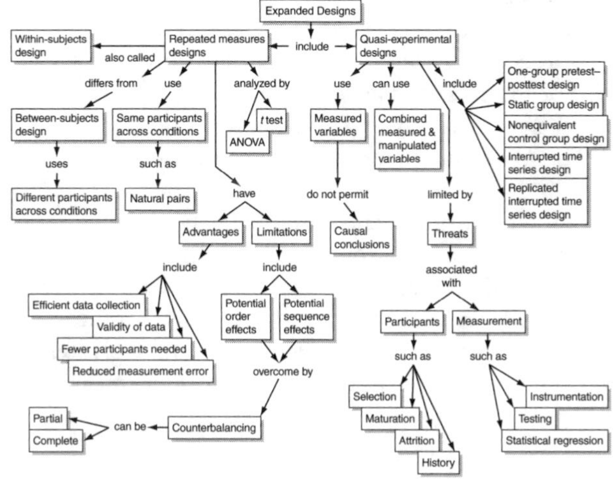

KEY TERMS

Asymmetric transfer, p. 225
Attrition (mortality) threat, p. 230
Baseline, p. 235
Between-groups design, p. 219
Complete counterbalancing, p. 226
Counterbalancing, p. 226
History threat, p. 231
Instrumentation threat, p. 231
Interrupted time series design, p. 236
Maturation threat, p. 230
Natural pairs, p. 223
Nonequivalent control group design, p. 235
One-group pretest–posttest design, p. 233
Order effects, p. 225
Partial counterbalancing, p. 226
Repeated measures (within-subjects) design, p. 219
Replicated interrupted time series design, p. 238
Selection threat, p. 230
Sequence effects, p. 225
Static-group comparison design, p. 235
Statistical regression threat, p. 231
Symmetric transfer, p. 225
Testing threat, p. 231
Transfer, p. 225

CHAPTER PREVIEW

You already know the basic elements of experimental research. The ideas in this chapter will fill in some of the gaps when you need to expand on the basics of experimental design.

Throughout a research project you have to make many practical decisions about how you intend to carry out the project. One of the decisions includes whether you want to observe participants more than once, an approach called a repeated measures design. There are quite a few advantages to such a strategy: You are certain that participants are comparable across groups (because they are the same people being measured in different conditions), you can get a lot of information from a smaller number of participants, and you are more likely to detect small differences between groups.

Researchers frequently make use of repeated measures designs because they are very efficient and because the advantages often outweigh the disadvantages significantly. No method is without its disadvantages, though. For instance, in a repeated measures design, you have to worry that one treatment will have effects that persist, affecting later behaviors.

Another extension of the experimental design is the quasi-experiment. This approach involves comparing groups that may differ in critical ways at the outset of your study. For instance, if you compare women and men, you might conclude that they differ is a particular way, but you cannot conclude that your treatment caused a difference. The two groups may have come into your study already differing in important ways.

Although quasi-experiments resemble experimental designs, they lack random assignment of participants to groups. As a result, you can make meaningful and accurate descriptions and predictions, but it is hard to identify the cause of differences.

Researchers have created quite a large number of different quasi-experimental designs. As the studies get more complex, they require greater investments in time and energy, so you have to decide how to maximize your research results and to minimize your costs.

REPEATED MEASURES DESIGNS

Setting up a research project is time consuming; carrying it out may be even more so. As a result, as an experimenter you want to maximize the amount of information you get from your work.

Repeated measures (within-subject) design—A research design in which the same individuals provide data in more than one group, essentially serving as their own control group.

Between-groups design—A research design in which a single individual does not provide data for more than one condition or group.

One obvious way to increase information is by manipulating more than one independent variable in a single study, that is, by using a factorial design. This approach might not save a lot of time or energy, though. You will have saved some time and effort in planning only one study, but you may need to test the same number of participants as if you had carried out two separate projects.

A different way to increase the economy of your work is to set up an experiment in which you test the same individuals in more than one condition in a single setting. When you collect data from the same people more than once in the same experiment, you are using a **repeated measures design**; this approach is also called a **within-subjects design.** It is called a within-subjects design because you are trying to find out if there are any differences in the way the participants within a single sample behave. You can contrast it with a **between-groups design** in which you test different participants in different groups. The goal is to see if there are any differences between groups.

ADVANTAGES OF REPEATED MEASURES DESIGNS

There are several advantages associated with repeated measures designs, some purely practical regarding carrying out your project and others statistical. There are also some limitations.

Increasing Efficiency in Data Collection

One advantage with a repeated measures design is that you might be able to increase the amount of data without a marked increase in time and effort. If your design involved three groups and you wanted to test 50 in each group, you would need a total of 150 participants. By using a repeated measures design, you could still test 50 but get the benefits of using 150.

In some studies, you may gain a great deal of extra information with repeated measures. For instance, if you wanted to know whether people could remember a list of words better with fast versus slow presentation, you could use a repeated measures design, with each participant learning the words in each presentation condition. If the experiment takes 45 minutes for one condition, it might only take 15 more minutes to add the second condition. Thus, the experiment would be 33 percent longer, but you would get 100 percent more data. When there are small numbers of potential participants, it can be very helpful to test them repeatedly.

If you added a second IV and tested the same participants on each level of that variable as well, you would still need only the 50 participants, but the amount of data you collected could be much greater. Thus, you have effectively created two experiments with only a small increase the amount of time you spend testing participants.

As you can see in Table 9.1, if you had a 2×3 design with no repeated measures, you would need to test many more people than if you use repeated measures. You could

TABLE 9.1 Example of How Repeated Measures Lead to Greater Amounts of Data Without Increases in the Number of Participants for a Hypothetical 2×3 Design

In this example, the researcher wants 50 data points in each of the six cells.

Number of Participants Required for Independent (Nonrepeated) Measures. Participants experience only one of the six conditions.

Independent Variable B	**Independent Variable A** **Group A_1**	 **Group A_2**	**Total Number of Participants**
Group B_1	50 different people	50 different people	100 for B_1
Group B_2	50 different people	50 different people	100 for B_2
Group B_3	50 different people	50 different people	100 for B_3
Total Number of Participants	150 for Group A_1	150 for Group A_2	300 Participants

Number of Participants Required for Repeated Measures on Variable B. Participants experience B_1, B_2, and B_3, but only one of the groups for Variable A.

Independent Variable B	**Independent Variable A** **Group A_1**	 **Group A_2**	**Total Number of Participants**
Group B_1	50	50	100 for B_1
Group B_2	50	50	100 for B_2
Group B_3	50	50	100 for B_3
Total Number of Participants	50 for Group A_1 because each person participates in B_1, B_2, and B_3	50 for Group A_2 because each person participates in B_1, B_2, and B_3	100 Participants (The same 100 people are in B_1, B_2, and B_3)

Number of Participants Required for Repeated Measures on Variables A and B. Every participant experiences B_1, B_2, and B_3, and also A_1 and A_2. That is, each person is in all conditions.

Independent Variable B	**Independent Variable A** **Group A_1**	 **Group A_2**	**Total Number of Participants**
Group B_1	50	50	50 for B_1 because the same people are in A_1 and A_2
Group B_2	50	50	50 for B_2 because the same people are in A_1 and A_2
Group B_3	50	50	50 for B_3 because the same people are in A_1 and A_2
Total Number of Participants	50 for Group A_1 because the same people are in B_1, B_2, and B_3	50 for Group A_2 because the same people are in B_1, B_2, and B_3	50 Participants (The same 100 people are in B_1, B_2, and B_3; likewise, the same people are in A_1 and A_2)

reduce the number of people you test from 300 to 50, which can be an immense savings of your time and a notable reduction in the number of people you have to recruit.

Increasing Validity of Data

A second advantage to using repeated measures is that you may have greater confidence in the validity of your data. Sometimes participants in different groups approach the same task very differently. Their behaviors may look as if the IV has made a difference when the participants' pre-existing perspectives are causing the changes. A repeated measures approach can remedy this problem.

One clever experiment reveals how this problem could occur. Birnbaum (1999) recruited participants via the Internet, asking them to serve in a "1-minute judgment study." They were asked to "judge how large is the number 9" or ". . . the number 221." A rating of 1 reflected "very, very small," whereas a 10 reflected "very, very large."

Figure 9.1 reflects the participants' judgments. Surprisingly, the results showed that people believe that 9 is larger than 221. What is going on? Most likely, according to Birnbaum, people in the "Judge 9 Group" were comparing 9 to single-digit numbers or to small numbers in general; in that context, 9 is pretty large. On the other hand, the participants in the "Judge 221 Group" were comparing it to much larger numbers, so it seemed relatively small (Figure 9.2).

When you ask different people to provide ratings, you need to make sure that they are all using the same context. Thus, for this judgment task, you could provide an anchor for the participants; that is, you could say that for this judgment, 1 would be considered very, very small and 1,000 would be considered very, very large. Would this solve the

FIGURE 9.1 The surprising results of the study in which participants rated the size of "9" and "221" on a scale of 1 (*very, very small*) to 10 (*very, very large*). The study involved independent assignment to conditions rather than repeated measures. That is, different people judge the size of 9 and of 221.

Source: M. H. Birnbaum. (1999). How to show that 9 > 221: Collect judgments in a between-subjects design. *Psychological Methods, 4,* 243–249. Copyright © 1999 American Psychological Association. Used with permission.

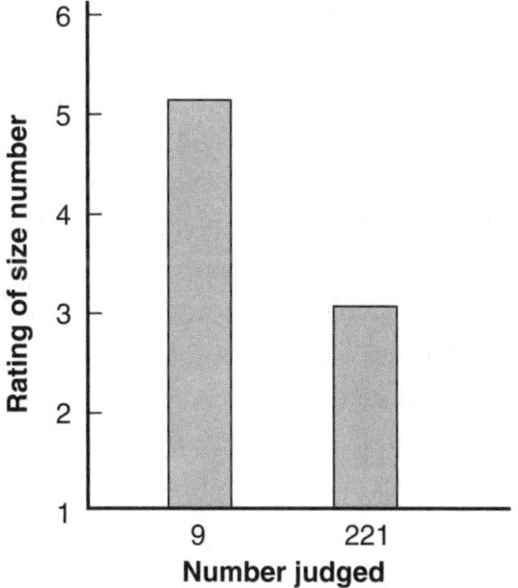

FIGURE 9.2 Relative ratings can be misleading when based on subjective criteria. A value like 9 might seem big in comparison with small numbers and 221 might seem small compared to big numbers.

Source: M. H. Birnbaum. (1999). How to show that 9 > 221: Collect judgments in a between-subjects design. *Psychological Methods, 4,* 243–249. Copyright © 1999 American Psychological Association. Used with permission.

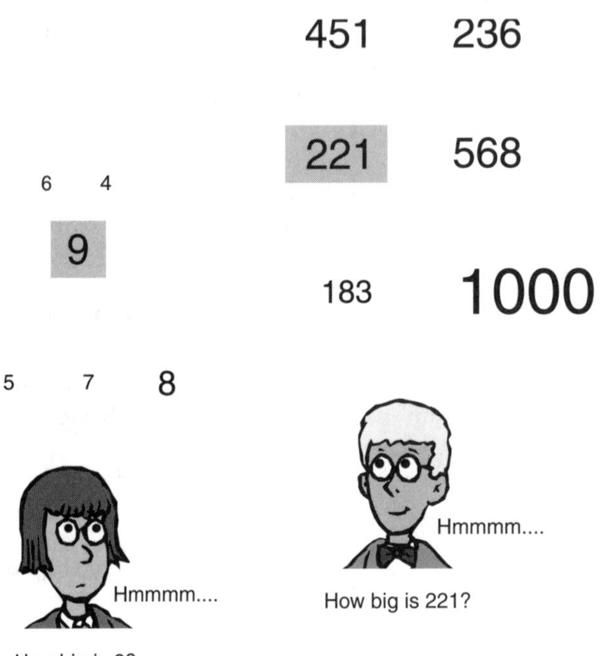

problem? According to Birnbaum (1974), even when you do this, participants can rate smaller numbers as being bigger than larger ones. Participants rated 450 as larger than 550 when he provided anchors. Thus, when there are no objective guidelines for responses, it may be a good idea to include repeated measures in the research design. With repeated measures, it's the same person being measured in each condition, so changes in behavior are more likely to be due to the IV than to differing perspectives.

This problem of different contexts by raters occurs only for subjective judgments, not for objective measures, like grades or other concrete measurements.

Sometimes it makes the most sense to use repeated measures. For instance, Leirer, Yesavage, and Morrow (1991) investigated the effects of marijuana use in airline pilots over 48 hours. The researchers legally obtained marijuana and administered controlled doses to pilots who engaged in simulated flights. The investigators were interested in how long marijuana affected the pilots' performance and whether the pilots were aware of any effects of the marijuana on their behaviors. They discovered that most of the pilots experienced residual effects of marijuana after 24 hours, but they typically were not aware of the effects.

Finding Enough Participants

A third advantage of repeated measures designs is that if the group you wanted to test was rare, such as airline pilots or other highly trained experts in some field, you might not be able to find many such people. By using the repeated measures design, you can avoid the problem of running out of participants.

On the other hand, you may not have to worry about the availability of participants if they are plentiful, like students from large introductory psychology classes. If your testing sessions require a lot of time and effort, it may be better not to use a repeated measures design because your participants may be fatigued, bored, or otherwise worn out by the time they finish one condition.

Reducing Error in Measurement

Another advantage with repeated measures designs is that, in general, your groups are equivalent at the outset because they are the same people in each group. The participants are serving as their own control group. Any characteristic that helps or hurts a person's performance is going to be the same across conditions. Further, you are increasing the number of data points in your analysis, which increases the power of your analysis, that is, the likelihood of rejecting the null hypothesis when you should (Vonesh, 1983).

A different design related to repeated measures involves matching participants in different groups. If you were going to investigate how long it takes for people to interact with a single stranger versus a group of strangers, you might initially measure your participants regarding their levels of introversion and extroversion. Then you could match two people on introversion–extroversion, assigning one to the "single stranger" condition and the other to the "multiple stranger" conditions.

Natural pairs—A pairing of individuals, like twins, who are similar to one another in some way and are useful for comparison after being exposed to different levels of an independent variable.

In addition, researchers sometimes use **natural pairs** in a matched design. This could involve twins, siblings, or other pairs that share a variable that is important in the research. You can see how repeated measures and matching are conceptually related; the big difference is that in repeated measures, the participant is identical in all conditions whereas with matching, there is similarity across conditions, but the match is imperfect.

Matching is a less frequently used strategy in experimental, laboratory work. It is more likely in psychiatric or clinical research. In a psychiatric research project, Coverdale and Turbott (2000) assessed sexual and physical abuse among psychiatric patients compared to medical patients. They matched 158 psychiatric outpatients with 158 medical outpatients; the match was based on gender, age, and ethnicity.

The benefit of matching here is that if there are differences in rates of abuse associated with gender, age, and ethnicity, the researchers could be confident that these variables were equated across the two types of outpatient participants. These researchers discovered that the two groups did not differ in the incidence of childhood abuse, whereas as adults psychiatric patients were more susceptible to both physical and sexual abuse.

Laboratory researchers often stay away from matching because matching participants well can be difficult, especially if you want to use more than one variable. Consider the situation in which you have three variables you want to match, for example, age, years of education, and family income. If you are interested in creating two groups in which the first person in Group A is matched closely with the first person in Group B, you will find that it is easy to pair people on the first variable (e.g., age), but the matches get worse as you continue because you lose some flexibility in later pairings.

You have two basic options when you have poor matches. One is to live with the best matches possible, even if they aren't very good. The problem here is that you lose the statistical advantages of matching. The second option is to discard matched pairs that are not good and to conduct your study with the pairs that remain. The drawback here is that you may end up with a small sample size that greatly reduces the chance that you will spot small but real differences across groups.

Because of these problems, psychologists do not use matching very frequently. Further, if you match your participants, you need to make sure that the matching variable is reliably associated with your dependent variable.

LIMITATIONS TO REPEATED MEASURES DESIGNS

Some research projects do not lend themselves to repeated measures designs and some variables make repeated measures impossible. If you conduct a study in which you compare people according to an existing personal characteristic, you will not be able to use repeated measurements. If you want to compare the study habits of high and low achieving students, it would be impossible to use repeated measures because each student would fall into only one category.

Another consideration about testing the same person repeatedly is that, if you test participants over time, you have a big investment in each one. If they fail to return, you have committed time and effort that will not be repaid.

Possible, but Unlikely, Repeated Measures Designs

Other projects could conceivably be carried out using repeated measures, but it would not be a good idea. If you are planning a study on the acquisition of study skills with a new technique compared to a control group, it is pretty clear that you wouldn't want to use repeated measures. Once the students learned a skill in the experimental group, they would no longer be naïve, so their performance in the control condition would have been influenced by the exposure to the experimental treatment.

Other research projects using repeated measures might be possible and would lead to valid results, but they would not be practical. For example, suppose you want to see whether young adults and older adults could complete a learning task with equal speed. This study might require many years with repeated measures because you would have to wait for participants to age.

You can see an example of this situation in research by May, Hasher, and Stoltzfus (1993). They investigated learning in people of different ages, using one set of young people and one set of old people. They could have waited for the young people to age for fifty years, but that isn't very reasonable.

Sequence effects—The result of multiple or repeated measurements of individuals in different experimental conditions such that they behave differently on later measurements as a result of having undergone the earlier measurements.

Order effects—The result of multiple or repeated measurements of individuals in different experimental conditions such that a particular behavior changes depending on which condition it follows.

Transfer—A change in behavior in a repeated measures design that results from learning that takes place in an earlier condition.

Symmetric transfer—A change in behavior in a repeated measures design that results from learning in an earlier condition, with the same degree of change in later behaviors, regardless of the order of conditions.

Asymmetric transfer—A change in behavior in a repeated measures design that results from learning in an earlier condition, with differences in the amount of transfer in a later condition depending on which conditions occur first.

Unfortunately, people growing up in different eras may simply be very different. This is particularly important in longitudinal studies (e.g., Schaie, 2000).

In addition, age may not be the best explanatory variable. For instance, May et al. (1993) found that when young and old people engaged in a learning task during their best time of the day (which tends to be in the morning for older people but later in the day for younger people), there was remarkably little difference in performance; and Ryan, Hatfield, and Hofstetter (2002) discovered that caffeine eliminates the decline in performance from morning to afternoon. Sometimes the obvious variable is not the only variable to consider.

Subject (Participant) Variables

In addition to age, there are other subject or participant variables that you will see frequently in psychological research. You generally can't use repeated measures when you examine pre-existing characteristics, such as sex, political affiliation (e.g., Democrat versus Republican), religious affiliation (Protestant, Catholic, Jewish, Muslim, etc.), sexual behavior (homosexual, heterosexual, bisexual, or none). You can't assign people to be Democrats, Protestants, etc. They are what they are.

Another case in which repeated measure would not be desirable is when the participants' behavior in one condition is essentially independent of their behavior in the other. As a general rule, if the correlation between participants' scores in two groups is less than about .25, repeated measures designs are not warranted (Vonesh, 1983).

Sequence and Order Effects

Another situation that limits the desirability of repeated measurements is when there may be **sequence effects** in testing, which occur when different treatment sequences (e.g., A-B-C versus B-A-C) lead to different outcomes. If a particular treatment, no matter where in the sequence of treatments it occurs, affects performance in subsequent conditions, this would involve sequence effects.

There are also potential **order effects**, which are progressive effects of testing when an individual is tested repeatedly. Fatigue that sets in after repeated testing is an example of an order effect.

When early behavior effects later behavior, it is called **transfer**; there are two types of transfer, **symmetric transfer** and **asymmetric transfer**. If people are tested twice (A-B), they may simply improve after the first exposure. If the improvement in A when it occurs second equals the improvement in B when it occurs second, we have symmetric transfer. If A helps later performance on B, but B doesn't help a later performance on A, we have asymmetric transfer.

Counterbalancing—In a repeated measures design, the changing of the order of conditions across individuals to avoid contamination of data because of systematic sequence, order, or transfer effects.

Complete counterbalancing—In a repeated measures design, the use of all possible orders of experimental conditions to avoid contamination of data because of systematic sequence.

Partial counterbalancing—In a repeated measures design, the use of a subset of all possible orders of experimental conditions to avoid contamination of data because of systematic sequence, order, or transfer effects.

Most psychological research on sequence effects has involved short-term effects in the laboratory. In reality, long-term sequence effects can also occur. In market research involving grocery store retailing, Paksoy, Wilkinson, and Mason (1985) suggested that researchers provide a "rest" week in their studies so that the effects of advertising and sales in week one of a study will not affect consumers' choices in week two, when a different IV is manipulated.

Overcoming Sequence and Order Effects. When sequence effects are likely, researchers often use **counterbalancing** to avoid mistaking sequence or order effects for treatment effects. If you created a project with two conditions, A and B, you would want to test some participants in the AB order and other participants in the BA order. If you had three conditions, A, B, and C, you could order them ABC, ACB, BAC, BCA, CAB, and CBA if you wanted to use all possible orderings. This approach reflects **complete counterbalancing** because you use all possible orders.

As you add conditions, the number of orderings grows quickly and requires that you test a large number of participants. Thus, with three conditions, you have six orders; with four conditions, it grows to 24; with five, you have 120. Normally, you would test multiple participants in each order; so if you had four conditions (i.e., 24 orders) and if you wanted to include three participants per order, you would need to test 72 people. In addition, you would need a multiple of 24 participants (e.g., 48, 72, 96) in your study because there are 24 orders to repeat in each block.

Fortunately, there is no need to use complete counterbalancing. **Partial counterbalancing** can help keep experiments manageable. Only a subset of all orders is needed.

DATA ANALYSIS WITH REPEATED MEASURES DESIGNS

When you create an experiment that uses repeated measures, you will be faced with choices about statistics that can become pretty complicated.

Many of the issues are beyond the scope of this book but you can see some common approaches to data analysis with repeated measures in the statistics appendix. Before you carry out a study with repeated measures, you should consult with somebody who knows the field. The last thing you want to do is to collect data that you won't be able to analyze properly. When investigators employ repeated measures designs, they often carry out data analyses that are not optimal, causing researchers either to miss differences between groups that are small, but real, or to conclude that there are differences when there aren't (Gaito, 1961; Pollatsek & Well, 1995; Reese, 1997).

A common statistical approach is to compare pretest and posttest scores with either a *t*-test or an analysis of variance (ANOVA), depending on how many groups and independent variables are involved. A closely related approach involves assessing change scores, which means subtracting a person's score at the end from the score at the beginning.

QUASI-EXPERIMENTAL DESIGNS

You have already had some exposure to quasi-experiments in the last chapter. Now you will learn about some of the specific issues associated with this approach.

In a quasi-experiment, researchers typically compare groups to see if they differ in a behavior of interest. That is, does this group of people differ from that group? Quasi-experiments can provide valuable information about group differences, but such designs are not ideal for assessing cause and effect.

The researcher cannot randomly assign people to groups but can only assign participants to groups based on their characteristics.

Questions that researchers address with quasi-experiments could include whether women and men differ in their behavior, whether young and old people are alike, whether beagles and German shepherds respond differently to children, etc. As you can imagine, there are many interesting questions that we can address with quasi-experiments. The fact that unites these examples is that participants and subjects belong in a category (female or male, young or old, beagles or German shepherds), and nothing that the researcher does is going to permit them to be placed in a different category. What differentiates a true experiment from a quasi-experiment is that, in true experiments, the researcher randomly assigns a participant to a given group. These independent variables are thus measured rather than manipulated variables.

Causation and Quasi-Experimental Designs

Quasi-experiments based on measured variables are really correlational in nature, so they do not allow you to identify causation. So if you compare female and male participants with respect to the way they act, you cannot conclude that any differences are due to sex. The problem is that from birth onward, parents (and everybody else) treat female and male babies differently. Through childhood and adolescence, and into adulthood, women and men experience the world around them in countlessly different ways.

We have different stereotypical images of women and men. These stereotypes may reveal a degree of truth, but we cannot tell why the differences emerge.

It is important to remember that sex can be a causal variable. For instance, the adult height of men and women is partially a function of their sex. (Multiple factors will influence any complex development, though, so there is more to your adult height than whether you are a woman or a man.) We have to remember that even though an independent variable in a quasi-experiment might be a causal variable, we just don't have enough information to conclude that.

In order to say that A causes B, three conditions must exist: A has to precede B, they have to covary (i.e., B must occur when A does), and A must be the most plausible cause of B with other potential causes ruled out. In a quasi-experiment, a failure to satisfy the last condition, ruling out alternate explanations, is the source of the problem.

Unfortunately, in a quasi-experiment we don't know when we have excluded all of the relevant variables, so we can't be completely confident in our conclusions. In general, you should be very cautious about making causal statements with quasi-experiments, just as you should be cautious with any correlational approach.

Combining Experimental and Quasi-Experimental Designs

Researchers quite commonly use a mixture of true and quasi-experiments because there are many interesting questions that can only be addressed with such a combination. For instance, it appears that highly neurotic people are more likely to associate sex with death than are less neurotic people (Goldenberg et al., 1999).

If you wanted to study the effect of neuroticism on reactions to different independent variables, you would have to use a quasi-experimental design because you cannot assign people to a level of neuroticism. They bring it with them on their own. You

CONTROVERSY: Sex and Death

Psychologists have speculated on the link between sex and death (e.g., Becker, 1973). Although the connection may not be obvious, it surfaces at times. For instance, as Goldenberg et al. (1999) point out, one term for orgasm in French is *le petite mort* (the little death, p. 1175).

The issue that these psychologists have dealt with is that thinking about the physical act of sex reminds people of their mortality. The result, according to Terror Management Theory (TMT), is that people seek to control their fear of death by changing the way they think about sex, removing it from the realm of death. One way to do this is to adopt a new view of sex; if we can imbue it with value that extends beyond the physical, perhaps sex can be a more spiritual experience, not a death-related phenomenon.

Goldenberg et al. combined true and quasi-experimental variables to explore this question. They identified people who were high versus low in neuroticism, generating a quasi-experimental variable. The researchers then exposed these participants to questionnaires focused either on the sexual or the romantic aspects of sex, which was a true experimental manipulation. Thus, participants were either high or low in neuroticism and were primed either to the physical or to the romantic view of sex.

The researchers then gave the participants word stems (e.g., COFF__) and asked them to complete the word. The stems could be completed with death-related words (e.g., coffin) or non-death words (e.g., coffee).

Highly neurotic people were significantly more likely to complete the word stems with death-related words when they were exposed to the prime that focused on the physical aspects of sex; interestingly, these people were the least likely to generate death-related words when exposed to the romantic prime. You can see the interaction between level of neuroticism and type of prime in Figure 9.3.

In this mixture of a true and a quasi-experiment, Goldenberg et al. provide support for their hypothesis that for people who have anxieties toward both sex and death (i.e., highly neurotic people), thinking about the physical nature of sex makes them think of death. We need to remember that it is not necessarily the neuroticism that makes people link sex and death. Whatever has made them neurotic may have also made them link sex and death. The connection is predictable, but we don't know exactly why it occurs.

As Goldenberg et al. have shown, though, the neurotic individuals can break this link by directing their attention to the romantic rather than to the physical nature of sexual behavior.

Question for Discussion: Would there be any way to induce neuroticism experimentally? How could you justify it ethically?

FIGURE 9.3 The relation between neuroticism and type of sex prime. According to Terror Management Theory, thoughts of sex are often linked with thoughts of death. People who are highly neurotic are more likely to think of the two together than are those with lower levels of neuroticism. That is, death-related words are more accessible to highly neurotic people after thinking of sex. The link can be broken, though, if the highly neurotic people are primed to change their thoughts of sex from physical to romantic.

Source: J. L. Goldenberg et al. (1999). Death, sex, love, and neuroticism: Why is sex such a problem? *Journal of Personality and Social Psychology*, 77, 1173–1187. Copyright © 1999 American Psychology Association. Reprinted with permission.

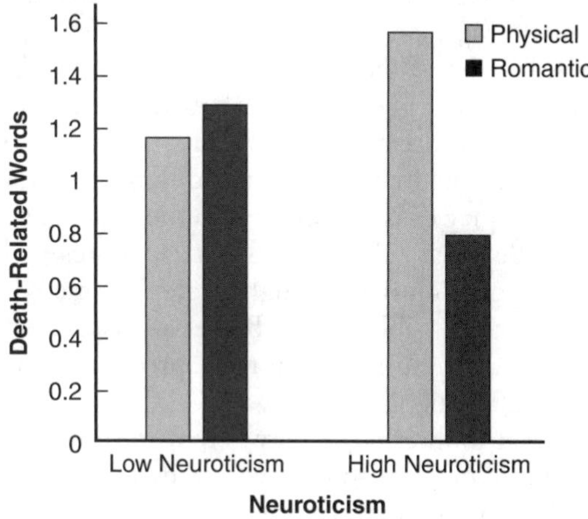

can manipulate other variables, though, and see how those variables affect people with different levels of neuroticism.

Goldenberg et al. discovered an interesting connection between a person's level of neuroticism and the individual's tendency to connect sex and death. To do so, they developed a mixture of true and quasi-experimental variables. You can see what happened regarding this sex, death, and neuroticism study in the Controversy on sex and death.

Threats to Internal Validity

The internal validity of a research project is critical to the level of confidence you have in your conclusions. The greater the internal validity, the more you can have faith that you know what factors cause an individual to act in a certain way.

The major threats to internal validity were initially elucidated by Campbell and Stanley (1966). Researchers now recognize that we have to take these potential problems very seriously. Such problems are common in applied research that takes place outside of the laboratory.

The reason that non-laboratory studies are more prone to these problems than other research is because we generally have less control over the research setting outside the lab. When we conduct theoretical or applied research in a laboratory, we can simplify

Selection threat—A threat to the internal validity of a study such that groups to be compared differ before being exposed to different experimental treatments, so any differences after treatment could be due to the initial differences rather than to the independent variable.

Maturation threat—A threat to the internal validity of a study due to short- or long-term changes in a participant because of psychological changes like boredom or fatigue, for example, or because of physical maturation.

Attrition (Mortality) threat—A threat to the internal validity of a study when participants drop out of a study, leading to a change in the nature of the sample.

the environment so that only a few easily identifiable differences exist between groups. If the groups then behave differently, we assume that a variable or a combination of variables that we manipulated had an effect.

If you create a study in a retail establishment, for instance, the company still wants to make money, so you have to work around the business that takes place. As such, you make compromises and conduct your study differently than if you could manipulate the situation to your liking.

Threats Associated with Participants. Several of the threats to internal validity pertain to the characteristics of the research sample. The first threat involves **selection**. Whenever we design a study that does not involve random assignment of participants to group, the selection threat may be a problem. This threat reflects the fact that if we compare two groups with predetermined characteristics, differences other than the independent variable may cause differences in the dependent variable.

For example, Bell et al. (2000) noted that a lot of research has found that women suffer sports injuries at a higher rate than men. Conclusions have been drawn about possible causes. Bell et al. discovered that initial fitness levels among Army inductees was more predictive of future injury than sex was, leading to causal ambiguity.

A second threat to internal validity is **maturation**. People change the way they act for a lot of reasons. If you study individuals over time, they may not be the same at the end as they were at the start. Their behavior with respect to your DV might change because of the changes in the participants, not because of your IV.

Maturation is more clearly a problem if you study children over time because they mature physically and psychologically in dramatic ways. But maturation can also come into play with adults. They may not change physically in obvious ways over a short period, but they can change psychologically. In this case, maturation does not only mean maturation of the kind from infancy to older childhood to adolescence; it means any physical or psychological changes, including fatigue, boredom, having learned about the study, for example.

A third threat, **attrition** (also called subject mortality), can affect your results. If you test people over time, some may not return for later tests. You can't be sure that the people who drop out are like the ones that remain when it comes to your DV. For instance, if you are studying the development of skill over time, the participants who are progressing slowly may drop out, leaving you only with those people who are competent. Any conclusions you draw about your research will thus be based on a sample consisting of more proficient people.

The issue is not attrition in and of itself. Rather, problems arise because of nonrandom attrition. That is, the participants in one group who drop out may exhibit different characteristics from those who remain, so groups may look like they differ because of the IV; in reality, they may differ because of the effect of those who left the study.

A fourth threat to validity is **history**. Events during the course of a study may affect one group and not another. Even if you started with randomly assigned groups,

History threat—A threat to the internal validity of a study that results when some event outside the research project affects participants systematically.

Instrumentation threat—A threat to the internal validity of a study that results from changes in the way the dependent variable is measured, due to factors like poor calibration of mechanical equipment or changes in the way researchers record subjective observations.

Testing threat—A threat to the internal validity of a study that results when participants' behavior changes as a function of having been tested previously.

Statistical regression threat—A threat to the internal validity of a study that results when participants are categorized or selected for research participation on the basis of an initial observation that involves significant measurement error that is not likely to repeat itself on later measurements, giving the false impression that change is due to a treatment when it is really due to the difference in measurement error.

this could happen. But if you are conducting a study with two different groups, like young people versus old people, one group may be affected by some event outside your research so their behaviors change. If you concluded that your IV is the reason for the differences across groups, you would be victimized by the history threat.

Threats Associated with Measurement. A fifth threat to internal validity is **instrumentation**. This means that there is a problem in the way you measure your dependent variable over time. If you asked different questions to a group in the initial and final research sessions, your data would not be comparable because changing the questions might lead your participants to interpret them differently. Another situation in which instrumentation could be a problem would be if you used two different people to collect data at the beginning and at the end of the project; the second set of data collectors might introduce changes in the research environment, leading to changes in the way participants respond.

The instrumentation threat could also come into play if you were measuring behaviors with mechanical instruments. Sometimes these instruments need calibration or readjustment; if you don't do that, two measurements that should be the same could be different because of the machinery you are using.

A sixth threat to internal validity is **testing**. Sometimes, initial testing of your participants can sensitize them to the reasons for your research. As a result, they may act differently because they know too much about the nature of your research question, and it biases their responses.

A seventh threat to internal validity is **statistical regression**. A researcher might want to compare good and poor students who are admitted to a special program. In order to make the groups seem equivalent, the researcher might take the poorest students from the higher level group and the best students from the lower level group. This would mean that the two groups would seem equivalent to begin with.

Unfortunately, the better students who score low in their group may really be typical students who, for no systematic reason, scored poorly. Similarly, the poorer students at the top of their group may not be all that different from their peers; they just scored higher, also for unknown reasons.

So, in later testing, these better students' scores are likely to be closer to the mean of their group then they were on the initial testing. The poorer students' scores also go back where they belong, toward the low end of the scale.

This means that the average scores of the two groups would quite likely be different on the retest even if there were no independent variable at all. This phenomenon is sometimes called regression to the mean.

When researchers attempt to match participants in nonequivalent groups, there is a high likelihood of statistical regression. Consequently, if you are not going to randomly assign matched pairs to the different treatment conditions, you probably should not use matching as a strategy to equate groups because statistical regression can obscure the effects of your treatment.

These threats to internal validity, which are summarized in Table 9.2, reduce our confidence in the conclusions we draw about our results.

TABLE 9.2 Major Threats to the Internal Validity of a Research Project

Threat	Description
Selection	When participants are not randomly assigned to conditions, groups to be compared may differ before the experimental treatment is applied. Any difference between groups may be due to initial differences, not the treatment.
Maturation	In the short term, people become fatigued or bored, or they may learn how to perform better with practice on a task, so behaviors may differ due to changes in psychological states. In the long term, people change physical and psychologically; such changes may affect behavior, not a treatment.
Mortality (Attrition)	When researchers monitor participants over time, some participants may leave a study. If people with certain characteristics drop out, there may be a biasing effect so that the remaining sample contains people who are very different from the original sample. Differences in behaviors may not be due to the research variables.
History	An event may occur outside the study during the course of a research project that leads to a change in behavior. If one group is differentially affected, it may appear that a treatment was responsible for the differences between groups when, in fact, it was a particular event that influenced one of the groups.
Instrumentation	If the way a researcher measures the DV varies over time due to changes in equipment or to changes in subjective judgments by the researcher, differences in measurements may have nothing to do with the research variables.
Testing	When people go through a research protocol multiple times, they may change their behaviors because they are sensitized to the testing situation itself.
Statistical regression	When people exhibit extreme scores on an initial test, one of the reasons for the extreme score may be random error. On a subsequent test, that random component of the score is no longer so prominent and the person's score regresses, that is, moves back toward the average of the group.

TYPES OF QUASI-EXPERIMENTAL DESIGNS

There are several quasi-experimental designs that psychologists regularly use. Some approaches resemble the typical experiment we have already discussed, with two or more groups being compared. Others depart from the typical model by incorporating measurements over a longer period of time than we generally see in an experiment.

Some researchers use quasi-experiments for laboratory studies, as we saw in the Goldenberg et al. (1999) study linking sex, neuroticism, and thoughts of death. But quasi-experiments are also frequently used in applied research outside the lab.

One-group pretest–posttest design—A quasi-experimental research design in which a single group is measured before a treatment is applied, then again afterward.

One-Group Pretest–Posttest Design

The simplest of the quasi-experimental designs is the **one-group pretest–posttest design**. As its name suggests, there is a single group of participants who are measured both before and after the application of a treatment. As you can see in the schematic outline below, it might be very easy to conduct this type of research.

Schematic Outline of a One-Group Pretest–Posttest Design

Single Group of Participants ⇒ Observation ⇒ Treatment ⇒ Observation

Commonly cited examples of this type of research include weight loss programs and test preparation courses. In theory, there would be no problem with this kind of design if we could determine that nothing of interest happens in people's lives between observations other than the treatment. In reality, a lot happens between the "before" and the "after." What transpires in a person's life, not the treatment, may very well affect the measurements taken at the second observation.

Although there is no selection threat to internal validity here because there is no comparison across groups, the second observation could be affected by history, maturation, testing, and instrumentation.

Let's consider a weight loss program. If researchers wanted to know if keeping a diary made a difference in weight loss, they could weigh a group of participants, ask them to keep a diary of food (and calories) consumed over eight weeks, then weigh them again after eight weeks. If the participants weighed significantly less at the end, it would be tempting to conclude that knowing how many calories you consumed made you more aware of your eating habits, so you cut down on your intake. Unfortunately, there could be a problem with history. If the research were done between mid-April and mid-June, the arrival of summer with its skimpy clothing might have motivated the people to lose weight; the diary may have been completely irrelevant.

This type of design is also prone to problems due to the threat of maturation. Between the start of the study and the final weigh-in, participants might become more motivated because they begin exercising and start to enjoy it.

The third threat in a one-group pretest–posttest design is testing. If an educator wanted to see if a test preparation course was effective in improving students' SAT scores, the researcher might see a gain in scores that was due to increases in familiarity with the test after taking it the first time. Sometimes the hardest part of a test is figuring out how to take it, not what the answers are. Continuing with the SAT example, if the students took a test at the end that just happened to be a little easier, they would score higher. The threat to internal validity here is called instrumentation, which means that changes in the measurement system are problematic.

We can also easily imagine the history threat. Perhaps students became more motivated by an inspiring teacher. The validity of the conclusions about test preparation courses based on such a situation may be suspect.

It's important to remember that these threats are quite possible, but we don't know if problems are really present or not.

Could you actually demonstrate that nothing important outside your study happened? You probably couldn't, but you might be able to make a convincing argument that history was unlikely. The same is true for the other threats to validity. They could affect your final observations, but you might be able to persuade others that they weren't likely. The best strategy, though, is to create a design in which these problems are minimized.

Static-Group Comparison Designs

A somewhat more useful design expands on the one-group pretest–posttest design by adding a second group. This type of design, called the **static-group comparison design,** can be useful because it allows the researcher to assess different groups. Still, there is a selection threat in this design. The selection of participants is not randomized, so you don't know if your groups differed from the start.

Static-group comparison design—A quasi-experimental research design in which two groups that differ on some pre-existing dimension (i.e., participants are not randomly assigned to conditions) are compared.

An example of a static-group comparison design comes from a study that assessed the validity of a new test of mental functioning for people with visual impairments (Beauvais, Woods, Delaney, & Fein, 2004). The researchers studied three groups, adults with (a) visual impairments and normal mental functioning, (b) visual impairment and neurological (i.e., mental) impairment, and (c) no impairment (the control group). When the investigators evaluated people in the three groups, the result showed that people with no impairment and with only visual impairment scored comparably on the test, which is what you would expect because people with visual problems perform cognitively just like anyone else. But those with neurological and visual impairment scored more poorly.

Beauvais et al. (2004) concluded that the test was valid for discriminating between people with neurological problems and those without, as they had predicted. The limitation here is that participants were not randomly assigned to groups, so characteristics other than neurological impairment may have affected the test scores. There is no particular reason to believe that variables other than neurological impairment affects participants' performances, but it is always a possibility. That possibility is always present with static-group comparison designs.

You can see the schematic outline of the static-group comparison design below. The outline shows two groups, but you could include additional groups, as Beauvais et al. did.

Schematic Outline of a Static-Group Comparison Design

Nonrandom Placement in Group 1 ⇒ (Treatment ⇒) Observation
Nonrandom Placement in Group 2 ⇒ (No Treatment ⇒) Observation

Nonequivalent Control Group Designs

One way to compensate for the selection threat, at least in part, would be to collect data before applying an experimental treatment as well as after it. If you did this, you would be using a pretest–posttest design.

Nonequivalent control group design—A quasi-experimental research design in which two groups that differ on some pre-existing dimension (i.e., participants are not randomly assigned to conditions) are measured on a pretest, exposed to a treatment, and measured on a posttest.

Baseline—A series of measurements recorded before a treatment is applied to see the normal course of behavior prior to an intervention.

When you measure nonrandomly assigned participants on your dependent variable at the beginning of the study, apply the treatment, then measure them again, you are using a **nonequivalent control group design**. As the label suggests, your treatment and control groups may differ in important ways; that is, they are nonequivalent, even at the beginning of your study. But if you obtain a **baseline** measurement of each group, you can see if they differ at the start.

Ochocka, Nelson, Janzen, and Trainor (2006) uses this design to study the effect of peer counseling and mentoring among people experiencing psychological problems. The researchers evaluated participants who actively sought mental health counseling in a community-based system that included mentoring by people who had used the mental health system previously, called a consumer/survivor initiative (CSI). At baseline, active users and nonusers were fairly similar. One group participated in the CSI, but the other group chose not to participate. After the participation, those who were active in the CSI showed better functioning and less stress. The investigators concluded that the CSI helped the people seeking treatment.

One limitation, though, is that the people in the two groups were different. After all, one group chose to participate and the other didn't; there must have been some reason for that difference. Maybe those who did not participate in the CSI were destined not to improve and their nonparticipation reflected that. Nonetheless, this nonequivalent control group design provides useful information about what might constitute an effective program. A schematic outline of this type of design appears below.

Schematic Outline of a Nonequivalent Control Group Design

Nonrandom Placement in Group 1 ⇒ Observation ⇒ Treatment ⇒ Observation
Nonrandom Placement in Group 2 ⇒ Observation ⇒ No Treatment ⇒ Observation

One of the reasons that the question of equivalence is so important is because when you measure people in existing categories over time, you don't know what change they would undergo over that period, even if you didn't apply a treatment.

If you look at Figures 9.4 and 9.5, you can see how you could be deceived regarding your results. In Figure 9.4, the results show that participants were measured twice.

FIGURE 9.4 Illustration of possible result with a nonequivalent control group design. The inequality at the start and the different rate of change for the two groups leads to problems with interpretation of the results.

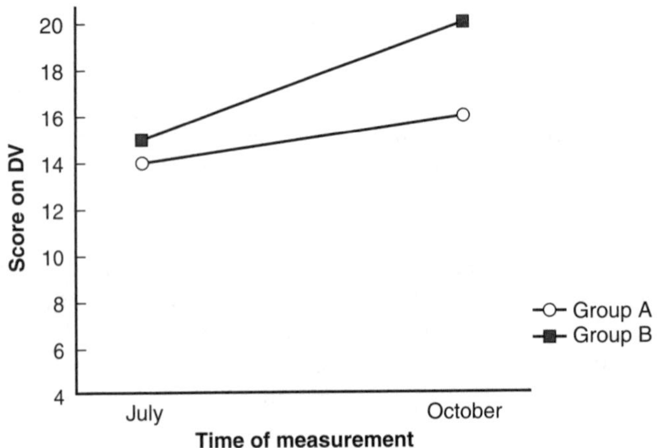

It appears that one group always scores higher than the other. However, if you had measured the participants earlier, you would have noted that the course of change of one group is markedly different from that of the other.

If this hypothetical study had included earlier measurements, a very different pattern of results would be apparent. Group A initially had higher scores that wouldn't be seen if only the last two measurements were made.

Interrupted Time Series Designs

In the one-group pretest–posttest design, one of the major problems is its simplicity. We measure participants only twice, but we don't know what has come before the first measurement nor what will follow the second one. We would be better off if we observed and measured the participants more than twice.

Interrupted time series design—A quasi-experimental research design in which a group is measured at different times, with a treatment applied at some point, resulting in baseline measurements and post-treatment measurements.

Simpson et al. (2006) used an **interrupted time series design** to study treatment for bulimia. They treated five women and one man who were experiencing eating disorders. Because of difficulties in the participants' abilities to travel to the therapist, each one experienced therapy via remote video sessions. The investigators assessed each participant multiple times prior to the start of the treatment, then again during the course of the therapy. Each person began treatment at a different point in time.

The researchers found that the intervention via videoconferencing was beneficial. The episodes of bulimic behavior diminished with the onset of treatment.

An interrupted time series design like the one used by Simpson et al. (2006) provides multiple measurements. It solves some of the problems of the pretest–posttest design. You can see a schematic outline of the interrupted time series design below.

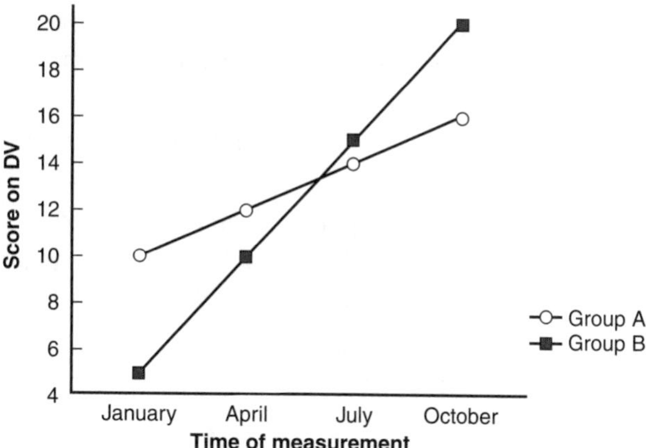

FIGURE 9.5 Illustration of possible pattern of results in a nonequivalent control group design. The final two measurements in this figure match those in Figure 9.3. If you only measured your participants in July and October (as in Figure 9.3), you would get a very different impression than if you assessed them in January and April as well. When you do not use random assignment of participants to groups, you cannot assume that they are equal to begin with; you also cannot assume that their patterns of change are going to be the same.

Schematic Outline of an Interrupted Time Series Design*

Group or Participants ⇒ Obs ⇒ Obs ⇒ Obs ⇒ Treatment ⇒ Obs ⇒ Obs ⇒ Obs

*Obs = Observation

In this example, we see three observations before the treatment and three afterward, although you could decide to use different numbers of observations before and after the treatment. This type of design reduces the threats of maturation and testing. It is unlikely that you would be so unlucky in your research as to test your participants so that the only maturation occurs exactly when your treatment is in place.

In addition, when participants become sensitized because of an initial exposure to the measurement process, they are likely to be affected right away. As a result, in the schematic example, we would probably conclude that by the time they were observed and measured three times, any sensitization would have occurred. Again, you could be very unlucky and the testing effect might take hold only after your third observation, but this possibility is also pretty remote. If you thought it might happen, you could insert more observations prior to applying the treatment. Designs like this are useful because they allow researchers to establish a baseline of behavior against which behaviors after the treatment can be compared.

The threat that still exists is history. So you might be unlucky, seeing the effect of history just when your treatment goes into effect; it would be hard to spot.

Replicated interrupted time series design—A quasi-experimental research design in which different groups are measured in an interrupted time series design, with a treatment being applied at a different time for each group.

Replicated Interrupted Time Series Designs

If you added a control group to an interrupted time series design, you would have a more complicated methodology, but it would be associated with fewer threats to internal validity. The **replicated interrupted time series design** provides a control group and reduces the chance that your results will be affected by history. The schematic outline below is an extension to the simpler interrupted time series design.

Schematic Outline of a Replicated Interrupted Time Series Design*

Group 1 ⇒ Obs ⇒ Obs ⇒ Obs ⇒ Treatment ⇒ Obs ⇒ Obs ⇒ Obs
Group 2 ⇒ Obs ⇒ Obs ⇒ Treatment ⇒ Obs ⇒ Obs ⇒ Obs ⇒ Obs
Control Group ⇒ Obs ⇒ Obs ⇒ Obs ⇒ No Treatment ⇒ Obs ⇒ Obs ⇒ Obs

*Obs = Observation

There are different replicated designs. One approach is to apply the treatment at different times to the two groups. This will overcome many of our concerns about the history threat because a single historic episode is unlikely to affect the two groups at two different times. The selection threat is also reduced because we are observing the same people over time and can see a stable pattern of behaviors that is interrupted by the treatment.

A second design involves applying a treatment to one group but not to a control group. Here also the history threat is reduced. The reason we don't have to worry about it so much is that, if one occurs, it should happen to both groups, so its effects should be obvious.

This replicated interrupted time series design is not perfect, but even if the groups are not randomly assigned, the results are often amenable to a tentative causal analysis. For example, Hennigan et al. (1982) addressed an issue more than two decades ago that originated with the beginning of television broadcasting and continues today: Does television affect behavior in negative ways?

Although most people today grew up with television, it has not always existed. In fact, for some of us, radio was initially the dominant mass medium during childhood. In the early years of commercial television in the late 1940s, it was established in a number of cities in the United States, then Congress imposed a freeze that restricted its expansion. Because of the freeze, television became widespread in homes in some cities while others remained out of broadcasting range. Hennigan et al. used the results of this freeze to create an interrupted time series design. They looked at larceny rates (i.e., theft that does not involve violence or force) in cities before and after 50 percent of the homes in those cities had televisions.

The researchers reasoned that if television crime shows influenced actual crime, cities with early television stations should have an increase in larceny while the cities without television shouldn't. On the other hand, when the freeze on new stations was lifted, the cities that then gained television stations should show an increase in larceny, but the initial cities would not.

Figure 9.6 shows the results of the study. Crime was inching upward in the absence of television, but you can see that from 1949 to 1950, when television was introduced

FIGURE 9.6 Introduction of television and incidence of larceny (cases per million population) in cities. Television became widespread by 1949 in the prefreeze cities; it was widespread in postfreeze cities around 1954. In each case, larceny increased following introduction of television (Hennigan et al., 1982). The arrows indicate the approximate time at which 50 percent of households in the two types of cities had televisions. Copyright American Psychological Association. Adapted with permission.

Source: K. M. Hennigan et al. (1982). Impact of the introduction of television on crime in the United States: Empirical findings and theoretical implications. *Journal of Personality and Social Psychology, 42,* 461–577. Copyright © 1982 American Psychological Association. Adapted with permission.

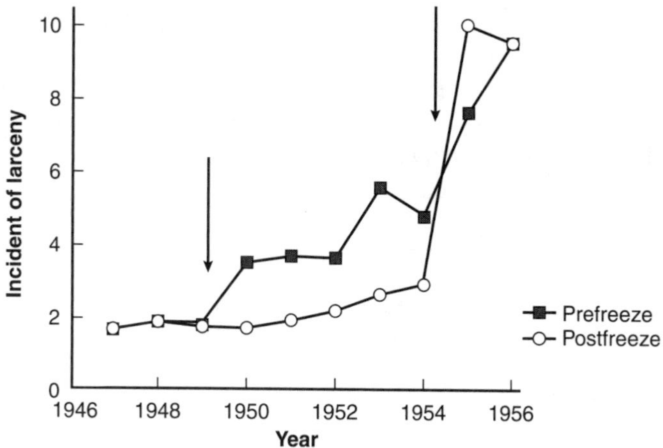

to the early cities, there was an increase in larceny in those cities. The areas without television did not show an upsurge. When the freeze set by Congress was lifted, the later cities showed an upsurge, whereas the initial cities did not. In 1946 and in 1956, the cities had comparable crime rates, which reassures us that the cities in the two conditions were roughly equivalent with respect to the DV of crime rate. They diverged when TV became prevalent in the different cities, then became similar again after they all had easy access to television.

Hennigan et al. concluded that television had a causal effect on the incidence of larceny. Television programs generally depicted middle- and upper-class individuals who owned desirable possessions. The investigators suggested that perhaps viewers were frustrated because their lives were more impoverished, so they pilfered items that they couldn't afford.

As you should recognize by now, though, this research was not experimental. The investigators did not randomly assign people to groups; rather, factors in everyday life that were beyond the control of the researchers determined a person's group.

One way to reduce the worries about the validity of the research findings is to use an experimental approach that will complement the nonexperimental research. Each approach will answer slightly different questions, but if the data point in the same direction, we will have convergent validity and can have faith in the overall validity of the research.

Since the Hennigan et al. study, the data have shown pretty clearly that exposure to violent media can increase aggressive tendencies. One such study involved participants who listened to music that either had or did not have violent lyrics (Anderson, Carnagey, & Eubanks, 2003). After hearing violent lyrics in an experiment, college students displayed higher levels of aggressive thought and more hostility compared to the students who heard nonviolent lyrics.

Researchers frequently use time-series designs for applied research where experiments are not practical or possible. It is typical to see these applications in studies of intervention programs, such as attempts to reduce the incidence of violence among adolescents at a runaway shelter (Nugent, Bruley, & Allen, 1998). This approach is also used in less traumatic circumstances, such as the effectiveness of psychological skills training in athletes (Brewer & Shillinglaw, 1992).

CONTROVERSY: Using Laws to Change Behavior

Legislators create laws to change behaviors or to punish the people who engage in them. Laws are enacted all the time, but seldom repealed. When laws outlive their usefulness, people simply tend to ignore them. We all know of laws that are not enforced vigorously.

For example, drinking by people under 21 in the United States is illegal, but it is so widespread that we can only conclude that, as a society, we are not overly concerned with it. The public service campaigns to restrict young people's drinking might have impact on some, but the drinking is still fairly widespread.

It might be illustrative to see if laws actually change what people do. Researchers have used time-series designs to find out. Levitt and Leventhal (1986) studied whether the New York State bottle return bill has reduced the amount of litter in New York. This bill mandated that consumers pay a five-cent deposit on beer and soda bottles and cans; the deposit is refunded when they return the container. Has it made a difference? This is an important question given that over a decade, if nothing were done to reduce litter, Americans could generate a billion tons; this litter would cost taxpayers a trillion dollars to clean up over the decade.

The researchers walked along highway entrance ramps and railroad tracks, counting the number of bottles and documenting the general level of litter. They chose sites in New York before and after the bottle bill passed and in New Jersey, which had no such law.

About a year after the bill became law, the researchers found that on the highway entrances there was significantly less litter in New York than in New Jersey for cans and bottles that were returnable in New York. The amount of nonreturnable litter (i.e., general garbage and trash) did not change. The picture was a little more complex on the railroad sites, but the law seemed to be effective as well. Thus, the bottle bill seemed to have changed behaviors; consumers didn't litter cans and bottles for which they paid a deposit. Unfortunately, other kinds of litter persisted.

On the west coast of the United States, a different set of researchers (Stolzenberg & D'Alessio,

1997) studied the effect of a very different California law using a time-series design. The California state legislature passed a "Three Strikes and You're Out" law; this law mandates extended prison terms for repeat criminals. In one well-publicized example, a California man who had previously committed a felony received a mandatory prison sentence of 25 years to life after being convicted of stealing a slice of pizza from a group of children.

Stolzenberg and D'Alessio looked at the crime index for felonies and for petty theft from 1985 to 1994, when the law was passed, then monitored the crime rate for another year. California officials claimed that the law was successful; the felony crime rate was lower after the law was passed.

The researchers discovered, however, that for a year or so prior to the law, the crime rate had begun to decline. They concluded that the continued decline after the law took effect only reflected a trend that had begun well before the law was in existence.

Stolzenberg and D'Alessio suggested that if other research supports their findings, it might be a good idea to repeal such "Three Strike" laws. For one thing, they are costly; it is expensive to incarcerate people. Another reason is that there may be other programs that actually will work for no greater cost. A third reason is that we may be wasting human talent and human lives by keeping people in prison for decades. The researchers are not proposing that criminals not be punished; they are saying that everybody in society will be better off when we have a logical criminal justice system.

This type of research can provide useful information for society. Well-designed investigations can tell us if we are making progress in dealing with societal issues and, if not, how we might be able to improve the situation.

Question for Discussion: How could you generate a quasi-experimental design to decrease cell phone use during driving?

SUMMARY

After reading this chapter, you should recognize the benefits of repeated measures designs. Psychologists rely on this approach because of its notable advantages. When you conduct research that involves repeated measures, you can have confidence that your groups are comparable from the start because each group has the same people. Thus, any differences that emerge are likely to be due to your treatments.

In addition, repeated measures designs are efficient, allowing researchers to double or triple (or more) the data they collect with minimal increases in costs. Further, if you are studying a relatively rare population, you can benefit by collecting all the data you can with your few participants. An added benefit is that your research design is more sensitive to small differences between groups. This means that if your treatment really has an effect, even if it is a small one, you are more likely to find a significant difference.

The drawback to repeated measures designs is that exposure to a treatment may have a long-lasting effect on the participant. In later observations, the person may be tired or bored, or the individual might perform better because he or she learned how to be more effective in the experimental task. These sequence effects can obscure a real difference or make a small difference look more important than it really is. Fortunately, there are ways to overcome these problems.

Another extension to the basic experimental design is the quasi-experiment. It is set up like an experiment, with different groups that are compared to see if they show the same behaviors. Quasi-experiments differ from true experiments in that quasi-experiments do not employ random assignment of participants to groups.

The participants differ on some characteristic to begin with, and it is this difference that leads them to be assigned to different groups. The problem here is that people in each group differ from the start, so if they differ at the end, your IV may have had an effect, but differences may have resulted from something other than your IV.

Researchers have devised quasi-experimental designs to overcome many of the problems that can affect the validity of the results. As we move from simple static-group comparison designs with one group to the replicated time-series design, we can gain confidence that the various threats to internal validity are unlikely.

With the sophistication of some of the quasi-experimental designs, we can begin to form tentative, causal conclusions. We should continue to show caution about deciding that our treatment actually causes some behavior, though, because quasi-experiments are really variants on correlational designs.

REVIEW QUESTIONS

Multiple Choice Questions

1. Another name for a repeated measures design is a
   a. within-subjects design.
   b. between-groups design.
   c. nonequivalent control group design.
   d. longitudinal design.
2. If you wanted to collect data from 50 participants and in each of three conditions, you wouldn't need to recruit 150 people if you used a
   a. nonequivalent control group design.
   b. replicated interrupted design.
   c. within-subjects design.
   d. between-subjects design.
3. If you are interested in studying how quickly people learn in early adulthood compared to old age, you would probably choose which design?
   a. Repeated measures design
   b. Between-groups design
   c. Interrupted time series design
   d. Partially counterbalanced design
4. Green and Vaid (1986) reported that when participants engage in two tasks at the same time, finger tapping and reading, it makes a difference if they start tapping with the left hand or the right hand. This is an example of a potential problem with
   a. order effects.
   b. counterbalancing effects.

c. sequence effects.
d. symmetric transfer effects.

5. When order effects occur in the same way regardless of whether the order is A-B or B-A, this is a case of
a. incomplete counterbalancing.
b. symmetric transfer.
c. selection effect.
d. latency effect.

6. Studies using a within subjects design can analyze data on differences in performance at the start and end of the session through
a. correlations.
b. descriptive statistics.
c. baseline analysis.
d. change scores.

7. Goldenberg et al. (1999) discovered that highly neurotic people tend to associate sex with death. When they compared high and low neurotic people, they were using
a. a time series design.
b. a quasi-experimental variable.
c. a within-subjects design.
d. asymmetric transfer.

8. Bell et al. (2000) found that people who are more physically fit suffer athletic injuries less often than people who are less fit. This threat to internal validity that keeps us from concluding that fitness is a causal variable is
a. selection.
b. maturation.
c. statistical regression.
d. history.

9. If research participants are assessed with a particular questionnaire early in a study, but the researchers change the questions for later assessment so participants can't simply repeat answers, what potential thread to internal validity would be at work here?
a. instrumentation.
b. testing.
c. selection.
d. history.

10. A study that looked at grades in a history class before and after students learned a memory technique would likely be a
a. static-group comparison design.
b. one-group pretest–posttest design.
c. nonequivalent control group design.
d. time series design.

11. If your research plan started with a static-group comparison design, then you added a pretest to the design, your new plan would involve a
    a. nonequivalent control group design.
    b. one-group pretest–posttest design.
    c. static-group comparison design.
    d. time series design.
12. If your research design involved collecting data on several different occasions before you applied your experimental treatment, followed by a series of additional measurements, you would be using
    a. a static-group comparison design.
    b. a one-group pretest–posttest design.
    c. an interrupted time series design.
    d. a nonequivalent control group design.

Essay Questions

13. Explain why repeated measures designs can be more useful than nonrepeated measures designs when participants provide subjective ratings. Why are objective measures less problematic in nonrepeated designs?
14. Why would counterbalancing help overcome problems of order effects?
15. What are the four threats to internal validity that are associated with participants?

ANSWERS TO REVIEW QUESTIONS

Multiple Choice Questions

1.	a	5.	b	9.	a
2.	c	6.	d	10.	b
3.	b	7.	b	11.	a
4.	c	8.	a	12.	c

Essay Questions

13. Explain why repeated measures designs can be more useful than nonrepeated measures designs when participants provide subjective ratings. Why are objective measures less problematic in nonrepeated designs?

    When participants engage in subjective ratings, as on a Likert-type scale, each person brings his or her own perspective to the judgment task. There is no guarantee that two different people will have the same subjective rating perspective. With objective measures, we rely less on personal perspectives and instead focus on more externally verifiable behaviors.

14. Why would counterbalancing help overcome problems of order effects?

    Counterbalancing helps overcome sequence and order effects by spreading the results of those effects across condition. Thus a participant who goes through condition A then B might perform differently in B because of the experience with A. Another participant who goes through B then A will have his or her performance affected in condition A rather than B. Thus, order effects will be spread out over the different conditions.

15. What are the four threats to internal validity that are associated with participants?
    a. Selection—people in the groups to be compared differ from one another at the outset of the study.
    b. Maturation—people change over the course of a study either physically or psychologically.
    c. Attrition (Mortality)—different types of people may leave a study before it is completed.
    d. History—events not specifically associated with the treatment may affect the outcome for one group.

CHAPTER TEN

PRINCIPLES OF SURVEY RESEARCH

CHAPTER OVERVIEW

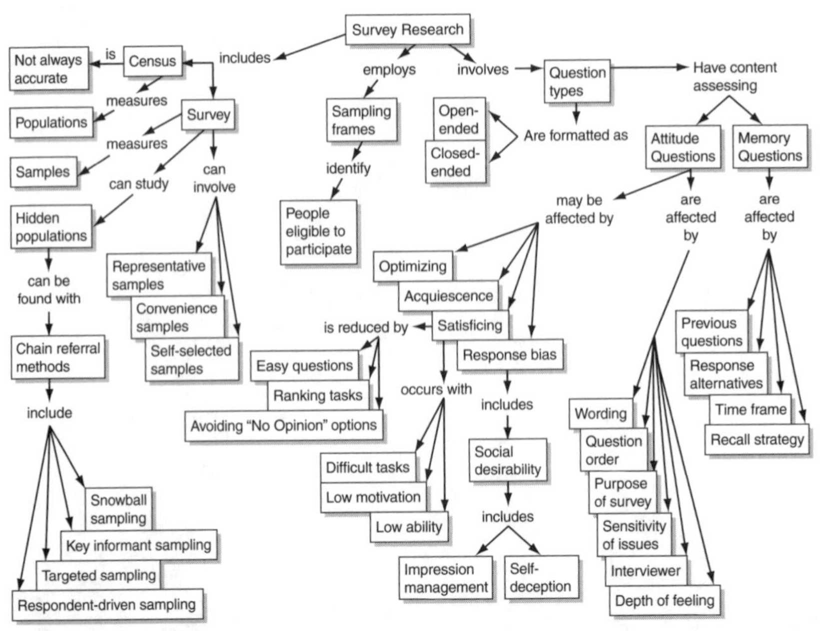

KEY TERMS

Acquiescence, p. 262
Census, p. 249
Chain-referral methods, p. 265
Chronically accessible information, p. 256
Closed-ended question, p. 252
Hidden population, p. 265
Impression management, p. 260
Key informant sampling, p. 266
Nondifferentiation, p. 264
Open-ended question, p. 252
Optimizing, p. 263
Population, p. 249
Respondent-driven sampling, p. 266
Response bias, p. 259
Sampling frame, p. 252
Satisficing, p. 263
Self-deception positivity, p. 260
Self-selected samples, p. 265
Snowball sampling, p. 265
Social desirability bias, p. 260
Survey, p. 248
Targeted sampling, p. 266
Telescoping, p. 255
Temporarily accessible information, p. 257

CHAPTER PREVIEW

Asking questions in survey research is an important aspect of research methodology. Surveys have become a fixture in modern life, with professional pollsters examining details of our lives and social scientists uncovering trends in attitudes and patterns of behavior. Most surveys rely on samples rather than on an exhaustive questioning of the entire population, which is a census.

Surveyors can choose from among different question types and content. The construction of the questions is probably the hardest part of a project because the form of a question influences responses, depending on the wording. In addition, respondents don't want to be seen in unfavorable light, so they may alter responses to make themselves look good and may tailor their answers to meet what they think are the expectations of the researcher. Fortunately, there are ways to avoid the obvious pitfalls in asking questions.

Finally, survey researchers prefer probability samples and are wary of self-selected convenience samples that do not represent the entire population. Researchers continue to develop new sampling strategies to overcome potential problems in current strategies.

SURVEYS: ANSWERING DIVERSE QUESTIONS

Beginning a little over half a century ago, investigators began developing the theory and techniques of survey research. Early in the 1900s, surveys took place that increased our information base on various topics, but by today's standards they were methodologically suspect. For instance, in 1936, the now defunct magazine *Literary Digest* inaccurately predicted that Franklin Roosevelt would lose the U.S. presidential election in a landslide. This may be the most famous error in the history of research. The problem was that the editors of that magazine used a sampling method that led to an unrepresentative picture of the voting population.

A little more than a decade later, a newspaper proclaimed that Thomas Dewey had defeated Harry Truman in the 1948 presidential election. The problem there was that in the forecasting, the newspaper also used a sampling technique that was prone to error in depicting the population as a whole.

Today's researchers can also make mistakes, as they did in the 2000 presidential election when they declared that Al Gore won the state of Florida. In spite of this recent major mistake, current survey techniques provide very useful information most of the time. After all, in the 2000 presidential election, the pollsters called 49 of the 50 states correctly.

The implication here is that using samples to understand populations can lead to mistakes because we are using incomplete information to draw conclusions, but if researchers use proper techniques, the number of misjudgments and the magnitude of error are small.

Survey—A research method in which an investigator asks questions of a respondent.

Surveys are one of the most widely used forms of research. When a company considers developing a new product, it hires survey marketing researchers to find out whether the product could compete in the marketplace. When politicians want to know what the voters think, surveys are the best way to find out. When social researchers want to know about behaviors and attitudes, they often design surveys.

Surveys Versus Junk Mail

Just as survey researchers want you to complete their questionnaires, retailers who send out junk mail disguised as scientific surveys want to capture your attention. And just as researchers have evaluated different strategies to increase response rates, marketers have also addressed that issue (Headden, 1997). It turns out that many of the same tactics that work for scientific surveys lead to greater responsiveness by consumers.

Researchers and junk mailers both try get your attention. Their goals differ, however. Researchers want information, junk mailers want your money. By considering the content and purposes of surveys, you may be able to spot those associated with research and those with money-making intent. As you can see in Table 10.1, research surveys tend to be personally directed and involve fewer gimmicks.

TABLE 10.1 Characteristics Differentiating Survey Research and Junk Mail That Simulates Survey Designs

Researchers	Junk Mailers
Letters addressed to a specific person	Letters addressed to a specific person after an individual responds to an initial, less personal mailing
Real signatures at the end of the letter	Fake handwritten notes and fake signatures
Monetary incentives	Gifts like decorative stamps or offers of free gifts
Sincere statements of appreciation	Appeals to fear, greed, guilt, and exclusivity; association with high-status individuals or organizations
Distinctive envelopes and surveys	Envelopes that appear to be from the government

Census Versus Sample

When researchers conduct survey research, they must decide whether to contact everybody in the population of interest or to sample a subset. Probably the most famous example of the former in the United States is the census. The Constitution of the United States mandates a decennial **census**, that is, a complete counting of everybody living in the country. The basic purpose of the census is to inform the Congress about how many people live in each state so there can be proportional representation in the House of Representatives. There are also other uses for the results, like figuring out where the population is growing so adequate highways can be built or where to build hospitals to meet the needs of an aging populace.

Census—Data collection that includes every member of a population of interest.

The 2000 census had a price tag of about $7 billion, or about $25 to count each person. Mailing a census form to every household in the country alone is an enormous expense; when people don't reply, a personal followup takes place, which is also expensive. We also know that many people are missed in the census, particularly people who have no fixed address, people from countries where they may have had an appropriate fear of the government, and others. In addition, some people are counted twice, like those who own multiple homes.

The census has never been completely accurate, beginning with the first one in 1790. Even with our increasing technical sophistication, the accuracy of the census is probably worse than it used to be. As you can see in the Controversy on the U.S. census, there are scientific ways to reduce the error, but they face political obstacles.

One difference between the Census Bureau and most other researchers is that, generally, researchers are content to survey a portion of the population, that is, a sample, rather than take a census.

Accuracy of Survey Results

On a national level, there are about 100 million potential voters in the United States. It would make no sense to try to ask each of them about their views; it would take too long and cost too much money. If you wanted to characterize 100 million possible voters with reasonable accuracy, how many would you have to sample? Typically, political polls sample about 1,000 people; ranging from 700 or 800 to perhaps 1,500. These numbers reflect about .001 percent of the voting population.

How accurate are these polls? After every election, the vote count provides a test. In the 2000 U.S. presidential election, the predictions in the final pre-election polls differed from the actual vote by an average of only about 1.1 percent (High accuracy found, 2001). The polls are not error-free, but they are pretty impressive.

You can get a pretty good picture of your population by sampling a relatively small number of people. As you increase your sample size, the accuracy of your information grows, but for a population as large as 100 million voters, once you reach a sample size of about 1,000, your accuracy doesn't grow very much for each new person you sample.

If the **population** from which you want to sample is relatively small, you might need a larger proportion in order to end up with accurate results, but the actual number will not be all that large.

Population—A set consisting of every person or data point that would be of interest to a researcher.

CONTROVERSY: The U.S. Census

It would be natural to think that if the government used a census to count everybody in the country, we would know how many people reside in our land. In truth, the census never achieves the ideal of counting everybody. In fact, in the first set of mail returns for the 2000 census, about 2 out of every 5 households failed to return the form, in spite of the fact that it is required by law. Consequently, the Census Bureau dispatched over half a million workers to follow up the nonresponses.

The incomplete count is nothing new. According to Anderson and Fienberg (2000), none of the 22 census counts done since the inception of the United States has actually found everybody, even with the current $7 billion price tag.

One of the most contentious debates about the 2000 census was whether the Bureau would be able to use statistical sampling to estimate the number of people who had not responded. According to every panel of statisticians commissioned by the National Research Council, statistical sampling would at least partially remedy the undercounts, even if some error remained in the count. Some statisticians did not favor statistical sampling, but they were in the minority.

As a group, Republicans opposed correcting the undercount with statistical sampling, whereas the Democrats favored it. The Supreme Court ruled that the sample data could not be used for apportionment of seats to the House of Representatives, but could be used for all other purposes.

Political considerations are nothing new in the census. In 1920, Congressional Republicans refused to recognize the results because potential changes in reapportionment would not favor them. As a result, they continued to use results of the 1910 census, even though it did not accurately represent the country. Finally, in 1929, Republican President Herbert Hoover resolved the impasse as he pressured members of his party to pass a census bill for the 1930 count. By doing this, Hoover averted a Constitutional crisis.

What all this means is that simply counting people in this country involves error. The statistical, scientifically based methods designed to eliminate some of the error are affected by social and political considerations. Once again, we see that scientific research is affected by the same factors as every other aspect of our lives.

Question for Discussion: Do we really need a complete census? Why don't we just use samples?

ETHICS IN SURVEY RESEARCH

All research carries the requirement of ethical behavior on the part of the investigator. With regard to survey research, we have to pay attention to two critical, related considerations—anonymity and confidentiality.

It is standard practice to completely guarantee both the anonymity and confidentiality of responses. This means that nobody who is not part of the research will have access to information about whether an individual participates or what his or her responses might have been.

If a researcher is tracking whether people have responded and wants to send a reminder to those who have not completed a survey, some kind of identification is necessary. In the rare event that an investigator needs to keep identification information over a long period of time, the data cannot be anonymous. There is nothing wrong with such procedures in and of themselves, although at the end of the project, the researcher should destroy any information that could link a respondent with participation in the study.

When researchers cannot guarantee anonymity, they can at least assure respondents that participation will be kept confidential. Confidentiality means that nobody will be able to connect a given person with their data. This is typically assured by reporting the data only in aggregate, that is, in a summarized form so that nobody can tell who responded in one way or another. For surveys that ask sensitive questions, you must provide such assurances because your respondents will either decline to respond or will not tell the whole truth.

Ironically, if you make a big point of assuring confidentiality and anonymity, it may arouse suspicions in those you survey (Singer, Von Thurn, & Miller, 1995). In a situation involving mundane questions, it might be more reasonable to play down the confidentiality and anonymity aspects because they may distract a participant from the real purpose of the study. If you are going to ask sensitive questions about behaviors that are otherwise disapproved of, you should make sure that the person knows about confidentiality and anonymity.

A further ethical constraint is that your respondents must know that they do not have to participate in your research and that they can terminate their responses at any time. This constitutes voluntary participation. If you stand over their shoulder or are even in their presence, you may be influencing a person's behavior; your respondent may feel compelled to enter answers because you are watching. You may also pay a price in the data. People may not respond honestly.

You can see in Table 10.2 the professional code of the Council for Marketing and Opinion Research. This code provides good guidance about ethical behavior in survey

TABLE 10.2 The Ethics Code Promulgated by the Council for Marketing and Opinion Research

What Are Your Rights If You Are Surveyed?

Your participation in a legitimate marketing or public opinion research survey is very important to us, and we value the information you provide. Therefore, our relationship will be one of respect and consideration, based on the following practices:

- Your privacy and the privacy of your answers will be respected and maintained.
- Your name, address, phone number, personal information, or individual responses won't be disclosed to anyone outside the research industry without your permission.
- You will always be told the name of the person contacting you, the research company's name, and nature of the survey.
- You will not be sold anything, or asked for money, under the guise of research.
- You will be contacted at reasonable times, but if the time is inconvenient, you may ask to be recontacted at a more convenient time.
- Your decision to participate in a study, answer specific questions, or discontinue your participation will be respected without question.
- You will be informed in advance if an interview is to be recorded and of the intended use of the recording.
- You are assured that the highest standards of professional conduct will be upheld in the collection and reporting of information you provide.

research. Naturally, you would want to follow APA's ethics code and state and federal laws as well.

SELECTING YOUR METHODOLOGY

Most research projects begin with a general question that needs an answer. After that, practical issues arise. In the case of surveys, the critical issues include identifying the sampling frame. The **sampling frame** is the entire list of people from which the sample is drawn. In psychological research, we seldom have a list of all possible respondents; in fact, we usually do not even have any way to detail the population of interest to us.

Sampling frame— A subset of a population from which a sample is actually selected.

Researchers who conduct surveys prefer to use probability samples, which you learned about in Chapter 5. There are several different methods of constructing a probability sample. If the process is done properly, researchers can be confident that the sample is likely to represent the entire population. With poorly created samples, the results will reflect the sample, but not necessarily any other group of people.

Researchers also spend considerable time developing the questions. Creating survey questions seems as if it should be easy but is probably the most difficult part of survey research and requires the greatest creativity and insight.

One important issue that has arisen in the past decade is the use of computers to collect self-report data. Switching from paper and pencil to a computer might seem like a minor issue, but there is no guarantee that people will respond the same way for both. Fortunately, at least for some measurements, respondents have shown comparable behavior (Vispoel, 2000). Any time you change methodologies, you don't know if the new and the old method will result in the same outcome until you research the question. Computerized data collection appears to lead to results that are as valid as those in traditional methods.

Throughout the entire process of survey research, the investigators must make a series of very practical decisions. The type of question you ask has to meet your needs, the way you word your questions should not distort the responses, and the format of your instrument has to promote people's willingness to complete the task.

One practical example of the difficulty in answering even a simple question involves the determination of how many adolescents in the United States smoke. A generally accepted answer based on survey research is about 4 million, but this number can be deceiving because the definition of "smoking" makes a big difference in the number that you accept as valid. The Controversy on adolescent smoking at the end of this section illustrates this problem.

Open-ended question— In survey research, a question that respondents answer using their own words, unconstrained by choices provided by the researcher.

Closed-ended question—In survey research, a question that contains a set of answers from which a respondent chooses.

Question Types

In terms of question and response structure, there are two main types of survey items: **open-ended questions**, which allow respondents to generate an answer without limitations regarding length or content, and **closed-ended questions**, which require respondents to select from a set of answers already provided. Each type has its own advantages and disadvantages. Table 10.3 shows how a researcher might develop different types of questions to investigate a topic.

If you attempted to answer an open-ended question about drinking alcohol, as illustrated in Table 10.3, you could discuss many different aspects of drinking behavior.

TABLE 10.3 Examples of Questions in Open- Versus Closed-Ended Formats That Relate to the Same General Topic, Alcohol Consumption

Open-Ended Question:

Describe the situations in which you consume alcoholic beverages and what you drink. (Note: You would only ask this question after you have established that the individual does consume alcohol.)

Closed-Ended Questions:

1. On how many days per week do you consume alcohol?
   - ☐ None
   - ☐ 1-2 times per week
   - ☐ 3-4 times per week
   - ☐ 5 or more times per week
2. When you drink alcoholic beverages, what do you drink most frequently?
   - ☐ I do not drink alcoholic beverages
   - ☐ Beer
   - ☐ Wine
   - ☐ Liquor (Gin, Vodka, Scotch, Bourbon)
3. Which of the following statements describes the most likely situation when you drink alcoholic beverages?
   - ☐ I do not drink alcoholic beverages
   - ☐ I am alone
   - ☐ I am with one other person
   - ☐ I am in a small group (2 to 5 people)
   - ☐ I am in a larger group (6 or more people)
4. Do you think it is easier, no different, or harder for teenagers to obtain alcohol compared to ten years ago?
   - ☐ Easier
   - ☐ No different
   - ☐ Harder
5. The minimum legal age for drinking alcoholic beverages in the United States is 21 years. Do you agree with the statement, "The minimum legal age for drinking should remain at 21 years"?
   - ☐ Strongly agree
   - ☐ Agree
   - ☐ Disagree
   - ☐ Strongly disagree
   - ☐ No opinion

You would determine what you thought was important and what was irrelevant, then respond accordingly. The advantage of such questions is that they provide a rich body of information. The disadvantage is that they can be harder to categorize, sort, and summarize because the responses can go in any direction the participant wants to take them.

On the other hand, researchers can use closed-ended questions. These items do not permit free responding. There is a set of responses from which to choose, such as *yes–no* or *strongly agree/somewhat agree/somewhat disagree/strongly disagree*. The information provided by such questions is not as rich as with open-ended questions, but they are much easier to score and summarize. Further, with closed-ended questions, the investigator can make sure that the respondent has the chance to answer questions of critical importance to the research project. For example, if the investigator wants to know whether teenagers drink alone or with others, the closed-ended question may provide that information from every respondent. Few people may address that issue in the open-ended question.

Although research has shown that both types of question format lead to answers of comparable validity, since the 1940s, researchers have preferred closed-ended questions because such a format lends itself to easier scoring.

However, recent evaluation of closed-ended questions has revealed some of their limitations. For instance, if people can choose from among answers prepared by the surveyor or can generate their own, they will often pick one of the surveyor's responses, even if they can provide their own, better answer (Krosnick, 1999). One reason is that people generally don't want to work any harder than they have to; it is easier to select a response that somebody else provides than to work to find your own. This phenomenon of selecting the first acceptable answer, even if it is not the best, is called satisficing.

Question Content

A key difference among questions involves what the researcher is trying to measure. In general, we can divide the purpose of the questions into three domains: measures of memory and behavior, measures of attitude and opinion, and demographics.

Memory Questions. Most of the time in our lives, when we converse with people, we assume that they are telling us the truth. This is usually a reasonable assumption. The same is probably true regarding answers on a questionnaire. At the same time, we all know that we don't always tell the whole truth, and sometimes we lie outright. This pattern is also true for responses to surveys.

People may not be lying when they misreport their behaviors. They may not know the answer to a question, but they give it their best guess (maybe a bad one), trying to be helpful. When you want people to tell you how often they have engaged in mundane behaviors that don't stand out in memory, they are prone to significant error (Rockwood, Sangster, & Dillman, 1997). For example, for many students, it would be difficult to answer precisely the question, "How often in the past two months have you eaten pizza?" The episodes individually do not stand out in memory because they are so normal. Thus, it may be difficult to come up with an accurate response.

Sometimes researchers ask respondents to answer questions that require the person to remember something. For instance, Kleck and Gertz (1995) wanted to know the extent to which people report having protected themselves with handguns against burglars. Their analysis revealed 2.5 million instances of such protection, implying that handguns in such situations exert a positive effect. Hemenway (1997) argued that the problem with Kleck and Gertz's data is that more people claim to have protected themselves with guns during burglaries than were actually burglarized.

Hemenway argued that whenever you ask a sample to remember relatively rare events of any kind, a small increase in false positives (i.e., saying something happened when it did not) leads to an inappropriately large estimate when you generalize to the population.

Hemenway's point about the reporting of rare events was reinforced by further research. Cook and Ludwig (1998) noted that reports of defensive gun use (DGU) in studies with relatively small samples suggest greater rates of DGU than are likely to be true. This doesn't mean that there is not significant defensive gun use, only that we may not know how often it occurs. Considering less controversial topics, Wentland and Smith (1993) noted that people have trouble with remembering if they have a library card.

We can identify four particularly troublesome problems associated with memory questions. First, people use different strategies to recall events from the recent past and distant past in some cases. When Winkielman, Knäuper, and Schwarz (1998) inquired of people how often they have been angry either in the last week versus in the last year, the respondents interpreted the meaning of the question differently. In the "last week" group, participants decided that the surveyor wanted a report of minor irritations, whereas the "last year" group focused on major irritations.

A second source of problems is that, when a question involves a time span (e.g., "How many times in the last year have you ..."), people may engage in a memory phenomenon called **telescoping**. When you look through a telescope, distant objects do not seem as far away as they really are; similarly, when people try to remember events from the past, things that happened a long time ago tend to be remembered as having happened more recently than they actually did.

Telescoping—A phenomenon of memory in which events that occurred in the distant past are remembered as having occurred more recently than they actually did.

A third difficulty is that the nature of previous questions affects the responses to later ones. People want to appear consistent in their responses, so they may use previous answers to help them form responses to new questions. Todorov (2000) discovered that people reported different levels of vision problems in a health survey depending on what questions had been asked just before a critical question.

A fourth concern involves the nature of alternatives presented in a closed-ended question. Schwarz (1999) and others have reported that the scale of alternatives can make a big difference in a person's response.

For example, Schwarz, Hippler, Deutsch, and Strack (1985) asked people how much daily television they watched. Respondents saw one of two scales for their response. One set of options provided response options in half-hour increments starting at zero (0 to .5, .5 to 1, 1.0 to 1.5, 1.5 to 2, 2 to 2.5, and 2.5 or more); this was the low-frequency condition. A different set of respondents saw options that began at 2.5

hours; that is, the lowest response category was 2.5 to 3 hours. This was the high-frequency condition. Over a third of those who answered using the high-frequency scale replied that they watched television more than two and a half hours a day. Less than half that number using the low-frequency scale reported such television watching.

Why would there be such a discrepancy? For the high-frequency television watching scale, respondents are likely to conclude that the surveyor is asking a reasonable question and that numbers in the middle of the scale are typical. Accordingly, if they think they watch a "normal" amount of television, their answers will gravitate toward the numbers that are in the middle of this scale, which are relatively high.

People responding to the low-frequency scale expressed a belief that the typical person watched 2.7 hours of television a day, whereas those responding on the high-frequency scale suggested that the typical person watched 3.2 hours.

Do the respondents watch a lot of television or not? To gain confidence in your data, you should rely on pretesting your questions, on your best judgment, and on the strategies that successful researchers before you have employed.

Table 10.4 provides some guidelines about asking questions when you want people to recall something. You will notice that some of the points seem to contradict one another. For example, one element says to ask for specific information and another says not to. When you are preparing survey questions, you need to make decisions about each question in the context in which it is asked. Sometimes you will want to ask specific questions, sometimes you will not.

Understanding the people you query and the behaviors you want to assess is critical to developing a useful survey. Pilot testing can help you decide if you have made good decisions. One noted expert once reported generating 41 different versions of a question before he arrived at one he considered "passable" (Payne, 1951, cited in Dillman, 2000).

Attitude Questions. People have attitudes on many different issues and they are often willing to share them. But asking about attitudes is difficult. There are seven major concerns that researchers have to ponder.

One prime concern with questions about attitudes, just as with memory questions, is the wording of the item. For example, emotionally laden terms can result in answers that are more likely to be responses to the wording than to the meaning of the question. For instance, a question that refers to sexual material as "hard-core pornography" is likely to elicit negative responses because of the attitude to the words, even if those words do not describe that sexual material very well.

Professional researchers are likely to be sensitive to the biasing factor of the words they use, but sometimes the effects are subtle. Rasinski (1989) pointed out that people voiced less support for "welfare" for the poor than they did for "assistance to the poor."

A second variable that can affect responses is the order of the questions. People feel one way when thinking about certain things, but they feel another way when thinking about other things. Memories and feelings about a topic that always surface when a respondent addresses some topic are **chronically accessible**. This means that respondents call some information to mind very readily; this information will affect their responses.

Chronically accessible information—Memories that are available for retrieval at any time.

TABLE 10.4 Elements for Constructing Survey Questions Involving Respondents' Memory

Guideline	Comment
Do not ask for details of mundane activities that are beyond a person's ability to remember (e.g., "How many people are usually in the library when you study there?").	Some people are better at remembering details than others are; asking for too much recall of detail may lead some groups to produce low-quality data based on faulty estimates.
If possible when you ask people how frequently they have engaged in a behavior, request the respondent to provide as specific a number as possible.	If you give respondents a series of alternatives to choose from, the scale you use will influence the answer to this question and possibly to others.
If you need to ask about specific periods of time, make sure that the respondent can accurately gauge behaviors in the time frame you specify.	People are better at the recent past than the distant past. Further, respondents are more accurate for behaviors they engage in on a regular schedule.
Avoid questions that have vague quantifiers (e.g., "rarely" or "sometimes"); instead, use more specific quantifiers (e.g., "twice a week").	Vague quantifiers like "frequently" differ depending on the person and on the event being judged. For example, "frequent headaches" means something different than "frequent brushing of teeth."
Avoid questions that require overspecific quantifiers (e.g., "How many times have you eaten at a restaurant in the past year?"); instead give ranges (e.g., "0-1 times," "2-3 times," etc.).	When people engage in commonplace activities on an irregular basis, precise estimates are little more than guesses.
Do not ask questions using words that might distract the respondent (e.g., offensive or inflammatory words).	Respondents may use negative or emotionally charged words as a cue to how often they should report a behavior, trying to avoid a negative evaluation of such behavior.

Temporarily accessible information—Memories that are available for retrieval only when cued by exposure to information that cues those memories.

Other memories and feelings might be **temporarily accessible**. This information also affects responses, but only if it has been recently brought into awareness, as by an earlier question on the survey.

Such accessibility may explain why, in nationwide polls, people generally claim that their own school systems are doing a good job, but that the nation's schools as a whole are not doing well (e.g., Satisfaction with local schools, 2005). When events in educational settings are especially troubling, news reports highlight the problem. So people compare their own schools with the negative reports and conclude that their own system is just fine.

A third feature that guides participants' responses is their perceptions of the purpose of the interview or questionnaire. In one study, participants completed a questionnaire that had printed on the top "Institute for Social Research," whereas others saw "Institute for Personality Research." The responses of the two groups differed, with the first group concentrating on social variables in their answers and the second group concentrating on personality issues (Norenzayan & Schwarz, 1999).

A fourth possible variable influencing the expression of attitudes is the sensitivity of the issue being investigated. People may be reluctant to admit to drunken driving, illegal drug use, some sexual behaviors, and other such issues. There are two likely sources of invalidity for analysis of responses to these items. One source is nonresponse. That is, people simply ignore the question. The problem is that if too many people fail to answer the item, you may have problems with the representativeness of the answers you actually get. A second likely source of invalidity is simple lying.

A fifth factor that may come into play in personal interviews is the nature of the person doing the questioning. For example, Finkel, Guterbok, and Borg (1991) discovered that White respondents were more likely to express support for a Black candidate when an interviewer was Black rather than White, even though the interview was over the telephone.

In considering a sixth possible source of problems with the quality of data, it is important to distinguish between attitudes and opinions that people already have, as opposed to attitudes that they create when a researcher asks them a question. Some people might not actually have an opinion on some topic until the surveyor asks them about it. They then construct one. Sometimes people even report attitudes on fictional topics.

People might foolish about saying they don't know about a topic. Another reason for making up an opinion is that respondents assume that the surveyor is asking a reasonable question, so they draw from their knowledge of apparently related topics and give an answer that would be consistent with their attitudes in general (Schwarz, 1999).

Researchers have discovered that when people have pre-existing attitudes, their response times to a question are shorter than when the respondent is creating an attitude to report (Powell & Fazio, 1984). Thus, if researchers are worried about differentiating between existing and newly created attitudes, keeping track of response times might be a useful strategy.

A seventh concern about obtaining high-quality data with attitudinal questions is that people may hold a positive or a negative attitude about some topic, but it is not always clear how deeply they hold that attitude. Thus, a lot of people may favor gun control laws, but they might not hold that conviction deeply enough to write a letter to their political representatives. There may be fewer people who oppose such laws, but they may be more committed to act on their beliefs. These seven concerns are summarized in Table 10.5.

RESPONSE BIAS

Surveyors have long known that people may hesitate to tell you the truth when they fear a negative reaction to their answers. This should come as no surprise; as social beings, we all consider how much to reveal to another person, whether we are talking to a friend or to a stranger. As long as people think that they are going to be evaluated, they will tailor their responses in a survey.

Sometimes respondents show certain patterns in their answers, regardless of the content of the question. One person may be likely to agree with questions most of the

TABLE 10.5 Seven Major Concerns About Surveys That Investigate Respondents' Attitudes

Concern	Reason for Concern
Wording of the question	Wording that predisposes a respondent to answer in a particular way (e.g., an item that is emotionally loaded) does not give valid information about an attitude because the person is responding on the basis of wording.
Order of the question	Early questions may prime a respondent to think about issues in a given way or may bring information into memory so that it affects responses to a later question.
Perceived purpose of the survey	Respondents may interpret the meaning of questions differently, depending on what they believe the is the underlying purpose of the survey.
Sensitivity of the issue being investigated	People may alter their responses or simply lie when asked about issues that might be embarrassing or otherwise make the respondent uncomfortable. Respondents may also omit answers to such questions.
The nature of the surveyor	People may respond more frankly to a researcher who is similar to them, particularly when the survey involves sensitive issues.
Respondents may not have pre-existing attitudes about a topic	Sometimes people are not aware of the issues being surveyed, so they don't have attitudes about them. They may make up their attitudes on the spot, sometimes on the basis of previous questions and their responses to them.
Surveys may not reveal the intensity with which a respondent holds an attitude	We can identify the extent of agreement with an issue, but we don't know the depth of feeling or commitment associated with that issue.

time; another person might be likely to disagree most of the time. When people engage in such patterns of behavior, they are showing **response bias**.

Response bias—A tendency for a respondent to answer in predictable ways, independent of the question content, such as always agreeing with a statement or always providing high or low ratings on a Likert scale.

Studying Sensitive Issues

Sometimes the best way to get information from people is simply to ask them. Surprisingly, many people are willing to give researchers reports of intimate details of their lives. In fact, some people are willing to do it on national television. However, professional researchers are more interested in good data than in good television drama. One approach is simply to guarantee anonymity to respondents. In many cases, this promise will suffice; naturally, it relies on trust between the researcher and the respondent.

Researchers have documented the fact that, in some cases, it does not make much of a difference whether people complete questionnaires anonymously. Clients at a substance abuse clinic responded to questions about their satisfaction and their motivation related to the treatment program. The clients generated the same patterns of response across three administrations of the same questionnaire; one administration was anonymous, whereas for the other two, the clients gave the survey directly to a therapist (Leonhard et al., 1997).

Are Telephone Surveys Appropriate for Sensitive Issues? Researchers are appropriately concerned that telephone interviews may not generate high-quality data. However, studies show that telephone surveys can be highly effective when done properly. Johnson and colleagues (2000) found that when respondents think that an interviewer is different from them, they are less forthcoming in reporting drug use in a telephone survey. A respondent talking to somebody of the same relative age, gender, race, and educational level may be more likely to report sensitive behaviors than when the interviewer is seen as different.

In a comparison of telephone and other survey techniques, McAuliffe et al. (1998) reported that researchers can get very high-quality data with telephone surveys, even when the topic involves an issue like substance abuse, and suggested that telephone surveys can be as useful as any other mode.

Social desirability bias—The tendency of respondents to answer questions in ways that generate a positive impression of themselves.

Social Desirability

In an attempt to look good (or to avoid looking bad), people do not always tell the truth. Researchers have written extensively about this problem, referred to as **social desirability bias**. It can take two forms. One is **impression management**, which involves active deception by respondents to keep the researcher from forming a negative impression of the them. A second component of social desirability bias is **self-deception positivity**, which occurs when people do not consciously give inappropriate responses but, rather, give a generally honest but overly positive self-report.

Impression management—A form of social desirability bias in which respondents actively deceive a researcher in order to generate a positive impression of themselves in the researcher's eyes.

Self-deception positivity—A form of social desirability bias in which respondents provide generally honest, but overly optimistic, information about themselves that generates a positive impression of them.

One domain that has received considerable attention regarding social desirability bias is self-concept and its relation to sex differences. The stereotypical belief is that women are more likely to excel in verbal and artistic areas, whereas men are more proficient in math and physical domains. In some research, female and male students report such differences in expertise on questionnaires even when performance is comparable across groups. The gender differences in beliefs seemed to occur because of impression management, the intentional form of social desirability bias, suggesting that differences in self-concept across sexes may occur because of a desire to report conformity to the stereotype (Vispoel & Forte Fast, 2000).

Researchers have found socially desirable responses to be problematic in a number of different domains, including marketing (King & Bruner, 2000), self-concept (Vispoel & Forte Fast, 2000), sexual behav-

CONTROVERSY: Adolescent Smoking

The U.S. government regularly conducts surveys on health-related matters. The National Household Survey on Drug Abuse specifically investigates the use of various legal and illegal drugs. Based on the results of such surveys, various prominent people (e.g., then-President Bill Clinton) have publicly stated that 4 million adolescents (aged 12–17) smoke (Kovar, 2000).

This figure may be alarming and, if true, signals potentially serious health issues. In order to figure out what to do about such apparently prevalent smoking behavior, we need to understand what the data really signify. What constitutes an "adolescent"? What do we mean when we say that a person is a "smoker"?

An adolescent is somebody from age 12 to 17. A 12-year-old is very different from a 17-year-old on many dimensions. As it turns out, very few 12-year-olds smoke, so to believe that 12-year-olds are being lured into smoking is not accurate. Most of the smoking occurs toward the top of the age range.

When it came to defining a smoker in the survey, anybody who had had even one puff within the past 30 days was considered a smoker. One puff on one day is very different from a pack-a-day smoker.

About 25 percent of the adolescent smokers were heavy smokers. The survey defined "heavy" as indicating that the person smoked 10 cigarettes a day or more for over 20 days in the past month.

Of the middle group of smokers (41 percent of adolescents), most used 1 to 5 cigarettes on the days when they smoked, and they smoked relatively infrequently. The results also revealed that 31 percent of the "smokers" had less than one cigarette when they did smoke.

What do these data tell us? The sad news is that the heavy smokers are probably already addicted in adolescence; many report smoking more than they really want to. The better news is that about 2 in 5 of these teen smokers have had less than half a pack of cigarettes in their entire lifetime and are unlikely to become addicted.

Knowing the complete picture, which means understanding the definitions used in the survey, will allow us to generate public health policies that do what we want them to.

Question for Discussion: Why does knowing the details of this research lead to more useful information?

ior (Meston, Heiman, Trapnell, & Paulhus, 1998), mathematics ability (Zettle & Houghton, 1998), attendance at religious services (Presser & Stinson, 1998), and personality reports (Francis & Jackson, 1998).

How can you deal with social desirability bias? Enlightening respondents about the existence of such response biases can help (Hong & Chiu, 1991). Another strategy is to create forced-choice questions so that respondents must select from among a number of equally attractive or unattractive choices (Ray, 1990). Another approach to reducing social desirability bias is to give both sides of an attitude in the question stem. Table 10.6 gives an example of how to present both sides of an issue in the question.

Finally, some researchers (e.g., Krosnick, 1999) believe that social desirability may not occur to the extent that other researchers claim. For instance, when people complete surveys on voting behavior, the percentage of respondents who report voting in the most recent election exceeds the proportion of the population that actually did. Researchers have interpreted this discrepancy to reflect social desirability bias by participants.

TABLE 10.6 Representing Both Sides of an Issue in a Potential Survey Question and How to Reduce the Likelihood of Response Bias to It

Poor Item: **To what extent to you agree that the Statistics course should be eliminated as a required course for a Psychology major?**

_____ Strongly agree
_____ Somewhat agree
_____ Somewhat disagree
_____ Strongly disagree

Problem: Only one side of the issue (i.e., eliminating Statistics) is represented. A respondent might think that the interviewer is stating his or her own opinion and might consequently give an "agree" reply, acquiescing with the interviewer.

Better Item: **Do you think that the Statistics course should be eliminated as part of the Psychology major or do you think that the Statistics course should be kept as part of the Psychology major?**

_____ Eliminate the Statistics course
_____ Keep the Statistics course
_____ No Opinion

Note: The "No Opinion" option should be at the end rather than between the other two options so that the respondent does not confuse it with a neutral response.

Newer research, however, suggests two alternate interpretations. First, people who vote are more likely to respond to surveys than those who don't vote. So the discrepancy in percentages who say they voted and who actually did may reflect a bias in the survey sample, not social desirability bias. A second interpretation is that people with a habit of voting and who did not vote in the most recent election may think (erroneously), "I always vote, so I must have voted in the most recent election." This type of response indicates a memory problem, not a social desirability bias.

Acquiescence

When somebody asks you, "How are you?" your tendency is probably to respond that you are fine. In general conversation, our tendency is to provide responses that are in line with others' expectations. As a rule, when people ask, "How are you?" they are really only extending a greeting. Most of the time, they don't expect (or even want) a litany of your woes.

A related dynamic can occur with surveys. Sometimes it is just easier to respond "yes" or to agree with a question. So that's what respondents may do, engaging in **acquiescence**, the tendency to agree with the assertion of a question, regardless of what it is. When the same question appears in two forms on a survey (e.g., "I enjoy socializing" and "I don't enjoy socializing"), respondents often agree with both, even though the people are directly contradicting themselves (Krosnick, 1999).

Acquiescence—In survey research, the tendency to agree with the assertion of a question, regardless of its content.

Krosnick (1999) described several explanations for people's tendency to acquiesce. One reason has to do with personality characteristics. Some people's personalities simply predispose them to want to agree with an assertion. Another explanation is that respondents often view surveyors as having higher status, so they feel compelled to agree with an assertion that the surveyor presents because we are "supposed to" agree with our superiors. Acquiescence can also be explained through the concept of satisficing, which we encounter below.

Satisficing Versus Optimizing

Suppose you are taking a test and you encounter a difficult question. You might spend a few moments trying to conjure up the answer and as soon as you identify a possibility, you go for that answer without considering other possibilities. If you have ever done this, you have engaged in **satisficing**, which means that you adopted the first acceptable answer, even if it wasn't the best answer.

Satisficing—The tendency of respondents to be satisfied with the first acceptable response to a question or on a task, even if it is not the best response.

Optimizing—The tendency of respondents to search for the best response to a question.

This tactic occurs regularly when people answer survey questions. Respondents often decide to reply with the first thing that sounds plausible to them or with an easy answer. Obviously, what works for the respondent can be a problem for the researcher.

According to Krosnick (1999), satisficing is likely to occur for any of three general reasons: (a) high task difficulty, (b) lower respondent ability, and (c) low respondent motivation. **Optimizing** is the complement to satisficing. When a respondent optimizes, the person works to generate the best possible answer.

Why would a survey question pose difficulties? Understanding a question and responding to it is actually a complex process. First, respondents must work to understand the point of the question.

Second, respondents have to search through memory to find relevant information. We know that the context in which a question is asked affects a person's response. Regarding surveys, it may be hard for somebody to remember events being probed in the context of the research setting because those events are neither chronically nor temporarily accessible.

A third task required of a respondent for generating good answers to survey questions is organizing everything that has been recalled.

Finally, in order to generate a high-quality response to a question, a person must choose from among the alternatives presented on a questionnaire. When people listen to an interviewer give a series of alternatives, there can be a tendency to select the later alternatives because they are easier to remember. When a questionnaire is on paper, there is a tendency for a respondent to pay more attention to the first alternatives (Krosnick, 1999).

If a person's cognitive processes fail at any step in this chain of events, a respondent will provide lower-quality information.

A related factor that leads to satisficing is the participant's level of ability. Researchers have discovered that respondents with lower ability levels tend to satisfice because they are unable to generate high-quality responses. Further, after the participant has answered a few questions, the motivation to respond may decrease. You may have participated in a psychology experiment either as a requirement for a course or for extra credit. Many students in such situations are in a hurry to complete this activity, so they are often less motivated to spend time on a response or to think deeply about a question. Many people have the same experience, engaging in satisficing as a result.

Minimizing the Occurrence of Satisficing

There will probably always be tension between the desires of the respondent and the needs of the researcher. If you conduct survey research, you will want to encourage people to optimize. How can you do this?

One way to minimize the possibility of satisficing is to create survey questions that are easily understood. In addition, when you ask people to remember events, it may help to ask several related questions so the information is more accessible. People may generate more accurate responses when the surveyor encourages them to remember events related to or close in time to the critical event, rendering obscure memories temporarily accessible.

Another path to reducing the incidence of satisficing is for the researcher to consider using ranking a group of items rather than rating them individually. Asking respondents to use a rating scale may lead them to identify a point on the scale and generally to respond with that value (e.g., giving a rating of 3 on a scale of 1 to 5) on virtually every item. This way of responding is called **nondifferentiation** because people fail to provide different responses across questions.

Nondifferentiation—The tendency of respondents to give the same answer to questions, regardless of content.

Some researchers have suggested that you can reduce the probability of acquiescence and satisficing by not giving respondents a "No Opinion" option (O'Muircheartaigh, Krosnick, & Helic, 2000). The logic is that if you want participants to think about their responses and give high-quality answers, you should not allow them to say "No Opinion." Other investigators have suggested just the opposite, that allowing a "No Opinion" option leads to more valid data (Krosnick et al., 2002).

As you can see, it isn't clear whether it is a good idea to give people a choice to say they have no opinion or are neutral about an issue. Sometimes people really are neutral, but sometimes they take the "No Opinion" option as an opportunity not to think about an issue. The research against including the "No Opinion" option indicates that people may use that option inappropriately when they are low in cognitive skills and motivation (Krosnick et al., 2002); that is, they may be satisficing.

Finally, if you can keep your respondents motivated, such as by establishing a positive atmosphere and by making sure they know that their answers are important, you may be able to decrease satisficing.

SAMPLING ISSUES

Most psychological research involves students, groups of people who are easily available, which is why this approach involves what is called a convenience sample, as you learned in Chapter 5.

Self-selected samples—In survey research, a nonrandom, biased sampling technique in which people choose to participate in the research rather than being selected by the investigator.

Hidden population—Population of interest that is hard to study because the people in that group are engaged in activities that may be embarrassing or illegal (e.g., drug users), so they do not want to be recognized as members of that population.

Chain-referral methods—A set of sampling techniques that relies on people who know about a population or are members of a that population to gain access to information about the group.

Snowball sampling—A chain-referral sampling technique in which one person from a population of interest identifies another person from that population to a researcher who contacts that second person, then that new individual refers yet another person, for as many stages as desired by the researcher.

However, there are also drawbacks with this approach. If you are interested in claiming that your research results are typical of people, you have to make sure that the people you study are typical of people in general.

Popular surveys rely on **self-selected samples**. These are groups of people who volunteer to participate without having been contacted by the researchers. They may see a notice on the Internet, for example, and decide it would be interesting to participate. Or they may be willing to call a 900-number, which costs them money, in order to express their opinion. Or they may respond to a talk show host. The types of people who engage in this responding are different from the population as a whole. In fact, professional researchers regard such polls as entirely nonscientific, therefore useless in telling us what the population thinks about a topic. Some investigators refer to such polls by the derogatory acronym SLOP (i.e., SeLf-Selected Opinion Poll; Horvitz et al., 1995).

Finding Hidden Populations

In survey research, some groups of people are difficult to study because they don't want to be found. Such groups are referred to as **hidden populations**. Two characteristics typify hidden populations: First, it is impossible to establish who constitutes the population and, second, there are strong privacy issues associated with the groups (Heckathorn, 1997).

If we want to find out about such groups, we can't use probability samples because probability samples require that we be able to identify the entire pool of possible respondents. So researchers have to make compromises in collecting data. Researchers studying hidden populations have turned to a class of techniques called **chain-referral methods**.

One chain-referral method for contacting respondents involves **snowball sampling**, which relies on the fact that an individual from a hidden population is likely to know others from that group. The volunteer identifies a certain number of people that the researcher will contact; the researcher will then ask each of these second-stage individuals to provide the names of yet others. The process continues through as many stages as the researchers determine desirable. Kaplan, Korf, and Sterk (1987) studied heroin use among addicts in the Netherlands. They identified a single user and asked for names of others who fit their target categories, either prostitutes or foreigners. These referrals then identified others, and so on.

Snowball samples often contain more cooperative volunteers who have a large social network. They are a variation on convenience samples, so it is not always clear to whom the researchers can generalize their findings.

Key informant sampling—A sampling technique that relies on getting information from people who know about a population of interest rather than from members of that population themselves.

A second approach to contacting respondents from hidden populations is to use **key informant sampling**. This technique relies on information from knowledgeable individuals rather than from members of the target population itself.

For example, a researcher might contact social workers to get information about patterns of sexual behavior in the population the social workers serves. Key informant sampling may reduce the respondent's reluctance to report unusual behaviors, but it may introduce the biases of that individual and is based on the limited number of people the social worker sees.

Targeted sampling—A sampling technique that relies on finding locations that attract members of the population of interest and getting information from these people at such locations.

A third approach is **targeted sampling**. With this technique, researchers work in advance to identify their population as well as possible, then to find out the different places that attract the widest range of people from that population. The results will only be as good as the researcher's knowledge of where to find members of the target population.

Respondent-driven sampling—A sampling technique in which a researcher uses a member of the population of interest to actively recruit others, often with some incentive like money for engaging in this recruiting.

Recently, Heckathorn (1997) has developed a new approach called **respondent-driven sampling**. In this approach, researchers use two types of incentives to attract participants. Primary incentives are offered to individuals; one such incentive may be money. The difference between this technique and other chain-referral methods involves the presence of secondary reward for getting others to join. When a participant identifies a potential candidate for the research, that participant uses peer pressure and social approval to induce a new person to join the project. That is, the researcher doesn't actively recruit the next person; that task is performed by the first participant.

Your choice of which chain-referral methods to use depends on the practical issues involved in your particular study. If the population is very closed, you may need to use respondent-driven samples, as Heckathorn did with the heroin users he studied. On the other hand, if the population is only somewhat hidden, snowball sampling might be adequate. For example, Frank and Snijders (1994) were able to use snowball sampling in their study of heroin use in the Netherlands because heroin use is more open there.

SUMMARY

Professional surveyors and pollsters have developed techniques that allow researchers to use small samples to make accurate predictions and descriptions of a larger population. As a result, the more economic practice of sampling typically means that researchers don't need a census.

The most common technique in scientific survey research is the telephone survey. For most questions, people who are available by phone adequately represent the entire population. Researchers who use probability sampling can generate a good picture of the population with a relatively small set of responses.

Researchers also have to painstakingly create survey questions that lead to valid responses. This is often the most difficult part of conducting good survey research. Whether you are asking for attitudes or for people to remember past behaviors, subtle differences in the way questions are worded and presented can make a notable difference in the responses that a person makes.

Sometimes different respondents interpret the same question in different ways. They may also show response biases that will either make them look better or make it easier for them to complete a questionnaire without really thinking about the issues at hand. Researchers must work hard to overcome these tendencies on the part of respondents.

Finally, some populations don't want to be found, like those involved in criminal activity or other undesirable or embarrassing behaviors. Investigators have developed techniques designed to make contact with these hidden populations. The samples may not be probability samples, but they often provide useful information.

REVIEW QUESTIONS

Multiple Choice Questions

1. Psychologists typically do not use a census in their research because
   a. a census often leads to telescoping of responses.
   b. census responses often result in nondifferentiation.
   c. respondent-driven sampling leads to better generalization.
   d. a census is generally too costly.
2. Researchers have greatest confidence in being able to generalize the results of research based on
   a. sampling frames.
   b. surveys.
   c. probability samples.
   d. randomly selected questions.
3. On the U.S. census that everybody has to complete, people identify their racial/ethnic status by selecting from among options provided on the form. This type of a question is
   a. a closed-ended question.
   b. almost always responded to accurately.
   c. part of the sampling frame.
   d. used because respondents are from a self-selected sample.
4. Researchers may avoid open-ended items on questionnaires because such items
   a. are not very scientific.
   b. permit too limited a range of responses.
   c. can result in responses that are difficult to code and categorize.
   d. generally provide details about behaviors but not the context in which they occur.
5. One of the difficulties surveying people about rare events is that
   a. those events are likely to involve sensitive issues that people are reluctant to discuss.

b. a small increase in the rate of false positives leads to a very large, inaccurate estimate when generalized to the population.
c. people have very different attitudes about rare events, so accurate responses are to get.
d. people are likely to show high levels of acquiescence about such items.

6. By the time a person is near the end of a questionnaire, the responses
   a. have probably shifted from optimizing to acquiescence.
   b. will no longer show telescoping.
   c. will be affected by how the respondent answered earlier questions.
   d. will show high levels of self-deception positivity.
7. When people are able to retrieve information from memory only after being primed by an earlier question on the topic, we say that the memory is
   a. targeted.
   b. nondifferentiated.
   c. temporarily accessible.
   d. respondent driven.
8. When respondents make up an attitude on the spot while answering a question,
   a. the researcher can find out by asking the respondent to answer the question again.
   b. the respondents respond more quickly when they have a pre-existing attitude.
   c. they usually claim to hold that attitude firmly and deeply.
   d. they may engage in impression management tactics.
9. Sometimes, respondents engage in active deception to keep the researcher from forming a negative image of the respondent. This behavior is called
   a. self-deception positivity.
   b. impression management.
   c. acquiescence.
   d. satisficing.
10. Research has revealed that we can reduce social desirability bias by
    a. telling respondents that we will be able to detect false responses on their part.
    b. avoiding forced choice responses and creating open-ended questions instead.
    c. educating respondents about social desirability bias.
    d. presenting only one side of an issue in a given question so respondents cannot focus on only the positive response.
11. When a person responds the same way to just about every item on a rating scale, this respondent is engaging in
    a. nondifferentiation.
    b. telescoping.
    c. acquiescence.
    d. satisficing.
12. It could be useful to know about illegal immigrants and how they live, but such people are reluctant to participate in anything they think might be associated with the government. These immigrants constitute a
    a. sampling frame.
    b. chronically inaccessible, self-selected sample.

   c. hidden population.
   d. a nondifferentiated sample.

13. Researchers sometimes use a member of a hidden population to provide names of other members of that population to recruit participants in research. The resulting sample would involve
   a. chain-referral method.
   b. sampling frame.
   c. probability sample.
   d. self-selected sampling.
14. When researchers try to contact members of hidden populations by finding out where such people congregate, the sampling technique they are using is
   a. key informant sampling.
   b. snowball sampling.
   c. targeted sampling.
   d. probability sampling.

Essay Questions

15. Why do open-ended questions provide more information to survey researchers than closed-ended questions? What drawbacks are associated with open-ended questions?

16. Identify the seven major problems associated with survey questions about attitudes.

17. Why does the research on how many adolescents smoke reflect the difficulty in creating good survey research?

18. What two characteristics typify hidden populations?

ANSWERS TO REVIEW QUESTIONS

Multiple Choice Questions

1.	d	6.	c	11.	a
2.	c	7.	c	12.	c
3.	a	8.	b	13.	a
4.	c	9.	b	14.	c
5.	b	10.	c		

Essay Questions

15. Why do open-ended questions provide more information to survey researchers than closed-ended questions? What drawbacks are associated with open-ended questions?

    Open-ended questions allow a respondent to provide the best answer to a question, whereas closed-ended questions force the respondent to choose from a selected set. The open-ended questions may lead to answers that the researcher doesn't anticipate, which could be positive, leading to more valid answers; such answers could be problematic, though, because they are hard to code and summarize when respondents take very different paths to their answers.

16. Identify the seven major problems associated with survey questions about attitudes.
    a. The wording of a question can lead a respondent in a particular direction, especially with emotionally sensitive topics.
    b. Previous questions have an effect on what kind of information people have in mind when they respond to a later item.
    c. The respondents' beliefs about what the interview is supposed to be about will lead them to tailor their responses so as to be more helpful to the surveyor.
    d. The sensitivity of an issue is critical to whether and how people respond.
    e. The characteristics of the person doing the interview can be important; respondents are more forthcoming with people who are similar to them.
    f. It is hard to distinguish between attitudes that have an attitude already held from those that the respondent has just made up.
    g. It is hard to differentiate between attitudes that are deeply and shallowly held.

17. Why does the research on how many adolescents smoke reflect the difficulty in creating good survey research?

    The research on adolescent smoking is difficult because adolescence spans the ages of 12 to 17 years. The younger adolescents are different in physical, psychological, and others ways from the older ones. The younger adolescents were quite unlikely to smoke anything at all. So categorizing all adolescents together may distort the results.

    In addition, the definition of what it means to smoke is hard. If an adolescent had had even a puff of a cigarette, it was considered smoking and would be categorized (for some data analysis) the same way as a pack-a-day smoker. Most of the infrequent smokers had less than one cigarette when they smoked.

    Depending on how you define adolescents and how you categorize them and depending on how you define smoking can lead to different pictures of who smokes and how much.

18. What two characteristics typify hidden populations?
    a. It is impossible to establish exactly who constitutes the population.
    b. There are privacy issues associated with the population.

CHAPTER ELEVEN

CORRELATIONAL RESEARCH

CHAPTER OVERVIEW

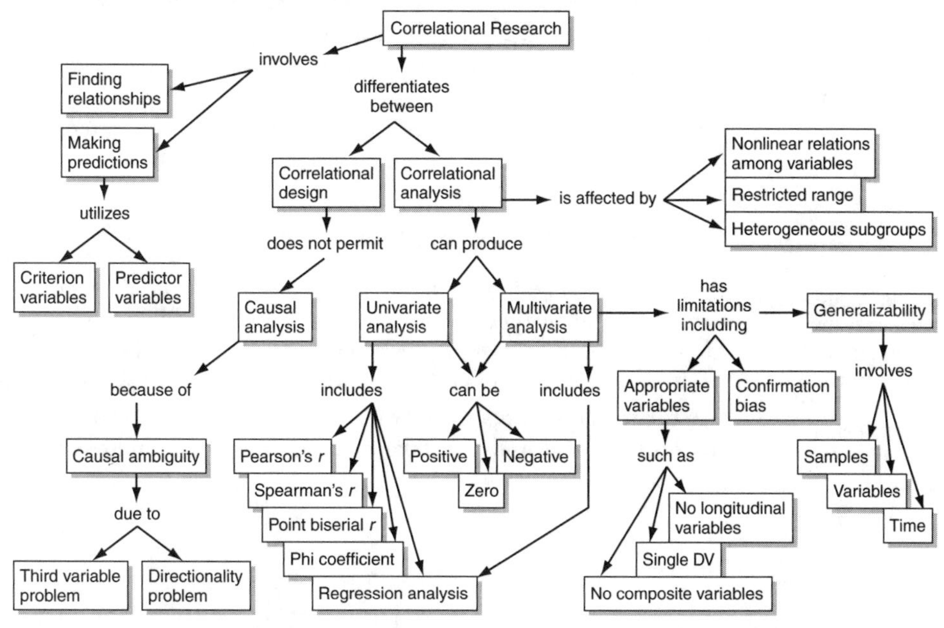

KEY TERMS

Bivariate correlation, p. 286
Correlational analysis, p. 275
Correlational study, p. 275
Criterion variable, p. 274
Directionality problem, p. 275
Heterogeneous subgroup problem, p. 280
Higher-order correlation, p. 287
Linear relationship, p. 280
Multiple regression, p. 288
Negative (indirect) correlation, p. 277
Nonlinear relationship, p. 280
Pearson product–moment correlation, p. 280
Positive (direct) correlation, p. 277
Prediction study, p. 274
Predictor variable, p. 274
Restricted range problem, p. 280
Scatter diagram, p. 277
Third variable problem, p. 275
Zero-order correlation, p. 287

CHAPTER PREVIEW

Psychologists use correlational studies to investigate the relationships among variables when there is a lot of complexity in the behavior and when experimental approaches are not feasible. Correlational studies permit us to find relationships and to make accurate predictions about behavior.

There are different correlational approaches. The simplest involves bivariate relationships between two variables. Researchers typically employ the standard, well-known Pearson product–moment correlation in such circumstances, although we also use several other correlational tests associated with it.

When we want to see how variables interconnect, we rely on more complex approaches. Multivariate tests, which involve at least three variables, allow us to see a more complex picture of behavior. Some of the newer multivariate correlational approaches actually move us in the direction of making tentative statements about causation.

These varied approaches are useful, but we must use them appropriately for arriving at helpful descriptions of behavior. Many of the multivariate models of behavior are quite complex, so it is important to know how to use them and to be able to identify their limitations.

In this chapter, you will encounter the critical aspects of different correlational approaches so you can understand how we employ them in research.

CORRELATIONAL STUDIES

Correlational study—An approach to research that involves measuring different variables to see whether there is a predictable relationship among the variables.

Psychologists, like most scientists, search for causes. We want to know why people act as they do, although this can be an elusive goal. In some cases, we are not able to identify what variables affect behavior directly, but we can find patterns and relationships that make behavior predictable. **Correlational studies** tell us which variables and behaviors are related. In a correlational study, we take what nature gives us and see how things interconnect.

Finding Relationships

Many students don't like to take classes that meet early in the morning. Many professors only like to meet early in the morning. This unfortunate mix of preferences suggests that either students or professors will not be working at their best times.

Is there any reason to believe that students' peak performance is related to their preferred times? Guthrie, Ash, and Bendapudi (1995) have verified that there is a relationship between students' tendencies toward morningness and their overall semester grade point average (GPA). This is an example of correlational research in a relationship study, a project that aims to determine whether two variables are related to one another.

In the Guthrie et al. study, we can see that there is a relationship between morningness and class performance. The correlation is based on students' preferences for morning activities and their performance in classes. When students are not morning people, they tend to earn lower grades in classes that begin at 8:00 or 8:30 A.M. The overall relationship between students' morningness scores and their GPAs is not very strong but it is reliable. This weak relation means that even night owls can perform adequately in the morning, even if it isn't their preference.

Let's briefly go over the concept of correlations. We can make predictions about students' grades based on multiple variables: the amount of time they study, the percentage of time they go to class, the amount of time required for family activities, how many hours a week they work, how much partying they do, and on and on indefinitely. These variables might be associated with better or worse grades. Hypothetically, if we knew about all possible sources associated with grades, we could identify the relation each one had with grades. Each variable would provide some amount of information. Ultimately, we could predict grades perfectly, accounting for 100 percent of the difference among students.

How did Guthrie et al. discover this relationship? They conducted a relationship study in which they looked at the associations among variables like GPA, when students tended to study, and other factors. They assessed morningness by means of a simple 13-item scale devised by Smith, Reilly, and Midkiff (1989). Then they computed the correlation coefficients among variables.

This kind of relationship study is useful for preliminary investigations in which a researcher does not yet know if variables are related to one another. There are two important points to remember when considering relationship studies. The first is that your variables have to have construct validity. That is, they have to relate meaningfully to what you are measuring. In the case of the morningness study, you would need to have a good measure of morningness. Guthrie et al. used a scale validated by other researchers.

The second thing to remember is that if you compute correlation coefficients on a lot of different variables, you will get some significant relationships that are meaningless. Five percent of the time, variables with no relationship will appear significant. So if you are going to compute multiple correlations, you should remember that some of them will be significant when they don't mean anything.

In general, it is not a wise idea to compute correlations just to compute them; you should look for associations between variables when you expect there to be a relation, not just throw variables together and see what happens.

Making Predictions

Prediction study—A correlational study in which the goal is to predict the value of one variable given the level of another variable, with the predictor variable often occurring before the criterion variable rather than simultaneously.

Criterion variable—In a prediction study, the variable that an investigator is trying to predict.

Predictor variable—In a prediction study, the variable that an investigator is using to predict another variable.

When you find relationships between variables, sometimes you can go a step further and make predictions regarding the variables and behaviors of interest to you. Colleges and universities do this each year when they decide which students to accept. A project designed to predict some outcome variable in correlational research is called a **prediction study**.

Many variables may help predict student success in college, including SAT scores and high school grades. In prediction studies, the outcome that interests us is the **criterion variable**, which we want to predict. The variable that we use to make the prediction is called the **predictor variable**. As such, SAT scores are one of the predictor variables that colleges use, while first-year GPA is the criterion variable. SAT scores are moderately correlated to first-year GPA. About 25 percent of the difference from one person to the next is predictable on the basis of GPA. This is not too bad when you consider all the factors related to student achievement in college.

The remaining 75 percent of the difference across students might be predictable based on as-yet unknown factors. Thus, when applicants complain that others with lower SAT scores have been admitted to a college and that they haven't, it is appropriate to keep in perspective that variables other than SAT scores predict more of the variability among students than the standardized test does.

Further, grades are not the only way to measure achievement; growth in ability to engage in critical thinking and to synthesize and communicate complex information, tendencies to engage in civic activities that strengthen the community, awareness of the implications of scientific and political issues in our lives, and so on are also critical components of education that are not always reflected in grades.

If making such predictions were easy, admissions officers would have little difficulty deciding which students to admit. And the outcome would be that each student who enrolled would succeed, whereas each student who did not gain admission would not have succeeded. This is far from the truth. SAT scores may be one predictor of future performance, but an imperfect and incomplete predictor.

USING THE CORRELATIONAL APPROACH

It is important to distinguish between correlational studies and correlational analyses. A correlational study relies on making measurements without controlling or trying to manipulate variables. The purpose is to identify connections among variables.

On the other hand, **correlational analysis** is an approach to extracting information from a data set; it doesn't necessarily tell you anything about whether the study is experimental or correlational in design.

Correlational analysis—A statistical approach used in research that uses any of a variety of correlational tests, regardless of whether the research is a correlational study.

Correlational Studies

A correlational study involves the investigation of factors that might be connected to one another. For instance, two variables that are related are the amount of time you study for a test and your grade on that test. A researcher studying the two might be able to guess your test score reasonably well given knowledge of how long you studied. Still, the relationship is associative, not necessarily causal. Students who are very interested in a class may study a long time and may earn a high score on a test. It might ultimately be their interest in the material that leads to better scores, not simply their study time.

Third variable problem—In correlational studies, the problem in assessing cause and effect due to the fact that when two variables are correlated, an outside (or third) variable is responsible for any causation.

When you perform a correlational study, you can logically conclude that variables are associated, but not that one causes another. Keep in mind that there may really be a causal connection; the problem is that correlational studies don't give you enough information to let you know. There may be a third factor that is really the cause; psychologists refer to this as the **third variable problem**.

Directionality problem—In correlational studies, the problem in assessing cause and effect when two variables are correlated when a researcher does not know which of two variables has a causal effect on the other.

Another problem with assessing causation with correlational data is that you don't know which way the causation proceeds. This problem is one of **directionality**. Logically, in a correlational analysis A could cause B or B could cause A. Consider the morningness scale (Guthrie et al., 1995). It could be that students do well in early classes because they are morning people, as indicated on their responses to the scale. On the other hand, they might conclude that they are morning people because they do well in early classes.

It is important not to fall for an apparent cause–effect relationship that is not valid. One area of research that has been prone to criticism that causal relationships are not real is whether watching violence on television leads to violent behavior. Seeing violence could lead to violence. However, you could argue that people prone to violence like to watch violence on television. There is a real possibility of a problem with directionality.

In the Controversy on the media and violence, you will see the current scientific status of the argument. A great many media researchers have concluded that there is a causal relationship here: Media violence leads to violent behavior.

Correlational Analysis

Correlational analyses are not the same as correlational studies. A correlational analysis uses correlations as a statistical approach, but if the research design is experimental, we can draw causal conclusions. This is easy to grasp by considering a hypothetical two-group study. If we create two groups, randomly assign participants to them to generate equivalent groups, and apply a treatment to only one of the two groups, we have a basic experiment. If the two groups differ at the end, we assume the treatment made the difference.

The normal approach to data analysis with such a design is to compute a *t*-test, which lets us know if two groups differ reliably. However, we could legitimately compute a correlation coefficient. It would tell us exactly what the *t*-test does. If you look at Figure 11.1, you can see how comparable the two tests are.

It is important to remember that the research design, not the statistical test, determines the type of conclusion you can draw. If you employ a correlational study, no matter what statistical test you compute, it does not allow you to assess causation; similarly, if you use an experimental approach, doing a correlational analysis does not keep you from drawing causal conclusions.

Suppose you have two groups with 10 participants in each. Let's label them simply Group 1 and Group 2. If you compute a *t*-test for independent groups, you get:
$t(18) = -3.55, p = .002$

Group 1	6	8	7	5	6	9	7	4	8	9
Group 2	5	6	3	7	2	3	1	5	4	5

You can rearrange the data, as follows, showing each score next to its appropriate group:

6	8	7	5	6	9	7	4	8	9	5	6	3	7	2	3	1	5	4	5
1	1	1	1	1	1	1	1	1	1	2	2	2	2	2	2	2	2	2	2

Now we can compute the familiar Pearson product–moment correlation coefficient on the two variables, Group and Score. (When one variable is ordinal, interval, or ratio, and the second variable is dichotomous [i.e., it can take one of two values], the Pearson *r* is called a point-biserial correlation.) When we do this, we get: $r\,(18) = -.642, p = .002$. The next step in a correlational analysis is to see if the correlation is significant, for which we use a *t*-test with the following formula:

$$t = \frac{r\sqrt{N-2}}{\sqrt{1-r^2}}$$

$$t - \frac{(-.642)(4.243)}{.767} = -3.55$$

If you notice, the value of *t* here is the same as when you completed your *t*-test. The analyses from the correlational and experimental approaches provide the same information.

FIGURE 11.1 llustration of how correlational and experimental analyses lead to the same conclusions.

Positive and Negative Correlations

Correlations can be either positive (direct) or negative (indirect) or nonexistent. Perfect positive correlations have a value of +1.00; perfect negative correlations, –1.00. Sometimes correlations are so close to zero that we conclude that two variables have no bearing on one another. For instance, Lang and Heckhausen (2001) discovered that life satisfaction and age are not correlated. The value of their correlation coefficient was .05. This value is so close to zero that, among their participants who ranged in age from 20 to around 70, knowing their age doesn't help you predict how satisfied they are with their lives. (This may surprise students who are 20, but it won't surprise students who are 40 or older.)

Positive (direct) correlation—A relation between two variables such that when the value of one variable increases, so does the value of the second variable, and when the value of one variable decreases, so does the value of the second.

Negative (indirect) correlation—A relation between variables such that when the value of one variable increases, the value of the second variable decreases and vice versa.

A **positive or direct correlation** implies that when the value of one of the two variables being correlated gets larger, so does the other. According to another analysis by Lang and Heckhausen (2001), perceived control over life is positively correlated with life satisfaction. This means that, in general, the more control people felt in their lives, the more satisfied they were.

A **negative or indirect correlation** arises when the value of one of the two variables being correlated gets larger, the value of the other variable gets smaller. Lang and Heckhausen observed a negative correlation between the number of negative events in people's lives (like losing something or having a small accident) and their perception of control. When people experience many negative events, they are likely to feel lower levels of control.

Strength of Association

The strength of the association between variables is reflected in the absolute value of the correlation coefficient. Consequently, coefficients of –.50 and +.50 reflect equally strong correlations. Further, a correlation of –.80 reveals a stronger association than does a correlation of +.50 because the absolute value of this negative correlation is .80, which is larger than .50.

You can change a negative correlation into a positive correlation simply by changing the scale on which you measure one of the variables. Returning to the example of the relation between the amount of time you spend studying for a test and your score on the test, we would expect a positive correlation. You could create a negative correlation by changing one variable to the number wrong on the test instead of the number right. The absolute value of the correlation coefficients would be the same, but the sign would change. You would have the same predictability associated with each one. In Figure 11.2, you can see graphically what happens.

Scatter diagram—A graphical representation showing the relationship between two quantitative variables, with one variable represented on the horizontal (X) axis and the other on the vertical (Y) axis.

If you create a **scatter diagram** to represent the relation between two variables, as the correlation coefficient approaches 1.0 or to –1.0, the points in the graph appear to form a straight line. As the correlation heads

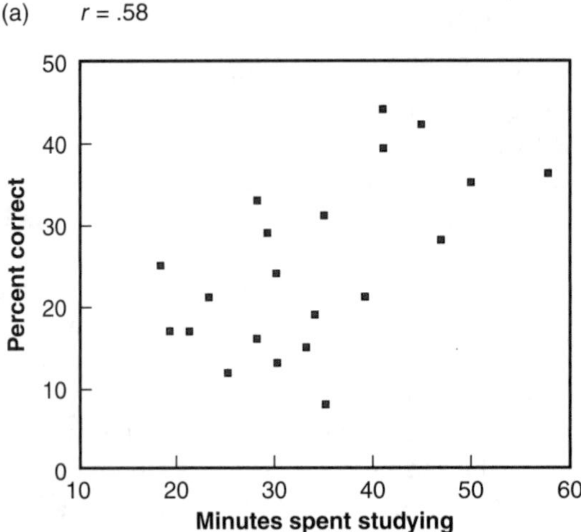

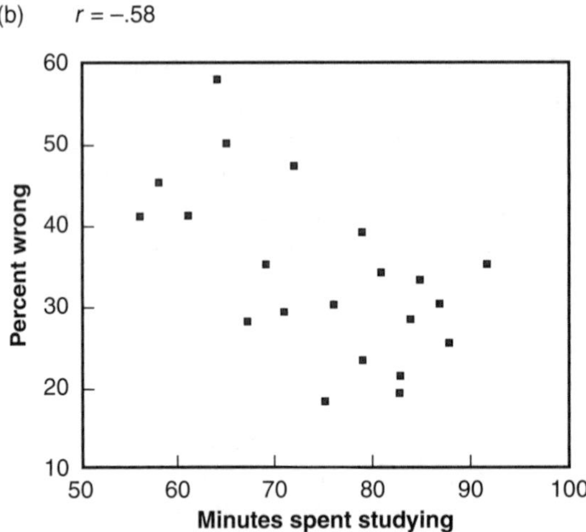

FIGURE 11.2 Hypothetical example illustrating how a single data set can lead to a negative or to a positive correlation, depending on how the variable is defined: (a) shows that more studying is associated with a higher number correct, (b) shows that more studying is associated with fewer errors. Both correlations are legitimate and provide the same information. The only change is in the way information is labeled on the Y-axis. In both cases, the strength of the correlation is the same.

toward zero, the pattern becomes rounder until, when r = 0, the display of data points is nearly circular, reflecting poor predictability. These relationships are demonstrated in Figure 11.3. When r is close to 1.0 or –1.0, the value of Y is clearly predictable from the value of X.

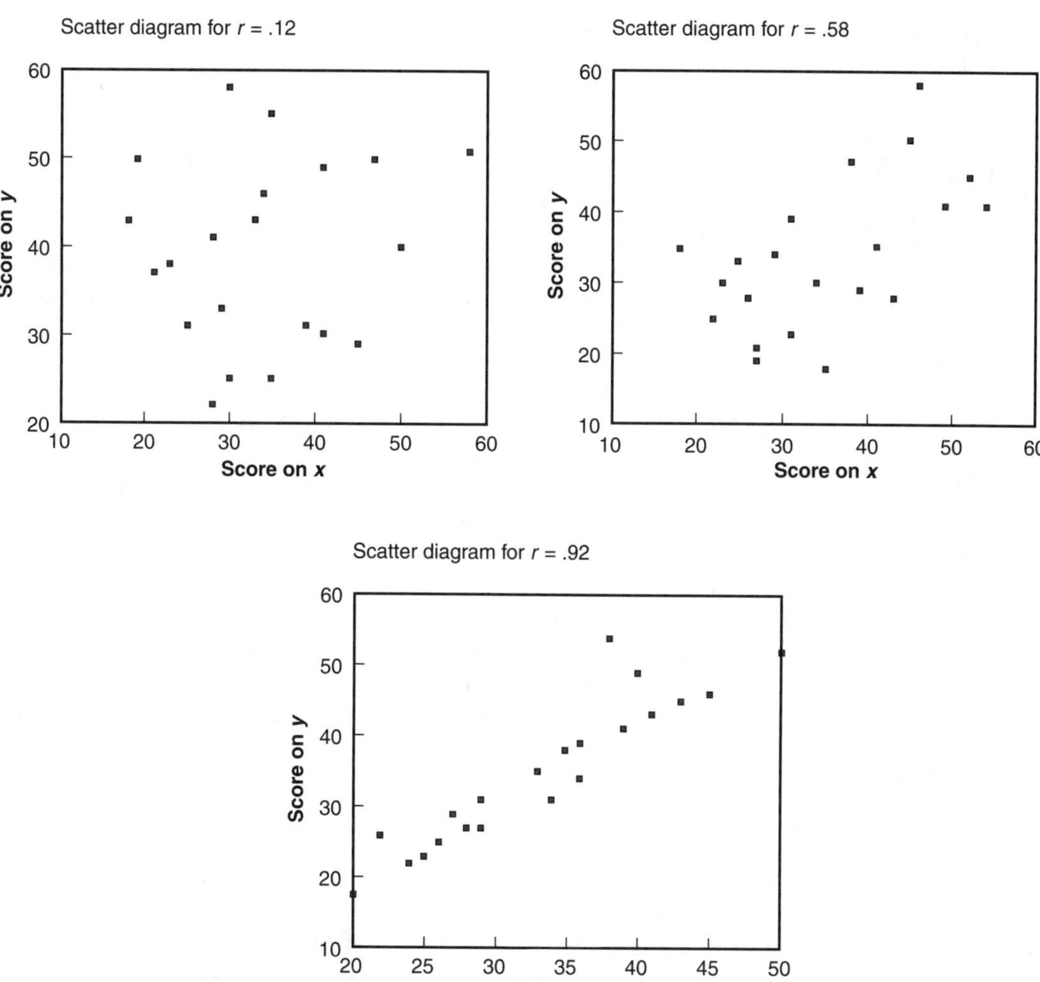

FIGURE 11.3 Scatter diagrams for different values of the Pearson product–moment correlation coefficient. Notice that with higher correlations, the scores tend to resemble a straight line where Y values rise predictably with X values. When the correlation decreases, the scores tend to become more scattershot and Y scores no longer change as predictably with X values. As the correlation coefficient approaches zero, meaningful predictability vanishes.

Factors Affecting the Size of a Correlation Coefficient

We use correlation coefficients to see if two variables are associated. Sometimes the correlational tests we typically use can lead us to believe that variables are unrelated. One problem is that our sample might turn out not to represent the entire population. When that happens, we are pretty much out of luck. We may have collected data flawlessly, but

Linear relationship—A relationship between two variables that can be represented graphically as a straight line, with the increase in value of one unit on the first variable being systematically associated with a constant increase or decrease on the second variable.

Nonlinear relationship—A relationship between two variables that can be represented graphically as a curved line, reflecting the fact that a change in value of one unit on the first variable is associated with different amounts of change on the second variable, depending on the value of the first.

Pearson product–moment correlation—A bivariate, correlational measure that indicates the degree to which two quantitative variables are related.

Restricted range problem—In a correlational analysis, the failure to spot a real relationship between variables because the range of scores on at least one of the variables obscures that relationship.

if the sample is not representative, there is nothing we can do about it, and we may never know about it. All we see is a lack of a relationship without knowing why.

However, there are other, more predictable reasons why two variables are correlated in reality, but a statistical analysis doesn't reveal it.

Nonlinearity. The typical correlations we use work best when the data show a **linear relationship**, that is, when a particular amount of change in the value of X is associated with a stable amount of change in the value of Y, no matter where on the X axis the change occurs. Figure 11.4a shows a simple example of how the same change in X is associated with a different amount of change in Y, depending on the values of X. In Figure 11.4a, for lower values of X, a change of one unit on X is related to a small change in Y; for higher values of X, the same change is associated with large changes in Y. This pattern of change reflects a **nonlinear relationship**.

For example, LaHuis, Martin, and Avis (2005) measured speed and accuracy of job-related tasks of clerical workers along with their conscientiousness as measured on a 17-item inventory. The results indicated a nonlinear relation between job performance and conscientiousness. At low levels of conscientiousness, workers showed relatively poor performance; as conscientiousness increased, so did performance. But after a point, performance stopped increasing even when conscientiousness rose. The performance measures just leveled off.

This nonlinear relation provides a good example of how a nonlinear pattern can obscure a real relation between variables. LaHuis et al. (2005) reported that the linear relation was nonsignificant. If they had computed only a **Pearson product-moment correlation,** which is only useful with linear relations, they would have concluded that conscientiousness was not related to job performance when, in fact, there is a predictable and reliable association between the two variables, as shown in Figure 11.4b. If you collect data that are nonlinear, the frequently used Pearson r may still result in a significant correlation, but it will suggest a less predictable relationship than actually exists.

Restrictions in Range. Sometimes there may be a legitimate relationship between two variables, but you may compute a lower correlation coefficient in your sample than you would have if you had access to the entire population. The problem may be with a **restricted range**.

Take a look at Figure 11.5, which represents a hypothetical population. You can see a clear, but imperfect, relation between X and Y. A problem can arise if you sample from the middle range of scores and neglect extreme scores. For instance, if you plotted the association between SAT scores and school grades for the entire population, you would see a clear pattern.

(a)

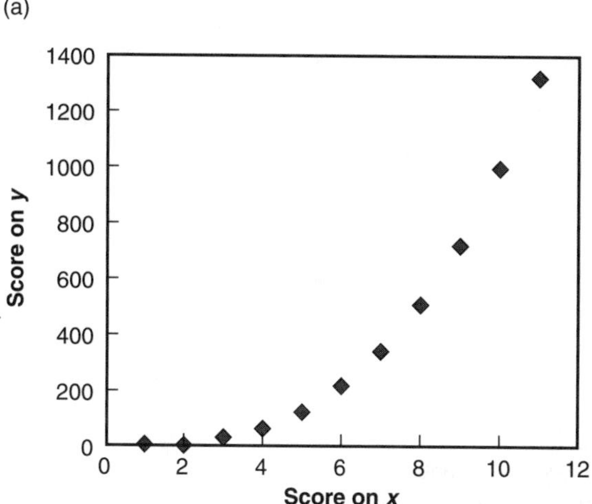

(b)

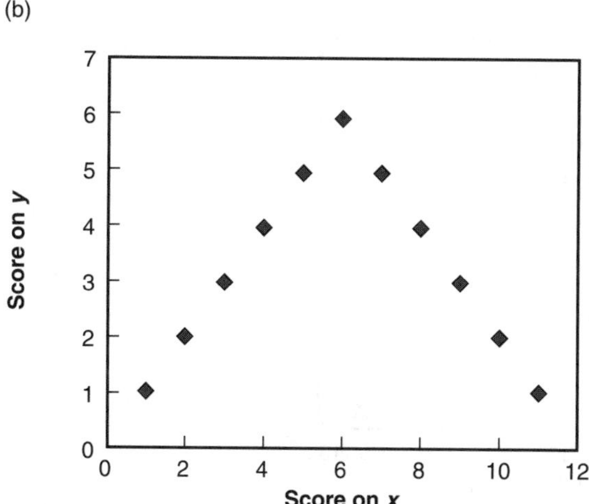

FIGURE 11.4 Examples of nonlinear relationships that obscure the strength of the association between two variables. In (a) we have a perfect nonlinear relationship, but the Pearson correlation coefficient is less than 1.0 ($r = .92$). A change in X from 1 to 4 is associated with a change in Y of 63, whereas the same size change on X from 8 to 11 is associated with a change of 819. This reflects one of many types of nonlinear relationships; you can see how the line curves. In (b) the relationship is again perfectly predictable, but the Pearson r is 0 because the Pearson r is maximally useful for linear relationships.

If you sampled from your fellow students, though, you would probably not find many with extremely low SAT scores (because they haven't been admitted to your school) or with extremely high SAT scores (because they are rare and may go to other schools). So you are stuck with the middle group of people, which is most of us.

(a)

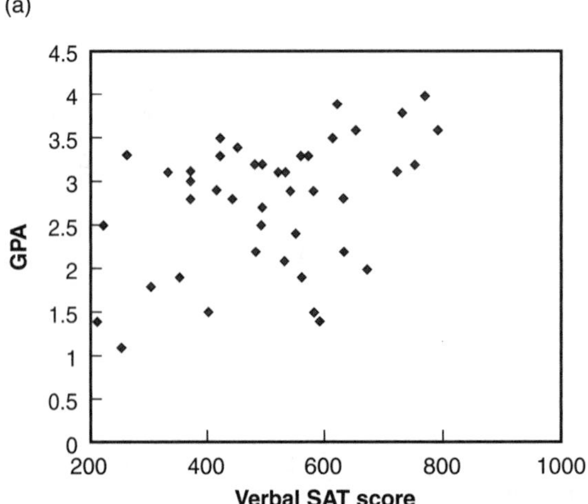

(b)

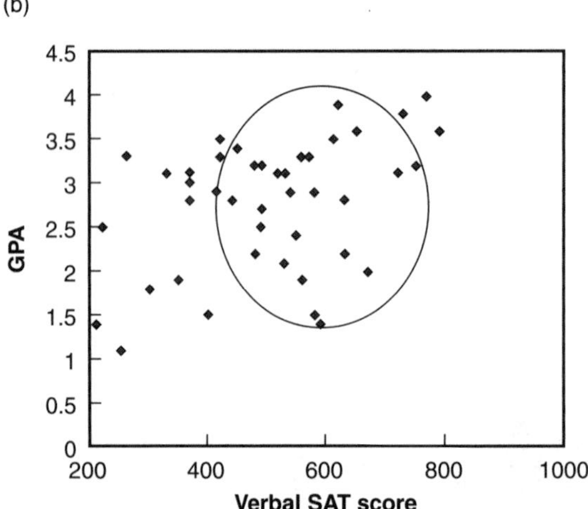

FIGURE 11.5 Fictitious example of the relation between SAT scores and GPA and how the correlation coefficient is affected by a restricted range. This scatter diagram in (a) depicts a correlation with $r = .45$ for this population. If there is a restricted range of SAT scores, which would not be uncommon at many schools, the trend toward higher GPAs as SAT scores are larger tends to disappear. The correlation coefficient for (b) is .29, which would not be significant in this example.

The population pattern shows a trend, but the sample inside the circle shows what would happen with a restricted range of SAT scores. One of the problems is that if you wind up with a small correlation coefficient, you can't tell whether there is no relation between variables or whether you have a restricted range problem.

Heterogeneous subgroup problem—In a correlational analysis, the appearance of a positive correlation in an overall data set and a negative correlation in subgroups or vice versa.

Heterogeneous Subgroups. A third problem that affects the size of the correlation coefficient is the presence of distinct subgroups within your sample that differ from one another; the problem is one of **heterogeneous subgroups**. If you are measuring groups that have different means on the variables you measure, your correlation coefficient showing the association between the two variables could be artificially high. Statisticians recognized this a century ago (e.g., Pearson, 1896) and described the mathematics over a quarter of a century ago (Sockloff, 1975).

Howell (2007) pointed out that for one particular data set that correlated men's and women's heights, the correlation coefficient between height and weight was .78 when the data for both sexes were pooled. The correlation between these two variables for men alone was .60 and for women alone was .39 (p. 265). Figure 11.6 illustrates how nonzero correlations could arise even when correlations within individual groups are zero. As you can see if the figure, the scatter diagram for each group is circular, suggesting no correlation. But the means for each group differ, so the pattern when the three are combined shows an oval shape that suggests that the correlation is greater than zero.

Another counterintuitive effect of heterogeneous subgroups can occur when individual groups have a positive (or negative) correlation, but when combined, the correlation is in the opposite direction. Consider an extreme, hypothetical situation where you want to find out if the anxiety among elementary school children changes as reading proficiency increases. Suppose that, as reading skills improve, children do become more comfortable and less anxious. But suppose also that, as children get older, their anxiety levels start out higher early in the school year, then decrease.

You might end up with the pattern shown in Figure 11.7. When all the data are combined, the overall pattern seems to indicate a positive correlation, whereas each

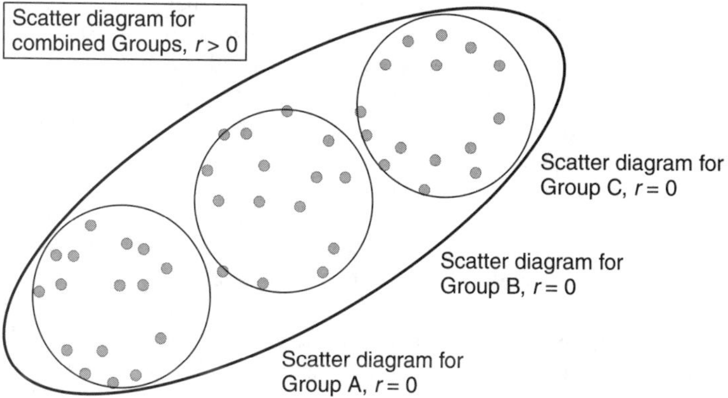

FIGURE 11.6 Illustration of how combining with different average scores can lead to an increase in values of the correlation coefficient. The scatter diagram for the three groups combined reflects a nonzero correlation because it is oval shaped, even though the groups providing the data each show correlations of zero.

individual group shows a negative correlation. This reversal of the sign of the correlation is likely to be fairly rare, but combining heterogeneous subgroups can have an impact on your correlation coefficients.

CONTROVERSY: The Media and Violence

A persistent societal question is the effect of media violence on behavior. Do people who people see violence enacted on television, in the movies, or in video games become violent and aggressive in their own lives?

Researchers in this area have concluded that there is a causal link: Exposure to violence leads to violent behavior (Carnagey, Anderson, & Bartholow, 2007). Over the past decades, investigators have accumulated evidence addressing this question. For instance, the introduction of television, with its violence, was associated with an increase in burglaries in the 1950s in a large number of cities in the United States (Hennigan et al., 1982). Exposure to realistic crime programs among adolescents in the United States can be associated with risk taking, including vandalism and trespassing (Kremar & Greene, 2000). In India, attitudes toward violence changed after exposure to violent television programming (Varma, 1999).

The problem with many such studies is that they don't really inform us about the causes of violent behavior. The research is usually correlational. With respect to specific types of violence (i.e., homicides), other variables like divorce rates and other social factors (Jensen, 2001) may be better predictors than media violence.

This question of causation is fundamental to psychologists who study complex behavior. How do we handle the dilemma of relying on correlational data when we want to determine causation?

Researchers use different types of studies to paint a complete picture of the situation. Substantial correlational research has revealed a clear link between media violence and actual violence. In addition, experiments have consistently demonstrated a causal link between exposure to violence and self-reports of aggression and hostility (e.g., Scharrer, 2001), even though this research doesn't deal with actual violence. And the evidence keeps increasing. For example, Anderson, Gentile, and Buckley (2007) showed that exposure to a violent video game increased the level of aggressive behavior among children and college students. Future directions in this experimental research could include an examination of physiological effects of exposure to violence in the growing area of social neuroscience (Carnagey, Anderson, & Bartholow, 2007).

The picture is not perfect, but we can draw conclusions based on the best evidence available. The overall analysis of correlational and experimental research affirms that the causal link between media violence and aggressiveness is nearly as strong as the link between smoking and cancer, and stronger than the connection between condom use (or non-use) and AIDS transmission, exposure to lead and lower IQ scores, and homework and academic achievement. The connection is apparent both in correlational and in experimental research (Anderson & Bushman, 2001; Bushman & Anderson, 2001).

Interestingly, over the last quarter century, as the science has become clearer, the news media have ignored the research. News outlets are less likely to report the strength of the connection between media violence and actual violence than before (Bushman & Anderson, 2001).

Question for Discussion: How can correlational and experimental approaches each help overcome the the limitations of the other approach?

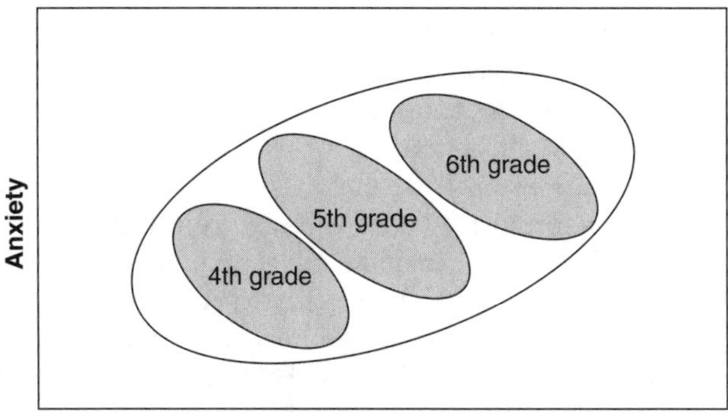

FIGURE 11.7 Example of the effect of heterogeneous subgroups on the correlation coefficient. Each subgroup in the fictitious example shows less anxiety as the school year progresses, which could lead to negative correlations within each grade, while the overall correlation would be positive.

TRADITIONAL CORRELATIONAL TESTS

The first correlation coefficients were invented about a century ago; we now call them bivariate correlations. They involved two (bi-) variables. The most common such test is the Pearson *r*.

Generally, when we talk about finding relations among variables, if the data are dichotomous (i.e., they can take only two values, like 0 or 1 or female and male), we talk about tests of association. When the data fall on a continuum, we refer to tests of correlational measures. This semantic difference gives us information about the nature of our data, but the underlying mathematics are often identical.

The Pearson Product–Moment Correlation

We use the Pearson product–moment correlation when we have two variables that are on an interval or ratio scale of measurement.

The Pearson *r* is useful for assessing the degree to which scores on two different variables show a linear relation. For example, there is a linear relation between frequency of parents spanking their children and children's antisocial behavior; more spanking is associated with higher rates of antisocial behavior (Straus, Sugarman, & Giles-Sims, 1997). This result means that there is a predictable relationship between the variables: Greater spanking is associated with greater antisocial behavior. Remember, though, that the relationship here is correlational, so we cannot determine causation.

Alternate Bivariate Correlations

Since Karl Pearson invented the correlation coefficient, there have been important extensions to it. The main differences between Pearson's *r* and the others might come in applications that are beyond our considerations (Howell, 2007). Sometimes researchers choose different versions of the correlation coefficient. Other widely used **bivariate correlations** are the Spearman correlation for ranked data (r_s), the point–biserial correlation for relating one dichotomous and one continuous variable (r_{pb}), and the phi coefficient (Φ), a measure of association for two dichotomous variables.

These tests are all variations on the Pearson product–moment correlation, for which you can use the Pearson formula. There are other formulas that researchers sometimes use, but they are merely algebraic manipulations of the standard formula.

Bivariate correlation—A correlational analysis relating only two variables.

The formula typically used for the Spearman correlation will result in the same numerical value as the Pearson formula. The Pearson formula is actually more generally useful because scores with tied ranks make the Spearman formula inaccurate, whereas the Pearson formula is still applicable.

Linear Regression

One statistical approach that has been around for quite a long time because its computations are relatively straightforward is multiple regression. If you can remember back to your high school algebra class, you may recall the formula for a straight line, Y = a + bX, where a is the Y-intercept and b is the slope. That simple formula lets you plot a straight line on a graph such that for every increase of 1 unit on X, you get a particular increase on the Y variable. So if b = 2, every increase in X leads to an increase of 2 on Y.

You can see an example in Figure 11.8. If you bought 5 lottery tickets at $1.00 each, the cost is predictable. In linear regression analysis, we use the concept of predicting Y from X, but it gets more complicated than buying lottery tickets because behavior is not as perfectly predictable as the cost of lottery tickets.

For example, Benfante and Beins (2007) measured the sense of humor of participants using the Multidimensional Sense of Humor Scale (MDSHS, Thorson &

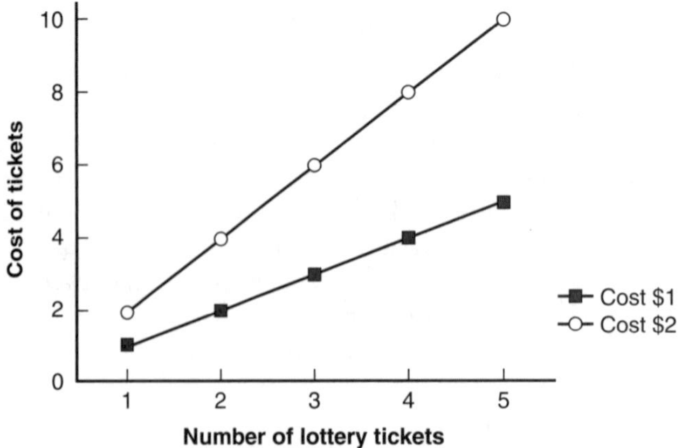

FIGURE 11.8 Simple example to illustrate Y = a + bX, with the Y-intercept = 0 and the slope (b) changing from 1 to 2. When b increases, the slope of the line does, too. This means that when b increases, every change in X means a big change in Y.

Powell, 1993) and asked the participants to rate the funniness of a set of jokes on a scale of 1 (*not very funny*) to 7 (*very funny*). One question is whether knowing the level of a person's sense of humor would let us predict how they rated the jokes. This research questions lends itself to regression analysis. The general formula for linear relationships is

Average Rating = Constant + Slope × Sense of Humor Score

The value of the slope was 0.76; the value of the Y-intercept (the constant) was 1.84. Analysis of the data indicated that the score on the MDSHS was correlated with joke ratings. The value of the correlation coefficient was .29, which signals a reliable but not a perfect correlation: The better the sense of humor, the higher a person rated the jokes.

The regression analysis led to the following equation that we can use to predict joke ratings. If somebody's sense of humor score on a scale of 1 to 5 was a 4.0, the best prediction based on the data is as follows:

Average Rating = 1.84 + .76 × Sense of Humor Score
Average Rating = 1.84 + (.76 × 4.0)
Average Rating = 1.84 + 3.04
Average Rating = 4.88

Thus, for the set of jokes used in the study, if we knew that a person's sense of humor score was 4, that person is likely to have rated the jokes, on average, with a score of 4.88.

The predictions are not perfect because the correlation between MDSHS score and average joke rating is not perfect. Still, the prediction would be better than just guessing that the person's rating would be at the average for the group, which would be a reasonable guess because most people are somewhere around the average. If the correlation were not significant, your best prediction of the participant's rating of the jokes would have been the mean rating of all participants, which was 4.29. As you can see, there is a noticeable discrepancy between a prediction based on the mean and the prediction based on regression analysis. The stronger the association between variables, the better the prediction.

Zero-order correlation—A correlational analysis involving two variables.

Higher-order correlation—A correlational analysis involving more than two variables.

CORRELATIONS WITH MULTIPLE VARIABLES

As a first step in finding out how variables relate to one another, the bivariate correlations we've encountered are quite helpful. At some point, though, we are likely to decide that behavior is too simple to be handled by two variables. So we begin to assemble the puzzle of behavior using many pieces (i.e., variables) and we move from the bivariate, or **zero order correlations**, to **higher-order correlations** that relate multiple variables simultaneously.

Fortunately, we have quite a number of useful statistical tools to help us begin to fathom the interrelationships among sets of variables. Many of these tools have been around for decades, but it hasn't been until computers have eased the tedium of calculation that psychologists have adopted them.

Multivariate statistics—Statistical approaches that can accommodate simultaneous analysis of multiple variables.

Today, **multivariate statistics** are a common tool in correlational research. The critical component in using them is no longer accuracy in computation because computerized statistical packages have eliminated that problem. Now we have to worry about using these statistics appropriately and interpreting them meaningfully.

Multiple regression—A correlational technique that employs more than one predictor variable to estimate the value of a criterion variable.

Multiple Regression

In **multiple regression**, we use more than one predictor variable to estimate the outcome. Your equation for two predictor variables would be as follows:

$$\mathbf{Y = Constant + (Slope_1 \times Score_1) + (Slope_2 \times Score_2),}$$

which tells you that the Y score you are trying to predict, the criterion variable, will be a function of the score on the first predictor variable, Score_1, and the slope associated with it, plus the score on the second predictor variable, Score_2, times its slope. The formula may look intimidating, but the logic is the same as for the simple, one-variable equation: Given the value of your X variables, you can generate a prediction of Y.

In the humor study by Benfante and Beins (2007), they wanted to know if they could predict how funny people thought they were based on how extraverted the participants were and how the participants rated the jokes. That is, do people who score high on a scale of extraversion think they are funnier than people who score low? And do people who rate jokes as being very funny rate themselves as funnier than those who rate jokes lower?

These questions lend themselves to multiple regression analysis. In this case, the participants' score on an extraversion scale and their average joke ratings were the two predictor variables; their self-rating of how funny they were on a scale of 1 (*I'm not very funny*) to 10 (*I'm very funny*) was the criterion variable that the researchers were trying to predict.

The data revealed that both of these predictor variables were useful is estimating the participants' self ratings as to how funny they thought they were. That is, both variables predicted significantly how funny people thought they were.

The values of the Y-intercept and the slopes for the two variables appear in Table 11.1. The regression equation for a participant whose extraversion score is low (2) and whose self-rating of funniness is low (3) is as follows:

$$\mathbf{Self\text{-}Rating\ of\ Funniness = Constant + (Slope_{extraversion} \times Extraversion\ Score) + (Slope_{ratings} \times Joke\ Rating)}$$

$$\mathbf{Self\text{-}Rating\ of\ Funniness = 3.48 + (0.35 \times 2) + (0.52 \times 3)}$$

$$\mathbf{Self\text{-}Rating\ of\ Funniness = 3.48 + 0.70 + 1.56}$$

$$\mathbf{Self\text{-}Rating\ of\ Funniness = 5.74}$$

TABLE 11.1 The Values of the Constant (the Y-intercept) and the Slopes in the Regression Analysis Designed to Predict People's Self-Ratings About How Funny They Think They Are on a Scale of 1 (*I'm not very funny*) to 10 (*I'm very funny*) Based on Their Extraversion Scores and the Ratings They Gave to a Set of Jokes (Benfante & Beins, 2007)

	Coefficient
Constant (Y-intercept)	3.483
Extraversion	0.521
Ratings of jokes	0.348

CONTROVERSY: The Mental Health of College Students

College students generally show good mental health. The suicide rates of college students, for example, are consistently lower than those of the general population of the same age. Still, there are high rates of suicidal ideation among young people, with 30 to 40 percent of high school and college students seriously thinking about it (Gutierrez et al., 2000).

In the past, institutions have sometimes taken the action of sending the students home for help. Recently, schools have tried to take a more proactive role, working to prevent the situation from deteriorating to the point of tragedy. We can use the information that psychologists have provided. Often their research involves complex, correlational analyses because life and death are very complex matters. There aren't going to be simple answers because the problem isn't simple.

Gutierrez et al. worked to develop the simplest model possible to predict suicidal ideation. Using the multivariate approach called factor analysis, they identified two factors associated with risk assessment among students. One factor was associated with negative themes, like repulsion by life, hopelessness, low survival and coping beliefs, and negative self-evaluation. Higher levels on these dimensions were associated with greater thought of suicide. A second factor was associated with less suicide risk. This factor included such protective variables as fear of social disapproval, fear of suicide, and a sense of responsibility to one's family.

Based on these results, a therapist or counselor might be able to spot potential problems before they get out of hand. But this strategy relies on students seeking help in the first place. Fortunately, psychologists have also identified variables correlated with student attitudes toward seeking psychological help.

Komiya, Good, and Sherrod (2000) used multiple regression to identify important variables associated with seeking help, which include gender, the stigma associated with seeking help, emotional openness, and severity of symptoms. Women were more likely to seek help; part of this tendency is that women are often more emotionally open. As symptoms grow more severe, students are more likely to see a therapist or counselor. Finally, students are more likely to get help if there is less stigma associated with therapy.

These results can suggest options for increasing student use of counseling centers. Psychological research can be an important component in identifying ways to maximize student use of mental health resources.

Question for Discussion: Why would multivariate research lead to better predictions than bivariate research?

Thus, our best prediction of a person's self-rating of funniness in this case would be 5.74. If these variables were not significant predictors of the self-rating, our best prediction would be the mean of the entire group, which is 6.85. Again, the prediction will not be perfect because the correlations are not perfect; but knowledge of how people rate jokes and how extraverted they are can help us predict how funny they feel they are.

LIMITATIONS OF MULTIVARIATE CORRELATIONAL ANALYSIS

Most tools can be used for many purposes. However, it is important recognize when they should and should not be applied. There are limitations to the use of these approaches.

Generalizability

The problem of generality is such that we first need to concern ourselves with the representativeness of our samples. There is more to generalizability, though, than the people who participate in our research. A second concern is whether our measures will generalize.

The models that we develop from a single study are based on specific measurements. Those measurements might be excellent for our purposes, but there are other approaches that might be just as good. It is an empirical question as to whether those other measures would lead to the same conclusions. Once again, the issue of replication is critical.

A third aspect of generalizability to consider involves the effects of time on our measurements. If researchers make measurements over time, the results may change depending on how long the study lasts. Some researchers have found that time between measurements is an important consideration. For example, Sher, Wood, Wood, and Raskin (1996) studied alcohol use among college students. These researchers looked at alcohol use and what students expected to gain from drinking (e.g., "drinking makes me feel less shy").

The investigators found that across one year, the students' past drinking pattern predicted the gain they expected from drinking. That is, the students' drinking patterns predicted their expectations about the benefits of drinking. Over three years, however, a reversal occurred: Students' expectations predicted their drinking pattern. This is a good example of how our research conclusions may be dependent on the time frame of measurements.

Confirmation Bias

One of the strengths of correlational modeling is that the approach allows us to create models that link important variables to the behaviors that we are interested in. The goal of investigators is to find models that fit the data.

One potential problem, however, is confirmation bias. As McCallum and Austin (2000) have pointed out, a model that results from the data we collect is only one possible model. They noted that all models are, to some degree, incomplete; the most we can hope for is a reasonably good fit between our data and the unknown reality. This is true because human behavior is much more complicated than even the most complex models we have developed. Thus, no matter how good the match between the data and the model, there are generally other models that provide just about as a good a fit with the data.

Researchers are sometimes led toward particular conclusions because of their preconceptions, just as all people are. This tendency may cause them to ignore perfectly good models that, in the long run, may be better than the one they choose.

Most of us show a confirmation bias in our lives, looking to support our beliefs rather than refuting them. The same can happen in the development of models. McCallum and Austin (2000) encourage researchers to take a more active role in considering alternate models, although too often, published research tends to confine itself to testing a single model.

SUMMARY

We have seen how psychologists use correlational approaches to study complex behavioral patterns. Experimental approaches are useful and often preferred, but correlational studies may actually provide a better means of understanding complex aspects of behavior.

By using correlational approaches, we can see how different behaviors interrelate and we can often apply this knowledge to predicting behavior. When we recognize the power (and limitations) of the approaches, we can begin to understand the complex interconnections among variables that we may miss in simplified experimental settings.

Researchers use correlational approaches to spot associations among variables and to make predictions about behavior. The reason that we cannot use such analyses to be certain about causation is that there may be other variables influencing the ones we are investigating and that if there is a causal relationship, we don't always know which variable is the cause and which is the effect.

The first correlation coefficient was invented about a century ago. Afterward, different correlational statistics flourished and newer approaches have emerged. One of the commonly used approaches includes multiple regression, which allows us to make better predictions about behavior based on more information, that is, based on more variables. When used appropriately, these techniques provide us with power tools for understanding and predicting behavior.

REVIEW QUESTIONS

Multiple Choice Questions

1. When Guthrie, Ash, and Bendapudi (1995) investigated whether students' grades and their tendency to be morning or evening people are associated, these investigators conducted
   a. a prediction study.
   b. a relationship study.
   c. confirmatory factor analysis.
   d. multiple regression.

2. If you were studying ten variables to see whether they were correlated, and if you computed all possible correlation coefficients,
   a. 5 percent of your correlations would be significant but actually meaningless.
   b. you would want to pay attention to higher-order correlations more than to zero-order correlations.
   c. by choosing the proper variables, you could begin to identify causal relationships.
   d. your best approach to examining the correlations would be to create a third variable problem.
3. A clinician might want to know whether a psychological inventory would predict future levels of depression in clients. Those future levels of depression would constitute a
   a. predictor variable.
   b. criterion variable.
   c. confirmatory variable.
   d. manipulated variable.
4. Psychologists have discovered that people high in neuroticism associated sex with death more than people low in neuroticism do. We can't conclude that neuroticism causes people to associated sex with death because the outside variables that lead to neuroticism could also lead to thoughts sex and death. This illustrates the
   a. directionality problem.
   b. third variable problem.
   c. restricted range problem.
   d. latent variable problem.
5. When two variables are related in such a way that when one increases, so does the other, you can conclude that
   a. there is no problem with directionality.
   b. factor analysis is inappropriate.
   c. the relation between variables is positive.
   d. there are no latent variables affecting the relationship.
6. If a researcher wanted to know whether certain behaviors are associated with income, he or she might be reluctant to travel of a poor part of town that has a high crime rate. As a result, the data would not include very low values of income levels and the correlation coefficient would be lower than if such data were included. The potential problem in this case is
   a. heterogeneous subgroups.
   b. nonlinear relationships.
   c. the presence of latent variables.
   d. a restricted range.
7. The Pearson product–moment correlation and the Spearman correlation both involve
   a. higher-order correlations.
   b. multiple regression.
   c. bivariate correlations.
   d. nonlinear correlations.

8. When you try to predict the value of an outcome variable from several variables, you are likely to be using
   a. multiple regression.
   b. the Pearson product–moment correlation.
   c. the analysis of variance.
   d. heterogeneous subgroups.
9. In correlational modeling, a researcher selects a set of variables to predict some behavior. The results from that set of variables may not be the same as if a different set of variables had been used. This limitation reflects a problem with
   a. zero-order correlations.
   b. restricted range.
   c. directionality.
   d. generalizability.
10. The research showing that people who watch violent television and movies also engage in more aggressive behavior involves
   a. confirmation bias.
   b. unstable predictor variables.
   c. correlational studies.
   d. heterogeneous subgroups.

Essay Questions

11. What is the difference between a relationship study and a prediction study? Which one is likely to be more preliminary? Why?
12. Why is it important to recognize if your variables are related in a nonlinear way?
13. In what situations would multiple regression be inappropriate?

ANSWERS TO REVIEW QUESTIONS

Multiple Choice Questions

1. b
2. a
3. b
4. b
5. c
6. d
7. c
8. a
9. d
10. c

Essay Questions

11. What is the difference between a relationship study and a prediction study? Which one is likely to be more preliminary? Why?

    A relationship study involves establishing which variables are reliably related to one another. A prediction study involves using a predictor variable to predict a criterion variable.

    A relationship study might precede a prediction study because we need to understand which variables are related before we can make useful predictions based on those relationships.

12. Why is it important to recognize if your variables are related in a nonlinear way?

    If your variables are nonlinearly related, you should be cautious about using the standard Pearson correlation. You might need to test for nonlinearity and use a different correlational approach to identify whether the relation between variables is reliable.

13. In what situations would multiple regression be inappropriate?
    a. Multiple regression is not appropriate when researchers employ repeated measures on the DV.
    b. Multiple regression can be used with only one DV.
    c. Multiple regression is useful only with measured variables; it can't be used with latent variables.

CHAPTER TWELVE

STUDYING PATTERNS IN THE NATURAL WORLD

Observational Approaches

CHAPTER OVERVIEW

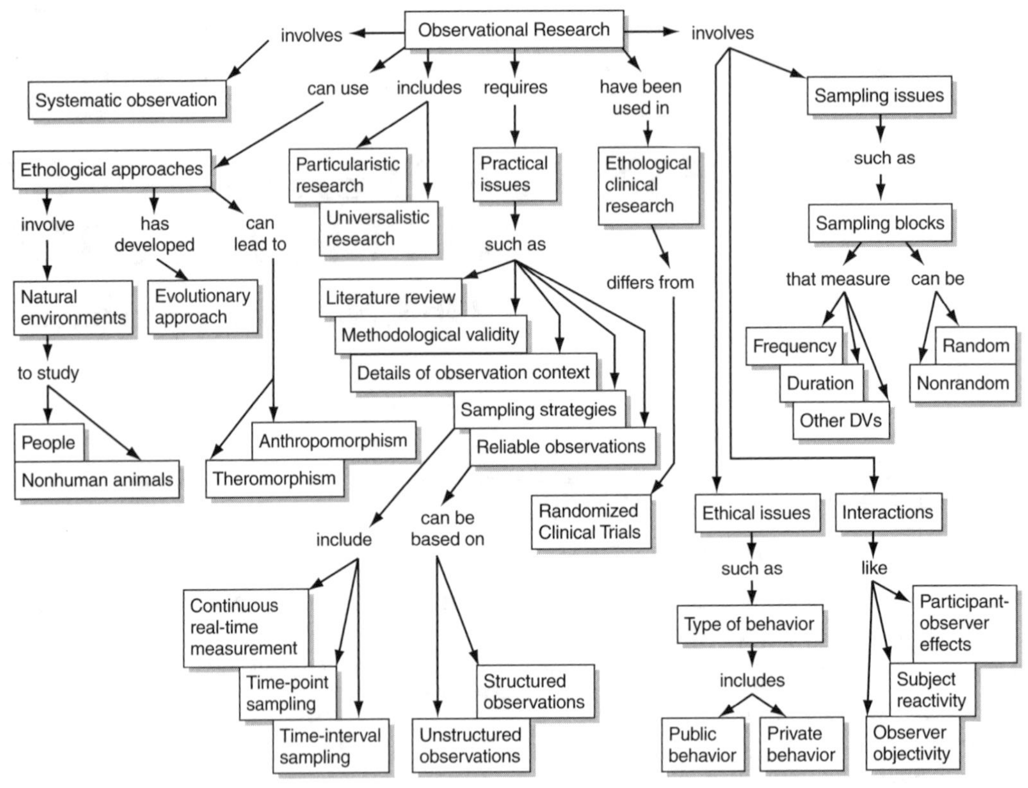

KEY TERMS

Anthropomorphism, p. 301
Behavior checklist, p. 315
Cluster sampling of behaviors, p. 307
Continuous real-time measurement, p. 303
Ethologist, p. 300
Evolutionary psychology, p. 301
Interobserver (interrater) reliability, p. 315
Naturalistic observation, p. 298
Observational research, p. 297
Observer bias, p. 315
Observer drift, p. 315
One/zero sampling, p. 308
Particularistic research, p. 298
Subject reactivity, p. 314
Systematic observation, p. 298
Theromorphism, p. 301
Time-interval sampling, p. 303
Time-point sampling, p. 303
Universalistic research, p. 299

CHAPTER PREVIEW

One of the most pronounced differences between the way scientists study the world and the way that most people observe their world involves the degree to which the observations are systematic and focused. Most of the time, people (including scientists who are "off duty") manage to ignore most of the things that go on around them. If something catches our eye or attracts some interest, we pay attention to it. Otherwise, we ignore it.

In scientific research, we observe certain behaviors or events with meticulous care, trying not to miss occurrences that are critical to our research topic. Depending on the research, a scientist will pay attention to one set of behaviors and ignore others.

In this chapter, you will see how scientists set up the strategies of their research and collect data in the natural world. The approaches discussed here rely on phenomena that exist regardless of whether a researcher studies it. For example, a soccer game will take place whether a scientist decides to investigate the degree to which players are prone to break the rules under certain conditions. Given that the activity to be observed will take place, it is the observer's responsibility to identify which behaviors to attend to and to define them appropriately.

In addition, researchers have to consider issues of sampling. With observational studies, the question of sampling refers to when, where, and how to select the events to be recorded, not only whom to study. There are several strategies that researchers use in setting up their procedures. Very often there is a tradeoff between what is practical and what is ideal. Observational techniques may require extensive time commitments that involve resources in excess of what the researcher can devote to the project. Thus, compromises have to be made that will make the research possible without affecting too greatly the validity of the data.

Another important element in planning observational research is that of ethics. Is it appropriate to observe people without getting their consent or debriefing them? There are some circumstances where these ethical issues pose no problems, but in other conditions, there are notable ethical considerations.

Observational approaches have a distinct set of advantages and disadvantages, just like any other scientific method. Researchers still have to pay attention to issues of reliability and validity, because when the researchers interpret the data to find out what they mean, the conclusions are meaningless if the data are not reliable and valid. There are also some very practical questions that investigators have to address in setting up their research.

OBSERVATIONAL APPROACHES

Researchers can search for patterns of behavior and relationships among behaviors by directly recording how human and nonhuman animals behave in their natural environments. This approach is called **observational research**. Scientists who make use of observational approaches do not typically create experimental situations to study; in many cases, they try their best to remain completely unnoticed by those they study. Observational researchers try to record behaviors as accurately as they can, noting the context in which those behaviors occur. Observational research seems as if it would be easy to conduct, but there are many pitfalls to avoid.

In this chapter, we will cover various aspects of observational research. Psychologists do not use observational research as extensively as some other behavioral scientists like sociologists and anthropologists. Nonetheless, these methods can provide a wealth of information about human behavior and attitudes.

Observational Research—A methodology in which investigators are trained to record human or nonhuman behavior exactly as it occurs, attempting to avoid interpretation or subjective evaluation.

SCIENTIFIC VERSUS CASUAL OBSERVATION

In everyday life, we observe behavior and make predictions all the time. For instance, if you are driving your car on the highway, you monitor the way others are driving, anticipating what they are likely to do. Such casual observation is very important. But it differs from scientific observation. In research we engage in **systematic observation**. This means that we make note of behavior exactly how and when it occurs, without trying to interpret it. Systematic observation generally takes place in the preliminary stages of research, before the investigators develop hypotheses.

Systematic observation—A form of observational research in which an investigator records behavior as it naturally occurs, attempting to note every behavior exactly as it emerges, often in a laboratory as an initial stage of research and prior to the development of hypotheses.

Naturalistic observation—A form of observational research involving the recording of behavior as it naturally occurs, without any attempt at intervention, often without the knowledge of those being observed.

It is impossible to record accurately every behavior a person or animal engages in, so observational researchers limit themselves to certain behaviors that are important in the current research project. Think of the behavior of referees in soccer (or any other sporting event). In a very real sense, they are acting like scientists who are engaged in systematic observation. While on the field, they watch for certain patterns of behavior on the part of the players; in this example, the officials focus on behaviors that relate to the rules of the game. Referees do not take detailed notes as scientists do, but the referees keep track of important behaviors just as scientists do.

On the other hand, parents are likely to observe their own children in great detail, ignoring other occurrences on the field. Parents are notorious for showing low levels of objectivity: Any contact with their children should be called fouls, whereas their children seldom violate the rules.

Sports officials are supposed to maintain objectivity, just as scientists are. The events that occur are what they are; neither scientists nor referees are supposed to inject their own values or desires into their work. However, scientists and referees do bring their own biases into their work. After all, they are human like the rest of us. The unfortunate outcome can be either poor science or poor sport. The advantage in science is that other researchers may try to replicate the findings; therefore, invalid scientific findings can ultimately be corrected.

STUDYING NATURAL BEHAVIORS

The term natural behavior in research refers to behaviors that psychologists, sociologists, anthropologists, and others study in a natural setting as opposed to in a laboratory. Scientists call such research **naturalistic observation**. In many cases, those being observed are unaware that a researcher is recording behaviors.

Particularistic research—Investigation taking place at a specific time and place that focuses on a single question and that is not oriented toward general questions.

For investigators who have a specific, practical goal in their research, like solving a problem of communication among co-workers, the naturalistic approach might work best. Researchers refer to this type of research as **particularistic** because it addresses a particular or specific question that might be limited to a single setting.

Just because the research is naturalistic, we can't assume that it provides us with a high degree of external validity. If you conduct an observational study on your campus of whether men hold doors open for women more than vice versa, the results may or may not apply to any other campus, to older populations, to people in other parts of the country, or any other groups. You have a particular result in a natural setting, but you don't know if the same thing would happen with other people elsewhere.

Universallistic research—Investigation whose goal is to address a general question that extends beyond the specific time and place where the research itself occurs.

When the investigators are more interested in addressing general principles, like the conditions that lead people to engage in helping behavior, it is easier to test hypotheses in a controlled environment. We refer to the research goal here as **universalistic**, meaning that we don't intend to limit our conclusions to what happens in the simple laboratory setting. Rather, it will have more general, theoretical implications.

Observational techniques constitute a small, but important, domain in psychology. You are likely to encounter it in three particular types of research, involving the study of children, psychiatric populations, and nonhumans. In many cases, observational research is not experimental; that is, researchers don't generally manipulate anything in the environment. Rather, they observe an organism as it behaves in a particular environment.

Studying Complex Human Behavior

People are complex; so are our behaviors. When psychologists use laboratory studies to investigate behaviors, the research generally involves relatively simple observations and measurements. For instance, how long does it take to solve a problem, how much money would a mock jury award a plaintiff in a trial, how long will an animal persist in a nonrewarded behavior, or can people be primed to conform to a group's views? Each of these topics may involve complex behavior, but the measurements that researchers make are pretty simple: number of seconds to solve the problem, a dollar amount given to a plaintiff, number of nonreinforced bar presses, and the percentage of the time a person agrees with a group.

The value of laboratory studies is that they can remove many of the effects of factors that are not of interest to the researcher. What remains is a simplified version of reality that allows complex behavior to be broken into individual elements.

Observational research, on the other hand, involves behavior in its complexity. One disadvantage is that the researcher cannot always tell what causes the behavior to occur because so many things are happening at the same time; the advantage is that the researcher can determine realistically what behaviors occur in a given situation because they indeed naturally happened.

For example, Snowden and Christian (1999) wanted to find out how parents of gifted students fostered their children's development. The researchers asked the parents to complete a questionnaire, then followed up with a visit to their home for purposes of an interview and naturalistic observation. During the observation and interview, the researchers discovered (among other things) that the parents were affectionate, allowed the children freedom of self-expression, and provided materials for creativity.

An important component of the research was finding out how the parents and children really interacted. The only way to do this is to observe directly. As you already know, a household with children is a busy, complex environment, with a lot happening that is out of control of the researchers. Consequently, the investigators could identify what factors in the household might be involved in fostering the children's intellectual growth, but it is impossible to say which specific factors or combination of factors may be critical.

Schools provide a natural environment for observation. Increasing numbers of children are enrolled in preschools because parents have jobs that prevent them from caring for their children during daytime hours. Thus, with children in the preschools and parents who may not have a lot of time to take the children to a psychologist or psychiatrist, it can make sense for the professional to observe the child in the preschool itself. Further, this setting is a more natural environment than a clinic or office, so the assessment and evaluation can be based on more valid observations. Finally, the preschool setting may be the cause, in part, of problems that develop. When these reasons are combined with the fact that it is easier to discuss the problems with teachers on site, we can see that naturalistic observation may be an effective means to document difficulties among preschoolers (Kaplan, 1999).

Ethology

Most of our discussion of observational research will involve studies of human behavior. However, there are various traditions in studying natural behavior in nonhuman animals. For instance, **ethologists**, scientists who investigate broad or general patterns of behavior of organisms in a natural environment often study nonhumans, although their techniques are appropriate for the study of human behavior as well.

As you saw in Chapter 2, there are ethical arguments concerning research with animals that need consideration prior to beginning an investigation. Researchers who think that animal research is appropriate are legally and ethically required to keep ethical considerations in mind in planning their work with captive animals. When animals are captive, it isn't clear that their behaviors are really normal, although we don't always know what normal means. If we choose to study animals in laboratories, as behavioral psychologists tend to do, we may be observing behaviors that an animal might seldom display in the wild.

Ethologist—A researcher who studies behavior, usually of animals, in their natural environment.

Ethological studies of people can be very instructive as well. For instance, Troisi (1999) pointed out that although people with schizophrenia show poorer prognosis for recovery than most psychiatric disorders, there are wide individual differences in recovery. Troisi speculated that there may be a way, using ethological approaches, to identify early in treatment those patients who are less or more likely to recover normal behavior. Based on the ethological data, Troisi and colleagues (1991) reported that schizophrenic patients who made less eye contact with an interviewer and who closed their eyes more had poorer prognoses than other patients. Not only is this type of research useful in predicting treatment outcomes, but it can also shed light on particular behaviors, like disturbed social behavior.

Describing the Behavior of Nonhuman Animals

Depending on what kind of animal a researcher investigates, we see different terminology in descriptions and interpretations of the results. When an investigator studies nonhuman animals, explanations of how the animals act in the presence of others might invoke the idea of territoriality. For instance, birds that alight on railings or power lines tend to maintain a "comfortable" distance between themselves and their neighbors. When the distance between two birds becomes small, they begin to peck at one another, gradually separating to an acceptable distance (Dixon, 1998). Imagine two children in a car who are taking a long trip. They show the same "pecking" behavior with one another.

When the investigator studies people in this kind of situation, results are likely to be characterized in terms of an individual's personal space or comfort zone. Researchers tend to describe the behavior of animals, but to discuss the motives and thoughts of people.

Even though researchers may be studying the same underlying phenomenon, they often use different terms that reflect the history and traditions of the field. When research involves nonhuman animals, we tend to avoid developing explanations that make use of internal, mental processes. Thus, many investigators who study animal behavior may give a description of how an animal responds to the presence of another, but you will seldom see a statement that the animal is "uncomfortable." Discomfort is a human feeling that we can describe because we have language; we can't tell if an animal is experiencing the same emotion that we would in a similar situation.

Anthropomorphism—The attribution of human characteristic to nonhuman animals, such as an animal being called lonely.

Theromorphism—The attempt to understand the behavior of nonhuman animals by speculating about the behavior within the context of the animal's perspectives.

Evolutionary psychology—A relatively recent branch of psychology whose focus is human behavior from the perspective of its evolutionary development.

Part of the reason for this tendency is that psychologists began studying animal behavior in great depth when behavioral theory dominated. Behaviorists were loath to invoke mental concepts for human or nonhuman behavior. Behaviorists studied behavior, not thought processes that were unobservable and therefore not thought to be scientific.

Another reason for a cautious approach in describing animal behavior is that, prior to the behaviorists, scientists would too freely attribute human emotions to nonhuman animals. Such attribution is called **anthropomorphism**. If you were to say that your dog runs to you when you get home because it likes you, you would be anthropomorphizing. That is, you would be attributing a human emotion to a nonhuman animal. Researchers often prefer **theromorphism**, which focuses more on the animal's perceptions and behaviors than on the way a human would respond.

The distinction between anthropomorphism and theromorphism is an interesting one because it can dramatically affect the way we view behaviors. In the Controversy on rape in animals, you will see why it makes a difference in the terms we use.

Ethological approaches can be useful in comparing behaviors across species. In fact, ethologists have a long tradition of such comparative research. Currently, the domain of **evolutionary psychology** attempts

CONTROVERSY:
Rape in Animals

Rape is a vicious offense against another person. It is associated with contempt for the victim, a desire for power, or other inappropriate emotions. Can animals engage in rape? At times, researchers have used this term to describe animal behavior.

Does it make sense to call it rape when a male animal forces himself sexually on a female? Estep and Bruce (1981) argued that we should not use such anthropomorphic terms when describing animal behavior. In describing human forms of rape, we can gain insight into causes and into the motivations of the perpetrator. We can't do that with animals.

Further, in some animals, resistance to sexual intercourse is a normal part of the species behavior. Cox and LeBoeuf (1977) pointed out that female elephant seals normally resist the advances of the male, even when they are willing to mate. Thus, does it make sense to say that elephant seal bulls rape the cows? To do so would be to engage in inappropriate anthropomorphism.

Another reason for taking care in our terminology, according to Estep and Bruce, is that the term rape as a human assault carries with it notable emotional and ethical implications. Is it reasonable to talk about animal behavior using human standards? In humans, rape results in severe psychological and, often, physical trauma; it is an egregious break with societal ethics. Our feelings about resistance against mating are probably not the same as those in other species, for whom evolution may have led to such resistance as a natural and normal part of the continuation of the species.

Question for Discussion: How can the terminology that researchers use reveal their biases and assumptions? Can this be avoided?

to provide an overriding theoretical approach to explaining the behaviors of people with an evolutionary focus. This approach may also be useful in understanding the interrelatedness of behaviors of different species.

Although virtually all scientists recognize the explanatory power of the theory of evolution in biological sciences, the field of evolutionary psychology is still controversial; we do not know how useful it will ultimately be in explaining human behavior. At the same time, that is what science is all about. Hypotheses are generated and tested. If the results of research support the hypothesis and the theory, we increase our confidence in the explanatory power of the theory, at least until a better set of explanations comes along.

APPROACHES TO OBSERVATIONAL RESEARCH

As with any research project, observational investigators have to make some very practical decisions. These decisions are important because they can affect the outcome and conclusions of the research. Some decisions revolve around how to collect observational data. Some techniques require that the observer record behaviors simply and descriptively. Other approaches lead to categorization and summarizing behaviors that occur.

Five Practical Steps in Observational Research

Observational strategies differ from laboratory approaches in a number of ways. One commonality is that you have to make decisions about exactly how you want to carry out your study. Some decisions are similar to those in laboratory studies, but there are some unique determinations as well.

First, you need to find out what others have already done that relates to your project. Replication is useful, but you don't really want to devote a lot of time and energy to research that only repeats what others have done.

Second, you should develop and employ specific methods that experts in the area will recognize as valid. This means you should develop ways to measure the hypothetical constructs of interest to you. If published research has provided you with tools, make use of them. For instance, Troisi's (1999) Ethological Coding System for Interviews (ECSI) could give you the means for documenting behaviors when people talk. The ECSI was developed for Troisi's work with psychiatric populations, but you could adapt it to your own nonpsychiatric population.

Third, you must determine the details of your observations. You have to identify the settings in which you will observe behaviors. This will involve the location or locations where you will collect data, the times of day and days of the week you will do it, and the duration of data collection.

Continuous real-time measurement—The measurement of the duration of behaviors as they occur.

Time-point sampling—The measurement of the occurrence of a behavior by selecting specific points in time and recording whether the behavior is occurring at that instant.

Time-interval sampling—The measurement of behavior by noting whether it has occurred within a specified time interval or intervals.

Sometimes these decisions may be nearly fixed. For instance, if you are going to set up a videotape recorder and complex instrumentation, you may have to determine which location you want to use and stay there. Similarly, if you are going to monitor behaviors in places where you have limited access, you will be constrained by the realities of the situation.

A fourth step is to determine your sampling strategy. In most psychological research, sampling is largely concerned with the participants who provide the data. In observational studies, you also have to consider what events you are going to code and what your strategy will be during observation.

For instance, with respect to temporal aspects of collecting data, you may engage in continuous real-time measurement, time-point sampling, or time-interval sampling. **Continuous real-time measurement** involves monitoring how long behaviors of interest last. Each time the observed person engages in the behavior being studied, the researcher records how long the behavior persists over the course of the recording session. On the other hand, in **time-point sampling**, observers determine points in time when they look to see whether a behavior is or is not occurring. In **time-interval sampling**, the observer notes whether a behavior has occurred within a predetermined interval.

The fifth step is to train the observers so that data collection is reliable. Because observational research often takes place in the field, there are going to be a lot of distractions; it will help for observers to know exactly what they are supposed to pay attention to. Further, the observers must follow a strict protocol in observing, judging, and recording relevant behaviors. If all the observers are not doing the same thing, reliability and validity will suffer.

By following these steps, you will be able to create a study that will result in high-quality data. The effect will be that you will have more useful information about behavior in natural settings.

Structured and Unstructured Observations

When you observe behavior as it naturally unfolds, you have to make decisions about what to record. If you are using the traditional approach of watching and recording in a notebook, it will be impossible in most situations to identify every behavior your subject engages in. There will be large and small movements, changes in facial expressions, vocalizations, and so on. They are so numerous and varied that you won't be able to keep track of them all accurately.

In the past several decades, researchers have made increasing use of videotaping (e.g., Pepler & Craig, 1995) or audiotaping (e.g., Mehl, 2006; Tapper & Boulton, 2002) to capture behaviors. This technology allows the investigator to view the behaviors as many times as necessary to provide a complete description of what is happening. Even this approach will not solve all observational problems because the camera angle emphasizes some behaviors but misses others.

As an example, you only need to watch replays of a major college or professional football game. All too often, even with the multiple camera angles they employ, it isn't entirely clear what happened in a play. There is also room for subjectivity and interpretation. Two people who cheer for different teams will see the same play and interpret it quite differently. The advantages of videotaping and audiotaping are that they can reduce (but not eliminate) the ambiguity of observation and can preserve a record of the behavior permanently.

Some researchers prefer to make relatively unstructured observations. Such observations entail as complete a description as possible of relevant behaviors that occur. The observer does not categorize or interpret the activity, but only records what happens simply and descriptively.

Ethologists often refrain from developing initial categories of behaviors to record, focusing instead on descriptions of behaviors of interest. The point is to find out what is happening, not necessarily to test hypotheses or confirm prior expectations.

On the other hand, other researchers may decide to focus on specific behaviors from the start. In this situation, behaviors are identified prior to the observational period. These behaviors are categorized and precisely defined so the investigator can keep an accurate and reliable record of behaviors that occur.

SAMPLING ISSUES IN OBSERVATIONAL RESEARCH

In observational research, the question of sampling can be quite complex. The investigator needs to worry about samples of people, of behaviors, and of times during which behaviors are sampled.

Most research does not use random sampling either of people or of behaviors. That is, we decide what materials the participants will see and we collect convenience samples of college students or laboratory rats, then we observe behaviors that are convenient for one reason or another (e.g., others used them in their research). For example, Jenni (1976) and Jenni and Jenni (1976) studied differences in the way female and male students carry their books on campus. This behavior is one of many behaviors that the investigators could have investigated.

Number of Sampling Blocks

Moore (1998) provided a good example of how much data is needed to represent behavior accurately, at least in the observation of problem students in school. He observed three students continuously through the day on 20 different days, collecting data in 8-minute blocks. He monitored several target behaviors: on/off task, isolating self, verbal refusal, daydreaming, inappropriate verbalization, noncompliance, disruptive behavior, and aggression.

He then investigated what the results would have been like with smaller amounts of sampling. Using the data he had collected, he took randomly selected groups of 4, 8, 12, 16, 20, and 30 blocks from the population of forty-eight 8-minute blocks and compared the subsamples to the entire set of 48 blocks. This process simulated a large number of studies with 4, 8, etc. observation periods.

When he used relatively few (4 or 8) observations, he found notable discrepancies between the samples and the criterion. Keep in mind that a researcher who used eight 8-minute blocks would devote over an hour's worth of time to the task. Moore studied three students with four independent observers during actual observations. If a researcher observed three children, the time commitment would be over three hours. Multiply this by the number of different observers used. In Moore's study, the observation time rose to over 12 hours.

What happens with twelve 8-minute blocks? Such a study would involve over four and a half hours of data collection per observer on three students. This is a lot of time and energy to expend gathering questionable data. According to Moore, the quality of the data even at twelve observation periods is still suspicious. Figure 12.1 shows the degree of difference between the smaller samples and the criterion value based on forty-eight 8-minute blocks. The dependent measure is the number of times that the students engaged in group activity.

As you can see in the figure, the deviations are striking. If this study had been done with only four 8-minute observation periods, then, according to the data collected by the investigators, the researchers would, on average, be wrong in their estimate of group activity by 50 percent.

How long do researchers actually observe behavior in their studies? According to the data by Odom and Ogawa (1992), researchers collected data over a wide range of periods, but sometimes as little as 6 minutes. The implication of such a small observation period is that we may not be able to place much faith in the data generated. Moore (1998) pointed out that if researchers are interested in studying changes in behavior over time, small numbers of sampling blocks may provide inaccurate baseline data and followup data. The result would be an undesirably low level of both reliability and of validity.

This type of problem is why some researchers spend extensive periods of time observing behaviors. For instance, Troisi spent 263 hours observing grooming

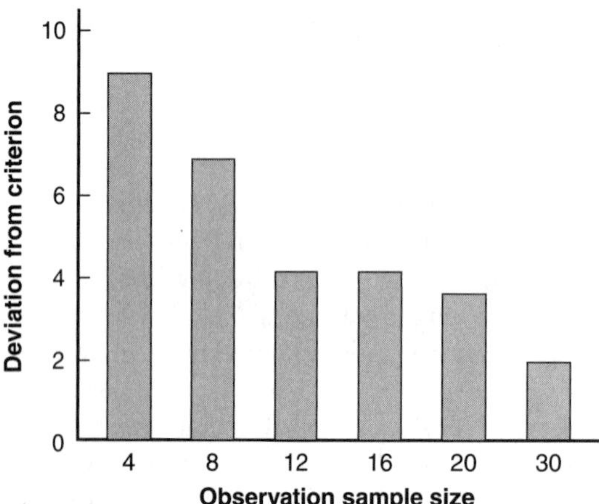

FIGURE 12.1 The degree to which samples showed deviations from the number of instances of actual group activity. The estimates of group activity deviated from a valid criterion of about 17, with greater error associated with fewer observations sampled. With only four observation periods, the estimate of the amount of group activity was off by about 50 percent; with 30 observations, the error fell to about 13 percent. The greater the number of 8-minute blocks sampled, the more accurate the estimate of activity.

Source: S.R. Moore. (1998). Effects of sample size on the representativeness of observational data used in evaluation. *Education and Treatment of Children, 21,* 209–226. Adapted with permission from *Education and Treatment of Children.*

behavior in female monkeys. They found that the monkeys tended to spend time grooming other monkeys that were aggressive toward them. Without this sizable expenditure of time, the actual patterns of behavior might not be clear.

Methods of Sampling Events During Observation

The goal of making observations is to understand behavior beyond the time of data collection. We hope that our sample of observed behaviors is representative of the larger population. One way to increase the likelihood that the behaviors we sample are representative of the population is to use random sampling of behaviors. In the case of observational research, the population is the entire set of behaviors of interest. Random sampling of behaviors is as important as random sampling of people.

One implication of random sampling of behaviors is that the researchers need to be able to monitor them at any time, in any place, and under any conditions (Peregrine, Drews, North, & Slupe, 1993). This is an unlikely combination. Researchers have personal lives and don't want to be in the field all the time; those who are observed are unwilling to let researchers invade their privacy.

In order to see the implications of various random and nonrandom sampling techniques on research results, Peregrine et al. (1993) monitored touching behavior of children in a child development center on a college campus. They videotaped 32 hours of interaction, recorded the action taking place, and counted the number of touches and their duration.

Every time they rewound and reviewed the tape, it increased their time commitment. If they had to watch each event twice, they would have needed 64 hours of viewing time to code the data, plus the time to stop and rewind the tape and to enter the data. Two coders watched all the tapes so they could estimate their reliability in coding. In the end, they divided the tape into 32 hours of 3-second intervals, generating over 38,000 time intervals, each one with several pieces of data.

Once this gigantic task was completed, the investigators sampled from among the 3-second intervals, simulating what would happen with different observational techniques.

When the researchers randomly sampled 10 percent of the data, the results were very similar to the data from the entire population. This means that if the investigators randomly sampled 3,800 3-second periods, they would capture the same basic information as they had when they used all the data. Systematic sampling of 10 percent also worked well. For this, they sampled every tenth time interval.

They concluded that if they were interested in touching behavior within a child development center, they could sample 3,800 random 3-second intervals and end up with a representative sample. It would not be representative of touching behavior in different settings, though.

Peregrine et al. also looked at what would happen if they restricted their observations to a single type of activity, like playing with blocks. The result was that their estimates of touching behavior were higher than had actually occurred through the entire set of 3-second intervals. As they pointed out, playing with blocks involves reaching for them, which might result in greater accidental or cooperative touching than other behaviors.

The implication here is that if researchers select some activity and monitor behavior only during that activity, they might end up with a distorted picture of what happens in general; their results might pertain only to the particular event they sampled. Suppose, for example, that instead of choosing to observe while the children were playing with blocks, they observed during a reading period. The point is that you have to sample across a variety of behaviors if you want to make general statements about what people do in a variety of situations.

They also employed a third sampling technique, **cluster sampling of behaviors.** In cluster sampling, researchers pick a start time and watch for some predetermined time period. So instead of 3-second intervals, the researchers investigated what would happen if they observed behavior during fewer, but longer, time intervals.

They found out that cluster sampling is a poor way to collect data. The results from of 15-, 30-, and 60-minute clusters was unlike that from the entire population of 3-second intervals. In fact, Peregrine et al. discovered that in order to generate valid data, they needed to sample 57 percent of the entire 32 hours. This is more than a fivefold increase over the 10 percent needed for random sampling. The researchers noted that the effect of using long clusters is to increase the variability of the meas-

Cluster sampling of behaviors—In naturalistic observation, the recording of behaviors in specified, extended time periods, a method that can lead to biased estimates of how often particular behaviors occur over the long run.

urements, so it is possible that estimates of the occurrence of a given behavior will be either very high or very low.

We can see that random sampling is the most efficient way to collect valid data. The drawback is that sometimes it is difficult to do. The tradeoff is time and energy versus quality of the data. As such, you have to decide on the best compromise for your own research.

Estimating the Frequency and Duration of Behaviors

When you observe behavior naturalistically, you could be overwhelmed with choices about what behaviors to study and how to study them. For example, Zinner, Hindahl, and Schwebbe (1997) studied observed behaviors in a group of baboons (*Papio hamadryas*). The researchers recorded frequency and duration of locomotion (moving about), grooming, approaches to another baboon, and threats.

One/Zero sampling—In naturalistic observation, the recording of whether a behavior occurs (earning a score of one) or not (earning a score of zero), a technique that tends to overestimate the amount of time a behavior is exhibited but underestimates the frequency of its occurrence.

The researchers engaged in an enormous initial data collection task. Their database consisted of 324 videos of 45 minutes of continuously videotaped activity in several different settings. They counted how often the target behaviors occurred and for how long.

One technique they investigated was **one/zero sampling**, which is used with time sampling. It involves recording whether a target behavior occurs at all in an interval. If it appears, the interval gets a score of 1; otherwise, the score for that interval is 0. Zinner et al. reported that one/zero sampling tends to overestimate the amount of time an animal engages in a behavior and underestimates how frequently it occurs. Still, they noted that one/zero sampling can be an effective strategy for short intervals; its reliability decreases as the sampling interval increases.

ETHOLOGICAL OBSERVATIONS IN CLINICAL RESEARCH

Ethological research tends not to involve real-life applications, although some interesting research by Troisi and colleagues (1999, 2007) reveals how this approach can be used to study human behavior. In different studies, he recorded behaviors of schizophrenics during an interview using structured observations. He employed the Ethological Coding System for Interviews (ECSI), a 37-item list of definitions of behavior for analyzing the data after interviews. Table 12.1 shows some of the behaviors and how they were defined. You can see that the definitions vary in detail. For example, the definition of a laugh allowed him to differentiate among different facial expressions, like grins, smiles, and so forth.

Could you differentiate in recording a smile versus a grin? Although in everyday life we can do it, it is not easy to come up with a formal definition of each one that will fit all people and that will result in reliable and valid coding. Troisi et al. (2007) found that nonverbal behaviors like facial expressions were good predictors of social disabilities among people with schizophrenia. Beyond this, Troisi, Spalletta, and Pasini (1998) concluded on the basis of ethological coding that schizophrenics tend to show less

TABLE 12.1 Examples of Definitions from the Ethological Coding System for Interviews (ECSI)

Specific definitions are critical in allowing observers to record and code data reliably and accurately, especially when there are behaviors that can be closely related to one another, like a laugh and a grin. The ECSI has 37 defined behaviors that measure affiliation, submission, prosocial behavior, flight, assertion, displacement, and relaxation.

Source: Troisi, A. (1999). Ethological research in clinical psychiatry: The study of nonverbal behavior during interviews. *Neuroscience and Biobehavioral Reviews, 23*, 905–913. Reprinted with permission of Elsevier Science.

Behavior	**Definition**
Facial Expressions	
Smile	The lip corners are drawn back and up.
Laugh	The mouth corners are drawn up and out, remaining pointed, the lips parting to reveal some of the upper and lower teeth.
Twist mouth	The lips are closed, pushed forward, and twisted to one side.
Head Movements	
Look at	Looking at the interviewer.
Look away	Looking away from the interviewer.
Head to side	The head is tiled to one side.
Bob	A sharp upwards movement of the head, rather like an inverted nod.
Thrust	A sharp forward movement of the head towards the interviewer.
Other Movements	
Shrug	The shoulders are raised and dropped again.
Wrinkle	A wrinkling of the skin on the bridge of the nose.
Groom	The fingers are passed through the hair in a combing movement.
Yawn	The mouth opens widely, roundly and fairly slowly, closing more swiftly. Mouth movement is accompanied by a deep breath and often closing of the eyes and lowering of the brows.

friendliness and less gesturing than a control group. They also pointed out that some schizophrenics had ethological profiles that were essentially the same as those of people in the control group, which is typical of research on schizophrenia. Interestingly, this type of behavior coding could have practical implications for people prior to the onset of schizophrenia. Troisi et al.'s (1998) results are consistent with earlier research findings that preschizophrenic children showed some of the same abnormal patterns of facial expression that occur after schizophrenic symptoms appear (Walker, Grimes, Davis, & Smith, 1993).

Psychiatric researchers typically do not employ ethological methods. Instead, they use randomized clinical trials (RCTs) and rating scales to study their patients. This typical approach often involves creating two or more groups that receive different treatments and perhaps a placebo; the investigator usually records changes in behavior or degree of improvement in people exposed to different treatments. The RCTs and rating scales are simply more efficient, taking perhaps 10 percent of the time that ethological approaches would require (Troisi & Moles, 1999). Investigators have to balance the extra time and money that ethological approaches require against the added information that is gained. As Troisi and Moles demonstrated, though, ethological approaches provide information that RCTs and clinical rating scales do not.

For instance, gender differences among depressed patients are clear with the ethological approach. Troisi and Moles (1999) found that their depressed female participants showed greater hostility as reflected in the ethological profiles. This leads to the hypothesis that women would be less likely to respond to antidepressant medications than men are. In fact, research has revealed this to be true (e.g., Overall, Hollister, Johnson, & Pennington, 1966). This type of research is important because we know that hostile people are less likely to respond to psychotropic medication than are others.

Further support for the use of ethological methods is shown by the fact that depressed patients had higher levels of assertion during psychiatric interviews than controls did. In addition, women showed greater levels of assertion than men, particularly when depressed women and men were compared. The pattern appears in Figure 12.2.

Troisi and Moles (1999) suggested that interpersonal factors underlie women's depressions more so than men's and that it is important for therapists to be aware of this fact if therapy is to be successful. Ethological studies will reveal such patterns, they argued. RCTs and simpler clinical rating scales will not.

THE HUMAN SIDE OF OBSERVATIONAL RESEARCH

As with any method, there are details that we have to consider when planning observational studies. The issues include the setting in which we will observe the behaviors, the means of recording behavior, and how long we will observe and how we sample the events. We also have to consider the ethics of observing behavior, the investigators' relationships with those being observed, and how personal and social issues affect both the researcher and the subject.

Ethics

Any time you study people, you may have an impact on them. In a controlled, laboratory study you are sure that participants know what is going on because you provide them with sufficient information in advance to decide if they want to participate, then you debrief them at the end. At the conclusion of an experimental session, you can be confident that they know as much as they should know and that you have answered all of their questions.

FIGURE 12.2 Differences in level of assertion (a) and submission (b) by depressed men and women compared to controls. The data were collected using an ethological approach that allows coding of behaviors that are not easily obtained with rating scales. This type of information can be important because patients with interpersonally based depression, which will have a large component related to assertion and submission, are less likely to respond to medical intervention than are others (Troisi & Moles, 1999). Reprinted with permission.

Source: Reprinted from *Journal of Psychiatric Research, 33,* A. Troisi & A. Moles, Gender differences in depression: An ethological study of nonverbal behavior during interviews, pp. 243–350, copyright © 1999, with permission from Elsevier Science.

(a)

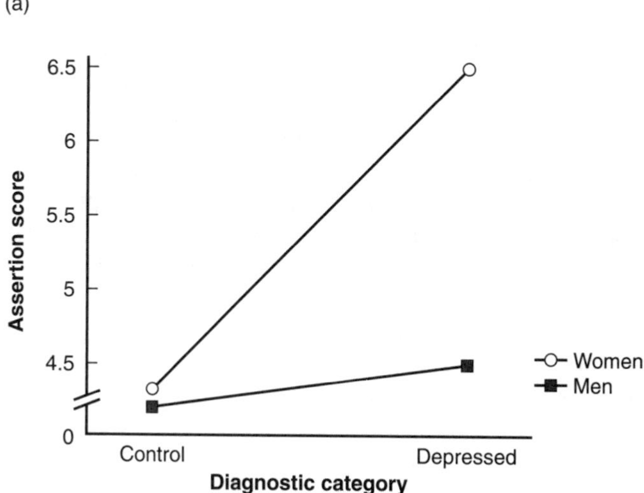

(b)

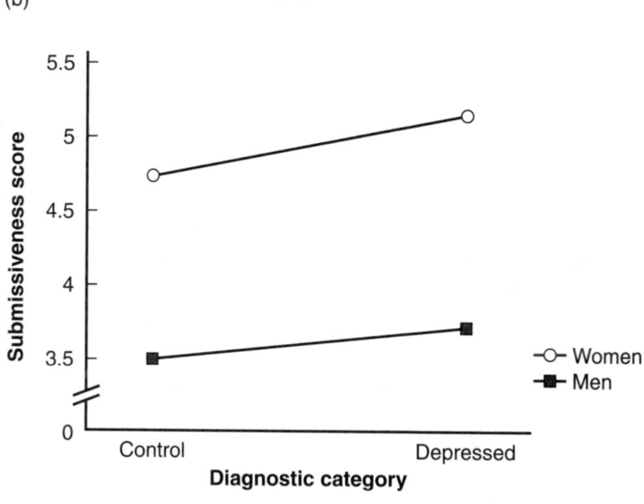

Observational studies are somewhat different. The people being monitored do not necessarily know that they are the subjects of study. In most cases, they neither give informed consent nor receive a debriefing.

In the abstract, the ethical issues of observational research are very clear and straightforward. In general, researchers (and the federal officials who issue governmental guidelines) agree that there is no problem in observing public behavior when the researcher doesn't manipulate any variables or intervene in the situation.

So if you are going to observe people's behaviors as they walk down the street or in any public setting, you don't need their permission. If you intend to manipulate any variables or intervene in the situation, though, the situation changes. At this point, you are not merely an observer of public behavior. You are a researcher who is changing the course of people's behavior, even if in an apparently trivial way. As such, you should seek approval from your Institutional Review Board (IRB).

Another important issue is defining what constitutes public behavior. A commonsense rule can sometimes be all we need. For example, we would probably get no disagreement if we concluded that any behavior in a public park, on a public beach, or at a sporting event is public behavior. We would also be likely to get little argument if we were to maintain that when people engage in sexual behavior in their homes, they can expect to be left unobserved.

The problem, of course, is that life doesn't involve only clear-cut cases. Ambiguity is all too predictable in our lives. One notorious example of research that has generated serious controversy involved an investigator who studied men who engaged in sexual activity (which you could consider private behavior) in a men's restroom in a public park (which might make it public, at least to men). Humphreys (1975) studied the behavior of men who engaged in anonymous sex in a generally public area. The ethical status is complicated (Reynolds, 1982).

You might not want to conduct such research yourself, but that is not the issue here. Our personal sensibilities differ, so what one person thinks is unsavory, another might not object to. The critical issue is whether research like that of Humphreys is within ethical boundaries. Such a proposal would probably not be approved by any IRB now; at the time the research took place, in the late 1960s, IRB approval was not mandated; in fact, there were no IRBs at all. In the Controversy on public versus private sex, you will see some of the issues associated with the ethics of this research.

In discussing controversies like this, you should remember that most psychological research is completely within the boundaries of ethical guidelines. Sometimes extreme cases can illustrate the issues that we have to deal with, but these extreme cases are just that—extreme. They don't resemble the kind of research that the overwhelming majority of scientists engage in. The point to consider here is that we ultimately want to treat people with respect. By discussing cases that are potentially troublesome, we can get a sense of how our own research should proceed.

Participant–Observer Interactions

An ethical issue that is closely allied to practical issues is the extent to which an observer interacts with those being watched. In the classical observational study, researchers are removed from the subjects of their study.

For instance, a quarter of a century ago, a researcher used a non-interactive approach to see how students carried their books (Jenni, 1976). She observed 2,626 people in the United States, Canada, and Central America and found that girls and women carried books with their arms wrapped around the books and held near their chest; boys and men held the books on their hips. She attributed the differences to psychological, social, and biological factors.

The investigator had no need to interact with a student; she merely noted how the students carried their books. The situation involved public areas and public behaviors; there would be no particular ethical issues with this research. But sometimes we can't get the type of information we want by using simple, remote observation. It can be helpful to be part of a group in order to see how it functions. This raises ethical questions. If you joined a group in order to study them, you would be creating relationships with the group members. We could argue that you are deceiving them. Further, we could argue that you are invading their privacy. You might be putting them at risk of psychological harm if they discover your true purposes after they form a close friendship with you. Is it ethical to establish such a relationship with people simply to be able to study them?

We can depict observational research according to whether the investigator interacts with the group and whether the subjects know they are being observed. Table 12.2 indicates some of the ethical issues associated with the different approaches.

TABLE 12.2 Relationship Between Observer and Participant in Observational Research

There are different ethical considerations associated with each approach.

	Researcher Interacts with People Being Observed	Researcher Does Not Interact with People Being Observed
People know they are being observed	Ethical considerations are minimal as long as those being observed are aware of the nature of the research.	Ethical considerations may be minimal if behavior is public. If behaviors are normally considered private, however, there may be ethical issues associated with this research, depending on whether those being observed consent to such observation.
People don't know they are being observed	The researcher might be invading the privacy of the group, deceiving them, and putting them at psychological risk if they discover that a friendship has been based on such deception. The researcher may need to seek IRB approval before undertaking this research.	Ethical considerations may be minimal if behavior is public. Because people don't give know they are being observed, they may engage in private behaviors, raising potential ethical issues.

Subject Reactivity

When we are aware that others are watching us, we often act differently than when we are confident of being unobserved. When people know that a researcher is investigating them, the problem of **subject reactivity** arises. With subject reactivity, people act in unusual ways, so the researcher may not be getting a realistic depiction of the way behavior unfolds.

Subject reactivity—The tendency people being observed to act differently than normal as a result of their awareness of being monitored.

Psychologists who study behavior in laboratories are aware that participants can purposefully change their behaviors, but in the lab, we can control the environment so as to minimize the effects of reactivity. Because observational research does not involve manipulation or intervention most of the time, we can't control reactivity as well. This is why investigators like to keep subjects unaware that they are being observed.

When people know that researchers are monitoring their behaviors, it sometimes does not affect their activities. For example, Jacob et al. (1994) monitored two types of families, distressed and nondistressed. In the distressed families, the father was diagnosed either as alcoholic or as depressed; in the nondistressed families, there were no major psychiatric problems among the parents. The researchers arranged the methodology so that the families did not always know whether their behaviors were being recorded. They discovered little reactivity in either type of family. Why would the families not change their behaviors, given that we know that reactivity is a potentially major problem in observational studies? According to Jacob et al., there are three possible reasons.

First, families have developed routine ways of interaction; it may be hard for them to reliably change the dynamics of their interactions. Second, because families are routinely very busy, they may not have the luxury of trying to figure out how to change their behaviors during monitoring. Third, there may be little motivation for them to change their behaviors. After all, the families have limited interaction with the researchers and no deep, personal relationships with them. So there is little reason for the family to invest energy in changing their behaviors for a group of strangers.

We can't count on such natural behavior, though. As Pepler and Craig (1995) have pointed out, when children move into adolescence, aggressive behaviors may change when the children know they are being observed. Pepler and Craig videotaped and audiotaped children on a playground. The video was remote, but the children wore wireless microphones. The younger children seemed to act naturally during the monitoring. As such, reactivity can be important.

Observer Effects

There are two noteworthy observer effects that can occur in naturalistic observation. When people have to monitor behavior and make decisions about it, there is ample opportunity for the individual to selectively observe or remember some behaviors and to ignore others. This may not represent a lack of integrity by the researcher, just an unwitting human tendency. Still, it is a real research dilemma.

Observer bias—The tendency on the part of observers to bring their biases and predispositions to the recording of data, a process that may be unintentional.

Behavior checklist—A list of behaviors to be recorded in naturalistic observation.

Observer drift—The tendency on the part of an observer to change criteria for recording behaviors over time.

Interobserver (Interrater) reliability—The degree to which two or more observers agree in their coding and scoring of behaviors they are observing and recording.

One problem involves **observer bias**. Just like the rest of us, observers have their own points of view that can affect the way they observe and record information. We all know that any given behavior could be interpreted in very different ways. As objective as observers try to be, we know that people are going to insert their predispositions into everything they do. One way to reduce the effects of observer bias is to create a **behavior checklist** with objective definitions of behaviors to be coded. When Troisi (1999) observed the behaviors of schizophrenics, he used a checklist that would enhance the reliability of measurements. Some of the behaviors he studied are shown in Table 12.1. With explicit definitions on such a checklist, researchers have little latitude for letting their predispositions interfere with the data collection.

The second problem is **observer drift**, in which the coding scheme used by an observer changes over time. This is similar to the threat to validity called instrumentation that you encountered with regard to quasi-experimental designs. Basically, the criteria used by the observer change from the beginning to the end of data collection.

One of the ways that we try to avoid a lowering of the reliability of our observations is to use multiple observers. We assess the reliability of their measurements to see if they are doing the same thing in their coding by assessing **interobserver reliability** (also called **interrater reliability**), the extent to which they agree in their coding. Unfortunately, at times two (or more) observers may begin to code in the same idiosyncratic way. They unknowingly change their way of looking at things so that they are engaged the same inappropriate coding patterns. If we compared two observers whose coding strategies had drifted, we would find that, although they tended to agree with each other, their data would not be consistent with that of other observers.

We can minimize the effects of observer drift by taking these steps:

- Using objective criteria.
- Systematic training of observers.
- Retraining observers.
- Looking at interobserver reliability.
- Changing pairs of observers so the same people don't always collect data together.

CONTROVERSY: Public Versus Private Sex

Normally, we think of sexual behavior as being an intimate and private affair. This feature makes sex difficult to study, especially when the sexual activity is relatively unusual. In spite of this limitation, one particular researcher (Humphreys, 1975) managed such research. It was a highly controversial study of sexual behavior that generated a great deal of debate regarding its ethics.

Humphreys wanted to find out how men who engaged in anonymous homosexual behavior differed from men who were not known to have done so. He went to a certain restroom in a public park

(*continues*)

Public Versus Private Sex (*Continued*)

where men would go to engage in anonymous homosexual sex. His role was to act as a lookout in case the police or rowdy teenagers approached. While acting as the lookout, he recorded the nature of the sexual activity.

After they had finished, he noted their license plate numbers, then went to the police and, using a cover story, obtained their names and addresses. Eighteen months later, he went to their homes to interview them, surveying them regarding other topics.

Is this research ethical? Should he have been watching them engage in sexual activity? You could argue that he invaded their privacy, he lied to the police, he helped them engage in illegal activities. If he had ever had to turn his records over to the police and the men's names became public, they might have been put at risk for psychological harm (embarrassment and ostracism) or physical harm (legal prosecution).

Consider this, though. You could argue that he wasn't deceiving them because he agreed to act as a lookout, and he did. (He actually got arrested a couple of times while doing it.) You could also maintain that he didn't invade their privacy. After all, they were engaging in behavior with a total stranger that they would never again see and were doing it in a public facility in front of a lookout.

What about the possible physical or psychological risk? Humphreys took great pains to keep his records out of the hands of others. He rented a safe deposit box in another state that would have been inaccessible to police in just about any foreseeable case. In reality, there was little chance of harm befalling the men due to his research.

Finally, what did he find? Humphreys discovered that the men who engaged in this behavior did not differ in any systematic ways from men who were not known to have done it. That is, there was remarkably little difference between "them" and "us."

Question for Discussion: Is it possible to argue that the benefits of this research outweigh its ethical problems?

DATA ANALYSIS IN OBSERVATIONAL RESEARCH

Data analysis in observational research spans the range from simple descriptions of behavior to complex statistical analysis. In a naturalistic observation study of children on a playground at school, Pepler and Craig (1995) relied on simple Pearson product–moment correlations, whereas in an ethological comparison of differences in schizophrenics and controls, Troisi et al. (1998) conducted analyses of variance. Some researchers prefer to use qualitative descriptions instead of or in addition to quantitative analysis (e.g., Henwood, 1996; Krahn & Putnam, 2003).

You can find about as many different statistical approaches in observational studies as you will in any other form of research. Because there is no control of variables, though, the research is correlational.

SUMMARY

Observational research provides us with interesting ways to understand behavior. In the most basic form, a researcher simply monitors and records the behaviors of interest. It is a good way to study human and nonhuman activity as it naturally unfolds. Although observational studies are conceptually fairly simple, they actually require attention to a considerable number of details. In order to guarantee reliability and validity, researchers have to develop very specific definitions of variables and to define precisely those conditions in which the behaviors will be observed.

Depending on the nature of the research, observations can be structured or unstructured. Structured observations entail paying attention only to a very restricted set of behaviors; unstructured observations are wider in scope. The investigators need to decide who they will observe, for how long, whether they want to count the number of behaviors or the duration of those behaviors (or both), and the time and location of observation. All of these factors can play critical roles in the results of the research.

Most (but not all) observational studies are field studies because laboratory environments are generally too simple to capture complex behaviors and complex interaction. So when researchers begin their planning, they need to consider the ethical issues associated with observing people who may not know they are under scrutiny. The problems don't disappear if you tell people they are being observed because the subjects of your study may begin to act differently when they know you are watching. We need to take great care so that personal characteristics of the subjects and the observers don't produce misleading results.

REVIEW QUESTIONS

Multiple Choice Questions

1. The study of the behavior of human and nonhuman animals in the natural environment, without any manipulation of variables, is called
   a. subjective research.
   b. anthropometric research.
   c. observational research.
   d. quasi-experimental research.
2. When researchers do not know exactly what behaviors to expect in their observational research, they can set up an artificial situation in a lab and observe behaviors in a preliminary study. Based on the preliminary data, the researchers can then generate hypotheses about behavior in the actual study. The preliminary study would involve
   a. systematic observation.
   b. observational research.
   c. anthropomorphic research.
   d. quasi-experimental research.
3. If researchers wanted to study how long museum visitors looked at various displays in order to learn more about how to set up the displays, the investigators could monitor the behaviors of the visitors. Such research would be called
   a. universalistic.
   b. continuous.
   c. reactive.
   d. particularistic.

4. Researcher Jane Goodall observed the behaviors and social structures of chimpanzees in the wild for many years. Her research could be classified as
   a. experimental.
   b. a case study.
   c. systematic observation.
   d. ethological.
5. The relatively new area of psychology that focuses on human behavior by focusing on the development of our species is called
   a. evolutionary psychology.
   b. anthropomorphism.
   c. theromorphism.
   d. universalism.
6. If a researcher monitored how long a person kept smiling or laughing after seeing a person slip on a banana peel, the data collection would involve
   a. time-point sampling.
   b. time-interval sampling.
   c. continuous real-time sampling.
   d. cluster sampling.
7. If a researcher observes whether a behavior of interest occurs during short, randomly selected intervals, the approach to data collection is
   a. continuous real-time sampling.
   b. time-interval sampling.
   c. cluster sampling.
   d. time-point sampling.
8. One way to increase the likelihood that behaviors of interest in observational research are representative of behaviors in general is to
   a. observe a few behaviors at great length.
   b. take a random sample of behaviors at different times and places.
   c. use universalistic research techniques.
   d. create a comprehensive behavior checklist for observers to use.
9. In observational research, using a small number of long observation times rather multiple short intervals is called
   a. cluster sampling.
   b. one/zero sampling.
   c. time-point sampling.
   d. time-interval sampling.
10. In naturalistic observation, the practice of dichotomous recording whether a behavior occurs or not constitutes
    a. cluster sampling.
    b. one/zero sampling.
    c. continuous real-time sampling.
    d. time-interval sampling
11. Walker et al.'s (1993) research with ethological coding among children

   a. revealed that preschizophrenic children showed some of the same abnormal patterns of facial expression that occur after schizophrenic symptoms appear.
   b. led to the finding that schizophrenics seldom had ethological profiles that resembled those of people in a control group.
   c. showed that behaviors that were similar, like smiling versus grinning, were hard to differentiate reliably.
   d. led to extensive use of ethological approaches in clinical research.

12. If people are observed by a researcher who has joined their organization in order to be able to study them, the researcher must
   a. consider the possibility that there may be an invasion of privacy even if the people engage in lawful public behavior.
   b. get informed consent for studying any behavior members engage in while part of the group.
   c. get approval from an Institutional Review Board even if the people in the group know they are being observed.
   d. consider whether deceiving participants about his or her membership in the group might put group members at risk if they discovered that a friendship has been based on deception.
13. The tendency of researchers to bring their biases and predispositions to the recording of data is called
   a. reactivity.
   b. observer drift.
   c. lack of interrater reliability.
   d. observer bias.
14. When two different researchers code the same behavior in the same setting, they
   a. can assess interobserver reliability.
   b. can rely on subjective criteria for coding.
   c. may eliminate systematic training of observers.
   d. reduce the likelihood of subject reactivity.
15. Some researchers previously labeled aggressive sex on the part of a male animal rape. This type of labeling reflects
   a. theromorphism.
   b. observer bias.
   c. subject reactivity.
   d. anthropomorphism.

Essay Questions

16. Identify the advantages of conducting on-site observations of children in schools when those children have behavior problems.
17. What crucial decisions are associated with sampling in observational research?
18. How do ethological and randomized clinical trials differ in the study of psychiatric patients? What are the advantages and disadvantages of each?

ANSWERS TO REVIEW QUESTIONS

Multiple Choice Questions

1. c	6. c	11. a
2. a	7. b	12. d
3. d	8. b	13. d
4. d	9. a	14. a
5. a	10. b	15. d

Essay Questions

16. Identify the advantages of conducting on-site observations of children in schools when those children have behavior problems.

Because of hectic parental schedules, it may be difficult for them to arrange appointments with a clinician. Observation in the school may be more convenient. In addition, the setting is a natural one for a child, so observations can take place in a place that is normal for the child. The clinician is also able to observe more complex interactions that are apparent in an office visit. Finally, the school may be part of the problem; observing behavior in that setting may give a clue to the source of the difficulty.

17. What crucial decisions are associated with sampling in observational research?

Sampling in observational research involves three different elements. First, who will be observed? The nature of the population needs to be determined. Second, what specific behaviors will be the focus of observations? Third, what kind of temporal sampling will be done: continuous, intermittent, time of day, etc.

18. How do ethological and randomized clinical trials differ in the study of psychiatric patients? What are the advantages and disadvantages of each?

A randomized clinical trial (RCT) typically involves creating two or more groups that receive different treatments, either qualitatively different therapies or different dosages of a medication. One group usually involves the accepted treatment for the problem being studied. The dependent measure typically includes relatively simple measurements, such as numbers on a rating scale and degree of improvement in behavior.

An ethological approach would involve studying a more extensive set of behaviors that are more "natural," that is, that the participants are likely to show in everyday behavior.

A RCT usually requires a smaller commitment of time by the researcher. On the other hand, the ethological approach provides a richer data set involving naturally occurring behaviors.

CHAPTER THIRTEEN

RESEARCH IN DEPTH

Longitudinal and Single-Case Studies

CHAPTER OVERVIEW

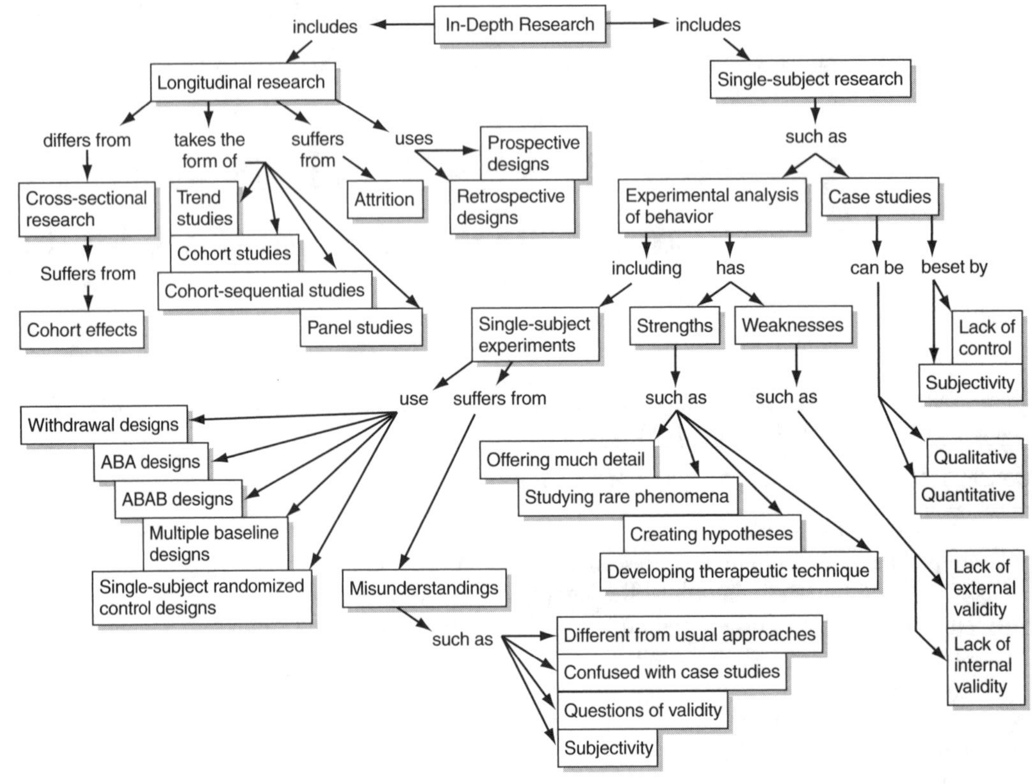

KEY TERMS

ABA design, p. 337
ABAB design, p. 338
Case study, p. 342
Cohort effects, p. 324
Cohort sequential design, p. 327
Cohort study, p. 327
Cross-sectional research, p. 324
Grounded theory, p. 343
Longitudinal research, p. 323
Multiple baseline design, p. 338
N of 1 randomized clinical trial (RCT), p. 339
Panel study, p. 328
Prospective study, p. 331
Retrospective study, p. 331
Trend study, p. 325
Withdrawal design, p. 337

CHAPTER PREVIEW

In this chapter we will cover some techniques that deal with different types of research questions than we have encountered previously. The approaches here are typically employed by researchers with questions that involve in-depth study of people.

Each of these domains has developed its own traditions that sometimes differ from the ones we have already covered. This research may also answer different types of questions. Both of them have added to our understanding of behavior.

Psychologists who study development across time make use of longitudinal research. In this field, we have to deal with change over a long period, sometimes years and decades. As a result, there are special considerations to ponder. When our studies are temporally compact and can be created and completed within a matter of weeks, we think differently from when our studies will not be over for a very long time.

A second specialized research design involves single-participant research. In applied fields, particularly in psychotherapeutic settings and in theoretical work, we may be interested in studying a single individual in depth. We can do so in a quantitative way, with N of 1 randomized clinical trials and experimental analysis of behavior that often entails animal research. We can also use the relatively rare case study approach that tends to be more qualitative.

LONGITUDINAL RESEARCH

If you observe people long enough, you will see that they change in predictable ways. Sometimes the changes take place fairly quickly. Infants 1 year old are very different than they were even a month or two before. College students become much more sophisticated thinkers between the start of their college careers and their graduation. More mature adults show consistent developmental changes as they progress from being the "young-old," the "old," and finally, the "old-old."

Longitudinal research—A design in which an investigator studies the same people or the same population (but different individuals) over time, sometimes across decades.

Psychologists have developed techniques to study people at different stages in their lives. One such approach is called longitudinal research. In psychology, **longitudinal research** refers to the study of the same individuals over time. Within psychology, developmental psychologists make greatest use of longitudinal research. A developmental psychologist, or developmentalist, is interested in the nature and causes of change.

Common Themes in Longitudinal Research

When researchers study change over either a short or a long time span, they investigate the psychological and physiological causes of development. We can conveniently categorize the sources of difference among people into three general groups. First, some researchers may focus on genetic differences that underlie behavior. Scientists recognize that genetic factors can affect behaviors that psychologists study, but the extent to which genes control behavior is overwhelmed by other factors. Genetic factors may explain up to 25 percent of the variability in cognitive ability across different people, but much less for personality characteristics (Schaie, 2000).

A second potential cause for individual differences is environmental. Thus, a person's education, family structure, socialization, and access to good nutrition and healthcare have an effect on behavior and attitudes. Not surprisingly, these situational factors are important for the emergence of most of the variability in behavior. Another environmental (i.e., social) aspect of change involves cohort effects, that is, the effects of one's peers, which begin to exert pronounced consequences beginning with school years, but less so during infancy and toddlerhood.

Research on environmental causes of change is complex because it is virtually impossible to identify all of the individual factors that affect even the simplest of behaviors. Further, almost all longitudinal research is descriptive, not experimental. This correlational approach allows us to spot relationships among variables, but not causes.

A third domain involves the interaction between genetics and environment. The reason for complexity here is that we still have a very incomplete knowledge base related to how genes and the environment interact for different people. For some behaviors, we will probably ultimately conclude that a complete understanding requires knowledge both of genetic and of environmental factors, particularly for some psychological disorders.

Cross-Sectional Versus Longitudinal Research

When we discuss contemporary research, it is easy to assume that psychologists have always used the methods we now use. In reality, research strategies have to be invented. Normally, we persist in using the approach with which we are most comfortable. It is likely to be the approach that our peers and contemporaries use. That is why so many research reports describe similar methods.

Psychologists who study developmental processes have developed increasingly useful strategies. Initially, the approach to developmental questions, particularly for studying aging, did not include longitudinal research. Instead, researchers used **cross-sectional research** (Schaie, 2000). From the beginning of the 1900s and for the subsequent several decades, if investigators wanted to know how younger and older adults differed in their intellectual functioning, they would locate two samples, one younger and one older, and assess differences in their abilities.

Cross-sectional research—A design in which an investigator studies groups differing on some characteristic (e.g., age) at the same time, in contrast to a longitudinal approach that studies the same individuals over time.

Although cross-sectional studies dominated, not all psychologists used them exclusively. Lewis Terman's longitudinal study of gifted people from childhood into old age is a case in point. The research began in the 1920s, when cross-sectional studies were the norm.

Although a cross-sectional plan seemed like a reasonable approach for the first three decades of the twentieth century, after a while some cracks appeared in the foundation. For instance, researchers discovered that they could not replicate the well-documented decline in cognitive functioning across the lifespan that early cross-sectional studies reported (Jones & Conrad, 1933). Gradually, through the 1930s, longitudinal studies became more common.

Researchers began to realize that in a nonequivalent groups design that investigates groups of people who grew up in different eras, the participants differed in more than just age. They experienced life from a different viewpoint and may have had different opportunities for education and healthcare.

Cohort effects—Differences across age groups having to do with characteristics of the era in which a person grew up rather than to age effects specifically.

Differences between groups that result from participants having had quite different life experiences are called **cohort effects**. A cohort is a population whose members have some specific characteristic in common, like a birth cohort, a group of people born about the same time. A cohort doesn't have to rely on age; studying psychology majors as compared to other majors will also involve cohorts.

Once researchers accepted the notion of studying the same people over time, investigators often used two-point studies, with researchers observing their participants twice. One of the problems with two-point studies is statistical regression, sometimes called regression to the mean. It refers to the fact that when people are measured and show extreme scores, they often have less extreme scores the next time. In many cases, extreme scores include a large amount of measurement error. That error is unlikely to repeat itself in subsequent measurements. So when changes in scores occur, the result might represent only a change in measurement error.

Further, some variables that researchers measure show different results in cross-sectional and longitudinal studies, with longitudinal studies sometimes failing to replicate cross-sectional studies and sometimes showing greater differences (Schaie, 1992).

The methodological innovation that has allowed greater understanding of the developmental process is the longitudinal approach.

VARIETIES OF LONGITUDINAL RESEARCH

Researchers generally categorize longitudinal research according to the way participants are selected for a study. In some longitudinal research, the measurements at each time interval involve the same people. In other designs, the measurements include different people across time. Psychological research is more likely to include the same people in each observation frame. Other research may sample from a population without concerns as to whether the same individuals are included. Such studies often involve large, perhaps national, samples.

Trend Studies

When investigators assess a general population across time, they sometimes sample randomly at each data-collection point. Depending on the nature of the study, this approach can result in a completely different sample each time. This total replacement of participants is characteristic of **trend studies**.

One example of a trend study involves the prevalence of suicidal thoughts in young people. Late adolescence and young adulthood seem like precarious times for youth in the United States. One manifestation of the problem is suicides on college campuses. Such tragedies are in the news all too frequently.

Trend study—A variety of longitudinal research in which an investigator samples randomly from a generally defined population over time, with different individuals constituting each sample.

One report noted that six students at New York University had committed suicide within a one-year period (Caruso, 2004) (www.suicide.org/joann-mitchell-levy-nyu-suicides.html). In other well-publicized news, three Massachusetts students (at MIT, Harvard, and the University of Massachusetts at Amherst) died during a single week in 1998 amid suspicion that the deaths were suicides, according to a story in the *Christian Science Monitor* (April 7, 1998). MIT and Harvard lead the nation in student suicides, as noted in the University of Illinois's Daily

Illini (February 14, 2001). As of several years ago, Penn State suffered an average of two student suicides a year, according to its online student newspaper, *The Digital Collegian* (July 24, 1997).

Any suicide is a calamity for the friends and family of the victim, but we don't know whether collegiate suicide rates are going up or down or staying the same. Colleges only began keeping track of suicides in 1990. Over the past decades, suicides among the young have increased dramatically, though.

We can figure the suicide rate among students, but how many students actually think about suicide? Fortunately, researchers in Vermont, in an attempt to anticipate and prevent problems in the state, have collected data from middle- and high-school students over time that may shed light on the question. This data set can form a trend study sampled from the state's population of high school students in every two years since the mid 1990s.

The percentage of students who have had suicidal ideation (i.e., thoughts of suicide) in the twelve months prior to the survey was alarmingly high, as shown in Figure 13.1. As many as a quarter of the students in middle and high school thought about suicide in the mid 1990s. Luckily, many fewer make plans or attempt suicide (Vermont Youth Risk Behavior Survey: Statewide Report, 1997, 2001, 2005). The results of this trend study suggest that we cannot ignore the problems of the young. In fact, David Satcher, former Surgeon General of the United States, has declared that suicide is a public health crisis. College officials have begun to pay significant attention to ways of preventing student deaths.

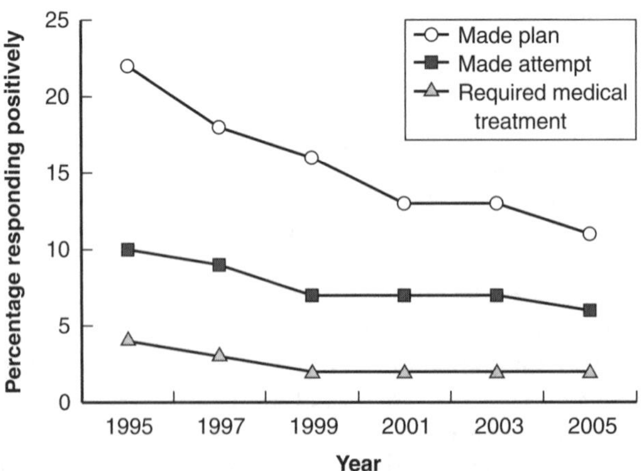

FIGURE 13.1 Incidence of suicide ideation and attempts among students in Vermont. Thoughts of suicide occurred to up to 25 percent of students, while decreasing numbers actually made a plan, attempted suicide, and required medical attention after an attempt. [*Made Plan* = Actually made a plan to commit suicide; *Attempted* = Carried out a suicide attempt; *Medical* = Carried out an attempt that required medical intervention]

Another type of trend study might, in repeated assessments, include some of the same participants. If we were interested in the extent to which eighth-grade teachers include novels in their reading assignments, we could sample from that population of teachers periodically. Some teachers might appear in both samples. As long as the sample is large, though, the instances of such overlap will be minimal. In any case, if the sampling is random, we will likely generate a representative sample each time, regardless of the degree of overlap among participants.

Cohort Studies

When researchers study a specific, well-defined population over time but sample different people at each data collection point, they are using a **cohort study**. (Trend studies examine more general populations.)

Cohort study—A variety of longitudinal research in which an investigator samples randomly from a population selected because of a specific characteristic, often age.

One of the most well-known cohort studies is the Nurses Health Study, which began in 1976. It involves about 122,000 nurses from the original cohort, followed by a new generation of nurses in 1989. (This research design is known in the medical field as an observational epidemiology study.) The project began in order to study the long-term effects of using oral contraceptives. Every two years, cohort members receive a survey with questions about health-related topics. At the request of the participants, the investigators began adding questions on a variety of topics, like smoking, nutrition, and quality-of-life issues. The researchers even collected toenail clippings so they could identify minerals in food that the participants ate. Psychologists do not use trend studies or cohort studies very extensively. These approaches are more within the province of medical research, although studies like the Nurses Health Study include quality-of-life information that might help us answer behavioral and attitudinal questions.

Cohort Sequential Studies

If you wanted to compare people of different ages, you could use a cross-sectional design wherein you select samples of such individuals and investigate differences that might exist between them. The problem in interpretation, as mentioned before, is that the people have different life experiences because of the particular environment in which they grew up. You may not be able to attribute differences to age alone.

Cohort sequential design—A variety of longitudinal research in which an investigator repeatedly measures a cohort group (e.g., people 60 years of age) over time, adding a new cohort (e.g., new 60-year-olds) in each wave in order to differentiate between cohort effects and age effects.

One solution to this problem is the **cohort sequential design**. This technique involves measuring samples of people at a selected age and testing them on a regular basis. In this approach, you study people of a given age, for example, 60 years old, then study them at some later point, like when they are 67. During the second test, you could also investigate a new group of 60-year-olds.

This gives you the opportunity to test 60-year-olds from slightly different eras to see if there is something special about being 60. You can also see how people change over time. The cohort sequential design mixes the cross-sectional approach with the longitudinal. The strength of the cohort sequential design is that it can help you spot changes due to age as well as to differences in the environment in which people develop.

A classic example of this research began in the 1950s by Warner Schaie. He selected a group of elderly people and tested them on their cognitive ability every seven years. At the second testing phase, he assessed the original group but also included a new group of people that he tested every seven years. This second group was as old when tested as the first group was at its initial testing. Then, at the third testing phase, he included a new group that was as old as his first group at their initial testing. So he started with a group of 60-year-olds. Seven years later, he tested these people who were now 67 and began assessment of a new group of 60-year-olds. After another seven years, he brought in a new group of 60-year-olds to compare with the second group, now aged 67, and the first group, now aged 74.

Over four decades, he tested different groups at the same age in their lives but who grew up in different times. He was able to spot changes in their behavior as they aged and was also able to look for differences that might be attributable to cohort effects.

People performed very differently depending on when they were born. Earlier birthdates were associated with poorer performance for the same age. When people born in 1896 were tested at age 60, their performance was clearly lower than the cohorts from all other birth years when those cohorts were tested at age 60. In fact, with each successive cohort, performance at age 60 was higher than that of the previous cohort.

Thus, there is nothing special about the absolute test scores at age 60 (or at any other age); it is more reasonable to believe that having been born later led to different experiences, perhaps involving education, nutrition, healthcare, etc. that would be important in development and maintenance of their cognitive skill.

Bray, Adams, Getz, and Baer (2001) used this design to study alcohol use in children over a three-year period. In the first year, one cohort was in the sixth grade, the second cohort was in the seventh grade, and the third cohort was in the eighth grade. In the second year, the previous sixth graders were now in the seventh grade, so their alcohol use could be compared with that of the children who had been in the seventh grade the year before (and who were now in the eighth grade). In the third year, the original sixth graders were in the eighth grade, so their drinking could be compared to those children who were in the eighth grade in the first year of the study. Their results appear in Figure 13.2. Although the research lasted three years, the investigators ended up with data on children as young as sixth grade and as old as tenth grade, a five-year span.

Other researchers have also used this approach to study alcohol use in children. For example, Duncan, Duncan, and Strycker (2006) studied even younger children (i.e., fourth graders). Drinking had already begun by some children that young.

Panel Studies

Another general category of longitudinal studies is the **panel study**. In this design, the same participants are followed throughout the course of the study. The most famous study of people throughout their lifespan was initiated by Lewis Terman in the 1920s.

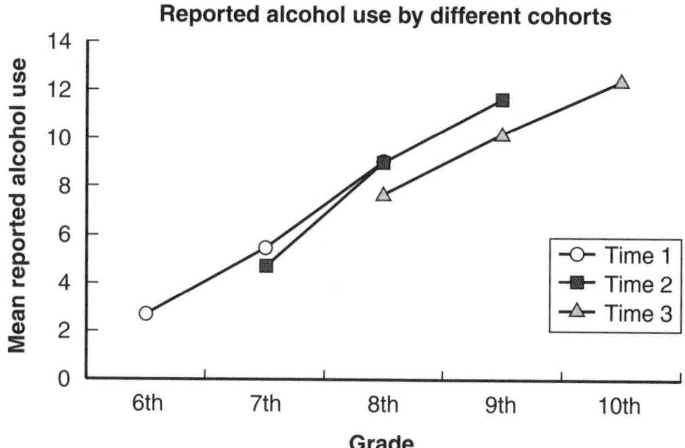

FIGURE 13.2 Example of a cohort-sequential analysis of alcohol use by children. The researchers studied children for the same three-year period. One cohort was in the sixth grade at the start of the research, the second cohort was in the seventh grade, and the third cohort was in the eighth grade. The results reflect an increase in alcohol use as the children get older, with similar but not identical patterns across the three years.

Source: Bray, J. H., Adams, G. J., Getz, J. G., & Baer, P. E. (2001). Developmental, family, and ethnic in influences on adolescent alcohol usage: A growth curve approach. *Journal of Family Psychology, 15*, 301–314. Copyright © 2001 by the American Psychological Association. Adapted with permission

Panel study—A variety of longitudinal research in which an investigator studies the same individuals over time.

When he began, he didn't suspect that it would become a lifelong enterprise for him. At his death in 1956, the research was still going strong. In fact, his successors have kept it alive into its ninth decade.

Terman was born in Indiana in 1877 but moved to Los Angeles after contracting tuberculosis. (Ironically, the relocation was for the clean air that he could expect in Los Angeles at that time.) While teaching there, he identified 1,528 children with IQ scores over 135 and compared them to a comparable group of unselected children, a typical cross-sectional approach. Many writers have detailed the research (e.g., Holahan & Sears, 1995), but, in essence, the gifted children and adolescents matured into adults who tended to be happy, healthy, successful, and productive.

A more typical example of a longitudinal study involved a project that investigated the effects of bullying on young teenagers. This project lasted through one school year and into a second (Bond et al., 2001). Investigators have documented that being bullied is strongly associated with depression (Hawker & Boulton, 2000). Unfortunately, the cross-sectional studies comparing depression in bullied and non-bullied groups do not allow assessment of causality because these nonequivalent control groups designs are correlational.

Bond and colleagues (2001) examined bullying among high-school students in Australia in three waves, that is, at three data collection points. They administered questionnaires to 2,680 students, twice in grade 8 and once in grade 9. The investigators

CONTROVERSY: Student Achievement

Each generation of parents seems to be worried that their children are not learning as much in school as they did when they were students. It doesn't matter that the parents of the current group of parents had the same worry, as did each previous generation before them. It is an empirical question as to whether current students are less capable than previous students; that is, we can use data to answer the question.

The National Assessment of Educational Progress (NAEP) project is an example of a trend study. Since 1971, students at grades 4, 8, and 12 have been tested in a variety of subject areas, such as reading, mathematics, and science. The results are often called the "nation's report card."

In Figure 13.3, you can see how 17-year-olds (i.e., twelfth-grade high school students) have fared in their reading since 1971. In spite of complaints about how students cannot read as well as they used to, it is pretty clear that student scores remained relatively stable over thirty-three years. If you look at the scores of the high school girls, their average performance rose dramatically in 1984 and stayed more or less the same. Boys, on the other hand, peaked in 1988 and declined somewhat, although their scores are about the same as those of boys in 1971. Since 1973, math scores have actually increased.

At each NAEP testing, there will be a different set of students because when the test is administered every two or three years, the students in the twelfth grade will have changed. The samples used in NAEP can be considered to involve different cohorts in one sense because the actual participants differ each time, but they involve the same cohort in the sense that they sample twelfth graders each time.

What do these numbers say about the current generation of students? Should we believe the comments people make about how deficient students are today? The answer is that, although the situation in some schools, some neighborhoods, and some states is in dire need of remedy, the picture is not all that bleak. There is certainly room for improvement, but it appears that we are no worse off now than we were in the 1970s.

Question for Discussion: If the NAEP scores have not declined, why do you think people believe that education has deteriorated?

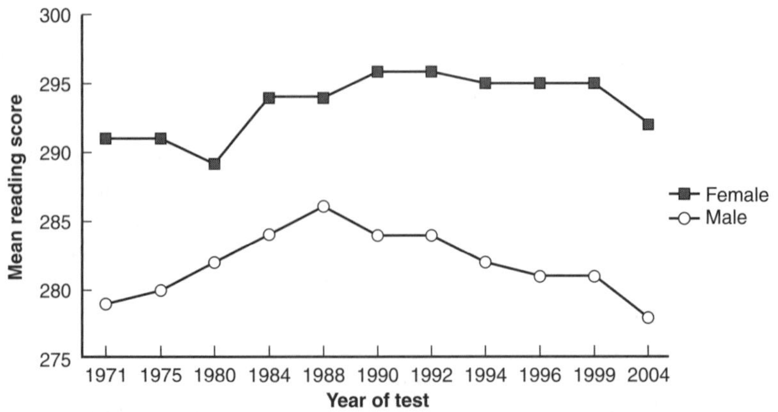

FIGURE 13.3 Reading scores by gender on the National Assessment of Educational Progress (NAEP) test for students 17 years of age since 1971. The assessment uses a random sample of students at each data collection point so there is little or no overlap among participants. This is an example of a trend study.

found that recurrent victimization like being teased or excluded, having rumors spread about them, and being physically threatened predicted depression for girls, but not for boys.

One tentative conclusion was that being bullied might cause depression. The researchers noted that previous depression did not predict being bullied; that is, depressed students were not singled out for bullying because they appeared fragile or vulnerable. Students with no sign of depression who were bullied subsequently showed depression, so bullying might be a causal agent.

ISSUES IN LONGITUDINAL DESIGNS

Longitudinal designs have provided us with a wealth of information about the ways we develop over time. They can be adapted for use with populations ranging from neonates and infants to the very old. If you are patient enough, you can monitor changes over months, years, and even decades. As with any design, though, longitudinal research has weaknesses as well strengths.

Retrospective and Prospective Studies

When we want to see how people change over time, it is generally easier to ask them about critical events at a single point in time, relying on their memories for past events. This happens in a **retrospective study**. It is certainly more convenient for the researcher. Unfortunately, it is also prone to distortions from memory lapses. An additional consideration regarding retrospective research is that it cannot involve experimental manipulation of variables, so it is always quasi-experimental or ex post facto. Consequently, it is not possible to identify causal relationships among variables with confidence.

Retrospective study—An approach to studying change over time that relies on people's memories and recollections of the past.

Prospective study—An approach to studying change over time that identifies research participants at the beginning of the project who are followed throughout the course of the research.

We have trouble with mundane information. For instance, Wentland and Smith (1993) found that a significant percentage of people have a hard time remembering if they had a library card. As an example of faulty memories for major events, Cannell, Fisher, and Bakker (1965, cited in Judd, Smith, & Kidder, 1991) demonstrated that people erred in determining how many times they had been hospitalized in the past year.

We are also likely to reconstruct details of the past, in effect creating memories that fit the overall structure of what we are trying to recall. We don't do this intentionally, but it happens just the same. In longitudinal research, we shouldn't expect people to show high levels of mnemonic accuracy for remote events, even for significant events.

The alternative to a retrospective study is a **prospective study**. In this approach, researchers identify the participants they want to observe and follow them forward in time. Sometimes this is relatively easy, as in Bond et al.'s (2001) study of bullying behavior. They identified their population, created a sample, and questioned them while the events of interest were likely to be fresh in memory.

Other prospective studies rely on some event whose impact the researchers want to assess. Researchers sometimes initiate research when something of interest happens in society. For instance, Hurricane Andrew hit Florida in 1992, causing massive damage and suffering. A team of psychologists used that event to study the course of posttraumatic stress in children.

La Greca, Silverman, Vernberg, and Prinstein (1996) studied 442 elementary school children after the hurricane. The investigators administered the Posttraumatic Stress Disorder Reaction Index for Children (RI), the Hurricane-Related Traumatic Experiences (HURTE) measure, the Social Support Scale for Children (SSSC), the Kidcope survey, and the Life Event Schedule (LES). Measurements were obtained three, seven, and ten months after the hurricane. They found that 12 percent of the children experienced severe to very severe levels of posttraumatic stress disorder (PTSD) at ten months.

You can see that it would be nearly impossible to obtain valid data with a retrospective study of the effects of the hurricane. You can't go back in time to administer the RI (or any of the other scales). It is also unreasonable to think that the children could reconstruct their reactions from seven or ten months previously. In order to know how feelings and emotions change over time, the only viable approach is prospective.

As in the latter example, the decision to use a prospective or a retrospective design is sometimes not under the control of the researcher. Prospective research is possible when the investigators identify a question and have a group that they can follow into the future. Retrospective research is called for when the answer to a research question lies, at least in part, in what has already happened.

Attrition

The single largest methodological concern in longitudinal studies is the fact that some people will stop participating. The study of bullying by Bond et al. (2001) began with 2,680 students, but by the end of their data collection, only 2,365 remained.

The biggest issue associated with this loss of participants, known as attrition, is that you don't always know whether those who disappear differ from those who remain. Bond et al. (2001) reported that the attrition rate in their bullying study was higher for boys than for girls. They also noted in their results that boys showed a lower incidence of depression associated with bullying. Could it be that a significant proportion of the boys who left the study experienced depression from bullying and those who remained did not? Further, attrition was greater for students with single-parent families. Thus, conclusion by the researchers that boys experience less depression may have been biased to reflect the remaining participants, who could very well differ from those who departed.

Sometimes it is hard to anticipate whether attrition will affect outcomes. Hayslip, McCoy-Roberts, and Pavur (1998–99) conducted a three-year study of how well adults cope after the death of a loved one. They reported, first of all, that attrition at six months was associated with an active decision to leave the study whereas at three years, the researchers had simply lost track of the individuals, some of whom might have participated if found.

The investigators also discovered that attrition did not seem to affect the nature of the results of their research on the effects of the death of a spouse. The results and conclusions would have been pretty much the same regardless of whether those who left had been included.

On the other hand, Hayslip et al. (1998–99) noted that those who had suffered a nonconjugal loss (i.e., somebody other than a husband or wife) and who dropped out were younger, less active in their coping, were in better health, and were less lonely at the beginning of the study. The researchers pointed out poorer psychological recovery after the death of a spouse or other loved one is associated with younger age, poorer health, and more loneliness. Given that nonconjugal dropouts were younger, they might be expected to show poorer outcomes. Their attrition might affect conclusions greatly because those remaining in the sample were the types of people you would expect to do well.

Dropouts were also in better health and less lonely, factors associated with better psychological outcomes. If your study experienced attrition by those who were healthy and not lonely, you would lose people who typically recover well. As a result, your sample would look bleak, not because people can't recover from bereavement, but because the people who agree to be studied are likely to have worse outcomes than those who leave.

Hayslip et al. (1998–99) concluded that we need to be very sensitive to the nature of those who leave longitudinal projects. There is a realistic chance that dropouts lead to biased results, therefore less valid conclusions. Given the potential importance of attrition, it is common for researchers to report the degree of attrition in their reports. The reality of longitudinal research is that you can count on losing people. An important question is whether those who leave a study differ in relevant ways from those who remain.

When LaGreca and her colleagues (1996) studied students over ten months who suffered through Hurricane Andrew, they recorded the dropouts, documented the reasons for the attrition, and formally compared participants and nonparticipants. Figure 13.4 displays the percentage of the initial 568 students in the Hurricane Andrew study who departed and the general reason for having done so. As you can see, over 8 percent had departed by seven months and a total of about 22 percent by ten months. These attrition figures are not unusual for such research.

Fortunately, La Greca et al. discovered that those who dropped out did not differ from those who remained in terms of grade, gender, ethnicity, or initial symptoms of PTSD. It is likely that the students who participated throughout the study were representative of the entire set of 568 who began the project.

We have found ways to reduce the attrition rates, although they are not without cost. The tactics involve a commitment of time and expense on the researcher's part. Wutzke and colleagues (2000) studied a group of 554 people who engaged in heavy drinking in Australia. The project extended for ten years, a period of time that generally leads to notable attrition among highly educated and cooperative participants, and extremely high levels among people with substance abuse problems. At the end of their ten years, Wutzke et al. randomly sampled and reviewed 20 percent (n = 109) of the records to see how well contact had been maintained. Surprisingly, 72.5 percent of the 109 people had been successfully located for the study; over 78 percent of the total group of 554 had been located.

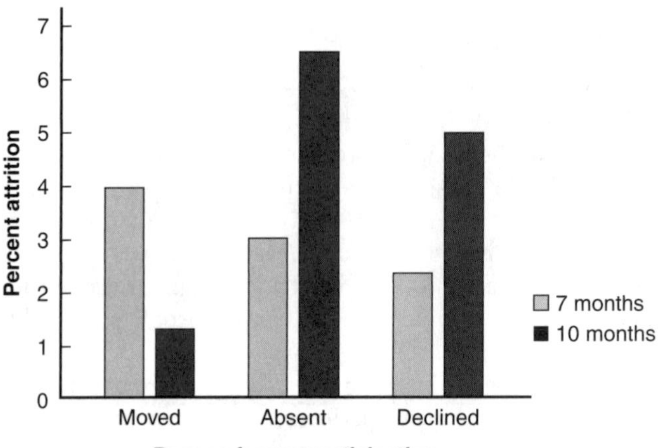

FIGURE 13.4 Reason for nonparticipation in the Hurricane Andrew study of posttraumatic stress disorder (PTSD). The researchers documented the reasons for nonparticipation and compared those who left the study with those who remained. Of the initial 568 elementary school students, just over 22 percent dropped out of the study for reasons that were sometimes clear (e.g., they had moved) or vague (e.g., they simply declined). Those who participated did not differ from those who dropped out.

Source: A. M. LaGreca et al. (1996). Symptoms of posttraumatic stress in children after Hurricane Andrew: A prospective study. *Journal of Counseling and Clinical Psychology, 64,* 712–723. Copyright © 1996 American Psychological Association. Adapted with permission.

The researchers had prepared well and worked diligently throughout the study to keep in touch with the participants. They enhanced their success by taking a number of steps as they initiated their project and as they conducted it. Table 13.1 presents their strategies to avoid losing track of people and maintaining the participants' motivation to continue in the project. Some of these steps are seemingly obvious, like getting participants' full names and people related to them; others are less obvious, like maintaining participants' motivation by sending birthday cards. As obvious as they might be, researchers have not always carried them out.

Finally, when you are studying older people, an additional reason for attrition is likely, namely, the death of the participant. In the study begun by Terman in 1921, there has been considerable attrition, as you might expect. However, in the thirty-fifth year of the study (1955), over 88 percent of the women and over 87 percent of the men remained in the project.

When Terman died in 1956, the attrition rate increased, possibly because the participants had felt a very strong personal connection with him. Between 1955 and 1960, the number who actively declined to participate exceeded the total attrition since 1921 (Holahan & Sears, 1995). Since 1972, attrition has been more likely due to death than to a choice to drop out. Remarkably, only 8 percent of the women and 6 percent of the men have been "lost," the researchers term for loss of contact because they can't find the person.

TABLE 13.1 Steps Taken by Researchers to Decrease Attrition of Participants in a Longitudinal Study Involving Heavy Drinkers (Wutzke et al., 2000)

Preparation

- Ensuring that dates of birth and middle names were collected (to make later tracing easier).
- Identifying a contact person who lived at a different address.
- Maintaining contact throughout the project with such mailings as birthday cards or regular newsletters.

Persistence

- Beginning a trace of the person as soon as contact is lost.
- Making multiple phone calls to set up appointments for interviews.
- Showing willingness to conduct interviews at times and locations convenient for the respondent.
- Providing incentives to offset the inconvenience of participation.

It is ironic that the exceedingly low attrition in the Terman study is fairly unimportant in some ways. The sample he chose in 1921 wasn't representative either of the population generally or of gifted children specifically. As a result, we don't know exactly to whom we can generalize the results of the research.

DATA ANALYSIS IN LONGITUDINAL RESEARCH

Because measurements in longitudinal research are not fundamentally different than those in other types of research, we see the same statistical approaches in long-term projects that we do in cross-sectional studies. You can review the common techniques for data analysis in the statistics appendix.

Most longitudinal research is correlational, so data analyses reflect that fact. Research that involves multiple variables of interest typically involves correlation or regression analysis. Such tests give us critical information about what variables are associated with one another and what variables are useful in predicting outcomes.

For instance, Hayslip et al. (1998–99) used a sophisticated correlational approach called discriminant analysis to combine the effects of variables such as health, adjustment, loneliness, and distress so they could examine how people cope with the death of a loved one. La Greca et al. (1996) used simple regression analysis to find the associations of posttraumatic stress symptoms and other variables that included exposure to a hurricane, the amount of loss or disruption, demographics, and social support afterward.

Sometimes researchers use tests related to the analysis of variance (ANOVA) in longitudinal research. Such use typically occurs when the design involves nonequivalent control group designs. For example, Bosworth and Schaie (1999) used the database associated with Schaie's Seattle Longitudinal Study to compare the cognitive functioning of two groups of older adults. The researchers compared performance over the years of a group of people who had subsequently died versus a comparable group of survivors. Bosworth and Schaie found that the deceased group had shown declines on some measures years prior to their death. To spot differences between groups, Bosworth and Schaie employed repeated measures analysis of covariance (ANCOVA), a variation of the ANOVA that removes the effects of variables that may correlate with the DV.

Hoekstra-Weebers, Jaspers, Kamps, and Klip (2001) studied the psychological adaptation among parents of children with cancer over one year. They used a simple repeated measures ANOVA to see if they could identify factors associated with the way parents cope with their children's cancer.

In short, you can expect to see just about any type of statistical approach in longitudinal research that you see in other varieties of research. An important reminder about interpreting the results of the statistical tests is that, even if we use tests like an ANOVA, we can't make conclusions about causation if we haven't manipulated an independent variable. In longitudinal studies, the data are usually correlational, so we can't make causal statements.

SINGLE-SUBJECT EXPERIMENTATION

In the past century, psychologists have developed the tradition of conducting studies with groups of participants, ignoring the behavior of single individuals. As a discipline, psychology was not always oriented toward this approach. In the early years of psychology, researchers often studied a single person intensively.

Experimentalists and clinicians shared this methodology. Freud used single-participant studies in his clinical work, as did John Watson (e.g., Little Albert) in his research on learning. Then in the early decades of the twentieth century, experimental psychologists gravitated toward the study of groups. Single-subject experimental research did not return until the middle of the century. When it was resurrected, researchers often conducted long-term studies of single subjects, often rats and pigeons. The research reports were largely devoid of statistical analysis; visual displays of data replaced statistics. The behaviorists who resurrected single-subject research believed that enough data over many experimental trials would reveal important patterns of behavior, so statistical treatment wasn't necessary. Today, single-subject studies with people tend to involve those with psychological problems.

Experimental Analysis of Behavior

The experimental analysis of behavior reflects a unique tradition in research. It arose from the behaviorist tradition and had significant focus on the study of reinforcement contingencies. Because one of the major tenets of behaviorism was that we can discover general principles and laws of behavior, researchers believed that studies with large numbers of subjects were not only unnecessary, but also undesirable. By using many subjects and averaging the data on their performance, the behaviorists thought that we would lose sight of individual details.

Consequently, the tradition of using one or a few subjects emerged. Psychologists who may rely on visual presentation of results rather than on complex statistical analysis. These researchers are not immune to psychological culture, though, so even these psychologists have altered their traditions somewhat, using some statistical analysis to help them understand their research results.

Within the realm of experimental analysis of behavior, two distinct paths have developed. Some experimenters rely on studies of animal behavior; their work is largely theoretical. Investigations with people often involve clinical settings and tend to be more applied although clearly based on behavioral theory. The experimental analysis of behavior is likely to be highly objective and quantitative.

METHODS OF SINGLE-CASE DESIGNS

Studies with single individuals, whether human or nonhuman, do not differ in concept from many of the other approaches we have already covered. The biggest difference involves the number of people or animals tested, not necessarily the methodology. In fact, this difference in the number of participants is not necessary; single-case research can involve multiple cases. The researchers are likely to report on them individually, though. Case studies can involve controlled observations, like experiments. They can also rely on questionnaires and naturalistic observation.

Another difference between single-case analyses and group analyses is that single-case research involves continuous monitoring of behavior over time. In this sense it resembles time-series or longitudinal designs more than the typical cross-sectional design.

Withdrawal Designs

Single-case research can take many different forms. The general process involves assessing the behavior or behaviors of interest to monitor the baseline rate of the behaviors. Then a treatment begins. After that, different designs lead to different steps.

Withdrawal design—A research method in which an investigator observes a baseline of behavior, applies a treatment, and assesses any behavioral change, then removes or withdraws the treatment to see the degree to which the behavior reverts to baseline levels.

ABA design—A type of withdrawal design in which a treatment is applied only once, then withdrawn.

One design, the **withdrawal design**, entails a baseline phase, a treatment phase, then a return to a baseline phase. It is represented as an **ABA design** because researchers refer to the baseline period with the letter A and the treatment with the letter B. If treatment is effective, a simple withdrawal design should document that there is movement toward the desired outcome during the treatment phase. In medical or psychiatric research that assesses whether a drug stabilizes a person's condition, a return of the symptoms to the original level when the treatment is withdrawn may be entirely predictable, even desirable for assessing the effectiveness of a treatment. This design is most useful when researchers expect that after a treatment is removed, the original pattern of behavior will recur. In such a case, the ABA design permits the researchers to identify cause and effect relationships.

In much psychological research, it isn't clear what will happen in the second baseline phase. After a behavioral treatment phase ends, we hope that the desired behavior change is going to persist. So in the second baseline phase, we hope there isn't a return to the first level. Consequently, an ABA design and its variations may not be useful for studying the effects of psychological therapy.

ABAB Designs

In order to strengthen the internal validity of single-case research, investigators sometimes withdraw a treatment to see if a person's condition worsens, then they introduce a second baseline phase, followed by a reintroduction of the treatment, creating an **ABAB design**. If the individual's behavior changes predictably every time the treatment is applied and removed, it shows that the treatment is having the desired effect. Naturally, this design only makes sense if the researcher expects behavior to revert to an original state after the treatment ends.

ABAB design—A type of withdrawal design that uses a baseline period followed by application of a treatment, the withdrawal of the treatment (as in an ABA design), and reapplication of the treatment.

We can see how this type of single-case design works in a study of head injury patients. Hall, MacDonald, and Young (1992) assessed motor responses and eye movements of five individuals with serious head injury, four resulting from automobile accidents and one from a fall. In the baseline phase, the researchers monitored the behaviors of interest, then applied either directed multisensory stimulation or nondirected stimulation. This means that they exposed the patients to auditory, visual, tactile, and smell/taste stimuli and requested certain behaviors, like eye movements, from them. Directed multisensory stimulation (SDS) involved tailoring the nature of the stimuli to the individual. The researchers stimulated the patient with things that were personally meaningful for the individual. Non-directed stimulation (NDS) entailed stimulation that did not have personal relevance for the patient.

The researchers' version of the ABAB design was a single day of baseline recording, followed by alternating SDS, baseline, and NDS on a weekly basis for four to six weeks. The investigators discovered that simply providing stimulation was not particularly effective in increasing the person's awareness of the environment compared to providing stimuli that were relevant to that particular person.

Multiple Baseline Designs

Sometimes clinicians are interested in changing several behaviors of a client or in changing a behavior across different settings. These psychologists can work on such changes one at a time. For instance, for the first phase, the psychologist and the client work on one behavior. When the client's behavior reaches the desired state, they will work on a second behavior, continuing until they have worked with all relevant behaviors.

Multiple baseline design—A research design that studies multiple behaviors that may change across baseline, treatment, and withdrawal phases.

Changing successive behaviors or the same behavior in different settings is part of the **multiple baseline design**. These designs follow the same logic as the withdrawal and ABAB designs. The investigator monitors baseline levels of the behavior of interest, then applies the treatment.

As an example of how this design is applied, let's consider the study of a woman who had been in an automobile accident and who was experiencing posttraumatic stress disorder (PTSD) as a result (Kellett & Beall, 1997). She was having recurrent nightmares; the therapist used psychodynamic-interpersonal psychotherapy to try to eliminate the dreams.

The investigators used an AB design, that is, baseline observation of nightmares followed by psychotherapy and monitoring of the nightmares. It was a multiple baseline design because the therapist was looking at multiple target variables: frequency of the nightmares, intensity of the nightmares, extent of fear and of upset, and how long it took the client to recover from the nightmare (as measured by the number of book chapters she read before returning to sleep).

The baseline period extended for fourteen days, with the treatment phase covering the next forty-nine days and a followup at six months. The number of nightmares and the degree of fear both immediately diminished, only to increase temporarily three weeks into the treatment; then the nightmares and the fear again decreased. At six weeks, her distress and her nightmares again took an upswing before declining further. At six months, the symptoms of distress were minimal.

This type of change is not unusual in applied research with people who have severe, complex problems. There is improvement followed by relapse, then greater improvement. Sometimes idealized graphs show consistent improvement with the application of a treatment. In an ideal world, a client's progress would be continuous, but life doesn't always unfold this way.

The strength of the multiple baseline design is that as the clinician works with multiple behaviors, the effect of the therapy can be noted in each one independently. If the treatment is working, each application should change the new behavior being studied.

Single-Subject Randomized Controlled Trials

In medical or psychiatric research, large-scale studies may not be feasible. When an investigator wants to assess treatment with a single person, one option is the **N of 1 randomized clinical trial (RCT)**. In this approach, the researcher studies the effect of treatment on a single individual by exposing the individual to a treatment and a placebo in random order over time (e.g., ABBABAABBAB).

This approach makes sense only when several criteria are met. First, the patient's problem must be chronic but relatively stable. If the symptoms are too variable or time-limited, it is difficult to attribute any changes to the treatment. Second, the treatment (usually a drug in this kind of study) should have a rapid effect and also a rapid cessation of effect. This criterion is important because the researcher doesn't want to have carryover effects that can interfere with conclusions about the effectiveness of the different approaches. Finally, there needs to be a clear and objective outcome that can be measured reliably (Cook, 1996).

N of 1 randomized clinical trial—A research design involving the study of a single person over multiple trials, with trials involving application of the treatment and trials with no application of the treatment occurring in random order.

An example of this approach is illustrated in the case of a 55-year-old man who sustained brain injury in a motorcycle accident. After six months, his psychometric performance included above-average IQ scores, excellent memory, and good motor performance. Unfortunately, he complained of difficulty with concentration.

The researchers used an N of 1 RCT to see if different medications could help with this problem with a preselected, random order of each of two drugs (Bleiberg et al., 1993). They prescribed the drugs lorazepam (treatment days 1 and 4) and dextroamphetamine sulfate (treatment days 3 and 5) and also used a placebo (treatment day 2) in a double-blind procedure. In addition, there was a day between treatments to eliminate carryover effects from the drugs.

The results revealed that dextroamphetamine led to higher levels of performance and greater stability as well. When the patient took lorazepam or the placebo, performance deteriorated relative to the dextroamphetamine; in addition, with lorazepam and the placebo, the patient showed greater variability, that is, inconsistency, in his performance on mental tasks. The N of 1 RCT design can help tailor treatment for individuals in ways that group, cross-sectional designs cannot.

Strengths of Single-Participant Designs

Just like any other method of research, single-case studies help fill in the gap in our knowledge of behavior. These approaches have some notable strengths. First, one of the most pronounced advantages is the amount of detail reported about a person. Entire books can be (and have been) written about exceptional people. These designs are time and labor intensive; you can easily see why an investigator might limit the research to a single person. The amount of detail to sort through would be overwhelming if the researcher studied many people. Second, case studies and single-case experiments are also useful when we want to investigate rare phenomena. Researchers may not be able to locate a large group of individuals if the phenomena of interest seldom occur.

A third strength of single-case studies relates to creating and evaluating research hypotheses. We can use the results of single-participant studies to generate hypotheses that can be tested with larger numbers of people. Single-case studies can also test hypotheses based on existing theory.

A further advantage of single-case studies is that they provide help in developing and assessing therapeutic or intervention techniques. The causes of psychological difficulties in clients and patients may be unique to each person. As a result, using large numbers of research participants may actually obscure the effectiveness of a therapeutic technique that might be helpful for a particular person.

Whenever we want to know about behaviors that are particular to a single person, single-case designs can be highly beneficial. In addition to the realm of clinical psychology, single-case research can be important in areas like sports psychology (Hrycaiko & Martin, 1999). In clinical psychology, the aim is to improve a person's psychological state; in sports psychology, the goal is to enhance performance. In both cases, there are likely to be individual characteristics that are critical to change; group research would probably not be optimal in either field.

Weaknesses of Single-Participant Designs

Probably the biggest limitation of single-subject studies involves the question of external validity. In one sense, they have a high degree of external validity. There is generally nothing artificial about them. Thus, the studies tell us about a person in his or her natural environment.

Another component of external validity is relevant here, though. We cannot be sure that conclusions based on a single person will generalize to anybody else. In fact, because this research often involves rare phenomena, it is not clear that there are many others to whom we would be able to generalize. The results might pertain to only one person.

In addition to questions of external validity, we are also faced with potential problems with internal validity. Causal conclusions about the person's behaviors are risky if there is no controlled manipulation of variables in the research.

Misunderstandings About Single-Case Research

Single-case research is fairly rare in psychological and psychiatric research. There are several possible reasons.

First, the tradition in psychology is cross-sectional research involving comparisons between groups. Most training in graduate programs therefore focuses on research with groups rather than with individuals. For many researchers, single-case studies don't look like normal, psychological research, and the psychologists may not be well versed in the details of single-case approaches.

Second, researchers may confuse the relative subjectivity of some case-study approaches and the relative objectivity of single-subject experiments that are highly controlled. Furthmore, most psychologists and other researchers have little training in qualitative approaches. A qualitative study can provide a lot of information about behavior, but it is likely to be different information from that produced in a quantitative study.

Third, some researchers believe that the levels of internal and external validity are low in single-participant research. There is some truth to this claim, but the same can be said for cross-sectional designs. Most behavioral research involves convenience samples, so concerns about generalizability (i.e., external validity) exist for all types of data collection. Further, given that much experimentation occurs in laboratories, the question of external validity arises again. The issue of internal validity may be notable in case studies, but is less relevant for N of 1 RCT studies. Experiments with a single case may have levels of internal validity that are as high as in cross-sectional research.

Fourth, some researchers claim that the data analysis in single-case research is too subjective. It is true that there will be some subjectivity when an investigator works with subjective phenomena, like emotional states. But this is no different than with cross-sectional research. For researchers interested in the experimental analysis of behavior, they may avoid statistical analyses, but when the data are objective and when objective criteria for drawing conclusions are set ahead of time, data analysis is simply different, not necessarily less valid.

CASE STUDIES

Case studies are investigations that focus on a single individual (occasionally a few people) in great detail. Historically, case studies did not include controlled observations and took place in the context of psychotherapy (Kazdin, 1998). In contemporary applications, though, investigators make use of interventions and control (e.g., Cytowic, 1993; Mills, Boteler, & Oliver, 1999).

Case study—A research design involving the in-depth study of one or a few people, historically with no manipulation of variables, although such manipulations can occur in contemporary designs.

This approach to research is often seen as having more problems than other techniques. In fact, even though a new journal has appeared that deals only with case studies, some journals do not accept them as research papers. In other journals, case studies are for teaching purposes rather than research questions (Gawrylewski, 2007a). Questions of causation, generalizability, and interpretation biases are among the most notable concerns. At least one medical journal has decided to eliminate them altogether (Gawrylewski, 2007a).

In case studies, it is hard to see what factors lead to certain behaviors and which are merely correlated with those behaviors. In essence, there is the problem of too many rival hypotheses and no way to see which ones are best. A second caution about case studies concerns whether we can generalize from a particular patient or client to others.

An additional concern about single-case research in general is interpretive. That is, what does the information mean? It is possible for researchers to ignore viable explanations for behaviors because those explanations do not fit with their theoretical position. This is not an attempt to deceive. Rather, it is a natural inclination on our part to accept information that supports what we believe and to ignore information that doesn't. The problem is exacerbated by the fact that studies of a single person often rely on clinical judgment and subjectivity that another person may not be able to replicate objectively.

Because of these problems, case studies are fairly rare in the research literature. At the same time, it is easy to see why clinicians use this approach. People with ailments that are interesting (in the research sense) are likely to be rare, at least when they first appear. As a case in point, AIDS was initially a puzzle to the medical community; young, healthy people were contracting unusual, fatal diseases for no apparent reason. Initial research could only involve case studies because there were so few instances.

When the numbers began to grow, preliminary studies showed patterns. Initially, physicians thought that the disease was limited to gay men, which accounts for its initial label, Gay Related Immune Deficiency (GRID). Without continued research with larger numbers of people, it would have been impossible to understand the nature of what was ultimately renamed AIDS. But the initial case studies provided critical clues to the disease.

Within psychology, case studies can give us a lot of compelling information about individual people. The clinical researcher can then try to understand an individual's behavior by fitting a large number of puzzle pieces together. For example, how would you react if somebody told you that he knew that the food being cooked for dinner wasn't done yet because "there aren't enough points on the chicken"? Is this the utterance of a delusional person? What do "points" have to do with how well done a chicken is? You can see how an interesting case study shed light on the perceptions of the man for whom flavors had shapes (Cytowic, 1993), shapes that were as real to him as the flavor of chicken is to us.

Researchers have estimated that as few as one person in about 100,000 has such experiences, known as synesthesia (Cytowic, 1997), although some have produced higher estimates of one person in 2,000 (Baron-Cohen et al., 1996). Obviously, if you wanted to study synesthesia, you would have a hard time finding a group to study. Case studies make the most sense. You can see in the next section how Cytowic used a case study to investigate a synesthete he met.

We can see an example of the attempt to capture experience and feeling in a case study that investigated women's changes in identity during their first pregnancy (Smith, 1997). The investigator used interviews, diaries, and retrospective accounts, then created a case study to which the women responded. The researcher then wrote a final case study report. Smith generally relied on qualitative data in this research. One advantage of this phenomenological, experiential approach is that he was able to see how the women felt and how they reacted on a personal level.

He discovered that the four women in his case studies engaged in reconstruction of their memories during pregnancy. He suggested that women generate a series of different stories at various points during pregnancy. The result is that there is a more positive memory of pregnancy than one might expect based on the actual course of the pregnancy. These results gave us some interesting information about how we remember events. In addition, the research told us something about emotions and feelings during and after pregnancy.

Grounded theory—An approach to theory development in which an investigator makes systematic observation free of prior hypotheses, generates facts, then uses those facts for development of the theory.

This qualitative approach makes use of **grounded theory**, an approach in which we start with hypotheses that help us construct meaningful descriptions of what people do and feel as we observe them. Thus, the theories are grounded in information or data that researchers have provided. Proponents of grounded theory believe that theories are assembled based on the information available, but that there is no single best version of reality.

By combining various types of rich and complex data in a case study, we try to understand psychological experiences that would be unavailable if we used cross-sectional psychological research methods.

A CASE STUDY: Tasting Pointed Chickens and Seeing Colored Numbers

When somebody scratches his or her fingernails on a blackboard, the sound can send shudders down our spines, even though we have not been touched. This effect is an analogue to that of people who experience synesthesia, or the mixing of different sensory modalities. This mixing is so bizarre from our perspectives that descriptions sound like they are coming from delusional people.

Should we believe people who claim that the sound of a pager causes them to see "blinding red jaggers" or that the poison strychnine and angel food cake have the same "pink smell" (Cytowic, 1993, p. 48). Or that the number 257 induces "a swirl that consists of yellowish orange as the dominant color, green as the next most dominant, and lastly there is a small amount of pink" (Mills, Boteler, & Oliver, 1999, p. 183)?

Synesthesia can take many different forms. In the case of the man Cytowic studied, flavors had shapes. The most famous synesthete in the psychological literature experienced shapes and colors when he heard words; for him, a particular tone looked like fireworks tinged with a pink-red hue, an unpleasant taste, and was rough enough to hurt your hand (Luria, 1968).

In another documented case, the synesthete converted visually presented numbers to colors, but also experienced synesthesia to spoken numbers, music, voices, emotions, smells, and foods (Mills, Boteler, & Oliver, 1999). When she saw a written number, she perceived different colors in front of her eyes. For example, a 1 was white, 2 was yellowish orange, 5 was kelly green, 7 was pink. Each of the single digits had its own, consistent color. Multiple-digit numbers combined colors, with the color associated with the first digit predominating.

Synesthetes respond to the world in ways that are very consistent for them, even if they are strange to us. This is an ideal situation for a case study. Cytowic (1993) met a synesthete, Michael, and spent an extended period studying his perceptions. Cytowic became aware of how special this person was when the synesthete didn't want to serve the chicken he was cooking yet because it was round, without enough points. He also reported being able to smell a tree because his brain processed its visual components and sent information to the part of his brain that dealt with smell.

Over the course of two years, Cytowic exposed Michael to different manipulations to see how he reacted. During the development of the case study, the researcher found that quinine, a bitter liquid, felt like polished wood, whereas another liquid had "the springy consistency of a mushroom, almost round, . . . but I feel bumps and can stick my fingers into little holes in the surface" (Cytowic, 1993, p. 64).

The functioning of the brain is complex in synesthesia, as it is for everything else, but Cytowic used the results of his study with Michael to discover some important elements of the phenomenon. He presented various liquids to see what shapes and colors they generated. He also investigated the effects of amphetamines and alcohol on synesthesia; amphetamines blocked synesthesia whereas alcohol enhanced it. Cytowic also injected radioactive gas to identify the parts of the brain involved in synesthesia; he found that during synesthesia, there was minimal blood flow to Michael's cortex. At the same time, blood flow to the emotional center of the brain, the limbic system, increased greatly.

Cytowic provided an extended case study of the experiences of the synesthete and wound up with a description not only of Michael's feelings and perceptions but also of patterns of brain activity. Such research is only possible in case-study form.

SUMMARY

Psychologists have created specialized approaches to research to answer questions about behavior when traditional experiments may not suffice. Developmental psychologists use longitudinal approaches to study how people change over time. Some longitudinal research in psychology has continued for over eighty years. With research like this, the investigators have to contend with considerably different issues than they do in typical, short-term cross-sectional experiments. Psychologists have developed a variety of methods to maximize the validity of the information obtained in these long-range projects.

Longitudinal projects often involve studying the same people over time. For example, Terman's multi-decade study followed a set of people identified in childhood as gifted throughout their lives. Sometimes, researchers investigate groups whose members change over time. The National Assessment of Educational Progress studies twelfth graders across time, so there is a new group of students for each phase of the research. Other research follows the same people over time, but also brings new people into the study at regular intervals.

Sometimes researchers study the same individual over time, concentrating on one person (or a few) rather than on a group. Like longitudinal studies, single-case studies involve observing the same person over time, with multiple repeated measures. Depending on the specific research question, investigators might introduce a treatment, then withdraw it, sometimes multiple times. Psychologists are often not well trained in the use of single case designs, one of the reasons that this approach is relatively rare in psychology.

REVIEW QUESTIONS

Multiple Choice Questions

1. Lewis Terman's study of gifted children that continued to follow them through adulthood and into old age constitutes
   a. multiple baseline research.
   b. cross-sectional research.
   c. trend research.
   d. longitudinal research.
2. A researcher who wants to know if elderly people are more health conscious than younger people could study a group of elderly people and a group of young people to assess any differences. Such an approach would involve
   a. multiple baseline research.
   b. cohort research.
   c. longitudinal research.
   d. cross-sectional research.
3. To avoid cohort effects, researchers can
   a. conduct cross-sectional studies.
   b. use multiple baseline studies.

c. make use of panel studies.
d. conduct retrospective studies.

4. To find out if using nightlights affected the development of nearsightedness, a group of researchers asked parents whether their teenaged children had slept with nightlights on as infants. This research illustrates a
   a. retrospective design.
   b. cohort design.
   c. cross-sectional design.
   d. longitudinal design.
5. The single largest methodological concern in longitudinal studies is
   a. cohort effects.
   b. attrition.
   c. trend effects.
   d. retrospective errors.
6. Wutzke et al. (2000) studied ways to reduce attrition in longitudinal research on heavy drinkers. They found that they could reduce attrition by
   a. promising the participants total confidentiality and anonymity in their participation.
   b. increasing internal motivation rather than relying on incentives to the participants.
   c. maintaining a strict policy of participation in order to establish routines for participation.
   d. maintaining contact throughout the project by sending birthday cards or regular newsletters.
7. Studies in the experimental analysis of behavior rely on
   a. case studies.
   b. cohort-sequential studies.
   c. trend studies.
   d. single-subject studies.
8. An ABA design would not be useful in research if
   a. a treatment had a permanent effect.
   b. a researcher expected a high level of attrition.
   c. the research is prospective.
   d. participants form a cohort.
9. Single-subject research that involves a series of measurements of a dependent variable during periods when a treatment is applied and also when the treatment is not given could be classified as
   a. an N of 1 randomized clinical trial.
   b. a multiple baseline design.
   c. a trend study.
   d. a panel study.
10. The most notable weakness of single-subject designs is
    a. they are not useful for generating hypotheses that can be tested with larger groups.
    b. they are not helpful in studying rare phenomena.

c. the results from such designs may not be generalizable to others.
d. they are susceptible to cohort effects.

11. The use of systematic observations free of prior hypotheses and collection of facts, followed by the an integration of the ideas, refers to
    a. grounded theory.
    b. retrospective research.
    c. cohort effects.
    d. randomized clinical trials.
12. The state of Vermont tried to anticipate the degree to which middle- and high-school students contemplated suicide. The state collected data from students every two years from 1993 to 2007. This approach reflects
    a. a cohort study.
    b. a trend study.
    c. a cross-sectional study.
    d. a retrospective study.

Essay Questions

13. What are the advantages of longitudinal designs and cross-sectional designs?
14. How does a panel study differ from a trend study? What are the advantages of each?
15. In the Bond, Carlin, Thomas, Rubin, and Patton (2001) study on bullying in schools and depression, why could attrition have influenced their results?
16. Why would an ABA design not be appropriate for behavioral (as opposed to drug) treatment for depression?
17. What are the advantages of single-case research?

ANSWERS TO REVIEW QUESTIONS

Multiple Choice Questions

1.	d	5.	b	9.	a
2.	d	6.	d	10.	c
3.	c	7.	d	11.	a
4.	a	8.	a	12.	b

Essay Questions

13. What are the advantages of longitudinal designs and cross-sectional designs?

    Longitudinal designs permit the study of change in an individual over time, avoiding cohort effects that could confuse change over time in a person with change due to different environments. Cross-sectional designs are quicker to complete, allowing assessment of different populations in a short time period.

14. How does a panel study differ from a trend study? What are the advantages of each?

A panel study typically involves the study of the same people in successive waves of data collection. A trend study involves studying the same population over time, but not necessarily the same people.

The advantages of panel studies include the fact that you are studying the same people, so the nature of the sample doesn't change.

The advantages of trend studies include the fact that you don't have to worry about keeping track of the same people or about attrition because you sample from the population at each measurement.

15. In the Bond, Carlin, Thomas, Rubin and Patton (2001) study on bullying in schools and depression, why could attrition have influenced their results?

    In the Bond et al. study, they found that boys showed less depression as a result of bullying. However, the attrition rate for boys was larger than for girls. This might mean that boys who were affected by the bullying by becoming depressed may have dropped out of the study, whereas boys not so affected did not drop out. It would have distorted the effect of bullying on boys.

    Further, there was more attrition for students from single-parent families. Perhaps people in such families are differentially susceptible to depression than are students from two-parent (or other) families.

16. Why would an ABA design not be appropriate for behavioral (as opposed to drug) treatment for depression?

    An ABA design presupposes that at the second baseline phase (i.e., the second *A* phase), the individual's behavior will return to the way it was before the treatment. In behavioral treatment for depression, if therapy is successful, the person will not return to his or her original depressed state. Thus, an ABA design will not be appropriate.

17. What are the advantages of single-case research?
    a. Single-case research provides a wealth of detail, much more than for a group design, where in depth information would be too much to evaluate.
    b. Single-case research is also good for studying rare phenomena.
    c. Single-case research can be used for creating and testing research hypotheses.
    d. Single-case research is useful for studying clinical interventions on single people whose specific symptoms are unique.

CHAPTER FOURTEEN

PEOPLE ARE DIFFERENT

Considering Cultural and Individual Differences in Research

CHAPTER OVERVIEW

CONCEPT MAP ▪ KEY TERMS ▪ CHAPTER PREVIEW

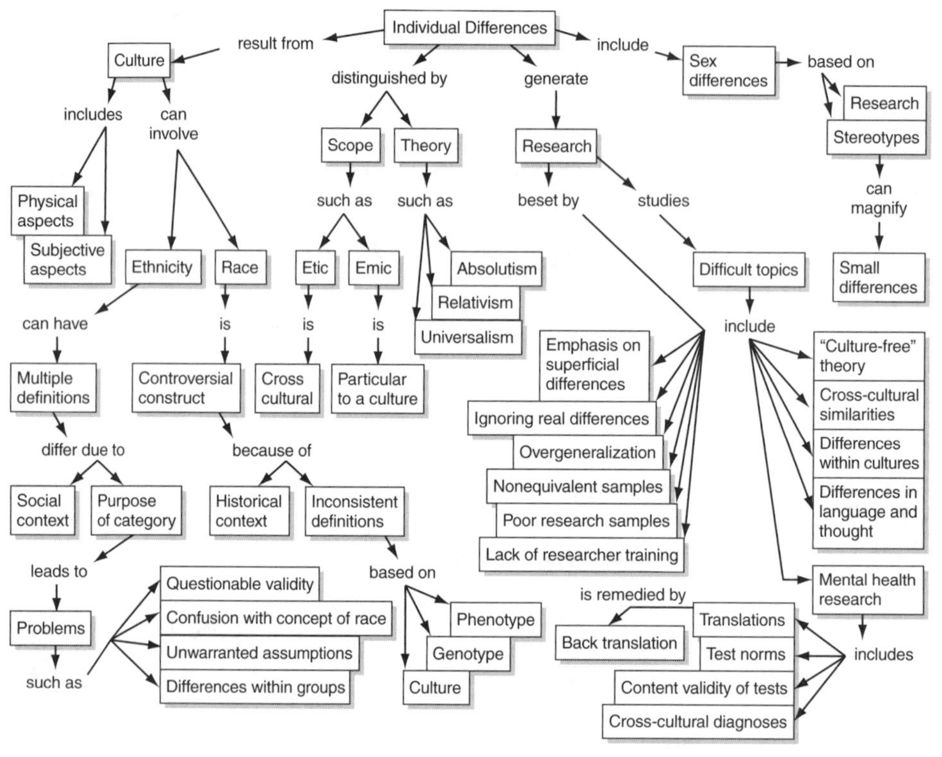

KEY TERMS

Absolutism, p. 356
Back translation, p. 367
Content validity, p. 366
Culture, p. 356
Emic, p. 356
Ethnicity, p. 352
Etic, p. 356
Interpretation paradox, p. 357
One-drop rule (hypodescent), p. 359
Race, p. 352
Relativism, p. 356
Univeralism, p. 356

CHAPTER PREVIEW

Most psychologists would agree that our attitudes and beliefs affect the way we make judgments. When we draw a conclusion about somebody's behavior, our judgments may reflect us as much as the people we observe. That is, we see others in a particular way because of who we are. If we share the same culture as those we study, we may be able to gain insights into why they act as they do. On the other hand, when we observe behaviors of those in other cultures, we may not understand what motivates them.

Understanding the effects of culture on behavior requires detailed knowledge of the person being observed as well as that person's culture, which is not easy. The issues we have to consider are complex. For instance, how do culture, ethnicity, and race affect behavior? The answer is certainly complex. Even though most people firmly believe that there are several easily definable races of people, many scientists have come to the conclusion that the concept of race is a social construction, not a biological fact. According to a great number of anthropologists, sociologists, psychologists, biologists, and geneticists, race is not a particularly useful biological concept. Yet many people believe that it exists.

Even though a concept like race may be scientifically invalid, we can still identify behaviors associated with culture or ethnicity, although we need to take care in the ways we classify people. Research participants are often assigned to categories in simplistic and contradictory ways from one study to another. Fortunately, more researchers are coming to the realization that we need to have good cross-cultural knowledge if we are going to understand people.

Finally, studying differences between women and men poses problems in research. Sometimes, investigators find ways to reinforce pre-existing beliefs by failing to acknowledge what might be considered cultural differences between the sexes. The researchers may believe in myths that are not true, so their research may be flawed.

Throughout this chapter, your beliefs will be challenged, and you will have to deal with controversies that, ultimately, may make you view people differently and change the way you think about studying them.

DIFFERENT CULTURAL PERSPECTIVES

It would be a mistake to assume that all people think as we do. As a result, we should be cautious in interpreting why people act as they do when these people come from a culture that is different from ours.

For example, Stiles, Gibbons, and Schnellman (1990) asked Mexican and U.S. adolescents to characterize members of the opposite sex. Mexican adolescents relied on stereotypes and talked about internal characteristics. U.S. adolescents were more likely to use physical and sexual descriptors. In addition, the girls who participated in the study tended to make different drawings, depending on their culture. Mexican girls depicted men helping them more than U.S. girls did. If we wanted to study attitudes of Mexican and of U.S. adolescents, we might have a hard time comparing their responses because they would be using different worldviews to generate their responses.

Cohen and Gunz (2002) have documented that people born in Western and Eastern countries have quite different memories of events in their lives. Those from Asia tended to remember events in the first person (e.g., "I did this") when the memories did not involve their being at the center of attention; when they were the center of attention, their memories were in the third person (e.g., "he did this"). People born in the Western world showed memories that were just the opposite, with the center of attention being associated with the first person. The researchers concluded that the differential perspectives on the world actually dictated the way information is processed and the form of subsequent memory.

If the investigators are correct, we can expect people from different cultures to think about things very differently, so if we give them the same task to complete, they may be engaged in quite different mental processes. As such, comparisons about performance may be difficult.

What Is Culture?

Sometimes we think that we understand a concept, but when we try to express our ideas in words, it is very difficult. **Culture** is one such concept. We all know people who act differently than we do because of cultural differences. If somebody asked you to identify differences between your culture and that of another person, you would probably discuss differences in religious beliefs, eating habits, clothing, and so on. This is typically what we mean by "culture" (Matsumoto, 1994). At the same time, we have only identified some of the signs associated with cultural differences; we haven't defined culture itself.

Culture—The customs, behaviors, attitudes, and values (psychological culture) and the objects and implements (physical culture) that can be used to identify and characterize a population.

Throughout this chapter it will become apparent that our concepts of culture, ethnicity, and race are quite vague and subjective. Unfortunately, the research literature is at times just as confusing. Different investigators use the same term but define it differently.

Culture. We can identify two distinct components of culture. Physical culture relates to objects like tools and buildings. Subjective culture, which is of interest to psychologists, refers to such things as familial patterns, language habits, attire, and a wide range of other characteristics that pass from one generation to the next (Betancourt & Lôpez, 1993; Matsumoto, 1994).

Other psychologists have defined culture somewhat differently from Matsumoto (1994), involving the notion that culture is not something "out there," but rather that it is a cognitive response a person makes on the basis of his or her interactions with others (Segall, Lonner, & Berry, 1998). For example, it seems unlikely that Americans are overtly conscious of being Americans on a daily basis; this categorization makes sense only when they want to make some contrast. In their communities, they are simply who they are. Similarly, think about Mexican citizens. People living in Mexico City feel no need to identify themselves as Mexicans or as Hispanics because on a daily basis, it is not a relevant consideration. On the other hand, when people live in a country different from that of their birth, they would likely describe themselves according to place of birth because that information might be relevant to understanding their behavior and because it draws a contrast between them and others.

Race—A controversial concept with very limited construct validity about classification of people based on real or imagined biological traits, most often centering on skin color.

Ethnicity—A concept related to a person's identification with a particular group of people, often based on ancestry, country of origin, or religion.

Race and Ethnicity. **Race** and **ethnicity** are also difficult concepts. When discussing race, researchers (and people in general) often think of biological characteristics. On the other hand, ethnicity is often thought of as a more subjective concept. A person's ethnicity is associated with affiliation. That is, to what group do people think they belong or what group has affected the way an individual thinks and acts?

It doesn't help researchers that the concept of ethnicity itself is somewhat unclear. For instance, Phinney (1996) noted that "ethnicity is most often thought of as culture. . . . To understand the psychological implications of ethnicity, it is essential to identify the specific cultural characteristics associated with an ethnic group and with the outcomes of interest such as educational achievement or mental health" (p. 920).

Matsumoto (1993) depicted ethnicity differently, suggesting that ethnicity "is defined most often by biological determinants; culture, however, must be defined by sociopsychological factors. . . . Defined in this way, the parameters of culture are 'soft,' and perhaps more difficult to distinguish, than the parameters of ethnicity, which are set in biology and morphological differences" (p. 120).

As Betancourt and Lôpez (1993) stated, in research, people often use culture interchangeably with race, ethnicity, and nationality. On surveys, people often must indicate race by selecting categories that really encompass ethnicity or nationality, not race. Latinos, for instance, can be White, Black, Asian, American Indian, or any combination thereof.

DEFINING AN INDIVIDUAL'S CULTURE, ETHNICITY, AND RACE

Scientific designations should be based on valid, objective, and stable scientific criteria. The categories researchers use often reflect social and political conditions. For example, in record keeping, the Census Bureau is not trying to be scientific; it is trying to describe the population of the United States. Still, scientific research relies on Census Bureau categories. Berreby (2000) has pointed out that the utility of racial classifications depends in part on how well people define the categories they use.

Further, Rodriguez (2000) pointed out that the concept of race or ethnicity may not help us understand behavior because an individual may fall into different categories, depending on who is doing the assessment. For instance, when the U.S. government collects data on an individual, the Bureau of the Census does not regard Hispanics as constituting a race, whereas federal agencies that deal with civic rights issues do have a separate racial category for Hispanics. Suppose you wanted to carry out a research project to see if people in different racial categories achieve different educational levels. Would your data include a racial category for Hispanics? With governmental categories, you could argue either way, if you consider that the government has sanctioned both approaches.

Another concern in categorizing research participants is that a researcher may use terms that are clear in the context of an investigation but that might be unclear to others. For instance, Selten et al. (2001) examined psychotic disorders among Turkish, Moroccan, and Hindustani people who had migrated to The Netherlands. But Bhui and Bhugra (2001) pointed out that the terms Turkish and Moroccan reflect place of birth, whereas Hindustani refers to religion. Such a mixture of categories can cause confusion in cross-cultural comparisons. Further, the degree to which a person identifies with a given ethnic group often changes over the course of the person's life. For all these reasons studying the effect of ethnicity is very difficult.

Criteria for Inclusion in a Group

The criteria for inclusion in a group change over time. For instance, over the years the United States census has classified people into ethnic groups on the basis of what language they spoke, then their last name, then their place of origin, and now, through self-identification.

In some cases, people classify themselves differently depending on what is at stake. Phinney (1996) cited research in which 259 university students self-identified as American Indian or Alaska Native. Only 52 could provide confirmation that they belonged in those categories. If tuition aid depends on ethnic status, people might classify themselves differently. Research often relies on data resulting from these self-classifications.

In addition, as Phinney (1996) pointed out, when we try to categorize people according to ethnicity, the labels we create are not particularly useful when people come from mixed backgrounds. Beyond that, Phinney noted that "a common practice is to interpret empirical results or clinical observations in terms of cultural characteristics that are assumed to exist but that are not directly assessed" (p. 921). That is, researchers make assumptions about behaviors of the groups they are studying, but the researchers often do not check to make sure that their assumptions are valid. Research has shown that researchers' assumptions are misguided.

As an example of a difficulty in categorization, consider the Chinese, a group that has recently been studied extensively in cross-cultural psychology. Chang (2000) noted that the Chinese are not easy to characterize because being Chinese can mean an enormous number of things. For one thing, there is no single "race" because of the genetic and anthropological variability among the Chinese, who can count over 50 ethnic minorities encompassed under the overarching term "Chinese." In addition, the diversity in language is so great that you could find two languages labeled "Chinese" that are as different from one another as German is from French.

Researchers studying Chinese people living outside China sometimes use the family name as an indicator of being Chinese. This is a problematic strategy. Chang pointed out that the name Lee can be Chinese and has been used to signify Chinese ethnicity even though Lee is also a Korean and a Vietnamese name. Lee can also be a Western name—there is no evidence that the Confederate General Robert E. Lee was Chinese. Further, the most common Chinese surname, Chang, is also a Korean name.

Sometimes, researchers are even broader in their categorization schemes. Cohen and Gunz (2002), in studying the difference between Eastern and Western thought, simply included a participant in the Eastern category if he or she had been born in Asia. The range of ethnicity in such a strategy is vast. Participants in the Asian group were probably as different from one another as they were from the participants who grew up in North America. In other research, Kim and colleagues (1999) put into one category Asian Indians, Cambodians, Filipinos, Hmong, Japanese, Koreans, and others. This represents a stereotype that all people from Eastern cultures share significant attitudes and behaviors and that they all differ from people in the West.

To add to the confusion, Kim and colleagues (1999) have suggested that as people from Asian countries become acculturated to the United States, their behaviors change more quickly than their attitudes, which may not change even across generations. So in one sense, they are attitudinally still members of an ethnic group but behaviorally they are not. When we describe people within some arbitrarily determined category, we may be talking about very different types of people as though they were the same.

FIGURE 14.1 High school dropout rates according to ethnicity/race in the United States (Kaufman, Kwon, Klein, & Chapman, 2000).

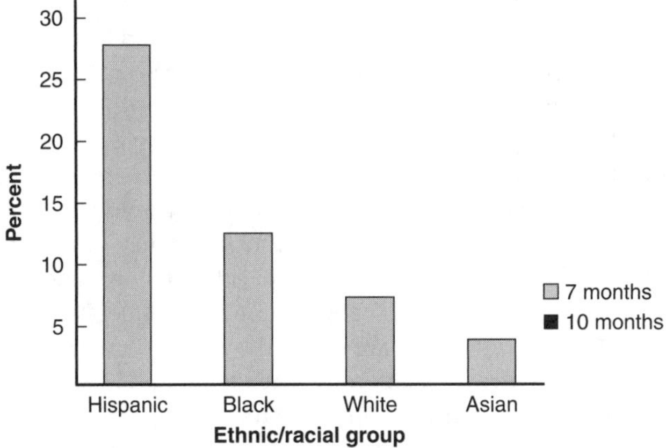

Social Issues and Cultural Research

The way we categorize people has implications for the way we think of social issues. As you can see in Figure 14.1, the National Center for Educational Statistics reported that high school dropout rates for Hispanics are very high (Kaufman, Kwon, Klein, & Chapman, 2000). What should we conclude from the fact that Hispanics are nearly seven times as likely to drop out of high school than Americans of Asian descent? This question is too simplistic because dropout rates for Hispanics drop by two-thirds for families who have been in the United States for two generations or more. As such, ethnic categories are less important than degree of acculturation.

Rather than concentrating on ethnicity, it might make more sense to talk about other variables, like the number of years people have lived in a given culture, socioeconomic status, fluency in English, nature of one's peers, and so forth (Watkins, Mortazavi, & Trofimova, 2000).

Yee, Fairchild, Weizmann, and Wyatt (1993) summarized the problems nicely: They noted that psychologists themselves use common stereotypes and rely on self-identification. The use of stereotypes suffers from four notable problems: It (a) neglects important differences among people in the same group, (b) assumes with no proof that behaviors that differ across groups are based on racial or cultural differences, (c) inappropriately depicts race and other variables as being related, and (d) relies on ideas for which there is no scientific consensus.

CROSS-CULTURAL CONCEPTS IN PSYCHOLOGY

Historically, psychologists have not concerned themselves with cultural differences. From the first decades of the 1900s into the 1960s, most psychologists were behaviorists who thought the causes of behavior were the same universally. We now recognize that this idea is too simplistic.

Are Psychological Constructs Universal?

Early cross-cultural researchers imposed their own cultural viewpoints on the behaviors of the people they studied, which meant that they failed to understand the subtleties of other cultures. After a while, it became clear that things were not as simple as people had hoped.

Etic—A research finding that appears to be universally true across cultures.

Emic—A research finding that is valid only within a given culture.

Absolutism—In discussions of cultural research, the concept that maintains that behavioral phenomena can be viewed from the same perspective, regardless of the culture in which they appear.

Relativism—In discussions of cultural research, the concept that maintains that behavioral phenomena can be understood only within the context of the culture in which they occur.

Universalism—A moderating view in cultural research that maintains that behavioral phenomena may be based on invariant psychological processes but that each culture will induce different manifestations of those underlying processes.

One of the distinctions that resulted from critical analysis of the research was between an etic and an emic. An **etic** refers to findings that result from studies across cultures and that may hold true cross-culturally. Thus, many people might regard the taboo against incest or cannibalism as an etic. On the other hand, an **emic** refers to a finding that is particular to a single culture that is being studied and understood in local terms. Although these two terms are gaining wider recognition in psychology, they are still controversial because the distinction between etic and emic perspectives are not always clear (Lonner, 1999).

In the study of different cultures, Berry, Poortinga, Segall, and Dasen (1992, cited in Segall et al., 1998) identified three orientations in cross-cultural psychology: absolutism, relativism, and universalism.

The first orientation, **absolutism**, assumes that behavioral phenomena are basically the same, regardless of cultures. In this view, depression will be depression; it does not differ from one locale to another. Should we believe this? Price and Crapo (1999) illustrate the difficulty with accepting the concept of depression as a single, unvarying construct across cultures. For example, the Hopi do not have a single category that corresponds to the Western view of depression; they have five different categories. Further, the hopelessness of major depression would be accepted by some Buddhists as simply being "a good Buddhist" (p. 126). In a Buddhist culture, hopelessness is part of the world and salvation arises, in part, in recognition of this hopelessness.

A second orientation is **relativism**. A relativistic approach stands in contrast to absolutism in that relativists make no attempts to relate psychological constructs across cultures. A researcher with this orientation would undertake only emic research, believing that the phenomena of any culture stand independently from those in any other. According to Segall et al. (1998), few psychologists favor either the extreme of absolutism or of relativism. Most fall between these two poles.

The final orientation is **universalism**. This approach strikes a balance between absolutism and relativism, accepting the idea that there may be universal psychological processes, but that they manifest differently, depending on the particular culture. For example, Segall, Campbell, and Herskovits (1966) found that susceptibility to perceptual illusions was widespread and suggested universal, underlying cognitive processes. At the same time, reactions differed depending on a person's life experience.

According to the absolutist viewpoint, if perceptual illusions are caused by universal sensory processes, we should all experience illusions the same way. But that usually doesn't happen. According to the relativist viewpoint, there could be little or no similarity in perceptions across cultures because perception in this orientation arises only from experience. That, too, doesn't seem very common. According to the universalist perspective, the same internal processes take place but lead to different interpretations because of experience. The truth is likely to fall somewhere between the extreme viewpoints.

Although scientists hope for psychological constructs that are valid across cultures, careful examination of behaviors so far leads us to be careful to avoid falling prey to our own cultural biases. In the Controversy on culture and neurological diagnosis, we see that something as objective as medical diagnosis is susceptible to cultural influences.

Issues in Cross-Cultural Research

When researchers pursue cross-cultural research, they can fall prey to certain problems in interpreting their data. Van de Vijver and Leung (2000) have identified four major concerns in research on people from different cultural groups.

- First, although some behavioral differences across cultures reflect important cross-cultural differences in thought and behavior, some differences in behavior are quite superficial and do not relate to important, underlying psychological processes.
- Second, sometimes psychological tests legitimately generate different patterns of scores across cultures. There is often a tendency to treat them as artifacts of measurement error, that is, to see the test as deficient rather than as identifying true differences between groups. In other words, when we indeed find cultural differences, it might be tempting to ignore them rather than share unpopular results.
- Third, researchers are prone to overgeneralization from their results. That is, differences due to small sample biases or poor measurement instruments may lead researchers to make more of their data than they should.
- Fourth, differences across groups may reflect lack of equivalence across samples. The differences could occur because the samples contain different types of people who differ in critical ways, not because the cultures differ.

Interpretation paradox—In cultural research, the fact that large differences between groups are easy to spot but hard to understand because there are so many factors that could be responsible, whereas small differences are harder to spot but easier to explain.

These difficulties imply what van de Vijver and Leung (2000) call the **interpretation paradox** of cross-cultural research. Large differences between very diverse cultures are easy to obtain but hard to interpret because the reasons for the differences may be caused by any of a number of multiple factors. On the other hand, small differences between people of similar cultures may be hard to spot, but when observed, are easy to interpret because the groups being assessed share many features, so the reasons for differences stand out and are easy to identify.

CONTROVERSY: Culture and Neurological Diagnosis

Diagnosing a medical or psychiatric condition resembles the formal research process quite closely. Physicians initially ask enough questions to allow them to form hypotheses about a problem. They then make observations and draw conclusions. If they still don't have enough information to identify the source of a patient's problems, they generate more hypotheses and ask more questions. Finally, the physician comes to a conclusion and treats the patient. In many cases, the ultimate diagnoses are correct, but sometimes they are wrong. This is exactly what happens in research.

The neurologist Harold Klawans (2000) described a case from the 1970s in which a patient with neurological problems was initially misdiagnosed because of cultural factors. The patient, who had suffered repeated blackouts due to carbon monoxide poisoning in the workplace, was brought to a Chicago hospital.

As part of the diagnostic process, an attending neurologist asked the patient who the mayor of Chicago was. The patient responded correctly, but was unable to identify any other previous mayors, asking if there ever had been any other mayors. He was also unable to name the current president or any previous presidents. The patient did not know that President John Kennedy had been assassinated, and had no knowledge of the Vietnam war, which was a very controversial aspect of U.S. culture at the time.

The neurologist finally asked the patient to identify which of four objects was different from the others: hammer, wood, chisel, wrench. The patient replied that none of them was different; they were all the same. At that point, the doctor concluded that the patient had suffered severe brain damage.

As Klawans discovered through further questioning, though, the patient's memory for some things (like baseball) going back forty years was very acute. The trouble with the initial diagnosis was that the first doctor had not taken culture into account. The patient, who had grown up in Mississippi in the 1930s, had gone to school for two years and had never learned to read. As a result, the patient's memories rested on what he had experienced directly. He didn't watch the news on television, so it is no surprise that he didn't know about the president, about Vietnam, about politics. None of these things had ever entered his world.

Klawans stated that people who don't read don't classify objects the way that literate people do. The task of categorizing the hammer, wood, chisel, and wrench is a foreign concept to them. It is only relevant to those of us who use written words to designate objects. The ability to read brings a set of skills that we take for granted, like classifying, but that ability is very closely bound to literacy.

In the end, it was clear that the patient's mental faculties were as sharp as anyone else's. Had Klawans not been attuned to this cultural difference, the patient might have been diagnosed with severe brain damage.

Question for Discussion: What kinds of psychological questions might be affected by culture? Are there any that would not be?

IS THERE A BIOLOGICAL BASIS FOR RACE?

Psychologists in the United States have studied one particular ethnic group to a great extent, Blacks or African Americans. Very often, the research does not appear to center around culture or ethnicity. Rather, investigators cast their studies in terms of race.

You probably imagine a person's race as something that is clearly defined; many people do. The problem lies in the process we use to classify a person. In the United States,

One-drop rule (hypodescent)—One means by which a person is racially categorized as a member of a low-status group such that if he or she has "one drop" of blood from a given group (i.e., any ancestor, no matter how remote, from that group), the individual is automatically classified as being from that group, used specifically with people of African descent who live in the United States.

we have had a tradition of calling a person "Black" or African American if the person has any African ancestry, no matter how remote or how little. This pattern is known colloquially as the **one-drop rule**, also known as **hypodescent**. A person is Black if he or she has "one drop of black blood." In Brazil, a person with any Caucasoid features is regarded as "White" (Zuckerman, 1990). The validity of such racial categorization is suspect if a person's race changes simply because he or she enters a different country.

Psychologists continue to use race as a conceptual category in research, despite good arguments for not doing so (e.g., Helms et al., 2005). For instance, racial categories can reflect researchers' beliefs more than actual characteristics of participants. As Helms et al. reported, researchers sometimes classify people of Asian descent as minorities and sometimes as "White," even in the same study. Liang, Li, and Kim (2004) suggested that this multiple categorization occurs in everyday life and may cause stress, independent of the supposed racial category.

The Criteria for Race

Race is clearly a strange concept scientifically. Why does a single ancestor determine race when there are so many ancestors who are ignored? And why does a single Black ancestor make a person Black, when a single White ancestor does not make a person White? The concept of race in scientific research is troublesome; race-determining characteristics fall on a continuum, but people create all-or-none categories. Whenever you have a continuum, but you try to make discrete categories, you have to make a decision as to where to put the cutoff for inclusion into different categories. Such decisions are arbitrary, and another person could make a different decision that has as much validity (or lack thereof) as yours.

The use of the concept of race, even among the educated, has sometimes been very loose. For instance, *The Mother's Encyclopedia* (1942) discussed rheumatic fever, asserting that "some races who live in New York are especially prone to it, particularly Italians and Jewish people" (p. 1028). Further, in the United States, there used to be a greater belief in the nature of the continuum regarding Black and White, even if there was no real scientific basis for it. Historically, an individual with one Black grandparent was classified as a quadroon; a person with one Black great-grandparent was listed as an octoroon. These "races" were considered as real as any others.

The problem with race as a construct that might help us understand behavior is that individual differences within races overwhelm the biological differences between races. In other words, if you look at the variability between any two people in the same culture, they show much more variability in genetic makeup than do two "average" people with ancestors on different continents.

At the phenotypical level, race is often defined in terms of features like skin color, but also hair type, eye color, and facial features. These turn out to be unreliable markers for race; in fact, they are not correlated with one another, meaning that just because a person shows one "racial" characteristic, it doesn't mean that he or she will show the others (Zuckerman, 1990). In addition, there are people in the so-called Negroid groups who are lighter in skin color than others in the so-called Caucasoid groups.

Current Biological Insights Regarding Race

Scientists working on the Human Genome Project, which is an attempt to identify the genetic makeup of human beings, have brought attention to this issue. According to Harold Freeman of North General Hospital in Manhattan, the percentage of genes that reflect differences in external appearances associated with race is about 0.01 percent (Angier, 2000).

Since the emergence of humans in present form, there have been about 7,000 generations. This is not a sufficiently large number to lead to clear differentiation of one group from another, according to geneticists. Further, there has always been mixing of genes of various groups when they come in contact with one another, intermarry, and reproduce. Biological variables may differentiate groups in a general way, but these variables are not, in and of themselves, markers for race because a person from any group could show them. "For instance, Afro-Americans are at a higher risk [for essential hypertension] than Anglo-Americans. From our perspective, what is of scientific interest is not the race of these individuals, but the relationship between the identified biological factors . . . and hypertension" (Betancourt & Lôpez, 1993, p. 631). The biological factors contribute causally to the hypertension; race is a correlational variable.

Still, some psychologists argue that real racial differences exist. They cite the notion that brain sizes, on average, are largest in Asians, middle-sized in Whites, and smallest in Blacks, a pattern that reflects trends in IQ scores. That is, the claim is that IQ score and brain size are positively correlated. At the same time, Peters (1993) noted that in studies of brain size and IQ, measurement error as small as one millimeter could account for the observed difference across races.

Historical Error

Unfortunately, from the beginning, research that investigated brain size and intelligence suffered from fatal flaws (Gould, 1996). In the 1840s, Samuel George Morton found that Whites had the largest brains, Indians were in the middle, and Blacks were on the bottom. As it turns out, his sample of skulls was egregiously poor. He specifically included a large number of Peruvian Inca skulls; these people were small of stature. He had very few Iroquois Indians, whose skulls were large. As a result, the mean skull size of Indians was artificially low.

Morton also decided to eliminate some Caucasian skulls, of Hindus who were small, thereby raising the average of Caucasians. There is no evidence that Morton thought he was doing anything inappropriate, because he kept meticulous records that others could investigate. He assumed that white Europeans had greater intelligence than others; the use of skull and brain size was simply meant to quantify what "everybody knew to be true."

Current Controversies

Modern psychologists (e.g., Cernovsky, 2000) have countered the argument about brain size and intelligence with the fact that mean brain size of groups living near the equator is less than that of groups nearer the poles, so that brain size is correlated with geog-

CONTROVERSY: Different Races

How many races are there? Many people in the United States would list White, Black, Hispanic, Native American, and Asian, believing that these categories are valid, discrete groupings. That is, you are White or you are not; you are Black or you are not; etc. Everybody falls into one and only one category.

The truth is not so simple. In reality, there do not seem to be biologically based markers that separate people conveniently and reliably. For example, skin color, which many people use to define inclusion in a racial category, is inconsistent. There are Black people who are lighter than White people. Similarly, people of Asian and Hispanic descent span many different skin colors.

People are very hard to classify precisely and objectively. One reason is that the differences among people are usually on a continuum. One person has more or less of this or that trait. When you have such continua, any point on the continuum that you use to create categories is going to be arbitrary.

Once scientists decided that racial differences were interesting, there were always problems defining race. In the 1920s, scientists agreed that there were three European races; in the 1930s, they changed it to ten European races. At the same time, there was a single African-based racial category. Africa is a big continent (over 11 million square miles); Europe is a small continent (about 4 million square miles). Not surprisingly, Africans show much greater genetic diversity than Europeans do. Why then was there only one African race? The categorization process was based on socially derived beliefs, not scientific measurement.

In terms of psychological research, we see again and again that behaviors and characteristics attributed to race generally have their causes in social or environmental factors. When researchers account for these factors, the effect of "race" generally diminishes or vanishes.

If a fine analysis eliminates effects of "race" on behavior in most of situations that have been studied, a critical thinker might conclude that the remaining differences could well be due to factors that researchers have not yet identified.

Nobody has yet identified scientifically reliable and valid definitions of race based on biology or genetics. As Yee et al. (1994) and others have pointed out, even in scientific research, depictions of race are generally made from a layperson's point of view, with no real scientific backing.

Question for Discussion: In studying differences across groups, how should researchers create different classifications?

raphy of one's ancestors and not much else. Besides, women's brains are smaller than men's, even after body size is taken into consideration. There is no evidence that women are less intelligent than men.

Another problem arises when we equate a score on a standardized test with intelligence. An IQ score is just that, a test score. It relates to behaviors that the test makers regard as important, like how well you do in school. It is true that your grades in school will correlate pretty well with your IQ score, but much of that may be due to the fact that IQ scores are based, to a degree, on tasks that are valued in educational settings.

Flynn (1999) has refuted a number of arguments that relate IQ and race, concluding that environmental, not genetic, differences explain differences in scores on IQ tests. The controversy will undoubtedly persist for a long time because the issues remain socially controversial and complex and the arguments multifaceted.

PRACTICAL ISSUES IN CULTURAL RESEARCH

Sue (1999) has pointed out some of the major issues in carrying out cross-cultural research. One of them is that many researchers may have difficulty finding participants from different cultural groups.

The result is that when they plan their own research, they make use of student participants because of availability. The truth is that it would take a considerable amount of time, money, and energy to find the diverse samples that are desirable. Given the practical considerations, researchers generally feel that they have to live with the samples they can access, even if it limits how well their results apply to different groups.

Lack of Appropriate Training Among Researchers

In addition to having access to fairly homogeneous samples, researchers may simply not have the knowledge or training needed to conduct high quality, cross-cultural research. Fortunately, the Council of National Psychological Associations for the Advancement of Ethnic Minority Interests has developed guidelines published by the American Psychological Association for research with ethnic minority communities (Council of National Associations, 2000). Some of their major points appear in Table 14.1.

TABLE 14.1 Important Considerations Regarding Research with People of Ethnic Groups (Council of National Psychological Associations, 1999)

Personal Characteristics	Develop awareness of the culture of the group you study
	Become aware of the effects of the culture and oppression and discrimination
	Recognize multiple linguistic and communication styles
	Recognize the heterogeneity that exists within any simple ethnic label
	Identify the degree to which an individual is acculturated
Research Considerations	Recognize cultural assumptions and biases in creating methods and materials
	Make sure all measurement instruments make sense from the cultural viewpoint of the group you study
	Use measurement instruments that are appropriately normed and that have established reliability and validity
	Determine if the research is culturally relevant to the group you study
	Establish appropriate comparison (control) groups
	Use adequately translated materials to maximize effectiveness of communication
	Conduct a cost/benefit analysis to make sure the research is worth doing
Outcomes	Interpret results within the appropriate cultural context
	Consider alternate explanations
	Remember that difference does not mean deviance
	Request help from community members in interpreting your research results
	Increase mainstream outlets for minority research
	Recognize the existence of confounding variables like educational level and socioeconomic status

These considerations are important in any research project. They just happen to be particularly relevant to research with ethnic populations. If you keep these points in mind, any research with any population will be better.

WHY THE CONCEPTS OF CULTURE AND ETHNICITY ARE ESSENTIAL IN RESEARCH

After the long discussion about the controversial concepts of race and ethnicity, you may wonder why we should consider it in our research. The reason is that various groups of people differ from one another in many ways. These groups just don't differ in the simplistic ways we normally think. We need to identify what differences occur across groups, as well as what differences occur within groups.

Differences Due to Language and Thought Processes

One research project that revealed the importance of culture on psychological processes involved asking people to rate the intensity of emotions on the faces of people in photographs. Matsumoto and Assar (1992) showed a series of photos of people displaying the so-called universal emotions of anger, fear, happiness, sadness, or surprise. Research participants rated the apparent emotion displayed in each picture. Participants were students in India who were bilingual in English and Hindi.

The most interesting manipulation here was that in one testing session, the research took place entirely in English; in another session, everything was in Hindi. The results showed that the students recognized emotions more accurately when they used English than Hindi. According to Matsumoto and Assar, people who speak English come from cultures in which people are used to talking openly about emotions. This cultural effect may lead English speakers to greater recognition and accurate judgment of emotions. Further support for the importance of language in thought came from research by Marian and Neisser (2000), who demonstrated that bilingual people have easier access to memories when they try to recall those memories using the language they would have used when they initially experienced the event. Language involves more than different word use. In fact, Ball, Giles, and Hewstone (1984) suggested that in order to learn a second language, you must also learn the culture of that language. You won't understand the language completely unless you know its context.

Language may also influence thought in other ways. Hedden et al. (2002) noted that Chinese speakers have an advantage over English speakers in some numerical tasks because the Chinese words representing numbers are shorter, thus easier to remember. They found no such advantage on a visuo-spatial task involving completing visual patterns. Thus, language may affect not only what you think but also how you think. Cross-cultural research needs to take such differences into account.

Differences in Simple and Complex Behaviors

Even simple responses may differ as a function of culture. When Chinese and U.S. students indicated how often they engaged in certain behaviors, the Chinese participants may have had better memories than U.S. students did because, as members of a collectivist society, the Chinese are expected to monitor their own behaviors closely (Ji, Schwarz, & Nisbett, 2000). The Americans, on the other hand, did not seem to have as reliable a memory for their behaviors and had to estimate them. Thus, even a simple memory task may lead to fundamentally different ways of responding, depending on your culture.

Not surprisingly, differences in behaviors also occur in more complex situations. For instance, people in China seem to have a different approach to problem solving than people in the Western world. Peng and Nisbett (1999) studied Chinese students and U.S. students in several experiments to see how they responded to contradictory statements in decision making. Chinese students were generally more comfortable accepting two contradictory statements as involving partial truths; U.S. students were more likely to look for a single, logical truth.

These differences reflect fundamentally different views of the world. In problem solving, the emphasis in most research is on logic and rationality that arrives at a single, logically coherent response. Before we claim that such approaches are a good general characterization of problem solving, we should remember that more than a billion people in this world may disagree with our representation of thought and decision making.

If we want to generate a complete description of the way people think and solve problems, we cannot ignore the fact that our approach to problem solving reflects ways that we are comfortable with, but they are not the only ways that are valid. Knowing about culture helps us know about thought. Ignoring the effects of culture will mean that we have incomplete knowledge about thought and behavior.

Is Culture-Free Theory Really Free of Culture?

The importance of understanding cultural effects on behavior emerges when we look at the studies of how babies attach themselves to parents. Rothbaum and colleagues (2000) described the general tenets of attachment theory and assessed whether the theory is more culturally relevant in the Western hemisphere than elsewhere. This is an important discussion because some psychologists view attachment theory as evolutionarily based, thus free of cultural biases.

Three of the important tenets of attachment are as follows: First, there is a connection between maternal sensitivity and security of attachment. Second, secure children are more socially and emotionally competent than insecure children. Third, infants who show higher levels of adaptation are more likely to explore when they feel secure. These notions seem pretty straightforward. The research on attachment has typically involved middle-class U.S. children. If attachment were strictly a part of evolutionary development, this would not be a problem. However, cultural differences may be important

As Rothbaum et al. (2000) note, when parents or teachers identify potentially problematic behavior, the Japanese may identify one set of behaviors as appropriate and a different set as troublesome. The Americans could reverse the pattern. Rothbaum et al. maintain that in order to understand the nature of children's attachment, we have to understand the culture because attachment theory is not as culture-free as psychologists have traditionally believed.

These researchers may raise valid points, but not all psychologists agree. For instance, Chao (2001) suggested that Rothbaum didn't define the term culture adequately, equating it with nations. Van Ijzendoorn and Sagi (2001) and Chao also argued that there is too much variability within Japanese and within U.S. cultures for easy generalizations about Japanese people and U.S. people. The disagreements aren't reconciled easily because of the difficulties associated with cultural research.

Similarities and Differences Within the Same Culture

People who grow up in the same culture share attitudes, values, and behaviors, but such people are not merely clones of one another. Part of the problem is that people in a group may show similarities on one dimension but not on another. Matsumoto (1993) investigated differences in emotion among Americans of various ethnic groups.

He asked his research participants to identify the emotion displayed in facial photographs and rate its intensity. They also indicated how appropriate a display of the emotion was. He discovered that some differences existed among Asian Americans, Blacks, Hispanics, and Whites, but the differences were inconsistent. Sometimes the different groups rated emotions in the pictures the same, but sometimes not. For example, Americans of Asian ancestry looked at a given picture and saw less anger than an American of African ancestry. But the Asian Americans saw an equal amount of sadness as African Americans. In addition, African Americans saw more intense emotions generally in pictures of White people than did Asian, Hispanic, or White Americans.

This pattern of findings suggests that if we are studying emotions, we could sometimes treat all Americans as more or less similar (e.g., for happiness and sadness), but not all the time (e.g., for fear). Simple research like this can reflect the complexity of cross-cultural studies.

CULTURAL FACTORS IN MENTAL HEALTH RESEARCH

Psychologists continue to make progress in mental health research, documenting the effectiveness of various therapies for different problems and identifying variables associated with normal and abnormal behavior. As we have recognized the diversified culture in the United States, we have begun to pay attention to the different needs of people of varying backgrounds, although we still know much less than we need to know.

One type of research that clinical psychologists conduct involves assessing the validity of psychological tests across cultural boundaries. If we cannot translate tests into different languages to convey the same ideas as they do in English, we cannot be confident that test results signify the same psychological processes. A poorly translated test will not assess the same thing in both languages. Problems also occur when clinicians try to use a test with minority or immigrant populations when that test is created for and standardized on a White population born in the United States and raised to speak English. In either case, the scores might mean different things.

Content Validity

The process of ensuring that psychological tests serve diverse populations is difficult (Rogler, 1999). Diagnostic and research instruments need to make sense from the viewpoint of those who use them; that is, the tests must show, among other things, **content validity**. The questions should, in expert judgment, relate to what the test assesses. When psychologists create tests, they have to decide what questions to ask. This is where their expert judgment comes in. The problem is that potential patients or clients may not share the same culture as the psychologist, so the patient or client may be answering a different question than the clinician is asking.

Content validity—The degree to which the material contained in a test relates to the concept being assessed.

Rogler (1999) illustrated this point through a particular question on the Diagnostic Interview Schedule (DIS), which he noted is the most influential test in psychiatric epidemiology. The question asks, "Do you often worry a lot about having clean clothes?" This question might be useful in identifying whether people are overly distressed about unreasonable things. The problem with this question is that it assumes that the person answering it has access to running water. If you have all the water you need, then worrying about clean clothes might be a sign of psychological distress. On the other hand, if you do not have access to running water, laundry facilities, and so forth, such a worry becomes a reasonable preoccupation. As it turns out, many Plains Indians in the United States do not have access to running water. As such, to respond that they do not worry about clean clothes would probably be more indicative of a problem than if they replied that they do worry.

Translation Problems

If questions pose difficulties within the same language, imagine what problems arise if we try to translate the test into a different language for use by people whose cultural outlook does not match ours. Rogler (1999) provided another example from the DIS.

He identified the question that reads, "I felt I could not shake off the blues even with help from my family or friends." In trying to translate this apparently simple and straightforward item into Spanish, he encountered great difficulty. In translation, an individual tries to stay as close to the original wording as possible, but there were no suitable Spanish equivalents. One problem here is that in English, "the blues" has a particular meaning that does not survive in a translation to the Spanish word *azul*, the color blue. Rogler also noted that in the United States, we often think that it would be possible, by force of will, to "shake off" an unwanted mood. Is this concept shared by Spanish speakers? If so, what Spanish verb would be appropriate? He wondered whether the word *sacudir* would be a good translation. It means to shake off vigorously like a dog shakes water off its body. He decided that *sacudir* would not be appropriate.

He eventually translated the item by rewording the original English sentence to read "I could not get over feeling sad even with help from my family or friends." Normally, a translator tries not to deviate from the original form of an item, but in this case, there was probably no alternative. Table 14.2 provides other examples that Rogler generated to illustrate the cultural biases of the DIS.

TABLE 14.2 Examples Reflecting a Strong Effect of Culture That May Cause Problems Across Cultures (Rogler, 1999)

Example	Reason for the Problem
In assessing dissociation, the Dissociative Experience Scale asks about the following: "Some people have the experience of driving a car and suddenly realizing that they don't remember what has happened during all or part of the trip."	The question assumes that the person taking the test takes long car trips. This kind of factual assumption is a problem because people living in the inner city rarely, if ever, drive in places that do not have heavy traffic. As such, an answer to the question will not provide useful information.
Translation of the Clinical Analysis Questionnaire into Spanish.	Thirty-six percent of test items contained grammatical errors and involved direct translation of colloquialisms that made no sense in Spanish. With these translation problems, we could conclude that the questions in the different languages did not have the same meaning.
How does schizophrenia affect decision making among married couples in San Juan, Puerto Rico?	Among the people studied, decision making was not a critical aspect of familial interactions, as it is in the United States. In Puerto Rico, the corresponding dimension was how "men's work" and "women's work" was divided. Knowing about decision making would not help in understanding problems or devising treatments.
Description of symptoms of bipolar disorder in the Amish.	The typical examples that clinicians look for include buying sprees, sexual promiscuity, and reckless driving, which are not applicable to the Amish. Instead, relevant symptoms involve behaviors like excessive use of public telephones, treating livestock too roughly, or giving gifts during the wrong season of the year.

Back translation—In cross-cultural research, the process by which comparable testing instruments are developed, by translating from an original language to a second language, then back to the first to ensure that the original version and the translation back into that language produce comparable meanings.

One useful technique for ensuring comparability of items across languages is **back translation** (Banville, Desrosiers, & Genet-Volet, 2000). In this process, an item is translated from one language to a second. Then a blind translator converts it back to the first language. For example, an item might start in English, be translated into Spanish, then back again into English. If the original version in the first language is equivalent in meaning to the version that has been translated out of, then back into, English, the item is likely to capture the same concepts in both languages.

Cross-Cultural Norms

Relatively few distress inventories have received scrutiny on a cross-cultural basis; none have involved norms with college students (Cepeda-

Benito & Gleaves, 2000). Ironically, although college students form the typical research participant in psychology, the clinical literature seems to underrepresent them.

When researchers have investigated cross-cultural equivalence of inventories, they have revealed a complex picture. For instance, the complete version of the Center for Epidemiologic Studies–Depression scale seems valid for Americans of African, European, and Mexican descent (Aneschensel, Clark, & Frerichs, 1983), although the short version produces differences between Americans of African and European descent (Tran, 1997, cited in Cepeda-Benito & Gleaves, 2000).

In one study, Cepeda-Benito and Gleaves (2000) investigated the generalizability of the Hopkins Symptom Checklist-21 (HSCL-21) across Blacks, Hispanics, and Whites. This test is a short, 21-item version of a longer, 57-item inventory designed to measure distress. The HSCL-21 shows validity across a wide array of cultural groups, including Italian, Vietnamese, Latino, and European Americans, and among college students. Not every U.S. ethnic group was represented in the research, but its generality across the three disparate groups tested provided cautious optimism. Unfortunately, the number of psychological tests that have been normed for varied groups is still uncomfortably small.

Cross-Cultural Diagnoses

One consequence of the lack of information on the validity of psychological tests for minority populations is that the tests might lead to diagnoses that are based more on ethnicity than on problematic behavior. As Iwamasa, Larrabee, and Merritt (2000) have shown, people may be predisposed to classify individuals of different ethnic groups in predetermined ways.

Iwamasa et al. (2000) identified the criteria for personality disorders listed in the Diagnostic and Statistical Manual (DSM; American Psychiatric Association, 1987). In clinical work, mental health workers observe an individual and make note of behaviors that occur. If a person shows a certain, well-specified group of behaviors, he or she may be diagnosed with a particular personality disorder as a result. In Iwamasa et al.'s study, the researchers asked their participants to sort these diagnostic criteria in three different ways: according to their presence in men versus women, by ethnicity, and by self (i.e., is this characteristic of you?). Some of the statements that the participants rated appear in Table 14.3. The participants did not know that they were dealing with clinical diagnostic criteria. Rather, they simply identified their stereotypes of the "normal" behaviors of people of different types.

The results suggest that strong cultural effects could occur in diagnosing personality disorders. The college students' beliefs about normal characteristics of Blacks are the same as the criteria used by psychologists and psychiatrists to diagnose antisocial and paranoid personality disorders. Similarly, the students' depiction of the typical behavior of Asian Americans reflects what clinicians look for in people who are schizoid. According to the research results, people of European descent showed a wide range of behaviors associated with different pathologies.

These results suggested that when people think of the behavior of Blacks, Whites, Asian Americans, and Native Americans, those behaviors are the same ones used by

TABLE 14.3 Examples of Descriptions from DSM-III-R That Participants Rated as Typical in Men Versus Women, in Different Ethnic Groups, and of the Participants Themselves (Iwamasa, Larrabee, & Merritt, 2000)

Examples of Description	Personality Disorder with Which the Description Is Associated	Group in Which the "Symptoms" Are Considered Typical
Has no regard for the truth Has never sustained a totally monogamous relationship for more than one year	Antisocial	African American
Is easily hurt by criticism or disapproval Fears being embarrassed by blushing, crying, or showing signs of anxiety in front of other people	Avoidant	European American
Inappropriate, intense anger or lack of control of anger, e.g., frequent displays of temper, constant anger, recurrent physical fights Chronic feelings of emptiness or boredom	Borderline	European American
Feels devastated or helpless when close relationships end Allows others to make most of his or her important decisions, e.g., where to live, what job to take	Dependent	European American
Is overly concerned with physical attractiveness Is uncomfortable in situations in which he or she is not the center of attention	Histrionic	European American
Reacts to criticism with feelings of rage, shame, or humiliation (even if not expressed) Believes that his or her problems are unique and can be understood only by other special people	Narcissistic	European American
Perfectionism that interferes with task completion, e.g., inability to complete a project because own overly strict standards are not met Inability to discard wornout or worthless objects even when they have no sentimental value	Obsessive-Compulsive	European American
Expects, without sufficient basis, to be exploited or harmed by others Bears grudges or is unforgiving of insults or slights	Paranoid	African American
Neither desires nor enjoys close relationships, including being part of a family Is indifferent to the praise and criticism of others	Schizoid	Asian American

(*continues*)

TABLE 14.3 continued

Examples of Description	Personality Disorder with Which the Description Is Associated	Group in Which the "Symptoms" Are Considered Typical
Odd or eccentric behavior or appearance Inappropriate or constricted affect, e.g., silly, aloof, rarely reciprocates gestures or facial expressions, such as smiles or nods	Schizotypal	Native American

mental health practitioners to diagnose psychological disorders. The problem is not with Americans of various heritages. The problem is with people's biases and assumptions. That could lead to differential diagnoses for what might be normal behavior.

Iwamasa et al. studied undergraduate volunteers, not clinicians. In addition, the undergraduates did not assign the diagnostic criteria in the same way that clinicians do. Would the results generalize to clinical psychologists and psychiatrists? Only when research takes place in a clinical setting will we know how cultural biases affect the ways that practitioners diagnose people.

SEX AND GENDER: DO MEN AND WOMEN COME FROM DIFFERENT CULTURES?

Much has been made of the behavioral differences between men and women. Is it really true that *Men Are from Mars and Women Are from Venus* (Gray, 1992)?

If we regard culture the way that Matsumoto (1994) defined it, as "the set of attitudes, values, beliefs, and behaviors, shared by a group of people, communicated from one generation to the next via language or some other means of communication" (p. 4), we might very well argue that men and women are culturally different in some important ways. In addition, people stereotype men and women differently, just as people stereotype Whites and Blacks differently.

Iwamasa et al.'s (2000) research on the perception of stereotypically female or male behaviors also shed light on the fact that people have certain expectations about behaviors across the sexes. The investigators found that normal but stereotypically female behavior was associated with certain disorders (e.g., avoidant personality, paranoia) and normal but stereotpyically male behavior with others (antisocial personality, schizoid personality). Some important issues about gender differences appear in the Controversy on men, women, and math.

Stereotypes and Gender-Related Performance

Could stereotypes of women negatively affect their performance in the same way that stereotypes affect the performance of African Americans and Asian Americans (Cheryan

& Bodenhausen, 2000; Steele & Aronson, 1995)? According to Inzlicht and Ben-Zeev (2000), when women attempt to solve difficult math problems in the presence of men, they are less successful than when they are in the presence of other women only. These researchers suggest that, in the presence of men, women act out the stereotype of poorer

CONTROVERSY: Men, Women, and Math

It is a very widely held belief that women have better verbal abilities than men. Conversely, many people believe that men show better mathematical abilities than women do. In fact, among the general public, you don't hear much argument about it. Just take a look at high school math courses: Boys like them and are more likely to enroll in them. On the other hand, girls like poetry and literature and are more willing to enroll in them. Given that most people will gravitate toward things they do better in, doesn't this say something about the relative abilities of boys and girls in math and English?

The patterns of enrollment in math and in English definitely give us important information, but not necessarily the information we think. Maybe ability doesn't have as much to do with enrollment and success in classes as other factors like encouragement and discouragement. Consider the fact that, at one point, talking Barbie dolls complained how hard mathematics is. Is there a message here? Perhaps years of emphasizing that girls don't like math but boys do, and that boys don't like English but girls do takes its toll.

As Caplan and Caplan (1999) have noted, the popular media have reported about male superiority in mathematics. Should we believe these accounts of sex differences in mathematical abilities?

Two decades ago, Benbow and Stanley (1980, 1983) claimed that hormonal differences in math performance may have been responsible for the differences between men and women. As Caplan and Caplan pointed out, however, nobody bothered to measure hormonal levels of the men or women in the research. Thus, the argument that hormones affect performance goes something like this: Men have higher testosterone levels than women. The men scored higher than the women. Thus, higher testosterone levels lead to higher math scores. Logically, you cannot use two true, but unrelated, statements to prove an argument. There doesn't seem to be any reliable evidence that testosterone levels bear any relationship to math ability.

According to Caplan and Caplan, people are predisposed to believe in male superiority in math. As such, they are likely to accept plausible-sounding arguments ("the difference is hormonal") even though those arguments are not based on research. When people are predisposed to believe in this difference between the sexes, they tend to ignore potentially potent factors like parents' and teachers' expectations, and responses to society's stereotypes.

We also have to take into consideration the dynamics of the testing situation. As Inzlicht and Ben-Zeev (2000) have shown, the context in which women take tests can influence their performance. Another point to remember is that research has consistently documented female strengths in quantitative courses (e.g., Schram, 1996). Before we accept facile explanations based on questionable theory, we should rely on well-documented information and explanations that research has provided.

Finally, how do we explain the fact that recent research has revealed that the gap in women's and men's scores is narrowing? Are women becoming more masculine? Are men becoming more feminine? Are men's and women's hormonal levels changing? These are generally unlikely explanations. Greater emphasis on female success in math courses, increased encouragement to take math courses, higher motivation levels, and the nature of the testing situation are probably better explanations.

Question for Discussion: If women perform better in math when men are not around, how can we create workplaces in which women perform well?

female performance in mathematics, just as members of minority groups fulfill stereotypes. Moving back to the question of possible cultural differences between men and women, it seems that some psychologists might be comfortable with the idea. Women see themselves as different from men in some respects; men see themselves as different from women in some respects.

SUMMARY

In order to understand why people act as they do, we need to understand the cultural context in which those behaviors occur. The effects of culture, race, and ethnicity all surface in our behaviors. The problem that researchers face in considering these contextual questions is that the terms people use every day and even in scientific research are often quite vague. One researcher may refer to ethnicity in describing a behavior, whereas a different researcher may refer to culture in describing the same thing. Because of the problems with definitions, the conclusions that people draw about causes of behavior are sometimes suspect.

One persistent controversy in this area involves the questionable concept of race. There are quite a number of supposed racial categories. The problem is that these categories aren't scientifically defensible. The recent work in genetics indicates that genes are not going to be a useful way of defining races. Still, some scientists maintain that racial categories are useful in their research, even if they cannot define the concept very well.

Because of the complexities of culture, race, and ethnicity, scientific researchers have to work hard to understand the relationship between these constructs and people's behaviors. Research across cultures can be difficult because cultural factors may cause people to understand even simple situations differently. Judgments made by two people from the same cultural background may differ greatly; judgments across cultural boundaries may be nearly impossible to understand without research into those factors. Within the United States, differences between men and women have provided a good deal of controversy, with many questions yet unanswered.

REVIEW QUESTIONS

Multiple Choice Questions

1. The customs, values, and attitudes that can be used to characterize and identify a population refer to
   a. an etic.
   b. an emic.
   c. culture.
   d. relativism.
2. The notion that a person identifies with a particular group of people based on ancestry, religion, or country of origin involves the concept of
   a. ethnicity.
   b. race.
   c. physical culture.

d. psychological culture.

3. When researchers try to study potential differences across racial and ethnic groups, the categories they use
   a. now rely on well-specified biological and genetic differences.
   b. generally overlap with religious categories, making comparisons difficult.
   c. are unchanging for a single individual over that person's lifespan.
   d. often rely on governmental rather than scientific criteria.
4. When researchers have study differences between Hispanic and Anglo residents of the United States,
   a. the research shows few reliable differences between the groups.
   b. the research relies on categories recognized by behavioral scientists.
   c. the research often ignores the differences among people within each group itself.
   d. the research typically uses categorization data from several decades ago, so the results are questionable.
5. The virtually universal taboo against cannibalism would be regarded by researchers as
   a. a universal construct.
   b. a hypothetical construct.
   c. an etic.
   d. an emic.
6. The concept that internal, psychological processes may be universal but that they are expressed differently across cultures is associated with
   a. absolutism.
   b. etics.
   c. universalism.
   d. ethnic constructs.
7. The concept of race is controversial scientifically because
   a. the social history of the races has always been troublesome.
   b. the genetic differences between some races is larger than it is between other races.
   c. depending on the categorization process used, an individual could be placed in different racial categories.
   d. scientists have not been able to determine exactly where the different races fall on the racial continuum.
8. According to the Council of National Psychological Associations, investigators conducting cultural research should note that
   a. the differences across cultural groups are usually much larger than the differences within groups.
   b. developing test norms for a new culture is often costly and is not worth the cost most of the time because the norms change slowly.
   c. understanding the degree of acculturation of participants is critical to interpreting results.
   d. it is most useful to develop a single interpretation of research results and to avoid the complication of seeking alternate explanations.

9. Matsumoto and Assar (1992) tested participants who spoke English and Hindi on their abilities to recognize emotions of people in photographs. They concluded that
   a. the participants were engaged in the same types of mental processing regardless of language.
   b. the participants' thought processes were more conducive to thinking about emotions when they spoke English.
   c. speakers of English had less willingness to deal with the emotions depicted in the photographs.
   d. the same ideas and emotions are expressed easily in either language.
10. If U.S. research participants were asked to identify the emotion in a facial photograph and rate its intensity, the results might be hard to interpret because
    a. there is little agreement on what behaviors are associated with different emotions.
    b. Americans of different cultural backgrounds show similar responses to some emotions but different responses to others.
    c. people often label the emotion depicted in a photograph very differently and with little consistency.
    d. people from different parts of the country label emotions in consistently different ways.
11. When a test is successfully back translated, it
    a. can be retranslated into virtually any new language.
    b. retains the same meaning in the initial language and the language into which it is translated.
    c. will have validity with respect to cross-cultural norms.
    d. cannot be forwarded translated afterward.
12. Iwamasa et al. (2000) studied differences in stereotypical female and male behaviors and found that
    a. there are really few consistent differences in behaviors across genders, even though many people perceive differences.
    b. the differences in math and verbal performances between women and men are consistently large.
    c. the stereotypes about male and female differences are true for most high school and college students.
    d. stereotypically female behaviors were associated with certain disorders and stereotypically male behaviors were associated with other disorders.
13. In the discussions of female–male differences in math ability, researchers
    a. have tended not to publish the studies showing female superiority.
    b. measured hormonal differences between women and men and found that the hormones played a part in the higher scores of men.
    c. discovered that if women are tested with men, the women use the situation competitively to raise their math performance.
    d. have reported that the differences between sexes is, on average, small and is getting smaller.

Essay Questions

14. Why is it so hard to distinguish among the effects of culture, race, and ethnicity in our research?
15. Why should we differentiate between etics and emics in our explanations of behavior?
16. Why are culture, race, and ethnicity hypothetical constructs? In what sense are they useful and in what sense are they limited?
17. What are some difficulties that scientists have had in categorizing people by race and in defining race?
18. Why is content validity a critical concept to consider in conducting research on tests administered by mental health workers when working with people from different backgrounds and cultures?

ANSWERS TO REVIEW QUESTIONS

Multiple Choice Questions

1. c	6. c	11. b
2. a	7. c	12. d
3. d	8. c	13. d
4. c	9. b	
5. c	10. b	

Essay Questions

14. Why is it so hard to distinguish among the effects of culture, race, and ethnicity in our research?

    People, including psychologists, use the terms culture, race, and ethnicity very imprecisely. One researcher might refer to a person's culture but a second researcher might refer to race or ethnicity in explaining the same behaviors; the researchers might mean the same thing, but they use different terms. Or they might really mean different things when they use the terms differently. Unfortunately, there is no consistent agreement about what the terms mean. In addition, the concept of race is problematic because there are not characteristics that we can use to reliably categorize people racially; there will always be confusion because some people resist easy categorization. Many scientists regard race as a social construction rather than as a biological fact.

    It is important to distinguish among them because they can refer to useful construct. For instance, ethnicity is often associated with affiliation (e.g., who you think you belong with), whereas culture pertains to the objects we use (physical culture) or to behaviors (subjective culture).

15. Why should we differentiate between etics and emics in our explanations of behavior?

    Etics are research results that hold true across cultures; emics are research results pertaining to a single culture. It is important to differentiate between them because we need to pay attention to the fact that behaviors in different societies may have very different causes and explanations.

16. Why are culture, race, and ethnicity hypothetical constructs? In what sense are they useful and in what sense are they limited?

    Culture, race, and ethnicity are hypothetical constructs because they are concepts that psychologists have constructed to help explain and understand behavior. They are hypothetical because we hypothesize that they exist and that they are going to be useful, explanatory concepts.

    Sometimes these constructs are helpful because, when measured appropriately, they might be helpful in our understanding of why people in some groups act one way, whereas people in another group act differently. Not everybody in a group acts and thinks the same way, but the hypothetical constructs of culture and ethnicity can give some insights into group processes.

    On the other hand, none of these concepts can be precisely defined and measured, which is why we rely on external markers (e.g., skin color) to represent them. These external markers may not really be very helpful in understanding behavior because they are only imperfectly correlated with thought and behavior. People within a given group differ from one another in many ways, so trying to figure out how a single person thinks is not feasible.

17. What are some difficulties that scientists have had in categorizing people by race and in defining race?

    a. Skin color has often been a means by which people are racially categorized. This is unreliable because sometimes people with darker skin will be considered "White" while people with lighter skin will be considered "Black."
    b. Race is seem as involving discrete, mutually exclusive categories; a person falls in one and only one category. In reality, the characteristics associated with the categories fall on a continuum, so the cutoff points are arbitrary.
    c. Scientists have not reached consensus about what racial categories there might actually be. There is no set number of racial categories that scientists agree on.
    d. Geographical criteria for race is unreliable because there are many people whose birthplace is not a reliable indicator of their ancestry, which is likely to be mixed in any case.
    e. When scientists did create racial categories, they were based on subjective, nonscientific criteria.

18. Why is content validity a critical concept to consider in conducting research on tests administered by mental health workers when working with people from different backgrounds and cultures?

Content validity relates to the questions that clinicians ask when working with a client. In order to draw good conclusions, the clinician must ask appropriate questions. What will be appropriate in one setting or with one group may not be useful in another context.

People with different lifestyles may not share the same perspective, so a simple question might indicate something quite different across groups. Similarly, a certain behavior will reflect normal functioning in one culture, abnormal functioning in a second, and be completely irrelevant in a third. The potential problems are compounded when a clinician wants to translate a question into a different language; there may not be corresponding ideas in different languages.

In order for test items to be valid for different groups, the concepts have to address the appropriate ideas using appropriate words. Without content validity, answers to individual questions on a test may mislead a clinician entirely.

APPENDIX A

WRITING A RESEARCH REPORT

Most research reports in psychology appearing in journals have a standard format, which is specified in the *Publication Manual of the American Psychological Association* (5th ed.). The use of a consistent style makes it easier for readers to locate critical information. In addition, once writers learn the basics of APA style, it can be easier to write up a report because it is clear where to put various kinds of information.

In general, APA style papers have the following components in this order:

- Title Page
- Abstract
- Introduction
- Methods
- Results
- Discussion
- Discussion
- References
- Tables
- Figure Captions
- Figures

Occasionally, there are deviations from this listing. For instance, if a manuscript reports on two or more studies, the author might combine the Results and Discussion section for each study rather than creating two sections. Then there might be a General Discussion after the final study. Following APA style isn't difficult, but you have to pay attention to a lot of small details.

As with any writing you do, it is important to communicate well. The former editor of the journal *Teaching of Psychology*, Charles Brewer, has commented that writers should strive for "clarity, conciseness, and felicity of expression." This means that you should be clear in making your points; you should use economy in your writing, keeping it as short as you can while still getting your message across; and you should write so that your readers doesn't have to fight their way through a tangled thicket of words to get your point.

This appendix is designed to help you learn appropriate formatting so your reader knows where to find information. It will also be somewhat useful in giving you guidance on writing style. Remember that this guide to APA style only highlights the material in the *Publication Manual of the American Psychological Association.* The information here will be useful for creating a basic APA-formatted manuscript. There are many other details in the publication manual itself.

FORMATTING YOUR MANUSCRIPT

There are a few general considerations involved in formatting an APA-style manuscript. To begin with, you should set your margins at one inch on the top, bottom, and sides. Then leave them that way. In addition, everything in the manuscript should be double spaced. Set your word processor's line spacing at double spaced. Then leave it that way.

Another aspect of APA style is that every page should be numbered in the upper right-hand corner, next to the page header. The best way to display the header and to paginate appropriately is with your word processor's function for creating a page header. By using the header function, you guarantee that this information appears where it needs to on every page. If you type in the header and the page number manually, any time you add or eliminate material in your manuscript, the header and page number will wind up in the wrong place.

When you are typing your manuscript, you will create several different sections (e.g., Introduction, Methods, Results, Discussion). Do not begin a new section on a new page. As a rule, just continue to type, using normal double spacing between lines. There are some exceptions to this; they are explained below.

In addition, you have to create headings for each section. There are different levels of headings, depending on the complexity of your manuscript. For most single-study manuscripts, you will use two different types of headings.

When you finish typing the main body of the manuscript and the references, you then add any tables that you want to include. The tables do not appear on the pages with the normal text. They are put at the end, right after the references. Each table goes on a separate page. Following the tables is a page that has the figure captions. All of the figure captions go on the same page, followed by the figures themselves. Graphs, charts, and pictures are all classified as figures. When you prepare them, you put only the figure on a sheet, not the caption.

The general points in this section appear in Figure A-1. Remember that this is a primer on APA style. There are other guidelines that are relevant to more complex manuscripts than you are likely to produce. You can refer to the *Publication Manual* for those details. You can also learn from reading and referring to journal articles that have been published.

TITLE PAGE

The title page is pretty simple to construct, but it is important to include all the information that is required. You can see the general format in Figure A-2. There are three main components of the title page: the short title, the running head, and the title and author information.

Page Header

The short title consists of the first two or three words of the paper's title, followed by the page number. The short title helps others keep your manuscript together and in the right order if the pages become separated. If the title of your paper is "Study habits of

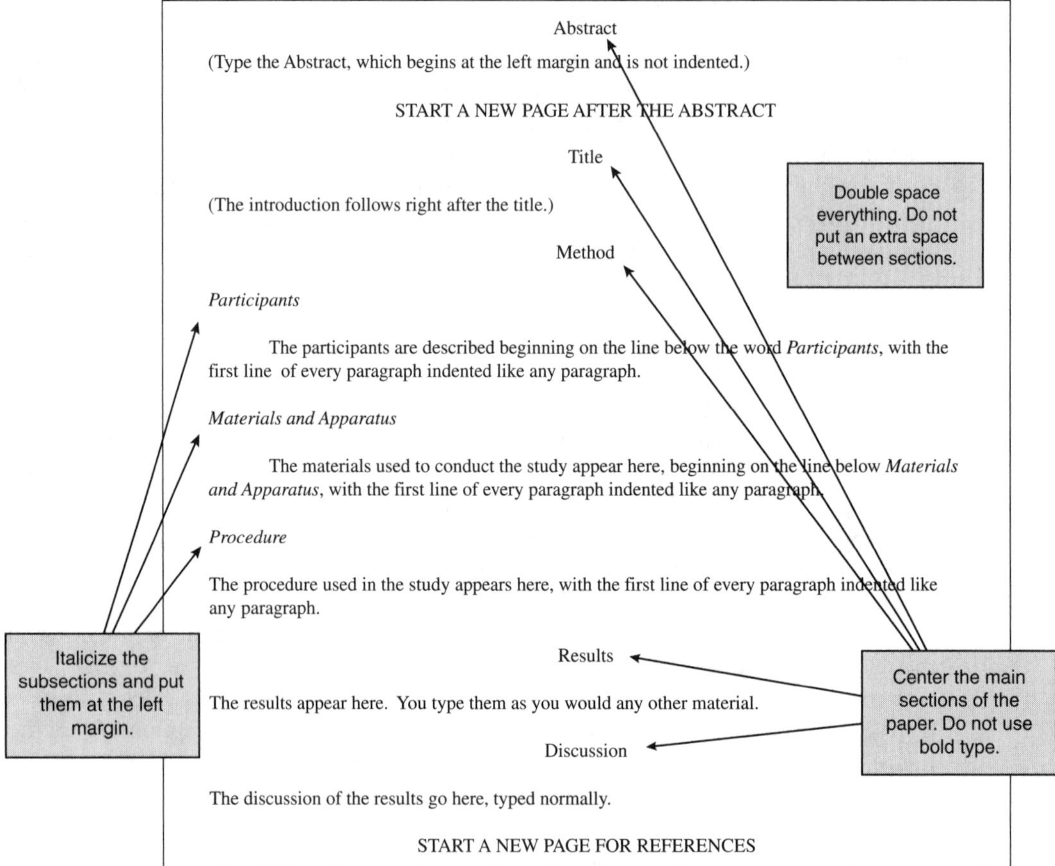

FIGURE A-1 General format of an APA-style research report.

college students over four years," the short title would be *Study habits of.* (You should not italicize it. The examples in this appendix appear in italics so you can see them, but you rarely use italics in a research report.)

The short title appears on every page of the manuscript, so it is best to use your Header/Footer capability on your word processor to create it. In this way, your computer will make sure that the pages are numbered correctly and that the short title is in place, even if you revise your paper, adding or eliminating material.

Running Head

The running head is like an abbreviated title. It should explain the general nature of your project. It is limited to a maximum of 50 characters (i.e., letters and spaces). If your full title is "Study habits of college students over four years," an abbreviated title for the running head could be *STUDENT STUDY HABITS.* (It should be in capital letters.)

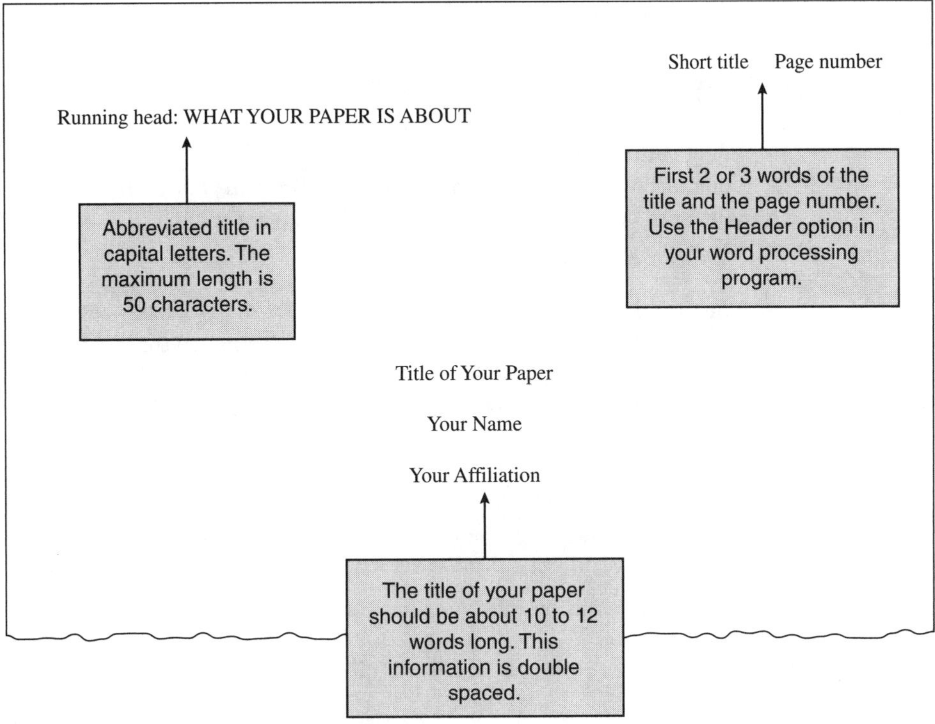

FIGURE A-2 Format of a title page in APA style.

Title and Author Information

The title of the paper should clue the reader into the nature of your project. The recommended length is 10 to 12 words. Your name and your affiliation, which will be your school (unless your instructor tells you otherwise for a class paper), appear just below the title of the paper. They let the reader know who you are and where you come from.

ABSTRACT

The abstract is a brief description of the purpose of the project, what methods the author used to address the issues of interest, the results of data collection, and the conclusions and interpretations the author drew. This section gives the reader a general sense of the paper so he or she can decide whether to read the entire paper.

The abstract is typed on its own page, immediately after the title page. It appears as a block. That is, the first line is not indented. According to APA style, the abstract should be about 120 words.

INTRODUCTION

The Introduction section begins with the title of the article you are writing. The word *Introduction* does not appear. So type the title, then begin the introduction itself. As with the rest of your manuscript, use double spacing, with no extra space between the title and the beginning of the introduction. This section addresses several questions that prepare the reader for the ideas discussed throughout the manuscript:

- What is the general topic of the research article?
- What do we know about this topic from previous research?
- What are you trying to demonstrate in your research?
- What are your hypotheses?

You are likely to make your first mention of the work of previous researchers in the introduction. There is a general format for referring to that work. When you cite a published journal article, you typically use the authors' last names and indicate the year of publication or presentation of their work. As you see in Figure A-3, you might men-

The first time you mention a reference, list the last names of the authors, but cite all of them. Put the year of publication in parentheses.

If you wanted to discuss whether people equate sex and death, you could refer to the research by Goldenberg, Pyszczynski, McCoy, Greenberg, and Solomon (1999). They provided evidence about the sex-death link. Or you could cite the research questioning the effectiveness of the so-called "three strikes" laws that mandate lengthy prison sentences (Stolzenberg & D'Alessio, 1997)

If your first citation of a work appears in parentheses, give the last names of all authors, using an ampersand (&) instead of the word *and* prior to the last author's name. The year of publication goes last, following a comma after the last author.

The second time you refer to work done by three or more authors, cite only the first author. So when mentioning the work linking sex and death by Goldenberg et al. (1999), you use the first author's last name and the Latin abbreviation *et al.*, which stands for *and others* (but you do not use italics). The year goes in parentheses. If you refer to work by two authors, you cite them both any time you mention them, such as the work on prison sentences (Stolzenberg & D'Alessio, 1997). If you mention work done by six authors or more, like the work by Hennigan et al. (1982), you include only the first author's name, even the first time you cite it.

If a work has six or more authors, list only the first author's last name, followed by the designation et al., with a period after al. You do this even the first time you mention it.

FIGURE A-3 Reference formats for citing work in a manuscript in APA style.

tion names in the text per se or in parentheses. The APA *Publication Manual* describes the conventions in detail for citing authors. The highlights are in Figure A-3.

METHOD

This section of the manuscript contains several subparts. Each one is pretty much self-contained. The purpose of the Method section is to let the reader know how you actually carried out your project. There should be enough detail so another person could read your words and reproduce your study in nearly identical form. You should present only those details that would be relevant to the purpose and outcome of the study. The different segments of the method section describe who took part, what materials and implements were important in carrying out the study, and the procedure used to complete the research.

Participants

In this subsection, you tell the reader who participated in the study, how many people (or rats, mice, pigeons, etc.) were involved, and the demographics of your sample (e.g., age, ethnicity, educational level, etc. as appropriate). The information that gives you reader appropriate information about your participants include the following:

- How many humans or nonhumans were studied?
- If there were nonhuman animals, what kind were they?
- If there were people, what were their characteristics (e.g., average and range of age, gender, race or ethnicity, were they volunteers or were they paid, etc.)?

Apparatus and Materials

The basic issues in this subsection involve what you needed to carry out your study. Sometimes you have used machines, computers, or other instrumentation. Much psychological research also requires materials that participants read, learn, memorize, and so on. When you have created your own apparatus, you should describe it in great detail. If you used commercially available apparatus, you can simply mention the type of apparatus (with make and model), the company that provided it, and any other relevant details that would be useful for somebody who might want to replicate your or simply to understand your approach. Important information about materials and apparatus include:

- How many and what kind of stimuli, questions, etc. were used?
- What instrumentation, if any, was used to present material to participants and to record their responses?

Procedure

This subsection addresses the issue of what the participants actually did during the research session. The details here should give a complete account of what your participants did from the time the study began until the debriefing was done. The important elements of the procedure are as follows:

- After the participants arrived, what did they do?
- What did the experimenters do as they interacted with participants?

RESULTS

In this section, you give a verbal description of your results, accompanied by appropriate quantitative information (e.g., means and standard deviations, statistical analyses). It is often difficult for a reader to understand your results if you simply list all of them without describing them. A long series of means, for instance, can be hard for a reader to comprehend without some narrative to accompany them. The critical questions in the Results section include the following:

- What were patterns of behaviors among participants?
- Did behaviors differ when groups were compared?
- What type of behaviors are predictable in the different testing conditions?
- Were there predictable relationships among variables?
- What were the results of any statistical tests?

Your Results section can also include tables and figures. Sometimes a table or a figure can present important information much more simply than you can describe it in words. When that is the case, make good use of tables and figures. At the same time, try to avoid using tables and figures that do not contain enough useful information. You probably don't want to use a graph, for example, if you have only two data points to compare.

In detailing your results, make sure that you give enough of a verbal description so the reader has a good idea of what you found. If you only present numerical information, the reader may have difficulty understanding which results were most important and how they related to one another.

Tables

Tables can present data very effectively and efficiently. They are relatively easy to create with the Tables function in your word processing program. Figure A-4 outlines some of the main considerations in the use of a table.

At times, tables can get quite complex, especially when there are many groups being compared or when researchers use complex statistical analyses. The basic format is pretty simple, though. The table consists of a label that gives enough information to the readers so they don't have to refer back to the text to comprehend the contents of the table. The table also contains data, often organized by conditions or groups. Sometimes, mean values appear in the margins of the tables, the so-called marginal means. In some cases, tables may not contain numbers, but involve only words and text. This type of table follows the same general principles as numeric tables.

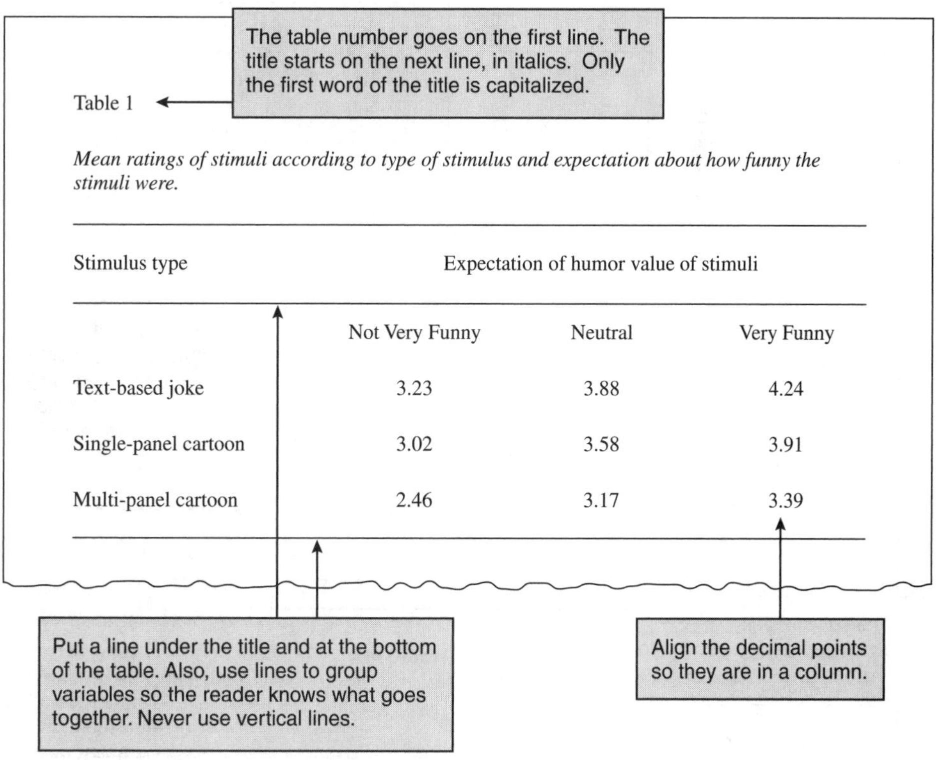

Table 1

Mean ratings of stimuli according to type of stimulus and expectation about how funny the stimuli were.

Stimulus type	Expectation of humor value of stimuli		
	Not Very Funny	Neutral	Very Funny
Text-based joke	3.23	3.88	4.24
Single-panel cartoon	3.02	3.58	3.91
Multi-panel cartoon	2.46	3.17	3.39

FIGURE A-4 Example of a results table in APA style.

Figures

Graphs and charts used to be difficult to construct when an author had to draw them by hand. Currently, however, data analysis software and spreadsheets permit easy construction of graphs. It is important to remember that when you use graphic presentations, you should make sure that they convey the information you want in a manner that is easy for the reader to comprehend. It takes some practice in creating effective visual presentations; you can learn how to construct them by looking at published figures to see which ones are effective and which are not.

The main types of figures used in research articles are line graphs, bar graphs, and scatter diagrams. Line graphs show the relation between two quantitative variables. Bar graphs are often used to represent relations among categorical variables. Scatter diagrams usually reflect correlational analyses. Figures A-5 and Figure A-6 provide examples of line graphs that look slightly different, but that convey the same information. The two graphs show that the depiction can look different depending on which independent variable you put on the X-axis and which variable you place in the graph.

You can represent your data in bar graphs. Typically, bar graphs represent categorical data, but the example in Figure A-7 is based on the same continuous data we've

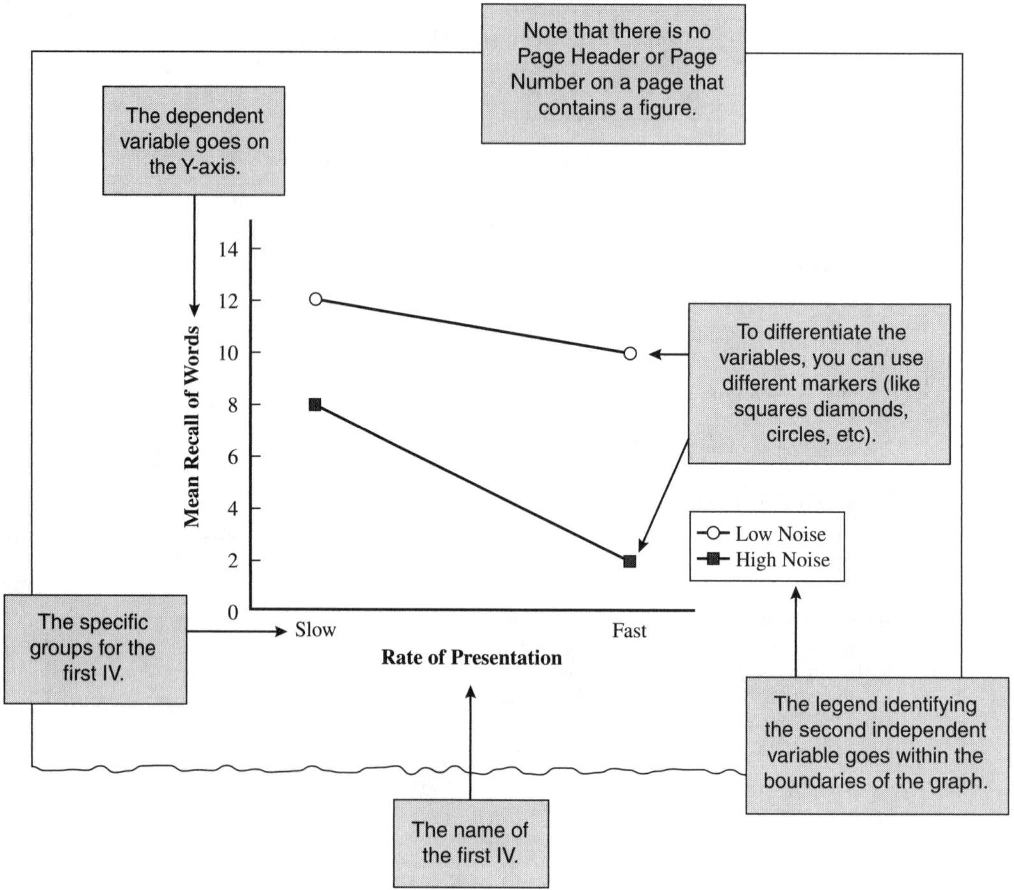

FIGURE A-5 Example of a line graph in APA style.

been working with in these examples. You can see that the visual representation of the bar graph shows the same pattern that you saw in Figure A-5.

If you have completed a correlational analysis, you might want to present a scatter diagram that reveals the relation between two variables. The basic format of this type of figure is the same as for line graphs and bar graphs. The type of information in a scatter diagram is different in an important way, though. Unlike line and bar graphs, which present data at the level of groups, a scatter diagram includes data points from each individual on two variables being measured.

Statistical Results

The statistics that you are most likely to use in your research report are the analysis of variance, the Student's *t*-test, the Pearson product-moment correlation, and the chi-square test. When you type your research results, you need to follow specific guidelines about including necessary information. Figure A-8 gives the formatting for these tests.

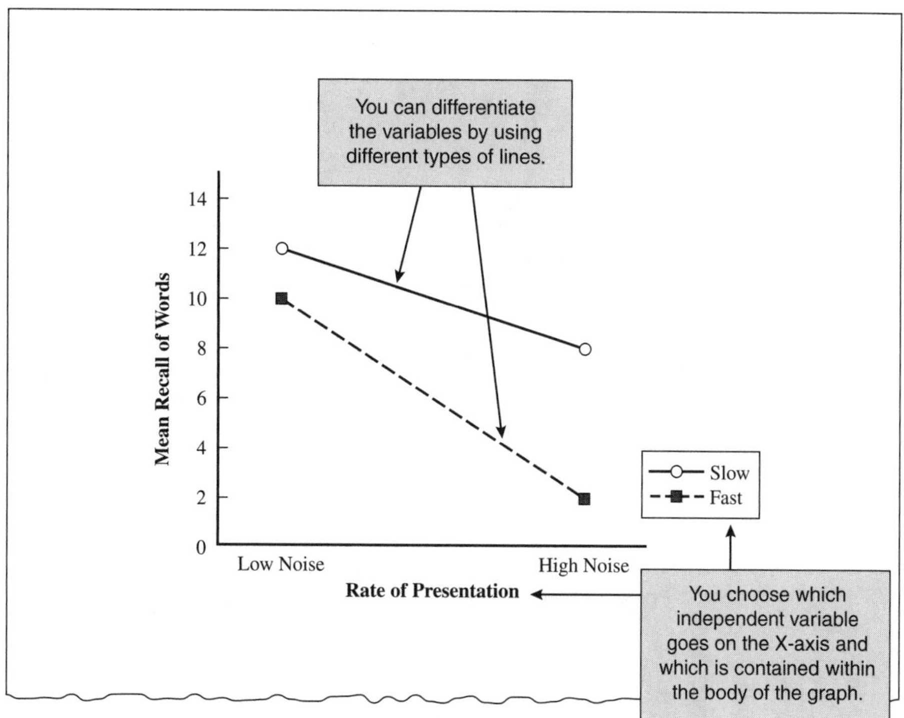

FIGURE A-6 Example of a line graph in APA style.

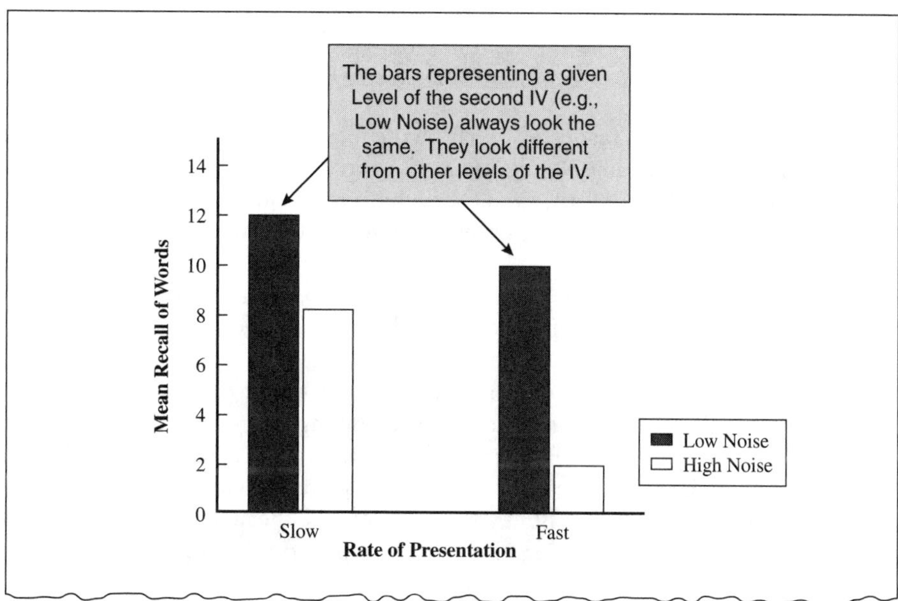

FIGURE A-7 Example of a bar graph in APA style.

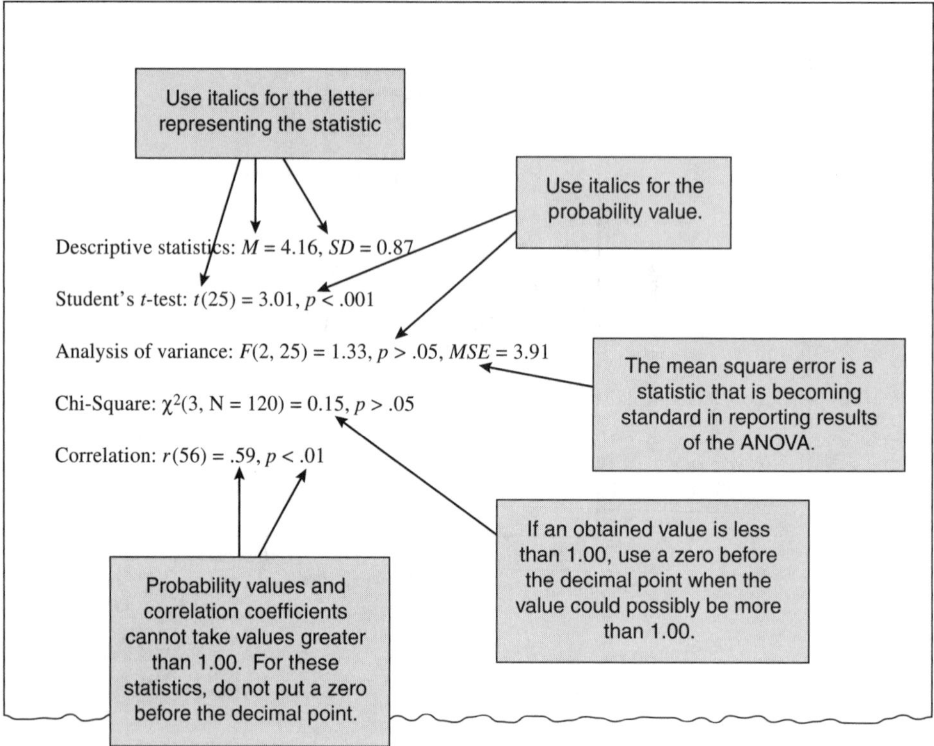

FIGURE A-8 Format for presenting statistical results in APA style.

DISCUSSION

After you tell the reader what has happened, you need to spend some time explaining why it happened. The Results section is simply a description of the results, without much explanation. By contrast, the Discussion section offers you the opportunity to explain why your results occurred as they did and why they are important to the psychological community.

When you discuss your findings, it is important to relate them to the ideas you presented in your Introduction section. The introduction set the stage for the research, so your reader will expect you to show why those ideas are important to your ideas. This is the section of the manuscript that allows you to draw inferences about important psychological processes that are taking place among your participants. It is perfectly appropriate for you to speculate on the meaning of your data. If others disagree, they can always do their own research to provide for support their ideas. When you speculate, you should give the logic behind your arguments. Otherwise, you are only giving an opinion, not logical speculation. The Discussion section addresses the following questions:

- What do the results mean?
- What explanations can you develop for why the participants responded as they did?

- What psychological processes help you explain participants' responses?
- What questions have not been answered fully?
- How do your results relate to the research cited in the introduction?
- How do your results relate to other kinds of research?
- What new ideas emerge that you could evaluate in a subsequent experiment?

REFERENCES

The reference section includes the full citation for any work that you referred to in your writing. This section is only for works cited in your paper; it is not a general bibliography related to your topic. The rule is that if something was referred to in the manuscript, it belongs here; if a work was not mentioned in your writing, it does not appear here.

The reference section is actually fairly easy to create because you know exactly what the section must contain. The only difficulty is making sure that you use the correct format in the citation. You may be familiar with styles other than APA's, like MLA (from the Modern Language Association) or the Chicago style. They are considerably different from APA style. Fortunately, in your manuscripts, you are likely to use only a few of the many types of sources available, so it is easy to become familiar with the rules for citing references. Examples appear in Figures A-9 through A-12.

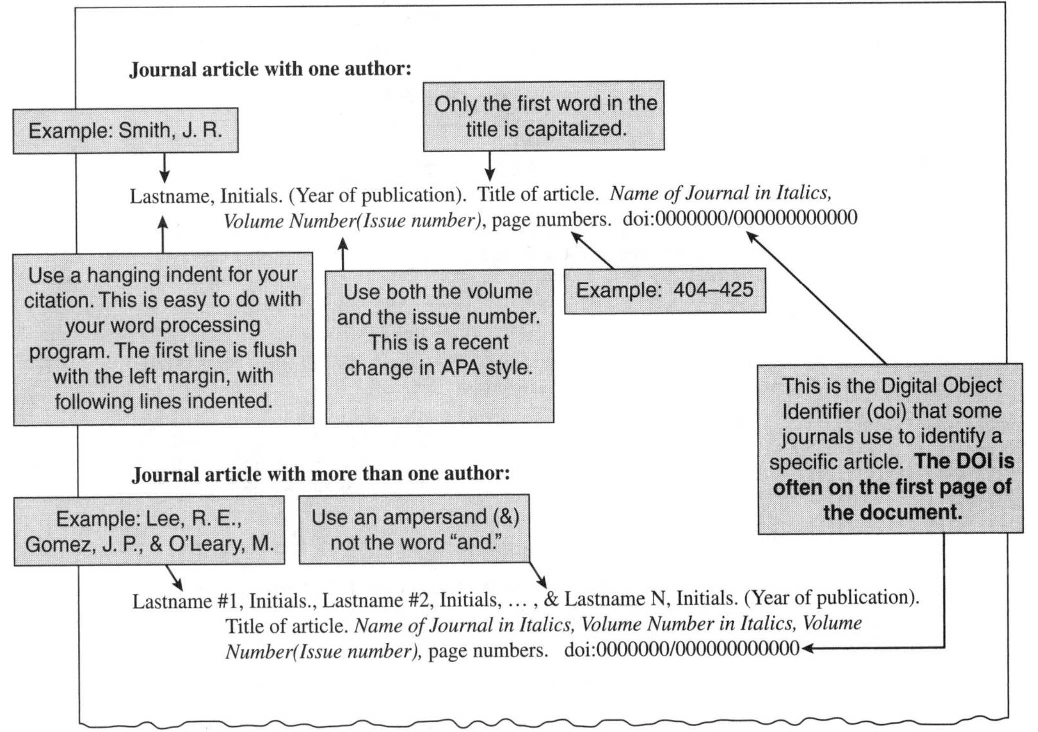

FIGURE A-9 Format for journal article references in APA style.

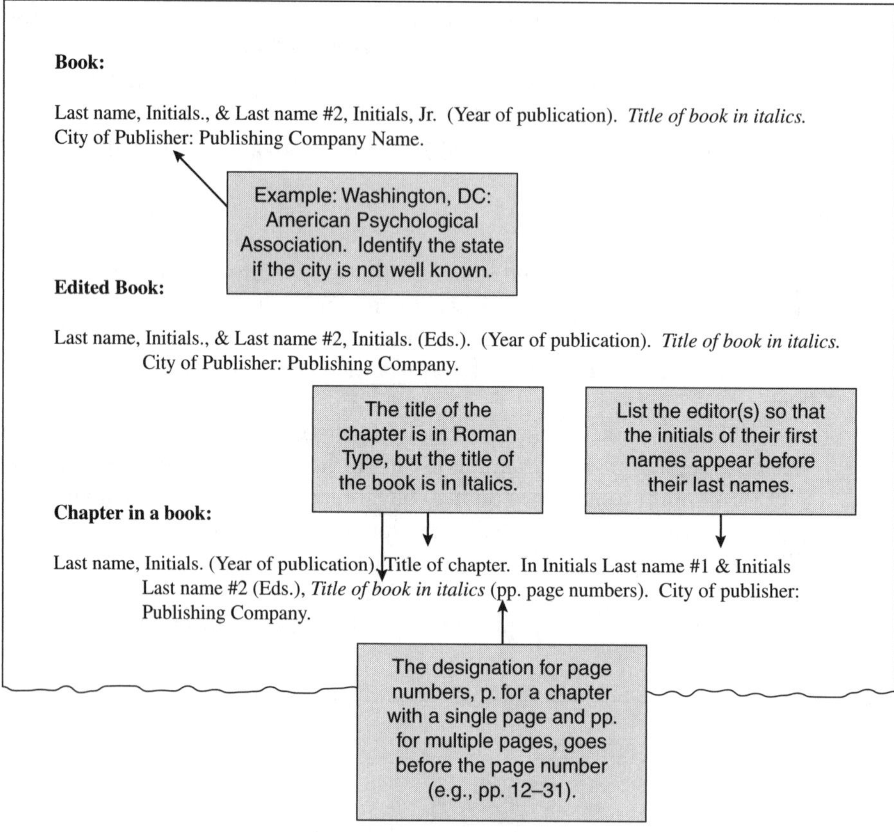

FIGURE A-10 Format for book references in APA style.

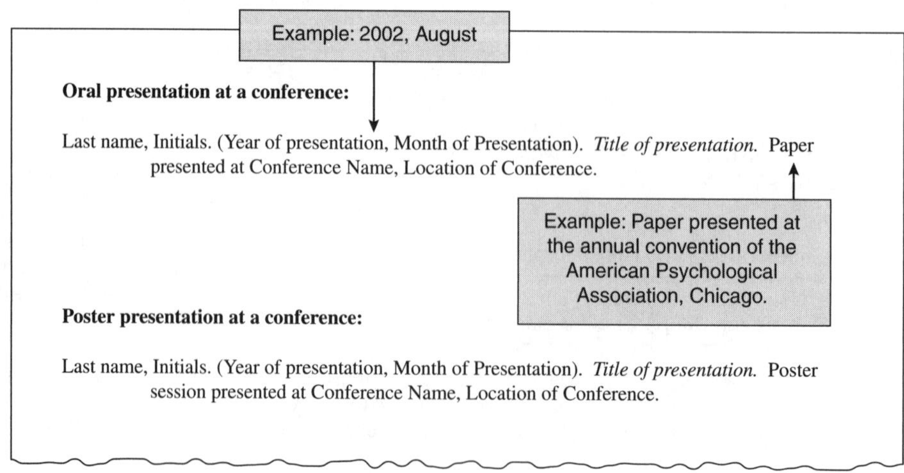

FIGURE A-11 Format for oral and poster presentation references in APA style.

Electronic Reference from an online-only journal article with no DOI:

Lastname, Initials (Year, Date). Title of article, *Online Journal Name in Italics,* Volume #(Issue number), Article number. Retrieved from <URL—web address>.

Electronic Reference from an online-only journal article with DOI:

Lastname, Initials (Year, Date). Title of article, *Online Journal Name in Italics,* Volume #(Issue number), Article number. doi:0000000/000000000000

This is the Digital Object Identifier (doi) that some journals use to identify a specific article. **The DOI is often on the first page of the document.**

Electronic reference from a print journal that was accessed online:

Lastname, Initials. (Year). Title of article. *Journal Name in Italics,* Volume #(Issue number), page numbers. doi:0000000/000000000000

Online Document:

Last name, Initials (Year). *Title of work in italics.* Retrieved <Month, day, year> from <URL— web address>.

Provide the entire web address, beginning with **http://**
Don't use the pointed brackets when you type the references.

FIGURE A-12 Format for electronic references in APA style.

The most common sources are journal articles, books and book chapters, presentations at conferences, and electronic resources. You can see how to format them in Figures A-9 through A-12. Specific examples appear in Table A-1. Each of these can come in several different varieties, so you will have to make sure that you are following the APA guidelines exactly. For details on the less common types of references, you can consult the *Publication Manual of the American Psychological Association.* There are also numerous web sites that provide help. The technical information about the citations tells the reader:

- What research was cited in the report (e.g., work published in journals or other written sources, research presentations, personal communications)?
- Where was the information made public?

TABLE A-1 Examples of reference formats in APA style.

Journal articles:

Adair, J. G. (1984). The Hawthorne effect: A reconsideration of the methodological artifact. *Journal of Applied Psychology, 69,* 334-345.

Aronson, J., Lustina, M. J., Good, C., Keough, K., Steele, C. M., & Brown, J. (1999). When white men can't do math: Necessary and sufficient factors in stereotype threat. *Journal of Experimental Social Psychology, 35,* 29-46.

Article from a print journal with DOI assigned:

Kazdin, A. E. (2008). Evidence-based treatment and practice: New opportunities to bridge clinical research and practice, enhance the knowledge base, and improve patient care. *American Psychologist, 63*(3), 146–159, doi:10.1037/0003-066X.63.3.146

Book:

Cytowic, R. E. (1993). *The man who tasted shapes.* New York: G. P. Putnam & Son.

Edited book:

Davis, S. F., & Buskist, W. (Eds.) (2002). *The teaching of psychology: Essays in honor of Wilbert J. McKeachie and Charles L. Brewer.* Mahwah, NJ: Erlbaum.

Chapter in an edited book:

Gardner, H., Krechevsky, M., Sternberg, R. J., & Okagaki, L. (1994). Intelligence in context: Enhancing students' practical intelligence for school. In K. McGilly (Ed.), *Classroom lessons: Integrating cognitive theory and classroom practice* (pp. 105, 127). Cambridge: MIT Press.

Ball, P., Giles, H., & Hewstone, M. (1984). Second language acquisition: The intergroup theory with catastrophic dimensions. In H. Tajfel (Ed.), *The social dimension* (Vol. 2, pp. 668, 694). Cambridge, UK: Cambridge University Press.

Online document:

Lloyd, M.A. (2001, January 20). *Marky Lloyd's careers in psychology page.* Retrieved February 13, 2003 from http://www.psywww.com/careers/index.htm.

Oral presentation at a conference:

Loftus, E. F. (2003, January). Illusions of memory. Presented at the National Institute on the Teaching of Psychology. St. Petersburg Beach, FL.

Poster presentation at a conference:

Wimer, D. J., & Beins, B. C. (2000, August). Is this joke funny? Only if we say it is. Poster session presented at the annual convention of the American Psychological

WRITING STYLE

As the *Publication Manual of the American Psychological Association* points out, scientific writing is different from fiction or other creative writing. Scientific writing benefits from clear and direct communication, whereas creative writing benefits from the creation of ambiguity, abrupt changes in perspective, and other literary devices. When you write a research report, you should concentrate on making your point clearly, avoiding prose that doesn't contribute to the logic of your arguments.

This section presents some common problems in writing that you should note. Much of your writing to this point has probably been more literary than scientific, so you might have to unlearn some habits that you have developed.

Precision of Expression

When you write, avoid using more words than you need and avoid words that are more technical than necessary. Sometimes communication is better when you use a technical term because it has a specific meaning that the term transmits very efficiently. On the other hand, when you use complex wording to describe a simple situation, the reader can get confused. Using impressive terminology may not help you get your point across.

Just as you should avoid being too technical, you have to make sure that you are not too informal in your language. If an experiment has some methodological flaws, for example, and the results might be confounded, you should not make vague statements like *The methodological flaws skewed the results* because the word *skew* could mean just about anything. You would want to be more specific, suggesting that *The methodological flaws led to higher mean scores in Groups A and B*, or something equally explanatory. Or if your participants engaged in a behavior in some circumstances, you should specify how often the behavior occurred; ill-defined statements like *most of the time* do not communicate as precisely as you want in a research report.

Another grammatical feature that leads to problems is the use of passive voice verbs (e.g., *they were asked to move* instead of *I asked them to move*). For one thing, such verbs make for dull prose. Another problem is that passive voice verbs lead to lack of clarity. That is, to say that *The participants were given the materials* means that you are not telling your reader who did the giving. When you use passive voice verbs, the actor is often hidden. In some cases, it is important to know who completed the action. In virtually all cases, active voice verbs make more your prose more interesting.

Avoiding Biased Language

When you describe or refer to people in your writing, use language that gets your point across but also shows sensitivity to the individuals and groups to which you refer. For example, sexist language can be problematic. If you make a statement that *The pioneers, their wives, and their children who settled the western states experienced hardships we cannot even imagine*, you are showing bias in your language. The implication is that the men were the pioneers, whereas the women and children were not.

Another type of bias that we see less than we used to regarding the sexes is the use of the word *man* to refer to people in general. The convention of using *man* to refer to people also led to the use of male pronouns (i.e., *his*, *him*) when the meaning supposedly included women. This change has led to the use of plural pronouns in referring to a single person (e.g., *A student can be rude when they use their cell phones in class*). Although this has gained acceptance in speech, it is not appropriate in formal writing because if you use a pronoun to refer to *a student*, the pronoun must be singular. One solution is to use plural nouns (e.g., *students*) so the use of plural pronouns is grammatically consistent. The use of *he or she*, *his or her* or other double pronouns can also solve the problem if you use a singular noun.

A further issue regarding pronouns involves the use of first-person pronouns (e.g., *I* or *we*). Many students have learned to avoid using the personal pronoun *I*. Teachers have said to use passive voice verbs or to use *we* in their writing when they mean only a single person, that is, themselves. According to APA style, it is appropriate to use *I* when referring to yourself (although not in the Abstract). Using *I* also avoids the use of passive voice verbs, which you should keep to an absolute minimum.

Another issue involves sensitivity to diverse groups, particularly with respect to the labeling of those groups. It is impossible to state a set of unchanging rules because the terms we use to denote people in various groups change. It may not be possible to satisfy everybody in every group, but you should be aware of the terms that any particular time are appropriate for describing them. Incidentally, if you use the words *Black* and *White* as racial or ethnic terms, these words should be capitalized.

Recently, authorities on writing have concluded that it is not appropriate to refer to people as though a single characteristic defined them completely. For example, in discussing people with handicaps, you should avoid calling them *the handicapped* because such a term implies that the handicap is perhaps their most significant characteristic. Noting that they are either *handicapped people* or *people with handicaps* highlights the fact that they are, first and foremost, people. For a task as difficult as writing well, these few rules will not suffice by themselves. But they provide a good start.

The following section presents a brief example of an APA-style paper based on research conducted by students and presented at the annual convention of the New England Psychological Association in 2007.

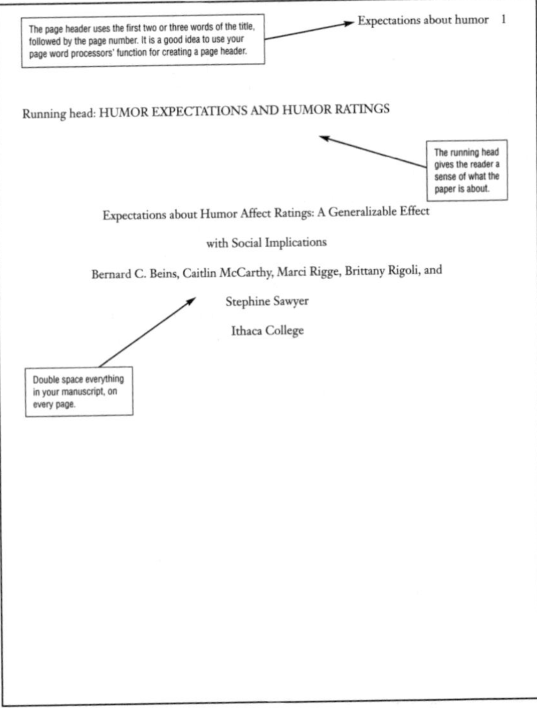

The page header uses the first two or three words of the title, followed by the page number. It is a good idea to use your page word processors' function for creating a page header.

Expectations about humor 1

Running head: HUMOR EXPECTATIONS AND HUMOR RATINGS

The running head gives the reader a sense of what the paper is about.

Expectations about Humor Affect Ratings: A Generalizable Effect

with Social Implications

Bernard C. Beins, Caitlin McCarthy, Marci Rigge, Brittany Rigoli, and

Stephine Sawyer

Ithaca College

Double space everything in your manuscript, on every page.

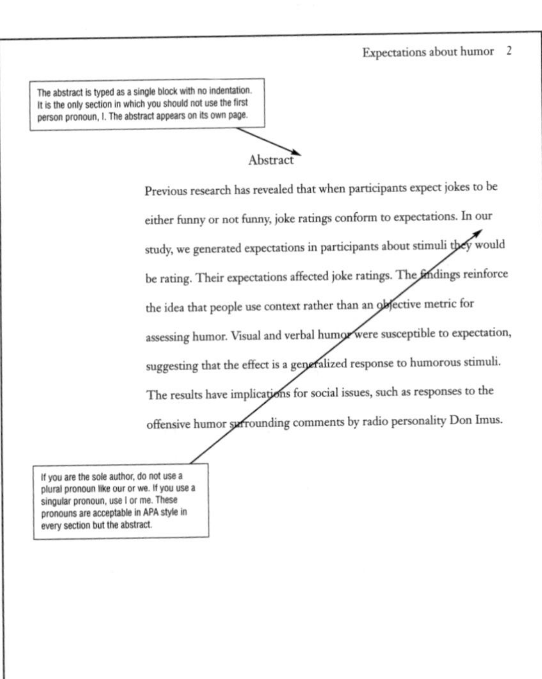

Expectations about humor 2

The abstract is typed as a single block with no indentation. It is the only section in which you should not use the first person pronoun, I. The abstract appears on its own page.

Abstract

Previous research has revealed that when participants expect jokes to be either funny or not funny, joke ratings conform to expectations. In our study, we generated expectations in participants about stimuli they would be rating. Their expectations affected joke ratings. The findings reinforce the idea that people use context rather than an objective metric for assessing humor. Visual and verbal humor were susceptible to expectation, suggesting that the effect is a generalized response to humorous stimuli. The results have implications for social issues, such as responses to the offensive humor surrounding comments by radio personality Don Imus.

If you are the sole author, do not use a plural pronoun like our or we. If you use a singular pronoun, use I or me. These pronouns are acceptable in APA style in every section but the abstract.

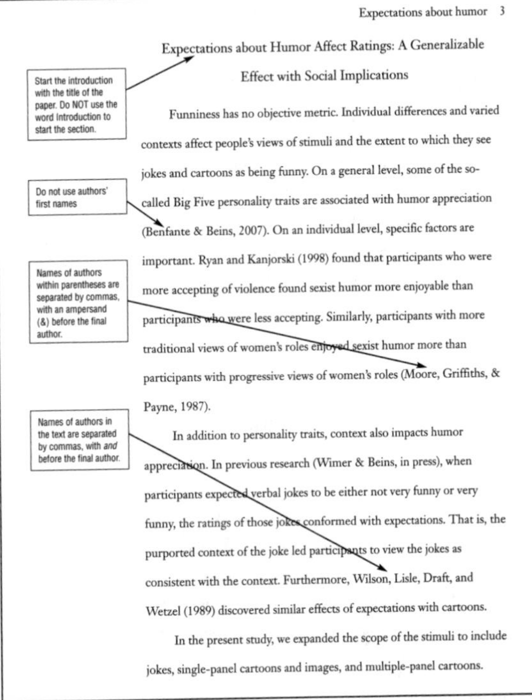

Expectations about humor 3

Start the introduction with the title of the paper. Do NOT use the word Introduction to start the section.

Expectations about Humor Affect Ratings: A Generalizable

Effect with Social Implications

Funniness has no objective metric. Individual differences and varied contexts affect people's views of stimuli and the extent to which they see jokes and cartoons as being funny. On a general level, some of the so-called Big Five personality traits are associated with humor appreciation (Benfante & Beins, 2007). On an individual level, specific factors are important. Ryan and Kanjorski (1998) found that participants who were more accepting of violence found sexist humor more enjoyable than participants who were less accepting. Similarly, participants with more traditional views of women's roles enjoyed sexist humor more than participants with progressive views of women's roles (Moore, Griffiths, & Payne, 1987).

Do not use authors' first names

Names of authors within parentheses are separated by commas, with an ampersand (&) before the final author.

In addition to personality traits, context also impacts humor appreciation. In previous research (Wimer & Beins, in press), when participants expected verbal jokes to be either not very funny or very funny, the ratings of those jokes conformed with expectations. That is, the purported context of the joke led participants to view the jokes as consistent with the context. Furthermore, Wilson, Lisle, Draft, and Wetzel (1989) discovered similar effects of expectations with cartoons.

Names of authors in the text are separated by commas, with *and* before the final author.

In the present study, we expanded the scope of the stimuli to include jokes, single-panel cartoons and images, and multiple-panel cartoons.

Start the introduction with the title of the paper. Do NOT use the word Introduction to start the section.

Names of authors within parentheses are separated by commas, with an ampersand (&) before the final

Based on the findings of Wimer and Beins (in press) with jokes and of Wilson et al. (1989) with cartoons, we hypothesize that participants will conform to expectations in their ratings of the stimuli.

It is an open question at this point whether participants will react to the varying types of stimuli in the same way. Single-panel stimuli have greater immediacy than do jokes that require reading from start to finish. Multiple-panel cartoons may be midway between the other two types of stimuli with regard to how much cognitive processing must take place prior to getting the point of the humor. If participants develop an overall mindset based on their expectations, they may show the same pattern of rating for all types of humor, regardless of cognitive effort required for understanding it. On the other hand, if the pattern of elevated or depressed ratings emerges after complete processing of a stimulus, the single-panel cartoons may show less effect of expectation.

In a paper reporting a single study, two levels of headings are usually sufficient. The major headings are centered. The minor headings are on the left margin and are italicized.

Method

Participants

We recruited 94 participants from psychology classes. They volunteered in exchange for extra credit in those classes. Participants were predominately White (84%), but also included students from various other groups, including Asian (9.6%), Hispanic (3.2%), and Black (1.1%). Some students chose the "Other" category (2.1%). The mean age was 19.13 years (*SD* = 1.12).

Do not start sentences with numerals. If you have to start a sentence numerically, write out the number. Generally, try to put the number somewhere within the sentence.

Materials and Apparatus

The stimuli included 10 jokes, 10 single-panel images or cartoons, and 10 multiple-panel cartoons. We found them on various sites on the Internet. The stimuli were in randomized blocks of three such that each block had one stimulus of each type. Participants viewed the stimuli as we projected them onto a screen using PowerPoint.

Procedure

After completing informed consent forms, the participants learned that previous participants had rated the stimuli and that we wanted to get their ratings. In one group, participants heard, embedded in the general directions, that previous participants had rated the jokes as not very funny. A second group learned that participants had rated the stimuli as very funny. In a control group, they only learned that others had already rated the stimuli. Participants rated the stimuli on a scale of 1 (*Not very funny*) to 7 (*Very funny*).

When you use rating scales, put the verbal anchors within parentheses, in italics.

When presenting statistics, if it uses a Roman letter (e.g., M for the mean, F for the results of an analysis of variance, or p for a probability value), italicize the letter.

Results

As hypothesized, participants conformed to the message they had received about whether the jokes were funny. Participants in the Very funny group produced the lowest mean ratings (M = 2.88, SD = 0.876), followed by Control participants (M = 3.54, SD = 0.993), and Not very funny participants (M = 2.90, SD = 0.917). The mean for the Not very

funny condition was significantly lower than the other two, which did not differ significantly, $F(2, 91) = 11.263, p < .001, \eta^2 = .198$. The results appear in Figure 1.

When presenting statistics, if it uses a Greek letter, do not italicize the letter.

If you create a figure or a table, make sure you refer to it in the text.

The type of stimulus was significant. Participants rated jokes as funniest (M = 3.79, SD = 1.02), followed by single-panel stimuli (M = 3.52, SD = 1.04), and multiple-panel cartoons (M = 3.04, SD = 0.98). All three differed significantly, $F(2, 182) = 40.123, p < .001, \eta^2 = .306$. The interaction between variables was not significant, $F(4, 182) = 0.141, p = .967$.

The results reveal that the effects of priming were the same for a given expectation, regardless of type of stimulus. It made no difference regarding ratings whether the participant was assessing a text-based joke, a single-panel cartoon, or a multipanel cartoon. These results appear in Table 1.

Discussion

Once again, the results indicate that people are susceptible to context when they respond to humor. The same stimulus can be seen as very funny or not very funny, depending on the setup. And the effect seems generalizable: The same effect emerges, regardless of stimulus type.

This susceptibility to a message has implications for the use of humor in everyday life. When the radio personality Don Imus made racially offensive comments on his program, he intended it to be

embedded in a humorous context. That is, he was saying, "This is funny," with the expectation that the audience would find it so.

As it turned out, although a message can sway people in a particular direction, people will reject improbable messages about humor (Wimer & Beins, in press). Furthermore, individual characteristics of a (large) subset of listeners may lead them to find an attempt at humor to be offensive (e.g., Moore et al., 1987; Ryan & Kanjorski, 1998).

In the Discussion section, it is a good idea to talk about the research you mentioned in your introduction.

Interestingly, even though people find some humor to be offensive, they may also find it funny (Beins et al., 2005) and may be inclined to repeat it even when they find it offensive (Ryan & Kanjorski, 1998). So for situations like those of Don Imus, he may encounter contradictory responses: Some people may find his statements funny because of expectations, but they may also find them so offensive. Those who experience extreme reactions and outrage are probably not likely to find the attempt at humor actually to be funny. But the dynamics of who will find something funny are complicated enough that a potentially offensive statement will lead to a variety of reactions. And, as Wimer and Beins (in press) showed, if the humor is outrageous enough, people will cease to accept the message that it is funny.

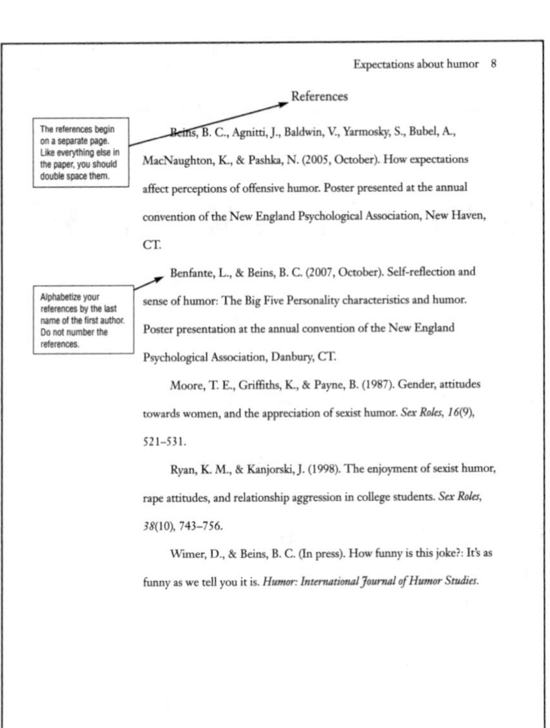

Expectations about humor 8

References

The references begin on a separate page. Like everything else in the paper, you should double space them.

Alphabetize your references by the last name of the first author. Do not number the references.

Beins, B. C., Agnitti, J., Baldwin, V., Yarmosky, S., Bubel, A., MacNaughton, K., & Pashka, N. (2005, October). How expectations affect perceptions of offensive humor. Poster presented at the annual convention of the New England Psychological Association, New Haven, CT.

Benfante, L., & Beins, B. C. (2007, October). Self-reflection and sense of humor: The Big Five Personality characteristics and humor. Poster presentation at the annual convention of the New England Psychological Association, Danbury, CT.

Moore, T. E., Griffiths, K., & Payne, B. (1987). Gender, attitudes towards women, and the appreciation of sexist humor. *Sex Roles, 16*(9), 521–531.

Ryan, K. M., & Kanjorski, J. (1998). The enjoyment of sexist humor, rape attitudes, and relationship aggression in college students. *Sex Roles, 38*(10), 743–756.

Wimer, D., & Beins, B. C. (In press). How funny is this joke?: It's as funny as we tell you it is. *Humor: International Journal of Humor Studies.*

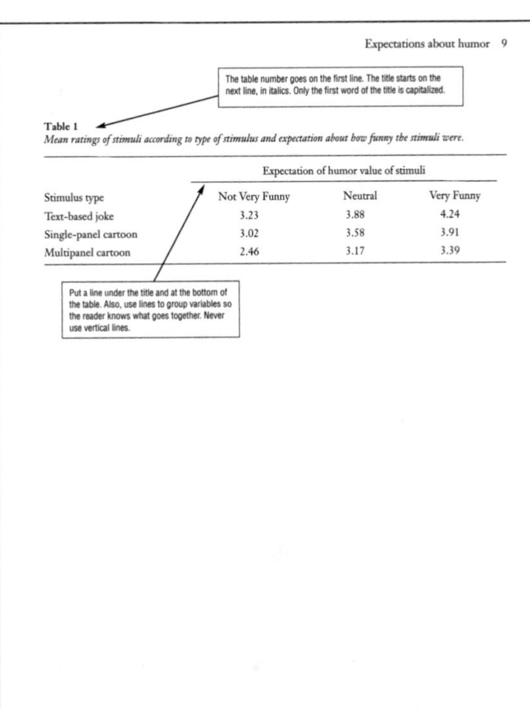

Expectations about humor 9

The table number goes on the first line. The title starts on the next line, in italics. Only the first word of the title is capitalized.

Table 1
Mean ratings of stimuli according to type of stimulus and expectation about how funny the stimuli were.

	Expectation of humor value of stimuli		
Stimulus type	Not Very Funny	Neutral	Very Funny
Text-based joke	3.23	3.88	4.24
Single-panel cartoon	3.02	3.58	3.91
Multipanel cartoon	2.46	3.17	3.39

Put a line under the title and at the bottom of the table. Also, use lines to group variables so the reader knows what goes together. Never use vertical lines.

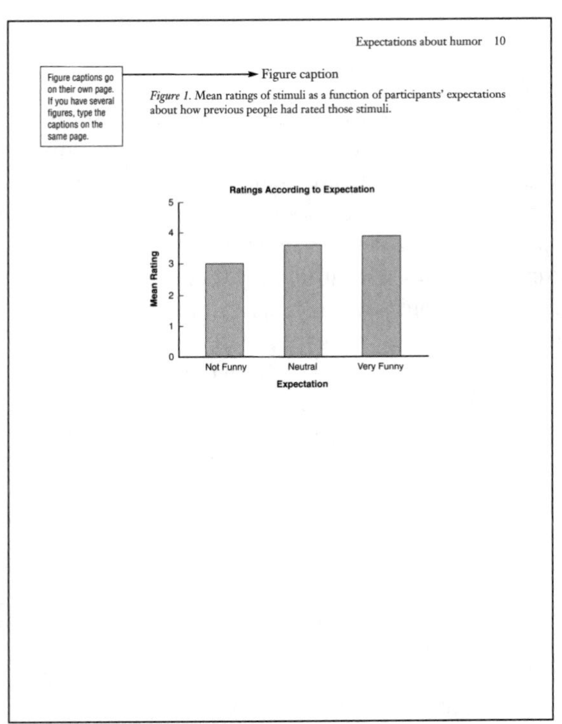

Expectations about humor 10

Figure captions go on their own page. If you have several figures, type the captions on the same page.

Figure caption

Figure 1. Mean ratings of stimuli as a function of participants' expectations about how previous people had rated those stimuli.

APPENDIX B

STATISTICS REVIEW

INTRODUCTION

In this appendix, you can review basics of how psychologists use statistics. The most common approaches include the *t*-test, analysis of variance and its related tests, and correlational tests. If you are interested in exploring different approaches or the theory that underlies statistical usage, you should consult a statistics textbook.

You should develop your statistical plan during the design of your research. There are few things as frustrating as finding out after completing a lengthy study that your design is not amenable to statistical analysis. You have results but you can't analyze them; as a result, you won't have as good a grasp of the question you are investigating as you would like.

You may discover that, after you design your research, you have to make changes because your initial design does not lend itself to easy analysis. Perhaps, your design doesn't lend itself to any analysis that an experienced researcher would have confidence in. What it comes down to is that you have to know what kinds of questions your methodology permits and what statistical tests will help you answer them.

THE USE OF STATISTICS

A century ago, psychologists used descriptive statistics like correlations, means, and standard deviations. An advanced test was the *z*-test, which let investigators understand probability analysis. The statistical tests that we take for granted had yet to be invented.

At the end of the nineteenth century, Karl Pearson invented the correlation coefficient as we know it after Francis Galton proposed the initial concept. In the first decade of the twentieth century, William F. Gossett invented the *t*-test. By the 1930s, Ronald Fisher (1932, 1935) devised the analysis of variance; the *F* value of the analysis of variance stands for Fisher.

Fisher is responsible for the use of the null hypothesis testing that dominates psychology today. He argued that a null hypothesis of equality between means could never be proven, but it could be disproven. So he argued that we should set up a test to see if the null hypothesis is universally true; if the difference across groups was large enough, we could use that fact as a demonstration that the null hypothesis of no difference was false. The only option left is to accept the idea that the groups were not universally equal.

Fisher showed us how we can demonstrate, through manipulation of variables, that we can reliably show that scores in different groups vary. Differences were said to be significant, which doesn't necessarily mean important. It just means that we can expect them to occur reliably. Significant as used by statisticians doesn't mean the same thing as significant in everyday language.

With the advent of these ideas, the way was paved for refinement of statistical approaches. By the middle of the twentieth century, the statistics most commonly used today were becoming increasingly well known.

When computers made complex data analysis feasible, the highly complex statistical designs of today became practical. Theoretical and applied statisticians continue to work on new approaches, most of which have their theoretical basis in the initial work of Fisher and Pearson.

Common Statistics

As you read research reports, you will see that certain statistics appear repeatedly. These include the ANOVA, *t*-tests, correlations, and regressions. This set constitutes most of the tests known as **parametric statistics**. When you use these tests, you generally want to have equal sample sizes, equal variances, and normally distributed scores.

With equal samples sizes and variances and with normally distributed scores, the answers we arrive at will be statistically sound. Our decisions about whether to reject the null hypothesis will be relatively free of Type I and Type II errors. The tests are robust, though, that they can withstand some notable departures from these assumptions. For instance, as long as the number of data points in any cell is not more than about twice as large as the smallest, the use of these tests will lead to decent conclusions. Similarly, as long as the ratio of the largest variance to the smallest is not more than about four or five, we can have confidence in our conclusions. If the distribution of scores is not normal, the tests can still be remarkably useful (Howell, 2007). Problems arise if we begin to violate all of the requirements. Sometimes we will need to select different tests of the null hypothesis that do not have these requirements.

Even so, some psychologists have criticized the use of tests of the null hypothesis altogether (e.g., Falk, 1986; Falk & Greenberg, 1995; Wilcox, 1998), although you can still find cogent arguments in its favor (Frick, 1996).

Recently, the American Psychological Association created a task force to investigate the use of statistics and to provide guidance for researchers. The task force concluded that null hypothesis testing was appropriate for answering some questions, but that the standard parametric statistics should be supplemented with other information.

An important point raised by the task force is that we should rely on the simplest statistical test that will allow us to answer our questions. Complex analyses might needlessly obscure the concepts we are dealing with. That being said, we need to realize that there is sometimes a need for very complex statistical analyses because the psychological questions we ask are often complex.

In this appendix, you can review basics of how psychologists use statistics. The most common approaches include the *t*-test, analysis of variance and its related tests, and correlational tests. If you are interested in exploring different approaches or the theory that underlies statistical usage, you should consult a statistics textbook.

Effect Size

Researchers are increasingly reporting a statistic that gives an assessment of how powerful the independent variable is in its effects on the dependent variable. That is, how much of the difference in scores across groups is due to the effect of the IV and how much is due to the effect of random variation and measurement error. Such an analysis involves a concept called effect size. For the *t*-test, the statistic that gives information on effect size is *d*. It is simple to compute. By convention, psychologists regard values of *d* around .20 as small, around .50 as moderate, and around .80 as large. The effect size represented in this example would be considered quite large.

When we use analysis of variance, we often use different measures of effect size, notably eta-squared (η^2) and omega-squared (ω^2). We will use eta-squared for our worked examples. The values for small to large effect size have not been standardized in complex, factorial designs.

Confidence Intervals

When we conduct statistical analyses, the results are based on samples that we hope will represent the population. Unfortunately, it is virtually always the case that the mean value of a sample will differ from that of the population, even if only by a small amount. As a result, we often include in our data analysis a statement of a confidence intervals, which is the range of values that has a certain likelihood of containing the population mean.

If we speak of a 95% confidence interval, we can identify the range of scores in which we are 95% confident that we would find the population mean. (It is possible to compute a confidence interval for any statistical parameter, but psychologists typically limit this analysis to means or differences between means.) A large confidence interval indicates uncertainty because it says that the true value of the population mean could be anywhere within a large span.

Our estimates are generally closer to the population mean when we use large samples. When sample sizes are small, one or two extreme data points can affect the size of the mean greatly. Consequently, your measurements can easily be affected by outliers.

As a result, with small samples there will be greater uncertainty about whether your sample mean is a good estimate of the population mean; this is reflected in the large confidence interval. Conversely, a few aberrant data points will not affect the mean of large samples, so your sample mean is not likely to be affected by outliers, and your estimate of the population mean is likely to be near the actual value. Thus, confidence intervals are smaller for large samples.

To compute a 95% confidence interval for estimating the population mean, you can use the following formula:

$$\mu = Mean \pm t_{.05/2}\,(s/\sqrt{n})$$

where you insert the mean of your sample (*Mean*), the critical value of the two-tailed t statistic ($t_{0.05}$) that is appropriate for your sample size (df = 24), the standard deviation of the sample (s), and the square root of the sample size (n).

If you recorded data for 25 participants, and the mean and standard deviation were 50 and 10, respectively, you would compute your confidence interval as follows:

$$\begin{aligned}\mu &= 50 \pm 2.064(10/\sqrt{25}) = 50 \pm 2.064(2) = 50 \pm 4.128\\ &= 50 + 4.128 = 54.128\\ &= 50 - 4.128 = 45.872\end{aligned}$$

So the 95% confidence interval would be 45.872 to 54.128.

Steps for calculating the confidence intervals for individual tests appear below.

Power

When we analyze our data for statistical significance, our decision can go in one of two directions. We could reject the null hypothesis and claim that we have discovered a reliable relation among or difference between variables. Or we could decide that we do not have enough evidence to support such a claim.

It can be helpful to determine how likely we are to correctly reject the null hypothesis, when it is false. This probability is known as power. The power of our statistical analysis, that is, the probability of rejecting the null hypothesis when we should, depends on several factors.

One factor is the alpha level we use. Typically, we are satisfied with the knowledge that we will wrongly reject the null hypothesis only 5% of the time, which is the alpha value we choose. If we choose a larger value of alpha, say 10%, we are more likely to say that an effect is significant because we are setting a looser criterion. We will appropriately reject the null hypothesis more often, thereby avoiding a Type I error. But we will also be more likely to reject the null hypothesis when we should not, committing a Type II error. With a larger alpha, we are simply more willing to reject the null hypothesis, regardless of whether it is true.

Conversely, we can set a tighter criterion, perhaps with alpha at 1%. We will be less likely to reject the null hypothesis, whether or not we should. When we use a loose criterion for rejecting the null hypothesis, our power increases because we are simply more likely to conclude that there is an effect. The price we pay is that we are more likely to reject the null when we should not.

A second factor affecting power is effect size. If we are comparing the means of two groups that come from very different populations, we are likely to see a large effect size. On the other hand, if the means come from two similar populations, the difference between the means of our samples will likely be small, reflecting the small effect size.

A third factor related to power is sample size. The larger the sample size, the more likely we are to spot an effect, even if it is a small one. Thus, small differences of a few points in SAT scores from one year to the next are likely to be significant because of the very large national samples. If you are conducting research and have reason to believe that your samples are really different but that the differences are not large, you will be less likely to spot the difference with small samples. Choosing large samples helps you spot small differences that are reliable.

It is possible to conduct a power analysis in advance of your research to see how large a sample you need to have high confidence that you will be able to spot differences that may be large or small. Some statistics packages, like SPSS, include a statement of retrospective power based on data already corrected; this statistic is useful for planning future studies but, as Howell (2007) has noted, not for explaining the outcome of a study you may have just conducted. He provides an accessible discussion of the computations of power.

INDEPENDENT GROUPS *T*-TEST

The independent groups *t*-test compares two samples to see if they differ from one another reliably. That is, is the difference between the two groups large enough to convince us that if we repeated our data collection, we would end up with similar results the second time.

You can also use the ANOVA to compare two groups. Your decision to reject or not to reject the null hypothesis will be the same regardless of whether you use a *t*-test or the ANOVA because the *t*-test is the algebraic equivalent to an ANOVA comparing two independent groups. Historically, we have used the *t*-test for two groups; this tradition continues for studies with a single IV and only two groups to compare.

The formula for the **independent groups *t*-test** appears below. When the two groups show unequal variances, you should consult a statistics text for guidance.

$$t = \frac{M_A - M_B}{\sqrt{s_p^2\left(\frac{1}{N_A} + \frac{1}{N_B}\right)}}$$

where M = means of groups A and B
N = number of observations in groups A and B
s^2 = the pooled variance given in the equation below

$$s_p^2 = \frac{(N_A - 1)s_A^2 + (N_B - 1)s_B^2}{N_A + N_B - 2}$$

where s^2 = variance of the group based on the unbiased estimate of the population variance.

Worked example for independent groups *t*-test.

Participants are tested either in Condition A or Condition B	**A**	**B**	
Data for Groups A and B	6	4	t = [**(1)** – **(2)**]/**(7)**
5	8	= (6.3 – 3.7) / 1.75	
8	3	= 2.6 / 1.75	
3	3	= 1.48	
6	5		
7	3		
7	4		
6	2		
9	3		
	2		
Mean	**(1)** 6.3	**(2)** 3.7	
Standard Deviation	1.73	1.77	
St. Deviation Squared (Variance)	**(3)** 2.99	**(4)** 3.13	
N	9	10	
Pooled Variance			[**(5)** * **(3)** + **(6)** * **(4)**]/[**(5)** + **(6)**]
			[(8 * 3.00) + (9 * 3.12)] / 17
			= (23.92 + 28.17) / 17
			= 3.06
Square root of pooled variance			= **(7)** 1.75
Degrees of Freedom	**(5)** 8	**(6)** 9	**(5)** + **(6)** = 17
Critical *t*-value (α = .05, two tails)			2.11
Decision		**Do not reject the null hypothesis. The obtained value of *t* is less than the critical value. Do not conclude that the two groups are significantly different.**	

In the example above, there are two groups, one having 9 data points, the other having 10. After finding the means and standard deviations for each group separately, it is easy to enter the values into the formula and compute your value of *t*. You then compare your obtained value with the critical value from the table of *t* values. If your obtained value is greater than the critical value in the table, reject the null hypothesis. If your obtained value is less than the critical value in the table, do not reject the null hypothesis.

Supplemental Analysis: Effect size:

$$d = \frac{Mean_A - Mean_B}{s},$$

$$s = \sqrt{s_A^2 + s_B^2} = \sqrt{3.00 + 3.12} = \sqrt{6.12} = 2.47$$

$$d = \frac{6.3 - 3.7}{2.47} = \frac{2.6}{2.47} = 1.05$$

Confidence Interval. To compute the confidence interval to estimate how far apart two population means are, you can use the formula below:

$$\begin{aligned} \boldsymbol{CI_{.95}} &= \boldsymbol{Mean_1 - Mean_2 \pm t_{.05/2}(S_p^2)} \\ &= 2.6 \pm 2.11(1.3229) \\ &= 2.6 \pm 2.79 \\ &= -0.19 \\ &= 5.39 \end{aligned}$$

Thus the confidence interval is -0.19 to 5.39. When the *t* value is not significant, the confidence interval contains zero, which is true for this example.

MATCHED SAMPLES/REPEATED MEASURES T-TEST

When you have two groups of scores that are paired, you use a different formula for the *t*-test. You use this version of *t* when a score in one group is paired for a specific reason with a score in the second group. For instance, if you administer a memory test to a person working alone, then a similar test when that person is in a group, you can compare the individual's score in the two conditions. It makes sense to pair the two scores because they came from the same person.

When you test the same person on two different occasions, that participant is likely to score similarly each time. When you have paired scores that are likely to be correlated, it makes sense to use this version of *t* because there is a better chance of detecting small differences between conditions.

$$t = \frac{\overline{D}}{\frac{S_{\overline{D}}}{\sqrt{N}}}$$

D = Mean of the difference scores
S = Standard deviation of the difference scores
N = Number of **pairs** of scores (not the total number of scores)

Worked example of a Matched Samples/Repeated Measures *t*-test

Participants are tested in both conditions	A	B	Difference Score	
Participant 1	11	9	2	$t = (1) / [(2) / (3)]$
Participant 2	9	4	5	$t = 3.2/[2.39/2.24]$
Participant 3	12	12	0	$= 2.99$
Participant 4	5	2	3	
Participant 5	17	11	6	
Mean			(1) 3.2	
Standard deviation	4.38		(2) 2.39	
N			5	
Square root of N			(3) 2.24	
Standard error				= 2.39/2.24 = 1.07
Degrees of Freedom				= # Pairs – 1 = 4
Critical *t*-value (α =.05, two tails)				2.776
Decision				**Reject the null hypothesis. The obtained value of *t* is greater than the critical value. Conclude that the two groups are significantly different.**

How to Designate the *t*-value: $t(4) = 2.776, p<.05$

Supplemental Analyses: **Effect size.** Computing the effect size here is fairly simple.

$$d = \frac{\bar{D}}{S_i} = 3.2 \ / \ 4.38 = 0.73$$

where d reflects the effect size, $\bar{D}$ is the mean difference between the matched pairs, and S_1 reflects the standard deviation of the control group, although you can use the standard deviation of either group. The control group is normally the standard of comparison, so it is a reasonable choice.

ANALYSIS OF VARIANCE

The Analysis of Variance (ANOVA) permits us to test for differences among multiple groups at the same time. Unlike the *t*-test, which is limited to comparisons of two groups at a time, the ANOVA can assess as many groups as you care to compare. (If you have only two groups, the ANOVA is perfectly applicable, although traditionally researchers have used the *t*-test.)

The advantage of the ANOVA is that you can be confident that the number of Type I errors that occur is at the level that you set. These errors arise when you conclude that there is a difference between groups that really occurred by chance, not because of the effect of your independent variable. In most cases, researchers want to keep Type I errors at no more than five percent. If you used multiple *t*-tests, as the number of comparisons you make increased, so would the likelihood that you would conclude that there was a reliable difference that would actually be due to chance.

An additional strength of the ANOVA is that we can make comparisons involving more than one independent variable. When an analysis involves a single IV, we call the test a One-Way ANOVA; if there are two IVs, we have a Two-Way ANOVA; and so on. For tests involving two or more IVs, we often refer to the design as factorial ANOVAs. Factorial ANOVAs let us see if there are main effects for each IV separately and if there are interaction effects among variables.

The underlying concept is the same for them all. We identify the magnitude of the differences among groups that are due to treatment effects, that is, to the IV; then we assess the size of the differences due to error. Finally, we see how large the treatment effect is compared to the error effect. If the treatment effect is big enough relative to the error effect, we conclude that the IV had a reliable effect on the behavior we are assessing.

As with *t*-tests, we can perform ANOVAs for data sets involving either independent groups or repeated measures groups. In this section, you will see how to compute One-Way ANOVAs involving both independent groups and repeated measures. You will also see how to compute a Two-Way ANOVA involving independent groups. For analysis of Two-Way or higher ANOVAs with repeated measures, you should consult a higher level statistics text. In general, you would carry out such tests via computer

Worked example of one-way independent groups ANOVA:

Group 1					
X	X^2	Sum of Scores ΣX	Sum of Squared Scores ΣX^2	Sum of Scores Squared $(\Sigma X)^2$	N_1
		35	315	$35^2 = 1225$	4
7	49				
9	81				
8	81				
11	36				
Group 2					
X	X^2	Sum of Scores ΣX	Sum of Scores Squared $(\Sigma X)^2$	Sum of Squared Scores ΣX^2	N_2
		8+10+11+11	64+100+100+121	$40^2 = 1600$	4
		40	406		
8	64				
10	100				
11	100				
11	121				

Group 3		Sum of Scores Σ X	Sum of Squared Scores Σ X^2	Sum of Scores Squared $(\Sigma X)^2$	N_3
X	X^2	11+10+11+12	121+100+121+144	$44^2 = 1936$	4
11	121	44	486		
10	100				
11	121				
12	144				
Totals		Sum of Scores ΣX_{TOTAL}	Sum of Squared Scores ΣX^2_{TOTAL}	Sum of Scores Squared $(\Sigma X)^2_{TOTAL}$	N_{TOTAL}
		115	1139	4497	12

because the amount of calculation is extensive, particularly with repeated measures designs.

One-Way Independent Groups Analysis of Variance

When you have multiple groups in which the data are unrelated across groups, you have an independent groups design. This means that there is no particular reason to pair a score in one group with any specific score in another group. When you have different people in each group rather than repeating measurements of the same people participating in different groups, you are using an independent groups design.

Computing Sums of Squares

$$SS_{TOTAL} = 315 + 406 + 486 - \frac{(31 + 40 + 44)^2}{12}$$ Total Sum of Squares (SS_{TOTAL})

$$= 1207 - (119_2 / 12)$$
$$= 1207 - (14161/ 12)$$
$$= 1207 - 1180.08$$
$$= 26.92$$

$$\frac{X_1 + \Sigma X_1 + \Sigma X_1}{N}$$

Treatment Sum of Squares ($SS_{TREATMENT}$) [also called Between Groups Sum of Squares]

$$SS_{TREATMENT} = \frac{\left(\sum X_1\right)^2}{N_1} + \frac{\left(\sum X_2\right)^2}{N_2} + \frac{\left(\sum X_3\right)^2}{N_3} - \frac{\left(\sum X_1 + \sum X_2 + \sum X_3\right)^2}{N_{TOTAL}}$$

Error Sum of Squares (SS_{ERROR}) [also called Within Groups Sum of Squares]

$$SS_{ERROR} = SS_{TOTAL} - SS_{TREATMENT}$$
$$SS_{ERROR} = 26.92 - 10.17$$
$$= 16.75$$

Computing Degrees of Freedom

$$df_{TOTAL} = (N_{TOTAL} - 1) = (12 - 1) = 11$$
$$df_{TREATMENT} = (\#\ Groups - 1) = (3 - 1) = 2$$
$$df_{ERROR} = df_{TOTAL} - df_{TREATMENT} = 11 - 2 = 9$$

Computing Mean Squares:

$$MS_{TREATMENT} = \frac{SS_{TREATMENT}}{df_{TREATMENT}}$$

$$= 10.17/2$$

$$= 5.08$$

$$MS_{ERROR} = \frac{SS_{ERROR}}{df_{ERROR}}$$

$$= \frac{16.75}{9}$$

$$= 1.86$$

ANOVA Summary Table

Source of Variation	Sum of Squares	Degrees of Freedom	Mean Square	F	Prob.	Effect Size
TREATMENT (Between Groups)	10.17	2	5.08	2.73	>.05	.38
ERROR (Within Groups)	20.75	9	1.86			
TOTAL	26.92	11				

$$\eta^2 = \frac{SS_{TREATMENT}}{SS_{TOTAL}}$$

$$= \frac{10.17}{26.92} = .38$$

How to designate the *F* value: $F(2,9) = 1.34, p > .05$

Decision: Look up the critical value in the *F*-Table for 2 and 9 degrees of freedom. For an alpha value (Type I error rate) of 5 percent, the critical value is 4.26.

In order to conclude that there are differences across groups, we need a computed value of *F* equal to or greater than 4.26. Our computed value is smaller than that, 2.73. Thus, we can conclude that the groups differ from one another for unknown reasons, not because of the effects of the independent variable. If the computed *F*-value is less than one, the *F* will never be significant.

Supplemental Analysis: Effect size: In recent years, investigators have started reporting effect sizes. An effect size indicates the strength of the relationship you are assessing. A statistically significant effect can be small; likewise, a nonsignificant effect can be large. Effect sizes tell you the relative magnitude of strength of your independent variable on the dependent variable. According to the conventions adopted by psychologists, an effect size of about .20 is considered small; an effect size of about .50 is moderate; an effect size around .80 is large.

In general, a measure of effect size reflects how much of the variability in scores is due to your manipulation. Powerful IVs lead to large effect sizes; manipulations that are weak lead to small effect sizes. It is important to remember that a small effect size can be very real and can be very important.

One statistic that researchers use to assess effect sizes is eta-squared (0^2). It is useful when you are interested in describing the effect sizes for your own research project. If you want to generalize beyond your own data, other statistics are preferred (Howell, 1992).

An additional, supplemental approach involves determining which groups differ from one another when you are comparing multiple conditions. In this example, we have three groups. If there is a significant difference between some of the groups, based on the ANOVA alone, we don't know which groups differ from one another. Groups 1 and 2 might differ from one another, but Groups 2 and 3 might not. We also don't know if Groups 1 and 3 differ.

Several different statistical tests exist that let us determine which groups differ from one another. Because the details differ in their application, if you are interested in using such tests after computing a *F*-value, you should consult a statistics book or make use of appropriate options in a computerized statistical package.

Confidence Intervals. After an analysis of variance, we can compute pairwise confidence intervals. That is, we can establish confidence intervals for any two groups that will estimate how far the population means for the two groups are from one another. Psychologists rarely perform the computations to assess differences across multiple pairs of means.

Factorial Analysis of Variance

When we manipulate more than one independent variable in an experiment, we can assess the effects of the IVs through a factorial analysis of variance. This statistical approach allows us to see whether the main effects are significant; in addition, we can investigate whether the two variables interact in ways that are not predictable from either independent variable alone.

The computations for a factorial ANOVA aren't difficult, but they can be tedious with a large data set. Researchers invariably use computerized statistical packages for analyzing the results of factorial designs. The example here involves very small data sets for convenience. In actual research, it is unlikely that an investigator would carry out such a small scale study.

This statistical analysis involves computation of the same sums of squares as the other ANOVAs, with the addition of a new term, the interaction effect. The nature of the computations is similar, though. This example involves an independent groups design; the calculations for a repeated measures design are more involved. If you plan a study with repeated measures, you should refer to a statistics book because additional statistical issues complicate the analysis.

Worked example of a factorial ANOVA

This example involves a 2×3 design, which means that there are two IVs. Variable A has two levels, while Variable B has three. There is no limit to the number of levels that an IV can take, nor is there a limit to the number if IVs allowed.

	A_1B_1	$A_1B_1^2$	A_2B_1	$A_2B_1^2$	A_3B_1	$A_3B_1^2$	
B1	4	*16*	6	*36*	9	*81*	
	5	*25*	7	*49*	8	*64*	
	5	*25*	6	*36*	7	*49*	
	7	*49*	8	*64*	8	*64*	
	$\Sigma A_1B_1 = 21$ $(\Sigma A_1B_1)^2 = 441$ $\Sigma A_1B_1^2 = 115$ $N_{A1-B1} = 4$		$\Sigma A_2B_1 = 27$ $(\Sigma A_1B_1)^2 = 729$ $\Sigma A_2B_1^2 = 185$ $N_{A2-B1} = 4$		$\Sigma A_3B_1 = 32$ $(\Sigma A_1B_1)^2 = 1024$ $\Sigma A_3B_1^2 = 258$ $N_{A3-B1} = 4$		$\Sigma B_1 = 80$ $(\Sigma B_1)^2 = 6400$ $\Sigma B_1^2 = 2194$ $N_{B1} = 12$
	A_1B_2	$A_1B_2^2$	A_2B_2	$A_2B_2^2$	A_3B_2	$A_3B_2^2$	
B2	5	*25*	4	*16*	3	*9*	
	4	*16*	7	*49*	2	*4*	
	3	*9*	6	*36*	4	*16*	
	7	*49*	8	*64*	2	*4*	
	$\Sigma A_1B_2 = 19$ $(\Sigma A_1B_1)^2 = 361$ $\Sigma A_1B_2^2 = 99$ $N_{A1-B2} = 4$		$\Sigma A_2B_2 = 25$ $(\Sigma A_1B_1)^2 = 289$ $\Sigma A_2B_2^2 = 165$ $N_{A2-B2} = 4$		$\Sigma A_3B_2 = 11$ $(\Sigma A_1B_1)^2 = 121$ $\Sigma A_3B_2^2 = 33$ $N_{A3-B2} = 4$		$\Sigma B_2 = 55$ $(\Sigma B_2)^2 = 3025$ $\Sigma B_2^2 = 771$ $N_{B2} = 12$
	$\Sigma A_1 = 40$ $(\Sigma A_1B_1)^2 = 1600$ $\Sigma A_1^2 = 802$ $N_{A1} = 8$		$\Sigma A_2 = 52$ $(\Sigma A_1B_1)^2 = 1936$ $\Sigma A_2^2 = 1018$ $N_{A2} = 8$		$\Sigma A_3 = 43$ $(\Sigma A_1B_1)^2 = 1849$ $\Sigma A_3^2 = 291$ $N_{A3} = 8$		
							$\Sigma X_{TOTAL} = 135$ $(\Sigma X_{TOTAL})^2 = 18225$ $\Sigma X_{TOTAL}^2 = 1475$ $N_{TOTAL} = 24$

The analysis will involve seeing whether the main effects for the two variables are significant and whether the interaction is significant.

Calculate Sums of Squares:

Total Sum of Squares:

$$SS_{TOTAL} = \sum X_{TOTAL}^2 - \frac{\left(\sum X_{TOTAL}\right)^2}{N_{TOTAL}}$$

$$= 855 - \frac{(135)^2}{24} = 855 - \frac{18225}{24} = 95.63$$

$$= 855 - 759.38$$

95.63

Variable A Sum of Squares (SS_A):

$$SS_A = \frac{\left(\sum A_1\right)^2}{N_{A_1}} + \frac{\left(\sum A_2\right)^2}{N_{A_2}} + \frac{\left(\sum A_3\right)^2}{N_{A_3}} - \frac{\left(\sum X_{TOTAL}\right)^2}{N_{TOTAL}}$$

$$= \frac{(40)^2}{8} + \frac{(52)^2}{8} + \frac{(43)^2}{8} - \frac{(135)^2}{24}$$

$$= \frac{1600}{8} + \frac{2704}{8} + \frac{1849}{8} - 759.38$$

$$= 200 + 338 + 231.13 - 759.38$$

$$= 9.75$$

Variable B Sum of Squares (SS_B):

$$SS_B = \frac{\left(\sum B_1\right)^2}{N_{B_1}} + \frac{\left(\sum B_2\right)^2}{N_{B_2}} - \frac{\left(\sum X_{TOTAL}\right)^2}{N_{TOTAL}}$$

$$= \frac{(80)^2}{12} + \frac{(55)^2}{12} - \frac{(135)^2}{24}$$

$$= \frac{6400}{12} + \frac{3025}{12} - 759.38$$

$$= 533.33 + 252.08 = 759.38$$

$$= 26.03$$

Interaction Sum of Squares ($SS_{A\times B}$):

$$SS_{A\times B} = \frac{\left(\sum X_{A_1B_1}\right)^2}{N_{A_1B_1}} + \frac{\left(\sum X_{A_2B_1}\right)^2}{N_{A_2B_1}} + \frac{\left(\sum X_{A_3B_1}\right)^2}{N_{A_3B_1}} + \frac{\left(\sum X_{A_1B_2}\right)^2}{N_{A_1B_2}} + \frac{\left(\sum X_{A_2B_2}\right)^2}{N_{A_2B_2}} + \frac{\left(\sum X_{A_3B_2}\right)^2}{N_{A_3B_2}}$$

$$- \frac{\left(\sum X_{TOTAL}\right)^2}{N_{TOTAL}} - SS_A - SS_B$$

$$= \frac{(21)^2}{4} + \frac{(27)^2}{4} + \frac{(32)^2}{4} + \frac{(19)^2}{4} + \frac{(25)^2}{4} + \frac{(11)^2}{4} - 759.38 - 9.75 - 26.03$$

$$= 30.09$$

Error Sum of Squares (SS_{ERROR})

$SS_{ERROR} = SS_{ERROR} - SS_A - SS_B - SS_{A \times B}$
$= 95.63 - 9.75 - 26.03 - 30.09$
$= 29.76$

Calculating Degrees of Freedom:

$df_{TOTAL} = N_{TOTAL} - 1 = 24 - 1 = 23$
$df_A = \# \ Groups_A - 1 = 3 - 1 = 2$
$df_B = \# \ Groups_B - 1 = 2 - 1 = 1$
$df_{A \times B} = (df_A)(df_B) = (2)(1) = 2$
$df_{ERROR} = df_{TOTAL} - dfA - dfB - df_{A \times B} = 23 - 2 - 1 - 2 = 18$

Calculating Mean Squares

$MS_A = SS_A / df_A = 9.75/2 = 4.88$
$MS_B = SS_B / df_B = 26.03/1 = 26.03$
$MS_{A \times B} = SS_{A \times B} / df_{A \times B} = 30.09/2 = 15.04$
$MS_{ERROR} = SS_{ERROR} / df_{ERROR} = 29.76/18 = 1.65$

Calculating *F*-values:

$$F_A = \frac{MS_A}{MS_{ERROR}} = \frac{4.88}{1.65} = 2.96$$

$$F_B = \frac{MS_B}{MS_{ERROR}} = \frac{26.03}{1.65} = 15.78$$

$$F_{A \times B} = \frac{MS_{A \times B}}{MS_{ERROR}} = \frac{15.04}{1.65} = 9.12$$

ANOVA Summary Table

Source of Variation	Sum of Squares	Degrees of Freedom	Mean Square	F	Effect Size
Variable A	9.75	2	4.88	2.96	.25
Variable B	26.03	1	26.03	15.78	.47
Interaction of A × B	30.09	2	15.04	9.12	.50
Error	29.76	18	1.65		
Total	95.63	23			

How to Designate the *F* values:

***Variable A:* $F(2,18)=2.96$, $p>.05$**
***Variable B:* $F(1,18)=15.78$, $p<.01$**
***Interaction Effect:* $F(2,18)=9.12$, $p<.01$**

Decision: *Main effect of Variable A*: To find the critical *F* value for a 5 percent error rate, look on the appropriate table of *F* values for 2 and 18 degrees of freedom. This critical value in the table is 3.55. Our computed value, 2.96, is smaller than the critical value. The difference among groups is not significant, so we conclude that any differences are attributable to measurement error, not the effects of Variable A.

Main effect of Variable B: To find the critical *F* value for a 5 percent error rate, look in the *F* table for 1 and 18 degrees of freedom. The critical value in the table is 4.41. Our computed value, 15.78, is larger than the critical value. So we conclude that the difference among groups is attributable to the effect of Variable B.

Interaction between Variable A and Variable B: To find the critical *F* value for a 5 percent error rate, look in the *F* table for 2 and 18 degrees of freedom. The critical value in the table is 3.55. Our computed value, 9.12, is larger than the critical value. So we conclude that the pattern of scores on B changes depending on which group on Variable A you are considering. Figure 1 shows how the values of B change depending on which level of A is under consideration.

The significant main effect of Variable B may be due largely to the fact that one group, A_3B_2, has caused the overall average of Variable B to drop greatly. You should be

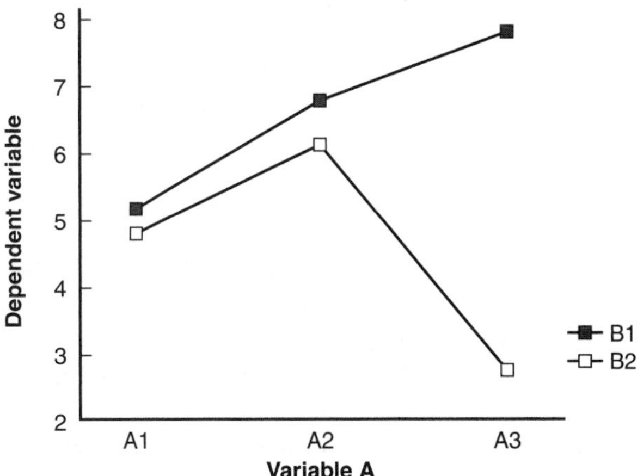

FIGURE 1 Figure Statistics Appendix 1. Illustration of interaction of Variables A and B. The pattern of results for Variable B differs depending on which level of Variable A is under consideration.

cautious about asserting that B_1 and B_2 really are all that different. Without the effect of the single, low group, B_1 and B_2 are not all that different.

Supplementary Analysis: You can assess effect size here with eta-squared (η^2). You find the effect size for each main effect and for the interaction.

There is an important computational difference in computing effect size for a factorial design compared to a one-way design. For a one-way ANOVA, you divided $SS_{TREATMENT}$ by SS_{TOTAL}. To compute eta-squared for a factorial design, you divide the $SS_{TREATMENT}$ term by the ($SS_{TREATMENT}$ + SS_{ERROR}).

$$\eta^2 = \frac{SS_{TREATMENT}}{SS_{TREATMENT} + SS_{ERROR}}$$

$$\eta^2_A = \frac{9.75}{(9.75 + 29.75)} = .25$$

$$\eta^2_B = \frac{26.03}{(26.03 + 29.75)} = .47$$

$$\eta^2_{A \times B} = \frac{30.08}{(30.08 + 29.75)} = .50$$

As these values are interpreted by researchers, the effect size for Variable A is small, whereas the effect sizes for Variable B and the interaction are moderate.

An additional supplemental analysis investigates where differences lie among multiple groups. When you employ an independent variable that has more than two levels, it is not immediately clear which groups differ significantly when you obtain a significant *F*-value. In this example, there is no main effect of Variable A. If there were, you would conduct a post hoc analysis to see which of the groups, when paired, differed significantly. You can consult a statistics book for details on the different tests you could use.

CHI SQUARE

There are two commonly used chi-square tests. (*Chi* sounds like *sky* with the *s* missing.) One provides information about whether the number of observations that you obtain in different categories matches your predictions. This is the **goodness of fit test**. Is there a good fit between what you expect and what you get? We use this test when we have one-dimensional tables.

A second chi-square provides information for two-dimensional tables about whether there is independence between two variables. For instance, is there independence between the number of women versus men majoring in psychology versus chemistry? Is major predictable from sex, which asks whether we can make a better than chance prediction about whether a student is majoring in psychology versus chemistry based on whether the person is female versus male? Is sex predictable from the major? This variety of chi-square test is a **contingency test.**

These chi square tests are useful only for nominal data. That is, you can only use these tests when you are counting the number of instances within a category. You can't use the tests for ordinal, interval, or ratio scale measurements.

Goodness of Fit Test

The chi-square goodness of fit test requires that you have categories into which individual observations fall. That is, you make a single observation and record that observation as belonging with category A, B, C, ... You repeat this for each observation. In order for chi-square to provide valid information, each observation must be independent of the others. You can't measure people repeatedly because one person's behavior at two different times may be highly related.

The idea of the chi-square test is to find out whether expected counts in each category match what you actually observe. In most psychological research, our null hypothesis specifies that there be equal numbers of observations in each category. You would depart from this strategy if you have specific expectations.

$$\chi^2 = \frac{\sum(O - E)^2}{E}$$

where O = Number of Observations and E = Expected Number of Observations.

Suppose you wanted to know if students had preferences for class times during the day. You could categorize the classes as early morning, late morning, early afternoon, and late afternoon. If you asked a randomly selected group of students to state a preference, you could then tally them and compute a value of chi-square to test whether all times are seen as equally desirable. For the fictitious data set below, you could answer this question.

	8 or 9 a.m.	**11 a.m. or noon**	**1 or 2 p.m.**	**3 or 4 p.m.**	**Total**
Observed Values	8	28	22	15	73
Expected Values	*18.25*	*18.25*	*18.25*	*18.25*	

Computing Expected Values: In this case, our assumption is that students don't have preferences for particular times of the day. Although in reality it is probably safe to assume that students wouldn't want early morning classes, we don't have good information about what percentage of students would prefer each category. So our null hypothesis at this point is that all times are equally desirable.

There are 73 observations in our sample. If we assume equal representation in each of the 4 time slots, we would compute the expected values as the total number of observations divided by the number of categories: 73/4 = 18.25. Using the formula for chi-square given above, we can compute our statistic.

$$\chi^2 = \sum \frac{(Observed - Expected)^2}{Expected}$$

$$= \frac{(8 - 18.25)^2}{18.25} + \frac{(28 - 18.25)^2}{18.25} + \frac{(22 - 18.25)^2}{18.25} + \frac{(15 - 18.25)^2}{18.25}$$

$$= \frac{105.06}{18.25} + \frac{95.06}{18.25} + \frac{14.06}{18.25} + \frac{10.56}{18.25}$$

$$= 5.76 + 5.21 + 0.77 + 0.58$$

$$= 12.32$$

Calculating Degrees of Freedom: For a Chi-Square Goodness of Fit test, the degrees of freedom is the number of categories minus one. There are four categories in this example, so the degrees of freedom is (4-1) = 3.

The Decision: To find the critical value of chi-square in the table for a Type I error rate of 5 percent, we use 3 degrees of freedom and the column labeled .05. The critical value is 7.815. Our computed value is larger than the critical value in the table, so we reject the null hypothesis and conclude that students do not prefer all times of the day for their classes. According to these fictitious data, we would conclude that students prefer middle of the day to early or late.

Test of Independence

The chi square test of independence, like the goodness of fit test, involves whether we can make accurate predictions about the number of observed events when we have two (or more) variables from which we make the predictions.

Jenni and Jenni (1976) observed college students carrying their books on campus and noted how the students held them. One category of carrying them was across the front of the body with one or both arms wrapped around the books; a second category was for the books to be held more toward the side, pinched from above or supported from below by the hand and/or arm. The researchers investigated whether book carrying was associated with sex.

They observed several hundred college students. If you conducted this study in 1976 with a smaller number of students, you might have obtained the fictitious data below, which you could analyze with a chi-square test of independence. There are two variables: sex of the student and category of carrying. The question is whether you can predict the sex of the carriers by knowing how they carry the books or, alternatively, whether you can predict how people will carry their books, given that you know their sex.

Observed Values	**Female Observed**	*Expected*	**Male Observed**	*Expected*	**(Total)**
Front	**21**	*12*	**3**	*14*	(24)
Side	**5**	*14*	**23**	*12*	(28)
(Total)	(26)		(26)		(52)

Computing Expected Values: For this 2×2 design, you need to compute expected values for each of the four conditions. As a rule of thumb, you should avoid computing chi-square values when a large percentage of your expected values are smaller then 5. It is probably not problematic as long as the number of such expectations is under 20 percent of the total number of cells (Howell, 1992). As you can see in this example, one of the cells has fewer than 5 observations, but the expected value is greater than 5. It is the expected value that is important to consider, not the observed value.

The expected value is computed by multiplying the row total for each cell times the column total for that cell, then dividing by the total number of observations. You do this for each cell. In the present example, you find the expected value for each of the four cells.

Once you have the set of observed and expected values, you can compute the value of chi-square, based on the formula above.

$$Expected = \frac{(Total_{Row}) \times (Total_{Column})}{N_{Total}}$$

$$Expected_{Female-Front} = \frac{24 \times 26}{52} = \frac{624}{52} = 12$$

$$Expected_{Female-Side} = \frac{28 \times 26}{52} = \frac{728}{52} = 14$$

$$Expected_{Male-Front} = \frac{24 \times 26}{52} = \frac{624}{52} = 12$$

$$\chi^2 = \sum \frac{(Observed - Expected)^2}{Expected}$$

$$= \frac{(21-12)^2}{12} + \frac{(5-14)^2}{14} + \frac{(3-14)^2}{14} + \frac{(23-12)^2}{12}$$

$$= 6.75 + 5.79 + 8.64 + 10.08$$

$$= 31.26$$

Calculating Degrees of Freedom: Degrees of freedom for this chi-square test equals the number of rows minus one times the number of columns minus one, or (R – 1)(C – 1). There are two rows and there are two columns in this design, so (R – 1)(C – 1) = (2– 1)(2 – 1) = (1)(1) = 1.

The Decision: When there is one degree of freedom and when you want your Type I error rate to be 5 percent, you look for the critical value in the Chi-Square table for the probability of .05 and 1 degree of freedom. The critical value is 3.841.

The value we computed is 31.26, which exceeds the critical value needed for significance. Thus we can conclude that there is a great deal of predictability regarding sex of students and the manner in which they carry their books.

This research took place over a quarter of a century ago. Virtually nobody had backpacks then. It would be interesting to see if the effect replicated today, with different means of conveying books from place to place and different types of students. Have women and men changed?

CORRELATIONAL ANALYSES

There are quite a few correlational analyses that researchers use to assess the relations among variables. The most common correlational analysis is the Pearson product-moment correlation. It provides information as to whether a linear relation exists between two variables. Curvilinear relations require more advanced statistics.

A second correlational approach is regression analysis, which allows us to identify the pattern of changes in scores and to make predictions of a criterion variable based on a single predictor variable. The linear regression analysis we will see here is based on the Pearson correlation for linear relationships.

Pearson Product-Moment Correlation

The Pearson Product-Moment Correlation is the most widely used correlation coefficient. In fact, some of the other correlations and tests of associations are merely algebraic manipulations of the Pearson *r*.

The formula for the Pearson Product-Moment Correlation appears below. There are several different ways to represent the formula. They will produce the same result, but this formula is fairly easy to use.

$$r = \frac{N\left(\sum AB\right) - \left(\sum B\right)\left(\sum B\right)}{\sqrt{\left[N\left(\sum A^2\right) - \left(\sum A\right)^2\right]\left[N\left(\sum B^2\right) - \left(\sum B\right)^2\right]}}$$

N = Number of pairs
Σ AB = Summed cross-product for each pair
Σ A = Sum of scores in Group A
Σ B = Sum of scores in Group B

In the worked example below, the obtained correlation coefficient is negative, which reflects the fact that scores in A that are high tend to be paired with scores in B that are low and vice versa. With a two-tailed, nondirectional test, the absolute value of *r* is compared with the critical value from the table.

	A	A^2	B	B^2	Cross-Product of A * B
	1	1	4	16	4
	3	9	8	64	24
	6	36	6	36	36
	7	49	2	4	14
	7	49	3	9	21
	8	64	2	4	16
	9	81	1	1	9
Number of Observations	**(1)**	7	**(1)**	7	
Sum of Cross-Products					**(2)** 124
Sum of Scores in Group	**(3)**	41	**(4)**	26	
Square of Sum of Scores	**(5)**	1681	**(6)**	676	
Sum of Scores Squared in Group	**(7)**	289	**(8)**	134	

Value of r

$$r = \frac{[(1)(2) - (3)(4)]}{\text{SQRT}\{[(1)(7) - (5)][(1)(8) - (6)]\}}$$

$$= \frac{(7)(124) - (41)(26)}{\text{SQRT}\{[7(289) - 1681][7(134) - 676]\}}$$

$$r = \frac{868 - 1066}{\text{SQRT}[(342)(262)]} = \frac{-198}{299.34}$$

$= -.66$

Note: SQRT = Square Root

Degrees of freedom: # Pairs – 2 = 5

Critical value (α = .05, two tails) from table of critical r values: **.7545**

Decision: **Do not reject the null hypothesis. The computed value is less than the critical value. There is not enough evidence to conclude that there is a relationship between a person's score in condition X and that person's score in condition Y.**

How to designate r values: $r(5)=.75, p<.05$

Other Correlation Coefficients:

The Pearson product-moment correlation is the most commonly used bivariate correlation (i.e., a correlation with two variables). There are other, specialized correlation coefficients that are related to the Pearson r. The most common of these are the point-biserial correlation, the Spearman correlation for ranks, and the phi coefficient.

Researchers use the point-biserial correlation with bivariate analyses involving one continuous variable and one dichotomous variable that can take only two values (e.g., male or female). In the past, authors have presented a specialized formula for computing the point-biserial correlation. In fact, there is no need for a special formula because we can use the formula for the Pearson r to obtain the point-biserial correlation coefficient.

To compute a point-biserial correlation, you simply number your dichotomous variable with any two numbers. (Usually we use 0 and 1 or 1 and 2, but the result will be the same no matter what numbers you use.) Then you compute the Pearson r using your two numbers paired with your continuous variable. So to investigate the relation between one's sex and one's grade point average, for example, you could code women as zero and men as one. Then you would calculate the correlation coefficient where each woman, scored as zero, would be paired with her GPA and each man, scored as one, would be paired with his GPA. And you would calculate the Pearson r. You can test the correlation for significance the same way you would for the standard Pearson r, with a t test.

A second correlation related to the Pearson r is the Spearman correlation for ranks. This correlation involves one variable that is continuous and the other ranked. As with the point-biserial correlation, one can simply use the formula for the Pearson r to compute the Spearman r. Authors have presented an alternate formula for the Spearman r, but that formula results in the same coefficient as the standard Pearson r when there are no tied ranks. When there are tied ranks, the alternate formula is inaccurate if you do not apply a correction factor (Howell, 2007).

After your computation, you can test the correlation for significance. As with the Pearson r, you test for significance using a t test.

Finally, when the data involve two dichotomous variables, researchers sometimes use the phi coefficient (Φ). For instance, if you wanted to see whether voting (or not voting) is related to gender, you could use two dichotomous variables, male-female and voted-did not vote.

You could code women as zero and men as one; you could also code not voting as zero and voting as one. So a woman who voted would have scores of 0, 1; a man who did not vote would be 1, 0. After coding the sex and voting pattern appropriately, you would have a series of paired scores consisting of some combination of one and zero. At this junture, you can simply compute the standard Pearson r, as you would with the point-biserial and ranked data.

Testing the significance of Φ is a little different than for the other tests. In this case, you compute a value of chi-square (χ^2). We will use a different version of the formula for Φ than we did for the Pearson *r*; the two equations lead to the same outcome. Because of the difference in testing for significance, however, we will work through an example.

Coding of Sex: Women = 0; Men = 1
Coding of Vote: Did not vote = 0; Voted = 1

Sex:	0	0	0	0	0	0	0	0	0	0	0	0	1	1	1	1	1	1	1	1
Vote?:	1	1	0	0	0	1	0	1	1	1	1	1	1	1	0	1	1	0	0	1

$$COVxy = \frac{\sum X - \frac{\sum X \sum Y}{N}}{N-1} = \frac{5 - \frac{(8)(13)}{20}}{19} = -0.2 / 19 = -0.0105$$

$$Sx = 0.5026$$

$$Sy = 0.4894$$

$$\Phi = r = \frac{COV_{xy}}{(s_x)(s_y)} = \frac{-0.0105}{(.5026)(.4894)} = .0432$$

In order to test for significance, we use χ^2 instead of *t*. The computation is simple. $\chi^2 = N\,\Phi^2 = 20(.0432^2) = 0.0373$.

In this test, there is one degree of freedom, so the critical value of χ^2 is 3.84. Our computed value is less than the critical value, so we declare that the value of Φ is non-significant. There is no relation between one's sex and whether one votes, according to these data. Incidentally, women typically do vote in higher percentages than men, with percentages generally in accord with what we see in this data set. But with the small sample size, the effect is not significant because the power is very small.

Supplementary Analysis: After computing a correlation coefficient, we can assess the size of the effect, just as we could do so for a test of differences between means. This analysis of effect size is generally done only for the Pearson *r* with two sets of continuous variables, not with the point-biserial or Spearman correlation for ranks, nor with Φ. The computation is extremely simple. All we need to do is to square the value of the correlation coefficient:

$$r^2 = (.66)^2 = .4356$$

This value represents the amount of variability in one factor that is predicted by the other factor. Thus, we can say that about 44% of the differences in Y scores is predictable from knowing the X scores. The other 56% of the variability is due to unknown causes. As the value of the correlation coefficient approaches 1.00, so does the value of *r* squared. If variables were perfectly correlated, our predictions would be perfect. Behavior is so complex, though, that we might be satisfied with predicting 10% of the variability or less.

Linear Regression Analysis

In many cases, researchers who conduct correlational analyses also generate predictions of a criterion variable (sometimes the dependent variable) given a particular value of the predictor variable (sometimes the independent variable). The terms independent and dependent variable are more likely to be used when the research is experimental but uses regression analysis.

The simplest of these involves linear regression on one variable. One predictor variable is used to estimate a criterion variable. For more advanced regression analysis, such as that using multiple predictor variables or nonlinear regression, you should consult a statistics book. We will use the values for the correlation example to generate the regression line that we use to make predictions about the Y value, the criterion, based on the X value, the predictor.

In predicting a value of the DV, we use the formula for a straight line:

$$Y = a + bX,$$

where

a = the Y-intercept
b = the slope of the line
X = the value of the predictor variable
Y = the value of the criterion variable

After completing a correlational analysis, we compute values of a and b based on statistical values from the correlation computations.

Calculating the slope (b):

$$b = r\frac{S_{criterion}}{S_{predictor}} = -.66\left(\frac{2.50}{2.85}\right) = (-.66)(.88) = -.58$$

The negative value of the correlation coefficient means that as the value of the predictor value increases, the value of the criterion variable decreases. The value of -.58 for the slope means that as the value of the predictor variable (usually the X value) increases by a value of one, the value of the criterion (usually the Y value) decreases by 0.58.

Calculating the Y-intercept:

$$a = Mean_{criterion} - b(Mean_{predictor})$$
$$= 3.71 - (-.58)(5.86) = 3.71 - (-3.40) = 7.11$$

According to this analysis, if the value of X is zero, the value of Y should be around 7.11. As the value of the predictor variable increases, our prediction of the value of the criterion variable will decrease because the slope is negative. So as the value of X goes from zero to larger numbers, the value of Y will diminish.

Estimating a value of Y based on X: If the predictor value, X, is 7, what is our best prediction of the criterion variable, Y?

$$Y = a + bX$$
$$Y = 7.11 + (-.58)X$$
$$= 7.11 + (-.58)7 = 7.11 + (-4.06) = 7.11 - 4.06 = 3.05$$

If the value of X is 7, our best prediction for the value of Y is 3.05, which is reasonably consistent with the data set, as you can see in Figure 2. The higher the value of the correlation coefficient, the better your prediction will be.

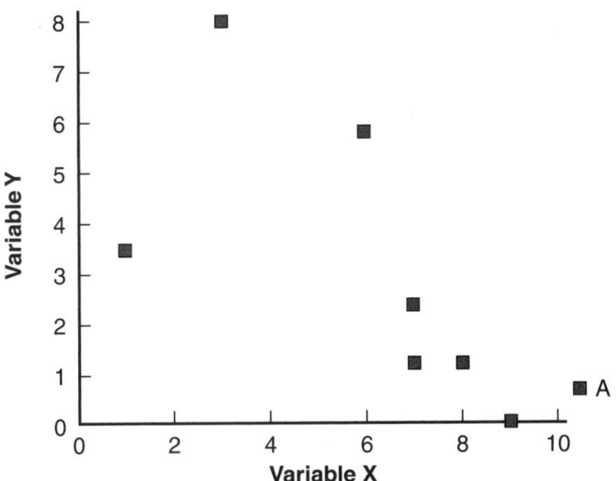

FIGURE 2 Figure Statistics Appendix 2. Scatterplot for correlation and regression data. The downward trend of the data when X increases reveals a negative correlation.

APPENDIX C

STATISTICAL TABLES

TABLE C.1 Significance values for the *t* distribution.

Computed values of *t* are significant if they are larger than the critical value in the table.

α LEVELS FOR DIRECTIONAL (ONE-TAILED) TESTS	*.05*	*.025*	*.01*	*.005*	*.0005*
α LEVELS FOR NONDIRECTIONAL (TWO-TAILED) TESTS					
df	*.10*	*.05*	*.02*	*.01*	*.001*
1	6.314	12.706	31.821	63.657	636.619
2	2.920	4.303	6.965	9.925	31.598
3	2.353	3.182	4.541	5.841	12.924
4	2.132	2.776	3.747	4.604	8.610
5	2.015	2.571	3.365	4.032	6.869
6	1.943	2.447	3.143	3.707	5.959
7	1.895	2.365	2.998	3.499	5.408
8	1.860	2.306	2.896	3.355	5.041
9	1.833	2.262	2.821	3.250	4.781
10	1.812	2.228	2.764	3.169	4.587
11	1.796	2.201	2.718	3.106	4.437
12	1.782	2.179	2.681	3.055	4.318
13	1.771	2.160	2.650	3.012	4.221
14	1.761	2.145	2.624	2.977	4.140
15	1.753	2.131	2.602	2.947	4.073
16	1.746	2.120	2.583	2.921	4.015
17	1.740	2.110	2.567	2.898	3.965
18	1.734	2.101	2.552	2.878	3.922
19	1.729	2.093	2.539	2.861	3.883
20	1.725	2.086	2.528	2.845	3.850
21	1.721	2.080	2.518	2.831	3.819
22	1.717	2.074	2.508	2.819	3.792
23	1.714	2.069	2.500	2.807	3.767
24	1.711	2.064	2.492	2.797	3.745
25	1.708	2.060	2.485	2.787	3.725
26	1.706	2.056	2.479	2.779	3.707
27	1.703	2.052	2.473	2.771	3.690
28	1.701	2.048	2.467	2.763	3.674
29	1.699	2.045	2.462	2.756	3.659
30	1.697	2.042	2.457	2.750	3.646
40	1.684	2.021	2.423	2.704	3.551
60	1.671	2.000	2.390	2.660	3.460
120	1.658	1.980	2.358	2.617	3.373
∞	1.645	1.960	2.326	2.576	3.291

TABLE C.2 Significance values for the analysis of variance (F test).

Degrees of freedom for treatments ($df_{between}$) appear in the left column. Degrees of freedom for the error term (df_{within} or df_{error}) are across the top. Computed values of F are significant if they are larger than the critical value in the table.

Values for α = .05 are in normal Roman type

Values for α = .01 are in bold type

Values for α = 0.001 are in italics

DF FOR THE NUMERATOR ($DF_{BETWEEN}$ OR $DF_{TREATMENT}$)

DF FOR THE DENOMINATOR (DF_{WITHIN} OR DF_{ERROR})		1	2	3	4	5	6	8	12	24
1	α =.05	161.4	199.5	215.7	224.6	230.2	234.0	238.9	243.9	249.0
	α = .01	**4052**	**4999**	**5403**	**5625**	**5764**	**5859**	**5982**	**6106**	**6234**
	α= .001	*405284*	*500000*	*540379*	*562500*	*576405*	*585937*	*598144*	*610667*	*623497*
2	α = .05	18.51	19.00	19.16	19.25	19.30	19.33	19.37	19.41	19.45
	α = .01	**98.50**	**99.00**	**99.17**	**99.25**	**99.30**	**99.33**	**99.37**	**99.42**	**99.46**
	α = .001	*998.5*	*999.0*	*999.2*	*999.2*	*999.3*	*999.3*	*999.4*	*999.4*	*999.5*
3	α = .05	10.13	9.55	9.28	6.12	9.01	8.94	8.84	8.74	8.64
	α = .01	**34.12**	**30.82**	**29.46**	**28.71**	**28.24**	**27.91**	**27.49**	**27.05**	**26.60**
	α = .001	*167.0*	*148.5*	*141.2*	*137.1*	*134.6*	*132.8*	*130.6*	*128.3*	*125.9*
4	α = .05	7.71	6.94	6.59	6.39	6.26	6.16	6.04	5.91	5.77
	α = .01	**21.20**	**18.00**	**16.69**	**15.98**	**15.52**	**15.21**	**14.80**	**14.37**	**13.93**
	α = .001	*74.14*	*61.25*	*56.18*	*53.44*	*51.71*	*50.53*	*49.00*	*47.41*	*45.77*
5	α = .05	6.61	5.79	5.41	5.19	5.05	4.95	4.82	4.68	4.53
	α = .01	**16.26**	**13.27**	**12.06**	**11.39**	**10.97**	**10.67**	**10.29**	**9.89**	**9.47**
	α = .001	*47.18*	*37.12*	*33.20*	*31.09*	*29.75*	*28.84*	*27.64*	*26.42*	*25.14*
6	α = .05	5.99	5.14	4.76	4.53	4.39	4.28	4.15	4.00	3.84
	α = .01	**13.74**	**10.92**	**9.78**	**9.15**	**8.75**	**8.47**	**8.10**	**7.72**	**7.31**
	α = .001	*35.51*	*27.00*	*23.70*	*21.92*	*20.81*	*20.03*	*19.03*	*17.99*	*16.89*
7	α = .05	5.59	4.74	4.35	4.12	3.97	3.87	3.73	3.57	3.41
	α = .01	**12.25**	**9.55**	**8.45**	**7.85**	**7.46**	**7.19**	**6.84**	**6.47**	**6.07**
	α = .001	*29.25*	*21.69*	*18.77*	*17.19*	*16.21*	*15.52*	*14.63*	*13.71*	*12.73*
8	α = .05	5.32	4.46	4.07	3.84	3.69	3.58	3.44	3.28	3.12
	α = .01	**11.26**	**8.65**	**7.59**	**7.01**	**6.63**	**6.37**	**6.03**	**5.67**	**5.28**
	α = .001	*25.42*	*18.49*	*15.83*	*14.39*	*13.49*	*12.86*	*12.04*	*11.19*	*10.30*
9	α = .05	5.12	4.26	3.86	3.63	3.48	3.37	3.23	3.07	2.90
	α = .01	**10.56**	**8.02**	**6.99**	**6.42**	**6.06**	**5.80**	**5.47**	**5.11**	**4.73**
	α = .001	*22.86*	*16.39*	*13.90*	*12.56*	*11.71*	*11.13*	*10.37*	*9.57*	*8.72*
10	α = .05	4.96	4.10	3.71	3.48	3.33	3.22	3.07	2.91	2.74
	α = .01	**10.04**	**7.56**	**6.55**	**5.99**	**5.64**	**5.39**	**5.06**	**4.71**	**4.33**
	α = .001	*21.04*	*14.91*	*12.55*	*11.28*	*10.48*	*9.92*	*9.20*	*8.45*	*7.64*

continued

TABLE C.2 Continued

DF FOR THE DENOMINATOR (DF_{WITHIN} OR DF_{ERROR})		DF FOR THE NUMERATOR ($DF_{BETWEEN}$ OR $DF_{TREATMENT}$) 1	2	3	4	5	6	8	12	24
11	α = .05	4.84	3.98	3.59	3.36	3.20	3.09	2.95	2.79	2.61
	α = .01	**9.65**	**7.20**	**6.22**	**5.67**	**5.32**	**5.07**	**4.74**	**4.40**	**4.02**
	α = .001	*19.69*	*13.81*	*11.56*	*10.35*	*9.58*	*9.05*	*8.35*	*7.63*	*6.85*
12	α =.05	4.75	3.88	3.49	3.26	3.11	3.00	2.85	2.69	2.50
	α = .01	**9.33**	**6.93**	**5.95**	**5.41**	**5.06**	**4.82**	**4.50**	**4.16**	**3.78**
	α = .001	*18.64*	*12.97*	*10.80*	*9.63*	*8.89*	*8.38*	*7.71*	*7.00*	*6.25*
13	α = .05	4.67	3.80	3.41	3.18	3.02	2.92	2.77	2.60	2.42
	α = .01	**9.07**	**6.70**	**5.74**	**5.20**	**4.86**	**4.62**	**4.30**	**3.96**	**3.59**
	α =.001	*17.81*	*12.31*	*10.21*	*9.07*	*8.35*	*7.86*	*7.21*	*6.52*	*5.78*
14	α = 5	4.60	3.74	3.34	3.11	2.96	2.85	2.70	2.53	2.35
	α = .01	**8.86**	**6.51**	**5.56**	**5.03**	**4.69**	**4.46**	**4.14**	**3.80**	**3.43**
	α =.001	*17.14*	*11.78*	*9.73*	*8.62*	*7.92*	*7.43*	*6.80*	*6.13*	*5.41*
15	α = .05	4.54	3.68	3.26	3.06	2.90	2.79	2.64	2.48	2.29
	α = .01	**8.68**	**6.36**	**5.42**	**4.89**	**4.56**	**4.32**	**4.00**	**3.67**	**3.29**
	α =.001	*16.59*	*11.34*	*9.34*	*8.25*	*7.57*	*7.09*	*6.47*	*5.81*	*5.10*
16	α =.05	4.49	3.63	3.24	3.01	2.85	2.74	2.59	2.42	2.24
	α = .01	**8.53**	**6.23**	**5.29**	**4.77**	**4.44**	**4.20**	**3.89**	**3.55**	**3.18**
	α = .001	*16.12*	*10.97*	*9.00*	*7.94*	*7.27*	*6.81*	*6.19*	*5.55*	*4.85*
17	α =.05	4.45	3.59	3.20	2.96	2.81	2.70	2.55	2.38	2.19
	α = .01	**8.40**	**6.11**	**5.18**	**4.67**	**4.34**	**4.10**	**3.79**	**3.45**	**3.08**
	α = .001	*15.72*	*10.66*	*8.73*	*7.68*	*7.02*	*6.56*	*5.96*	*5.32*	*4.63*
18	α = .05	4.41	3.55	3.16	2.93	2.77	2.66	2.51	2.34	2.15
	α = .01	**8.28**	**6.01**	**5.09**	**4.58**	**4.25**	**4.01**	**3.71**	**3.37**	**3.00**
	α = .001	*15.38*	*10.39*	*8.49*	*7.46*	*6.81*	*6.35*	*5.76*	*5.13*	*4.45*
19	α = .05	4.38	3.52	3.13	2.90	2.74	2.63	2.48	2.31	2.11
	α = .01	**8.18**	**5.93**	**5.01**	**4.50**	**4.17**	**3.94**	**3.63**	**3.30**	**2.92**
	α = .001	*15.08*	*10.16*	*8.28*	*7.26*	*6.62*	*6.18*	*5.59*	*4.97*	*4.29*
20	α = .05	4.35	3.49	3.10	2.87	2.71	2.60	2.45	2.28	2.08
	α = .01	**8.10**	**5.85**	**4.94**	**4.43**	**4.10**	**3.87**	**3.56**	**3.23**	**2.86**
	α =.001	*14.82*	*9.95*	*8.10*	*7.10*	*6.46*	*6.02*	*5.44*	*4.82*	*4.15*
21	α = .05	4.32	3.47	3.07	2.84	2.68	2.57	2.42	2.25	2.05
	α = .01	**8.02**	**5.78**	**4.87**	**4.37**	**4.04**	**3.81**	**3.51**	**3.17**	**2.80**
	α =.001	*14.59*	*9.77*	*7.94*	*6.95*	*6.32*	*5.88*	*5.31*	*4.70*	*4.03*
22	α = .05	4.30	3.44	3.05	2.82	2.66	2.55	2.40	2.23	2.03
	α = .01	**7.94**	**5.72**	**4.82**	**4.31**	**3.99**	**3.76**	**3.45**	**3.12**	**2.75**
	α =.001	*14.38*	*9.61*	*7.80*	*6.81*	*6.19*	*5.76*	*5.19*	*4.58*	*3.92*

TABLE C.2 Continued

DF FOR THE DENOMINATOR (DF_{WITHIN} OR DF_{ERROR})	DF FOR THE NUMERATOR ($DF_{BETWEEN}$ OR $DF_{TREATMENT}$)	1	2	3	4	5	6	8	12	24
23	α = .05	4.28	3.42	3.03	2.80	2.64	2.53	2.38	2.20	2.00
	α = .01	**7.88**	**5.66**	**4.76**	**4.26**	**3.94**	**3.71**	**3.41**	**3.07**	**2.70**
	α = .001	*14.19*	*9.47*	*7.67*	*6.69*	*6.08*	*5.65*	*5.09*	*4.48*	*3.82*
24	α =.05	4.26	3.40	3.01	2.78	2.62	2.51	2.36	2.18	1.98
	α = .01	**7.82**	**5.61**	**4.72**	**4.22**	**3.90**	**3.67**	**3.36**	**3.03**	**2.66**
	α =.001	*14.03*	*9.34*	*7.55*	*6.59*	*5.98*	*5.55*	*4.99*	*4.39*	*3.74*
25	α = .05	4.24	3.38	2.99	2.76	2.60	2.49	2.34	2.16	1.96
	α = .01	**7.77**	**5.57**	**4.68**	**4.18**	**3.86**	**3.63**	**3.32**	**2.99**	**2.62**
	α = .001	*13.88*	*9.22*	*7.45*	*6.49*	*5.88*	*5.46*	*4.91*	*4.31*	*3.66*
26	α = .05	4.22	3.37	2.98	2.74	2.59	2.47	2.32	2.15	1.95
	α = .01	**7.72**	**5.53**	**4.64**	**4.14**	**3.82**	**3.59**	**3.29**	**2.96**	**2.58**
	α = .001	*13.74*	*9.12*	*7.36*	*6.41*	*5.80*	*5.38*	*4.83*	*4.24*	*3.59*
27	α = .05	4.21	3.35	2.96	2.73	2.57	2.46	2.30	2.13	1.93
	α = .01	**7.68**	**5.49**	**4.60**	**4.11**	**3.78**	**3.56**	**3.26**	**2.93**	**2.55**
	α =.001	*13.61*	*9.02*	*7.27*	*6.33*	*5.73*	*5.31*	*4.76*	*4.17*	*3.52*
28	α = .05	4.20	3.34	2.95	2.71	2.56	2.44	2.29	2.12	1.91
	α = .01	**7.64**	**5.45**	**4.57**	**4.07**	**3.75**	**3.53**	**3.23**	**2.90**	**2.52**
	α =.001	*13.50*	*8.93*	*7.19*	*6.25*	*5.66*	*5.24*	*4.69*	*4.11*	*3.46*
29	α = .05	4.18	3.33	2.93	2.70	2.54	2.43	2.28	2.10	1.90
	α = .01	**7.60**	**5.42**	**4.54**	**4.04**	**3.73**	**3.50**	**3.20**	**2.87**	**2.49**
	α = .001	*13.39*	*8.85*	*7.12*	*6.19*	*5.59*	*5.18*	*4.64*	*4.05*	*3.41*
30	α = .05	4.17	3.32	2.92	2.69	2.53	2.42	2.27	2.09	1.89
	α = .01	**7.56**	**5.39**	**4.51**	**4.02**	**3.70**	**3.47**	**3.17**	**2.84**	**2.47**
	α =.001	*13.29*	*8.77*	*7.05*	*6.12*	*5.53*	*5.12*	*4.58*	*4.00*	*3.36*
40	α =.05	4.08	3.23	2.84	2.61	2.45	2.34	2.18	2.00	1.79
	α = .01	**7.31**	**5.18**	**4.31**	**3.83**	**3.51**	**3.29**	**2.99**	**2.66**	**2.29**
	α =.001	*12.61*	*8.25*	*6.60*	*5.70*	*5.13*	*4.73*	*4.21*	*3.64*	*3.01*
60	α =.05	4.00	3.15	2.76	2.52	2.37	2.25	2.10	1.92	1.70
	α = .01	**7.08**	**4.98**	**4.13**	**3.65**	**3.34**	**3.12**	**2.82**	**2.50**	**2.12**
	α =.001	*11.97*	*7.76*	*6.17*	*5.31*	*4.76*	*4.37*	*3.87*	*3.31*	*2.69*
120	α = .05	3.92	3.07	2.68	2.45	2.29	2.17	2.02	1.83	1.61
	α = .01	**6.85**	**4.79**	**3.95**	**3.48**	**3.17**	**2.66**	**2.34**	**1.95**	
	α = .001	*11.38*	*7.32*	*5.79*	*4.95*	*4.42*	*4.04*	*3.55*	*3.02*	*2.40*
×	α = .05	3.84	2.99	2.60	2.37	2.21	2.10	1.94	1.75	1.52
	α = .01	**6.64**	**4.60**	**3.78**	**3.32**	**3.02**	**2.80**	**2.51**	**2.18**	**1.79**
	α = .001	*10.83*	*6.91*	*5.42*	*4.62*	*4.10*	*3.74*	*3.27*	*2.74*	*2.13*

TABLE C.3 Significance values for the Pearson product–moment correlation (r).

Computed values of r are significant if they are larger than the value in the table.

α LEVELS FOR DIRECTIONAL (ONE-TAILED) TESTS	.05	.025	.01	.005	.0005
α LEVELS FOR NONDIRECTIONAL (TWO-TAILED) TESTS					
df (*# pairs - 2*)	*.1*	*.05*	*.02*	*.01*	*.001*
1	.9877	.9969	.9995	.9999	.9999988
2	.9000	.9500	.9800	.9900	.9990
3	.8054	.8783	.9343	.9587	.9912
4	.7293	.8114	.8822	.9172	.9741
5	.6694	.7545	.8329	.8745	.9507
6	.6215	.7067	.7887	.8343	.9249
7	.5822	.6664	.7498	.7977	.8982
8	.5494	.6319	.7155	.7646	.8721
9	.5214	.6021	.6851	.7348	.8471
10	.4973	.5760	.6581	.7079	.8233
11	.4762	.5529	.6339	.6835	.8010
12	.4575	.5324	.6120	.6614	.7800
13	.4409	.5139	.5923	.6411	.7603
14	.4259	.4973	.5742	.6226	.7420
15	.4124	.4821	.5577	.6055	.7246
16	.4000	.4683	.5425	.5897	.7084
17	.3887	.4555	.5285	.5751	.6932
18	.3783	.4438	.5155	.5614	.6787
19	.3687	.4329	.5043	.5487	.6652
20	.3598	.4227	.4921	.5368	.6524
25	.3233	.3809	.4451	.4869	.5974
30	.2960	.3494	.4093	.4487	.5541
35	.2746	.3246	.3810	.4182	.5189
40	.2573	.3044	.3578	.3932	.4896
45	.2428	.2875	.3384	.3721	.4648
50	.2306	.2732	.3218	.3541	.4433
60	.2108	.2500	.2948	.3248	.4078
70	.1954	.2319	.2737	.3017	.3799
80	.1829	.2172	.2565	.2830	.3568
90	.1726	.2050	.2422	.2673	.3375
100	.1638	.1946	.2301	.2540	.3211

TABLE C.4 Significance values for chi-square (χ^2).

Computed values of χ^2 are significant if they are larger than the value in the table.

	α LEVELS			
df	*.10*	*.05*	*.01*	*.001*
1	2.706	3.841	6.635	10.827
2	4.605	5.991	9.210	13.815
3	6.251	7.815	11.345	16.266
4	7.779	9.488	13.277	18.467
5	9.236	11.070	15.086	20.515
6	10.645	12.592	16.812	22.457
7	12.017	14.067	18.475	24.322
8	13.362	15.507	20.090	26.125
9	14.684	16.919	21.666	27.877
10	15.987	18.307	23.209	29.588
11	17.275	19.675	24.725	31.264
12	18.549	21.026	26.217	32.909
13	19.812	22.362	27.688	34.528
14	21.064	23.685	29.141	36.123
15	22.307	24.996	30.578	37.697
16	23.542	26.296	32.000	39.252
17	24.769	27.587	33.409	40.790
18	25.989	28.869	34.805	42.312
19	27.204	30.144	36.191	43.280
20	28.412	31.410	37.566	45.315
21	29.615	32.671	38.932	46.797
22	30.813	33.924	40.289	48.268
23	32.007	35.172	41.638	49.728
24	33.196	36.415	42.980	51.179
25	34.382	37.652	44.314	52.620
26	35.563	38.885	45.642	54.052
27	36.741	40.133	46.963	55.476
28	37.916	41.337	48.278	56.893
29	39.087	42.557	49.588	58.302
30	40.256	43.773	50.892	59.703

TABLE C.5 One thousand random numbers.

10801	69621	92008	13317	76917	21943	73624	80445	29832	36976
74959	65233	71968	87168	49732	01869	62348	31099	27069	48371
04613	70583	61117	90612	27112	01158	40970	13707	57074	68148
43119	10341	52504	17521	91658	65932	27217	27220	36299	18907
05196	58937	49852	05962	21349	22112	96044	51822	80307	48511
91846	14339	69334	41114	74998	67265	24494	94609	07506	41925
32611	04453	39706	93180	28343	65808	56739	35441	06383	48345
31612	64859	57247	48883	88849	12957	96368	59157	01457	32286
06811	56453	31190	40241	93777	05674	14878	98541	19978	62941
49156	18317	52290	57437	34766	15564	27358	88676	90462	01447
85083	29866	24889	75946	83452	05025	45481	38172	06556	95725
92686	83627	63324	76877	42736	18599	10076	18987	46692	83214
04153	87384	98578	37405	71255	76724	34331	18744	49206	88389
36264	00862	77603	18063	85971	93189	78687	87926	09703	18024
93188	81477	60543	71093	49282	95305	85972	18871	55505	67354
81856	61512	41926	55090	80158	50833	24492	84373	91432	73511
60993	75429	71568	64945	59296	65966	69284	44770	56988	42531
48760	55612	43419	41346	72776	03145	51665	93169	46002	12986
05686	49443	41186	29474	02306	80764	14764	71099	10101	99774
71131	17438	61830	52767	85360	99494	90297	05596	74534	35407

REFERENCES

Abreu, J. M., & Gabarain, G. (2000). Social desirability and Mexican American counselor preferences: Statistical control for a potential confound. *Journal of Counseling Psychology, 47*, 165–176.

ACHRE Report. (n.d.). Retrieved March 19, 2008, from www.hss.energy.gov/healthsafety/ohre/roadmap/achre/chap7_2.html

Adair, J. G. (1984). The Hawthorne effect: A reconsideration of the methodological artifact. *Journal of Applied Psychology, 69*, 334–345.

Adair, J. G., Dushenko, T. W., & Lindsay, R. C. L. (1985). Ethical regulations and their impact on research practice. *American Psychologist, 40*, 59–72.

Affsprung, E. H. (1998). Assessing for a history of serious depression among first-year college students. *Journal of College Student Psychotherapy, 12*, 61–65.

American Psychiatric Association. (1987). *Diagnostic and statistical manual of mental disorders* (3rd ed., revised). Washington, DC: Author.

American Psychological Association. (1994). *Publication manual of the American Psychological Association* (4th ed.). Washington, DC: Author

American Psychological Association. (2002). Ethical principles of psychologists and code of conduct. *American Psychologist, 57*, 1060–1073.

Americans felt uneasy toward Arabs even before September 11 (2001). Retrieved September 29, 2001, from http://www.gallup.com/poll/releases/pr010928.asp.

Anderson, C. A., & Bushman, B. J. (2001). Effects of violent video games on aggressive behavior, aggressive cognition, aggressive affect, physiological arousal, and prosocial behavior: A meta-analytic review of the scientific literature. *Psychological Science, 12*, 353–359.

Anderson, C. A., Carnagey, N. L., & Eubanks, J. (2003). Exposure to violent media: The effects of songs with violent lyrics on aggressive thoughts and feelings. *Journal of Personality and Social Psychology, 84*, 960–971.

Anderson, C. A., Gentile, D. A., & Buckley, K. E. (2007). *Violent video game effects on children and adolescents; Theory, research, and public policy.* New York: Oxford University Press.

Anderson, J., & Fienberg, S. E. (2000). Census 2000 controversies. *Chance, 13*(4), 22–30.

Anderson, K. C., & Insel, T. R. (2006). The promise of extinction research for the prevention and treatment of anxiety disorders. *Biological Psychiatry, 60*, 319–321.

Aneschensel, C. S., Clark, V. A., & Frerichs, R. R. (1983). Race, ethnicity, and depression: A confirmatory analysis. *Journal of Personality and Social Psychology, 44*, 385–398.

Angier, N. (2000, August 22). Do races differ? Not really, DNA shows. *New York Times on the Web* [http://www.nytimes.com/library/national/science/082200sci-genetics-race.html]. Retrieved August 22, 2000.

Anorexia may not have cultural roots. (2001). Retrieved April 28, 1998 from http://www.intelihealth.com.

Armitage, R., Smith, C., Thompason, S., & Hoffman, R. (2001). Sex differences in slow-wave activity in response to sleep deprivation. *Sleep Research Online, 4*, 33–41. http://www.sro.org/2001/Armitage/33/

Aronson, J., Lustina, M. J., Good, C., Keough, K., Steele, C. M., & Brown, J. (1999). When white men can't do math: Necessary and sufficient factors in stereotype threat. *Journal of Experimental Social Psychology, 35*, 29–46.

Austad, S. N. (2002). A mouse's tale. *Natural History, 111(3)*, 64–70.

Azar, B. (2000a, April). Online experiments: Ethically fair or foul? *Monitor on Psychology, 31*, 50–52.

Azar, B. (2000b, April). A web of research. *Monitor on Psychology, 31*, 42–44.

Babbie, E. (1995). *The practice of social research* (7th ed.). Belmont, CA: Wadsworth.

Bachorowski, J-A., & Owren, M. J. (2001). Not all laughs are alike: Voiced but not unvoiced laughter readily elicits positive affect. *Psychological Science, 12*, 252–257.

Ball, P., Giles, H., & Hewstone, M. (1984). Second language acquisition: The intergroup theory with catastrophic dimensions. In H. Tajfel (Ed.), *The social dimension* (Vol. 2, pp. 668–694). Cambridge, UK: Cambridge University Press.

Banville, D., Desrosiers, P., & Genet-Volet, G. (2000). Translating questionnaires and inventories using a cross-cultural translation technique. *Journal of Teaching in Physical Education, 19*, 374–387.

Barnett, W. S. (1998). Long-term cognitive and academic effects of early childhood education of children in poverty. *Preventive Medicine: An International Devoted to Practice & Theory, 27*, 204–207.

Baron-Cohen, S., Burt, L., Smith-Laittan, F., Harrison, J., & Bolton, P. (1996). Synaesthesia: Prevalence and familiarity. *Perception, 25*, 1073–1079.

Bartolic, E. I., Basso, M. R., Schefft, B. K., Glauser, T., & Titanic-Schefft, M. (1999). Effects of experimentally-induced emotional states on frontal lobe cognitive task performance. *Neuropsychologia, 37,* 677–683.

Basha, S., A., & Ushasree, S. (1998). Fear of success across life span. *Journal of Personality & Clinical Studies, 14,* 63–67.

Batson, C. D., Duncan, B., Ackerman, P., Buckley, T., & Birch, K. (1981). Is empathetic emotion a source of altruistic motivation? *Journal of Personality and Social Psychology, 40,* 290–302.

Baumrind, D. (1964). Some thoughts on ethics of research: After reading Milgram's "Behavioral study of obedience." *American Psychologist, 19,* 421–423.

Beach, F. A. (1950). The Snark was a Boojum. *American Psychologist, 5,* 115–124.

Beauvais, J. E., Woods, S. P., Delaney, R. C., & Fein, D. (2004). Development of a tactile Wisconsin card sorting test. *Rehabilitation Psychology, 49,* 282–287.

Becker, E. (1973). *The denial of death.* New York: Free Press.

Beins, B. C., McCarthy, C., Rigge, M., Rigoli, B., & Sawyer, S. (2007, October). Expectations about humor affect ratings: A generalizable effect with social implications. Poster presentation at the annual convention of the New England Psychological Association, Danbury, CT.

Bell, G., & Brady, V. (2000). Monetary incentives for sex workers. *International Journal of STD & AIDS, 11,* 483–484.

Bell, N. S., Mangione, T. W., Hemenway, D., Amoroso, P. J., & Jones, B. H. (2000). High injury rates among female Army trainees: A function of gender? *The American Journal of Preventive Medicine, 18*(3) Supplement 1, 141–146.

Benbow, C. P., & Stanley, J. C. (1980). Sex differences in mathematical ability: Fact or artifact? *Science, 10,* 1262–1264.

Benbow, C. P., & Stanley, J. C. (1983). Sex differences in mathematical reasoning ability: More facts. *Science, 222,* 1029–1030.

Benfante, L., & Beins, B. C. (2007, October). Self-reflection and sense of humor: The big five personality characteristics and humor. Poster presentation at the annual convention of the New England Psychological Association, Danbury, CT.

Benton, S. A., Robertson, J. M., Tseng, W-C., Newton, F. B., & Benton, S. L. (2003). Changes in counseling center client problems across 13 years. *Professional Psychology: Research and Practice, 34,* 66–72.

Berkowitz, L. (1992). Some thoughts about conservative evaluations of replications. *Personality & Social Psychology Bulletin, 18,* 319–324.

Berreby, D. (2000). Race counts. [Review of *Changing race: Latinos, the census and the history of ethnicity in the United States.*] *The Sciences, 40,* 38–43.

Betancourt, H, & Lôpez, S. R. (1993). The study of culture, ethnicity, and race in American psychology. *American Psychologist, 48,* 629–637.

Bhui, K., & Bhugra, D. (2001). Methodological rigour in cross-cultural research. *The British Journal of Psychiatry, 179,* 269.

Birnbaum, M. H. (1974). Using contextual effects to derive psychophysical scales. *Perception and Psychophysics, 15,* 89–96.

Birnbaum, M. H. (1999). How to show that 9 > 221: Collect judgments in a between-subjects design. *Psychological Methods, 4,* 243–249.

Bleiberg, J., Garmoe, W., Cederquist, J., Reeves, D., & Lux, W. (1993). Effects of dexedrine on performance consistency following brain injury: A double-blind placebo crossover case study. *Neuropsychiatry, Neuropsychology, and Behavioral Neurology, 6,* 245–248.

Bond, L., Carlin, J. B., Thomas, L., Rubin, K., & Patton, G. (2001). Does bullying cause emotional problems? A prospective study of young teenagers. *British Medical Journal, 323,* 480–484.

Bosworth, H. B., & Schaie, K. W. (1999). Survival effects in cognitive function, cognitive style, and sociodemographic variables in the Seattle Longitudinal Study. *Experimental Aging Research, 25,* 121–139.

Bowman, L., L., & Anthonysamy, A. (2006). Malaysian and American students' perceptions of research ethics. *College Student Journal, 40,* 11–24.

Bramel, D., & Friend, R. (1981). Hawthorne, the myth of the docile worker, and class bias in psychology. *American Psychologist, 36,* 867–878.

Bray, J. H., Adams, G. J., Getz, J. G., & Baer, P. E. (2001). Developmental, family, and ethnic in influences on adolescent alcohol usage: A growth curve approach. *Journal of Family Psychology, 15,* 301–314.

Brewer, N., Keast, A., & Rishworth, A. (2002). The confidence-accuracy relationship in eyewitness identification: The effects of reflection and disconfirmation on correlation and calibration. *Journal of Experimental Psychology: Applied, 8,* 46–58.

Brewer, B. W., & Shillinglaw, R. (1992). Evaluation of a psychological skills training workshop for male intercollegiate lacrosse players. *The Sport Psychologist,* 6, 139–147.

Bröder, A. (1998). Deception can be acceptable. *American Psychologist, 53,* 805–806.

Broman, C. L. (2005). Stress, race, and substance use in college. *College Student Journal, 39,* 340–352.

Budson, A. E., Desikan, R., Daffner, K. R., & Schachter, D. L. (2001). Perceptual false recognition in Alzheimer's disease. *Neuropsychology, 15,* 230–243.

Bull, R., & Stevens, J. (1980). Effect of unsightly teeth on helping behavior. *Perceptual and Motor Skills, 51,* 438.

Burtt, H. E. (1920). Sex differences in the effect of discussion. *Journal of Experimental Psychology, 3,* 390–395.

Bushman, B. J., & Anderson, C. A. (2001). Media violence and the American public: Scientific facts versus media misinformation. *American Psychologist, 56,* 477–489.

Byrnes, J. P., Miller, D. C., & Schafer, W. D. (1999). Gender differences in risk taking: A meta-analysis. *Psychological Bulletin, 125*, 367–383.

Cai, W-H., Blundell, J., Han, J., Greene, R. W., & Powell, C. M. (2006). Postreactivation glucocorticoids impair recall of established fear memory. *Journal of Neuroscience, 26*, 9560–9566.

Campbell, D. T., & Stanley, J. C. (1966). *Experimental and quasi-experimental designs for research.* Chicago: Rand McNally.

Caplan, P. J., & Caplan, J. B. (1999). *Thinking critically about research on sex and gender* (2nd ed.). New York: Longman.

Carnagey, N. L., Anderson, C. A., & Bartholow, B. D. (2007). Media violence and social neuroscience: New questions and new opportunities. *Current Directions in Psychological Science, 16*, 178–182.

Carr, S. C., Munro, D., & Bishop, G. D. (1995). Attitude assessment in non-Western countries: Critical modifications to likert scaling. *Psychologia, 39*, 55–59.

Carstens, C. B., Haskins, E., & Hounshell, G. W. (1995). Listening to Mozart may not enhance performance on the revised Minnesota paper form board test. *Psychological Reports*, 77, 111–114.

Caruso, K. (2004, September 6). Joann Mitchell Levy, sixth NYU student to die by suicide in the past year. Retrieved August 3, 2007, from http://www.suicide.org/joann-mitchell-levy-nyu-suicides.html

Case summaries. (2004). *Office of Research Integrity Newsletter, 12*(4), 5–7. Retrieved June 1, 2007, from http://ori.dhhs.gov/documents/newsletters/vol12_no2.pdf

Cepeda-Benito, A., & Gleaves, D. H. (2000). Cross-ethnic equivalence of the Hopkins Symptom Checklist-21 in European American, African American, and Latino college students. *Cultural Diversity and Ethnic Minority Psychology, 6*, 297–308.

Cernovsky, Z. Z. (2000). On the similarities of American blacks and whites. In B. Slife (Ed.), *Taking sides: Clashing views on controversial psychological issues.* Guilford, CT: Dushkin/McGraw Hill.

Chabris, C. F., Steele, K. M., Bella, S. D., Peretz, I., Dunlop, T., Dawe, L. A., et al. (1999). Prelude or requiem for the "Mozart effect"? *Nature, 400*, 826–828.

Chang, W. C. (2000). In search of the Chinese in all the wrong places! *Journal of Psychology in Chinese Societies, 1*, 125–142.

Chao, R. (2001). Integrating culture and attachment. *American Psychologist, 56*, 822–823.

Charges of fake research hit new high. (2005, July 10). Retrieved June 1, 2007, from http://www.msnbc.msn.com/id/8474936

Cheryan, S., & Bodenhausen, G. V. (2000). When positive stereotypes threaten intellectual performance: The psychological hazards of "model minority" status. *Psychological Science, 11*, 399–402.

Cho, H., & LaRose, R. (1999). Privacy issues in internet surveys. *Social Science Computer Review, 17*, 421–434.

Christensen, L. (1988). Deception in psychological research: When is its use justified? *Personality and Social Psychology Bulletin, 14*, 664–675.

CIA–The world factbook–United Kingdom. (2007). Retrieved July 11, 2007, from https://www.cia.gov/library/publications/the-world-factbook/geos/uk.html

Cialdini, R. B. (1980). Full-cycle social psychology. *Applied Social Psychology Annual, 1*, 21–47.

Cialdini, R. B., Darby, B. L., & Vincent, J. E. (1973). Transgression and altruism: A case for hedonism. *Journal of Experimental Social Psychology, 9* , 502–516.

Clark, D. M., & Teasdale, J. D. (1985). Constraints on the effects of mood on memory. *Journal of Personality and Social Psychology, 52*, 749–758.

Clawson, R. A., & Trice, R. (2000). Poverty as we know it: Media portrayals of the poor. *Public Opinion Quarterly, 64*, 53–64.

Cohen, D., & Gunz, A. (2002). As seen by the other . . . : Perspectives on the self in the memories and emotional perceptions of Easterners and Westerners. *Psychological Science, 13*, 55–59.

Cohen, S., Alper, C. M., Doyle, W. J., Treanor, J. J., & Turner, R. B. (2006). Positive emotional style predicts resistance to illness after experimental exposure to rhinovirus or influenza A virus. *Psychosomatic Medicine, 68*, 809–915.

Cohen, S., Tyrrell, D. A., & Smith, A. P. (1991). Psychological stress and susceptibility to the common cold. *New England Journal of Medicine, 325*, 606–612.

Coile, D. C., & Miller, N. E. (1984). How radical animal activists try to mislead humane people, *American Psychologist, 39*, 700–701.

Consumers in the 18-to-24 age segment view cell phones as multi-functional accessories; crave advanced features and personalization options. (2007, January 22). Retrieved July 24, 2007, from http://www.comscore.com/press/release.asp?press=1184

Cook, D. J. (1996). Randomized trials in single subjects: The N of 1 study. *Psychopharmacology Bulletin, 32*, 363–367.

Cook, P. J., & Ludwig, J. (1998). Defensive gun uses: New evidence from a national survey. *Journal of Quantitative Criminology, 14*, 111–131.

Council of National Psychological Associations for the Advancement of Ethnic Minority Interests. (2000). *Guidelines for research in ethnic minority communities.* Washington, DC: American Psychological Association.

Couper, M. P., Kapteyn, A. Schonlau, M., & Winter, J. (2007). Noncoverage and nonresponse in an Internet survey. *Social Science Research, 36*, 131–148.

Coverdale, J. H., & Turbott, S. H. (2000). Sexual and physical abuse of chronically ill psychiatric outpatients compared with a matched sample of medical outpatients. *Journal of Nervous and Mental Disease, 188*, 440–445.

Cox, C. R., & LeBoeuf, B. J.(1977). Female incitation of male competition: A mechanism in sexual selection. *American Naturalist, 111*, 317–335.

Crocker, P. R. E. (1993). Sport and exercise psychology and research with individuals with physical disabilities: Using theory to advance knowledge. *Adapted Physical Activity Quarterly, 10*, 324–335.

Croizet, J-C., & Claire, T. (1998). Extending the concept of stereotype and threat to social class: The intellectual underperformance of students from low socioeconomic backgrounds. *Personality & Social Psychology Bulletin, 24*, 588–594.

Croll, S., & Bryant, R. A. (2000). Autobiographical memory in postnatal depression. *Cognitive Therapy and Research, 24*, 419–426.

Cunningham, S. (1984). Genovese: 20 years later, few heed a stranger's cries. *Social Action and the Law, 10*, 24–25.

Cytowic, R. E. (1993). *The man who tasted shapes.* New York: G. P. Putnam & Son.

Cytowic, R. E. (1997). Synaesthesia: Phenomenology and neuropsychology–A review of current knowledge. In S. Baron-Cohen & J. E. Harrison (Eds.), *Synaesthesia: Classic and contemporary readings.* Cambridge, MA: Blackwell.

Davies, M., Stankov, L., & Roberts, R. D. (1998). Emotional intelligence: In search of an elusive construct. *Journal of Personality and Social Psychology, 75*, 989–1015.

Deese, J., & Hulse, S. H. (1967). *The psychology of learning* (3rd ed.). New York: McGraw-Hill

Demographics of internet users. (2007). Pew Internet & American Life Project, February 15-March 7, 2007 Tracking Survey. Retrieved July 17, 2007, from http://www.pewinternet.org/trends/User_Demo_6.15.07.htm

Diener, E., Matthews, R., & Smith, R. E. (1972). Leakage of experimental information to potential future subjects by debriefed subjects. *Journal of Experimental Research in Personality, 6*, 264–267.

Dillman, D. A. (2000). *Mail and internet surveys: The tailored design method.* New York: Wiley.

Dixon, A. K. (1998). Ethological strategies for defence in animals and humans: Their role in some psychiatric disorders. *British Journal of Medical Psychology, 71*, 417–445.

Dixon, W. A., & Reid, J. K. (2000). Positive life events as a moderator of stress-related depressive symptoms. *Journal of Counseling & Development, 78*, 343–347.

Dozois, D. J. A., Dobson, K. S., & Ahnberg, J. L. (1998). A psychometric evaluation of the Beck Depression Inventory–II. *Psychological Assessment, 10*, 83–89.

Dubowitz, G. (1998). Effect of temazepam on oxygen saturation and sleep quality at high altitude: Randomised placebo controlled crossover trial. *British Medical Journal, 316*, 587–589.

Duncan, S. C., Duncan, T. E., & Strycker, L. A. (2006). Alcohol use from ages 9 to 16: A cohort-sequential latent growth model. *Drug and Alcohol Dependence, 81*, 71–81.

Dunning, D., & Perretta, S. (2002). Automaticity and eyewitness accuracy: A 10–12 second rule for distinguishing accurate from inaccurate positive identifications. *Journal of Applied Psychology, 87*, 951–962.

Eagles, J. M., Andrew, J. E., Johnston, M. I., Easton, E. A., & Millar, H. R. (2001). Season of birth in females with anorexia nervosa in Northeast Scotland. *International Journal of Eating Disorders, 30*, 167–175.

Edwards, C. L., Fillingim, R. B., & Keefe, F. (2001). Race, ethnicity and pain. *Pain, 94*, 133–137.

Eichenwald, K., & Kolata, G. (1999, May 16). Drug trials hide conflicts for doctors. *New York Times.* Retrieved from http://www.nytimes.com/library/politics/051699drug-trials.html

Ellis, H. C., Thomas, R. L., & Rodriguez, I. A. (1984). Emotinoal mood states and memory: Elaborative encoding, semantic processing, and cognitive effort. *Journal of Experimental Psychology: Learning, Memory, and Cognition, 10*, 470–482.

Estep, D. Q., & Bruce, K. E. M. (1981). The concept of rape in non-humans: A critique. *Animal Behavior, 29*, 1272–1273.

Evans, S. W., Pelham, W. E., Smith, B. H., Burkstein, O., Gnagy, E. M., Greiner, A. R., Altenderfer, L., & Baron-Myak, C. (2001). Dose-response effects of methylphenidate on ecological valid measures of academic performance and classroom behavior in adolescents with ADHD. *Experimental and Clinical Psychopharmacology, 9*, 163–175.

Exline, J. J., & Lobel, M. (1999). The perils of outperformance: Sensitivity about being the target of a threatening upward comparison. *Psychological Bulletin, 125*, 303–337.

Fairburn, C. G., Welch, S. L., Norman, P. A., O'Connor, B. A., & Doll, H. A. (1996). Bias and bulimia nervosa: How typical are clinical cases? *American Journal of Psychiatry, 153*, 386–391.

Falk, R. (1986) Misconceptions of statistical significance. *Journal of Structural Learning, 9*, 83–96.

Falk, R., & Greenbaum, C. W. (1995) Significance tests die hard: The amazing persistence of a probabilistic misconception. *Theory & Psychology, 5*, 75–98.

Farley, P. (2003, January 21). Young scientist's paper gets him in hot water with colleagues. Retrieved January 23, 2003, from http://www.boston.com

Fausto-Sterling, A. (1993). The five sexes: Why male and female are not enough. *The Sciences, 33*(2), 20–25.

Felmingham, K., Kemp, A., Williams, L., Das, P., Hughes, G.. Peduto, A., et al. (2007). Changes in anterior cingulate and amygdala after cognitive behavior therapy of posttraumatic stress disorder. *Psychological Science, 18*, 127–129.

Fernandez, E., & Sheffield, J. (1996). Relative contributions of life events versus daily hassles to the frequency and intensity of headaches. *Headache, 36*, 595–602.

Finkel, S. E., Guterbok, T. M., & Borg, M. J. (1991). Race of interviewer effects in a preelection Poll: Virginia 1989. *Public Opinion Quarterly, 55*, 313–330.

Fisher, C. (2005). Deception research involving children: Ethical practices and paradoxes. *Ethics & Behavior, 15*, 271–287.

Fisher, C. B., & Fyrberg, D. (1994). Participant partners: College students weigh the costs and benefits of deceptive research. *American Psychologist, 49*, 417–427.

Fisher, M. L. (2004). Female intrasexual competition decreases female facial attractiveness. *Proceedings of the Royal Society B, 271*, S283–S285. (doi:10.1098./rsbl.2004.0160)

Fisher, R. A. (1932). *Statistical methods for research workers* (4th ed.). Edinburgh, Scotland: Oliver & Boyd.

Fisher, R. A. (1935). *The design of experiments.* Edinburgh, Scotland: Oliver & Boyd.

Flynn, J. R. (1999). Searching for justice: The discovery of IQ gains over time. *American Psychologist, 54*, 5–20.

Fosse, R., Strickgold, R., & Hobson, J. A. (2001). Brain-mind states: Reciprocal variation in thoughts and hallucinations. *Psychological Science, 12*, 30–36.

Francis, L. J., & Jackson, C. J. (1998). The social desirability of toughmindedness: A study among undergraduates. *Irish Journal of Psychology, 19*, 400–403.

Frank, O., & Snijders, T. (1994). Estimating the size of hidden populations using snowball sampling. *Journal of Official Statistics, 10*, 53–67.

French, S., & Stephen, J. (1999). Religiosity and its association with happiness, purpose in life, and self-actualisation. *Mental Health, Religion & Culture, 2*, 117–120.

Frick, R. W. (1996). The appropriate use of null hypothesis testing. *Psychological Methods, 1*, 379–390.

Gaito, J. (1961). Repeated measurements designs and counterbalancing. *Psychological Bulletin, 58*, 46–54.

Gaito, J. (1980). Measurement scales and statistics: Resurgence of an old misconception. *Psychological Bulletin, 87*, 564–567.

Gardner, H. (1999). *Intelligence reframed: Multiple intelligences for the 21st century.* New York: Basicbooks.

Gardner, H., Krechevsky, M., Sternberg, R. J., & Okagaki, L. (1994). Intelligence in context: Enhancing students' practical intelligence for school. In K. McGilly (Ed.), *Classroom lessons: Integrating cognitive theory and classroom practice* (pp. 105–127). Cambridge: MIT Press.

Gawrylewski, A. (2007a). Case reports: Essential or irrelevant? *The Scientist.* Retrieved May 14, 2007, from http://www.the-scientist.com/news/home/53192

Gawrylewski, A. (2007b). The trouble with animal models. *The Scientist.* Retrieved August 10, 2007, from http://www.the-scientist.com/article/home/53306

Gazdella, B. M., Masten, W. G., & Stacks, J. (1998). Students' stress and their learning strategies, test anxiety, and attributions. *College Student Journal, 32*, 416–422.

Gehrick, J-G., & Shapiro, D. (2000). Reduced facial expression and social context in major depression: Discrepancies between facial muscle activity and self-reported emotion. *Psychiatry Research, 95*, 157–167.

Gendall, P., Hoek, J., & Brennan, M. (1998). The tea bag experiment: More evidence on incentives in mail surveys. *Journal of the Market Research Society, 40*, 347–351.

Gladwell, M. (2002, March 13). John Rock's error. *The New Yorker*, 52–63.

Glaze, J. A. (1928). The association value of nonsense syllables. *Journal of Genetic Psychology, 35*, 255–269.

Glueck, W. F., & Jauch, L. R. (1975). Sources of ideas among productive scholars: Implications for administrators. *Journal of Higher Education, 46*, 103–114.

Goldenberg, J. L., Pyszczynski, T., McCoy, S. K., Greenberg, J., & Solomon, S. (1999). Death, sex, love, and neuroticism: Why is sex such a problem? *Journal of Personality and Social Psychology,* 77, 1173–1187.

Goleman, D. (1996). *Emotional intelligence.* New York: Bantam Books.

Goodman, A. H. (2000). Why genes don't count (for racial differences in health). *American Journal of Public Health, 90*, 1699–1702.

Goodman-Delahunty, J. (1998). Approaches to gender and the law: Research and applications. *Law and Human Behavior, 22*, 129–143.

Gorenstein, C., Andrade, L., Filho, A. H. G. V., Tung, T., & Artes, R. (1999). Pschometric properties of the Portugese version of the Beck Depression Inventory on Brazilian college students. *Journal of Clinical Psychology, 55*, 553–602.

Gosling, S. D., Vazire, S., Srivastava, S., & John, O. P. (2004). Should we trust web-based studies? A comparative analysis of six preconceptions about internet questionnaires. *American Psychologist, 59*, 93–104.

Gottschalk,A., Smith, D. S., Jobes, D. R., Kennedy, S. K., Lally, S. E., Noble, V. E., Grugan, K. F., Seifert, H. A., Cheung, A., Malkowicz, B., Gutsche, B. B., & Wein, A. J. (1998). Preemptive epidural analgesia and recovery from radical prostatectomy: A randomized controlled trial. *Journal of the American Medical Association, 279*,1076–1082.

Gould, S. J. (1996). *The mismeasure of man* (2nd ed.). New York: W. W. Norton.

Gray, J. (1992). *Men are from Mars, women are from Venus: A practical guide for improving communication and getting what you want in your relationships.* New York: HarperCollins.

Green, A., & Vaid, J. (1986). Methodological issues in the use of the concurrent activities paradigm. *Brain and Cognition, 5*, 465–476.

Green, C. W., & Reid, D. H. (1999). A behavioral approach to identifying sources of happiness and unhappiness among individuals with profound multiple disabilities. *Behavior Modification, 23*, 280–293.

Gruder, C. L., Stumpfhauser, A., & Wyer, R. S. (1977). Improvement in experimental performance as a result of debriefing about deception. *Personality and Social Psychology Bulletin, 3*, 434–437.

Gunewardene, A., Huon, G. F., & Zheng, R. (2001). Exposure to westernization and dieting: A cross-cultural study. *International Journal of Eating Disorders, 29*, 289–293.

Gunnell, D., Rogers, J., & Dieppe, P. (2001). Height and health: Predicting longevity from bone length in archaeological remains. *Journal of Epidemiology and Community Health, 55*, 505–507.

Guthrie, J. P., Ash, R. A., & Bendapudi, V. (1995). *Journal of Applied Psychology, 80*, 186–190.

Gutierrez, P. M., Osman, A., Kopper, B. A., Barrios, F. X., & Bagge, C. L. (2000). Suicide risk assessment in a college student population. *Journal of Counseling Psychology, 47*, 403–413.

Gwiazda, J., Ong, E., Held, R., & Thorn, F. (2000). Vision: Myopia and ambient night-time lighting. *Nature, 404*, 144.

Hahn, P. W., & Clayton, S. D. (1996). The effects of attorney presentation style, attorney gender, and juror gender on juror decisions. *Law and Human Behavior, 20*, 533–554.

Hall, M. E., MacDonald, S., & Young, G. C. (1992). The effectiveness of directed multisensory stimulation versus non-directed stimulation in comatose CHI patients: Pilot study of a single subject design. *Brain Injury, 6*, 435–445.

Halvari, H., & Kjormo, O. (2000). A structural model of achievement motives, performance approach and avoidance goals and performance among Norwegian Olympic athletes. *Perceptual & Motor Skills, 89*, 997–1022.

Harbluk, J. L., Noy, Y. I., Trbovich, Pl L., & Elizenman, M. (2007). An on-road assessment of cognitive distraction: Impacts on drivers' visual behavior and braking performance. *Accident Analysis and Prevention, 39*, 372–379.

Harris, B. (1980). The FBI's files on APA and SPSSI: Description and implications. *American Psychologist, 35*, 1141–1144.

Harris, G., & Roberts, J. (2007, June 3). After sanctions, doctors get drug company pay. *The New York Times* [Electronic version]. Retrieved October 5, 2007, from http://www.nytimes.com/2007/06/03/health/03docs.html

Hashemi, L., & Webster, B. S. (1998). Non-fatal workplace violence workers' compensation claims (1993–1996). *Journal of Occupational and Environmental Medicine, 40*, 561–567.

Hatfield, J., & Murphy, S. (2007). The effects of mobile phone use on pedestrian crossing behaviour at signalised and unsignalised intersections. *Accident Analysis and Prevention, 39*, 197–205.

Hawker, D. S. J., & Boulton, M. J. (2000). Twenty years' research on peer victimization and psychosocial maladjustment: A meta-analytic review of cross-sectional studies. *Journal of Child Psychology and Psychiatry, 41*, 441–455.

Hay, C. A., & Bakken, L. (1991). Gifted sixth-grade girls: Similarities and differences in attitudes among gifted girls, non-gifted peers, and their mothers. *Roeper Review, 13*, 158–160.

Hayslip, B., McCoy-Roberts, L., & Pavur, R. (1998–99). Selective attrition effects in bereavement research: A three-year longitudinal analysis. *Omega, 38*, 21–35.

Hazlett, R. L., & Hoehn-Saric, R. (2000). Effects of perceived physical attractiveness on females' facial displays and affect. *Evolution and Human Behavior, 21*, 49–57.

Headden, S. (1997, December 8). The junk mail deluge. *U.S. News & World Report*, 42–48.

Heckathorn, D. D. (1997). Respondent-driven sampling: A new approach to the study of hidden populations. *Social Problems, 44*, 174–199.

Hedden, T., Park, D. C., Nisbett, R., Ji, L. J., Jing, Q., & Jiao, S. (2002). Cultural variation in verbal versus spatial neuropsychological function across the lifespan. *Neuropsychology, 16*, 65–73.

Helms, J. E., Jernigan, M., & Mascher, J. (2005). The meaning of race in psychology and how to change it: A methodological perspective. *American Psychologist, 60*, 27–36.

Hemenway, D. (1997). The myth of millions of annual self-defense gun uses: A case study of survey overestimates of rare events. *Chance, 10*, 6–10.

Hennigan, K. M., Del Rosario, M. L., Heath, L., Cook, T. D., Wharton, J. D., & Calder, B. J. (1982). Impact of the introduction of television on crime in the United States: Empirical findings and theoretical implications. *Journal of Personality and Social Psychology, 42*, 461–577.

Henwood, K. L. (1996). Qualitative inquiry: Perspectives, methods and psychology. In J. T. E. Richardson (Ed.), *Handbook of qualitative research methods for psychology and the social sciences* (pp. 25–40). Malden, MA: BPS Blackwell.

Hertel, P. T. (1998). Relation between rumination and impaired memory in dysphoric moods. *Journal of Abnormal Psychology, 107*, 166–172.

Heuer, H., Spijkers, W., Kiesswetter, E, & Schmidtke, V. (1998). Effects of sleep loss, time of day, and extended mental work on implicit and explicit learning of sequences. *Journal of Experimental Psychology: Applied, 4*, 139–162.

High accuracy found in 2000 elections. (2001, January 4) *St. Petersburg Times*, 3A.

Hill, S. E., & Ryan, M. J. (2006). The role of model female quality in the mate choice copying behaviour of sailfin mollies. *Biology Letters, 2*, 203–205.

Hilts, P. J., & Stolberg, S. G. (1999, May 13). Ethical lapses at Duke halt dozens of human experiments. *New York Times*. Retrieved May 13, 1999, from http://www.nytimes.com/yr/mo/day/news/national/science/sci-duke-research.html.

Hoekstra-Weebers, J. E. H. M., Jaspers, J. P. C., Kamps, W. A., & Klip, E. C. (2001). Psychological adaptation and social support of parents of pediatric cancer patients: A prospective longitudinal study. *Journal of Pediatric Psychology, 26*, 225–235.

Holahan, C. K., & Sears, R. R. (1995). *The gifted group in later maturity*. Stanford, CA: Stanford University Press.

Holmes, J. D., Beins, B. C., & Lynn, A. (2007, June). Student views of psychology as a science: Findings and implications. Presented at the Eastern Conference on the Teaching of Psychology, Staunton, VA.

Holmes, T. H., & Rahe, R. H. (1967). The Social Readjustment Rating Scale. *Journal of Psychosomatic Research, 11*, 213–218.

Hong, Y., & Chiu, C. (1991). Reduction of socially desirable responses in attitude assessment through the enlightenment effect. *Journal of Social Psychology, 131*, 585–587.

Horvitz, D., Koshland, D., Rubin, D. Gollin, A., Sawyer, T., & Tanbur, J. M. (1995). Pseudo-opinion polls: SLOP or useful data? *Chance, 8*, 16–25.

Howell, D. C. (2007). *Statistical methods for psychology* (6th ed.). Wadsworth: Belmont, CA.

Hrycaiko, D., & Martin, G. L. (1999). Applied research studies with single-subject designs: Why so few? *Journal of Applied Sport Psychology, 8*, 183–199.

Humphreys, L. (1975). *Tearoom trade: Impersonal sex in public places* (2nd ed.). Chicago: Aldine.

Imrie, R., & Ramey, D. W. (2000). The evidence for evidence-based medicine. *Complementary Therapies in Medicine, 8*, 123–126.

Inzlicht, M., & Ben-Zeev, T. (2000). A threatening intellectual environment: Why females are susceptible to experiencing problem-solving deficits in the presence of males. *Psychological Science, 11*, 365–371.

Ioannidis, J. P. A. (2005). Why most published research findings are false. *PloS Medicine, 2*, e124, 696–701. Retrieved June 7, 2007, from http://www.plosmedicine.org

Iwamasa, G. Y., Larrabee, A. L., & Merritt, R. D. (2000). Are personality disorder criteria ethnically biased? A card-sort analysis. *Cultural Diversity and Ethnic Minority Psychology, 6*, 284–296.

Jacob, T., Tennenbaum, D., Seilhamer, R. A., Bargiel, K., & Sharon, T. (1994). Reactivity effects during naturalistic observation of distressed and nondistresed families. *Journal of Family Psychology, 8*, 354–363.

Jenni, D. A., & Jenni, M. A. (1976). Carrying behavior in humans: Analysis of sex differences. *Science, 194*, 859–860.

Jenni, M. A. (1976). Sex differences in carrying behavior. *Perceptual and Motor Skills, 43*, 323–330.

Jennings, C. (2000, May/June). [Letter to the editor.] *The Sciences, 40*, 3, 5.

Jensen, G. F. (2001). The invention of television as a cause of homicide: The reification of a spurious relationship. *Homicide Studies, 5*, 114–130.

Ji, L.J., Schwarz, N., & Nisbett, R. E. (2000). Culture, autobiographical memory, and behavioral frequency reports: Measurement issues in cross-cultural studies. *Personality and Social Psychology Bulletin, 26*, 585–593.

Johnson, T. P., Fendrich, M., Shaligram, C., Garcy, A., & Gillespie, S. (2000). An evaluation of the effects of interviewer charcteristics in an RDD telephone survey of drug use. *Journal of Drug Issues, 30*, 77–102.

Jones, B. C., DeBruine, L. M., Little, A. C., Burriss, R. P., & Feinberg, D. R. (2007). Social transmission of face preferences among humans. *Proceedings of the Royal Society B, 274*, 899–903.

Jones, H. E., & Contrad, H. S. (1933). The growth and decline of intelligence: A study of a homogeneous group between the ages of ten and sixty. *Genetic Psychology Monographs, 13*, 223–298.

Judd, C. M., Smith, E. R., & Kidder, L. H. (1991). *Research methods in social relations*. Fort Worth: Holt, Rinehart, & Winston.

Juhnke, R., Barmann, B., Cunningham, M., & Smith, E. (1987). Effects of attractiveness and nature of request on helping behavior. *Journal of Social Psychology, 127*, 317–322.

Kaneto, H. (1997). Learning/memory processes under stress conditions. *Behavioural Brain Research, 83*, 71–74.

Kaplan, C. D., Korf, D., & Sterk, C. (1987). Temporal and social contexts of heroin-using populations: An illustration of the snowball sampling technique. *Journal of Nervous and Mental Disease, 175*, 566–574.

Kaplan, M. D. (1999). Developmental and psychiatric evaluation in the preschool context. *Child and Adolescent Psychiatric Clinics of North America, 8*, 379–393.

Kasof, J. (1993). Sex bias in the naming of the stimulus person. *Psychological Bulletin, 113*, 140–163.

Kass, S. J., Cole, K. S., & Stanny, C. J. (2007). Effects of distraction and experience on situation awareness and simulated driving. *Transportation Research Part F, 10*, 321–329.

Katsev, R., Edelsack, L., Steinmetz, G., Walker, T., & Wright, R. (1978). The effect of reprimanding transgression on subsequent helping behavior: Two field experiments. *Personality and Social Psychology Bulletin, 4*, 326–329.

Kaufman, P., Kwon, J. Y., Klein, S., & Chapman, C. D. (2000.) Dropout rates in the United States: 1999. Washington, DC: National Center for Educational Statistics.

Kaur, M., Liguori, A., Lang, W., Rapp, S. R., Fleischer, A. B., & Feldman, S. R. (2006). Induction of withdrawal-like symptoms in a small randomized, controlled trial of opioid blockade in frequent tanners. *Journal of the American Academy of Dermatology, 54*, 709–711.

Kazdin, A. E. (1998). *Research design in clinical psychology* (3rd ed.). Boston: Allyn and Bacon.

Keith-Spiegel, P., & Koocher, G. P. (2005). The IRB paradox: Could the protectors also encourage deceit? *Ethics & Behavior, 15*, 339–349.

Keller, J. (2007). Stereotype threat in classroom settings: The interactive effect of domain identification, task difficulty and stereotype threat on female students' maths performance. *British Journal of Educational Psychology*, 77, 323–338.

Kellett, S., & Beall, N. (1997). The treatment of chronic post-traumatic nightmares using psychodynamic-interpersonal psychotherapy: A single-case study. *British Journal of Medical Psychology, 70*, 35–49.

Kennedy, D., & Norman, C. (2005, July 1). What we don't know. *Science, 309*, 75.

Kiecker, P., & Nelson, J. E. (1996). Do interviewers follow telephone survey instructions? *Journal of the Market Research Society, 38*, 161–176.

Kim, B. S. K., Atkinson, D. R., & Yang, P. H. (1999). The Asian Values Scale: Development, factor analysis, validation, and reliability. *Journal of Counseling Psychology, 46*, 342–352.

King, M. F., & Bruner, G. C. (2000). Social desirability bias: A neglected aspect of validity testing. *Psychology and Marketing, 17*, 79–103.

Klawans, H. (2000). *Defending the cavewoman and other tales of evolutionary neurology*. New York: W. W. Norton.

Kleck, G., & Gertz, M. (1995). Armed resistence to crime: The prevalence and nature of self-defense with a gun. *Journal of Criminal Law and Criminology, 86*, 150–187.

Komiya, N., Good, G. E., & Sherrod, N. B. (2000). Emotional openness as a predictor of college students' attitudes toward seeking psychological help. *Journal of Counseling Psychology, 47*, 138–143.

Korn, J. H. (1998). The reality of deception. *American Psychologist, 53*, 805.

Kovar, M. G. (2000). Four million adolescents smoke: Or do they? *Chance, 13*, 10–14.

Kozulin, A. (1999). Profiles of immigrant students' cognitive performance on Raven's Progressive Matrices. *Perceptual & Motor Skills, 87*, 1311–1314.

Krahn, G. L., & Putnam, M. (2003). Qualitative methods in psychological research. In M. C. Roberts & S. S. Ilardi (Eds.), *Handbook of research methods in clinical psychology* (pp. 176–195). Malden, MA: Blackwell.

Krantz, J. H., & Dalal, R. (2000). Validity of Web-based psychological research. In M. H. Birnbaum (Ed.), *Psychological experiments on the Internet* (pp. 35–60). San Diego: Academic Press.

Kremar, M., & Greene, K. (2000). Connections between violent television exposure and adolescent risk taking. *Media Violence, 2*, 195–217.

Krishnan, A., & Sweeney, C. J. (1998). Gender differences in fear of success imagery and other achievement-related background variables among medical students. *Sex Roles, 39*, 299–310.

Krosnick, J. A. (1999). Survey research. *Annual Review of Psychology, 50*, 537–67.

Krosnick, J. A., Holbrook, A. L., Sberent, M. K., Carson, R. T., Hanemann, W. M., Kopp, R. J., et al. (2002). The impact of "no opinion" response options on data quality: Non-attitude reduction or an invitation to satisfice. *Public Opinion Quarterly, 66*, 371–403.

Kumari, R. (1995). Relation of sex role attitudes and self-esteem to fear of success among college women. *Psychological Studies, 40*, 82–86.

Kwiatkowski, S. J., & Parkinson, S. R. (1994). Depression, elaboration, and mood congruence: Differences between natural and induced mood. *Memory & Cognition, 22*, 225–233.

LaGreca, A. M., Silverman, W. K., Vernberg, E. M., & Prinstein, M. J. (1996). Symptoms of posttraumatic stress in children after Hurricane Andrew: A prospective study. *Journal of Counseling and Clinical Psychology, 64*, 712–723.

LaHuis, D. M., Nicholas, R., & Avis, J. M. (2005). Investigating nonlinear conscientiousness-job performance relations for clerical employees. *Human Performance, 18*, 199–212.

Lane, J. D., Phillips-Bute, B. G., & Pieper, C. F. (1998). Caffeine raises blood pressure at work. *Psychosomatic Medicine*, 60, 327–330.

Lang, F. R., & Heckhausen, J. (2001). Perceived control over development and subjective well-being: Differential benefits across adulthood. *Journal of Personality and Social Psychology, 81*, 509–523.

Latané, B., & Darley, J. M. (1970). *The unresponsive bystander: Why doesn't he help?* New York: Appleton-Century-Crofts.

Lawson, C. (1995). Research participation as a contract. *Ethics and Behavior, 5*, 205–215.

Lee, Y-T., & Ottati, V. (1995). Perceived in-group homogeneity as a function of group membership salience and stereotype threat. *Personality & Social Psychology Bulletin, 21*, 610–619.

Lehman, D. R., Lempert, R. O., & Nisbett, R. E. (1988). The effects of graduate training on reasoning: Formal discipline and thinking about everyday-life events. *American Psychologist, 43*, 431–442.

Leirer, V. O., Yesavage, J. A., & Morrow, D. G. (1991). Marijuana carry-over effects on aircraft pilot performance. *Aviation, Space, and Environmental Medicine, 62*, 221–227.

Leonhard, C., Gastfriend, D. R., Tuffy, L. J., Neill, J., & Plough, A. (1997). The effect of anonymous vs. nonanonymous rating conditions on patient satisfaction and motivation ratings in a population of substance abuse patients. *Alcoholism: Clinical and Experimental Research, 21*, 627–630.

Levine, F. M., & De Simone, L. L. (1991). The effects of experimenter gender on pain report in male and female subjects. *Pain, 44*, 69–72.

Levitt, L., & Leventhal, G. (1986). Litter reduction: How effective is the New York State bottle bill? *Environment and Behavior, 18*, 467–479.

Lewis, C. A., McCollam, P., & Joseph, S. (2000). Convergent validity of the Depression-Happiness Scale with the Bradburn Affect Balance Scale. *Social Behavior & Personality, 28*, 579–584.

Liang, C. T. H., Li, L. C., & Kim, B. S. K. (2004). The Asian American Racism-Related Stress Inventory: Development, factor analysis, reliability, and validity. *Journal of Counseling Psychology, 51*, 103–114.

Lifton, R. J. (1986). *The Nazi doctors: Medical killing and the psychology of genocide.* New York: Basic Books.

Liston, C., & Kagan, J. (2002). Memory enhancement in early childhood. *Nature, 419*, 896.

Lockwood, K. A., Alexopoulos, G. S., Kakuma, T., & Van Gorp, W. G. (2000). Subtypes of cognitive impairment in depressed older adults. *American Journal of Geriatric Psychiatry, 8*, 201–208.

Loftus, E. F. (1975). Leading questions and the eyewitness report. *Cognitive Psychology, 7*, 560–572.

Loftus, E. F. (1979). *Eyewitness testimony.* Cambridge, MA: Harvard University Press.

Loftus, E. F. (1997). Memories for a past that never was. *Current Directions in Psychological Science, 6*, 60–65.

Loftus, E. F. (2003, January). Illusions of memory. Presented at the National Institute on the Teaching of Psychology. St. Petersburg Beach, FL.

Loftus, E. F., & Marburger, W. (1983). Since the eruption of Mount St. Helens, has anyone beaten you up? Improving the accuracy of retrospective reports with landmark events. *Memory and Cognition, 11*, 114–120.

Lonner, W. J. (1999). Helfrich's "principle of triarchic resonance": A commentary on yet another perspective on the ongoing and tenacious etic-emic debate. *Culture & Psychology, 5*, 173–181.

Lord, F. M. (1953). On the statistical treatment of football numbers. *American Psychologist, 8*, 750–751.

Luria, A. R. (1968). *The mind of a mnemonist.* New York: Basic Books.

MacGeorge, E. L., Samter, W., Feng, B., Gillihan, S. J., & Graves, A. R. (2004). Stress, social support, and health among college students after September 11, 2001. *Journal of College Student Development, 45*, 655–670.

Manucia, G. K., Baumann, D. J., & Cialdini, R. B. (1984). Mood influences on helping: Direct effects or side effects? *Journal of Personality and Social Psychology, 46*, 357–364.

Marans, D. G. (1988). Addressing researcher practitioner and subject needs: A debriefing-disclosure procedure. *American Psychologist, 43*, 826–828.

Marian, V., & Neisser, U. (2000). Language-dependent recall of autobiographical memories. *Journal of Experimental Psychology: General, 129*, 361–368.

Martinez-Ebers, V. (1997). Using monetary incentives with hard-to-reach populations in panel surveys. *International Journal of Public Opinion Research, 9*, 77–86.

Martinsen, E. W., Friis, S., & Hoffart, A. (1995). Assessment of depression: Comparison between Beck Depression Inventory and subscales of Comprehensive Psychopathological Rating Scale. *Acta Psychiatrica Scandinavica, 92*, 460–463.

Martinson, B. C., Anderson, M. S., & de Vries, R. (2005). Scientists behaving badly. *Nature, 435*, 737–738.

Matsumoto, D. (1993). Ethnic differences in affect intensity, emotion judgments, display rule attitudes, and self-reported emotional expression in an American sample. *Motivation and Emotion, 17*, 107–123.

Matsumoto, D. (1994). *Cultural influences on research methods and statistics.* Pacific Grove, CA: Brooks/Cole.

Matsumoto, D., & Assar, M. (1992). The effects of language on judgments of universal facial expressions of emotion. *Journal of Nonverbal Behavior, 16*, 85–99.

Matthews, G. A., & Dickinson, A. M. (2000). Effects of alternative activities on time allocated to task performance under different percentages of incentive pay. *Journal of Organizational Behavior Management, 20*, 3–27.

May, C. P., Hasher, L., & Stoltzfus, E. R. (1993). Optimal time of day and the magnitude of age differences in memory. *Psychological Science, 4*, 326–330.

Mayer, J. D., Salovey, P., Caruso, D. R., & Sitarenios, G. (2001). Emotional intelligence as a standard intelligence. *Emotion, 1*, 232–242.

Mazzoni, G. A., & Loftus, E. F. (1998). Dream interpretation can change beliefs about the past. *Psychotherapy, 35*, 177–187.

McAuliffe, W. E., Geller, S., LaBrie, R., Paletz, S., & Fournier, E. (1998). Are telephone surveys suitable for studying substance abuse? Cost, administration, cover and response rate issues. *Journal of Drug Issues, 28*, 455–481.

McCallum, R. C., & Austin, J. T. (2000). Applications of structural equation modeling in psychological research. *Annual Review of Psychology, 51*, 201–226.

McClung, H. J., Murray, R. D., & Heitlinger, L. A. (1998). The internet as a course for current patient information. *Pediatrics, 101*, e2 [online].

McGlone, M. S., & Aronson, J. (2007). Forewarning and forearming stereotype-threatened students. *Communication Education, 56*, 119–133.

McGuire, W. J. (1983). A contextualist theory of knowledge: Its implications for innovation and reform in psychological research. In L. Berkowitz (Ed.), *Advances in Experimental Social Psychology*, Vol 16. Orlando, FL: Academic Press.

Mehl, M. R. (2006). The lay assessment of subclinical depression in daily life. *Psychological Assessment, 18,* 340–345.

Meissner, C. A., Tredoux, C. J., Parker, J. F., & MacLin, O. H. (2005). Eyewitness decisions in simultaneous and sequential lineups. *Memory and Cognition, 33,* 783–792.

Melnik, T. A., Baker, C. T., Adams, M. L., O'Dowd, K., Mokdad, A. H., Brown, D. W., et al. (2002). Psychological and emotional effects of the September 11 attacks on the World Trade Center—Connecticut, New Jersey, and New York, 2001. *Mortality and Morbidity Weekly Report, 51,* 784–786.

Mendoza, M. (2005). Allegations of fake research hit new high. *Yahoo News.* Retrieved July 12, 2005, from http://www.news.yahoo.com

Mennella, J. A., & Gerrish, C. J. (1998). Effects of exposure to alcohol in mother's milk on infant sleep. *Pediatrics (online), 101,* e2.

Meston, C. M., Heiman, J. R., Trapnell, P. D., & Paulhus, D. L. (1998). Socially desirable responding and sexuality self-reports. *Journal of Sex Research, 35,* 148–157.

Milgram, S. (1963). Behavioral study of obedience. *Journal of Abnormal and Social Psychology, 67,* 371–378.

Milgram, S. (1964). Issues in the study of obedience: A reply to Baumrind. *American Psychologist, 19,* 848–852.

Milgram, S. (1974). *Obedience to authority: An experimental view.* New York: Harper & Row.

Miller, J. D. (2007a, February). The public understanding of science in Europe and the United States. Presented at the annual meeting of the American Association for the Advancement of Science, San Francisco, CA.

Miller, J. D. (2007b, February). Civic scientific literacy across the life cycle. Presented at the annual meeting of the American Association for the Advancement of Science, San Francisco, CA.

Miller, M. A., & Rahe, R. H. (1997). Life changes scaling for the 1990s. *Journal of Psychosomatic Research, 43,* 279–292.

Miller, N. (1985). The value of behavioral research on animals. *American Psychologist, 40,* 423–440.

Miller, R. S. (1995). On the nature of embarrassability: Shyness, social evaluation, and social skill. *Journal of Personality, 63,* 315–339.

Mills, C. G., Boteler, E. H., & Oliver, G. K. (1999). Digit synaesthesia: A case study using a stroop-type test. *Cognitive Neuropsychology, 16,* 181–191.

Miracle, A. D., Brace, M. F., Huyck, K. D., Singler, S. A., & Wellman, C. L. (2006). Chronic stress impairs recall of extinction of conditioned fear. *Neurobiology of Learning and Memory, 85,* 213–218.

Mobile web audience already one-fifth the size of PC-based internet audience in the U.K. (2007, May 14). Retrieved July 24, 2007, from http://www.comscore.com/press/release.asp?press=1432

Modern Language Association of America. (1995). *MLA handbook for writers of research papers* (4th ed.). New York: Author.

Mohr, D. C., Goodkin, D. E., Bacchetti, P., Boudewyn, A. C., Huang, L., Marrietta, P., Cheuk, W., & Dee, B. (2000). Psychological stress and the subsequent appearance of new brain MRI lesions in MS. *Neurology, 55,* 55–61.

Mook, D. G. (1983). In defense of external invalidity. *American Psychologist, 38,* 379–387.

Moonsinghe, R., Khoury, M. J., & Janssens, A. C. J. W. (2007). Most published research findings are false—but a little replication goes a long way. *PLoS Medicine, 4,* e28, 218–221.

Moore, D. W. (2005) Three in four Americans believe in paranormal. Gallup News Service. Retrieved May 17, 2007, from http://home.sandiego.edu/~baber/logic/gallup.html

Moore, S. R. (1998). Effects of sample size on the representativeness of observational data used in evaluation. *Education and Treatment of Children, 21,* 209–226.

Morgan, C. A., Hazlett, G., Doran, A., Garrett, S., Hoyt, G., Thomas P., et al. (2004). Accuracy of eyewitness memory for persons encountered during exposure to highly intense stress. *International Journal of Law and Psychiatry, 27,* 265–279.

Morris, J. S., Scott, S. K., & Dolan, R. J. (1999). Saying it with feeling: Neural responses to emotional vocalizations. *Neuropsychologia, 37,* 1155–1163.

The Mother's Encyclopedia. (1942). Vol. 5, New York: The Parents' Institute.

Müller, F. R. (2000, May/June). [Letter to the editor.] *The Sciences, 40,* 5.

Münsterberg, H. (1914). *Psychology and social sanity.* New York: Doubleday, Page, & Co.

Murray, L. A., Whitehouse, W. G., & Alloy, L. B. (1999). Mood congruence and depressive deficits in memory: A forced-recall analysis. *Memory, 7,* 175–196.

Muzzatti, B., & Agnoli, F. (2007). Gender and mathematics: Attitudes and stereotype threat susceptibility in Italian children. *Developmental Psychology, 43,* 747–759.

Newman, J., Rosenbach, J. H., Burns, K. L., Latimer, B. C., Matocha, H. R., & Vogt, E. E. (1995). An experimental test of "the Mozart effect." Does listening to his music improve spatial ability? *Perceptual and Motor Skills, 81,* 1379–1387.

The NIMH Multisite HIV Prevention Trial: Reducing HIV sexual risk behavior. (1998). *Science, 280,* 1889–1894.

Nisbet, M. (1998). New poll points to increases in paranormal belief. *Skeptical Inquirer, 22*(5), 9.

Norenzayan, A., & Schwarz, N. (1999). Telling what they want to know: Participants tailor causal attributions to researchers' interests. *European Journal of Social Psychology, 29,* 1011–1020.

North, C. S., Nixon, S. J., Shariat, S., Mallonee, S., McMillen, J. C., Spitznagel, E. L., & Smith, E. M. (1999). Psychiatric disorders among survivors of the Oklahoma City bombing. *Journal of the American Medical Association, 282*, 755–762.

Novi, M. J., & Meinster, M. O. (2000). Achievement in a relational context: Preferences and influences in female adolescents. *Career Development Quarterly, 49*, 73–84.

Nugent, W. R., Bruley, C., & Allen, P. (1998). The effects of aggression replacement training on antisocial behavior in a runaway shelter. *Research on Social Work Practice, 8*, 637–656.

O'Muircheartaigh, C., Krosnick, J. A., & Helic, A. (2000). Middle alternatives, acquiesence, and the quality of questionnaire data. Working paper, Harris School, University of Chicago.

Ochocka, J., Nelson, G., Janzen, R., & Trainor, J. (2006). A longitudinal study of mental health consumer/survivor initiatives: Part 3—A qualitative study of impacts of participation on new members. *Journal of Community Psychology, 34*, 273–283.

Odom, S. L., & Ogawa,, I. (1992). Direct observation of young children's social interactions with peers: A review of methodology. *Behavioral Assessment, 14*, 407–441.

Olkin, I. (1992). Reconcilable differences: Gleaning insight from conflicting scientific studies. *The Sciences, 32*, 30–36.

Orne, M. T. (1962). On the social psychology of the psychological experiment: With particular reference to demand characteristics and their implications. *American Psychologist, 17*, 776–783.

Orne, M. T., & Scheibe, K. T. (1962). The contribution of nondeprivation factors in the production of sensory deprivation effexts. *Journal of Abnormal and Social Psychology, 68*, 3–12.

Ornstein, R., & Sobel, D. (1987). *The healing brain.* New York: Simon and Schuster.

Ortmann, A., & Hertwig, R. (1997). Is deception acceptable? *American Psychologist, 52*, 746–747.

Ossorio, P., & Duster, T. (2005). Race and genetics: Controversies in biomedical, behavioral, and forensic sciences. *American Psychologist, 60*, 115–128.

Overall, J. E., Hollister, L. E., Johnson, M., & Pennington, V. (1966). Nosology of depression and differential response to drugs. *Journal of the American Medical Association, 195*, 946–948.

Paasche-Orlow, M. K., Taylor, A. A., & Barncati, F. L. (2003). Readability standards for informed-consent forms as compared with actual readability. *New England Journal of Medicine, 348*, 721–726.

Paksoy, C., Wilkinson, J. B., & Mason, J. B. (1985). Learning and carryover effects in retail experimentation. *Journal of the Market Research Society, 27*, 109–129.

Park, R. L. (2003). The seven warning signs of bogus science. *Chronicle of Higher Education, 49*(21), B20. Retrieved May March 3, 2003, from http://www.chronicle.com/free/v49/i21/21b02001.htm

Pearson, K. (1896). Mathematical contributions to the theory of evolution. III. Regression, heredity and panmixia. *Philosophical Transactions of the Royal Society (Series A), 187*, 253–318. Retrieved July 31, 2007, from http://links.jstor.org/sici?sici=02643952%281896%29187%3C253%3AMCTTTO%3E2.0.CO%3B2-%23

Peng, K., & Nisbett, R. E. (1999). Culture, dialectics, and reasoning about contradiction. *American Psychologist, 54*, 741–754.

Pepler, D. J., & Craig, W. M. (1995). A peek behind the fence: Naturalistic observations of aggressive children with remote audiovisual recording. *Develomental Psychology, 31*, 548–553.

Perceptions of foreign countries. Retrieved September 29, 2001, from http://www.gallup.com/poll/releases/pr010928.asp.

Peregrine, P. N., Drews, D. R., North, M., & Slupe, A. (1993). Sampling techniques and sampling error in naturalistic observation: An empirical evaluation with implications for cross-cultural research. *Cross-Cultural Research, 27*, 232–246.

Peters, M. (1993). Still no convincing evidence of a relation between brain size and intelligence in humans. *Canadian Journal of Experimental Psychology, 47*, 751–756.

Phillips, D. P., Christenfeld, N., & Ryan, N. M. (1999). An increase in the number of deaths in the United States in the first week of the month–An association with substance abuse and other causes of death. *New England Journal of Medicine, 341*, 93–98.

Phinney, J. S. (1996). When we talk about American ethnic groups, what do we mean? *American Psychologist, 51*, 918–927.

Plous, S. (1996a). Attitudes toward the use of animals in psychological research and education. *American Psychologist, 51*, 1167–1180.

Plous, S. (1996b). Attitudes toward the use of animals in psychological research and education: Results from a national survey of psychology majors. *Psychological Science*, 7, 352–358.

Pollatsek, A., & Well, A. D. (1995). On the use of counterbalanced designs in cognitive research: A suggestion for a better and more powerful analysis. *Journal of Experimental Psychology: Learning, Memory, and Cognition, 21*, 785–794.

Powell, M. C., & Fazio, R. H. (1984). Attitude accessibility as a function of repeated attitudinal expression. *Personality and Social Psychology Bulletin, 10*, 139–148.

Presser, S., & Stinson, L. (1998). Data collection mode and social desirability bias in self-reported religious attendance. *American Sociological Review, 63*, 137–145.

Price, W. F., & Crapo, R. H. (1999). *Cross-cultural perspectives in introductory psychology* (3rd ed.). Pacific Grove, CA: Brooks/Cole Wadsworth.

Quinn, G. E., Shin, C. H., Maguire, M. G., & Stone, R. A. (1999). Myopia and ambient lighting at night. *Nature, 399*, 113–114.

Quinn, R. P., Gutek, B. A., & Walsh, J. T. (1980). Telephone interviewing: A reappraisal and a field experiment. *Basic and Applied Social Psychology, 1*, 127–153.

Radford, B. (1998). Survey finds 70% of women, 48% of men believe in paranormal. *Skeptical Inquirer, 22*(2), 8.

Radner, D., & Radner, M. (1982). *Science and unreason.* Belmont, CA: Wadsworth.

Rasinski, K. A. (1989). The effect of question wording on public support for government spending. *Public Opinion Quarterly, 53*, 388–394.

Rauch, S. L., Shin, L. M., & Phelps, E. A. (2006). Neurocircuitry models of posttraumatic stress disorder and extinction: Human neuroimaging research—past, present, and future. *Biological Psychiatry, 60*, 376–382.

Rauscher, F. H., Shaw, G. L., Gordon, L. (1998). Key components of the Mozart effect. *Perceptual and Motor Skills, 86*, 835–841.

Rauscher, F. H., Shaw, G. L., & Ky, K. N. (1993). Music and spatial task performance. *Nature, 365*, 611.

Rauscher, F. H., Shaw, G. L., & Ky, K. N. (1995). Listening to Mozart enhances spatial-temporal reasoning: Towards a neurophysiological basis. *Neuroscience Letters, 185*, 44–47.

Ray, J. J. (1990). Acquiescence and problems with forced-choice scales. *Journal of Social Psychology, 130*, 397–399.

Recarte, M. A., & Nunes, L. M. (2000). Effects of verbal and spatial-imagery tasks on eye fixations while driving. *Journal of Experimental Psychology: Applied*, 6, 31–43.

Recarte, M. A., & Nunes, L. M. (2003). Mental workload while driving: Effects on visual search, discrimination, and decision making. *Journal of Experimental Psychology: Applied, 9*, 119–137.

Redelmeier, D. A., & Tibshirani, R. J. (1997). Association between cellular-telephone calls and motor vehicle collisions. *The New England Journal of Medicine, 336*, 453–458.

Reese, H. W. (1997). Counterbalancing and other uses of repeated-measures Latin-square designs: Analysis and interpretation. *Journal of Experimental Child Psychology, 64*, 137–158.

Renner, M. J., Mackin, R. S.(1998) A life stress instrument for classroom use. *Teaching of Psychology, 25*, 46–48.

Research ethics and the medical profession. (1996). Report of the Advisory Committee on Human Radiation Experiments. *Journal of the American Medical Association, 276*, 403–409.

Reynolds, P. D. (1982). *Ethics and social science research.* Englewood Cliffs, NJ: Prentice-Hall.

Richter, P., Joachim, W., & Bastine, R. (1994). Psychometrische eigenschaften des Beck Depressioninventars (BDI): Ein überblick. *Zeitschrift für Klinische Psychologie: Forschung und Praxis, 23*, 3–19.

Riley, J. L., Wade, J. B., Myers, C. D., Sheffield, D., Papas, R. K., & Price, D. D. (2002). Racial/ethnic differences in the experience of pain. *Pain, 100* , 291–298.

Ring, K., Wallston, K., & Corey, M. (1970). Mode of debriefing as a factor affecting subjective reaction to a Milgram-type obedience experiment: An ethical inquiry. *Representative Research in Social Psychology, 1*, 67–88.

Roberts, R. D., Zeidner, M., & Matthews, G. (2001). Does emotional intelligence meet traditional standards for an intelligence? Some new data and conclusions. *Emotion, 1*, 196–231.

Robins, R. W., & Gosling, S. D., & Craik, K. H. (1999). An empirical analysis of trends in psychology. *American Psychologist, 54*, 117–128.

Rockwood, T. H., Sangster, R. L., & Dillman, D. A. (1997). The effect of response categories on survey questionnaires: Context and mode effects. *Sociological Methods and Research, 26*, 118–140.

Rodriguez, C. E. (2000). *Changing race: Latinos, the census and the history of ethnicity in the United States.* New York: New York University Press.

Rogler, L. H. (1999). Methodological sources of cultural insensitivity in mental health research. *American Psychologist, 54*, 424–433.

Rosenberg, M. (1965). *Society and the adolescent self-image.* Princeton, NJ: Princeton University Press.

Rosenthal, R. (1979). The "file drawer problem" and tolerance for null results. *Psychological Bulletin, 86*, 638–641.

Rosenthal, R., & Fode, K. L. (1966). Three experiments in experimenter bias. *Psychological Reports, 12*, 491–511.

Rosenthal, R., & Rosnow, R. L. (1975). *The volunteer subject.* New York: Wiley.

Rosnow, R. L., & Rosenthal, R. (1997). *People studying people: Artifacts and ethics in behavioral research.* New York: W. H. Freeman.

Ross, L. M., Hall, B. A., & Heater, S. L. (1998). Why are occupational therapists not doing more replication research? *The American Journal of Occupational Therapy, 52*, 234–235.

Ross, L., Lepper, M. R., & Hubbard, M. (1975). Perseverance in self-perception and social perception: Biased attribution processes in the debriefing paradigm. *Journal of Personality and Social Psychology, 32*, 880–892.

Ross, M., & Wilson, A. E. (2002). It feels like yesterday: Self-esteem, valence of personal past experiences, and judgments of subjective distance. *Journal of Personality and Social Psychology, 82*, 792–803.

Rothbaum, F., Weisz, J., Pott, M., Kiyake, K., & Morelli, G. (2000). Attachment and culture: Security in the United States and Japan. *American Psychologist, 55*, 1093–1104.

Rothman, D. J. (1994, January 9). Government guinea pigs. *New York Times*, Section 4, 23.

Rothman, M. (1996). Fear of success among business students. *Psychological Reports*, *78*, 863–869.

Rowe, R. M., & McKenna, F. P. (2001). Skilled anticipation in real-world tasks: Measurement of attentional demands in the domain of tennis. *Journal of Experimental Psychology: Applied*, *7*, 60–67.

Rubin, Z. (1985). Deceiving ourselves about deception: Comment on Smith and Richardson's "Amelioration of deception and harm in psychological research." *Journal of Personality and Social Psychology*, *48*, 252–253.

Ryan, L., Hatfield, C., & Hofstetter, M. (2002). Caffeine reduces time-of-day effects on memory performance in older adults. *Psychological Science*, *13*, 68–71.

Sambraus, H. H. (1998). Applied ethology—Its task and limits in veterinary practice. *Applied Animal Behaviour Science*, *59*, 39–48.

Satisfaction with local schools. (2005). Survey Research Unit School of Public Affairs Baruch College/ CUNY. Retrieved February 9, 2007, from http:// etownpanel.com/results.htm

Schaie, K. W. (1992). The impact of methodological changes in gerontology. *International Journal of Aging and Human Development*, *35*, 19–29.

Schaie, K. W. (2000). The impact of longitudinal studies on understanding development from young adulthood to old age. *International Journal of Behavioral Develoment*, *24*, 257–266.

Scharrer, E. (2001). Men, muscles, and machismo: The relationship between television violence exposure and aggression and hostility in the presence of hypermasculinity. *Media Psychology*, *3*, 159–188.

Schiffman, S. S. (1997). Taste and smell losses in normal aging and disease. *Journal of the American Medical Association*, *278*, 1357–1362.

Schillewaert, N., Langerak, F., & Duhamel, T. (1998). Non-probability sampling for WWW surveys: A comparison of methods. *Journal of the Market Research Society*, *40*, 307–322.

Scholer, S. J., Hickson, G. B., & Mitchel, E. F., & Ray, W. A. (1998). Predictors of mortality from fires in young children. *Pediatrics*, *101*, e12. [online].

Schram, C. M. (1996). A meta-analysis of gender differences in applied statistics achievement. *Journal of Educational and Behavioral Statistics*, *21*, 55–70.

Schul, Y., & Goren, H. (1997). When strong evidence has less impact than weak evidence: Bias, adjustment, and instructions to ignore. *Social Cognition*, *15*, 133–155.

Schuller, R. A., & Cripps, J. (1998). Expert evidence pertaining to battered women: The impact of gender of expert and timing of testimony. *Law and Human Behavior*, *22*, 17–31.

Schulz, D., Buddenberg, T., & Huston, J. P. (2007). Extinction-induced "despair" in the water maze, exploratory behavior and fear: Effects of chronic antidepressant treatment. *Neurobiology of Learning and Memory*, *87*, 624–634.

Schwarz, N. (1999). Self-reports: How the questions shape the answers. *American Psychologist*, *54*, 93–105.

Schwarz, N., Hippler, H. J., Deutsch, B., & Strack, F. (1985). Response categories: Effects on behavioral reports and comparative judgments. *Public Opinion Quarterly*, *49*, 388–395.

Scientists should adopt codes of ethics, scientist-bioethicist says (2007, February 5). Retrieved May 31, 2007, from http://www.sciencedaily.com/releases/ 2007/02/070201144615.htm

Scriven, M., & Paul, R. (2007). Defining critical thinking. Retrieved March 19, 2008, from http://www.criticalthinking.org/aboutCT/define_cri tical_thinking.cfm

Sechrist, G. B., & Stangor, C. (2001). Perceived consensus influences intergroup behavior and stereotype accessibility. *Journal of Personality & Social Psychology*, *80*, 645–654.

Segall, M. H., Campbell, D. T., & Herskovits, M. J. (1966). *The influence of culture on visual perception*. Indianapolis, IN: Bobbs-Merrill.

Segall, M. H., Lonner, W. J., & Berry, J. W. (1998). Cross-cultural psychology as a scholarly discipline: On the flowering of culture in behavioral research. *American Psychologist*, *53*, 1101–1110.

Selten, J.-P., Veen, N., Feller, W., Blom, J. D., Schols, D., Camoenië, W., et al. (2001). Incidence of psychotic disorders in immigrant groups to the Netherlands. *British Journal of Psychiatry*, *178*, 367–372.

Shannon, E. R., Neibling, B. C., & Heckert, T. M. (1999). Sources of stress among college students. *College Student Journal*, *33*, 312–317.

Sher, K. J., Wood, M. D., Wood, P. K., & Raskin, G. (1996). Alcohol outcome expectancies and alcohol use: A latent variable cross-lagged panel study. *Journal of Abnormal Psychology*, *105*, 561–574.

Simpson, S., Bell, L., Britton, P., Mitchell, M., Morrow, M., Johnston, A. L., & Brebner, J. (2006). Does video therapy work? A single case series of bulimic disorders. *European Eating Disorders Review*, *14*, 226–241.

Singer, B., & Benassi, V. A. (1980, Winter). Fooling some of the people all of the time. *Skeptical Inquirer*, *5*, 17–24.

Singer, E., Von Thurn, D. R., & Miller, E. R. (1995). Confidentiality assurances and survey response: A review of the experimental literature. *Public Opinion Quarterly*, *59*, 266–277.

Singh, S. (1999). *The code book: The evolution of secrecy from Mary Queen of Scots to quantum cryptography*. New York: Doubleday.

Smith, C. S., Reilly, C., & Midkiff, K. (1989). Evaluation of three circadian rhythm questionnaires with suggestions for an improved measure of morningness. *Journal of Applied Psychology*, *74*, 728–739.

Smith, J. A. (1997). Developing theory from case studies: Self-reconstruction and the transition to motherhood. In N. Hayes (Ed.), *Doing qualitative analysis in psychology.* Hove, East Sussex, UK: Psychology Press.

Snowden, P. L., & Christian, L. G. (1999). Parenting the young gifted child: Supportive behaviors. *Roeper Review, 21,* 221.

Sockloff, A. L. (1975). Behavior of the product-moment correlation coefficient when two heterogeneous subgroups are pooled. *Educational and Psychological Measurement, 35,* 267–276.

Soliday, E., & Stanton, A. L. (1995). Deceived versus nondeceived participants' perceptions of scientific and applied psychology. *Ethics and Behavior, 5,* 87–104.

Sommers, S. R., & Ellsworth, P. C. (2001). White juror bias: An investigation of prejudice against black defendants in the American courtroom. *Psychology, Public Policy, and Law,* 7, 201–229.

Soto-Faraco, S., & Sebastián-Gallés, N. (2001). The effects of acoustic mismatch and selective listening on repetition deafness. *Journal of Experimental Psychology: Human Perception and Performance,* 27, 356–369.

Spencer, S. J., Steele, C. M., & Quinn, D. M. (1999). Stereotype threat and women's math performance. *Journal of Experimental Social Psychology, 35,* 4–28.

Steblay, N. M., Dysart, J., Fulero, S., & Lindsay, R. C. L. (2001). Eyewitness accuracy rates in sequential and simultaneous lineup presentations: A meta-analytic comparison. *Law and Human Behavior, 25,* 459–474.

Steele, K. M., Bass, K. E., & Crook, M. D. (1999). The mystery of the Mozart effect: Failure to replicate. *Psychological Science, 10,* 366–369

Steele, C. M., & Aronson, J. (1995). Stereotype threat and the intellectual test performance of African Americans. *Journal of Personality and Social Psychology, 69,* 797–811.

Steer, R. A., Rissmiller, D. J., & Beck, A. T. (2000). Use of Beck Depression Inventory-II with depressed geriatric inpatients. *Behaviour Research & Therapy, 38,* 311–318.

Steer, R. A., Rissmiller, D. J., Ranieri, W. F., & Beck, A. T. (1994). Use of the computer-administered Beck Depression Inventory and Hopelessness Scale with psychiatric inpatients. *Computers in Human Behavior, 10,* 223–229.

Steinberg, N., Tooney, N., Sutton, C., & Denmark, F. (2000, May/June). [Letter to the editor]. *The Sciences, 40,* 3.

Sternberg, R. J. (1985). *Beyond IQ: A triarchic theory of human intelligence.* New York: Cambridge University Press.

Sternberg, R. J. (1999). A triarchic approach to the understanding and assessment of intelligence in multicultural populations. *Journal of School Psychology, 37,* 145–159.

Sternberg, R. J., Grigorenko, E. L., & Kidd, K. K. (2005). Intelligence, race, and genetics. *American Psychologist, 60,* 46–59.

Stevens, J. C., Cruz, L. A., Hoffman, J. M., & Patterson, M. Q. (1995). Taste sensitivity and aging: High incidence of decline revealed by repeated threshold measures. *Chemical Senses, 20,* 451–459.

Stevens, S. S. (1946). On the theory of scales of measurement, *Science, 103,* 677–680.

Stevens, S. S. (1951). Mathematics, measurement, and psychophysics. In S. S. Stevens (Ed.), *Handbook of experimental psychology.* New York: Wiley.

Stiles, D. A., Gibbons, J. L., & Schnellman, J. D. (1990). Opposite-sex ideal in the U.S.A. and Mexico as perceived by young adolescents. *Journal of Cross-Cultural Psychology, 21,* 180–199.

Stokes, S. J., & Bikman, L. (1974). The effect of the physical attractiveness and role of the helper on help seeking. *Journal of Applied Social Psychology, 4,* 286–294.

Stolzenberg, L., & D'Alessio, S. J. (1997). "Three strikes and you're out": The impact of California's new mandatory sentencing law on serious crime rates. *Crime and Delinquency, 43,* 457–469.

Straus, M. A., Sugarman, D. B., & Giles-Sims, J. (1997). Spanking by parents and subsequent antisocial behavior of children. *Archives of Pediatrics and Adolescent Medicine, 151,* 761–767.

Strayer, D. L., Drews, F. A., & Crouch, D. J. (2006). A comparison of the cell phone driver and the drunk driver. *Human Factors, 48,* 381–391.

Strayer, D. L., Drews, F. A., & Johnston, W. A. (2003). Cell phone-induced failures of visual attention during simulated driving. *Journal of Experimental Psychology: Applied, 9,* 23–32.

Strayer, D. L., & Johnston, W. A. (2001). Driven to distraction: Dual-task studies of simulated driving and conversing on a cellular telephone. *Psychological Science, 12,* 462–466

Strober, M., Freeman, R., Lampter, C., Diamond, J. & Kaye, W. (2001). Males with anorexia nervosa: A controlled study of eating disorders in first-degree relatives. *International Journal of Eating Disorders, 29,* 263–269.

Strohmetz, D. B., & Moore, M. P. (2003, March). *Impact of a tattoo on a helping request.* Poster presented at the annual convention of the Eastern Psychological Association, Baltimore, MD.

Sue, S. (1999). Science, ethnicity, and bias: Where have we gone wrong? *American Psychologist, 54,* 1070–1077.

Sundblom, D. M., Haikonen, S., Niemi-Pynttaeri, J., & Tigerstedt, I. (1994). Effect of spiritual healing on chronic idiopathic pain: A medical and psychological study. *Clinical Journal of Pain, 10,* 296–302.

Swaddle, J. P., Cathey, M. G., Correll, M., & Hodkinson, B. P. (2005). Socially transmitted mate preferences in a monogamous bird: A non-genetic mechanism of sexual selection. *Proceedings of the Royal Society B, 272*, 1053–1058.

Takooshian, H., & O'Connor, P. J. (1984). When apathy leads to tragedy: Two Fordham professors examine "Bad Samaritanism." *Social Action and the Law, 10*, 26–27.

Tang-Martínez, Z., & Mechanic, M. (2000, May/June). [Letter to the editor.] *The Sciences, 40*, 5–6.

Tapper, K., & Boulton, M. J. (2002). Studying aggression in school children: The use of a wireless microphone and micro-video camera. *Aggressive Behavior, 28*, 356–365.

Taylor, S. J., & Bogdan, R. (1998). *Introduction to qualitative research methods.* New York: Wiley.

Teeter, P. A., & Smith, P. L. (1989). Cognitive processing strategies for normal and LD children: A comparison of the K-ABC and microcomputer experiments. *Archives of Clinical Neuropsychology, 4*, 45–61.

The score: Teens highly engaged online. (2006, March 16). Retrieved July 27, 2007, from http://www.imediaconnection.com/content/8691.asp

Thompson, J. K., & Heinberg, L. J. (1999). The media's influence on body image disturbance and eating disorders: We've reviled them, now can we rehabilitate them? *Journal of Social Issues, 55*, 339–353.

Thompson, J. K., & Stice, E. (2001). Thin-ideal internalization: Mounting evidence for a new risk factor for body-image disturbance and eating pathology. *Current Directions in Psychological Science, 10*, 181–183.

Thompson, W. F., Schellenberg, E. G., & Husain, G. (2001). Arousal, mood, and the Mozart effect. *Psychological Science, 12*, 248–251.

Thornhill, R., & Palmer, C. T. (2000). Why men rape. *The Sciences, 40*, 30–36.

Thorson, J. A., & Powell, F. C. (1993). Development and validation of a multidimensional sense of humor scale. *Journal of Clinical Psychology, 49*, 13–23.

Todorov, A. (2000). Context effects in national health surveys: Effects of preceding questions on reporting serous difficulty seeing and legal blindness. *Public Opinion Quarterly, 64*, 65–76.

Troisi, A. (1999). Ethological research in clinical psychiatry: The study of nonverbal behavior during interviews. *Neuroscience and Biobehavioral Reviews, 23*, 905–913.

Troisi, A., & Moles, A. (1999). Gender differences in depression: An ethological study of noverbal behavior during interviews. *Journal of Psychiatric Research, 33*, 243–350.

Troisi, A., Pasini, A., Bersani, G., Di Mauro, M., & Ciani, N. (1991). Negative symptoms and visual behavior in DSM-III-R prognostic subtypes of schizophreniform disorder. *Acta Psychiatria Scandinavia, 83*, 391–394.

Troisi, A., Pompili, E., Binello, L., & Sterpone, A. (2007). Facial expressivity during the clinical interview as a predictor functional disability in schizophrenia. A pilot study. *Progress in Neuro-Psychopharmacology & Biological Psychiatry, 31*, 475–481.

Troisi, A., Spalletta, G., & Pasini, A. (1998). Nonverbal behavior deficits in schizophrenia: An ethological study of drug-free patients. *Acta Psychiatrica Scandinavica, 97*, 109–115.

Trope, Y., & Fishbach, A. (2000). Counteractive self-control in overcoming temptation. *Journal of Personality and Social Psychology, 79*, 493–506.

Underwood, B. J., & Freund, J. S. (1970). Word frequency and short-term recognition memory. *American Journal of Psychology, 83*, 343–351.

Vadillo, M. A., Bárcena, R., & Matute, H. (2006). The internet as a research tool in the study of associative learning: An example from overshadowing [Electronic Version]. *Behavioural Processes, 73*, 36–40.

Varma, A. (2000). Impact of watching international television programs on adolescents in India. *Journal of Comparative Family Studies, 31*, 117–126.

Varvel, S. A., Wise, L. E., Niyuhire, F., Cravatt, B. F., & Lichtman, A. H. (2007). Inhibition of fatty-acid amide hydrolase accelerates acquisition and extinction rates in a spatial memory task. *Neuropsychopharmacology, 32*, 1032–1041.

Velleman, P. F., & Wilkinson, L. (1993). Nominal, ordinal, interval, and ratio typologies are misleading. *The American Statistician, 47*, 65–72.

Velten, E. (1968). A laboratory task for induction of mood states. *Behaviour Research and Therapy, 6*, 473–482.

Velten, E., Jr. (1997). A laboratory task for induction of mood states. In S. Rachman (Ed.), *Best of behavior research and therapy* (pp. 73–82). New York: Pergamon/Elsevier Science.

Vermont Youth Risk Behavior Survey: Statewide Report. (1997). Retrieved August 3, 2007, from http://healthvermont.gov/pubs/yrbs/yrbs_1997.pdf

Vermont Youth Risk Behavior Survey: Statewide Report. (2001). Retrieved August 3, 2007, from http://healthvermont.gov/pubs/yrbs/yrbs_2001.pdf

Vermont Youth Risk Behavior Survey: Statewide Report. (2005). Retrieved August 3, 2007, from http://healthvermont.gov/pubs/yrbs/yrbs_2005.pdf

Vink, T., Hinney, A., Van Elburg, A. A., Van Goozen, S. H. M., Sandkuijl, L. A., Sinke, R. J., Herpertz-Dahlmann, B-M., Hebebrand, J., Remschmidt, H., Van Engeland, H., & Adan, R. A. H. (2001). Association between an agouti-related protein gene polymorphism and anorexia nervosa. *Molecular Psychiatry, 6*, 325–328.

Vispoel, W. P. (2000). Computerized versus paper-and-pencil assessment of self-concept: Score comparability and respondent preferences. *Measurement and Evaluation in Counseling and Development, 33*, 130–143.

Vispoel, W. P., & Forte Fast, E. E. (2000). Response biases and their relation to sex differences in multiple domains of self-concept. *Applied Measurement in Education, 13*, 79–97.

Vonesh, E. F. (1983). Efficiency of repeated measures design versus completely randomized designs based on multiple comparisons. *Communications in Statistics–Theory and Methods, 12*, 289–302.

Wadman, M. (2005). One in three scientists confesses to having sinned. *Nature, 435*, 718–719.

Wagle, A. C., Ho, L. W., Wagle, S. A., & Berrios, G. E. (2000). Psychometric behaviour of BDI in Alzheimer's disease patients with depression. *International Journal of Geriatric Psychiatry, 15*, 63–69.

Wainer, H. (1999). The most dangerous profession: A note on nonsampling error. *Psychological Methods, 4*, 250–256.

Waldo, C. R., Berdahl, J. L., & Fitzgerald, L. F. (1998). Are men sexually harassed? If so, by whom? *Law and Human Behavior, 22*, 59–79.

Walker, E. F., Grimes, K. E., Davis, D. M., & Smith, A. J. (1993). Childhood precursors of schizophrenia: Facial expression of emotion. *American Journal of Psychiatry, 150*, 1654–1660.

Wallace, W. P., Sawyer, T. J., & Robertson, L. C. (1979). Distractors in recall, distractor-free recognition, and the word-frequency effect. *American Journal of Psychology. Vol 91*, 295–304.

Waller, G., Meyer, C., & van Hanswijck de Jonge, L. (2001). Early environmental influences on restrictive pathology among nonclinical females: The role of temperature at birth. *International Journal of Eating Disorders, 30*, 24–208.

Walsh, M., Hickey, C., & Duffy, J. (1999). Influence of item content and stereotype situation on gender differences in mathematical problem solving. *Sex Roles, 41*, 219–240.

Walsh, W. B. (1976). Disclosure of deception by debriefed subjects: Another look. *Psychological Reports, 38*, 783–786.

Wann, D. L., & Wilson, A. M. (1999). Relationship between aesthetic motivation and preferences for aggressive and nonaggressive sports. *Perceptual & Motor Skills, 89*, 931–934.

Watkins, D., Mortazavi, S., & Trofimova, I. (2000). Independent and interdependent conceptions of self: An investigation of age, gender, and culture differences in importance and satisfaction ratings. *Cross-Cultural Resarch: The Journal of Comparative Social Science, 34*, 113–134.

Weber, N., Brewer, N., Wells, G. L., Semmler, C., & Keast, A. (2004). Eyewitness identification accuracy and response latency: The unruly 10–12 second rule. *Journal of Experimental Psychology: Applied, 10*, 139–147.

Wells, G. L., Memon, A., & Penrod, S. D. (2006). Eyewitness evidence: Improving its probative value. *Psychological Science in the Public Interest*, 7(2).

Wentland, E. J., & Smith, K. W. (1993). *Survey responses: An evaluation of their validity*. Boston: Academic Press.

Westen, D. (1998). The scientific legacy of Sigmund Freud: Toward a psychodynamically informed psychological science. *Psychological Bulletin, 124*, 333–371.

Wilcox, R. R. (1998). How many discoveries have been lost by ignoring modern statistical methods? *American Psychologist*, 53, 300–314.

Wilkinson, L., & the Task Force on Statistical Inference. (1999). Statistical methods in psychology journals: Guidelines and explanations. *American Psychologist, 54*, 594–604.

Willimack, D. K., Schuman, H., Pennell, B-E, & Lepkowski, J. M. (1995). Effects of a prepaid nonmonetary incentive on response rates and response quality in a face-to-face survey. *Public Opinion Quarterly, 59*, 78–92.

Wilson, D. W. (1978). Helping behavior and physical attractiveness. *Journal of Social Psychology, 104*, 313–314.

Wimer, D. J., & Beins, B. C. (2000, August). *Is this joke funny? Only if we say it is.* Presented at the annual convention of the American Psychological Association. Washington, DC.

Wimer, D. J., & Beins, B. C. (in press). Expectations and perceived humor. *Humor: International Journal of Humor Studies.*

Winkielman, P., Knäuper, B., & Schwarz, N. (1998). Looking back at anger: Reference periods change the interpretation of (emotion) frequency questions. *Journal of Personality and Social Psychology, 75*, 719–728.

Wutzke, S. E., Conigrave, K. M., Kogler, B. E., Saunders, J. B., & Hall, W. D. (2000). Longitudinal research: Methods for maximizing subject follow-up. *Drug and Alcohol Review, 19*, 159–163.

Yee, A. H., Fairchild, H. H., Weizmann, F., & Wyatt, G. E. (1993). Addressing psychology's problem with race. *American. Psychologist, 48*, 1132–1140.

York, J., Nicholson, T., Minors, P., & Duncan, D. F. (1998). Stressful life events and loss of hair among adult women: A case-control study. *Psychological Reports, 82*, 1044–1046.

Zadnik, K., Jones, L. A., Irvin, B. C., Kleinstein, R. N., Manny, R. E., Shin, J. A., & Mutti, D. O. (2000). Vision: Myopia and ambient night-time lighting. *Nature, 404*, 143–144.

Zajonc, R. B. (1965). Social facilitation, *Science, 149*, 269–274.

Zeller, S., Lazovich, D., Forster, J., & Widome, R. (2006). Do adolescent indoor tanners exhibit dependency? *Journal of the American Academy of Dermatology, 54*, 589–596.

Zettle, R. D., & Houghton, L. L. (1998). The relationship between mathematics and social desirability as a function of gender. *College Student Journal, 32*, 81–86.

Zimbardo, P. G. (1973). On the ethics of intervention in human psychological research: With special reference to the Stanford prison experiment. *Cognition, 2*, 243–256.

Zinner, D., Hindahl, J., & Schwibbe, M. (1997). Effects of temporal sampling patterns of all-occurence recording in behavioural studies: Many short sampling periods are better than a few long ones. *Ethology, 103*, 236–246.

Zuckerman, M. (1990). Some dubious premises in research and theory on racial differences. *American Psychologist, 45*, 1297–1303.

Zusne, L., & Jones, W. H. (1989). *Anomalistic psychology: A study of magical thinking* (2nd ed.) Hillsdale, NJ: Erlbaum.

AUTHOR INDEX

SUBJECT INDEX